Dráma

Xánthi • Komotiní

ECE

THRACE

Kavála •

oníki

Alexandroúpoli

Aegean Sea

Northern Greece
Pages 236–261

AROUND
ATHENS

IENS •

ATTICA

• Lávrio

Athens
Pages 66–139

Around Athens
Pages 144–161

EYEWITNESS TRAVEL

GREECE
ATHENS & THE MAINLAND

Main Contributor **Marc Dubin**

DK

LONDON, NEW YORK,
MELBOURNE, MUNICH AND DELHI
www.dk.com

Project Editor Jane Simmonds
Art Editor Stephen Bere
Editors Isabel Carlisle, Michael Ellis, Simon Farbrother,
Claire Folkard, Marianne Petrou, Andrew Szudek
Designers Jo Doran, Paul Jackson, Elly King, Marisa Renzullo
Map Co-Ordinators Emily Green, David Pugh
Visualizer Joy Fitzsimmons
Language Consultant Georgia Gotsi

Contributors and Consultants
Rosemary Barron, Marc Dubin, Mike Gerrard, Andy Harris,
Lynette Mitchell, Colin Nicholson, Robin Osborne, Barnaby
Rogerson, Paul Sterry, Tanya Tsikas

Maps
Gary Bowes, Fiona Casey, Christine Purcell (ERA-Maptec Ltd)

Photographers
Joe Cornish, John Heseltine, Rob Reichenfeld, Peter Wilson,
Francesca Yorke

Illustrators
Stephen Conlin, Paul Guest, Steve Gyapay, Maltings Partnership,
Chris Orr & Associates, Paul Weston, John Woodcock

Printed in China

First published in Great Britain in 1997
by Dorling Kindersley Limited
80 Strand, London WC2R 0RL

17 18 19 20 10 9 8 7 6 5 4 3 2 1

Reprinted with revisions 1998, 1999, 2000, 2001, 2002,
2003, 2004, 2006, 2007, 2009, 2011, 2013, 2015, 2017

Copyright 1997, 2017 © Dorling Kindersley Limited, London

A Penguin Random House Company

MIX
Paper from
responsible sources
FSC™ C018179

Front cover main image: Parthenon, Acropolis, Athens

◀ The Medieval fort of Monemvasiá

Contents

How to Use
This Guide **6**

Black-figure bowl depicting
the god Dionysos

Introducing
Athens and
Mainland Greece

Discovering
Mainland Greece **10**

Putting Greece on
the Map **16**

A Portrait of
Mainland Greece **18**

The History
of Greece **28**

Athens and Mainland
Greece Through
the Year **48**

Ancient
Greece

Gods, Goddesses
and Heroes **56**

The Trojan War **58**

Greek Writers
and Philosophers **60**

Temple
Architecture **62**

Vases and Vase
Painting **64**

Athens Area by Area

Athens at
a Glance **68**

Central Athens
North **70**

Central Athens
South **86**

Shopping
in Athens **118**

Entertainment
in Athens **122**

Athens Street
Finder **126**

Three gateways at the entrance to Acrocorinth

Mainland Greece Area by Area

Mainland Greece at
a Glance **142**

Around Athens **144**

The Peloponnese **162**

Central and Western
Greece **206**

Northern Greece **236**

Travellers' Needs

Where to Stay **264**

Where to Eat and
Drink **274**

Fresco at Varlaám monastery at Metéora,
Central Greece

Shopping in Greece **292**

Specialist Holidays
and Outdoor
Activities **294**

Survival Guide

Practical
Information **300**

Travel Information **310**

General Index **324**

Phrase Book **344**

Road Map
Inside Back Cover

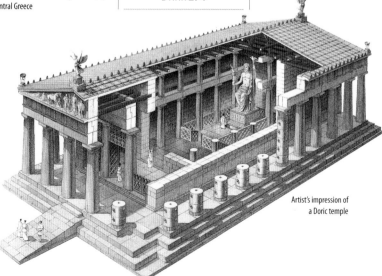

Artist's impression of
a Doric temple

HOW TO USE THIS GUIDE

This guide helps you to get the most from your visit to Mainland Greece. It provides expert recommendations and practical information. *Introducing Athens and Mainland Greece* maps the country and sets it in its historical and cultural context. *Ancient Greece* gives a background to the many remains and artifacts to be seen. The four regional chapters, plus *Athens*, describe important sights, with maps and illustrations. Restaurant and hotel recommendations can be found in *Travellers' Needs*. The *Survival Guide* has tips on everything from using a Greek telephone to transport.

Athens

Athens has been divided into two sightseeing areas. Each has its own chapter, opening with a list of the sights described. All sights are numbered on an area map, and are described in detail on the following pages.

Sights at a Glance gives a categorized list of the chapter's sights: Museums and Galleries; Squares, Parks and Gardens; Churches and Historic Buildings.

All pages relating to Athens have red thumb tabs.

A locator map shows you where you are in relation to the rest of Athens.

1 Area Map
The sights are numbered and located on a map. Sights in the city centre are also shown on the Athens Street Finder on *pages 126–39*.

2 Street-by-Street Map
This gives an overhead view of the key areas in central Athens. The numbering on the map ties in with the area map and the fuller descriptions that follow.

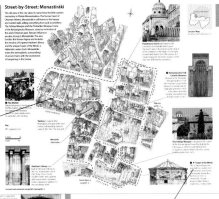

A suggested route for a walk is shown in red.

Story Boxes highlight special aspects of a particular sight.

Stars indicate the sights that no visitor should miss.

3 Detailed Information The sights within Athens are described individually. Addresses, telephone numbers, opening hours and information concerning admission charges and wheelchair access are given for each entry. Map references to the Athens Street Finder are also provided for orientation.

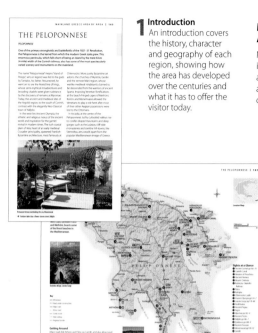

1 Introduction
An introduction covers the history, character and geography of each region, showing how the area has developed over the centuries and what it has to offer the visitor today.

Mainland Greece Area by Area

Mainland Greece has been divided into four regions, each of which has a separate chapter. A map of these areas can be found inside the front cover of the book.

Each region can be identified by its colour coding, shown on the inside front cover.

A locator map shows you where you are in relation to the other regions in the book.

2 Regional Map
This shows the region covered in the chapter. The main sights are numbered on the map. The major roads are marked and there are useful tips about the best ways of getting around the area.

3 Detailed Information
All the important towns and areas to visit are described individually. They are listed in order, following the numbering on the *Regional Map*. Within each entry, there is detailed information on all the major sights.

A Visitors' Checklist provides the practical information you will need to plan your visit.

4 Greece's Top Sights
These are given one or more full pages. Historic buildings are dissected to reveal their interiors. Many of the ancient sites are reconstructed to supplement information about the site as it is seen today.

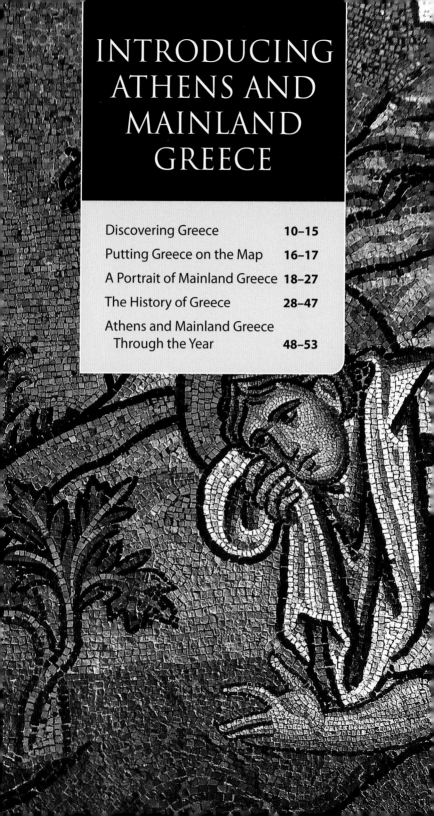

INTRODUCING ATHENS AND MAINLAND GREECE

Discovering Greece 10–15

Putting Greece on the Map 16–17

A Portrait of Mainland Greece 18–27

The History of Greece 28–47

Athens and Mainland Greece
  Through the Year 48–53

DISCOVERING GREECE

The following tours have been designed to take in as many of the country's highlights as possible, while keeping long-distance travel to a minimum. The first itinerary outlined here is a two-day tour of Athens, followed by five days spent in the Attica region and the Peloponnese. These itineraries can be followed individually or combined to form a week-long tour. Next, come two week-long tours, covering Central, Western and Northern Greece, including Thrace and Macedonia. Additional suggestions are included for those who want to extend their stay. Pick, combine and follow your favourite tours, or simply dip in and out and be inspired.

One Week in Central and Western Greece

- Explore the beautiful, rugged **Pílio** peninsula and visit its unspoilt villages.

- Admire the powerful mosaic, *Washing of the Apostles' Feet*, at the medieval **Monastery of Osios Loukás**.

- Imagine what life was like at **Ancient Delphi**, once considered the centre of the earth.

- Marvel at **Metéora's** huge sandstone towers topped by monasteries and hermitages.

- Enjoy a leisurely stroll along the theatre-shaped waterfront of **Párga** and see its Venetian fortress.

- See the spectacular scenery of the **Víkos Gorge**, carved over millions of years by the Voïdomátis river.

Key

— One Week in Central and Western Greece
— Five Days in Attica and the Peloponnese
— One Week in Northern Greece

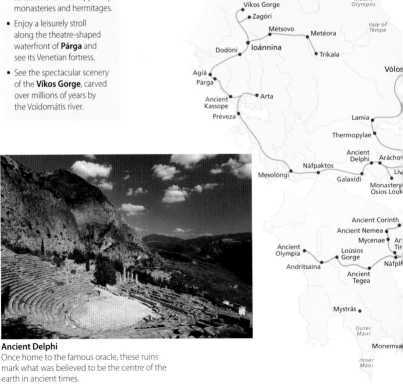

Préspa Lakes · Flórina · Edessa · Ancient Pella
Lefkádia
Kastoriá · Véroia · Thessaloní
Ancient Vergina
Siátista
Víkos Gorge
Zagóri
Métsovo · Metéora · *Mount Olympos*
Dodóni · Ioánnina · *Vale of Tempe*
Tríkala
Agiá · Párga · Vólos
Ancient Kassope · Arta
Préveza
Lamía
Thermopylae
Ancient Delphi · Arácho
Náfpaktos · Liv
Mesolóngi · Galaxídi
Monastery Osios Louk
Ancient Corinth
Ancient Nemea
Mycenae · Ar · Tir
Ancient Olympia · Loúsios Gorge · Náfpli
Andrítsaina
Ancient Tegea
Mystrás
Outer Máni
Monemva
Inner Máni

Ancient Delphi
Once home to the famous oracle, these ruins mark what was believed to be the centre of the earth in ancient times.

◀ The beautiful *Tranfiguration* mosaic depicting the apostles, Peter and John at the Monastery of Daphni

Thássos
Around 12 km (7 miles) from the mainland, this beautiful resort island is known for its sandy beaches and mountain villages.

One Week in Northern Greece

- Admire the distinctive Neo-Classical, Byzantine and Ottoman architecture of **Xánthi**.

- Visit the fascinating **Thessaloníki Archaeological Museum** to see its priceless gold treasures.

- Admire dramatic views of **Mount Athos** and explore the Orthodox monasteries around.

- Relax in the unspoilt wilderness of the **Olympos National Park** or the pretty **Préspa Lakes**.

- Enjoy rich avian life at **Lake Kerkíni**, Greece's premier birdwatching destination.

- Take a boat trip to the island of **Thássos**.

Xánthi
Famous for its annual spring carnival, the lively market town of Xánthi also has an interesting folk museum.

Five Days in Attica and the Peloponnese

- See the spectacle of dozens of ferries leaving Kentikó Limáni in **Piraeus** for the islands every morning.

- Discover the ancient sites of the Peloponnese, including **Mycenae**, **Epidaurus**, **Nemea** and **Olympia**.

- Explore well-preserved 19th-century architecture in the picturesque town of **Náfplio**.

- Be captivated by the magnificent mosaics at the **Monastery of Daphni**.

- Visit the **Attica Zoological Park**, home to one of the world's largest collections of birds.

- Admire the stunning medieval towns of **Monemvasiá** and **Mystrás** and wonder about the lives of the people who lived here.

Two Days in Athens

- **Arriving** Flights from around the world arrive everyday at the modern Elefthérios Venizélos – Athens International Airport, around 27 km (17 miles) from the city centre. A metro service links the airport with Plateía Syntágmatos and Monastiráki. Buses and taxis operate from outside the terminal to Athens and the ports of Piraeus and Rafína. Athens can also be reached by road.

- **Transport** The main sights of Athens are all within easy walking distance. The city also has an efficient bus and tram network.

- **Booking ahead** Some museums, including the Acropolis Museum, are closed on Mondays.

Day 1
Morning Start the day early with a trip to the **Acropolis** (see pp98–105). Follow the pathway up from the entrance and be sure to stop at the **Theatre of Herodes Atticus** (see p101), which dates from AD 161. Ascend the steps to the **Propylaia** (see p100). Take a minute to admire the **Temple of Athena Nike** (see p100), before moving on to see the mighty **Parthenon** (see pp102–103) dominating the scene ahead. Enjoy spectacular views of Athens and the coast from here. Later, make your way back down to pedestrianized Dionysíou Areopagítou, turn left and follow the path towards a selection of lunchtime eateries.

Afternoon Head for the ultra-modern **Acropolis Museum** (see p104), which is as stunning as the ancient treasures that are on display. Spend an hour here, and visit the Parthenon Gallery on the top floor, which has huge windows looking towards the Parthenon. Admire the outstanding exhibits. Next, explore vibrant **Pláka** (see pp106–107), but before losing

yourself in its labyrinth of tiny, picturesque lanes, take a quick detour to Hadrian's Arch and the **Temple of Olympian Zeus** (see p115). In the evening, dine at one of the locals' favourite tavernas in the central neighbourhoods of Psyrrí or Pangráti.

Day 2
Morning Spend the morning exploring the superb **Benáki Museum** (see pp82–3) or the nearby **Museum of Cycladic Art** (see pp78–9), both are full of interesting Greek treasures. Keep an eye on your watch so that you're in time outside the parliament building in **Plateía Syntágmatos** (see p116) to witness the pageantry of the changing of the guard. It begins at 11am and continues for about half an hour (longer on Sundays). From here, take a short walk to the **National Gardens** (see p116), one of the most peaceful spots in the city, before enjoying an early lunch in one of the area's restaurants.

Afternoon Make your way along Ermoú Street, lined with shops such as Gucci and Dolce & Gabbana, to **Monastiráki** (see pp88–9). Just off to your left, along Fokionos, is Plateía Mitropóleos, a bustling square dominated by the little 12th-century church, **Panagía Gorgoepíkoös** (see p109). Monastiráki is famous for its **Flea Market** (see p91) and the ruins of **Ancient Agora** (see pp94–5), where Athenians would once engage in bartering

goods. The marketplace dates from 600 BC. Among the ruins is the interesting octagonal **Tower of the Winds** (see p90). End the day with a romantic meal in Thiseío where some restaurants have a pretty view of the flood-lit Acropolis.

> **To extend your trip…**
> The **National Archaeological Museum** (see pp72–3) in the district of Exárcheia houses fabulous treasures from all over Greece, dating back to various eras.

Five Days in Attica and the Peloponnese

- **Arriving** Piraeus is just 10 km (6 miles) SW of Athens, and the two are connected by a line of the metro network.

- **Transport** The best way to explore Attica and the Peloponnese is by car.

Day 1: Piraeus to Soúnio
Explore **Piraeus** (see pp158–9), with its elegant Neo-Classical architecture, parks and museums. Follow the signs to Mikrolímano harbour and stop for a quiet lunch at any of the fish restaurants here before heading out of town and along the Attic Coast, strewn with marinas and resorts, to **Sounion** (see pp152–3). There is no village here – just a good beach with a few hotels nearby – but the magnificent ancient

The imposing Roman Theatre of Herodes Atticus

Temple ruins in Ancient Corinth

Temple of Poseidon at Sounion dominates the cape. Spend the night here.

Day 2: Sounion to Athens
Begin early from Sounion and make your way to **Ancient Brauron** *(see pp150–51)*, with its fine museum and sanctuary, via **Lávrio** *(see p152)* and the picturesque fishing harbour of **Pórto Ráfti** *(see p151)*. Continue along the coast to **Rafína** *(see p149)* and sample fresh fish for lunch. In the afternoon, take the road to Athens. Along the way, visit the **Attica Zoological Park** *(see p154)*, home to one of the world's largest collections of birds, and enjoy the peaceful countryside that inspired monks to build the **Moní Kaisarianís** monastery *(see pp154–5)* in the 11th century.

Day 3: Athens to Corinth
Just 10 km (6 miles) outside Athens is the **Monastery of Daphni** *(see p156–7)*, with its wonderful early 12th-century mosaics and later cloister. A few miles further on is **Ancient Eleusis** *(see pp160–61)*, which was once an important religious sanctuary. There's an interesting museum that tells its story. The Peloponnese "island" comes into full view as you make your way along the coastal road to the **Corinth Canal** *(see p171)*. Spend the afternoon visiting the site of **Ancient Corinth** *(see pp166–7)*, once a prosperous Roman city.

End the day in the village by the site, which has a good choice of accommodation.

Day 4: Corinth to Náfplio
Get acquainted with the Peloponnesian history by stopping first at **Ancient Nemea** *(see p171)*, then the mighty fortified palace of **Mycenae** *(see pp182–4)*. Next, move on to **Ancient Tiryns** *(see p185)* and, finally, **Epidaurus** *(see pp188–9)*, with its spectacular theatre. Arrive in time for dinner in charming **Náfplio** *(see pp186–7)* and spend the night here.

Day 5: Ancient Olympia
Set out very early to explore **Ancient Olympia** *(see pp174–7)*, one of the most important religious, political and athletic centres of the ancient world. From Náfplio, follow signs for Trípoli and **Ancient Tegea** *(see*

Bust of Roman Emperor Marcus Aurelius at Ancient Eleusis

p181). Opt to take the mountain road that passes above the **Loúsios Gorge** *(see pp178–80)*, then continue onwards via **Andrítsaina** *(see p181)*.

> **To extend your trip…**
> The medieval towns of **Monemvasiá** *(see pp190–92)* and **Mystrás** *(see pp196–7)* lie towards the south of the Peloponnese, as do the rocky plains of **Outer Máni** *(see pp198–9)* and **Inner Máni** *(see pp202–203)*.

One Week in Central and Western Greece

- **Arriving** Vólos is served by buses and railway from Athens and Thessaloníki, though you will have to change trains in Lárissa. The nearby airport at Nea Anchialos receives very few international flights at the moment.

- **Transport** The best way to explore Central and Western Greece is by car.

Day 1: Vólos to Argalastí
Before exploring the beautiful, rugged **Pílio** *(see pp222–3)* peninsula, do visit the **Vólos Archaeological Museum** *(see p224)*, which offers plenty of insight into the history of the region. Next, head southeast from Vólos and stop for the night at **Argalastí**. The route via **Miliés** will reveal unspoilt villages, such as cobbled **Vyzítsa**, and stunning scenery.

Day 2: Argalastí to Aráchova
Get an early start, take the coastal road back to Vólos and the motorway to **Lamía**, with its Catalan *kástro*, and **Thermopylae** *(see p228)*, site of the famous battle of 480 BC. After a break, continue on to Livadiá, with its riverside oracle of Trophonios, and nearby ancient Orchomenos. Enjoy a late-afternoon drive to **Aráchova**, which lies on the southern slopes of **Mount Parnassós** *(see p225)*. Soak up views of the Pleistos valley from here.

Pretty waterfront of the historic town of Galaxídi

Day 3: Aráchova to Galaxídi

Aráchova is famous for its wine, noodles and cheese, so be sure to buy some before backtracking slightly to the enchanting **Monastery of Osios Loukás** (see pp226–7). Look out for the wonderful mosaic *Washing of the Apostles' Feet*. Later, set out for **Ancient Delphi** (see pp232–5). Regarded as the mighty god Apollo's home, this ancient site was once considered the centre of the earth. Spend the night in historic **Galaxídi**, with its wonderfully preserved townscape and views back towards Mount Parnassós.

Day 4: Galaxídi to Párga

From Galaxídi, first head west, following the north coast of the **Gulf of Corinth** (see pp228–9), pausing for lunch en route at **Náfpaktos**, with its delightful old port and castle, or at **Mesolóngi** (see p229), where the fare offered is very likely to include smoked eel. Then, head northwest to **Préveza** (see pp216–17), with its castles and old town, perhaps taking a detour to Byzantine **Arta** (see p217). On the hillside between Arta and Párga are the ruins of the 3rd-century-BC city of **Kassope** (see p216).

Day 5: Párga to Ioánnina

Start the day with a leisurely stroll along the theatre-shaped waterfront of **Párga** (see p216). A Venetian fortress guards the harbour; there is another at **Agiá**, 5km (3 miles) north. Next, take the highway to **Dodóni** (see p215) with its theatre, one of the largest in Greece, and **Ioánnina** (see p214), the capital of the region. Take time out to explore Ioánnina before overnighting there, maybe even inside the castle.

Day 6: Around the Víkos Gorge

Get a dawn start to journey up to the trailhead for the **Víkos Gorge** (see p212), which has been carved by the Voïdomátis river over millions of years. Even if you don't actually hike in it, take the time to explore some of the more than 40 stone-built villages of **Zagóri** (see p211) that surround it. Return to your hotel in Ioánnina, or check into one of the many atmospheric village inns near the gorge.

Day 7: Ioánnina to Tríkala

Just off the motorway east, **Métsovo** (see p213) was once the main town of the region's Aroman shepherds and wealthy merchants, who benefited from the town's unusual tax status to build sumptuous mansions. Continuing east on a minor road, you'll notice huge sandstone towers topped by monasteries and hermitages. This is the peaceful and enchanting **Metéora** (see pp220–21). Spend the night in adjacent Kastráki village or nearby Kalambaka, with its fine Byzantine church. Otherwise, **Tríkala** (see p217), around 25 km (15 miles) away, is a possibility, with its pedestrian zones and riverside setting.

The awe-inspiring monasteries at Metéora

For practical information on travelling around Greece, see pp314–23

To extend your trip…
From Kalambáka or Tríkala, there are good express trains back to Athens or, with a change, to either Vólos or Thessaloníki. The rail line to Thessaloníki passes through the Vale of Tempe, where, according to legend, Apollo purified himself after slaying Python at Delphi.

One Week in Northern Greece

- **Arriving** Thessaloníki is the main international airport for northern Greece, with daily flights from many European countries, including the UK.
- **Transport** The best way to explore northern Greece is by car.

Day 1: Thessaloníki
Thessaloníki's *(see pp248–52)* city centre is a bustling place full of elegant buildings, fabulous Byzantine churches – including the largest church in Greece, **Agios Dimítrios** *(see p252)* – plush hotels and lively shopping areas. The **Thessaloníki Archaeological Museum** *(see pp250–51)* houses priceless treasures. Don't miss its collection of gold jewellery; some pieces are more than 2,000 years old.

Day 2: Thessaloníki to Edessa
Spend the morning exploring the ancient sites to the west of Thessaloníki. **Ancient Pélla** *(see p247)* has some of the best-preserved pebble mosaics in Greece, and it is also believed to have been where Alexander the Great was born in 356 BC. Nearby, **Vergína** *(see p246)* is a must-visit destination for its subterranean museum of tomb finds from the Macedonian royal dynasty. There are more tombs to visit at nearby **Lefkádia** *(see pp246–7)*. Afterwards, make your way to **Edessa** *(see p247)* for a late lunch, and enjoy the beautiful surrounding countryside with its waterfalls before overnighting here in the old quarter of Varósi.

Day 3: Edessa to the Préspa Lakes
Head west from Edessa, via **Flórina** – a potential lunch stop – then take the side road to the **Préspa Lakes** *(see pp240–41)*. The two lakes are a major wildlife habitat, especially for birds, and they offer also Byzantine and post-Byzantine monuments. Spend the night at an inn or, for more comfort, choose a hotel in nearby **Kastoriá** *(see p244)*.

Day 4: Kastoriá to Chalkidikí
Spend the morning examining the frescoed Byzantine churches of lakeside Kastoriá. Then, pass through **Siátista** *(see p244)* with its clutch of elegant, visitable mansions, en route to **Véroia** *(see p246)*, where you can have lunch, peek inside the Byzantine museum and stroll through the old Jewish quarter of Barboúta. Then spend the rest of the afternoon driving to your overnight base in **Sithonía** *(see p253)*, one of the three Chalkidikí peninsulas, with great evening views towards **Mount Athos** *(see pp256–8)*.

Day 5: Chalkidikí to Thássos
From Sithonía, take the back roads to ancient Amphipoli, with its famous carved lion and recently discovered, unlooted Macedonian tomb. Arrive in bustling **Kavála** *(see p259)* in time for lunch. Catch its museums before they close, stroll through the medieval Panagía quarter, then take an evening ferry to more peaceful Thássos to spend the night.

Day 6: Thássos to Néstos Valley
After a swim at one of Thássos's lovely beaches, take the ferry to mainland Keramotí, and drive to **Xánthi** *(see p259)*. Neo-Classical mansions, Byzantine churches and Ottoman mosques give this town a distinctive look. After lunch, detour slightly to the coast to see the ruins of ancient **Abdera** *(see p260)*. To the northwest lies the **Néstos Valley** *(see p259)*, where you can follow a trail on the wooded riverbank. Stay overnight in the characterful village of **Stavroúpoli**, gateway to the valley.

Day 7: Néstos Valley to Lake Kerkíni
Get an early start, and drive to **Lake Kerkíni** for a birdwatching tour. Relax, and then overnight at one of the inns around the lake before returning to Thessaloníki airport for your flight out.

To extend your trip…
Mount Olympos *(see p245)* and the unspoilt national park around it are about 80 km (50 miles) southwest of Thessaloníki. More than 1,700 plant species thrive here, along with wild boar, chamois and roe deer. Accommodation is within the park and in the village of Litóhoro, where information and maps are available. Before or after Olympos, pay a visit to the nearby museum and ancient site of Dion.

View of Mount Athos, known as the "monk's republic"

Putting Greece on the Map

Occupying the southernmost tip of the Balkan peninsula, Greece divides into over 2,000 islands stretching from the Ionian Sea in the west to the Aegean Sea in the east. The mainland has borders with Albania, Bulgaria, Turkey and the Former Yugoslav Republic of Macedonia and is home to most of Greece's 10.9 million people, with a third of these in Athens.

CZECH REPUBLIC

POLAND

Kraków
Ostrava
Brno

SLOVAKIA

Košic

Vienna
Bratislava

Budapest

HUNGARY

Oradea

Szeged

Milano

Torino

Venezia

Ljubljana

Zagreb

Trieste

Rijecka

CROATIA

Drava

Timişoara

Genova

Po

Bologna

Firenze

Sava

Belgrade

SERBIA

Nice

Pisa

Ancona

BOSNIA AND
HERZEGOVINA

Sarajevo

Niš

Calvi

Bastia

Split

Ajaccio

Corsica

*Adriatic
Sea*

MONTENEGRO

KOSOVO

Dubrovnik

Podgorica

Skopje

Rome

ITALY

FORMER
YUGOSLAV
REPUBLIC
MACEDON

Olbia

Tirana

Napoli

Bari

Brindisi

ALBANIA

Taranto

Sardinia

*Tyrrhenian
Sea*

Ioánnina

Corfu

Cagliari

Igoumenitsa

Préveza

Kefalloniá

Trapani

Palermo

Messina

Reggio di
Calabria

Pátra

Catania

SICILY

Zákynthos

*Ionian
Sea*

Tunis

Kalamá

TUNISIA

Sousse

Valletta

MALTA

Sfax

*Mediterranean
Sea*

Tripoli

Banghäzi

LIBYA

Key

═══ Motorway

─── Major Road

─── Railway line

----- Ferry route

▒▒▒ National boundary

For keys to symbols *see back flap*

Europe and North Africa

A PORTRAIT OF MAINLAND GREECE

Greece is one of the most visited European countries, yet one of the least known. The modern Greek state dates only from 1830 and bears little relation to the popular image of ancient Greece. At a geographical crossroads, Greece combines elements of the Balkans, Middle East and Mediterranean.

For a relatively small country, less than 132,000 sq km (51,000 sq miles) in area, Greece possesses marked regional differences in topography. Nearly three-quarters of the land is mountainous, uninhabited or uncultivated. Fertile agricultural land supports tobacco farming in the northeast, with orchard fruits and vegetables grown further south. A third of the population lives in the capital, Athens, the cultural, financial and political centre, in which ancient, medieval and modern stand side by side.

Rural and urban life in contemporary Greece have been transformed despite years of occupation and conflict, including a bitter civil war *(see p46)* that would surely have finished off a less resilient people. The society that emerged was supported with US aid, yet Greece remained relatively underdeveloped until the 1960s. Rural areas lacked paved roads and even basic utilities, prompting extensive, unplanned urban growth and emigration. It has been said, with some justice, that there are no architects in Greece, only civil engineers.

For centuries, numerous Greeks have lived abroad; currently there are an estimated 6 million Greeks outside the country. This diaspora occurred in several stages, prompted by changes in the Ottoman Empire late in the 17th century. Most post-war emigration was to Western Europe, the Americas and Australia. With the current economic crisis, emigration has increased again.

Backgammon players at the flea market around Plateía Avyssinías in Athens

◀ Leading a mule on the streets of Monemvasiá

The Pindos mountain range, from above the village of Vrysochóri

Religion, Language and Culture

During the centuries of domination by Venetians and Ottomans *(see pp42–3)*, the Greek Orthodox Church preserved the Greek language, and with it Greek identity, through its liturgy and schools. Today, the Orthodox Church is still a powerful force despite the secularizing reforms of the Panhellenic Socialist Movement (PASOK) government in the 1980s. The query *Eísai Orthódoxos* (Are you Orthodox?) is virtually synonymous with *Éllinas eísai* (Are you Greek?). While no self-respecting couple would dispense with a church wedding and baptisms for their children, civil marriages are now as equally valid in law. Sunday Mass is very popular with women, who often use the services as meeting places for socializing much in the same way as men do the *kafeneía* (cafés).

Parish priests, often recognizable by their tall stovepipe hats and long beards, are not expected to embody the divine, but to transmit it at liturgy. Many marry and have a

Votive offerings in the Pantánassas convent, Mystrás

second trade (a custom that helps keep up the numbers of entrants to the church). There has also been a renaissance in monastic life, perhaps in reaction to the growth of materialism since World War II.

The subtle and beautiful Greek language, another great hallmark of national identity, was for a long time a field of conflict between

Greek priests leading a religious procession in Athens

katharévousa, an artificial, written form hastily devised around the time of Independence, and the slowly evolved *dimotikí*, or everyday speech, with its streamlined grammar and words borrowed from several other languages. The

Tavernas in the town of Náfplio

dispute acquired political overtones, with the Right tending to champion *katharévousa* and the Left *dimotikí*, with blood even being shed at times. Today, the supple and accessible *dimotikí* is the language of the nation.

The art of storytelling is still as prized in Greece as in Homer's time, with conversation pursued for its own sake in *kafeneía* and at dinner parties. The bardic tradition has remained alive with poet-lyricists such as Mános Eleftheríou, Kóstas Vírvos and Níkos Gátsos. The continuous efforts made to produce popular and accessible art have played a key role in helping to keep *dimotikí* alive from the 19th century until the present day.

Both writers and singers, the natural advocates of *dimotikí*, have historically been important to the Greek public. During recent periods of censorship under the dictatorship or in times of foreign occupation, they carried out an essential role as one of the chief sources of coded information and morale-boosting.

Development and Diplomacy

Compared to most of its Balkan neighbours, Greece is a relatively wealthy country. However, by Western economic indicators, Greece is poor and languished at the bottom of the EU league table until the addition of ten new Eastern European countries in 2004. The persistent negative trade deficit is agg-ravated by imports of

An archaeologist helping to restore the Parthenon

luxury goods, an expression of *xenomanía* or belief in the inherent superiority of all things foreign. Cars are most conspicuous among these, since Greece is one of the very few European countries not to manufacture its own.

Greece still bears the hallmarks of a developing economy, with agriculture and the service sector accounting for two-thirds of the GNP. Blurred lines between work and living space are the norm, with professional brass plates alternating with personal bell-buzzer tags in any apartment block. There is a tenacious adherence, despite repeated campaigns against it, to the long afternoon siesta. As a result, some workers have to endure commuting twice a day.

Selling fish at Vólos harbour, the Pílio

Barrels in the Achaïa Klauss winery at Pátra

the largest hard-currency earner, offsetting the depression in world shipping and the fact that Mediterranean agricultural products are duplicated within the EU. Greece's geographical position and difficult-to-defend marine frontiers have long made it a magnet for refugees from the south and east, as well as for overland migration from Albania. But the country was unprepared for the huge number of people fleeing the conflicts in Syria, Iraq and Afghanistan in 2013–16. Early in 2016, a deal was struck with Turkey to forcibly return arrivals.

With EU membership since 1981 and a nominally capitalist orientation, Greece overcame its resemblance to pre-1989 Eastern Europe. After the turn of the millennium, Greece saw growth in its economy above the EU average, but due to uncontrolled government spending and the world financial crisis that started in the late 2000s, the Greek economy collapsed in 2010. Dependent on loans from international creditors offered in exchange for implementing harsh austerity measures, Greece has seen bankruptcies and a sharp rise in unemployment. Tourism remains

Statue of Athena standing beside the Athens Academy

The fact that the Greek state is less than 200 years old, and that it has had much political instability, means that there is little faith in government institutions. Life operates on networks of personal friendships and official contacts. The classic designations of Right and Left only acquired their conventional meanings in the 1930s. The dominant political figure of the first half of the 20th century was Elefthérios Venizélos, an anti-royalist Liberal. The years following World War II have been largely shaped by the influence of three men: the late 1960s premier Geórgios Papandréou (Centre Union); the late Andréas Papandréou, three times

Rooftops of Náfplio and Boúrtzi islet from the Palamídi fortress

House in the village of Psarádes, beside the Préspa lakes

The soliciting and granting of dowries, though officially banned, is still habitual, though arranged marriages are on the wane. Most single young people live with their parents or another relative until married, especially since the economic crisis began, though cohabiting unmarried couples are found everywhere except in small villages. Despite the renowned Greek love of children, the birth rate in the country ranks 21st in the EU and is less than half its pre-World War II levels. Owing in part to reforms in family and inheritance law, urban Greek women have been raised in status. Better represented in medicine and the law, many women run their own businesses. In the country, however, macho attitudes persist and women often forgo the chance of a career for the sake of the house and children. But the country's debt crisis has had a corrosive effect on traditions and values, and predictions as to future political and social trends are fraught with uncertainty.

premier as head of the PASOK; and the late conservative premier (and later president) Konstantínos Karamanlís. Since 2011, political instability has beset Greece, which currently has a coalition government headed by Alexis Tsipras and his anti-bailout Synaspismós Rizospastikís Aristerás (SYRIZA) party.

Since the end of the Cold War, Greece has been asserting its underlying Balkan identity. Relations with Albania have improved since the collapse of the Communist regime in 1990. Despite its economic woes, Greece remains one of the largest foreign investors in Bulgaria, with many Greek businesses relocating there to benefit from the low corporation tax rate. After a rapprochement with the Former Yugoslav Republic of Macedonia, Thessaloníki's port has potential as the future gateway to the southern Balkans.

Man with a shepherd's crook in the village of Métsovo

Home Life

The family is still the basic Greek social unit. Traditionally, one family could sow, plough and reap its own fields, without need of cooperative work parties. Today, family-run businesses are still the norm in urban settings. Family life and social life are usually one and the same, and tend to revolve around eating out, which – despite current straits – is still done more often than in most of Europe.

Wednesday market in Argos

Byzantine Architecture

Medieval churches are virtually all that have survived from
a millennium of Byzantine civilization in Greece. Byzantine
church architecture was concerned almost exclusively with
a decorated interior. The intention was to sculpt out a holy
space where the congregation would be confronted
with the true nature of the cosmos, cleared of all worldly
distractions. The mosaics and frescoes portraying the whole
body of the Church, from Christ downwards, have a dual
purpose: they give inspiration to the worshipper and are
windows to the spiritual world. From a mountain chapel
to an urban church, there is great conformity of design,
with structure and decoration united to a single purpose.

The Best of Byzantine Architecture

① Thessaloníki p252
② Mount Athos pp256–8
③ Arta p217
④ Monastery of Osios Loukás pp226–7
⑤ Metéora pp220–21
⑥ Moní Kaisarianís pp154–5
⑦ Monastery of Daphni pp156–7
⑧ Athens p84, p109, p112
⑨ Mystrás pp196–7
⑩ Geráki p193

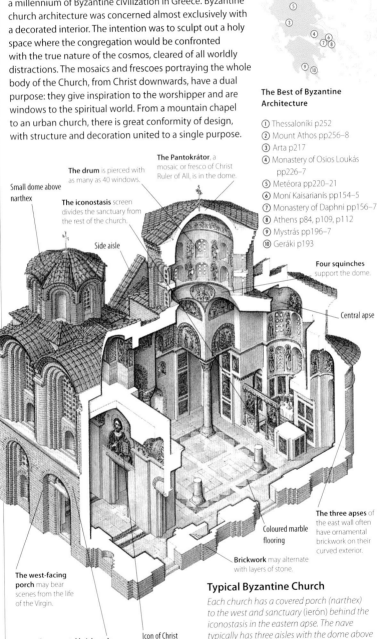

The drum is pierced with as many as 40 windows.

The Pantokrátor, a mosaic or fresco of Christ Ruler of All, is in the dome.

Small dome above narthex

The iconostasis screen divides the sanctuary from the rest of the church.

Side aisle

Four squinches support the dome.

Central apse

The three apses of the east wall often have ornamental brickwork on their curved exterior.

Coloured marble flooring

Brickwork may alternate with layers of stone.

The west-facing porch may bear scenes from the life of the Virgin.

Ornamental brickwork was a 10th-century Greek invention.

Icon of Christ above the main door

Typical Byzantine Church

Each church has a covered porch (narthex) to the west and sanctuary (ierón) behind the iconostasis in the eastern apse. The nave typically has three aisles with the dome above the central square space. In a monastery, the main church is known as the katholikón.

Understanding Frescoes in a Byzantine Church

The frescoes and mosaics in churches' interiors were organized according to a standard scheme. Symbolically, images descended from heaven (Christ Pantokrátor in the dome) to earth (the saints on the lowest level). The Virgin was shown in the semi-dome of the apse, with the fathers of the church below her.

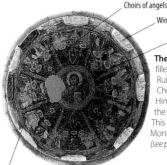

Choirs of angels

Windows in drum

Christ Pantokrátor

The dome is symbolically filled by the figure of Christ Ruler of All, the Pantokrátor. Choirs of angels swirl around Him, and outside them stand the Old Testament prophets. This dome comes from Moní Perivléptou in Mystrás *(see p196).*

Prophets

The Virgin and Child are in the curve of the apse, symbolically between heaven (the dome) and earth (the nave).

Archangels Michael and Gabriel, dressed like courtiers of a Byzantine emperor, honour the Virgin.

The Fathers of Orthodoxy, here in their episcopal robes, defined Orthodoxy in the early centuries.

Upper register of saints

The apse is often hidden from public view by an elaborate iconostasis screen, through whose doors only the clergy are admitted. This apse is from Agios Stratigós in the Máni *(see p203).*

Lower register of saints

Sand-filled tray for votive candles

The side walls are decorated in registers. On the lowest level stand life-size portrayals of the saints, their heads illuminated with haloes. More complex scenes portraying incidents from the Gospels or the Day of Judgment fill the upper walls and vaults. This church is at Miliés in the Pílio *(see pp222–4).*

The Virgin Mary

Icons of the Virgin Mary abound in every Orthodox church, where she is referred to as Panagía, the All Holy. Her exceptional status was confirmed in 431 when she was awarded the title Theotókos "Mother of God", in preference to just "Mother of Christ".

Eleoúsa, meaning "Our Lady of Tenderness", shows the Virgin Mary brushing cheeks with the Christ Child.

The Virgin seated on a throne, flanked by two archangels, is a depiction usually found in the eastern apse.

Odigítria, meaning "She Who Leads", shows the Virgin indicating the Christ Child with her right hand.

The Landscape of Mainland Greece

Greece is a land of rugged beauty. The narrow coastal belt is backed by cliffs in places, while inland, there are massive mountain ranges, gorges and cliffs, the haunt of eagles, hawks and vultures. The fantastic array of vegetation, including many species of spring wild flowers, is strongly influenced by the Mediterranean climate of long, hot and dry summers and mild, wet winters. Clearance of forests for agriculture and timber has produced a mosaic of flower-rich fields and areas of shrubs. This shrubland habitat is of two kinds: the dense aromatic bushes of *maquis* and the sparser *phrygana* with lower, more compact plants. Although the country's millions of goats destroy the vegetation with their constant grazing, one of the most romantic sights in Greece is that of flocks being herded through olive groves full of archaeological remains, as at Sparta in the Peloponnese.

Abandoned areas of cultivation soon revert to the wild. Larks and pipits feed and nest here and, in spring, wild flowers and butterflies are abundant.

Phrygana often covers bare slopes and rocky outcrops.

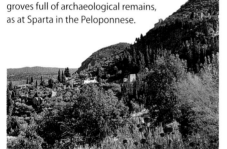

Hilly landscapes with stately cypress trees standing tall and dark against the steep slopes are closely associated with Greece's archaeological sites. These, including the Byzantine town of Mystrás above, are worth visiting for their wildlife alone, and in particular, the spring wild flowers that mix rare orchids with daisies, poppies and crocuses.

Olive trees harbour numerous birds and insects among their silvery-green foliage.

Spring flowers such as poppies and irises, have a brief but prolific season.

Maquis and Phrygana

Maquis *shrubland dominates the landscape in this view of Mycenae. It is a mixture of rockroses and aromatic herbs. The more barren* phrygana, *in the far distance, has clumps of spiny vetches.*

Olive groves are found all over Greece at low altitudes; this one is at Argalastí in the Pílio. In spring, flowers grow in profusion in the shade of trees and attract a wealth of butterflies and beetles. Lizards hunt for insects in the twisted trunks that also provide nesting places for birds such as masked shrikes.

Wetland areas, such as the margins of Lake Stymfalía in the Peloponnese, are often used for farming. Usually fairly dry underfoot, they are rich in birds, amphibians and plants.

Wild Flowers of Greece

Greece is blessed with an extraordinary wealth of flowering plants. At least 6,000 species grow in the country, quite a few of them found nowhere else in the world. The floral richness is due in part to the country's diversity of habitats, ranging from wetlands, coastal plains and lowland *maquis* to snow-capped mountain tops. The growing period for many plants is winter, the dampest, coolest season, and the flowering periods run from January to early June, and again in September to October. Coastal areas of the Peloponnese are perhaps the richest in wild flowers.

The wild gladiolus has several varieties that are among the most showy spring flowers.

The tassel hyacinth is aptly named for its appearance. It grows on open ground and flowers in May.

Cytinus hypocistus is a parasite plant found growing close to the base of colourful cistus bushes (*see below*).

Sage-leaved cistus is widespread in *maquis* habitats. Its colourful flowers attract pollinating insects.

White asphodel is often seen growing on roadside verges in many parts of Greece. Tall spikes of white flowers appear from April to June.

Areas of *maquis* provide ideal habitats for nesting birds such as warblers, serins and hoopoes.

Between the shrubs in open areas of *maquis*, orchids, tulips and other native flowers appear in the spring.

Orchids

One of the botanical highlights of a visit to Greece is the range of wild orchid species that can be found in bloom between late February and May. All have strangely shaped, and sometimes colourful, flowers whose purpose is to attract pollinating insects.

The four-spotted orchid has spots on the flower lip. A plant of open hillsides, it flowers in April.

The naked man orchid has a dense head of pale pinkish flowers and favours open woodland.

The Greek spider orchid looks more like a bumblebee than a spider. It is found in *maquis* in early spring.

THE HISTORY OF GREECE

The history of Greece is that of a nation, not of a land: the Greek idea of nationality is governed by language, religion, descent and customs, not so much by geography. Early Greek history is the story of internal struggles, from the Mycenaean and Minoan cultures of the Bronze Age to the competing city-states that emerged in the 1st millennium BC.

After the defeat of the Greek army by Philip II of Macedon at Chaironeia in 338 BC, Greece was absorbed into Alexander the Great's Asian empire. With the defeat of the Macedonians by the Romans in 168 BC, Greece became a province of the Roman Empire. As part of the Eastern Empire, she was ruled from Constantinople and in the 11th century became a powerful element within the new, Orthodox Christian, Byzantine world.

After 1453, when Constantinople fell to the Ottomans, Greece as a political entity disappeared altogether. Eventually, the realization that it was the democracy of Classical Athens which had inspired so many revolutions abroad gave the Greeks themselves the courage to rebel and, in 1821, to start the Greek War of Independence. In 1830, the Great Powers that dominated Europe established a protectorate over Greece which marked the end of Ottoman rule. Greece re-established itself as a sizeable state, but the "Great Idea" – the ambition to re-create Byzantium – ended after Greece's disastrous defeat in the Greco-Turkish War (1919–22).

The instability of the ensuing years was followed by the Metaxás dictatorship and then by the war years (1940–48), during which half a million people were killed. The present boundaries of the Greek state have only existed since 1948, when Italy returned the Dodecanese. Now, as an established, if still turbulent, democracy and member of the European Union, Greece's fortunes seem to have come full circle after 2,000 years of foreign rule.

A map of Greece from the 1595 Atlas of Abraham Ortelius called *Theatrum Orbis Terrarum*
◄ The 1821 Greek Revolution as shown in 1825 by Louis Dupré

Prehistoric Greece

During the Bronze Age, three separate civilizations flourished in Greece: the Cycladic, during the 3rd millennium; the Minoan, based on Crete but with an influence that spread throughout the Aegean islands; and the Mycenaean, which was based on the mainland but spread to Crete in about 1450 BC when the Minoans went into decline. Both the Minoan and Mycenaean cultures found their peak in the Palace periods of the 2nd millennium when they were dominated by a centralized religion and bureaucracy.

Prehistoric Greece

Areas settled in the Bronze Age

Neolithic Head (3000 BC)
This figure was found on Alónissos in the Sporades. It probably represents a fertility goddess who was worshipped by farmers to ensure a good harvest. These figures indicate a certain stability in early communities.

The town is unwalled, showing that inhabitants did not fear attack.

Multistorey houses

Cycladic Figurine
Marble statues such as this, produced in the Bronze Age from about 2800 to 2300 BC, have been found in a number of tombs in the Cyclades.

Minoan "Bathtub" Sarcophagus
This type of coffin, dating to 1400 BC, is found only in Minoan art. It was probably used for a high-status burial.

7000 Neolithic farmers in northern Greece

3200 Beginnings of Bronze Age cultures in the Cyclades and Crete

2000 Arrival of first Greek-speakers on mainland Greece

| 200,000 BC | 5000 BC | 4000 BC | 3000 BC | 2000 |

200,000 Evidence of Palaeolithic civilization in northern Greece and Thessaly

"Frying Pan" vessel from Sýros (2500–2000 BC)

2800–2300 Kéros-Sýros culture flourishes in the Cyclades

2000 Building of palaces begins in Crete, initiating First Palace period

Mycenaean Death Mask
Large amounts of worked gold were discovered at wealthy Mycenae, the city of Agamemnon. Masks like this were laid over the faces of the dead.

Forested hills

The inhabitants are on friendly terms with the visitors.

Cyclopean Walls
Mycenaean citadels, such as this one at Tiryns, were encircled by walls of stone so large that later civilizations believed they had been built by giants. It is unclear whether the walls were used for defence or just to impress.

Oared sailing ships

Minoan Sea Scene
The wall paintings on the island of Santoríni were preserved by the volcanic eruption towards the end of the 17th century BC. This section shows ships departing from a coastal town. In contrast to the warlike Mycenaeans, Minoan art reflects a more stable community which dominated the Aegean through trade, not conquest.

Mycenaean Octopus Jar
This 14th-century BC vase's decoration follows the shape of the pot. Restrained and symmetrical, it contrasts with relaxed Minoan prototypes.

1750–1700 Start of Second Palace period and golden age of Minoan culture in Crete

1620 Volcanic eruption on Santoríni devastates the region

1250–1200 Probable destruction of Troy, after abduction of Helen (see p58)

1450 Mycenaeans take over Knosós; use of Linear B script

Helen of Troy

| **1800 BC** | **1600 BC** | **1400 BC** | **1200 BC** |

1730 Destruction of Minoan palaces; end of First Palace period

1200 Collapse of Mycenaean culture

Minoan figurine of a snake goddess, 1500 BC

1600 Beginning of high period of Mycenaean prosperity and dominance

1370–50 Palace of Knosós on Crete destroyed for second time

The Dark Ages and Archaic Period

After 1200 BC, Greece entered a period of darkness. There was widespread poverty, the population decreased and many skills were lost. A cultural revival in about 800 BC accompanied the emergence of the city-states across Greece and inspired new styles of warfare, art and politics. Greek colonies were established as far away as the Black Sea, present-day Syria, North Africa and the western Mediterranean. Greece was defined by where Greeks lived.

Koúros (530 BC)
Koúroi were early monumental male nude statues *(see p74)*. Idealized representations rather than portraits, they were inspired by Egyptian statues, from which they take their frontal, forward-stepping pose.

Bronze breastplate

Locator Map
Areas of Greek influence

The double flute player kept the men marching in time.

Bronze greaves protected the legs.

Solon (640–558 BC)
Solon was appointed to the highest magisterial position in Athens. His legal, economic and political reforms heralded democracy.

Hoplite Warriors

The "Chigi" vase from Corinth, dating to about 750 BC, is one of the earliest clear depictions of the new style of warfare that evolved at that period. This required rigorously trained and heavily armed infantrymen called hoplites to fight in a massed formation or phalanx. The rise of the city-state may be linked to the spirit of equality felt by citizen hoplites fighting for their own community.

Vase fragment showing bands of distinctive geometric line patterns

900
Appearance of first Geometric pottery

1100 BC

1000 BC

900 BC

1100 Migrations of different peoples throughout the Greek world

1000–850 Formation of the Homeric kingdoms

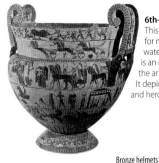

6th-Century Vase
This bowl *(krater)* for mixing wine and water at elegant feasts is an early example of the art of vase painting. It depicts mythological and heroic scenes.

Where to See Archaic Greece

Examples of *koúroi* can be found in the National Archaeological Museum *(pp72–75)* and in the Acropolis Museum *(p104)*, both in Athens. The National Archaeological Museum also houses the national collection of Greek Geometric, red-figure and black-figure vases. The first victory over the Persians in 490 BC was commemorated by the mound of Athenian dead which still dominates the plain at Marathon *(p149)*. The museum at Spárti *(p193)* contains a bust of Leonidas, the Spartan king, who with his 300 hoplite soldiers, was massacred by the Persians at Thermopylae in 480 BC.

Bronze helmets for protection

Spears were used for thrusting.

The phalanxes shoved and pushed, aiming to maintain an unbroken shield wall, a successful new technique.

Gorgon's head decoration

Characteristic round shields

Hunter Returning Home
(500 BC) Hunting for hare, deer, or wild boar was an aristocratic sport pursued by Greek nobles on foot with dogs, as depicted on this cup.

Darius I (ruled 521–486 BC)
This relief from Persepolis shows the Persian king who tried to conquer the Greek mainland, but was defeated at the battle of Marathon in 490.

776 Traditional date for the first Olympic Games

675 Lykourgos initiates austere reforms in Sparta

600 First Doric columns built at Temple of Hera, Olympia

Doric capital

490 Athenians defeat Persians at Marathon

800 BC	700 BC	600 BC	500 BC

770 Greeks start founding colonies in Italy, Egypt and elsewhere

750–700 Homer records epic tales of the *Iliad* and *Odyssey*

Spartan votive figurine

546 Persians gain control over Ionian Greeks; Athens flourishes under the tyrant Peisistratos and his sons

630 Poetess Sappho writing in Lésvos

480 Athens destroyed by Persians who defeat Spartans at Thermopylae; Greek victory at Salamis

479 Persians annihilated at Plataiai by Athenians, Spartans and allies

Classical Greece

The Classical period has always been considered the high point of Greek civilization. Around 150 years of exceptional creativity in thinking, writing, theatre and the arts produced the great tragedians Aeschylus, Sophokles and Euripides, as well as the great philosophical thinkers Socrates, Plato and Aristotle. This was also a time of warfare and bloodshed, however. The Peloponnesian War, which pitted the city-state of Athens and her allies against the city-state of Sparta and her allies, dominated the latter 5th century BC. In the 4th century, Sparta, Athens and Thebes struggled for power, only to be ultimately defeated by Philip II of Macedon in 338 BC.

Classical Greece, 440 BC

▦ *Athens and her allies*

☐ *Sparta and her allies*

Fish Shop
This detail is from a 4th- century BC Greek painted vase from Cefalù in Sicily. Large parts of the island were inhabited by Greeks who were bound by a common culture, religion and language.

Theatre used in Pythian Games

Temple of Apollo

Siphnian Treasury

The Sanctuary of Delphi
The sanctuary (see pp232–3), shown in this 1894 reconstruction, reached the peak of its political influence in the 5th and 4th centuries BC. Of central importance was the Oracle of Apollo, whose utterances influenced the decisions of city-states such as Athens and Sparta. Rich gifts dedicated to the god were placed by the states in treasuries that lined the Sacred Way.

Perikles
This great democratic leader built up the Greek navy and masterminded the extensive building programme in Athens between the 440s and 420s, including the Acropolis temples.

Detail of the Parthenon frieze

462 Ephialtes's reforms pave the way for radical democracy in Athens

431–404 Peloponnesian War, ending with the fall of Athens and start of 33-year period of Spartan dominance

c.424 Death of Herodotus, historian of the Persian Wars

475 BC

450 BC

425 BC

478 With the formation of the Delian League, Athens takes over leadership of Greek cities

451–429 Perikles rises to prominence in Athens and launches a lavish building programme

447 Construction of the Parthenon begins

Bust of Herodotus, probably of Hellenistic origin

Gold Oak Wreath from Vergína
By the mid-4th century BC, Philip II of Macedon dominated the Greek world through diplomacy and warfare. This wreath comes from his tomb.

Where to See Classical Greece

Athens is dominated by the Acropolis and its religious buildings, including the Parthenon, erected as part of Perikles's mid 5th-century BC building programme *(pp98–103)*. The Marmaria, just outside the sanctuary at Delphi, features the remains of the unique circular *tholos (p234)*. In the Peloponnese, the town of Messene dates from 396 BC *(p205)*; the best-preserved theatre is at Epidaurus *(pp188–9)*. Philip II's tomb can be seen at Vergína in Macedonia *(p246)*.

Votive of the Rhodians

Stoa of the Athenians

Sacred Way

Athenian Treasury

Slave Boy (400 BC)
Slaves were fundamental to the Greek economy and used for all types of work. Many slaves were foreign; this boot boy came from as far as Africa.

Athena Lemnia
This Roman copy of a statue by Pheidias (c.490–c.430 BC), the sculptor-in-charge at the Acropolis, depicts the goddess protector of Athens in an idealized rather than realistic way, typical of the Classical style in art.

387 Plato founds Academy in Athens

Sculpture of Plato

359 Philip II becomes King of Macedon

337 Foundation of the League of Corinth legitimizes Philip II's control over the Greek city-states

400 BC

375 BC

350 BC

399 Trial and execution of Socrates

371 Sparta defeated by Thebes at Battle of Leuktra, heralding a decade of Theban dominance in the area

338 Greeks defeated by Philip II of Macedon at Battle of Chaironeia

336 Philip II is killed at Aigai and is succeeded by his son, Alexander

Hellenistic Greece

Alexander the Great of Macedon fulfilled his
father Philip's plans for the conquest of the
Persians. He went on to create a vast empire that
extended to India in the east and Egypt in the
south. The Hellenistic period was extraordinary
for the dispersal of Greek language, religion and
culture throughout the territories conquered by
Alexander. It lasted from after Alexander's death
in 323 BC until the Romans began to dismantle
his empire, early in the 2nd century BC. For
Greece, Macedonian domination was replaced
by that of Rome in AD 168.

Relief of Hero-Worship
(c.200 BC) The worship
of heroes after death
was a feature of Greek
religion. Alexander,
however, was worshipped
as a god in his lifetime.

The Mausoleum of
Halikarnassos was one
of the Seven Wonders
of the Ancient World.

Issus, in modern Turkey,
was the site of Alexander's
victory over the Persian
army in 333 BC.

Pella was the birthplace of
Alexander and capital of Macedon.

Black Sea

• Pella

• Athens

• Issus

*Mediterranean
Sea*

Ammon •

Egypt

Red Sea

Arabia

Alexander Defeats Darius III
This Pompeiian mosaic shows the
Persian leader overwhelmed at Issus
in 333 BC. Macedonian troops are
shown carrying their highly effective
long pikes.

Alexander died in
Babylon in 323 BC.

The Ammon oracle
declared Alexander
to be divine.

Alexandria, founded by
Alexander, replaced Athens
as the centre of Greek culture.

Terracotta Statue
This 2nd-century BC
statue of two women
gossiping is typical of
a Hellenistic interest
in private rather than
public individuals.

Key

••• Alexander's route

▨ Alexander's empire

▨ Dependent regions

333 Alexander the Great defeats
the Persian king, Darius III, and
declares himself king of Asia

323 Death of Alexander,
and of Diogenes

301 Battle of Ipsus, between
Alexander's rival successors,
leads to the break-up of his
empire into three kingdoms

268–261
Chremonidean War,
ending with the
capitulation of Athens
to Macedon

325 BC | **300 BC** | **275 BC** | **250 BC**

322 Death
of Aristotle

287–275 "Pyrrhic
victory" of King Pyrros
of Epirus who defeated
the Romans in Italy but
suffered heavy losses

*Diogenes, the Hellenistic
philosopher*

331 Alexander founds
Alexandria after
conquering Egypt

Fusing Eastern and Western Religion

This plaque from Afghanistan shows the Greek goddess Nike and the Asian goddess Cybele in a chariot pulled by lions.

Where to See Hellenistic Greece

The royal palace at Pella (p247), capital of Macedon and birthplace of Alexander, and the palace of Palatítsia (p246) are exceptional. Pella has outstanding mosaics, one of which depicts Alexander. Goldwork and other finds are in the museum at Pella and the Archaeological Museum at Thessaloníki (pp250–51). In Athens, the Stoa of Attalos (p94) in the Greek Agora was given by Attalos of Pergamon (ruled 159 to 138 BC). The Tower of the Winds (pp90–91) in the Roman Agora, built by the Macedonian astronomer Andronikos Kyrrestes, incorporated a water clock.

Susa, capital of the Persian Empire, was captured in 331 BC. A mass wedding of Alexander's captains to Asian brides was held in 324 BC.

Alexander chose his wife, Roxane, from among Sogdian captives in 327 BC.

Battle elephants were used against the Indian King Poros in 326 BC.

Alexander's army turned back at the River Beas.

Caspian Sea

Sogdiani

Alexandropolis

Taxil

Bactria

Persia

Susa

Persian Gulf

Gedrosia

Indus

India

Arabian Sea

The Persian religious centre of Persepolis, in modern Iran, fell to Alexander in 330 BC.

Alexander's army suffered heavy losses in the Gedrosia desert.

The Death of Archimedes

Archimedes was the leading Hellenistic scientist and mathematician. This mosaic from Renaissance Italy shows his murder in 212 BC by a Roman.

Alexander the Great's Empire

In forming his empire, Alexander covered huge distances. After defeating the Persians in Asia, he moved to Egypt, then returned to Asia to pursue Darius, and then his murderers, into Bactria. In 326 BC, his troops revolted in India and refused to go on. Alexander died in 323 BC in Babylon.

---

227 Colossus of Rhodes destroyed by earthquake

Colossus of Rhodes

197 Romans defeat Philip V of Macedon and declare Greece liberated

146 Romans sack Corinth and Greece becomes a province of Rome

225 BC	**200 BC**	**175 BC**	**150 BC**

217 Peace of Nafpaktos: a call for the Greeks to settle their differences before "the cloud in the west" (Rome) settles over them

168 Macedonians defeated by Romans at Pydna

222 Macedon crushes Sparta

Roman coin commemorating Roman victory over the Macedonians in 196 BC

Roman Greece

After the Romans gained final control of Greece, with the sack of Corinth in 146 BC, Greece became the cultural centre of the Roman Empire. The Roman nobility sent their sons to be educated in the schools of philosophy in Athens *(see p61)*. The end of the Roman civil wars between leading Roman statesmen was played out on Greek soil, finishing in the Battle of Actium in Epirus in 31 BC. In AD 323, the Emperor Constantine founded the new eastern capital of Constantinople; the empire was later divided into the Greek-speaking East and the Latin-speaking West.

Roman Provinces, AD 211

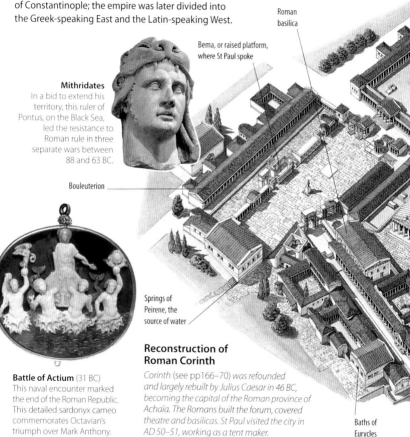

Roman basilica

Bema, or raised platform, where St Paul spoke

Mithridates
In a bid to extend his territory, this ruler of Pontus, on the Black Sea, led the resistance to Roman rule in three separate wars between 88 and 63 BC.

Bouleuterion

Springs of Peirene, the source of water

Battle of Actium (31 BC)
This naval encounter marked the end of the Roman Republic. This detailed sardonyx cameo commemorates Octavian's triumph over Mark Anthony.

Reconstruction of Roman Corinth

Corinth (see pp166–70) was refounded and largely rebuilt by Julius Caesar in 46 BC, becoming the capital of the Roman province of Achaïa. The Romans built the forum, covered theatre and basilicas. St Paul visited the city in AD 50–51, working as a tent maker.

Baths of Eurycles

A coin of Cleopatra, Queen of Egypt

49–31 BC Rome's civil wars end with the defeat of Mark Antony and Cleopatra at Actium, in Greece

AD 49–54 St Paul preaches Christianity in Greece

AD 124–131 Emperor Hadrian oversees huge building programme in Athens

100 BC

AD 1

AD 10[0]

86 BC Roman commander, Sulla, captures Athens

46 BC Corinth refounded as a Roman colony

AD 66–7 Emperor Nero tours Greece

St Paul preaching

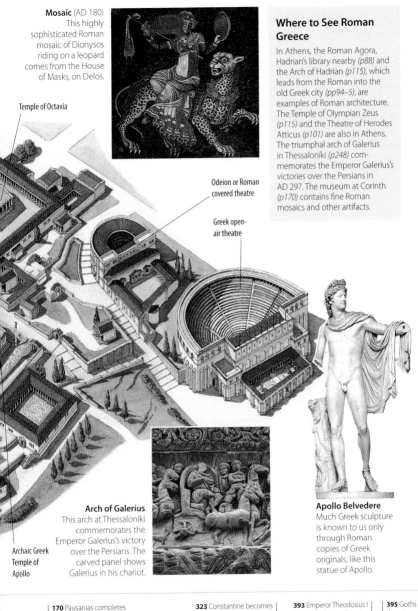

Mosaic (AD 180) This highly sophisticated Roman mosaic of Dionysos riding on a leopard comes from the House of Masks, on Delos.

Temple of Octavia

Where to See Roman Greece

In Athens, the Roman Agora, Hadrian's library nearby (p88) and the Arch of Hadrian (p115), which leads from the Roman into the old Greek city (pp94–5), are examples of Roman architecture. The Temple of Olympian Zeus (p115) and the Theatre of Herodes Atticus (p101) are also in Athens. The triumphal arch of Galerius in Thessaloníki (p248) commemorates the Emperor Galerius's victories over the Persians in AD 297. The museum at Corinth (p170) contains fine Roman mosaics and other artifacts.

Odeion or Roman covered theatre

Greek open-air theatre

Archaic Greek Temple of Apollo

Arch of Galerius This arch at Thessaloníki commemorates the Emperor Galerius's victory over the Persians. The carved panel shows Galerius in his chariot.

Apollo Belvedere Much Greek sculpture is known to us only through Roman copies of Greek originals, like this statue of Apollo.

170 Pausanias completes guide to Greece for Roman travellers

267 Goths pillage Athens

323 Constantine becomes sole emperor of Roman Empire and establishes his capital in Constantinople

393 Emperor Theodosius I bans all non-Christian religious practices, including the Olympic Games

395 Goths devastate Athens and Peloponnese

AD 200

AD 300

Coin of the Roman Emperor Galerius

293 Under Emperor Galerius, Thessaloníki becomes second city to Constantinople

395 Death of Theodosius I; formal division of Roman Empire into Latin West and Byzantine East

Byzantine and Crusader Greece

Under the Byzantine Empire, which succeeded the old Eastern Roman Empire at the end of the 4th century, Greece became Orthodox in religion and was split into administrative *themes*. When the capital, Constantinople, fell to the Crusaders in 1204, Greece was again divided, mostly between the Venetians and the Franks. Constantinople and Mystrás were recovered by the Byzantine Greeks in 1261, but the Ottomans' capture of Constantinople in 1453, and of Trebizond and Mystrás in 1460–61, meant the end of the Byzantine Empire. It left a legacy of hundreds of churches and a wealth of religious art.

Byzantine Greece in the 10th Century

Chapel

Watch-tower of Tsimiskís

Refectory

Great Lavra

This monastery is the earliest (AD 963) and largest of the religious complexes on Mount Athos (see pp256–8). Many parts of it have been rebuilt, but its appearance remains essentially Byzantine. The monasteries became important centres of learning and religious art.

Two-Headed Eagle
The double-headed eagle was an omnipresent symbol of the power of the Byzantine Empire in this era.

Defence of Thessaloníki
The fall of Thessaloníki to the Saracens in AD 904 was a blow to the Byzantine Empire. Many towns in Greece were heavily fortified against attack from this time.

578–86 Avars and Slavs invade Greece

Gold solidus of the Byzantine Empress Irene, who ruled AD 797–802

400	600	800

529 Aristotle's and Plato's schools of philosophy close as Christian culture supplants Classical thought

680 Bulgars cross Danube and establish empire in northern Greece

726 Iconoclasm introduced by Pope Leo III (abandoned in 843)

841 Parthenon becomes a cathedral

Constantine the Great
The first eastern emperor to recognize Christianity, Constantine founded the city of Constantinople in AD 324. Here, he is shown with his mother, Helen.

Where to See Byzantine and Crusader Greece

In Athens, both the Benáki (pp82–3) and the Byzantine and Christian (p80) museums contain sculpture, icons, textiles and metalwork. The medieval city of Mystrás (pp196–7) has a castle, palaces, houses and monasteries. The churches of Thessaloníki (p252) and the monasteries of Daphni (pp156–7) and Osios Loukás (pp226–7) contain fine Byzantine mosaics and frescoes, as do the monasteries of Mount Athos (pp256–8). Chlemoútsi (p173), built in 1223, is one of Greece's oldest Frankish castles. There are important fortresses at Acrocorinth (p170) and Monemvasiá (pp190–92).

Cypress tree of Agios Athanásios

Christ Pantokrátor
This 14th-century fresco of Christ as ruler of the world is in the Byzantine city and monastic centre of Mystrás.

Fortified walls

Chapel of Agios Athanásios, founder of Great Lavra

Combined library and treasury

The *katholikón*, the main church in Great Lavra, has the most magnificent post-Byzantine murals on Mount Athos.

1054 Patriarch of Constantinople and Pope Leo IX excommunicate each other

1081–1149 Normans invade Greek islands and mainland

Frankish Chlemoútsi Castle

1354 Ottoman Turks enter Europe via southern Italy and Greece

1390–1450 Turks gain power over much of mainland Greece

1000

1200

1400

Basil the Bulgar Slayer, Byzantine emperor (lived 956–1025)

1204 Crusaders sack Constantinople. Break-up of Byzantine Empire as result of occupation by Franks and Venetians

1210 Venetians win control over Crete

1261 Start of artistic and intellectual growth of Mystrás; Constantinople reoccupied by Byzantines

1389 Venetians in control of much of Greece and the islands

Venetian and Ottoman Greece

Following the Ottomans' momentous capture of Constantinople in 1453, and their conquest of almost all the remaining Greek territory by 1461, the Greek state effectively ceased to exist for the next 350 years. Although the city became the capital of the vast Ottoman Empire, it remained the principal centre of Greek population and the focus of Greek dreams of resurgence. The small Greek population of what today is modern Greece languished in an impoverished and underpopulated backwater, but even there, rebellious bands of brigands and private militias were formed. The Ionian Islands, Crete and a few coastal enclaves were seized for long periods by the Venetians – an experience more intrusive than the inefficient tolerance of the Ottomans, but one which left a rich cultural and architectural legacy.

Locator Map
- Areas occupied by Venetians
- Areas occupied by Ottomans

Battle of Lepanto (1571)
The Christian fleet, under Don John of Austria, decisively defeated the Ottomans off Náfpaktos, halting their advance westwards *(see p229)*.

Cretan Painting
This 15th-century icon is typical of the style developed by Greek artists in the School of Crete, active until the Ottomans took Crete in 1669.

Arrival of Turkish Prince Cem on Rhodes

Prince Cem, Ottoman rebel and son of Mehmet II, fled to Rhodes in 1481 and was welcomed by the Christian Knights of St John. In 1522, however, Rhodes fell to the Ottomans after a siege.

1453 Mehmet II captures Constantinople, which is renamed Istanbul and made capital of the Ottoman Empire

1503 Ottoman Turks win control of the Peloponnese apart from Monemvasiá

1571 Venetian and Spanish fleet defeats Ottoman Turks at the Battle of Lepanto

1500 **1550** **1600**

1460 Turks capture Mystrás

1456 Ottoman Turks occupy Athens

1522 The Knights of St John forced to cede Rhodes to the Ottomans

Cretan chain mail armour from the 16th century

Shipping
Greek merchants traded throughout the Ottoman Empire. By 1800, there were merchant colonies in Constantinople and as far afield as London and Odessa. This 19th-century embroidery shows the Turkish influence on Greek decorative arts.

Where to See Venetian and Ottoman Architecture

Náfplio (pp186–7) contains many examples of the Venetian presence, especially the Naval Warehouse (now a museum) and the Palamídi fortress (p187). Following a pattern familiar throughout the Balkan states, enormous efforts were made after Independence to remove or disguise all Ottoman buildings. However, Náfplio retains two mosques, in Athens there are small but well-preserved Ottoman buildings in the Pláka district, and the Tzistarákis Mosque (now the Ceramic Museum, p90) is also Ottoman. The White Tower in Thessaloníki (p248) was built by the Turks in the 16th century. In Kavála (p259), there is an aqueduct built during the reign of Suuleyman the Magnificent, and in Ioánnina (p214), the Aslan Pasha Mosque dates from 1618.

The Knights of St John defied the Ottomans until 1522.

The massive fortifications eventually succumbed to Ottoman artillery.

The Knights supported Ottoman rebel, Prince Cem.

Dinner at a Greek House in 1801
Nearly four centuries of Ottoman rule profoundly affected Greek culture, ethnic composition and patterns of everyday life. Greek cuisine incorporates Turkish dishes still found thoughout the old Ottoman Empire.

1687 Parthenon seriously damaged during Venetian artillery attack on Turkish magazine

1715 Turks reconquer the Peloponnese

Ali Pasha (1741–1822), a governor of the Ottoman Empire

1814 Britain gains possession of Ionian Islands

1650 | **1700** | **1750** | **1800**

1684 Venetians reconquer the Peloponnese

Parthenon blown up

1778 Ali Pasha becomes Vizier of Ioánnina and establishes powerful state in Albania and northern Greece

1801 Frieze on Parthenon removed by Lord Elgin

1814 Foundation of *Filikí Etaireía*, Greek liberation movement

The Making of Modern Greece

The Greek War of Independence marked the overthrow of the Ottomans and the start of the "Great Idea", an ambitious project to bring all Greek people under one flag. The plans for expansion were initially successful, and during the 19th century, the Greeks succeeded in doubling their national territory and reasserting Greek sovereignty over many of the islands. However, an attempt to take Asia Minor by force after World War I ended in disaster. In 1922, 1.5 million Greeks were expelled from Smyrna in Turkish Anatolia, ending thousands of years of Greek presence in Asia Minor.

The Emerging Greek State

Greece in 1832

Areas gained 1832–1923

Klephts (mountain brigands) were the basis of the Independence movement.

Massacre at Chíos
This detail of Delacroix's shocking painting *Scènes de Massacres de Scio* shows the events of 1822, when the Ottomans took savage revenge for the island having joined the War of Independence.

Weapons were family heirlooms or donated by philhellenes.

Declaration of the Constitution in Athens
Greece's Neo-Classical parliament building in Athens was the site of the Declaration of the Constitution in 1843. It was built as the Royal Palace for Greece's first monarch, King Otto, during the 1830s.

1824 The poet Lord Byron dies of a fever at Mesolóngi

1831 President Kapodístrias assassinated

1832 Great Powers establish protectorate over Greece and appoint Otto, Bavarian prince, as king

1834 Athens replaces Náfplio as capital

German archaeologist Heinrich Schliemann

1830   **1840**   **1850**   **1860**   **1870**

1827 Battle of Navaríno

1828 Ioánnis Kapodístrias becomes first president of Greece

King Otto (ruled 1832–62)

1862 Revolution drives King Otto from Greece

1874 Heinrich Schliemann begins excavation of Mycenae

1821 Greek flag of independence raised on 25 March; Greeks massacre Turks at Tripolitsá in Morea

1864 New constitution makes Greece a "crowned democracy"; Greek Orthodoxy made the state religion

Life in Athens

By 1836, urban Greeks still wore a mixture of Greek traditional and Western dress. The Ottoman legacy had not totally disappeared and is visible in the fez worn by men.

Where to See 19th-century Greece

Independence was proclaimed at Agías Lávras monastery, near Kalávryta (p172). Lord Byron died at Mesolóngi (p229). Ioánnis Kapodístrias was assassinated at the church of Agios Spyrídon in Náfplio (p186). Pýlos is the site of the battle of Navaríno (p204).

Flag Raising of 1821 Revolution

In 1821, the Greek secret society Filikí Etaireía *was behind a revolt by Greek officers which led to anti-Muslim uprisings throughout the Peloponnese. Tradition credits Archbishop Germanós of Pátra with raising the rebel flag near Kalávryta (see p172) on 25 March. The struggle for independence had begun.*

Corinth Canal

This spectacular link between the Aegean and Ionian seas opened in 1893 *(see p171).*

Elefthérios Venizélos

This great Cretan politician and advocate of liberal democracy doubled Greek territory during the Balkan Wars (1912–13) and joined the Allies in World War I.

1919 Greece launches offensive in Asia Minor

1893 Opening of Corinth Canal

1896 First Olympics of modern era, held in Athens

1908 Crete united with Greece

1917 King Constantine resigns; Greece joins Entente in World War I

1922 Turkish burning of Smyrna signals end of the "Great Idea"

1880	1890	1900	1910	1920

Spyrídon Loúis, marathon winner at the first modern Olympics

1899 Arthur Evans begins excavations at Knosós

1912–13 Greece extends its borders during the Balkan Wars

1920 Treaty of Sèvres gives Greece huge gains in territory

1923 Population exchange agreed between Greece and Turkey at Treaty of Lausanne. Greece loses previous gains

Modern Greece

The years after the 1922 defeat by Turkey were terrible ones for Greek people. The influx of refugees contributed to the political instability of the interwar years. The dictatorship of Metaxás was followed by invasion in 1940, then Italian, German and Bulgarian occupation and, finally, Civil War between 1946 and 1949, with its legacy of division. After experiencing the Cyprus problem of the 1950s to 1970s and the military dictatorship of 1967 to 1974, Greece is now an established democracy and a member of the European Union.

Barber shop in Marousi, a painting by Yannis Tsaroúchis

1938 Death of sculptor Giannoúlis Chalepás, best known for his *Sleeping Beauty* funerary statue

1946 Government institutes "White Terror" against Communists

1947 Internationally acclaimed Greek artist Yannis Tsaroúchis holds his first exhibition of set designs, in the Romvos Gallery, Athens

1957 Mosaics found by chance at Philip II's 300 BC palace at Pella

1933 Death of Greek poet Constantine (C P) Cavafy

1945 Níkos Kazantzákis publishes *Zorba the Greek*, later made into a film

1967 Right-wing colonels form Junta, forcing King Constantine into exile

1925	1935	1945	1955	1965

1925	1935	1945	1955	1965

1939 Greece declares neutrality at start of World War II

1951 Greece enters NATO

1955 Greek Cypriots start campaign of violence in Cyprus against British rule

1932 Aristotle Onassis purchases six freight ships, the start of his shipping empire

1948 Dodecanese becomes part of Greece

1963 Geórgios Papandréou's centre-left government voted into power

1960 Cyprus declared independent

1925 Mános Chatzidákis, who wrote music for the film *Never on Sunday*, is born

ΟΙ ΗΡΩΙΔΕΣ ΤΟΥ 1940

1940 Italy invades Greece. Greek soldiers defend northern Greece. Greece enters World War II

1946–9 Civil War between Greek government and the Communists who take to the mountains

1944 Churchill visits Athens to show his support for the Greek government against Communist Resistance

1993 Andréas Papandréou wins Greek general election for the third time

1980 Konstantínos Karamanlís becomes president, staying in office until 1995 (except for 1985–90)

1973 University students in Athens rebel against dictatorship and are crushed by military forces. Start of decline in power of dictatorship

1981 Andréas Papandréou's left-wing PASOK party forms first Greek Socialist government

2010 Economic crisis forces Greece to apply for financial support from the International Monetary Fund, European Central Bank and European Commission

2015 After early elections, Alexis Tsipras's hard-left SYRIZA party, which promises an end to austerity while remaining in the Eurozone, forms a coalition with far-right Europhobe ANEL. They accept a harsh bailout, despite this decision going against a referendum on the issue

1994 Because of the choking smog (néfos), central Athens introduces traffic restrictions

1974 Cyprus is partitioned after Turkish invasion

1988 Eight million visitors to Greece; tourism continues to expand

2005 The Greek Parliament ratifies the EU constitution

1975	1985	1995	2005	2015

1975	1985	1995	2005	2015

1975 Death of Aristotle Onassis

1990 New Democracy voted into power

2002 Euro becomes sole legal currency

2014 As conditions in war-torn Syria worsen, Greece's eastern frontier islands and mainland see the arrival of hundreds of thousands of refugees fleeing the conflict. They are joined by Iraqis, Afghans, Pakistanis, Sri Lankans and Eritreans.

1974 Fall of Junta; Konstantínos Karamanlís elected Prime Minister

2003 Greek presidency of EU (Jan–Jun)

2012 Greece's first coalition government in 60 years is formed by three parties, led by prime minister Antonis Samaras of the conservative New Democracy party

1981 Melína Merkoúri appointed Minister of Culture. Start of campaign to restore Elgin Marbles to Greece

2009 Left-wing PASOK party voted into Power; George Papandréou the Younger becomes Prime Minister

2007 Wildfires in Peloponnese cause the death of more than 70 people

1996 Andréas Papandréou dies; Kóstas Simítis succeeds him as party leader and Prime Minister

1973 Greek bishops give their blessing to the short-lived presidency of Colonel Papadópoulos

ATHENS AND MAINLAND GREECE THROUGH THE YEAR

Predominantly rural, Greece is deeply attached to locally produced food and wine, and chapels dotting the countryside serve as the focus for culinary, as well as religious, celebrations. Festivals of the Orthodox Church are deeply identified with Greekness, no more so than on 25 March, a date which commemorates both the Feast of the Annunciation and the start of the Independence uprising in 1821. Summer festivals are celebrated widely in rural villages, and expatriate Greeks return from across the globe. Organized cultural festivals are a more recent phenomenon, paralleling the rise of tourism.

Spring

Spring is a glorious time in Greece. The lowland landscape, parched for much of the year, luxuriates in a carpet of green, and wild flowers abound. But the weather does not stabilize until late spring, with rainy

25 March, Independence Day

or blustery days common in March and April. Artichokes ripen in March, and May sees the first strawberries. The fishing season lasts to the end of May, overlapping with the start of the tourist season. Spring festivities focus on Easter.

March
Apókries, Carnival Sunday *(first Sun before Lent)*. Carnivals take place during the week either side of this Sunday. There are parades and costume balls in many large cities, and the port of Pátra *(see p173)* hosts one of the most exuberant celebrations.

On *Tsiknopémpti* (Grill-Smell Thursday), tavernas are full of diners enjoying one last meaty feast before Lent. **Katharí Deftéra**, Clean Monday *(immediately after "Cheese Sunday" – seven Sundays before Easter)*. Kites are flown in the countryside. **Independence Day** and **Evangelismós** *(25 Mar)*. A national holiday, with parades and dances nationwide celebrating the 1821 revolt against the Ottoman Empire. The religious festival, one of the most important for the Orthodox Church, marks the Angel Gabriel's announcement to the Virgin Mary that she was to become the Holy Mother.

Celebrating Easter in Greece

Western Easter always falls before Greek Orthodox Easter – up to five Sundays earlier, though at times they may coincide. Easter is the most important religious festival in Greece, and Holy Week is a time for Greek families to reunite. It is also a good time to visit Greece, to see the processions and church services and to sample the Easter food. The ceremony and symbolism is a direct link with Greece's Byzantine past, as well as with earlier beliefs. The festivities reach a climax at midnight on Easter Saturday. As priests intone "Christ is risen", fireworks are lit, the explosions ushering in a Sunday devoted to feasting, music and dance. Smaller, more isolated towns, such as Andrítsaina and Koróni in the Peloponnese, and Polýgyros (the capital of Chalkidikí), are particularly worth visiting during Holy Week for the Friday and Saturday night services.

Priests in their richly embroidered Easter robes

Christ's bier, decorated with flowers and containing His effigy, is carried in solemn procession through the streets by each parish at dusk on Good Friday.

Candle lighting takes place at the end of the Easter Saturday mass. In pitch darkness, a single flame is used to light the candles held by worshippers.

Banners raised during a workers' May Day rally in Athens

April

Megáli Evdomáda, Holy Week *(Apr or May)*, including *Kyriakí ton Vaíon* (Palm Sunday), *Megáli Pémpti* (Maundy Thursday), *Megáli Paraskeví* (Good Friday), *Megálo Sávvato* (Easter Saturday), and the most important date in the Orthodox calendar, *Páscha* (Easter Sunday).

Agios Geórgios, St George's Day *(23 Apr)*. One of the major feast days in the Orthodox calendar, commemorating the patron saint of shepherds, and traditionally marking the start of the grazing season. Celebrations are nationwide, and are particularly festive at Aráchova, near Delphi *(see p225)*. If Easter falls on 23 April,

St George is honoured on the following Monday.

May

Protomagiá, May Day *(1 May)*. Also known as Labour Day, this is a national holiday. Traditionally, families go to the countryside

Firewalkers in a Macedonian village, 21 May

and pick wild flowers, which are made into wreaths with garlic. These are hung on doors, boats, balconies and even car bonnets to ward off evil. In towns and cities across the country, there are also parades and rallies led by the Communist Party.

Agios Konstantínos kai Agía Eléni *(21 May)*. A celebration throughout Greece for Constantine and his mother, Helen, the first Orthodox Byzantine rulers *(see p41)*. Firewalking ceremonies may be seen in some Macedonian villages.

Análipsi, Ascension *(40 days after Easter; usually late May)*. This is another important religious feast day.

Easter biscuits celebrate the end of Lent. Another Easter dish, *mageirítsa* soup, is made of lamb's innards and is eaten in the early hours of Easter Sunday.

The procession of candles in the very early hours of Easter Day, here at Lykavittós Hill in Athens, celebrates Christ's resurrection.

Tsourékia, made of sweet plaited dough, contain eggs with shells dyed red to symbolize the blood of Christ. They are baked on Maundy Thursday, the day of the Crucifixion.

Lamb roasting is traditionally done in the open air on giant spits over charcoal, for lunch on Easter Sunday. The first *retsína* wine from the previous year's harvest is opened. After lunch, young and old join hands to dance, Greek-style.

Summer

Warm days in early June signal the first sea-baths for Greeks (traditionally after Análipsi, Ascension Day). The peak tourist season begins, and continues until late August; after mid-July, it can be difficult to find hotel vacancies in the more popular resorts. June sees the arrival of cherries, plums and apricots, and the collection of honey from beehives can begin. The last green leaf vegetables are soon totally replaced by tomatoes, melons and cucumbers. By July, much of the Aegean is buffeted by the notorious *meltémi*, a high-pressure northerly wind, which – though more severe on the islands – can be felt along the mainland coast.

Various cultural festivals – programmed with an eye on the tourist audience, but no less impressive for that – are hosted in major cities and resorts. Outdoor cinemas are also well attended *(see p123)*. Urban Greeks retreat to mountain villages, often the venues for musical and religious fairs.

Beehives for summer honey production, near Mount Parnassós

June
Pentikostí, Pentecost or Whit Sunday *(seven weeks after Orthodox Easter)*. This important Orthodox feast day is celebrated throughout Greece.

Consecrated bread, baked for festivals

Agíou Pnévmatos, Feast of the Holy Spirit or Whit Monday *(the following day)*. A national holiday and three-day weekend.

Athens Festival *(mid-Jun to early Sep)*. A cultural festival encompassing a mix of modern and ancient theatre, ballet, opera, classical music and jazz. It takes place at various venues, including the Herodes Atticus Theatre *(see p123)* and the Lykavittós Theatre *(see p76)*.

The Herodes Atticus Theatre, on the slopes of the Acropolis, hosts performances of ancient tragedies, concerts by famous international orchestras or Greek performers and ballet.

The Lykavittós Theatre, spectacularly situated on Lykavittós Hill, with extensive views across Athens, hosts performances of modern music – jazz and folk – as well as drama and dance.

Epidaurus Festival *(Jun–Aug)*. Affiliated to the Athens Festival, though sited 150 km (90 miles) from the capital at the Epidaurus Theatre *(see p188)* in the Peloponnese, this festival includes open-air performances of Classical drama. The small, ancient theatre at nearby Palaiá Epídavros, on the coast, hosts a series of concerts in July.

Agios Ioánnis, St John's Day *(24 Jun)*. The birth of St John the Baptist is celebrated throughout Greece. However, it is on the evening of the 23rd that bonfires are lit in most areas, and May wreaths consigned to the flames. Older children jump over the fires. This is an equivalent celebration to midsummer's eve.

Agioi Apóstoloi Pétros kai Pávlos, Saints Peter and Paul *(29 Jun)*. A widely celebrated name day for Pétros and Pávlos.

July
Sáni Festival *(Jul–Aug)*, Kassándra, Chalkidikí. The best provincial festival on the mainland, with a mix of local and foreign artists.

Agía Marína *(17 Jul)*. This day is widely celebrated in rural areas, with feasts to honour the saint, an important protector of crops.

Profítis Ilías, the Prophet Elijah *(19–20 Jul)*. Widely celebrated at hill-top shrines, the best known being Mount Taÿgetos, near the town of Spárti. Name day for Ilías.

Agía Paraskeví *(26 Jul)*. There are many big village festivals on this day, but it is particularly celebrated in the Epirus region.

Musical performance at the illuminated Lykavittós Theatre

Agios Panteleímon *(27 Jul).*
As a doctor-saint, he is
celebrated as the patron of
many hospitals, and as a
popular rural saint, he is
celebrated in the countryside.
Name day for Pantelís
and Panteleímon.

Strings of tomatoes hanging out to dry in
the autumn sunshine

August
Metamórfosi,
Transfiguration of
Christ *(6 Aug).* For the
Orthodox church, this is
an important feast day.
Name day for Sotíris
and Sotiría.
Koímisis tis Theotókou,
Dormition of the
Virgin Mary *(15 Aug).*
A national holiday,
and an important and
widely celebrated
feast day. This is
traditionally a day
when Greeks return to
celebrate in their home
villages. It is also a name
day for Mary, María, Pános

and Panagiótis.
The Virgin Mary's
Assumption, on
23 August, is also
widely celebrated,
especially in the
Píndos Mountains.
Vlachopanagía
(23 Aug). This is a
day of celebration
in many Aroman
villages located in
Píndos Mountains.
**Apotomí Kefalís
Ioánnou Prodrómou,**
beheading of John
the Baptist *(29 Aug).*
The occasion for
festivals at the many
country chapels that
bear his name.

Autumn

By September, most
village festivals have
finished. The sea is
at its warmest for
swimming and, though the
crowds have gone, most
facilities are still available.
There is a second, minor
blooming of wild flowers,
and the fine, still days of
October are known as
the "little summer of
St Dimítrios", randomly
punctuated by
stormy weather.
Grapes, and the fat
giarmádes peaches,
are virtually the only fruit to
ripen since the figs of August,
and strings of onions, garlic and
tomatoes are hung up to dry for

Girl in national dress for
15 August festivities

the winter. The hills echo with
the sound of the September
quail shoot and dragnet fishing
resumes on 1 October.

Ceremonial dress
on Ochi Day

September
**Génnisis tis
Theotókou,** birth
of the Virgin
Mary *(8 Sep).*
An important
religious feast day
in the calendar of
the Orthodox church.
**Ypsosis tou
Timíou Stavroú,**
Exaltation of the
True Cross *(14 Sep).*
This is an important Orthodox
feast day, and, although it is
almost autumn, it is regarded
as the last of Greece's major
outdoor summer festivals.

October
Agios Dimítrios *(26 Oct).* This
marks the end of the grazing
season, when sheep are
brought down from the hills.
Celebrations for Dimítrios
are particularly lively in
Thessaloníki, where he is
the patron saint. Name day
for Dimítris and Dímitra.
Ochi Day *(28 Oct).* A national
holiday, with patriotic parades
in cities and plenty of dancing.
It commemorates the Greek
reply to the 1940 ultimatum
from Mussolini calling for Greek
surrender: an emphatic no *(óchi).*

November
**Ton Taxiarchón Archangélou
Michaïl kai Gavriíl** *(8 Nov).*
Ceremonies at the many rural
monasteries and churches
named after Archangels Gabriel
and Michael. It is also name day
for Michális and Gavriíl.
Thessaloníki Film Festival
(early to mid-Nov). One of
Europe's main cinematic events.
Eisódia tis Theotókou,
Presentation of the Virgin
in the Temple *(21 Nov).* An
important feast day in the
Orthodox calendar, celebrated
throughout Greece.
Agios Andréas, St Andrew's
Day *(30 Nov),* Pátra. A long
liturgy is recited for Pátra's
patron saint in the opulent
cathedral named after him.

Celebrating the Dormition of the Virgin Mary, 15 August

View over a snow-covered Herodes Atticus Theatre, Athens

Public Holidays

Agios Vasíleios (1 Jan)

Independence Day (25 Mar)

Protomagiá (1 May)

Megáli Paraskeví (Good Friday)

Pásha (Easter Sunday)

Deftéra tou Pásha (Easter Monday)

Koímisi tis Theotókou (Dormition) (15 Aug)

Christoúgenna (25 Dec)

Sýnaxis tis Theotókou (26 Dec)

Winter

Many mountain villages assume a ghostly aspect in winter, with their seasonal inhabitants returned to the cities. Deep snow accumulates at higher altitudes and skiing can begin; elsewhere, rain falls several days of the week. Fishing is in full swing, and at the street markets, kiwi fruits and exotic greens abound. Cheese shops display a full range of goat and sheep products, and olives are pressed for oil. The major festivals cluster to either side of the solstice. New Year and Epiphany are the most fervently celebrated festivals during winter.

Branch of olives

December

Agios Nikólaos, St Nicholas's Day *(6 Dec)*. The patron saint of seafarers, travellers, children and orphans is celebrated at seaside churches. The name day for Nikólaos and Nikolétta often marks the onset of cold, rainy weather.

Christoúgenna, Christmas *(25 Dec)*. A national holiday and, though less significant than Easter, it still constitutes an important religious feast day.

Sýnaxis tis Theotókou, meeting of the Virgin's entourage *(26 Dec)*. A religious celebration and national holiday.

January

Agios Vasíleios, also known as *Protochroniá*, or New Year *(1 Jan)*. A national holiday. Gifts are exchanged on this day and the traditional new year greeting is *Kalí Chroniá*.

Theofánia, or Epiphany *(6 Jan)*. A national holiday and major feast day. Blessing of the waters ceremonies take place by rivers, lakes and seaside locations throughout Greece. Youths dive to recover a cross that is thrown into the water by a priest.

Gynaikokratía *(8 Jan)*, various villages in Sérres province.

Gender role-swapping: men do the housework, while women go out carousing. The custom was brought by 1923 refugees from eastern Thrace.

February

Ypapantí, Candlemas *(2 Feb)*. An Orthodox feast day all over Greece, at a quiet time, prior to pre-Lenten carnivals.

Diving for a cross at a blessing of the waters ceremony, 6 January

Women playing cards on Gynaikokratía day, Sérres province

Name Days

Greeks celebrate their name day, or *giortí*, the day of the saint after whom they were named when baptized. Children are usually named after their grandparents, though in recent years, it has become fashionable to give children names deriving from Greece's history and mythology. When someone celebrates their name day, you may be told, *Giortázo símera* (I'm celebrating today), to which the traditional reply is *Chrónia pollá* (many years). Friends tend to drop in, bearing small gifts, and are given cakes and sweet liqueurs in return.

The Climate of Mainland Greece

The mainland climate varies most between the coastal lowlands and the mountainous inland regions. The mountains of western Greece and the Peloponnese get heavy snow in winter, rain during autumn and spring, and hot days in summer. The Ionian coast has milder temperatures, but is the wettest part of Greece. In Macedonia and Thrace, rainfall is spread more evenly across the year, with the North Aegean exerting a moderating influence on coastal temperatures. Around Athens, temperatures are hot in summer and rarely drop below freezing in winter, when rainfall is at its greatest.

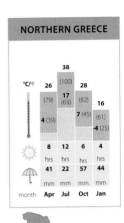

NORTHERN GREECE

°C/°F		38 (100)		
	26 (79)	17 (63)	28 (82)	16
	4 (39)		7 (45)	(61) -4 (25)
☀	8 hrs	12 hrs	6 hrs	4 hrs
☂	41 mm	22 mm	57 mm	44 mm
month	Apr	Jul	Oct	Jan

CENTRAL AND WESTERN GREECE

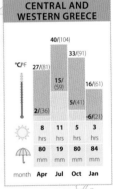

°C/°F		40/(104)	33/(91)	
	27/(81)	15/ (59)	16/(61)	
	2/(36)		5/(41)	-6/(21)
☀	8 hrs	11 hrs	5 hrs	3 hrs
☂	80 mm	19 mm	80 mm	84 mm
month	Apr	Jul	Oct	Jan

THE PELOPONNESE

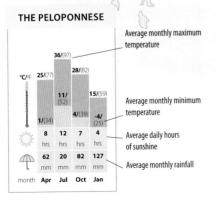

°C/°F		36/(97)	28/(82)	
	25/(77)	11/ (52)	15/(59)	
	1/(34)		4/(39)	-4/ (25)
☀	8 hrs	12 hrs	7 hrs	4 hrs
☂	62 mm	20 mm	82 mm	127 mm
month	Apr	Jul	Oct	Jan

Average monthly maximum temperature

Average monthly minimum temperature

Average daily hours of sunshine

Average monthly rainfall

ATHENS AND AROUND ATHENS

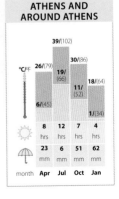

°C/°F		39/(102)	30/(86)	
	26/(79)	19/ (66)	18/(64)	
	6/(45)		11/ (52)	1/(34)
☀	8 hrs	12 hrs	7 hrs	4 hrs
☂	23 mm	6 mm	51 mm	62 mm
month	Apr	Jul	Oct	Jan

Northern Greece

Central and Western Greece

Around Athens

Athens

The Peloponnese

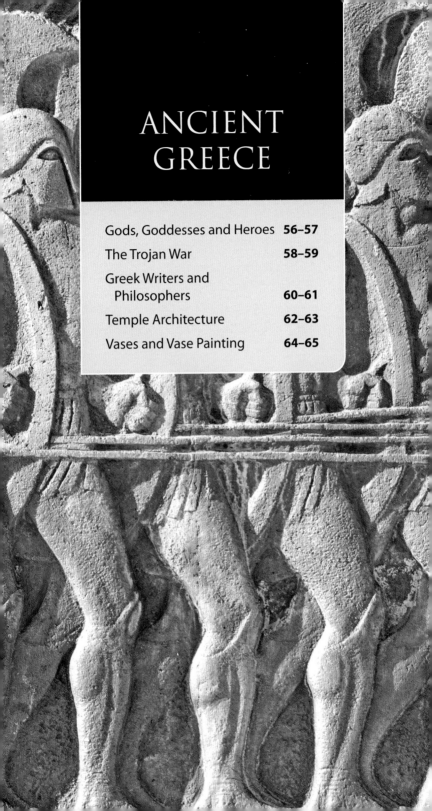

ANCIENT GREECE

Gods, Goddesses and Heroes   56–57

The Trojan War   58–59

Greek Writers and
   Philosophers   60–61

Temple Architecture   62–63

Vases and Vase Painting   64–65

Gods, Goddesses and Heroes

The Greek myths that tell the stories of the gods, goddesses and heroes date back to the Bronze Age when they were told aloud by poets. They were first written down in the early 6th century BC and have lived on in Western literature. Myths were closely bound up with Greek religion and gave meaning to the unpredictable workings of the natural world. They tell the story of the creation and the "golden age" of gods and mortals, as well as the age of semi-mythical heroes, such as Theseus and Herakles, whose exploits were an inspiration to ordinary men. The gods and goddesses were affected by human desires and failings and were part of a divine family presided over by Zeus. He had many offspring, both legitimate and illegitimate, each with a mythical role.

Hades and Persephone were king and queen of the Underworld (land of the dead). Persephone was abducted from her mother Demeter, goddess of the harvest, by Hades. She was then only permitted to return to her mother for eight months each year.

Eris was the goddess of strife.

Zeus was the father of the gods and ruled over them and all mortals from Mount Olympos.

Klymene, a nymph and daughter of Helios, was mother of Prometheus, creator of mankind.

Poseidon, one of Zeus's brothers, was given control of the seas. The trident is his symbol of power, and he married the sea-goddess Amphitrite, to whom he was not entirely faithful. This statue is from the National Archaeological Museum in Athens (see pp72–5).

Hera, sister and wife of Zeus, was famous for her jealousy.

Athena was born from Zeus's head in full armour.

Paris was asked to award the golden apple to the most beautiful goddess.

Paris's dog helped him herd cattle on Mount Ida where the Trojan prince grew up.

Dionysos, god of revelry and wine, was born from Zeus's thigh. In this 6th-century BC cup painted by Exekias, he reclines in a ship whose mast has become a vine.

A Divine Dispute

This vase painting shows the gods on Mount Ida, near Troy. Hera, Athena and Aphrodite, quarrelling over who was the most beautiful, were brought by Hermes to hear the judgment of a young herdsman, the Trojan prince, Paris. In choosing Aphrodite, he was rewarded with the love of Helen, the most beautiful woman in the world. Paris abducted her from her husband Menelaos, King of Sparta, and thus the Trojan War began (see pp58–9).

Artemis, the virgin goddess of the hunt, was the daughter of Zeus and sister of Apollo. She can be identified by her bow and arrows, hounds and group of nymphs with whom she lived in the forests. Although sworn to chastity, she was, in contrast, the goddess of childbirth.

Happiness, here personified by two goddesses, waits with gold laurel leaves to garland the winner. Wreaths were the prizes in Greek athletic and musical contests.

Helios, the sun god, drove his four-horse chariot (the sun) daily across the sky.

Hermes was the gods' messenger.

Aphrodite, the goddess of love, was born from the sea. Here, she has her son Eros (Cupid) with her.

Apollo, son of Zeus and brother of Artemis, was god of healing, plague and also music. Here he is depicted holding a lyre. He was also famous for his dazzling beauty.

The Labours of Herakles

Herakles (Hercules to the Romans) was the greatest of the Greek heroes, and the son of Zeus and Alkmene, a mortal woman. With superhuman strength, he achieved success, and immortality, against seemingly impossible odds in the "Twelve Labours" set by Eurystheus, King of Tiryns. For his first task, he killed the Nemean lion, and wore its hide ever after.

Killing the Lernaean hydra was the second labour of Herakles. The many heads of this venomous monster, raised by Hera, grew back as soon as they were chopped off. As in all his tasks, Herakles was helped by Athena.

The huge boar that ravaged Mount Erymanthos was captured next. Herakles brought it back alive to King Eurystheus who was so terrified that he hid in a storage jar.

Destroying the Stymfalían birds was the sixth labour. Herakles rid Lake Stymfalía of these man-eating birds, which had brass beaks, by stoning them with a sling, having first frightened them off with a pair of bronze castanets.

The Trojan War

The story of the Trojan War, first narrated in the *Iliad*, Homer's 8th-century BC epic poem, tells how the Greeks sought to avenge the capture of Helen, wife of Menelaos, King of Sparta, by the Trojan prince, Paris. The Roman writer Virgil takes up the story in the *Aeneid*, where he tells of the sack of Troy and the founding of Rome. Archaeological evidence of the remains of a city identified with ancient Troy in modern Turkey suggests that the myth may have a basis in fact. Many of the ancient sites in the Peloponnese, such as Mycenae and Pýlos, are thought to be the cities of some of the heroes of the Trojan War.

Achilles binding up the battle wounds of his friend Patroklos

Gathering of the Heroes

When Paris *(see p56)* carries Helen back to Troy, her husband King Menelaos summons an army of Greek kings and heroes to avenge this crime. His brother, King Agamemnon of Mycenae, leads the force; its ranks include young Achilles, destined to die at Troy.

At Aulis, their departure is delayed by a contrary wind. Only the sacrifice to Artemis of Iphigeneia, the eldest of Agamemnon's daughters, allows the fleet to depart.

Fighting at Troy

The *Iliad* opens with the Greek army outside Troy, maintaining a siege that has already been in progress for nine years. Tired of fighting, yet still hoping for a decisive victory, the Greek camp is torn apart by the fury of Achilles over Agamemnon's removal of his slave girl Briseis. The hero takes to his tent and refuses adamantly to fight.

Deprived of their greatest warrior, the Greeks are driven back by the Trojans. In desperation, Patroklos persuades his friend Achilles to let him borrow his armour. Achilles agrees and Patroklos leads the Myrmidons, Achilles's troops, into battle. The tide is turned, but Patroklos is killed in the fighting by Hector, son of King Priam of Troy, who mistakes him for Achilles. Filled with remorse at the news of his friend's death, Achilles returns to battle, finds Hector, and kills him in revenge.

King Priam begging Achilles for the body of his son

Patroklos Avenged

Refusing Hector's dying wish to allow his body to be ransomed, Achilles instead hitches it up to his chariot by the ankles and drags it round the walls of Troy, then takes it back to the Greek camp. In contrast, Patroklos is given the most elaborate funeral possible with a huge pyre, sacrifices of animals and Trojan prisoners and funeral games. Still unsatisfied, for 12 days Achilles drags the corpse of Hector around Patroklos's funeral mound until the gods are forced to intervene over his callous behaviour.

Priam Visits Achilles

On the instructions of Zeus, Priam sets off for the Greek camp holding a ransom for the body of his dead son. With the help of the god Hermes, he reaches Achilles's tent undetected. Entering, he pleads with Achilles to think of his own father and to show mercy. Achilles relents and allows Hector to be taken back to Troy for a funeral and burial.

Although the Greek heroes were greater than mortals, they were portrayed as fallible beings with human emotions who had to face universal moral dilemmas.

Greeks and Trojans, in bronze armour, locked in combat

Achilles Kills the Amazon Queen

Penthesileia was the Queen of the Amazons, a tribe of warlike women reputed to cut off their right breasts to make it easier to wield their weapons. They come to the support of the Trojans. In the battle, Achilles finds himself face to face with Penthesileia and deals her a fatal blow. One version of the story has it that as their eyes meet at the moment of her death, they fall in love. The Greek idea of love and death would be explored 2,000 years later by the psychologists Jung and Freud.

An early image of the Horse of Troy, from a 7th-century BC clay vase

Achilles killing the Amazon Queen Penthesileia in battle

The Wooden Horse of Troy

As was foretold, Achilles is killed at Troy by an arrow in his heel from Paris's bow. With this weakening of their military strength, the Greeks resort to guile.

Before sailing away, they build a great wooden horse, in which they conceal some of their best fighters. The rumour is put out that this is a gift to the goddess Athena and that if the horse enters Troy, the city can never be taken. After some doubts, but swayed by supernatural omens, the Trojans drag the horse inside the walls. That night, the Greeks sail back, the soldiers creep out of the horse and Troy is put to the torch. Priam, with many others, is murdered. Among the Trojan survivors

is Aeneas who escapes to Italy and founds the race of Romans: a second Troy. The next part of the story (the *Odyssey*) tells of the heroes' adventures on their way home to Greece.

Death of Agamemnon

Klytemnestra, the wife of Agamemnon, had ruled Mycenae in the ten years that he had been away fighting in Troy. She was accompanied by Aigisthos, her lover. Intent on vengeance for the death of her daughter Iphigeneia, Klytemnestra receives her husband with a triumphal welcome and then brutally murders him, with the help of Aigisthos. Agamemnon's fate was a result of a curse laid on his father, Atreus, which was finally expiated by the murder of both Klytemnestra and Aigisthos by her son Orestes and daughter Elektra. In these myths, the will of the gods shapes and overrides that of heroes and mortals.

Greek Myths in Western Art

From the Renaissance onwards, the Greek myths have been a powerful inspiration for artists and sculptors. Kings and queens have had themselves portrayed as gods and goddesses with their symbolic attributes of love or war. Myths have also been an inspiration for artists to paint the nude or Classically draped figure. This was true of the 19th-century artist Lord Leighton, whose depiction of the human body reflects the Classical ideals of beauty. His tragic figure of Elektra is shown here.

Elektra mourning the death of her father Agamemnon at his tomb

Greek Writers and Philosophers

The literature of Greece began with long epic poems, accounts of war and adventure, which established the relationship of the ancient Greeks to their gods. The tragedy and comedy, history and philosophical dialogues of the 5th and 4th centuries BC became the basis of Western literary culture. Much of our knowledge of the Greek world is derived from Greek literature. Pausanias's *Guide to Greece*, written in the Roman period and used by Roman tourists, is a key to the physical remains.

Hesiod with the nine Muses who inspired his poetry

Epic Poetry

As far back as the 2nd millennium BC, before even the building of the Mycenaean palaces, poets were reciting the stories of the Greek heroes and gods. Passed on from generation to generation, these poems, called *rhapsodes,* were never written down but were changed and embellished by successive poets. The oral tradition culminated in the *Iliad* and *Odyssey* (see pp58–9), composed around 700 BC. Both works are traditionally ascribed to the same poet, Homer, of whose life nothing reliable is known. Hesiod, whose most famous poems include the *Theogony*, a history of the gods, and the *Works and Days*, on how to live an honest life, also lived around 700 BC. Unlike Homer, Hesiod is thought to have written down his poems, although there is no firm evidence available to support this theory.

Passionate Poetry

For private occasions, and particularly to entertain guests at the cultivated drinking parties known as *symposia*, shorter poetic forms were developed. These poems were often full of passion, whether love or hatred, and could be personal or, often, highly political. Much of this poetry, by writers such as Archilochus, Alcaeus, Alcman, Hipponax and Sappho, survives only in quotations by later writers or on scraps of papyrus that have been preserved by chance from private libraries in Hellenistic and Roman Egypt. Through these fragments, we can gain glimpses of the life of a very competitive elite. Since *symposia* were an almost exclusively male domain, there is a strong element of misogyny in much of this poetry. In contrast, the fragments of poems discovered by the authoress Sappho, who lived on the island of Lésvos, are exceptional for showing a woman competing in a literary area in the male-dominated society of ancient Greece, and for describing with great intensity her passions for other women.

History

Until the 5th century BC, little Greek literature was composed in prose – even early philosophy was in verse. In the latter part of the 5th century, a new tradition of lengthy prose histories, looking at recent or current events, was established with Herodotus's account of the great war between Greece and Persia (490–479 BC). Herodotus put the clash between Greeks and Persians into a context, and included an ethnographic account of the vast Persian Empire. He attempted to record objectively what people said about the past. Thucydides took a narrower view in his account of the long years of the Peloponnesian War between Athens and Sparta (431–404 BC). He concentrated on the political history, and his aim was to work out the "truth" that lay behind the events of the war. The methods of Thucydides were adopted by later writers of Greek history, though few could match his acute insight into human nature.

Herodotus, the historian of the Persian wars

An unusual vase-painting of a *symposion* for women only

The orator Demosthenes in a Staffordshire figurine of 1790

Oratory

Public argument was basic to Greek political life even in the Archaic period. In the later part of the 5th century BC, the techniques of persuasive speech began to be studied in their own right. From that time on, some orators began to publish their speeches. In particular, this included those wishing to advertise their skills in composing speeches for the law courts, such as Lysias and Demosthenes. The texts that survive give insights into both Athenian politics and the seamier side of Athenian private life. The verbal attacks on Philip of Macedon by Demosthenes, the 4th-century BC Athenian politician, became models for Roman politicians seeking to defeat their opponents. With the 18th-century European revival of interest in Classical times, Demosthenes again became a political role model.

Drama

Almost all the surviving tragedies come from the hands of the three great 5th-century BC Athenians: Aeschylus, Sophocles and Euripides. The latter two playwrights had an interest in individual psychology (as in Euripides's *Medea*). While 5th-century comedy is full of direct references to contemporary life and dirty jokes, the "new" comedy developed in the 4th century BC is essentially situation comedy employing character types.

Vase painting of two costumed actors from around 370 BC

Greek Philosophers

The Athenian Socrates was recognized in the late 5th century BC as a moral arbiter. He wrote nothing himself but we know of his views through the "Socratic dialogues", written by his pupil, Plato, examining the concepts of justice, virtue and courage. Plato set up his academy in the suburbs of Athens. His pupil, Aristotle, founded the Lyceum, to teach subjects from biology to ethics, and helped to turn Athens into one of the first university cities. In 1508–11, Raphael painted this vision of Athens in the Vatican.

Aristotle, author of the *Ethics*, had a genius for scientific observation.

Plato saw "the seat of ideas" in heaven.

Euclid laid the rules of geometry in around 300 BC.

Epikouros advocated the pursuit of pleasure.

Socrates taught by debating his ideas.

Diogenes, the Cynic, lived like a beggar.

Temple Architecture

Temples were the most important public buildings in ancient Greece, largely because religion was a central part of everyday life. Often placed in prominent positions, temples were also statements about political and divine power. The earliest temples, in the 8th century BC, were built of wood and sun-dried bricks. Many of their features were copied in marble buildings from the 6th century BC onwards.

Pheidias, sculptor of the Parthenon, at work

Temple Construction

This drawing is of an idealized Doric temple, showing how it was built and used.

The cella, or inner sanctum, housed the cult statue.

The triangular pediment often held relief sculpture.

The cult statue was of the god or goddess to whom the temple was dedicated.

Fluting on the columns was carved *in situ*, guided by that on the top and bottom drums.

A ramp led up to the temple entrance.

The stepped platform was built on a stone foundation.

The column drums were initially carved with bosses for lifting them into place.

Detail of the Parthenon pediment

700 First temple of Poseidon, Ancient Isthmia (Archaic; *see p171*) and first Temple of Apollo, Corinth (Archaic; *see p166*)

550 Second temple of Apollo, Corinth (Doric; *see p166*)

520 Temple of Olympian Zeus, Athens, begun (Doric; completed Corinthian 2nd century AD; *see p115*)

6th century Temple of Artemis, Ancient Brauron (Doric; *see pp150–51*)

7th century Temple of Hera, Olympia (Doric; *see p174*)

460 Temple of Zeus, Olympia (Doric; *see p175*)

447–405 Temples of the Acropolis, Athens: Athena Nike (Ionic), Parthenon (Doric), Erechtheion (Ionic) (*see pp98–103*)

445–425 Temple of Apollo, Bassae (Doric with Ionic; *see p181*)

440–430 Temple of Poseidon, Sounion (Doric; *see pp152–3*)

4th century Temple of Apollo, Delphi (Doric; *see p233*); Temple of Athena Aléa, Tegea (Doric and 1st Corinthian capital; *see p181*)

700 BC   **600 BC**   **500 BC**   **400 BC**   **300 BC**

The gable ends of the roof were surmounted by statues, known as *akroteria*, in this case of a Nike or "Winged Victory". Almost no upper portions of Greek temples survive.

The roof was supported on wooden beams and covered in rows of terracotta tiles, each ending in an upright *akroterion*.

The Development of Temple Architecture

Greek temple architecture is divided into three styles, which evolved chronologically, and are most easily distinguished by the column capitals.

Doric temples were surrounded by sturdy columns with plain capitals and no bases. As the earliest style of stone buildings, they recall wooden prototypes.

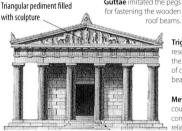

Triangular pediment filled with sculpture

Guttae imitated the pegs for fastening the wooden roof beams.

Triglyphs resembled the ends of cross beams.

Metopes could contain reliefs.

Doric capital

Ionic temples differed from Doric in their tendency to have more columns, of a different form. The capital has a pair of volutes, like rams' horns, front and back.

Akroteria, at the roof corners, could look Persian in style.

The Ionic architrave was subdivided into projecting bands.

The frieze was a continuous band of decoration.

The Ionic frieze took the place of Doric *triglyphs* and *metopes*.

Ionic capital

Stone blocks were smoothly fitted together and held by metal clamps and dowels: no mortar was used in the temple's construction.

The ground plan was derived from the megaron of the Mycenaean house: a rectangular hall with a front porch supported by columns.

Caryatids, or figures of women, were used instead of columns in the Erechtheion at Athens' Acropolis. In Athens' Agora (*see pp94–5*), tritons (half-fish, half-human creatures) were used.

Corinthian temples in Greece were built in Athens and Corinth under the Romans. They feature slender columns with elaborate capitals decorated with acanthus leaves.

The pediment was decorated with a variety of mouldings.

Akroterion in the shape of a griffin

The cella entrance was at the east end.

The entablature was everything above the capitals.

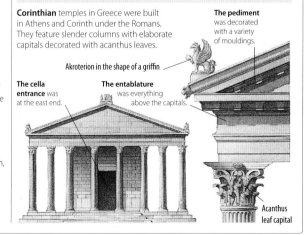

Acanthus leaf capital

Vases and Vase Painting

The history of Greek vase painting continued without a break from 1000 BC to Hellenistic times. The main centre of production was Athens, which was so successful that by the early 6th century BC it was sending its high-quality black- and red-figure wares to every part of the Greek world. The Athenian potters' quarter of Kerameikos can still be visited today *(see pp92–3)*. Beautiful works of art in their own right, the painted vases are the closest we can get to the vanished paintings with which ancient Greeks decorated the walls of their houses. Although vases could break during everyday use (for which they were intended), a huge number still survive intact or in reassembled pieces.

This 6th-century BC black-figure vase shows pots being used in an everyday situation. The vases depicted are *hydriai*. It was the women's task to fill them with water from springs or public fountains.

The white-ground lekythos was developed in the 5th century BC as an oil flask for grave offerings. They were usually decorated with funeral scenes, and this one, by the Achilles Painter, shows a woman placing flowers at a grave.

The naked woman holding a *kylix* is probably a flute-girl or prostitute.

The Symposion

These episodes of mostly male feasting and drinking were also occasions for playing the game of kottabos. On the exterior of this 5th-century BC kylix *are depictions of men holding cups, ready to flick out the dregs at a target.*

The Development of Painting Styles

Vase painting reached its peak in 6th- and 5th-century BC Athens. In the potter's workshop, a fired vase would be passed to a painter to be decorated. Archaeologists have been able to identify the varying styles of many individual painters of both black-figure and red-figure ware.

The body of the dead man is carried on a bier by mourners.

The geometric design is a prototype of the later "Greek-key" pattern.

Chariots and warriors form the funeral procession.

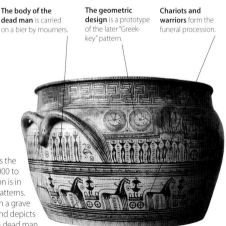

Geometric style characterizes the earliest Greek vases, from around 1000 to 700 BC, in which the decoration is in bands of figures and geometric patterns. This 8th-century BC vase, placed on a grave as a marker, is over 1 m (3 ft) high and depicts the bier and funeral rites of a dead man.

Eye cups
were given an almost magical power by the painted eyes. The pointed base suggests that they were passed around during feasting.

This kylix is being held by one handle by another woman feaster, ready to flick out the dregs at a *kottabos* target.

The rhyton, such as this one in the shape of a ram's head, was a drinking vessel for watered-down wine. The scene of the *symposion* around the rim indicates when it would have been used.

This drinker holds aloft a branch of a vine, symbolic of Dionysos's presence at the party.

Striped cushions made reclining more comfortable.

The drinking horn shape was copied in the pottery *rhyton*.

Black-figure style was first used in Athens around 630 BC. The figures were painted in black liquid clay on to the iron-rich clay of the vase which turned orange when fired. This vase is signed by the potter and painter Exekias.

Red-figure style was introduced in c.530 BC. The figures were left in the colour of the clay, silhouetted against a black glaze. Here, a woman pours from an *oinochoe* (wine jug).

Vase Shapes

Almost all Greek vases were made to be used; their shapes are closely related to their intended uses. Athenian potters had about 20 different forms to choose from. Below are some of the most commonly made shapes and their uses.

The amphora was a two-handled vessel used to store wine, olive oil and foods preserved in liquid such as olives. It also held dried foods.

This krater with curled handles or "volutes" is a wide-mouthed vase in which the Greeks mixed water with their wine before drinking it.

The hydria was used to carry water from the fountain. Of the three handles, one was vertical for holding and pouring, two horizontal for lifting.

The lekythos could vary in height from 3 cm (1 in) to nearly 1 m (3 ft). It was used to hold oil, both in the home and as a funerary gift to the dead.

The oinochoe, the standard wine jug, had a round or trefoil mouth for pouring, and just one handle.

The kylix, a two-handled drinking cup, was one shape that could take interior decoration.

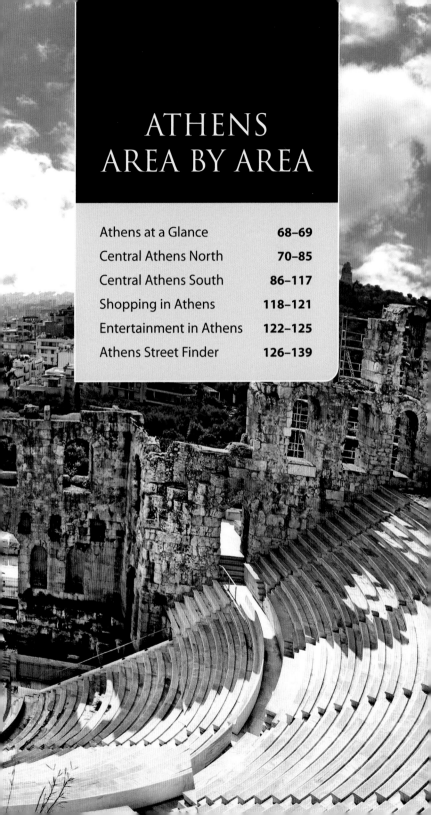

ATHENS
AREA BY AREA

Athens at a Glance	68–69
Central Athens North	70–85
Central Athens South	86–117
Shopping in Athens	118–121
Entertainment in Athens	122–125
Athens Street Finder	126–139

Athens at a Glance

Athens has been a city for 3,500 years but its greatest glory was during the Classical period of ancient Greece from which so many buildings and artifacts still survive. The 5th century BC in particular was a golden age, when Perikles oversaw the building of the Acropolis. Within the Byzantine Empire and under Ottoman rule, Athens played only a minor role. It returned to prominence in 1834, when it became the capital of Greece. Today, it is a busy and modern metropolitan centre.

Locator Map

The Kerameikos quarter *(see pp92–3)* was once the potters' district of ancient Athens and site of the principal cemetery, whose grave monuments can still be seen. Tranquil and secluded, it lies off the main tourist track.

The Agora *(see pp94–5)*, or market place, was the ancient centre of commercial life. The Stoa of Attalos was reconstructed in 1953–6 on its original, 2nd-century BC foundations. It now houses the Agora Museum.

The Tower of the Winds *(see pp90–91)* stands beside the Roman forum, but this small, octagonal building is Hellenistic in style. The tower – built as a water clock, with a compass, sundials and weather vane – has a relief on each side depicting the wind from that direction.

| 0 metres | 500 |
| 0 yards | 500 |

The Acropolis *(see pp98–105)* has dominated Athens for over 2,000 years. From the scale of the Parthenon to the delicacy of the Erechtheion, it is an extraordinary achievement.

◀ Ancient theatre in the Acropolis

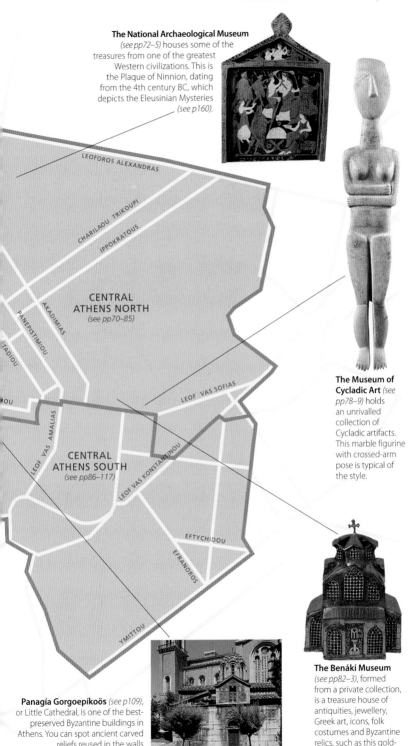

The National Archaeological Museum *(see pp72–5)* houses some of the treasures from one of the greatest Western civilizations. This is the Plaque of Ninnion, dating from the 4th century BC, which depicts the Eleusinian Mysteries *(see p160)*.

LEOFOROS ALEXANDRAS

CHARILAOU TRIKOUPI

IPPOKRATOUS

CENTRAL ATHENS NORTH *(see pp70–85)*

AKADIMIAS

PANEPISTIMIOU

STADIOU

LEOF VAS SOFIAS

LEOF VAS AMALIAS

CENTRAL ATHENS SOUTH *(see pp86–117)*

LEOF VAS KONSTANTINOU

EFTYCHIDOU

EFRANOROS

YMITTOU

The Museum of Cycladic Art *(see pp78–9)* holds an unrivalled collection of Cycladic artifacts. This marble figurine with crossed-arm pose is typical of the style.

The Benáki Museum *(see pp82–3)*, formed from a private collection, is a treasure house of antiquities, jewellery, Greek art, icons, folk costumes and Byzantine relics, such as this gold-plated incense holder.

Panagía Gorgoepíkoös *(see p109)*, or Little Cathedral, is one of the best-preserved Byzantine buildings in Athens. You can spot ancient carved reliefs reused in the walls of this tiny church.

CENTRAL ATHENS NORTH

Inhabited for 7,000 years, Athens was the birthplace of European civilization. It flourished in the 5th century BC when the Athenians controlled much of the eastern Mediterranean. The buildings from this era, including those in the ancient Agora and on the Acropolis, lie largely in the southern part of the city. The northern half has grown since the 1830s when King Otto made Athens the new capital of Greece. When the king's architects planned the new, European-style city, they included wide, tree-lined avenues, such as Panepistimíou and Akadimías, that were soon home to many grand Neo-Classical public buildings

and mansion houses. Today, these edifices still provide elegant homes for many major banks, embassies and public institutions, such as the University and the Library.

The chic residential area of Kolonáki is located in the north of the city centre, as is the cosmopolitan area around Patriárchou Ioakeím and Irodótou. These streets have excellent shopping and entertainment venues. Most of Athens' best museums, including the National Archaeological Museum, are also found in this area of the city. For information on getting around Athens, see pages 320–3.

Sights at a Glance

Museums and Galleries
1 National Archaeological Museum pp72–5
5 National Gallery of Art
6 War Museum
7 Byzantine and Christian Museum
8 Museum of Cycladic Art pp78–9
10 Benáki Museum pp82–3
11 Hadjikyriakos-Ghika Gallery
12 Museum of the City of Athens
13 National Historical Museum

Squares, Parks and Gardens
2 Exárcheia and Stréfi Hill
3 Lykavittós Hill
9 Plateía Kolonakíou

Churches
14 Kapnikaréa

Historic Buildings
4 Gennádeion

See also Street Finder maps pp126–139

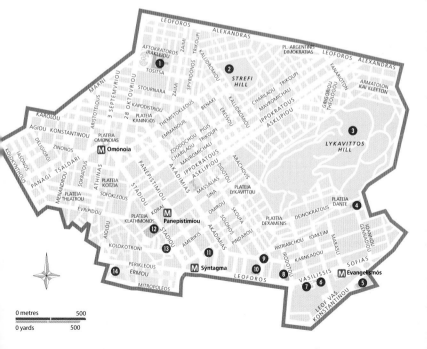

◄ The elegant pediment of the Neo-Classical University building *(see p85)*   **For keys to symbols** *see back flap*

❶ National Archaeological Museum

Εθνικό Αρχαιολογικό Μουσείο

Opened in 1891, this superb museum, often known simply as the National Museum, brought together a collection that had previously been stored all over the city. Additional wings were added in 1939. The priceless collection was then dispersed and buried underground during World War II to protect it from possible damage. The museum reopened in 1946, but it took a further 65 years of renovation and reorganization finally to do justice to its formidable collection. With the combination of such unique exhibits as the Mycenaean gold, along with the unrivalled amount of sculpture, pottery and jewellery on display, this is without doubt one of the world's finest museums.

Neo-Classical entrance to the National Archaeological Museum on Patissíon

Dípylon Amphora
This huge Geometric vase was used to mark an 8th-century BC woman's burial and shows the dead body surrounded by mourning women. It is named after the location of its discovery near the Dípylon Gate in Athens' Kerameikos *(see pp92–3)*.

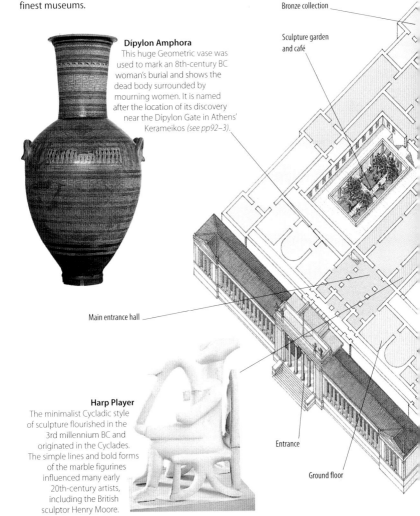

Bronze collection

Sculpture garden and café

Main entrance hall

Harp Player
The minimalist Cycladic style of sculpture flourished in the 3rd millennium BC and originated in the Cyclades. The simple lines and bold forms of the marble figurines influenced many early 20th-century artists, including the British sculptor Henry Moore.

Entrance

Ground floor

★ Mask of Agamemnon
Found at Mycenae by Schliemann, this gold death mask was originally thought to have belonged to the legendary king Agamemnon. It dates from the mid-1600s BC.

VISITORS' CHECKLIST

Practical Information
44 Patission, Exárcheia.
Map 2 E2. **Tel** 213 214 4800.
Open Apr–Oct: 8am–8pm Mon–Sun; Nov–Mar: 8am–3pm Tue–Sun, 1:30–8pm Mon. 🏛 📷
🛗 ♿ 🌐 namuseum.gr

Transport
Ⓜ Omónoia.

Eléni Stathátou jewellery collection

Egyptian collection

Thíra Frescoes

The Pottery Collection
contains a vast display of vases.

Stairs to first floor

Karapános collection

The Courtyard
has stairs leading to a basement café and shop.

★ Ephebe of Antikythera
This fine Hellenistic bronze statue was discovered off the island of Antikýthira in 1900. Larger than life, it stands proudly at approximately 2 m (7 ft) tall.

Aphrodite and Pan
This marble sculpture of Aphrodite, Eros and the goat-footed Pan was found on Delos and dates from c.100 BC.

Key to Floorplan
- Neolithic and Cycladic Art
- Mycenaean Art
- Geometric and Archaic Art
- Classical Sculpture
- Roman and Hellenistic Sculpture
- Other collections
- Thíra Frescoes
- Pottery Collection
- Temporary exhibitions
- Non-exhibition space

Gallery Guide
On the ground floor, Mycenaean, Neolithic and Cycladic finds are followed by Geometric, Archaic, Classical, Roman and Hellenistic sculpture. Smaller collections of bronzes, Egyptian artifacts, the Eléni Stathátou jewellery collection and the Karapános collection are also on the ground floor. The first floor houses a collection of pottery.

Exploring the National Archaeological Museum's Collection

Displaying its treasures in chronological order, the museum presents an impressive and thorough overview of Greek art through the centuries. Beginning with early Cycladic figurines and continuing through the Greek Bronze Age, the exhibits end with the glories of Hellenistic period bronzes and a collection of busts of Roman emperors. High points in between include the numerous gold artifacts found at Mycenae, the elegant Archaic *koúroi* statues and the many examples of fine Classical sculpture.

Neolithic and Cycladic Art

The dawning of Greek civilization (3500–2900 BC) saw primitive decorative vases and figures. This collection also contains terracotta figurines, jewellery and a selection of weapons.

The vibrant fertility gods and goddesses, such as the *kourotróphos* (nursing mother) with child, are particularly well preserved. Of exceptional importance are the largest known Cycladic marble figurine, from Amorgós, and the earliest known figures of musicians – the *Flute Player* and *Harp Player*, both from Kéros. Later finds from Mílos, such as the painted vase with fishermen, reveal the changes in pot shapes and colour that took place in the late Cycladic Bronze Age.

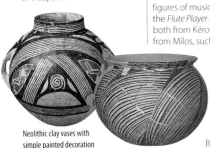

Neolithic clay vases with simple painted decoration

Mycenaean Art

It is not difficult to understand the allure of the museum's most popular attraction, the Hall of Mycenaean Antiquities, with its dazzling array of 16th-century BC gold treasures. Other exhibits in the collection include frescoes, ivory sculptures and seal rings made out of precious stones.

From the famous shaft graves *(see p184)* came a procession of daggers, cups, seals and rings as well as a number of regal death masks, including the justly famous *Mask of Agamemnon*. Two superb *rhytons*, or wine jugs, are also on display: one in the shape of a bull's head, made in silver with gold horns, and one in gold shaped like a lion's head. Equally rich finds from sites other than Mycenae have since been made. These include two gold bull cups found at Vafeió, in Crete, a gold phial entwined with dolphins and octopuses (excavated from a royal tomb at Déntra), clay tablets with the early Linear B script from the Palace of Nestor *(see p205)* and a magnificent sword from the Tomb of Staphylos on the island of Skópelos.

Mycenaean bronze dagger, inlaid with gold

The Development of Greek Sculpture

Sculpture was one of the most sophisticated forms of Greek art. We are able to trace its development from the early *koúroi* to the great works of named sculptors such as Pheidias and Praxiteles in Classical times. Portraiture only began in the 5th century BC; even then, most Greek sculptures were of gods and goddesses, heroes and athletes and idealized men and women. These have had an enormous influence on Western art down the centuries.

The Volomándra Koúros was
discovered in Attica and dates from the mid-6th century BC. The highly stylized *koúroi* (statues of naked youths) first appear in the mid-7th century BC. Derived from Egyptian art, these figures share a common pose and proportions. Clothed *kórai* are the female counterpart.

The Marathon Boy
(340 BC), like many other Greek bronzes, was found on the sea floor. The dreamy expression and easy pose of the figure are characteristic of the works of Praxiteles, the leading late Classical sculptor. An example of the "heroic nude", it shows a great naturalism and perfect balance.

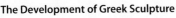

For hotels and restaurants see pp268–9 and pp282–5

Geometric and Archaic Art

Famed for its monumental burial vases, such as the *Dípylon Amphora*, the Geometric period developed a more ornate style in the 7th century BC with the introduction of mythological and plant and animal motifs. By the 6th century BC, the full artistry of the black-figure vases had developed. Two rare examples from this period are a *lekythos* depicting Peleus, Achilles and the centaur Cheiron, and the sculptured heads known as *aryballoi*.

Warrior from Boeotia, early 7th century BC

Hellenistic bronze known as the *Horse with the Little Jockey*

Classical Sculpture

The collection of Classical sculpture contains both fine statues and a selection of grave monuments, mostly from the Kerameikos. These include the beautiful *stele* (c.410 BC) of Hegeso (*see p92*). Classical votive sculpture on display includes parts of a statue of the goddess Hera, from the Argive Heraion in the Peloponnese, and many majestic statues of the goddess Athena, including the Roman *Varvakeion Athena*, a reduced copy of the original ivory and gold statue from the Parthenon (*see p103*).

Roman and Hellenistic Sculpture

Although a large number of Greek bronzes were lost in antiquity, as metal was melted down in times of emergency for making weapons, the museum has some excellent pieces on display. These include the famous bronzes *Poseidon* and the *Horse with the Little Jockey*, both found at Cape Artemísion on Evvoia, and the *Ephebe of Antikythera*, found in the sea off that island. Another of the best-known sculptures is the *Marathon Boy*.

Other Collections

The museum also houses several smaller collections, many donated by private individuals. Among these is the glittering **Eléni Stathátou jewellery collection**, which covers the Bronze Age through to the Byzantine period. The **Karapános collection**, which is composed mainly from discoveries made at the site at Dodóni (*see p215*), contains many fine bronzes, including *Zeus Hurling a Thunderbolt*. Also on display are small decorative and votive pieces, and strips of lead inscribed with questions for the oracle at Dodóni.

Other collections include the **Egyptian collection** and the **Bronze collection**, which comprises many small pieces of statuary and decorative items discovered on the Acropolis.

Thera Frescoes

Two of the famous frescoes discovered at Akrotíri on the island of ancient Thera (today Santoríni) in 1967, and originally thought to be from the mythical city of Atlantis, are displayed in the museum. The rest are on Santoríni. Dating from 1500 BC, they confirm the sophistication of late Minoan civilization. The colourful, restored images depict boxer boys, and animals and flowers symbolizing spring time.

Pottery Collection

The strength of this vast collection lies not only in its size, but in the quality of specific works, representing the flowering of Greek ceramic art. The real gems belong to the 5th century BC when red-figure vases and white-ground *lekythoi* became the established style (*see p64*) and were produced in vast numbers. Expressive painting styles and new designs characterize this period. The most poignant pieces are by the "Bosanquet Painter" and the "Achilles Painter" who portrayed young men by their graves.

This "valedictory stele" (mid-4th century BC) shows a seated woman bidding farewell to her family. The figures express a dignified suffering found in many Greek funerary reliefs.

Gold Hellenistic ring from the Eléni Stathátou collection

View northeast to Lykavittós Hill from the Acropolis

❷ Exárcheia and Stréfi Hill

Εξάρχεια Λόφος Στρέφη

Map 2 F2 & 3 A2. **M** Omónoia.

Until recently, the area around Plateía Exarcheíon was renowned as a hotbed of anarchist activity. Prior to the invasion of students, Exárcheia was a very attractive area and the 19th-century Neo-Classical buildings still stand as testament to this. Today, the area is picking up again and although parts of it are still rather run down, gentrification has brought many fashionable cafés, bars and *ouzerí* to the area. Themistokléous, which leads off the square down to Omónoia, is pleasant to wander along. The local food stores and small boutiques found on this street make a refreshing change from the noisy cafés in the square. Plateía Exarcheíon is especially lively at night when the outdoor cafés and the open-air cinemas, the Riviera and the Vox, in the adjoining streets, attract many visitors.

Every year, a demonstration takes place on 17 November, marking the date in 1973 when many students were killed by the Junta *(see p47)* during a sit-in.

The nearby park of Stréfi Hill, with its intriguing maze of paths, is quiet and peaceful by day but comes to life at night when nearby tavernas fill up.

Stréfi Hill is one of the many green areas in Athens that provide welcome relief from the noise and grime of the city, particularly in the oppressive heat of summer.

The restaurant on Lykavittós Hill, overlooking Athens

❸ Lykavittós Hill

Λόφος Λυκαβηττού

Map 3 B4. **Funicular**: from Ploutárchou. **Open** 9am–2:30am daily.

The peak of Lykavittós (also known as Lycabettus) reaches 277 m (910 ft) above the city, and is its highest hill. It can be climbed on foot by various paths or by the easier, albeit vertiginous, ride in the funicular from the top of Ploutárchou. On foot, it should take about 45 minutes. The hill may derive its name from a combination of the words *lýki* and *vaino*, meaning "path of light". The

ancient belief was that this was the rock once destined to be the Acropolis citadel, accidentally dropped by the city's patron goddess, Athena. Although it is without doubt the most prominent hill in Athens, surprisingly little mention is made of Lykavittós in Classical literature; the exceptions are passing refe-rences in Aristophanes's *Frogs* and Plato's *Kritías*. This landmark is a favourite haunt for many Athenians, who come for the panoramic views of the city from the observation decks that rim the summit.

The small whitewashed chapel of **Agios Geórgios** crowns the top of the hill. It was built in the 19th century on the site of an older Byzantine church, dedicated to Profítis Ilías (the Prophet Elijah). Both saints associated with the site are celebrated here on their name days (Profítis Ilías on 20 July and Agios Geórgios on 23 April). Another celebration is on the eve of Easter Sunday when a spectacular candlelit procession winds down the peak's wooded slopes *(see p49)*.

Lykavittós Hill is also home to a summit restaurant and café and the open-air **Lykavittós Theatre**, where contemporary jazz, pop and dance performances are held annually during the Athens Festival *(see p50)*.

❹ Gennádeion

Γεννάδειον

American School of Classical Studies, Souidías 54, Kolonáki. **Map** 3 C4. **Tel** 210 723 6313. Ⓜ Evangelismós. 🚌 3, 7, 8, 13. **Open** 8:30am–9pm Mon–Fri, 9am–2pm Sat. **Closed** Aug, main public hols.

The Greek diplomat and bibliophile Ioánnis Gennádios (1844–1932) spent a lifetime accumulating rare first editions and illuminated manuscripts. In 1923, he donated his collection to the American School of Classical Studies. The Gennádeion building, named after him, was designed and built between 1923 and 1925 by the New York firm Van Pelt and Thompson to house the collection. Above its façade of Ionic columns is an inscription which translates as "They are called Greeks who share in our culture" – from Gennádios's dedication speech at the opening in 1926.

Researchers need special permission to gain access to over 70,000 rare books and manuscripts and no items are allowed to be removed from the library. Casual visitors may look at selected exhibits that are on show, and books, posters and postcards are for sale at the souvenir stall.

Exhibits in the main reading room include 192 Edward Lear sketches purchased in 1929. There is also an eclectic mix of Byron memorabilia, including the last known portrait of the poet made before his death in Greece in 1824 *(see p153)*.

The imposing Neo-Classical façade of the Gennádeion

❺ National Gallery of Art

Εθνική Πινακοθήκη

Vasiléos Konstantínou 50, Ilísia. **Map** 7 C1. **Tel** 210 723 5937. Ⓜ Evangelismós. 🚌 3, 13. **Open** 9am–3:30pm Mon & Thu–Sun, 2–9pm Wed. **Closed** for renovation. 📷 ♿ 🆆 **nationalgallery.gr**

Opened in 1976, this gallery contains a permanent collection of European and Greek art. Upon completion of a new building on the site (in 2017 at the earliest), the following highlights should remain, but the floor plan may change. The ground floor opens out on to a sculpture garden. In addition to five impressive works by El Greco (1541–1614), there is a minor collection of non-Greek, European art. Alongside works of the Dutch, Italian and Flemish schools, there are studies, engravings and paintings by Rembrandt, Dürer, Brueghel, Van Dyck, Watteau, Utrillo, Cézanne and Braque, among others. These include Caravaggio's *Singer* (1620), Eugène Delacroix's *Greek Warrior* (1856) and Picasso's Cubist-period *Woman in a White Dress* (1939).

Other wings house modern Greek art from the 18th to the 20th century. The 19th century is represented mainly by numerous depictions of the War of Independence and seascapes, enlivened by portraits such as Nikólaos Gýzis's *The Loser of the Bet* (1878), *Waiting* (1900) by Nikifóros Lýtras and *The Straw Hat* (1925) by Nikólaos Lýtras. There are many fine works by major Greek artists including Theophilos, Hadjikyriakos-Ghikas, Kontoglou, Móralis and Tsaroúchis.

❻ War Museum

Πολεμικό Μουσείο

Corner of Vasilíssis Sofías & Rizári, Ilísia. **Map** 7 C1. **Tel** 210 725 2975. Ⓜ Evangelismós. 🚌 3, 7, 8, 13. **Open** May–Oct: 9am–7pm Mon–Sat, 9am–5pm Sun; Nov–Apr: 9am–5pm Tue–Sat, 9am–3pm Sun. **Closed** main public hols. ♿ 🆆 **warmuseum.gr**

The War Museum opened in 1975 after the fall of the military dictatorship *(see p47)*. The first nine galleries are chronologically ordered, and contain battle scenes, armour and plans from as far back as ancient Mycenaean times through to the more recent German occupation of 1941. Other galleries contain a miscellany of items, including a selection of different uniforms and Turkish weapons.

Spartan bronze helmet

There is a fine display of paintings and prints of leaders from the Greek War of Independence *(see pp44–5)*, such as General Theódoros Kolokotrónis (1770–1843). His death mask can also be seen in the museum. A sizeable collection of fine oils and sketches by the artists Flora-Karavía and Argyrós vividly captures the hardships of the two world wars.

Modern sculpture outside the National Gallery of Art

❾ Museum of Cycladic Art

Μουσείο Κυκλαδικής Τέχνης

Opened in 1986, this modern museum offers the world's finest collection of Cycladic art. It was initially assembled by Nikolaos and Dolly Goulandrís and has expanded with donations from other Greek collectors. The museum now has an excellent selection of ancient Greek and Cypriot art, the earliest from about 5,000 years ago. The Cycladic figurines, dating from the 3rd millennium BC, have never enjoyed quite the same level of popularity as Classical sculpture. However, the haunting simplicity of these marble statues has inspired many 20th-century artists and sculptors, including Picasso, Modigliani and Henry Moore.

Locator Map

Key

▨ Non-exhibition space

▨ Cycladic art

▨ Ancient Greek art

▨ Ancient Cypriot art

▨ Daily life in antiquity

▨ Temporary exhibitions

Terracotta Figurine
This elegant figure of a woman is one of many that were thought to have been produced at Tanágra, in Boeotia, Central Greece. It dates from 330–320 BC.

Second floor

First floor

Main entrance

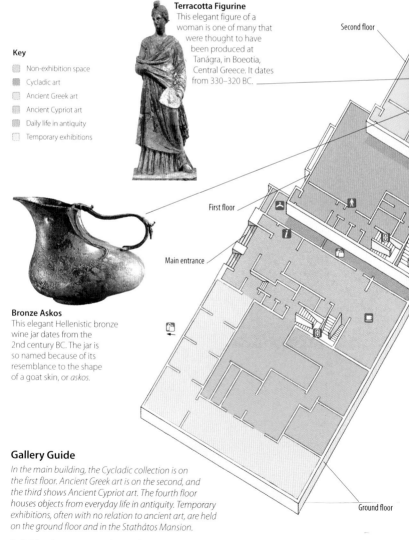

Bronze Askos
This elegant Hellenistic bronze wine jar dates from the 2nd century BC. The jar is so named because of its resemblance to the shape of a goat skin, or *askos*.

Ground floor

Gallery Guide

In the main building, the Cycladic collection is on the first floor. Ancient Greek art is on the second, and the third shows Ancient Cypriot art. The fourth floor houses objects from everyday life in antiquity. Temporary exhibitions, often with no relation to ancient art, are held on the ground floor and in the Stathátos Mansion.

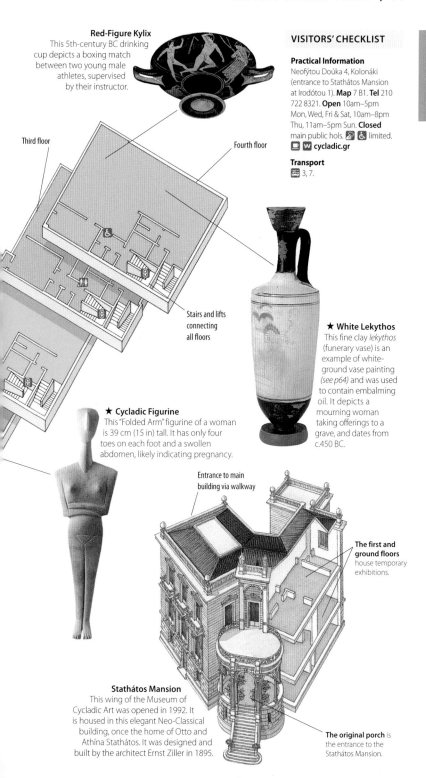

Red-Figure Kylix
This 5th-century BC drinking cup depicts a boxing match between two young male athletes, supervised by their instructor.

Third floor

Fourth floor

VISITORS' CHECKLIST

Practical Information
Neofýtou Doúka 4, Kolonáki (entrance to Stathátos Mansion at Irodótou 1). **Map** 7 B1. **Tel** 210 722 8321. **Open** 10am–5pm Mon, Wed, Fri & Sat, 10am–8pm Thu, 11am–5pm Sun. **Closed** main public hols. ♿ ♿ limited. ▣ ⓦ cycladic.gr

Transport
🚌 3, 7.

Stairs and lifts connecting all floors

★ White Lekythos
This fine clay *lekythos* (funerary vase) is an example of white-ground vase painting *(see p64)* and was used to contain embalming oil. It depicts a mourning woman taking offerings to a grave, and dates from c.450 BC.

★ Cycladic Figurine
This "Folded Arm" figurine of a woman is 39 cm (15 in) tall. It has only four toes on each foot and a swollen abdomen, likely indicating pregnancy.

Entrance to main building via walkway

The first and ground floors house temporary exhibitions.

Stathátos Mansion
This wing of the Museum of Cycladic Art was opened in 1992. It is housed in this elegant Neo-Classical building, once the home of Otto and Athína Stathátos. It was designed and built by the architect Ernst Ziller in 1895.

The original porch is the entrance to the Stathátos Mansion.

Icon of the Archangel Michael in the Byzantine and Christian Museum

❼ Byzantine and Christian Museum

Βυζαντινό και Χριστιανικό Μουσείο

Vasilíssis Sofías 22, Plateía Rigílis, Kolonáki. **Map** 7 B1. **Tel** 213 213 9500.
Ⓜ Evangelismós. 🚌 3, 8, 7, 13.
Open 9am–4pm Tue–Sun.
Closed main public hols. ♿
♿ ground floor only. ▢
🌐 byzantinemuseum.gr

Originally called the Villa Ilissia, this elegant Florentine-style mansion was built between 1840 and 1848 by Stamátis Kleánthis for the Duchesse de Plaisance (1785–1854). This eccentric woman, wife of the son of one of Napoleon's generals, was a key figure in Athens society during the mid-19th century and a dedicated philhellene.

Collector Geórgios Sotiríou converted the house into a museum in the 1930s with the help of architect Aristotélis Záchos. They transformed the entrance into a monastic court, incorporating a copy of a fountain from a 4th-century mosaic in Daphni (see pp156–7).

Following extensive renovations, the museum reopened with a modern open-plan, split-level exhibition space built underground, below the courtyard. The collection is organised into five main themes (including the role of women, burial practices and gold artifacts), divided into two chronologically ordered sections: section one, *From the Ancient World to Byzantium*, traces the rise of Christianity, while section two, *The Byzantine World*, runs from the 6th century AD up until the fall of Constantinople in 1453.

Section one is dominated by fragments of ornamental stone carvings and mosaics taken from basilicas, sarcophagi, and early religious sculpture such as the *Shepherd Carrying a*

Funerary stele showing Orpheus with his lyre

Lamb and *Orpheus Playing a Lyre*, both of which illustrate the way in which the Christian church absorbed and adapted pagan symbols. Section two presents an array of icons, frescoes and precious ecclesiastical artifacts. Fine pieces to watch out for include the Treasury of Mytilene (a horde of 7th century gold and silver jewellery, coins and goblets discovered buried), the Double-sided Icon of St George and the Mosaic Icon of the Virgin (both dating from the 13th century). There are also some magnificent frescoes that were rescued from the Church of the Episkopi and are cleverly displayed in the positions they would have been in the church, which was based on a cross in square plan with a dome and narthex.

In summer, there are often concerts in the courtyard. Year-round, there are frequent guided tours free of charge.

❽ Museum of Cycladic Art

See pp78–9.

The *Episkepsis*, from the Byzantine and Christian Museum, depicting the Virgin and Child

Icons in the Orthodox Church

The word icon simply means "image" and has come to signify a holy image through association with its religious use. Subjects range from popular saints such as St Andrew and St Nicholas to lesser-known martyrs, prophets and archangels. The image of the Virgin and Child is easily the most popular and exalted. Icons are a prominent feature in the Greek Orthodox religion and appear in many areas of Greek life. You will see them in taxis and buses, on boats and in restaurants, as well as in homes and churches. An icon can be in fresco, a mosaic, or made from bone or metal. The most common form is a portable painting, in egg tempera-based paints applied to wooden boards treated with gesso. The figures are arranged so that the eyes are clearly depicted and appear to be looking directly at the viewer of the icon. These works, often of great artistic skill, are unsigned, undated and share a rigid conformity, right down to details of colour, dress, gesture and expression (see pp24–5). The icon painter is careful to catch every detail of a tradition that stretches back hundreds of years.

Outdoor tables at a café on Kolonáki Square

❾ Plateía Kolonakíou

Πλατεία Κολωνακίου

Kolonáki. **Map** 3 B5. ▨ 3, 7, 8, 13.

Kolonáki Square and its neighbouring side streets are the most chic and sophisticated part of Athens. The area is often missed by those who restrict themselves to the ancient sites and the popular flea markets of Monastiráki. Also known as Plateía Filikís Etaireías, the square is named after a small ancient column *(kolonáki)* found in the area. Celebrated for its designer boutiques and fashionable bars and cafés, smart antique shops and art galleries and sumptuous *zacharoplasteía* (pastry shops), it revels in its status as the city's most fashionable quarter *(see p120)*.

❿ Benáki Museum

See pp82–3.

⓫ Hadjikyriakos-Ghikas Gallery

Πινακοθήκη Χατζηκυριάκου Γκίκα

Kriezótou 3, Athens. **Map** 2 F5. **Tel** 210 361 5702. Ⓜ Syntagma. ▨ 3, 8, 13. **Open** 10am–6pm Wed–Sun. **Closed** Aug, main public hols. ♿ limited. 📷

This annexe of the Benáki Museum *(see pp82–3)* is somewhat misnamed.

Although the gallery is situated in the former home of the great painter Hadjikyriakos-Ghikas, with his top-floor residence and atelier preserved as when he lived and worked here, most of the many galleries highlight just about everybody who has had an influence on 20th-century Greek cultural life. Such figures include archaeologist-architect Athanasios Orlandos, designer-architects Dimitris Pikionis and Aris Konstantinidis, photographers Nelly's, Takis Tloupas and Spyros Meletzis, the cartoonist Bost, and painters Yiannis Moralis and Yorgos Manousakis, to name but a few. Allow plenty of time for a pleasant and well-labelled survey of the greatest intellectual and cultural figures to have shaped modern Greece.

⓬ Museum of the City of Athens

Μουσείο της Πόλεως των Αθηνών

Paparrigopoúlou 7, Plateía Klafthmónos, Sýntagma. **Map** 2 E5. **Tel** 210 323 1387. Ⓜ Panepistímio. ▨ 1, 2, 4, 5, 9, 11, 12, 15, 18. **Open** 9am–7pm Mon & Wed–Fri, 11am–7pm Sat–Sun. **Closed** main public hols. 📷

King Otto and Queen Amalía *(see p44)* lived here from 1831 until their new palace, today's Voulí parliament building *(see p116)*, was completed in 1838. It was joined to the neighbouring house to create what was known as the Old Palace.

The palace was restored in 1980 as a museum devoted to royal memorabilia, furniture and family portraits, maps and prints. It offers a delightful look at life during the early years of King Otto's reign. Exhibits include the manuscript of the 1843 Constitution, coats of arms from the Frankish (1205–1311) and Catalan (1311–88) rulers of Athens, and a scale model of the city as it was in 1842, made by architect Giánnis Travlós (1908–85). The museum also has a fine art collection, including Nikólaos Gýzis's *The Carnival in Athens* (1892) and a selection of water-colours by the English artists Edward Dodwell (1767–1832), Edward Lear (1812–88) and Thomas Hartley Cromek (1809–73).

Upstairs sitting room recreated in the Museum of the City of Athens

⑩ Benáki Museum
Μουσείο Μπενάκη

This outstanding museum was founded in 1931 by Antónis Benákis (1873–1954), the son of Emmanouïl, a wealthy Greek who made his fortune in Egypt. Housed in an elegant Neo-Classical mansion, which was once the home of the Benákis family, the collection contains a diverse array of Greek arts and crafts, paintings and jewellery, local costumes and political memorabilia that spans over 5,000 years, from the Neolithic era to the 20th century.

Flag of Hydra
The imagery symbolizes the island of Hydra's supremacy in sea warfare as it was Greece's most powerful naval community.

Bridal Cushion
This ornate embroidered cushion comes from Epirus and dates from the 18th century. It depicts a bridal procession, with ornamental flowers in the background.

★ Detail of Wood Decoration
This intricately painted and carved piece of wooden panelling comes from the reception room of a mansion in Kozáni, in western Macedonia. It dates from the 18th century.

Silver Ciborium
Used to contain consecrated bread, this elegant piece of ecclesiastical silverware is dated 1667 and comes from Edirne, in Turkey.

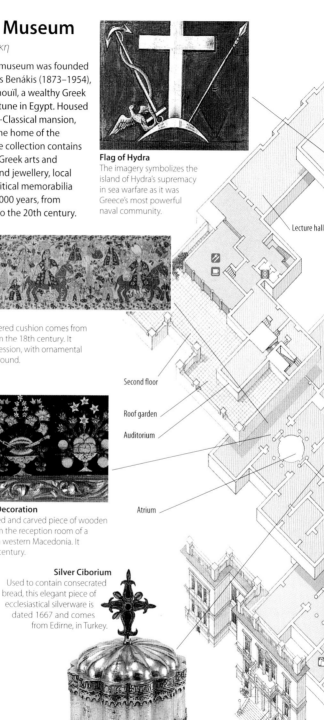

Lecture hall

Second floor

Roof garden

Auditorium

Atrium

Entrance

Key to Floorplan

- ☐ Ground floor
- ▦ First floor
- ▦ Second floor
- ☐ Third floor
- ▦ Non-exhibition space

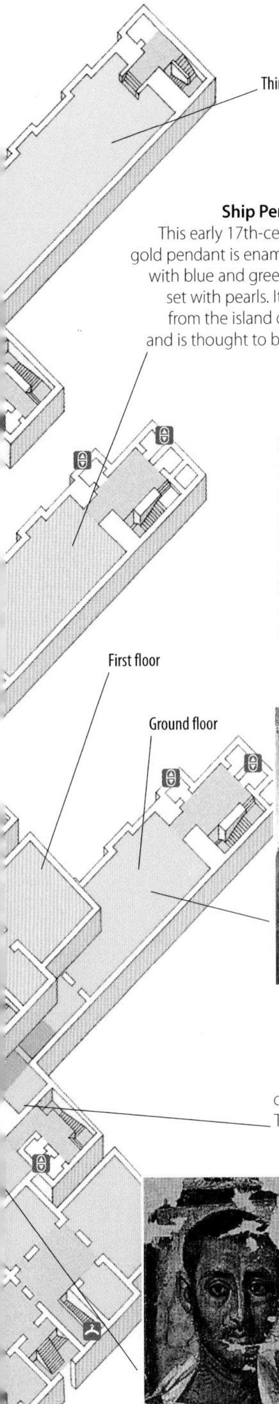

Third floor

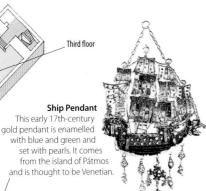

Ship Pendant
This early 17th-century gold pendant is enamelled with blue and green and set with pearls. It comes from the island of Pátmos and is thought to be Venetian.

Gallery Guide

The ground floor collection is arranged into different periods and ranges from Neolithic to late-Byzantine art and Cretan icon painting. The first floor exhibits are organized geographically and are from Asia Minor, mainland Greece and the Greek islands. There is also a collection of ecclesiastical silverware and jewellery. The second floor has items relating to Greek spiritual, economic and social life, and the third floor concentrates on the Greek War of Independence (see pp44–5) and modern political and cultural life, as well as having a wing for temporary exhibitions.

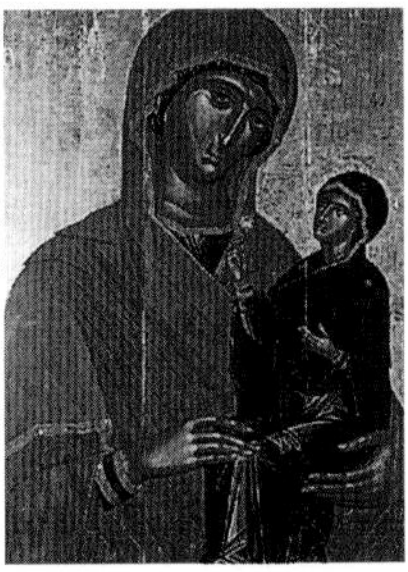

First floor

Ground floor

★ **Icon of St Anne with the Virgin**
A product of the Cretan School, this icon of St Anne was painted in the 15th century. St Anne is carrying the Virgin Mary as a child, who is holding a white lily, symbol of purity.

Bowl from Paphos
Dating from the 13th century AD, this colourful bowl originates from Cyprus. The dancing figure is holding rattles.

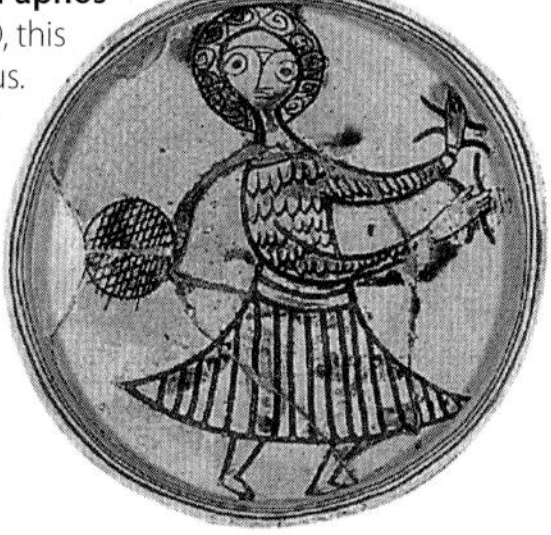

★ **El Faiyûm Portrait**
This Roman portrait of a man, painted on linen, dates from the 3rd century AD.

Neo-Classical façade of the National Historical Museum

⓭ National Historical Museum

Εθνικό Ιστορικό Μουσείο

Stadíou 13, Sýntagma. **Map** 2 F5. **Tel** 210 323 7617. Ⓜ Sýntagma. 🚌 1, 2, 4, 5, 9, 10, 11, 18. **Open** 8:30am–2:30pm Tue–Sun. **Closed** main public hols. 🅿 free Sun. 🌐 nhmuseum.gr

Designed by French architect François Boulanger (1807–75), this museum was originally built as the first home of the Greek parliament. Queen Amalía laid the foundation stone in 1858, but only 13 years later did it become the first permanent site of the Greek parliament. The country's most famous early prime ministers have sat in the imposing chamber of the Old Parliament of the Hellenes, including Chárilaos Trikoúpis and Theódoros Deligiánnis, who was assassinated on the steps at the front of the building in 1905. The parliament moved to its present-day site in the Voulí building on Plateía Syntágmatos *(see p116)* after the Voulí was renovated in 1935.

In 1961, the building opened as the National Historical Museum, owned by the Historical and Ethnological Society of Greece. Founded in 1882, the purpose of the society is to collect objects that illuminate the history of modern Greece.

Statue of General Theódoros Kolokotrónis

The museum covers the major events of Greek history from the Byzantine period to the 20th century. Venetian armour, regional costumes and figureheads from the warships used during the 1821 Revolution are some of the exhibits on show.

The collection also focuses on major parliamentary figures, philhellenes and leaders in the War of Independence, displaying such items as Byron's sword, the weapons of Theódoros Kolokotrónis (1770–1843), King Otto's throne and the pen used by Elefthérios Venizélos to sign the Treaty of Sèvres in 1920. The revolutionary memoirs of General Makrigiánnis (1797–1864) can also be seen. Among the paintings on view is a fine rare woodcut of the *Battle of Lepanto* (1571), the work of Bonastro. Outside the building is a copy of Lázaros Sóchos's equestrian statue of Kolokotrónis, made in 1900, the original of which is in Náfplio *(see pp186–7)*, the former capital of Greece. A dedication on the statue reads (in Greek): "Theódoros Kolokotrónis 1821. Ride on, noble commander, through the centuries, showing the nations how slaves may become free men." The Greek Communist Party used to have its headquarters across the street. A running joke stated that Kolokotronis's finger pointed that way to indicate his indignation.

⓮ Kapnikaréa

Καπνικαρέα

Corner of Ermoú & Kalamiótou, Monastiráki. **Map** 6 D1. **Tel** 210 322 4462. Ⓜ Monastiráki. **Open** 9am–2pm Mon–Sun. **Closed** main public hols.

This charming 11th-century Byzantine church was rescued from demolition in 1834, thanks to the timely intervention of King Ludwig of Bavaria. Stranded in the middle of a square between Ermoú and Kapnikaréa streets, it is surrounded by the modern office blocks and shops of Athens' busy garment district.

Traditionally called the Church of the Princess, its foundation is attributed to Empress Irene, who ruled the Byzantine Empire from AD 797 to 802. She is revered as a saint in the Greek church for her efforts in restoring icons to the Empire's churches.

The true origins of the name "Kapnikaréa" are unknown, although according to some sources, the church was named after its founder, a "hearth-tax gatherer" *(kapnikaréas)*. Hearth tax was imposed on buildings by the Byzantines.

Restored in the 1950s, the dome of the church is supported by four Roman columns. Frescoes by Phótis Kóntoglou (1895–1965) were painted during the restoration, including one of the Virgin and Child. Some of Kóntoglou's work is also on display in the National Gallery of Art *(see p77)*.

The dome and main entrance of the Byzantine church Kapnikaréa

Athenian Neo-Classical Architecture

Neo-Classicism flourished in the 19th century, when the architects who were commissioned by King Otto to build the capital in the 1830s turned to this popular European style. Among those commissioned were the Danish Hansen brothers, Christian and Theophil, and also Ernst Ziller. As a result of their planning, within 50 years a modern city had emerged, with elegant administrative buildings, squares and tree-lined avenues. In its early days, Neo-Classicism had imitated the grace of the buildings of ancient Greece, using marble columns, sculptures and decorative detailing. In later years, it evolved into an original Greek style. Grand Neo-Classicism is seen at its best in the public buildings along Panepistimíou; its domestic adaptation can be seen in the houses of Pláka.

Schliemann's House (also known as Ilíou Mélathron, the Palace of Ilium, or Troy) was built in 1878 by Ziller. The interior is decorated with frescoes and mosaics of mythological subjects. It is now home to the Numismatic Museum (**Map** 2 F5).

The National Theatre was built between 1882 and 1890. Ernst Ziller used a Renaissance-style exterior with arches and Doric columns for George I's Royal Theatre. Inspired by the Public Theatre of Vienna, its interior was very modern for its time (**Map** 2 D3).

The National Library was designed by Danish architect Theophil Hansen in 1887 in the form of a Doric temple with two side wings. Built of Pentelic marble, it houses over half a million books, including many illuminated manuscripts and rare first editions (**Map** 2 F4).

Athens Academy was designed by Theophil Hansen and built between 1859 and 1887. Statues of Apollo and Athena, and seated figures of Socrates and Plato, convey a Classical style, as do the Ionic capitals and columns. Inside the building, the Academy hall has beautiful frescoes that depict scenes from the myth of Prometheus (**Map** 2 F4).

The University of Athens was designed by Christian Hansen. This fine building, completed in 1864, has an Ionic colonnade and a portico frieze depicting the resurgence of arts and sciences under the reign of King Otto. A symbol of wisdom, the Sphinx is connected with Athens through the Oedipus legend (*see p225*). Oedipus, who solved the riddle of the Sphinx, later found sanctuary in enlightened Athens. Other statues on the façade include Patriarch Gregory V, a martyr of the War of Independence (**Map** 2 F4).

CENTRAL ATHENS SOUTH

Southern Athens is dominated by the Acropolis and is home to the buildings that were at the heart of ancient Athens. Pláka and Monastiráki still bask in their historical roots as the oldest inhabited areas of the city, and are full of Byzantine churches and museums. Nestling among the restored Neo-Classical houses are grocery stores,

icon painters and open-air tavernas. In the busy streets of Monastiráki's flea market, food vendors and street musicians provide the atmosphere of a Middle Eastern bazaar. Southeast of Plateía Syntágmatos are the National Gardens, the city centre's tree-filled park. For information on getting around Athens, see pages 320–23.

Sights at a Glance

Museums and Galleries
1 Kyriazópoulos Folk Ceramic Museum
4 Municipal Art Gallery
8 Ilías Lalaoúnis Jewellery Museum
9 Kanellópoulos Museum
10 University of Athens Museum
11 Museum of Greek Popular Musical Instruments
17 Frissiras Museum
18 Museum of Greek Folk Art
19 Jewish Museum of Greece

Ancient Sites
2 *Tower of the Winds pp90–91*
5 *Kerameikos pp92–3*
6 *Ancient Agora pp94–5*
7 *Acropolis pp98–105*
20 Temple of Olympian Zeus

Churches
12 *Panagía Gorgoepíkoös p109*
13 Mitrópoli
14 Agios Nikólaos Ragavás
21 Russian Church of the Holy Trinity

Historic Districts
15 Anafiótika

Markets
3 Flea Market

Squares and Gardens
16 Plateía Lysikrátous
22 Plateía Syntágmatos
23 National Gardens

Historic Buildings and Monuments
24 Presidential Palace
25 Kallimármaro Stadium

Cemeteries
26 First Cemetery of Athens

See also Street Finder map pp126–39

0 metres 500
0 yards 500

◀ The slender Ionic columns of the Erechtheion, Acropolis

For keys to symbols *see back flap*

Street-by-Street: Monastiráki

This old area of the city takes its name from the little sunken monastery in Plateía Monastirakíou. The former heart of Ottoman Athens, Monastiráki is still home to the bazaar and market stalls selling everything from junk to jewellery. The Fethiye Mosque and the Tzistarákis Mosque, home of the Kyriazópoulos Museum, stand as reminders of the area's Ottoman past. Roman influences are also strong in Monastiráki. The area borders the Roman Agora and includes the remains of Emperor Hadrian's library and the unique Tower of the Winds, a Hellenistic water clock. Monastiráki mixes the atmospheric surroundings of ancient ruins with the excitement of bargaining in the bazaar.

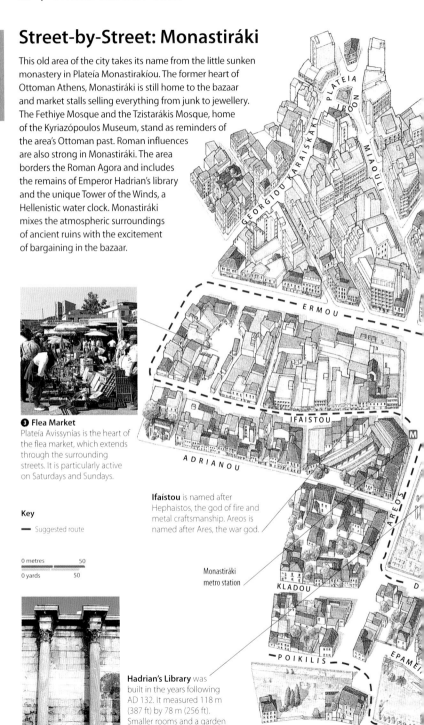

❸ **Flea Market**
Plateía Avissynías is the heart of the flea market, which extends through the surrounding streets. It is particularly active on Saturdays and Sundays.

Key

— Suggested route

```
0 metres          50
0 yards           50
```

Ifaístou is named after Hephaistos, the god of fire and metal craftsmanship. Areos is named after Ares, the war god.

Monastiráki metro station

Hadrian's Library was built in the years following AD 132. It measured 118 m (387 ft) by 78 m (256 ft). Smaller rooms and a garden with a pool were contained in the complex, in addition to the vast library itself.

Ancient Agora ↙
(see pp94–5)

Locator Map
See Athens Street Finder maps 2, 6

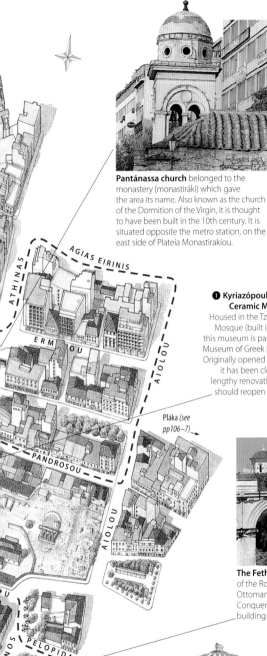

Pantánassa church belonged to the monastery (monastiráki) which gave the area its name. Also known as the church of the Dormition of the Virgin, it is thought to have been built in the 10th century. It is situated opposite the metro station, on the east side of Plateía Monastirakíou.

Pláka *(see pp106–7)* →

❶ Kyriazópoulos Folk Ceramic Museum
Housed in the Tzistarákis Mosque (built in 1759), this museum is part of the Museum of Greek Folk Art. Originally opened in 1974, it has been closed for lengthy renovations but should reopen in 2017.

The Fethiye Mosque is situated in the corner of the Roman Agora. It was first built by the Ottomans in 1458 to mark Mehmet the Conqueror's visit to Athens, but the current building dates from 1670.

❷ ★ Tower of the Winds
This octagonal structure was built as a water clock and weather vane by the astronomer Andrónikos Kyrrestes in the 1st century BC, though many scholars think it might be a century older.

❶ Kyriazópoulos Folk Ceramic Museum

Μουσείο Ελληνικής Λαϊκής Τέχνης, Συλλογή Κεραμικών Β. Κυριαζοπούλου

Tzistarákis Mosque, Areos 1, Monastiráki. **Map** 6 D1. **Tel** 210 324 2066. Ⓜ Monastiráki. **Closed** see website for updates. 🖼 🆔 **melt.gr**

This colourful collection of ceramics was donated to the Museum of Greek Folk Art *(see p114)* in 1974 by Professor Vasíleios Kyriazópoulos. Now an annexe of the Museum of Greek Folk Art, the Kyriazópoulos Folk Ceramic Museum is housed in the imposing Tzisdarákis Mosque (or the Mosque of the Lower Fountain). Of the hundreds of pieces on display, many are of the type still used today in a traditional Greek kitchen, such as terracotta water jugs from Aígina, earthenware oven dishes from Sífnos and storage jars from Thessaly and Chíos. There are also some ceramic figures and plates, based on mythological and folk stories, crafted by Minás Avramídis and Dimítrios Mygdalinós who came from Asia Minor in the 1920s.

The mosque itself is of as much interest as its contents. It was built in 1759 by the newly appointed Turkish *voivode* Tzistarákis. The *voivode* was the civil governor who possessed complete powers over the law courts and the police. He collected taxes for his own account, but also had to pay for the sultan's harem and the treasury. His workmen dynamited the 17th column of the Temple of Olympian Zeus *(see p115)* in order to make lime to be used for the stucco work on the mosque. Destruction of ancient monuments was forbidden by Turkish law and this act of vandalism was the downfall of Tzistarákis. He was exiled the same year. The mosque has been well restored after earthquake damage in 1981.

Ceramic of a young girl from Asia Minor

❷ Tower of the Winds

Αέρηδες

Within Roman Agora ruins, Pláka. **Map** 6 D1. **Tel** 210 324 5220. Ⓜ Monastiráki. **Open** Apr–Oct: 8am–8pm daily; Nov–Mar: 8:30am–3pm daily. **Closed** main public hols. 🖼 ♿

The remarkable Tower of the Winds is set within the ruins of the Roman Agora. Constructed from marble in the 2nd or 1st century BC by the Syrian astronomer Andrónikos Kyrrestes, it was built as a combined weather vane and water clock. The name comes from the external friezes, personifying the eight winds. Sundials are etched into the walls beneath each relief.

The tower is well preserved, standing today at over 12 m (40 ft) high with a diameter of 8 m (26 ft). Still simply called Aérides ("the winds") by Greeks today, in the Middle Ages it was thought to be either the school or prison of Socrates, or even the tomb of Philip II of Macedon *(see p246)*. It was at last correctly identified as the Horologion (water clock) of Andrónikos in the 17th century. All that remains today of its elaborate water clock are the origins of a complex system of water pipes and a circular channel cut into the floor which can be seen inside the tower.

The west and southwest faces of the Tower of the Winds

The west- and north-facing sides each contain a hole which lets light into the otherwise dark interior of the tower.

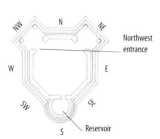

This interior floorplan of the tower shows the compass direction of the building's eight sides. External friezes personify each of the eight winds.

Northwest entrance

Reservoir

North

Boreas blows the cold north wind through a large conch shell.

Northwest

Skiron scatters glowing ashes from a bronze vessel.

West

Zephyros is a semi-naked youth scattering flowers.

❸ Flea Market

ΓΙΟΥΣΟΥΡΟΥΜ

From Plateía Monastirakíou to Plateía Avyssinías, Monastiráki. **Map** 5 C1. Ⓜ Monastiráki. **Open** 8am–2pm Sun.

Shoppers browsing in Athens' lively flea market

A banner welcomes visitors to Athens' famous flea market, past the ubiquitous tourist trinket shops of Adrianoú and Pandrósou streets. For the locals, the genuine flea market lies just west of Plateía Monastirakíou, in Plateía Avyssinías and its warren of surrounding streets.

On Sunday mornings, when many shops are closed, the market itself bursts into action. Traders set out their bric-a-brac on stalls and the pavement and many bargains can be found, everything from old East German alarm clocks to colourful old phone cards with scenic photos on them. More expensive items are also on sale, including brassware, leatherware and silverware.

During the week, all shops in the surrounding area are open, though they do not have the same range and quality of goods as the Sunday stalls. Individual shops each have their own specialities, so hunt around before making a purchase. You can buy almost anything, from antiques and old books to taverna chairs and army surplus gear.

The southwest wind, Lips, heralds a swift voyage. The reliefs show that each wind was given a personality according to its characteristics, and each promises different conditions. Gentle Zephyros and chilly Boreas, mentioned in Western literature and represented in art and sculpture, are the best known of these.

Howling dervishes used the tower as their *tekke* (lodge) in the mid-18th century. Members of the Rufa'i or Qadiri sect, the so-called "howling dervishes" became a popular attraction for visitors on the Grand Tour, who came to witness their weekly *sema* ritual of frenzied chanting and dancing.

| | | | Lines of sundial carved into wall of tower |
| | Relief carving of mythological figure | Metal rod casting shadow | |

Southwest	South	Southeast	East	Northeast

Lips holds the *aphlaston* (or stern ornament) of a ship as he steers.	**Notos** is the bearer of rain, emptying a pitcher of water.	**Euros** is a bearded old man, warmly wrapped in a cloak.	**Apeliotes** is a young man bringing fruits and corn.	**Kaïkias** empties a shield full of icy hailstones on those below.

Miss T K, by Giánnis Mitarákis, in the Municipal Art Gallery

❹ Municipal Art Gallery
Δημοτική Πινακοθήκη

Corner of Leonidíou & Myllérou, Metaxourgeíou. **Map** 1 B4.
Tel 210 324 3022. Ⓜ Metaxourgeíou.
Open 10am–9pm Tue, 10am–7pm Wed–Sat, 10am–3pm Sun. **Closed** main public hols. 🅿 ♿

This little-visited museum has one of the finest archive collections of modern Greek art. Designed by the architect Christian Hansen, originally as a silk workshop (hence the Greek name of the neighbour-hood, meaning "silk works"), since 2010 it has sheltered this museum. The old premises on Plateía Koumoundoúrou now only opens when there is a special exhibition.

The Municipality of Athens has been amassing the collection since 1923. It now offers a fine introduction to the diverse styles of modern Greek artists. Many paintings are passionate reflections on the Greek landscape, such as Dímos Mpraésas's (1878–1967) landscapes of the Cyclades, or Konstantínos Parthénis's (1882–1964) paintings of olive and cypress trees.

There are also portraits by Giánnis Mitarákis and still lifes by Theófrastos Triantafyllídis. Paintings such as Nikólaos Kartsonákis's *Street Market* (1939) also reveal the folk roots that are at the heart of much modern Greek art.

❺ Kerameikos
Κεραμεικός

This ancient cemetery has been a burial ground since the 12th century BC. The Sacred Way led from Eleusis *(see pp160–61)* to Kerameikos and the Panathenaic Way set out from the Dípylon Gate here to the Acropolis *(see pp98–101)*. Most of the graves remaining today are along the Street of the Tombs. The sculptures excavated in the early 1900s are in the Kerameikos Museum; however, plaster copies of the originals can be seen *in situ*.

Grave Stele of Hegeso
This is from the family burial plot belonging to Koroibos of Melite. It shows his wife, Hegeso, admiring her jewels with a servant and dates from the late 5th century BC.

Precinct of Aristion

The Precinct of Lysimachides contains a marble dog, originally one of a pair.

The Sanctuary of Hekate was sacred to the ancient goddess of the moon. It contained an altar and votive offerings.

★ Tomb of Dionysios of Kollytos
This fine tomb belongs to a rich treasurer. A bull often represents the god Dionysos.

South terrace

Oberlander ↘ Museum

Street of the Tombs
Most of the monuments in the Street of the Tombs date from the 4th century BC. The different styles, from the lavish (relief sculptures) to the simple kioniskoi (small columns), all reveal the dignity that is typical of Greek funerary art.

Locator Map

Stele of Dexileos
Dexileos was a young man killed in 394 BC during the Corinthian War. The son of Lysanias, he is seen on the relief slaying an enemy.

This tumulus was the burial place of an old Attic family dating from the 6th century BC.

Tomb of Hipparete

River Eridanos

The Sacred Way led from the Sacred Gate to Ancient Eleusis (see pp160–61).

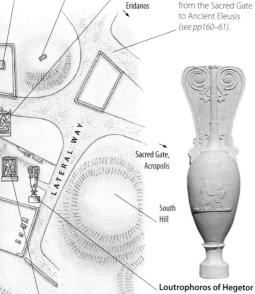

Sacred Gate, Acropolis

South Hill

Loutrophoros of Hegetor
The farewell scene depicted on this two-handled vase is typical of the less ornate style of commemorative funerary art.

★ **Stele of Demetria and Pamphile**
This moving sculpture shows the seated Pamphile with her sister Demetria behind her. This was one of the last ornate stelae to be made in the late 4th century BC.

🏛 Kerameikos Museum
This museum was formerly named after Gustav Oberlander (1867–1936), a German-American industrialist whose donations enabled the museum to open in 1937. In Gallery 1, some large fragments from grave stelae found incorporated into the Dípylon and Sacred Gates are exhibited. These include a marble sphinx (c.550 BC) that once crowned a grave stele. Galleries 2 and 3 offer an array of huge Proto-Geometric and Geometric amphorae and black-figure lekythoi (funerary vases). The most moving exhibits come from children's graves and include pottery toy horses and terracotta dolls. There are also examples of some of the 7,000 ostraka (voting tablets) (see p95) found in the bed of the river Eridanos. Among the superb painted pottery, there is a red-figure hydria (water vase) of Helen of Troy and a lekythos of Dionysos with satyrs.

Winged sphinx from grave stele

Geometric funerary amphora from the Kerameikos Museum

❻ Ancient Agora

Αρχαία Αγορά

The Agora, or marketplace, formed the political heart of ancient Athens from 600 BC. Democracy was practised in the *Bouleuterion* (Council) and the law courts, and in open meetings. Socrates was indicted and executed in the state prison here in 399 BC. The theatres, schools and stoas filled with shops also made this the centre of social and commercial life. Even the city mint that produced Athens' silver coins was here. The American School of Classical Studies began excavations of the Ancient Agora in the 1930s, and since then, the vast remains of a complex array of public buildings have been revealed.

Stoa of Attalos
This colonnaded building was reconstructed in the mid-20th century as a museum to house finds from the Ancient Agora site.

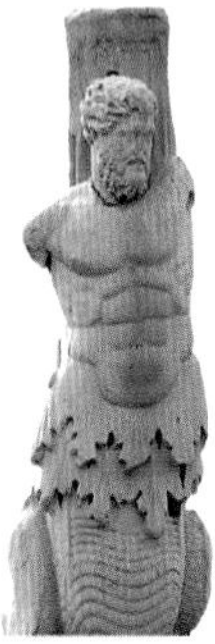

Odeion of Agrippa
This statue of a triton (half-god, half-fish) once adorned the façade of the Odeion of Agrippa. It dates from AD 150 and is now in the Agora museum.

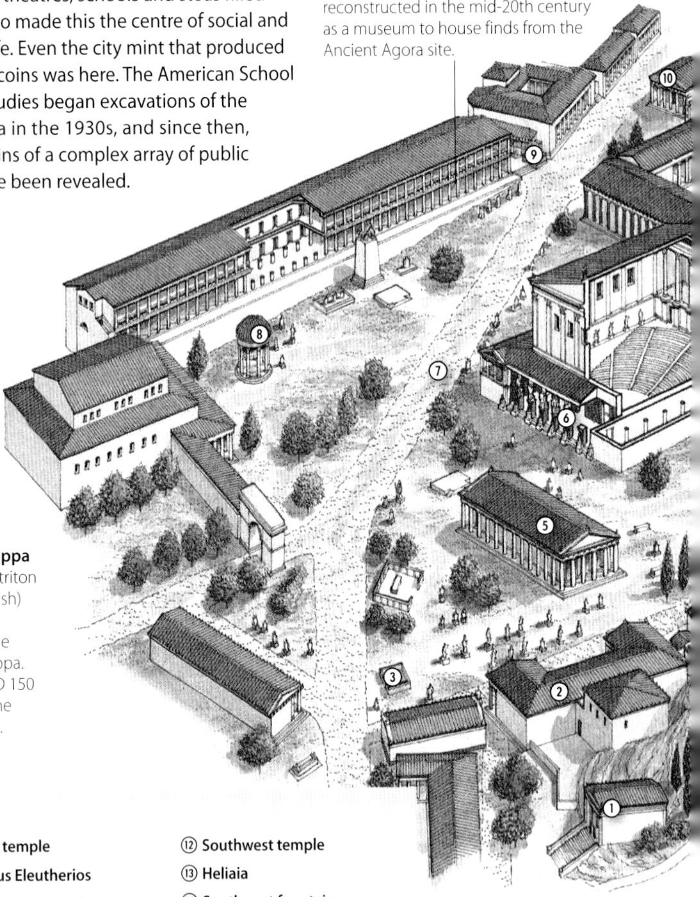

KEY

① Hellenistic temple

② Stoa of Zeus Eleutherios

③ Altar of the twelve gods

④ Temple of Apollo Patroös

⑤ Temple of Ares

⑥ Triton statues

⑦ **The Panathenaic Way** was named after the Great Panathenaia festival which took place every four years.

⑧ Monopteros temple

⑨ Library of Pantainos

⑩ Southeast temple

⑪ **The middle stoa** housed shops.

⑫ Southwest temple

⑬ Heliaia

⑭ Southwest fountain

⑮ Latrines

⑯ **The Tholos** was the Council headquarters.

⑰ **Bouleuterion or Council chamber**

⑱ Arsenal

⑲ Metroön

⑳ Monument of the Eponymous Heroes

㉑ Altar of Zeus

Reconstruction of the Ancient Agora

This shows the Agora as it was in c.AD 200, viewed from the northwest. The main entrance to the Agora at this time was via the Panathenaic Way, which ran across the site from the Acropolis in the southeast to the Kerameikos in the northwest.

View across the Agora from the south showing the reconstructed Stoa of Attalos on the right

0 metres 50
0 yards 50

Statue of Hadrian
Hadrian was Emperor of Rome from AD 117–38. Athens was under his authority. The statue dates from the 2nd century AD.

VISITORS' CHECKLIST

Practical Information
Main entrance at Adrianoú 24, Monastiráki. **Map** 5 C1. **Tel** 210 321 0185. **Open** 8am–8pm daily (to 3pm Nov–Mar). **Closed** 1 Jan, 25 Mar, Easter Sun, 1 May, 25 & 26 Dec. ♿ limited.
🌐 odysseus.culture.gr

Transport
Ⓜ Thiseío, Monastiráki.

Ostrakon condemning a man named Hippokrates to exile

🏛 Stoa of Attalos
This fine building was rebuilt between 1953 and 1956, helped by a huge donation from John D Rockefeller, Jr. An impressive two-storey stoa, or roofed arcade, founded by King Attalos of Pergamon (ruled 159–138 BC), it dominated the eastern quarter of the Agora until it was burnt down by raiding Germanic Heruli in AD 267. Reconstructed using the original foundations and ancient materials, it now contains a museum whose exhibits reveal the great diversity and sophistication of ancient life. Artifacts include rules from the 2nd-century AD Library of Pantainos, the text of a law against tyranny from 336 BC, bronze and stone lots used for voting and a *klepsýdra* (water clock) used for timing speeches. *Ostraka* (voting tablets on which names were inscribed) bear such famous names as Themistokles and Aristeides the Just, the latter banished, or "ostracized", in 482 BC. More everyday items, such as terracotta toys and portable ovens, and hobnails and sandals found in a shoemaker's shop, are equally fascinating. Also on display are some beautiful black-figure vases and an unusual oil flask moulded into the shape of a kneeling boy.

Kneeling-boy oil flask

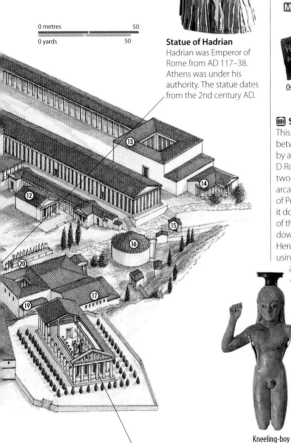

Hephaisteion
This temple, also known as the Theseion, is the best-preserved building on the site. It was built c.449–440 BC.

❼ Acropolis

Ακρόπολη

In the mid-5th century BC, Perikles persuaded the Athenians to begin a grand programme of new building work in Athens that has come to represent the political and cultural achievements of Greece. The work transformed the Acropolis with three contrasting temples and a monumental gateway. The Theatre of Dionysos on the south slope was developed under Lykourgos in the 4th century BC, and the Theatre of Herodes Atticus was added in the 2nd century AD.

Locator Map

★ **Porch of the Caryatids**
These statues of women were used in place of columns on the south porch of the Erechtheion. The originals, four of which can be seen in the Acropolis Museum *(see p104)*, have been replaced by casts, less vulnerable to harsh weather and pollution.

★ **Temple of Athena Nike**
This temple to Athena of Victory is on the west side of the Propylaia. It was built in 426–421 BC *(see p100)*.

KEY

① **An olive tree** now grows where Athena first planted her tree in a competition against Poseidon.

② **The Propylaia** was built in 437–432 BC to form a new entrance to the Acropolis *(see p100)*.

③ **The Beulé Gate** was the first entrance to the Acropolis *(see p100)*.

④ **Pathway to Acropolis from ticket office**

⑤ **Two Corinthian columns** are the remains of choregic monuments erected by sponsors of successful dramatic performances *(see p101)*.

⑥ **Panagía i Spiliótissa** is a chapel set up in a cave in the Acropolis rock *(see p101)*.

⑦ **Sanctuary of Asklepios**

⑧ **The Acropolis rock** was an easily defended site. It has been in use for nearly 5,000 years.

⑨ **Stoa of Eumenes**

Theatre of Herodes Atticus
Also known as the Odeion of Herodes Atticus, this superb theatre was originally built in AD 161. It was restored in 1955 and is used today for outdoor concerts *(see p101)*.

◀ The Caryatids in the Erechtheion temple ruins

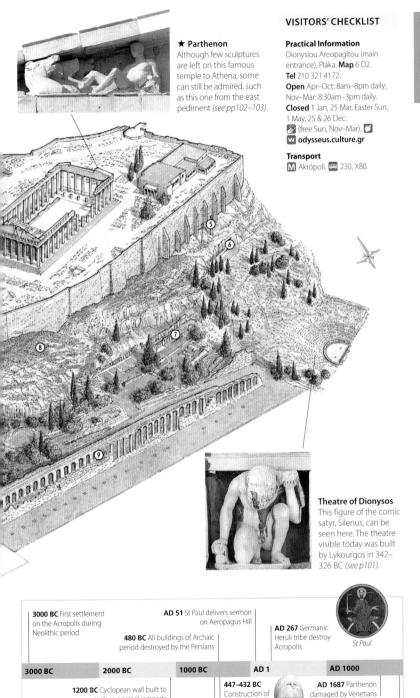

★ **Parthenon**
Although few sculptures are left on this famous temple to Athena, some can still be admired, such as this one from the east pediment (see pp102–103).

VISITORS' CHECKLIST

Practical Information
Dionysíou Areopagítou (main entrance), Pláka. **Map** 6 D2.
Tel 210 321 4172.
Open Apr–Oct: 8am–8pm daily; Nov–Mar: 8:30am–3pm daily.
Closed 1 Jan, 25 Mar, Easter Sun, 1 May, 25 & 26 Dec.
(free Sun, Nov–Mar).
odysseus.culture.gr

Transport
Akrópoli. 230, X80.

Theatre of Dionysos
This figure of the comic satyr, Silenus, can be seen here. The theatre visible today was built by Lykourgos in 342–326 BC (see p101).

3000 BC First settlement on the Acropolis during Neolithic period

AD 51 St Paul delivers sermon on Aeropagus Hill

480 BC All buildings of Archaic period destroyed by the Persians

AD 267 Germanic Heruli tribe destroy Acropolis

St Paul

3000 BC	2000 BC	1000 BC	AD 1	AD 1000

1200 BC Cyclopean wall built to replace original ramparts

447–432 BC Construction of the Parthenon under Perikles

AD 1687 Parthenon damaged by Venetians

510 BC Delphic Oracle declares Acropolis a holy place of the gods, banning habitation by mortals

Perikles (495–429 BC)

AD 1987 Restoration of the Erechtheion completed

Exploring the Acropolis

Once through the first entrance, the Beulé Gate, straight ahead is the Propylaia, the grand entrance to the temple complex. Before going through here, it is worth exploring the Temple of Athena Nike, on the right. Beyond the Propylaia are the Erechtheion and the Parthenon *(see pp102–103)*, which dominate the top of the rock. There are also stunning views of Athens itself from the Acropolis. Access to all the temple precincts is banned to prevent damage. On the south slope of the Acropolis are the two theatres, once used for drama festivals in honour of the god Dionysos. The striking Acropolis Museum and the hills immediately to the west are covered on pages 104–105.

View of the Acropolis from the southwest

Beulé Gate

The gate is named after the French archaeologist Ernest Beulé who discovered it in 1852. It was built in AD 267 after the raid of the Heruli, a Germanic people, as part of the Roman Acropolis fortifications. It incorporates stones from the *choregic* monument *(see p113)* of Nikias that was situated near the Stoa of Eumenes. Parts of the original monument's dedication are still visible over the architrave. There is also an inscription identifying a Roman, Flavius Septimius Marcellinus, as donor of the gateway. In 1686, when the Turks destroyed the Temple of Athena Nike, they used the marble to build a bastion for artillery over the gate.

Temple of Athena Nike

This small temple was built in 426–421 BC to commemorate the Athenians' victories over the Persians. The temple frieze has representative scenes from the Battle of Plataea (479 BC).

Designed by Kallikrates, the temple stands on a 9.5-m (31-ft) bastion. It has been used as both observation post and an ancient shrine to the goddess of Victory, Athena Nike, of whom there is a remarkable sculpture situated on the balustrade. Legend records the temple site as the place where King Aegeus stood waiting for his son Theseus to return from his mission to Crete to slay the Minotaur. Theseus had promised to swap his ships' black sails for white on his return, but he forgot his promise. When the king saw the black sails, he presumed his son to be dead and threw himself into the sea, which now bears his name (Aegean). Built of Pentelic marble, the temple has four Ionic columns 4 m (13 ft) high at

each portico end. It was reconstructed in 1834–8, after being destroyed in 1686 by the Ottomans. On the point of collapse in 1935, it was again dismantled and reconstructed according to information resulting from more recent research.

Propylaia

Work began on this enormous entrance to the Acropolis in 437 BC. Although the outbreak of the Peloponnesian War in 432 BC curtailed its completion, its architect Mnesikles created a building admired throughout the ancient world. The Propylaia comprises a rectangular central building divided by a wall into two porticoes. These were punctuated by five entrance doors, rows of Ionic and Doric columns and a vestibule with a blue-coffered ceiling decorated with gold stars. Two wings flank the main building. The north wing was home to the *pinakotheke*, an art gallery.

During its chequered history – later as archbishop's residence, Frankish palace, and Turkish fortress and armoury – parts of the building have been accidentally destroyed; it even suffered the misfortune of being struck by lightning in 1645, and later the explosion of the Ottoman gunpowder store *(see p102)*.

Erechtheion

Built between 421 and 406 BC, the Erechtheion is situated on the most sacred site of the Acropolis. It is said to be where Poseidon left his trident marks in a rock, and Athena's olive tree sprouted, in their battle for

The eastern end of the Erechtheion

The remains of the Theatre of Dionysos

patronage of the city. Named after Erechtheus, one of the mythical kings of Athens, the temple was a sanctuary to both Athena Polias, and Erechtheus-Poseidon.

Famed for its elegant and extremely ornate Ionic architecture and caryatid columns in the shape of women, this extraordinary monument is built on different levels. The large rectangular cella was divided into three rooms. One contained the holy olive-wood statue of Athena Polias. The cella was bounded by north, east and south porticoes. The south is the Porch of the Caryatids, the maiden statues which are now in the Acropolis Museum.

The Erechtheion complex has been used for a range of purposes, including a harem for the wives of the Ottoman *disdar* (commander) in 1463. It was almost completely destroyed by a Turkish shell in 1827 during the War of Independence *(see pp44–5)*. Restoration work here has caused heated disputes: holes have been filled with new marble, and copies have been made to replace original features that have been removed to the safety of the museum.

🔊 Theatre of Herodes Atticus (Iródio)
This small Roman theatre seats 5,000 spectators and is still in use today *(see p123)*. Built by the Roman consul Herodes Atticus between AD 161 and 174, in memory of his wife, the shape was hollowed out of the rocks on the southern slope of the Acropolis. The semicircular

orchestra in front of the stage was repaved with alternating blue and white marble slabs in the 1950s. Behind the stage, its distinctive colonnade once contained statues of the nine Muses. The whole theatre was originally enclosed by a cedarwood roof that gave better acoustics and allowed for all-weather performances.

🔊 Theatre of Dionysos
D. Areopagitou, Makrygiánni.
Tel 210 322 4625.
Open Apr–Oct: 8am–8pm daily; Nov–Mar: 8:30am–3pm daily. 📷

Throne from the Theatre of Dionysos

Cut into the southern cliff face of the Acropolis, the Theatre of Dionysos is the birthplace of Greek tragedy, and was the first theatre built of stone. Aeschylus, Sophokles, Euripides and Aristophanes all had their plays performed here, during the dramatic contests of the annual Dionysia festival, when it was little more than a humble wood-and-earth affair. The theatre was rebuilt in stone by the Athenian statesman Lykourgos between 342–326 BC, but the ruins that can be seen today are in part those of a much bigger structure, built by the Romans, which could seat 17,000. They used it as a gladiatorial arena, and added a marble balustrade with metal railings to protect spectators. In the 1st century AD, during Emperor Nero's reign, the orchestra was given its marble flooring, and in the 2nd century AD, the front of the stage was decorated with reliefs showing Dionysos's life. Above the theatre, there is a cave sacred to the goddess Artemis. This was converted into a chapel in the Byzantine era, dedicated to **Panagía i Spiliótissa** (Our Lady of the Cave), and was the place where mothers brought their sick children. Two large Corinthian columns nearby are the remains of choregic monuments erected to celebrate the benefactor's team winning a drama festival. The Sanctuary of Asklepios to the west, founded in 420 BC, was dedicated to the god of healing. Worshippers seeking a cure had to take part in purification rites before they could enter the temple precincts.

Interior of the Panagía i Spiliótissa chapel, above the Theatre of Dionysos

The Parthenon

Ο Παρθενώνας

One of the world's most famous buildings, this temple was begun in 447 BC. It was designed by the architects Kallikrates and Iktinos, primarily to house the 12-m (40-ft) high statue of Athena Parthenos (Maiden), sculpted by Pheidias. Taking nine years to complete, the temple was dedicated to the goddess in 438 BC. Over the centuries, it has been used as a church, a mosque and an arsenal, and has suffered severe damage. Built as an expression of the glory of ancient Athens, it remains the city's emblem to this day.

View of the Parthenon from the west

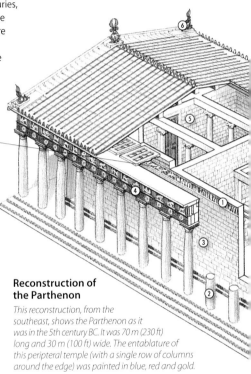

Parthenon Frieze
The frieze, designed by Pheidias, ran around the inner wall of the Parthenon. The metopes (sections of the frieze) depicted the Great Panathenaia festival, honouring Athena.

KEY

① **The Elgin Marbles** *(see p104)* were taken largely from the internal frieze.

② **Each column** was constructed from fluted drums of marble. The fluting was added once the columns were in place.

③ **Marble walls** concealed the cellas, or inner rooms.

④ **The external frieze** consisted of triglyphs and metopes.

⑤ **The west cella** was used as a treasury.

⑥ **Akroterion**

⑦ **The internal columns** were in two rows and Doric in style.

⑧ **The roof** was made from Pentelic marble tiles supported on wooden rafters.

⑨ **The steps** curved upwards slightly at the centre to make them appear level from a distance.

Reconstruction of the Parthenon

This reconstruction, from the southeast, shows the Parthenon as it was in the 5th century BC. It was 70 m (230 ft) long and 30 m (100 ft) wide. The entablature of this peripteral temple (with a single row of columns around the edge) was painted in blue, red and gold.

VEDUTA DEL CAST D'ACROPOLIS DALLA PARTE DI TRAMONTANA.

Explosion of 1687
During the Venetian siege of the Acropolis, General Francesco Morosini bombarded the Parthenon with cannon-fire. The Turks were using the temple as an arsenal at the time and the ensuing explosion demolished much of it, including the roof, the inner structure and 14 of the outer columns.

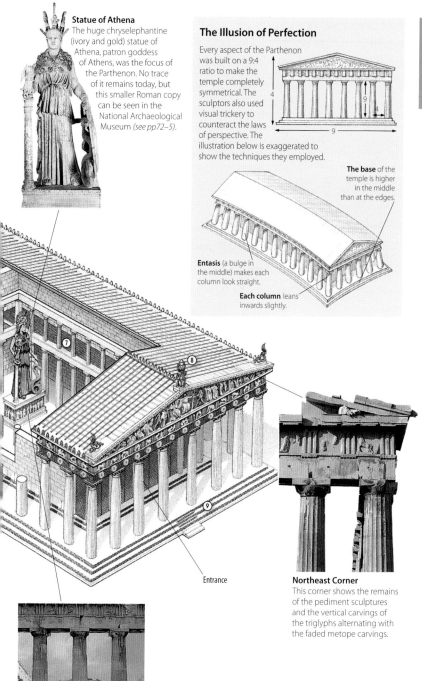

Statue of Athena
The huge chryselephantine (ivory and gold) statue of Athena, patron goddess of Athens, was the focus of the Parthenon. No trace of it remains today, but this smaller Roman copy can be seen in the National Archaeological Museum *(see pp72–5)*.

The Illusion of Perfection

Every aspect of the Parthenon was built on a 9:4 ratio to make the temple completely symmetrical. The sculptors also used visual trickery to counteract the laws of perspective. The illustration below is exaggerated to show the techniques they employed.

The base of the temple is higher in the middle than at the edges.

Entasis (a bulge in the middle) makes each column look straight.

Each column leans inwards slightly.

Entrance

Northeast Corner
This corner shows the remains of the pediment sculptures and the vertical carvings of the triglyphs alternating with the faded metope carvings.

View of the East Cella
The cella was the inner room of the temple. In the case of the Parthenon, there were two – east and west. The east cella contained the enormous cult statue of Athena and the offerings bestowed upon it. The west cella was the back room, reserved for the priestess.

Around the Acropolis

The area around the Acropolis was the centre of public life in Athens. In addition to the Agora in the north (see pp94–5), political life was largely centred on the Pnyx and the Areopagos, the hills lying to the west of the Acropolis; the Assembly met on the former and murder trials were heard by a council of ex-magistrates on the latter. Other ancient remains and the glittering Acropolis Museum, located at the foot of the Acropolis, provide a fascinating insight into what daily life was like in ancient Athens.

Excavation site at the Acropolis Museum

🏛 Acropolis Museum

Dionysiou Areopagitou 15, Akrópoli. **Tel** 210 900 0900. **M** Akrópoli. **Open** Apr–Oct: 8am–8pm daily (to 4pm Mon, to 10pm Fri); Nov–Mar: 9am–5pm daily (to 10pm Fri, to 8pm Sat & Sun). **Closed** 1 Jan, Easter Sun, 1 May, 25 & 26 Dec. 🚫🚫🖼🖥🚻 **W** theacropolismuseum.gr

After decades of planning and delays, the Acropolis Museum opened in 2008 in the historic Makrigiánni district, southeast of the Acropolis. The museum had been planned since the late 1970s to replace the old Acropolis Museum, next to the Parthenon, which was thought too small and dilapidated to do justice to the sculptures and architectural pieces found on the Acropolis hill. Today, the €130-million, multi-storey, all-glass showpiece designed by Bernard Tschumi, is undoubtedly a more fitting home for the hill's stunning treasures.

Tschumi had the added challenge of constructing the building over excavations of an early Christian settlement. Concrete pillars and a glass walkway allow the building to hover over the ruins, which are on view as you approach the entrance.

The rest of the collection is installed in chronological order and begins with finds from the slopes of the Acropolis. These include statues and reliefs from the Sanctuary of Asklepios.

The **Archaic Collection** is set out in a magnificent double-height gallery. Fragments of painted pedimental statues include mythological scenes of Herakles grappling with various monsters and the more peaceful votive statue of the Moschophoros, or Calf-Bearer, portraying a young man carrying a calf on his shoulders (c.570 BC).

The sky-lit **Parthenon Gallery** on the top floor is the highlight. Here, arranged around an indoor court and looking out on to the Parthenon, the remaining original parts of the Parthenon frieze still in Greece are displayed in the order in which they would have graced the Parthenon (plaster casts occupy the spaces of those held in London). The sculptures depict the Panathenaic procession, including the chariot and apobates (slaves riding chariot horses) and a sacrificial cow being led by youths.

On the level below, the **post-Parthenon Collection** comprises sculptures from the Temple of Athena Nike, and architectural features from the Propylaia and the Erechtheion, including five of the original six caryatids from the south porch; the sixth is in the British Museum.

The Elgin Marbles

These famous sculptures, also called the Parthenon Marbles, are held in the British Museum in London. They were acquired by Lord Elgin in 1801–12 from the occupying Ottoman authorities. He sold them to the British nation for £35,000 in 1816. There is great controversy surrounding the Marbles. While some argue that they are more carefully preserved in the British Museum, the Greek government does not accept the legality of the sale and many believe they belong in Athens. A famous supporter of this cause was the Greek actress and politician, Melína Merkoúri, who died in 1994.

The newly arrived Elgin Marbles at the British Museum, in a painting by A Archer

Areopagos Hill

There is little left to see on this low hill today, apart from the rough-hewn, slippery steps and what are thought to be seats on its summit. The Areopagos was used by the Persians and Turks during their attacks on the Acropolis citadel, and played an important role as the home of the Supreme Judicial Court in the Classical period. It takes its name, meaning the "Hill of Ares", from a mythological trial that took place here when the god Ares was acquitted of murdering the son of Poseidon. The nearby **Cave of the Furies** inspired the playwright Aeschylus (see p61) to set Orestes's trial here in his play *Eumenides* (The Furies). The hill also achieved renown in AD 51, when St Paul delivered his sermon "On an Unknown God" and gained his first convert, Dionysios the Areopagite, who subsequently became the patron saint of Athens.

Cross from Agios Dimítrios church

Pnyx Hill

If Athens is the cradle of democracy, Pnyx Hill is its exact birthplace. During the 4th and 5th century BC, the *Ekklesia* (citizens' assembly) met here to discuss and vote upon all but the most important matters of state, until it lost its powers during Roman rule. In its heyday, 6,000 Athenians gathered 40 times a year to listen to speeches and take vital political decisions. Themistokles, Perikles and Demosthenes all spoke from the *bema* (speaker's platform) that is still visible today. Carved out of the rock face, it formed the top step of a platform that doubled as a primitive altar to the god Zeus. There are also the remains of the huge retaining wall which was built to support the semicircular terraces that placed citizens on a level

with the speakers. It completely surrounded the auditorium, which was 110 m (358 ft) high.

Agios Dimítrios

Dionysíou Areopagítou, southwest slope of Acropolis. **Open** daily. except Sun.

This Byzantine church is often called Agios Dimítrios Loumpardiáris, after an incident in 1656. The Ottoman *disdar* (commander) at the time, Yusuf Aga, laid plans to fire a huge cannon called Loumpárda, situated by the Propylaia (see p100), at worshippers in the church as they celebrated the feast day of Agios Dimítrios. However, the night before the feast, lightning struck the Propylaia, miraculously killing the commander and his family.

Filopáppou Hill

The highest summit in the south of Athens, at 147 m (482 ft), offers spectacular views of the Acropolis. It has always played a decisive defensive role in Athens' history – the general Demetrios Poliorketes built an important fort here overlooking the strategic Piraeus road in 294 BC, and Francesco Morosini bombarded the Acropolis from here in 1687. Popularly called Filopáppou Hill after a monument still on its summit, it was also known

The Monument of Philopappus, AD 114–116

The Asteroskopeíon on the Hill of the Nymphs

to the ancient Greeks as the Hill of Muses or the Mouseion, because the tomb of Musaeus, a disciple of Orpheus, was traditionally held to be located here.

Built between AD 114–16, the Monument of Philopappus was raised by the Athenians in honour of Caius Julius Antiochus Philopappus, a Roman consul and philhellene. Its unusual concave marble façade, 12 m (40 ft) high, contains niches with statues of Philopappus and his grandfather, Antiochus IV. A frieze around the monument depicts the arrival of Philopappus by chariot for his inauguration as Roman consul in AD 100.

Hill of the Nymphs

This 103-m (340-ft) high tree-clad hill takes its name from dedications found carved on rocks in today's Observatory Garden. The Asteroskopeíon (Observatory) was built in 1842 by the Danish architect Theophil Hansen, with funds from philanthropist and banker Georgios Sínas. It occupies the site of a sanctuary to nymphs associated with childbirth. The modern church of Agía Marína nearby has similar associations of childbirth; pregnant women used to slide effortlessly down a smooth rock near the church, in the hope of an equally easy labour.

Street-by-Street: Central Pláka

Pláka is the historic heart of Athens. Even though only a
few houses date back further than the Ottoman period,
it remains the oldest continuously inhabited area of the
city. One explanation of its name comes from the word
pliaka (old), which was used to describe the area
by Albanian soldiers in the service of the
Turks who settled here in the 16th century.
Despite the crowds of tourists and the
many Athenians who come to eat in
the tavernas or browse in antique
shops, it still retains the feel of
a residential neighbourhood.

⓭ Mitrópoli
Athens' cathedral was
built in the second half
of the 19th century.

THOUKYDID

APOLLONOS

ADRIANOU

MNISIKLEOUS

LYSIOU

THEORIAS

Thoukydídou
is named after
the historian
Thucydides
(c.460–400 BC).

⓬ ★ Panagía Gorgoepíkoös
This tiny 12th-century church,
also known as the Little
Cathedral, has some
beautiful carvings.

**⓫ Museum of Greek Popular
Musical Instruments**
A range of folk instruments is
displayed in this museum,
which was opened in 1991.

Monastiráki
(see pp88–9)

Acropolis
(see pp98–105)

⓾ University of Athens Museum
Occupying the university's original home, this
museum has memorabilia from the institution's
early days, including these old medical artifacts.

Ancient Agora
(see pp94–95)

⓽ Kanellópoulos Museum
Privately owned, this museum
has exquisite works of art from
all areas of the Hellenic world.

For hotels and restaurants see pp268–9 and pp282–5

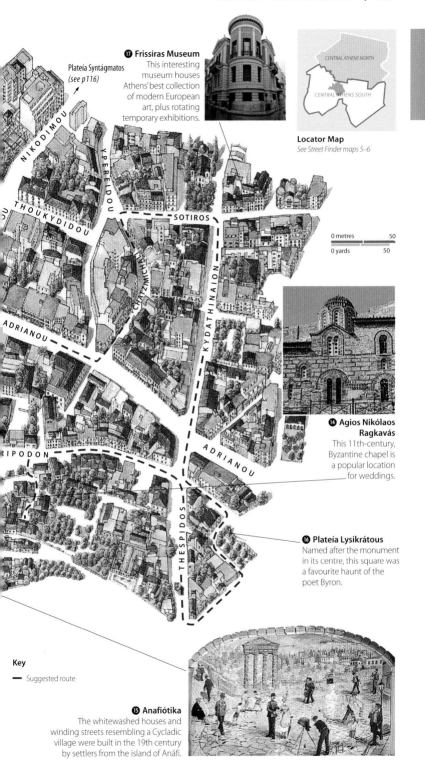

⑰ Frissiras Museum
This interesting museum houses Athens' best collection of modern European art, plus rotating temporary exhibitions.

Plateía Syntágmatos *(see p116)*

Locator Map
See Street Finder maps 5–6

CENTRAL ATHENS NORTH

CENTRAL ATHENS SOUTH

0 metres 50
0 yards 50

⑭ Agios Nikólaos Ragkavás
This 11th-century, Byzantine chapel is a popular location for weddings.

⑯ Plateía Lysikrátous
Named after the monument in its centre, this square was a favourite haunt of the poet Byron.

Key
— Suggested route

⑮ Anafiótika
The whitewashed houses and winding streets resembling a Cycladic village were built in the 19th century by settlers from the island of Anáfi.

❽ Ilías Lalaoúnis Jewellery Museum

Μουσείο Κοσμήματος Ηλία Λαλαούνη

Karyatidon & P. Kallisperi 12, Akrópoli. **Map** 6 D3. **Tel** 210 922 1044. Ⓜ Akrópoli. **Open** 9am–3pm Tue–Sat, 11am–4pm Sun. **Closed** main public hols. ✎ by prior written permission only. ♿ 🅿 Ⓦ lalaounis-jewelrymuseum.gr

Situated just below the Theatre of Dionysos, this small museum is a delight for anyone interested in decorative arts. The permanent collection comprises over 4,000 pieces spanning 60 years of jewellery making by designer Ilías Lalaoúnis, who is credited with the revival of Greek practice of the art in the 1950s.

❾ Kanellópoulos Museum

Μουσείο Κανελλοπούλου

Corner of Theorías & Pános 12, Pláka. **Map** 6 D2. **Tel** 210 324 4447. Ⓜ Monastiráki. **Open** 8am–3pm Tue–Sun (Jun–Oct: 9am–4pm). **Closed** 1 Jan, 25 Mar, Easter Sun, 25, 26 Dec. Ⓦ pacanellopoulosfoundation.org

In an immaculately restored Neo-Classical town house, this museum has a varied collection of artifacts from all over the Hellenistic world. On display are 6th-century BC helmets, 5th-century BC gold Persian jewellery and Attic vases. Also on view are Cycladic figurines, some unusual terracotta figures of actors in their theatrical masks, and a fine 2nd-century AD El Faiyûm portrait of a woman.

A huge block of stone that fell from the walls of the Acropolis can still be seen as an exhibit on the ground floor.

Rempétika musicians, Museum of Greek Popular Musical Instruments

❿ University of Athens Museum

Μουσείο Ιστορίας του Πανεπιστημίου Αθηνών

Thólou 5, Pláka. **Map** 6 D2. **Tel** 210 368 9502. Ⓜ Monastiráki. **Open** 9:30am–2:30pm Mon–Fri (Jun–Sep: also 6–9pm Mon & Wed).

This three-storey house was the first home of the University of Athens. It opened on 3 May 1837 with 52 students and 33 professors in its first year. In November 1841, the University moved to its new quarters, and from 1922, the building was home to many immigrant families. While they were there, a taverna known as the "Old University" was opened on the ground floor.

In 1963, the building was declared a National Monument. Later reacquired by the university, the old building was opened as a museum in 1974. Today, the "Old University", as it is still known, has an eclectic collection of memorabilia that were once used for study here such as corporeal body maps, anatomical models, scientific instruments and medicine jars.

⓫ Museum of Greek Popular Musical Instruments

Μουσείο Ελληνικών Λαϊκών Μουσικών Οργάνων

Diogénous 1–3, Pláka. **Map** 6 D1. **Tel** 210 325 0198. Ⓜ Monastiráki. **Open** 10am–2pm Tue–Sun, noon–6pm Wed. **Closed** 17 Nov, main public hols. Ⓦ instruments-museum.gr

Cretan musicologist Phoivos Anogianákis donated over 1,200 musical instruments to the Greek State in 1978. In 1992, this study centre and museum was opened, devoted to the history of popular Greek music, including Anogianákis's collection. The museum traces the development of different styles of island music and the arrival of *rempétika* (Greek "blues") from Smyrna in 1922.

Instruments from all over Greece are displayed, with recordings and headphones. The basement contains church and livestock bells, as well as water whistles, wooden clappers and flutes. Elsewhere, there are wind instruments including *tsampoúna* (bagpipes made from goatskin) and string instruments such as the Cretan *lýra*.

Sculpture of a triton from the Kanellópoulos Museum

⓬ Panagía Gorgoepíkoös

Παναγία η Γοργοεπήκοος

This domed cruciform church is built entirely from Pentelic marble, now weathered to a rich corn-coloured hue. Dating from the 12th century, it measures only 7.5 m (25 ft) long by 12 m (40 ft) wide. The size of the church is in scale with Athens when it was just a village in the 12th century. Adorned with friezes and bas-reliefs taken from earlier buildings, the exterior mixes the Classical and Byzantine styles. Although dedicated to Panagía Gorgoepíkoös (the Madonna who Swiftly Hears) and Agios Elefthérios (the saint who protects women in childbirth), it is often affectionately known as the Mikrí Mitrópoli (Little Cathedral).

VISITORS' CHECKLIST

Practical Information
Plateía Mitropóleos, Pláka. **Map** 6 E1. **Open** 7am–7pm daily.

Transport
Ⓜ Monastiráki.

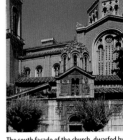

The south façade of the church, dwarfed by the giant Mitrópoli

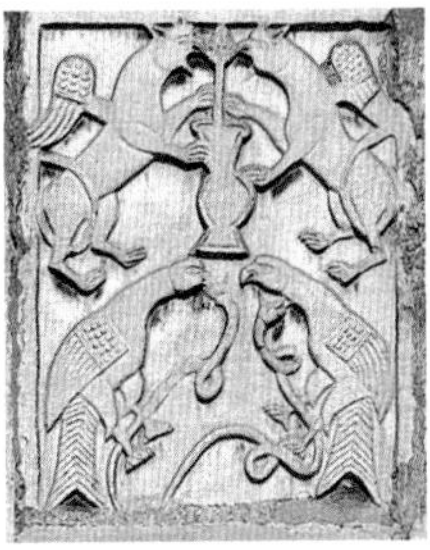

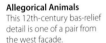

Allegorical Animals
This 12th-century bas-relief detail is one of a pair from the west façade.

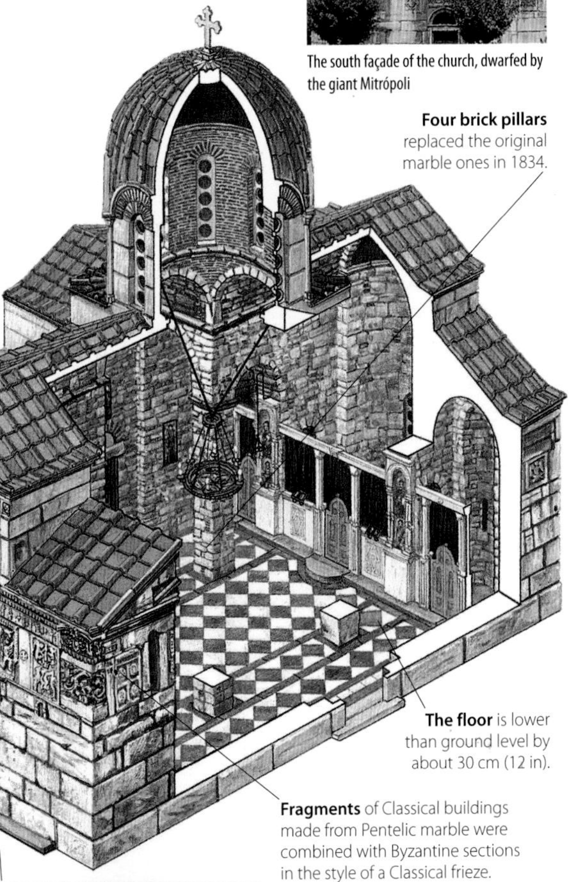

Four brick pillars replaced the original marble ones in 1834.

The floor is lower than ground level by about 30 cm (12 in).

Main entrance

Fragments of Classical buildings made from Pentelic marble were combined with Byzantine sections in the style of a Classical frieze.

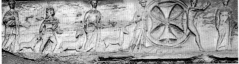

Lintel Frieze
This relief depicting personifications of the months of the year dates from the 4th century BC. The central cross was added in the 12th century.

Modern mosaics above the main entrance to Athens' cathedral, Mitrópoli

⓭ Mitrópoli
Μητρόπολη

Plateía Mitropóleos, Pláka. **Map** 6 E1. **Tel** 210 322 1308. Ⓜ Monastiráki. **Open** 7am–7pm daily.

Work began in 1840 on this huge cathedral, using marble from 72 demolished churches for its walls. The cornerstone was laid in a ceremony by King Otto and Queen Amalía on Christmas Day 1842. It took another 20 years to finish the building, using three different architects (François Boulanger, Theophil Hansen and Dimítrios Zézos), which may account for its slightly ungainly appearance. On 21 May 1862, it was formally dedicated to Evangelismós Theotókou (the Annunciation of the Virgin) by the king and queen. At 40 m (130 ft) long, 20 m (65 ft) wide and 24 m (80 ft) high, it is the largest church in Athens.

The cathedral is the official seat of the Bishop of Athens, and remains a popular city landmark that has been used for ceremonial events from the coronations of kings to the weddings and funerals of the rich and famous.

Inside, there are the tombs of two saints murdered by the Ottoman Turks: Agía Filothéi and Gregory V. The bones of Agía Filothéi, who died in 1589, are still visible in a silver reliquary. Her charitable works included the ransoming of Greek women enslaved in Turkish harems. Gregory V, Patriarch of Constantinople, was hanged and thrown into the Bosphorus in 1821. His body was rescued by Greek sailors and taken to Odessa. It was eventually returned to Athens by Black Sea (Pontic) Greeks 50 years later.

⓮ Agios Nikólaos Ragkavás
Αγιος Νικόλαος ο Ραγκαβάς

Corner of Tripodon & Prytaneíou 1, Pláka. **Map** 6 E2. **Tel** 210 322 8193. Ⓜ Monastiráki. 🚌 1, 2, 4, 5, 10, 11. **Open** 8am–noon, 5–8pm daily. ♿ limited.

This typical 11th-century Byzantine church, rebuilt in the 18th century and restored to some of its former glory in the late 1970s, incorporates marble columns and other remains of ancient buildings in its external walls. It is one of the favourite parish churches of Pláka, frequently used for colourful Greek weddings which spill out on to the street at weekends. It was the first church in Athens to have a bell after the War of Independence (1821), and the first to ring out after the city's liberation from the Germans on 12 October 1944.

⓯ Anafiótika
Αναφιώτικα

Map 6 D2. Ⓜ Akrópoli.

Nestling beneath the northern slopes of the Acropolis, this area is one of the oldest settlements in Athens. Today, its white-washed houses, cramped streets, lazy cats and pots of basil on windowsills still give it the atmosphere of a typical Cycladic village. Its first residents

Looking down on Agios Nikólaos Ragkavás church from Anafiótika

◀ Panoramic view of the Acropolis

were refugees from the Peloponnesian War *(see p34)*. By 1841, it had been colonized by workmen from Anáfi, in the Cyclades, who eventually gave the area its name. Part of the influx of island craftsmen who helped to construct the new city following Independence, they ignored an 1834 decree declaring the area an archaeological zone, and completed their houses overnight, installing their families by morning. By Ottoman law, this meant the authorities were powerless to knock the new houses down.

The area is bounded by two 17th-century churches: Agios Geórgios tou Vráchou to the east, which has a tiny courtyard filled with flowers, and Agios Symeón to the west, which contains a copy of a miraculous icon, originally brought from Anáfi.

Akrokérama, or terracotta sphinxes, on a roof in Anafiótika

⓰ Plateía Lysikrátous
Πλατεία Λυσικράτους

Lysikrátous, Sélley & Epimenídou, Pláka. **Map** 6 E2. 🚌 1, 5, 15.

Situated in the east of the Pláka district, this square is named after the monument of Lysikrates that dominates it. Despite Lord Elgin's attempts to remove it to England, the elegant structure is the city's only intact choregic monument. These monuments were built to commemorate the victors at the annual choral and dramatic festival at the Theatre of Dionysos *(see p101)*. They take their name from the rich sponsor *(choregos)* who produced the winning team. Built in 334 BC, this is the earliest known example where Corinthian capitals are used externally. Six columns rise in

a circle to a marble dome, decorated with an elegant finial of acanthus leaves which supported the winner's bronze trophy. It bears the inscription "Lysikrates of Kikynna, son of Lysitheides, was choregos; the tribe of Akamantis won the victory with a chorus of boys; Theon played the flute; Lysiades, an Athenian, trained the chorus; Evaineitos was archon". The Athenians elected nine magistrates known as archons each year, and referred to the year by the name of one of them, the "eponymous archon." A frieze above this

The monument of Lysikrates, named after the *choregos* of the winning team of actors

inscription, probably the theme of the winners' performance, depicts a battle between Dionysos, the god of theatre, and Tyrrhenian pirates. Surrounded by satyrs, the god transforms the pirates into dolphins and their ship's mast into a sea serpent.

Capuchin friars converted the monument into a library. Grand tour travellers, such as Chateaubriand (1768–1848) and Byron *(see p153)*, stayed at their convent, which was founded on the site in 1669.

Byron was inspired while staying there and wrote some of his poem, *Childe Harold*, sitting in the monument during his final visit to Athens in 1810.

Not far from the monument is the beautifully restored 11th-century Byzantine church of Agía Aikateríni (St Catherine). In 1767, it was given to the monastery of St Catherine of Mount Sinai. It was renovated, but in 1882, the monastery was forced to exchange it for land elsewhere and it became a local parish church.

Icon Painters in Pláka

Pláka is littered with small artists' studios where icons are still painted using traditional methods. The best are situated just south of Plateía Mitropóleos, among the ecclesiastical shops selling vestments

and liturgical objects, on Agías Filothéis and Apóllonos streets. In some workshops, painters still use the Byzantine method of painting in egg-based tempera on specially treated wood. Customers of all religions can order the saint of their choice in a variety of different sizes. A medium-sized icon depicting a single saint, 25 cm by 15 cm (10 in by 6 in) and copied from a photograph, takes about one day to complete.

Advertisement for a temporary exhibition at the Frissiras Museum

⓱ Frissiras Museum
Μουσείο Φρυσίρα

Monís Asteriou 3 & 7 **Map** 6 E2.
Tel 210 331 6027 Ⓜ Sýntagma.
🚌 2, 4, 9, 10, 11, 12, 15. **Open**
10am–5pm Wed–Fri, 11am–5pm Sat &
Sun 🅿 Ⓦ frissirasmuseum.com

Vlassis Frissiras started collecting
modern Greek art in 1978 but,
in the 1990s, he expanded his
collection to include art from
all of Europe. His acquisitions
centre on the human form and
its representation.

The Frissiras is split over two
buildings on the same street.
At no. 7, in a Neo-Classical
edifice designed by the
German architect Ernst Ziller,
the permanent collection
includes 3, 500 excellent
holdings of modern and
contemporary European
paitings and sculptures.
Familiar names here include
the likes of Paula Rego, R.B. Kitaj
and David Hockney. The
premises at no. 3 are devoted
to hosting rotating temporary
exhibits, sometimes including
up-and-coming Greek artists.

Decorative plate from Rhodes

⓲ Museum of Greek Folk Art
Μουσείο Ελληνικής Λαϊκής Τέχνης

Closed see website for updates.
Ⓦ melt.gr

This fascinating museum is set
to move from its Pláka location
and is currently closed to the
public. When it reopens,
visitors will again
be able to enjoy its
displays of Greek folk
art, including some
embroidery, ceramics
and costumes from
the mainland and
Aegean islands. The
collection also covers
the renaissance of
decorative crafts in
the 18th and 19th
centuries, to reveal
a rich Greek heritage
of traditional
techniques in skills
such as weaving, woodcarving
and metalwork.

The Bath House of the Winds
(Abdi Efendi Hamam) is the only
one of the three premises of the
Museum of Greek Folk Art that
is currently open to the public.
The bath house (Kirrýstou 8;
open 8am–3pm Wed–Mon; €2)
was built in phases from the
15th to the 17th centuries. At
first, it opened at different
times for men and women
but, in the 1870s, it was
extended and remodelled
so that there were separate
wings for men and women,
each with their own tepid
and hot rooms. It worked as
a public bath until 1956, and
has since been restored with
exceptional sensitivity. It is well
worth a visit.

⓳ Jewish Museum of Greece
Εβραϊκό Μουσείο της Ελλάδας

Nikis 39, Sýntagma. **Map** 6 F2.
Tel 210 322 5582. Ⓜ Sýntagma.
🚌 1, 2, 4, 5, 10, 11, 15. **Open**
9am–2:30pm Mon–Fri, 10am–2pm
Sun. **Closed** main public hols &
Jewish festivals. 🅰 📷
Ⓦ jewishmuseum.gr

This small museum traces the
history of Greece's Jewish
communities, which date
back to the 3rd century BC.
The exhibits present a
revealing portrait of both
Romaniot Jews, who had
always lived in Greece, and
Sephardic Jews, who fled Spain
and Portugal in the 15th century,
to settle throughout Greece
during the religiously tolerant
years of the Ottoman Empire.

Reconstruction of the ark
from Pàtra

Among the fine
examples of traditional
costumes, jewellery
and religious ceremonial
instruments on display,
one item of particular
interest is the recon-
struction of the *ehal*.
This is the ark contain-
ing the Torah from the
Pàtra synagogue,
which dates from
the 1920s. It
was rescued
by Nikólaos
Stavroulákis,
founder of the
museum, who has also written
several books about the Greek
Jews. These can be purchased
in the museum bookshop.

Moving displays of
documentation record the
German occupation of Greece
during World War II, when 87
per cent of the Jewish
population here was wiped
out. More than 45,000 Greeks
from Thessaloníki alone were
sent to the concentration
camp at Auschwitz during
a period of five months in
1943. Others were deported
as late as summer 1944.

Less than one third of the
museum's collection is
permanently on display,
so it hosts regular temporary
exhibitions to showcase the
remaining artifacts.

Hadrian's Arch, next to the Temple of Olympian Zeus

⑳ Temple of Olympian Zeus
Ναός του Ολυμπίου Διός

Corner of Amalías & Vasilíssis Olgas, Pláka. **Map** 6 F3. **Tel** 210 922 6330. Ⓜ Akrópoli. 🚌 2, 4, 11. **Open** 8am–8pm daily (Nov–Mar: to 3pm). **Closed** main public hols. 🎫 (free Sun, Nov–Mar.) ♿ limited.

The temple of Olympian Zeus is the largest in Greece, exceeding even the Parthenon in size. Work began on this vast edifice in the 6th century BC, in the reign of the tyrant Peisistratos, who allegedly initiated the building work to gain public favour. Although there were several attempts over many years to finish the temple, it was not completed until 650 years later.

The Roman Emperor Hadrian dedicated the temple to Zeus Olympios during the Panhellenic festival of AD 132, on his second visit to Athens. He also set up a gold and ivory inlaid statue of the god inside the temple, a copy of the original by Pheidias at Olympia *(see pp174–6)*. Next to it, he placed a huge statue of himself. Both these statues have since been lost.

Only 15 of the original 104 Corinthian columns remain, each 17 m (56 ft) high – but enough to give a sense of the enormous size of this temple, which would have been approximately 96 m (315 ft) long and 40 m (130 ft) wide.

Corinthian capitals were added to the simple Doric columns by a Roman architect in AD 174.

The temple is situated next to Hadrian's Arch, built in AD 131. It was positioned deliberately to mark the boundary between the ancient city and the new Athens of Hadrian.

The Russian Church of the Holy Trinity

㉑ Russian Church of the Holy Trinity
Ρωσική εκκλησία Αγίας Τριάδας

Fillelínon 21, Pláka. **Map** 6 F2. **Tel** 210 323 1090. Ⓜ Sýntagma. 🚌 1, 2, 4, 5, 9, 10, 11, 12, 15, 18. **Open** 7:30–10am Mon–Fri, 7–11am Sat & Sun. **Closed** main public hols. ♿ limited.

Still in use by the Russian community, this was once the largest church in the city. Built in 1031 by the Lykodímou family (also called Nikodímou), it was ruined by an earthquake in 1701. In 1780, the Turkish governor, Hadji Ali Haseki, partly demolished the church to use its materials for the defensive wall that he built around the city. During the siege of the city in 1827, it received more damage from Greek shells fired from the Acropolis.

The church remained derelict until the Russian government restored it 20 years later. It was then reconsecrated as the Church of the Holy Trinity. A large cruciform building, its most unusual feature is a wide dome, 10 m (33 ft) in diameter. Its interior was decorated by the Bavarian painter Ludwig Thiersch. The separate bell tower also dates from the 19th century, its bell a gift from Tsar Alexander II.

The Corinthian columns of the Temple of Olympian Zeus

The Tomb of the Unknown Soldier in Plateía Syntágmatos

㉒ Plateía Syntágmatos
Πλατεία Συντάγματος

Sýntagma. **Map** 6 F1. 🚌 1, 4, 5, 11, 12, 13, 15. Ⓜ Sýntagma.

This square (also known as Sýntagma Square) is home to the Greek parliament, in the Voulí building, and the Tomb of the Unknown Soldier, decorated with an evocative relief depicting a dying Greek hoplite warrior. Unveiled on 25 March 1932 (National Independence Day), the tomb is flanked by texts from Perikles's famous funeral oration. The other walls that enclose the space are covered in bronze shields celebrating military victories since 1821.

The National Guard *(évzones)* are on continuous patrol in front of the tomb, dressed in their famous uniform of kilt and pom-pom clogs. They are best seen at the changing of the guard, every Sunday at 11am.

㉓ National Gardens
Εθνικός Κήπος

Borders Vasilíssis Sofías, Iródou Attikoú, Vasilíssis Olgas & Vasilíssis Amalías, Sýntagma. **Map** 7 A1. Ⓜ Sýntagma. 🚌 1, 3, 5, 7, 8, 10, 13, 18. **Open** dawn–dusk. Botanical Museum, zoo, cafés: **Open** 8am–until dusk daily (Nov–Mar: to 3pm).

Behind the Voulí parliament building, this 16-ha (40-acre) park, cherished by all Athenians and formerly known as the "Royal Gardens", was renamed the National Gardens by decree in 1923. Queen Amalía ordered the creation of the park in the 1840s; she even used the fledgling Greek navy to bring 15,000 seedlings from around the world. The gardens were landscaped by the Prussian horticulturalist Friedrich Schmidt, who travelled the world in search of rare plants.

Although the gardens have lost much of their original grandeur, they remain one of the most peaceful spots in the city. Shady paths meander past small squares, park benches and ponds filled with koi. The feral cat colony that used to reside here is now much reduced. Remains of Roman mosaics excavated in the park and an old aqueduct add atmosphere. Modern sculptures of writers, such as Dionýsios Solomós, Aristotélis Valaorítis and Jean Moreas, can be found throughout the park. There is also a small **Botanical Museum** to visit, a ramshackle zoo, and cafés. South of the park lies the **Záppeion** exhibition

hall, an impressive building in use today as a conference centre. It was donated by Evángelos and Konstantínos Záppas, cousins who made their fortunes in Romania. Built by Theophil Hansen, architect of the Athens Academy *(see p85)*, between 1874 and 1888, it also has its own gardens. The elegant café next door to the Záppeion is a pleasant place to relax and refresh after a walk around these charming, peaceful gardens.

The tranquil and impressive National Gardens

㉔ Presidential Palace
Προεδρικό Μέγαρο

Iródou Attikoú, Sýntagma. **Map** 7 A2. Ⓜ Sýntagma. 🚌 3, 7, 8, 13. **Closed** to the public.

This former royal palace was designed by Ernst Ziller *(see p85)* in c.1878. It was occupied by the Greek Royal Family from 1890 until the deposition of King Constantine in 1967. It is still guarded by *évzones* whose barracks are at the top of the street. After the abolition of the monarchy, it became the official residence of the President of Greece, though now it is mostly used to receive foreign visitors. Due to security reasons, it is forbidden to approach the palace perimeter on foot or stop nearby in a car.

Voulí parliament building in Plateía Syntágmatos, guarded by *évzones*

㉕ Kallimármaro Stadium

Καλλιμάρμαρο Στάδιο

Vasileos Konstantinou Avenue.
Map 7 B3. **Tel** 210 752 2985. 3, 4, 10, 11. **Open** 8am–7pm daily (Nov–Feb: to 5pm).

This huge marble structure set in a small valley by Ardittós Hill occupies the exact site of the original Panathenaic Stadium built by Lykourgos in 330–329 BC. It was first reconstructed for gladiatorial contests during Hadrian's reign (AD 117–138), then rebuilt in white marble by the wealthy local benefactor Herodes Atticus for the Panathenaic Games in AD 144. Later neglected, its marble was gradually quarried for use in new buildings.

In 1895, Geórgios Avéroff funded the restoration of the stadium in time for the first modern Olympic Games on 5 April 1896. Designed by Anastásios Metaxás, the present structure is a faithful replica of Herodes Atticus's stadium, as described in the *Guide to Greece* by Pausanias *(see p60)*. Built in

Some of the ornate tombs in the First Cemetery of Athens

white Pentelic marble, it is 204 m (669 ft) long and 83 m (272 ft) wide and seats up to 60,000. Between 1869 and 1879, architect Ernst Ziller excavated the site. His finds included a double-headed statue of Apollo and Dionysos, one of many used to divide the stadium's running track down its length. The statue is on show in the National Archaeological Museum *(see pp72–5)*. During the 2004 Olympics, Kallimármaro hosted the marathon finish. It is now a popular summer concert venue.

㉖ First Cemetery of Athens

Πρώτο Νεκροταφείο Αθηνών

Entrance from Anapáfseos, Méts. **Map** 7 A4. **Tel** 210 923 6118. 2, 4, 10. **Open** 7am–sunset daily. limited.

Athens' municipal cemetery, which is not to be confused with the Kerameikos, the ancient cemetery *(see p92–3)*, is a peaceful place, filled with pine and olive trees and the scent of incense burning at the well-kept tombs.

Fine examples of 19th-century funerary art range from the flamboyance of some of the marble mausoleums to the simplicity of the belle époque *Oraía Koimoméni* or *Sleeping Beauty (see p46)*. Created by Tiniot artist Giannoúlis Chalepás, this beautiful tomb is found to the right of the main cemetery avenue where many of Greece's foremost families are buried.

Among the notable 19th- and 20th-century figures with tombs here are Theódoros Kolokotrónis *(see p84)*, British philhellene historian George Finlay (1799–1875), German archaeologist Heinrich Schliemann *(see p184)*, the Nobel Prize-winning poet Giórgos Seféris (1900–71) and the actress and politician Melína Merkoúri (1922–94).

In addition to the large number of tombs for famous people that are buried here, the cemetery contains a moving, single memorial to the 40,000 Athenians who perished through starvation during World War II.

A lone athlete exercising in the vast Kallimármaro Stadium

SHOPPING IN ATHENS

Shopping in Athens offers many delights. There are street markets, quiet arcades, traditional arts and crafts shops, and designer fashion boutiques to rival Paris and New York. Most Athenians go to the triangle which is formed by Omónoia, Sýntagma and Monastiráki squares to buy everyday household items, clothes and shoes. For leather goods, bargain hunters should head for Mitropóleos, Ermoú, Aiólou and nearby streets. Along smarter Stadíou and Panepistimíou, there are world-class jewellers and large clothing stores. The maze of arcades in the centre also houses smart leather-goods shops, booksellers, cafés and *ouzerís*. The most stylish shopping is to be found in Kolonáki where some of the city's most expensive art galleries are clustered among the foreign and Greek designer outlets selling the latest fashions. Around Athinás, Monastiráki and Pláka there is an eclectic mix of aromatic herb and spice stores, religious retailers selling icons and church candlesticks, second-hand bookshops with rare posters and prints, used vinyl and CD dealers, and catering stores packed with household goods such as pots and pans.

Opening Hours

Shops generally open from 9am–2:30pm, Monday to Saturday. On Tuesdays, Thursdays and Fridays, there is late shopping from 6–9pm (30 minutes earlier in winter). The exceptions to this rule are department stores, tourist shops, supermarkets, florists and *zacharoplasteía* (cake shops) which often open for longer. Many shops close every year throughout August, the time when many Greeks take their holidays.

Department Stores, Malls and Supermarkets

The main stores are **Attica** and **Notos Galleries**. They stock a wide range of beauty products, clothes, gifts, and household goods. Attica is not as big as

Notos Galleries, one of the largest department stores in Athens

Notos Galleries but, consciously modelled on London's Selfridges, it is more exclusive. The three biggest supermarket chains are **Carrefour Marinópoulos**, **Sklavenitis** and **AB Vasilópoulos**, with outlets across the city. **The Mall Athens** in Maroússi, near Neratziótissa station, and **Golden Hall**, also in Maroússi (car access only), are two of the city's largest covered shopping complexes, filled with outlets and restaurants. The Mall Athens also has a cineplex.

Markets

Athens is famous for its flea markets. **Monastiráki** market starts early in the morning every Sunday, when dealers set out their wears along Adrianoú and neighbouring streets.

The commercial tourist and antique shops of Pandrósou and Ifaístou, which collectively refer to themselves as "Monastiráki Flea Market", are open every day. Saturday and Sunday mornings are the best times to visit Plateía Avissynías. For food, the **Central Market** (Varvákeios Agorá), which takes place every day except Sunday, is excellent, as are the popular *laïkés agorés* (street markets) selling fresh fruit and vegetables, which occur 8am–2pm in different areas. Well-stocked central ones include Pagkráti (Tue and Fri), Exárcheia (Sat) and Kolonáki (Fri).

Greeks buy in bulk and stallholders will find it strange if you buy small quantities of less than half a kilo (1 lb) of a fruit or vegetable. In most cases, you will be given a bag to serve yourself – do not be afraid to touch, smell and – for stray grapes – even taste.

Art and Antiques

As authentic Greek antiques become increasingly hard to find, many shops are forced to import furniture, glassware and porcelain from around the globe. Fortunately, however, there are still reasonable buys in old Greek jewellery, brass and

Shoppers browsing the market stalls in Plateia Avyssinias

copperware, carpets and embroidery, engravings and prints. Some can be found at **Antiqua**, just off Plateía Syntágmatos. Kolonáki is a prime area for small, exclusive stores around Sólonos, Skoufá and their side streets. Try the **Gallery Skoufá** for a selection of fine art pieces and temporary exhibitions. Kolonáki is also the art centre with well-established galleries selling paintings and prints. The **Zoumpouláki Gallery** specializes in art and antiques.

Monastiráki also has many antique shops. Look out for **Martínos**, a store selling beautiful, ornate icons and silverware, and the **Athens Gallery**, which specializes in fine art and sculpture.

Antique jewellery and ornaments for sale in Monastiráki

Traditional Folk Art and Crafts

Affordable popular folk art, crafts and souvenirs are plentiful in Monastiráki and Pláka. There are innumerable stores filled with ecclesiastical ephemera and cramped icon painters' studios. Many shops stock elegant wood carvings, rustic painted wooden trays and richly coloured *flokáti* rugs *(see p293)*. **Amorgós** is packed with fine wood carvings and puppets, as seen in the Karagkiózis theatre in Maroúsi *(see p155)*. Among the more unusual shops offering unique services are **Melissinós Art** in Psyrrí and **Olgianna Melissinós** in

Pantelís Melissinós, son of the late shoemaker and poet Stávros Melissinós

Monastiráki. The son and daughter of the late self-styled poet sandal-maker continue to make a wide variety of sturdy sandals and leather goods.

Hellenic Art & Design sells a variety of affordable every-day objects designed by artists living in Greece. Beautiful carved shepherds' crooks from Epirus as well as a large variety of finely crafted ceramics can be found at the fascinating **Centre of Hellenic Tradition**.

Jewellery

Athens is justly famed for its jewellery stores. There is no shortage in Monastiráki and Pláka, which are full of small shops selling gold and silver. **Máris**, in Pláka, has a large selection of good-value classic and contemporary jewellery. Exclusive jewellers, such as **Elle Amber**, can be found in Voukourestíou. Window displays also dazzle at the designer of world-class fame **Zolótas**, whose own pieces copy museum treasures. Another famous name is that of the designer Ilías Lalaoúnis, whose collections, inspired by Classical and other archaeological sources, such as the gold of Mycenae, are eagerly sought by the rich and famous. At the **Ilías Lalaoúnis Jewellery**

Museum, over 3,000 of his designs are exhibited, and there is also a workshop where you can watch the craftsmen demonstrate the skills of the goldsmith and buy some of the jewellery.

Museum Copies

Museum shops provide some of the better buys in the city. Well-crafted, mostly tasteful copies draw on the wide range of ancient and Byzantine Greek art. They come in all shapes and sizes, from a life-size Classical statue to a simple Cycladic marble bowl. Many fine reproductions of the exhibits in the **Benáki Museum** *(see pp82–3)* can be bought from a collection of silverware, ceramics, embroidery and jewellery in the museum shop.

The **Museum of Cycladic Art** *(see pp78–9)* has some fine Tanagran and Cycladic figur-ines, bowls and vases for sale. There is a large selection of reproduction statues and pottery at the **National Archaeological Museum** *(see pp72–5)* souvenir shop. Apart from the museums, the Pláka shop **Orpheus** offers good quality marble and pottery copies of Classical Greek works as well as glittering Byzantine icons.

Display of reproduction red- and black-figure vases for sale

Periptero in Kolonáki selling English and Greek newspapers

Books, Newspapers and Magazines

Many *periptera* (kiosks) in the city centre sell foreign newspapers and magazines. Athens' wealth of bookshops includes many selling foreign language publications. For foreign books, go to the larger branches of **Eleftherou-dákis** or to **Papasotiriou** on Panepistimíou, with specialist floors concentrating on English and Greek fiction, academic genres and children's books. Try **Politeia** for books on history, archaeology and classics, and **Libro** for fiction and non-fiction books and stationery. There are currently no English-language papers or magazines being published in Greece.

One of the many designer stores to be found in Kolonáki

Clothes & Accessories

Although there are some renowned Greek fashion designers – not least **Parthénis**, whose hallmark is black and white minimalism – most clothing stores in Athens concentrate on imported garments. However, there are plenty of high-quality clothes; every designer label can be found in the city's main fashion centre, Kolonáki. There are branches of such famous names as **Gucci**, **Ralph Lauren** and **Max Mara**. Such upmarket stores as **Sótris**, **Bettina**, **Free Shop, Paul & Shark** and **Luisa** typify the area's urban chic. For good-quality high-street fashion, there is the Spanish chain **Zara**.

Kitchenware

Cavernous catering stores in the side streets around the Central Market specialize in classic Greek kitchen- and tableware. Here you will find tiny white cups and the copper saucepans *(mpríkia)* used to make Greek coffee, long rolling pins for making filo pastry, and metal olive oil pourers. **Cook-Shop** is a well-known Greece-based chain of quality kitchenware. It has two branches in central Athens selling everything from crockery and cutlery to arcane kitchen utensils. **Notos Home** in Omónoia stocks a good selection of kitchenware as well as furniture, homewares and other designer lifestyle products.

Food and Drink

There are myriad gourmet treats in Athens, including unusual *avgotáracho* (smoked cod roe preserved in bees-wax), herbs and spices, cheeses and wines. The bakeries and patisseries brim with delicious breads and biscuits, home-made ice cream and yoghurt. **Aristokratikón**, off Plateía Syntágmatos, sells luxurious chocolates and marzipan. One of Athens' best patisseries, **Karavan**, is full of decadent *mpaklavás* and crystallized fruits. **Loumidis** is the best place to buy freshly ground arabica coffee for Greek-style brews. For robusta beans, head to **Coffeeway**, which also serves coffee on the premises.

The Central Market on Athinás is one of the most enticing places for food shopping. It is surrounded by stores packed with cheeses, olives, pistachio nuts, dried fruits and pulses. You will find a range of herbs and spices at **Bahar**, in particular dried savory and sage, lemon verbena and saffron. Nearby, **Miran** sells delectable Armenian specialities and **Green Farm** is one of a new generation of organic supermarkets.

Two enterprising *káves* (wine merchants), **The Winebox** and **Cellier**, offer a broad range of wines and spirits from various small Greek wineries. **Vrettós** in Pláka has a varied display of own-label spirits and liqueurs, and it also operates as a bar.

A crammed Athenian housewares store

DIRECTORY

Department Stores, Malls and Supermarkets

AB Vasilópoulos
Spýrou Merkoúri 38,
Pagkráti. **Map** 7 C2.
Tel 210 725 8913. One
of several branches.

Attica
Panepistimíou 9,
Sýntagma. **Map** 2 F5.
Tel 211 180 2600.

Carrefour Marinópoulos
Kanari 9, Kolonáki. **Map** 3
A5. **Tel** 210 360 7708.

Golden Hall
Kifisías 37a, Maroúsi.
Tel 210 680 3450.

The Mall Athens
Andréa Papandréou 35,
Maroúsi.
Tel 210 630 0000.

Notos Galleries
Stadíou and Aiólou,
Omónoia. **Map** 2 E4.
Tel 210 324 5811.

Sklavenitis
Frýnis 48, Pagráti. **Map** 7
B3. **Tel** 210 751 6991.
One of several branches.

Markets

Central Market (Varvákios Agorá)
Athínás, Omónoia.
Map 1 D4.

Monastiráki
Adrianoú & Pandrósou,
Pláka. **Map** 6 E1.

Art and Antiques

Antiqua
Amaliás 2, Sýntagma.
Map 4 F2.
Tel 210 323 2220.

Athens Gallery
Pandrósou 14, Pláka. **Map**
6 D1. **Tel** 210 324 6942.

Gallery Skoufa
Skoufá 4, Kolonáki.
Map 3 A5.
Tel 210 364 3025.

Martínos
Pandrósou 50, Pláka.
Map 6 D1.
Tel 210 321 2414.

Zoumpouláki Gallery
Plateía Kolonakíou 20
& Kriezótou 6, Kolonáki.
Map 3 A5.
Tel 210 360 8278
& 210 364 0264.

Traditional Folk Art and Crafts

Amorgós
Kódrou 3, Pláka. **Map** 6
E1. **Tel** 210 324 3836.

Centre of Hellenic Tradition
Mitropóleos 59 (Arcade) –
Pandrósou 36,
Monastiráki. **Map** 6 D1.
Tel 210 321 3023.

Hellenic Art & Design
Chairefontos 10, Pláka.
Map 6 E2.
Tel 210 322 3064.

Melissinós Art
Ag. Theklas 2, Psyrrí. **Map**
2 D5. **Tel** 210 321 9247.

Olga Melissinós
Normánou 7, Monastiráki.
Map 1 C5.
Tel 210 331 1925.

Jewellery

Elle Amber
Voukourestíou 6,
Kolonáki. **Map** 2 F5.
Tel 210 324 9600.

Ilías Lalaoúnis Jewellery Museum
Karyatidon & P. Kallispéri
12, Akropoli. **Map** 6 D3.
Tel 210 922 1044.

Máris
Pandrósou 83,
Monastiráki. **Map** 6 D1.
Tel 210 321 9082.

Zolótas
Stadiou 9, Kolonáki.
Map 2 F5.
Tel 210 322 1222.

Museum Copies

Orpheus
Pandrósou 28B, Pláka.
Map 6 D1.
Tel 210 324 5034.

Books, Newspapers and Magazines

Eleftheroudákis
Panepistimíou 15. **Map** 2
F5. **Tel** 210 331 7609.

Libro
Pat. Ioakeim 8, Kolonáki.
Map 3 B5.
Tel 210 724 7116.

Papasotiriou
Panepistimíou 37. **Map** 2
E4. **Tel** 210 325 3232.

Politeia
Asklipiou 1–3 & Akadimías,
between Kolonáki &
Exárcheia. **Map** 2 F4.
Tel 210 360 0235.

Clothes & Accessories

Bettina
Anagnostopoúlou 29,
Kolonáki. **Map** 3 A5.
Tel 210 339 2094.

Free Shop
Voukourestíou 50,
Kolonçki. **Map** 3 A5.
Tel 210 364 1500.

Gucci
Tsakálof 27, Kolonáki.
Map 3 A5.
Tel 210 360 2519.

Luisa
Skoufá 15. **Map** 3 A4.
Tel 210 363 5600.

Max Mara
Kanari 2, Kolonáki.
Map 3 A5.
Tel 210 360 7300.

Parthénis
Dimokrítou 20, Kolonáki.
Map 3 A5.
Tel 210 363 3158.

Paul & Shark
Anagnostopoulou 6,
Athens. **Map** 3 B5.
Tel 210 339 2334.

Ralph Lauren
Voukourestíou 11,
Kolonáki. **Map** 3 A5.
Tel 210 361 1831.

Sótris
Anagnostopoúlou 30
& Voukourestíou 41,
Kolonáki. **Map** 3 A4.
Tel 210 363 9281
& 210 361 0662.

Zara
Skoufá 22, Kolonáki.
Map 3 A5.
Tel 210 363 6340.
One of several branches.

Kitchenware

Cook-Shop
Panepistimíou 41. **Map** 2
E4. **Tel** 210 322 5770.
Irodótou 26, Kolonáki.
Map 3 B5.
Tel 210 725 8989.

Notos Home
Kratínou 3–5, off Plateía
Kotzia, Omónoia. **Map** 2
D4. **Tel** 210 374 3000.

Food & Drink

Aristokratikón
Voulis 7, Sýntagma.
Map 2 E5.
Tel 210 322 0546.

Bahar
Evripídou 31, Omónoia.
Map 2 D4.
Tel 210 321 7225.

Cellier
Kriezótou 1, Kolonáki.
Map 3 A5.
Tel 210 361 0040.

Coffeeway
Stadíou 3, Sýntagma.
Map 2 F5.
Tel 210 322 2488.

Green Farm
Dimokrítou 13, Kolonáki.
Map 3 A5.
Tel 210 361 4001.

Karavan
Voukourestíou 11,
Kolonáki. **Map** 2 F5.
Tel 210 364 1540.

Loumidis
Aiólou 106, Omónoia.
Map 2 E4.
Tel 210 321 4608.

Miran
Evripídou 45, Psyrrí.
Map 2 D4.
Tel 210 321 7187.

Vrettós
Kydathinaíon 41, Pláka.
Map 6 E2.
Tel 210 323 2110.

The Winebox
Xenokrátous 25, Kolonáki.
Map 3 C5.
Tel 210 725 4710.

ENTERTAINMENT IN ATHENS

Athens excels in the sheer variety of its open-air summer entertainment. Visitors can go to outdoor showings of films both vintage and recent, spend lazy evenings in garden bars with the heady aroma of jasmine, or attend a concert in the atmospheric setting of the Herodes Atticus Theatre, which sits beneath the Acropolis.

The Mégaron Mousikís Concert Hall has given the city a first-class classical and jazz concert venue and draws some of the best names in the music world. For most

Athenians, however, entertainment means late-night dining in tavernas, followed by bar- and club-hopping until the early hours. Despite the economic crisis, many music bars and dance clubs still manage to survive across Athens, with door and cover charges sensibly reduced. Whatever your musical taste, there is something for everyone in this lively city. Sports and outdoor facilities are also widely available, in particular watersports, which are within easy reach of Athens along the Attic coast.

Listings Resources

The most comprehensive Greek weekly listings magazine is *Athinorama*, which is published on Thursdays. It lists events and concerts, and the latest bars and music venues – but it's in Greek only. There are no longer any English-language listings resources in print; nor any websites. The best strategy is to watch for posters on utility poles, usually in a mix of Greek and Latin lettering.

Booking Tickets

Although it is necessary to book tickets in advance for the summer Athens Festival (*see p50*) and for concerts at the Mégaron Concert Hall, most theatres and music clubs sell tickets at the door on the day of the performance. However, there is also a central ticket office

(Ticket Services, Panepistimíou 39, Tel: 210 723 4567), open Mon–Sat. The Athens Festival maintains its own ticket office in the same arcade (the Stoá Pesmázoglou), also with Mon–Sat opening hours (Tel: 210 327 2000). Festival tickets can also be purchased at Papasotiriou Books (Panepistimíou 37) or at Public (Karageórgi Servías 1, corner of Plateía Syntágmatos).

Theatre and Dance

There are many fine theatres scattered around the city centre, often hidden in converted Neo-Classical mansion houses or arcades. These include **Pallás**, the **Lampéti** and **Piraios 260**.

Some excellent productions of 19th-century Greek and European plays are staged at the **National Theatre**. Playhouses, such as the **Pántheon**, **Athinón**,

The façade of the National Theatre, Athens

Alfa and **Vretánia**, also mount Greek-language productions of works by well-known 19th- and 20th-century playwrights, as well as a few original-language presentations.

The major classical venues, including the National Theatre, put on contemporary dance and ballet as well as plays. The **Dóra Strátou Dance Theatre** on Filopáppou Hill performs traditional regional Greek dancing nightly between May and September.

The Dóra Strátou Dance Theatre performing traditional Greek dancing outdoors

The doorway to the outdoor Dexamení cinema

Cinema

Athenians love going to the cinema. All foreign-language films are subtitled, with the exception of children's films which are usually dubbed. The last showing is always at 11pm, which makes it possible to dine before seeing a movie.

The city centre has several excellent, large-screen cinemas showing the latest international releases. **Embassy Odeon** and **Village Centre** are large, comfortable, indoor cinemas equipped with Dolby Stereo sound systems. The **Asty**, **Elli** and **Petit Palais** show a comprehensive range of art-house and cult movies.

Athenians like to hang out at bars and tavernas next to the open-air cinemas that are open in the summers from May to late September, such as **Dexamení** in Kolonáki, the **Riviéra** and **Vox** in Exárcheia, **Zephyros** in Petrálona, **Oasis** in Pagkráti, **Cine Paris** in Pláka or **Aegli Village Cool** in Zappio before catching the last performance. The acoustics are not always perfect but the relaxed atmosphere, in the evening warmth, with street noises, typically cats and cars, permeating the soundtrack, is an unforgettable experience. These cinemas seem more like clubs, with tables beside the seats for drinks and snacks.

The outdoor **Thiseíon** cinema comes with the added attraction of a stunning view of the Acropolis.

Classical Music and Opera

The annual Athens Festival, held throughout the summer, attracts a few international ballet and opera companies, orchestras and theatrical troupes to the open-air **Herodes Atticus Theatre**, which seats 5,000 people, and to other venues around the city. This has always been the premier event of the classical music calendar. In 1991, the **Mégaron Mousikís Concert Hall** was inaugurated, providing a year-round venue for jazz, ballet and classical music performances. This majestic marble building contains two recital halls with superlative acoustics, an exhibition space,

Accordionist in Plateía Kolonakíou

a shop and a restaurant. The Olympia Theatre is home to the **Lyrikí Skiní** (National Opera), and stages excellent ballet productions as well as opera.

Greek Music, Rock and Jazz

The lively Greek music scene thrives in a variety of venues throughout central Athens. The large music halls of Syngróu and Ierá Odós advertise on omnipresent billboards around the city. **Vox, Gyalino Mousiko Theatro** and **Stavros tou Notou** attract the top stars and their loyal fans. For the haunting sounds of *rempétika* music, which draws its inspiration and defiant stance from the lives of the urban poor, head to the Exárcheia district, where small musical tavernas like **Tivoli** and **Efimeron** supply good food and live sessions several nights weekly. For more emphasis on the music, try **Makari**, with quality musicians led by George Makris, **Rempetikí Istoria**, with another established house band, and **Mpoemissa**, where a younger crowd is keener on dancing the night away than the quality of the music.

Athens' premier rock venue for home-grown or visiting bands is **Gagarin 205**, while the most durable jazz club, with exclusively touring acts, is **Half Note**.

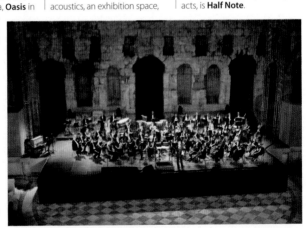

A classical concert at the ancient Herodes Atticus Theatre

Rock and Jazz Music

International acts usually perform at large stadiums or the open-air **Lykavittós Theatre** as part of the annual Athens Festival. The **Gagarin 205 Live Music Space**, a successfully converted cinema, also attracts the very cream of foreign and Greek rock bands. Greek bands can be enjoyed at the **An Club**, which offers patrons the intriguing prospect of Greek rock-and-roll dinner dancing.

The city's premier jazz venue is the **Half Note Jazz Club**. The club is housed in a former stonemason's workshop and is located opposite the First Cemetery. The Half Note is a cosy and popular venue, presenting the best of foreign contemporary jazz.

Live music in one of the city's popular rock clubs

Clubs and Polýchoroi

Athens is a hive of bars and nightclubs that come and go at an alarming rate. The up-and-coming areas of town are Gazi, Kerameikós and Rouf. However, the economic crisis has cut a swathe through the club scene. One of the few likely survivors is **B.E.D. (Before Every Dawn) Club**, on the beach in Glyfáda.

A big trend is the emergence of multipurpose spaces (polýchoroi), often in formerly derelict industrial premises, serving as venues for exhibits, concerts, film screenings and performing arts. The prime example of this is **Technopolis**, joined more recently by **GazARTE** and **Six d.o.g.s.**

Marathon runners in Athens retracing the path of their ancestors

Sport

Most taxi drivers will reel off their favourite football team to passengers before they have had a chance to mention their destination. Such is the Athenian passion for football that the two main rival teams, Panathenaïkós and Olympiakós, are always the subject of fervent debate. Each team is backed by a consortium of private companies, each of which also owns a basketball team of the same name. Football matches are played every Wednesday and Sunday during the September to May season. The basketball teams play weekly, in what is the latest popular national sport.

Lack of adequate parkland within the city means that joggers are a rare sight, despite the annual **Athens Open Marathon** every October. The athletes run from Marathon to the Kallimármaro Stadium in the centre of Athens (see p117). The **Olympiakó Stadium** in Maroúsi seats 80,000 and was built in 1982. Its glass roof was designed by Spanish architect Santiago Calatrava for the 2004 Olympic Games. The Panathenaïkós football team are based here. It has excellent facilities for all sports and includes an indoor sports hall, swimming pools and tennis courts in its 100 ha (250 acres) of grounds. The **Karaïskáki Stadium** in Néo Fáliro is the home of the Olympiakós football team. There are also facilities there for many other sports including volleyball and basketball. Another famous event is

the **Acropolis Rally**, a celebration of vintage cars, held around the Acropolis every spring. It attracts some 50 to 100 cars.

Outside the city centre, there are more facilities on offer, including bowling at the **Bowling Centre of Piraeus** and golf at the fine 18-hole **Glyfáda Golf Course**, which is located close to the airport. Tennis courts are available for hire at various places, including the **Politia Tennis Club**.

Proximity to the Attic coast means that a large variety of water sports is on offer. Windsurfing and water-skiing are widely available on most beaches. **Naftikos Omilos Vouliagmenis** offers water-skiing lessons for all ages and levels. One of the most renowned scuba-diving clubs is **Athina Diving**, which has lessons for all levels.

Basketball, an increasingly popular national sport among the Greeks

DIRECTORY

Theatre and Dance

Alfa
Patisíon 37 & Stournári, Exárcheia.
Map 2 E2.
Tel 210 523 8742.

Athinón
Voukourestíou 10, Kolonáki. **Map** 2 E5.
Tel 210 331 2343.

Dóra Strátou Dance Theatre
Filopáppou Hill, Filopáppou.
Map 5 B4.
Tel 210 324 4395.

Lampéti
Leof Alexándras 106, Neapoli.
Map 4 D2.
Tel 210 645 3685.

National Theatre
Agíou Konstantínou 22, Omónoia.
Map 1 D3.
Tel 210 528 8100.

Pallás
Voukourestíou 5, Sýntagma. **Map** 2 F5.
Tel 210 321 3100.

Pántheon
Peiraiós 166, Gázi.
Tel 210 347 1111.

Vretánia
Panepistimíou 7, Sýntagma. **Map** 2 E4.
Tel 210 322 1579.

Cinema

Aegli Village Cool
Garden of Zappio.
Map 7 A2.
Tel 210 336 9369.

Asty
Korai 4, Athens.
Map 2 E4.
Tel 210 322 1925.

Cine Paris
Kydathinaion 22, Pláka.
Map 6 E2.
Tel 210 322 2071.

Dexamení
Plateía Dexamenís, Kolonáki.
Map 3 B5.
Tel 210 362 3942.

Elli
Akadimias 64, Omónoia.
Map 2 E3.
Tel 210 363 2789.

Embassy Odeon
Patriárchou Ioakeím 5, Kolonáki. **Map** 3 B5.
Tel 210 721 5944.

Oasis
Pratínou 7, Pagkráti.
Map 8 C3.
Tel 210 724 4015.

Petit Palais
Rizári 24. **Map** 8 C2.
Tel 210 729 1800.

Riviéra
Valtetsíou 46, Exárcheia.
Map 2 F3.
Tel 210 384 4827.

Thiseíon
Apostólou Pávlou 7, Thiseío. **Map** 5 B2.
Tel 210 342 0864.

Village Centre
Ymittoú 110, Pagkráti.
Map 8 D3.
Tel 210 757 2440.

Classical Music

Herodes Atticus Theatre
Dionysíou Areopagítou, Acropolis. **Map** 6 C2.
Tel 210 324 1807.

Lyrikí Skiní, Olympia Theatre
Akadimías 59, Omónoia.
Map 2 F4.
Tel 210 366 2100.
w nationalopera.gr

Mégaron Mousikís Concert Hall
V Sofías & Kókkali, Ilísia.
Map 4 E4.
Tel 210 728 2333.
w megaron.gr. **Map** 1 A5. **Tel** 2.

Traditional Greek Music

Athinón Arena
Peiraios 166, Gazi. **Map** 1 A5. **Tel** 210 347 1111.

Gyalino Mousiko Theatro
Leoforos Andrea Syngrou 143, Nea Smýrni.
Tel 210 931 5600.

Makári
Zoödóchou Pigís 125, cnr Komninón, Exárcheia.
Map 2 B2.
Tel 210 645 8958.

Mpoémissa
Solomoú 13–15, Exárcheia. **Map** 2 D2.
Tel 210 383 8803.

Rempétiki Istoría
Ippokrátous 181, Neápoli. **Map** 3 C2.
Tel 210 642 4937.

Stavros tou Notou
Tharýpou 35–37, crn Frantzí, Néos Kósmos.
Tel 210 922 6975.

Tivoli
Emmanouíl Mpenáki 34, Exárcheia. **Map** 2 E3.
Tel 210 383 0919.

Vox
Ierá Odoós 16, Kerameikós. **Map** 1 A5.
Tel 210 341 1000.

Rock, Jazz and Ethnic music

An Club
Solomoú 13–15, Exárcheia. **Map** 2 E2.
Tel 210 330 5056.
w anclub.gr

Gagarin 205 Live Music Space
Liosíon 205, Athens.
Map 1 C1.
Tel 211 411 2500.
w gagarin205.gr

Half Note Jazz Club
Trivonianoú 17, Mets.
Map 6 F4.
Tel 210 921 3310.

Lykavittós Theatre
Lykavittós Hill.
Map 3 B4.
Tel 210 722 7209.

Clubs and Polýchoroi

B.E.D. Club
Poseidonos 58, Glyfáda.
Tel 210 894 7911.

GazARTE
Voutadon 32–34, Kerameikós. **Map** 1 A5.
Tel 210 346 0347.
w gazarte.gr

Six d.o.g.s.
Avramiótou 6–8, Monastiráki. **Map** 2 D5.
Tel 210 321 0510.

Technopolis
Peiraios 100, Gázi.
Map 1 A5.
Tel 210 347 5518.
w technopolis-athens.com

Sport

Athina Diving
38th km of Coastal Road, Athens–Sounio, Lagoníssi.
Tel 22910 25434.
w athinadiving.gr

Bowling Centre of Piraeus
Profítis Ilías, Kastélla.
Tel 210 412 7077.

Glyfáda Golf Course
Konstantínou Karamanlí, Glyfáda.
Tel 210 894 6820.

Karaïskáki Stadium
Néo Fáliro.
Tel 210 480 0900.

Naftikos Omilos Vouliagmenis
Laimós Vouliagménis.
Tel 210 896 2416.

Olympiakó Stadium
Leof Kifisías 37, Maroúsi.
Tel 210 683 4777.
w oaka.com.gr

Politia Tennis Club
Aristotélous 18, Politia, Kifisiá.
Tel 210 620 0003.
w politiatennisclub.gr

ATHENS STREET FINDER

Map references given for sights in Athens refer to the maps on the following pages. References are also given for Athens hotels (*see pp268–9*), Athens restaurants (*see pp282–5*) and for useful addresses in the *Survival Guide* section (*see pp300–23*). The first figure in the reference tells you which

Street Finder map to turn to, and the letter and number refer to the grid reference. The map below shows the area of Athens covered by the eight Street Finder maps (the map numbers are shown in black). The symbols used for sights and features are listed in the key below.

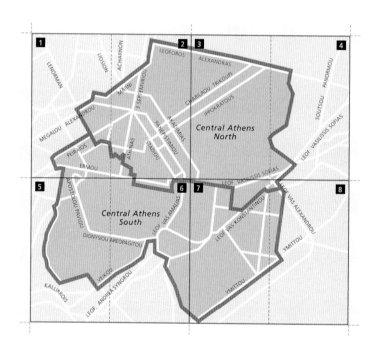

Key

Major sight	Church
Place of interest	Synagogue
Other building	Railway line
M Metro station	Pedestrianized street
Railway station	
Main coach or bus station	
Trolleybus stop	
Tram stop	
Funicular	
Tourist information	
Hospital with casualty unit	
Police station	

0 kilometres 1
0 miles 0.5

Scale of Map Pages

0 metres 250
0 yards 250

Street Finder Index

Abbreviations

Ag	Agios, Agía (saint)
Leof	Leofóros (avenue)
Pl	Plateía (square)

Note Squares and avenues are indexed by their name followed by Plateía or Leofóros.

A

Achaiou	3 B5
Acharnon	2 D2
Achilleos	1 A3
Achilleo Paraschou	3 B1
Acropolis	6 D2
Acropolis Museum	6 D2
Adanon	8 F2
Adrianou	5 C1
Adrianoupoleos	5 A1
Aetionos	6 F5
Afaias, Plateia	5 A1
Afroditis	6 E2
Aftokratoron Angelon	3 A1
Aftokratoros Irakleiou	2 E1
Aftomedontos	7 B2
Agaristis	7 A5
Agatharchou	1 C5
Agathiou	3 B2
Agathokleous	7 A5
Agathonos	2 D5
Agelaou	7 B5
Ag Artemiou	7 B5
Ag Paraskevis	7 C5
Agias Eirinis	2 D5
Agias Eleousis	2 D5
Agias Filotheis	6 E1
Agias Theklas	2 D5
Agias Varvaras	8 D5
Aginoros	5 A1
Agioi Theodoroi	2 D5
Agion Anargyron	1 C5
Agion Asomaton	1 B5
Agion Panton	4 E2
Agios Dionysios	2 F5
Agios Nikolaos Ragavas	6 E2
Agios Savvas	4 E2
Agiou Dimitriou	2 D5
Agiou Dimitriou	4 F1
Agiou Fanouriou	8 D3
Agiou Georgiou	8 F3
Agiou Isidorou	3 A3
Agiou Konstantinou	1 C3
Agiou Markou	2 D5
Agiou Nikolaou	5 B4
Agiou Nikolaou, Plateia	8 E3
Agiou Orous	1 A4
Agiou Pavlou	1 C2
Agiou Spyridonos	7 B2
Agisilaou	1 B4
Agkylis	6 E5
Aglaonikis	6 E4
Aglavrou	5 C5
Agnanton	5 A4
Agrafon	5 A4
Agras	7 B3
Aidesiou	7 B4
Aidonon	4 D1
Aigeiras	1 B1
Aiginitou	4 E5

Aigyptou	2 E1
Aigyptou	8 D2
Aineiou	8 D4
Ainianos	2 E1
Aioleon	5 A3
Aiolou	6 D1
Aischylou	2 D5
Aischynou	6 E2
Aisopou	1 C5
Aitherias	5 A3
Aixoneon	5 A1
Akadimias	2 E3
Akadimou	1 B4
Akakion	2 D1
Akamantos	5 B1
Akarnanos	7 B4
Akominatou	1 C3
Akronos	8 D3
Aktaiou	5 B1
Alamanas	1 A1
Alastoros	4 E1
Alchimou	6 D4
Aldou Manoutiou	4 E2
Alektoros	7 C4
Alexandrou Soutsou	3 A5
Alexandras	4 E4
Alexandras, Leofóros	2 E1
Alexandreias	1 A1
Alexandrou Palli	4 D1
Alexandroupoleos	4 F4
Alfeiou	4 E1
Alikarnassou	1 A3
Alitsis	2 D1
Alkaiou	4 F5
Alkamenous	1 C1
Alketou	7 C4
Alkidamantos	5 A2
Alkimachou	8 D1
Alkippou	1 B2
Alkiviadou	2 D2
Alkmaionidon	8 D2
Alkmanos	4 E5
Alkyonis	1 A1
Almeida	5 B4
Almopias	4 F4
Alopekis	3 B5
Alsos	4 E5
Alsos Eleftherias	4 D4
Alsos Pagkratiou	7 C3
Alsos Syngrou	8 E1
Alyos	4 E5
Amaliados	4 F2
Amazonon	1 A4
Amerikis	2 F5
Amfiktyonos	5 B1
Ampati	5 C4
Ampelakion	4 E2
Amvrosiou Frantzi	6 D5
Amynandrou	5 B4
Amynta	7 B2
Anacharsidos	7 B4
Anagnostopoulou	3 A4
Anakreontos	8 E5
Analipseos	8 E5
Anapiron Polemou	4 D4
Anastasiou Gennadiou	3 C1
Anastasiou Tsocha	4 E2
Anaxagora	2 D4
Anaxagora	8 F3
Anaximandrou	8 D4
Ancient Agora	5 C1
Andrea Dimitriou	8 E2
Andrea Metaxa	2 F3

Andrea Syngrou, Leoforos	5 C5
Andromachis	1 B2
Andromedas	8 E5
Androutsou, G	5 B5
Anexartisias	3 A2
Anexartisias, Plateia	2 D2
Angelikara	5 C3
Angelikis Chatzimichali	6 E1
Antaiou	5 A3
Anthidonos	1 A2
Anthippou	7 B4
Antifilou	4 E5
Antifontos	7 B3
Antilochou	1 A3
Antimachidou	6 D4
Antinoros	7 C1
Antiopis	8 E5
Antisthenous	6 D5
Antonio Fratti	5 C3
Apokafkon	3 B3
Apollodorou	6 E4
Apolloniou	5 A3
Apolloniou, Plateia	5 A3
Apollonos	6 E1
Apostoli	1 C5
Apostolou Pavlou	5 B1
Appianou	8 D3
Arachosias	4 F5
Arachovis	2 F3
Arakynthou	5 A4
Aratou	7 B3
Archelaou	7 C2
Archilochou	6 D5
Archimidou	7 A4
Archyta	7 B3
Ardittou	6 F3
Areos	6 D1
Aretaielon	4 E5
Aretaiou	4 F1
Argenti	6 D5
Argentinis Dimokratias, Pl	3 B1
Argolidos	4 F1
Argous	1 A1
Argyriou	5 C4
Argyroupoleos	4 D2
Arianitou	3 B2
Arionos	1 C5
Aristaiou	6 E5
Aristarchou	8 D3
Aristeidou	2 E5
Aristippou	3 B4
Aristodimou	3 C4
Aristofanous	1 C4
Aristogeitonos	2 D4
Aristogeitonos	5 A5
Aristokleous	8 E4
Aristonikou	7 A4
Aristonos	1 C3
Aristoteli Kouzi	4 E2
Aristotelous	2 D3
Aristotelous	5 A5
Aristoxenou	7 C3
Aritis	8 E4
Arkadon	5 A4
Arkados	3 B2
Arkesilaou	6 E5
Arktinou	7 B2
Armatolon Kai Klefton	4 D2
Armeni-vraila Petrou	3 A1
Armodiou	2 D4
Arnis	4 E5
Arrianou	7 B2
Arsaki	2 E4
Arsinois	8 E3
Artemonos	6 F5
Artis	7 C5

Artotinis	8 E4
Arvali	5 C4
Aryvvou	8 D5
Asimaki Fotila	2 F1
Asklipiou	2 F4
Asopiou	3 B1
Aspasias	7 C3
Asteroskopeion	5 B2
Astrous	1 A1
Astydamantos	8 D3
Athanasias	7 C3
Athanasiou Diakou	6 E3
Athens Academy	2 F4
Athens Megaron Concert Hall	4 E4
Athinaidos	2 D5
Athinas	2 D5
Athinogenous	8 D2
Athinon, Leoforos	1 A3
Avanton	5 A1
Averof	2 D2
Avgerinou	4 E1
Avissynias, Plateia	1 C5
Avlichou	7 A5
Avliton	1 C5
Avrammiotou	2 D5
Axariou	8 F5

B

Benaki Museum	7 A1
British Archaeological School	3 C5
Byzantine Museum	7 B1

C

Central Market	2 D4
Chairefontos	6 E2
Chalkidikis	1 A3
Chalkidonos	8 E2
Chalkokondyli	2 D2
Chaonias	1 A1
Charalampi	3 B2
Charidimou	7 C5
Charilaou	2 E4
Charilaou Trikoupi	5 B5
Charissis	1 C1
Charitos	3 B5
Chatzichristou	6 D3
Chatzigianni	4 D5
Chatzikosta	4 F3
Chatzimichali	6 D5
Chatzipetrou	6 E5
Chavriou	2 E4
Cheironos	7 C2
Chersonos	3 A4
Chionidou	7 B5
Chiou	1 C2
Chloridos	5 A1
Choida	3 C4
Chomatianou	1 C1
Chormovitou	1 C1
Chremonidou	8 D4
Christianoupoleos	6 D5
Christokopidou	1 C5
Christou Lada	8 F3
Christou Vournasou	4 E3
Chrysafi	7 B4
Chrysanthou Serron	3 B3
Chrysolora	3 A2
Chrysospiliotissis	2 D5
Chrysostomou	6 E2

Chrysostomou
  Smyrnis, Leof 8 D5
Chrysostomou
  Smyrnis 8 E3
Chrysoupoleos 8 F5
City of Athens
  Museum 2 E5

D

Dafnomili 3 A3
Daidalou 6 E2
Damagitou 7 A5
Damareos 7 B5
Damasippou 4 F4
Damaskinou 3 C2
Dameou 1 A4
Dania 5 B4
Daponte 3 B2
Daskalogianni 4 D2
Defner 6 F4
Deinarchou 5 C4
Deinocharous 5 A4
Deinokratous 3 B5
Deinostratou 6 E5
Dekeleias 8 E2
Delfon 3 A4
Deligianni 1 B2
Deligianni 2 F2
Deligiorgi 1 C3
Dervenion 2 F2
Dexileo 6 F4
Dexippou 6 D1
Diagora 7 B4
Didotou 3 A4
Didymou 2 D1
Digeni
  Akrita 3 B2
Dikaiarchou 7 B4
Dikaiou 5 C4
Dilou 8 F5
Dimis 1 C1
Dimitressa 4 E5
Dimitsanas 4 E2
Dimocharous 4 D4
Dimofontos 5 A2
Dimokratias,
  Leoforos 8 E3
Dimokritou 3 A5
Dimosthenous 1 A2
Dimoulitsa
  Pargas 4 E1
Diocharous 7 D1
Diofantou 7 B2
Diogenous 6 D1
Diomeias 6 E1
Dionysiou
  Aiginitou 5 B2
Dionysiou
  Areopagitou 5C2
Dionysiou
  Efesou 4 D1
Dionysiou
  Therianou 3 A1
Dioskoridou 7 B3
Dioskouron 6 D1
Dipylou 1 B5
Distomou 1 A1
Dodekanisou 8 E5
Doras
  D'istria 3 B4
Dorylaiou 4 E3
Dorou 2 E3
Douridos 7 C3
Doxapatri 3 B3
Doxatou 1 A3
Dragatsaniou 2 E5
Dragoumi 8 E1
Drakontos 8 D2
Drakou 5 C3
Dyovounioti 5 B4

E

Edouardou 2 F5
Efatosthenous 7 B3
Efesteion 1 A5

Efforionos 7 B3
Efmolpou 6 F2
Efpatorias 4 F2
Efpatridon 1 A4
Efroniou 7 C2
Efthimou 7 B5
Eftychidou 7 C3
Eirinis Athinaias 3 A2
Ekalis 7 B4
Ekataiou 6 E5
Ekfantidou 8 D4
Ekklision 8 E5
Elas Artemisiou 1 A4
Elefsinion 1 B2
Eleftheriou
  Venizelou 4 E3
Eleftheriou
  Venizelou 7 A1
Eleftheriou
  Venizelou, Pl 8 E5
Ellanikou 7 B2
Ellinos 7 B4
Ellis 2 E1
Emmanouil
  Benaki 2 E3
Empedokleous 7 B4
Epidavrou 1 A1
Epifanou 5 C3
Epikourou 1 C4
Epiktitou 7 C3
Epimenidou 6 E2
Epimitheos 7 B4
Eptachalkou 1 B5
Eratosthenous 7 B2
Eratyras 1 C1
Erechtheion 6 D2
Erechtheiou 6 D3
Erechtheos 6 D2
Eressou 2 F2
Eretrias 1 A2
Ergotimou 8 D2
Erifylis 8 D2
Ermagorou 1 A2
Ermionis 7 C2
Ermou 1 B5
Errikou
  Traimper 1 C2
Erysichthonos 5 A1
Erythraias 8 E5
Erythraias 8 F4
Eslin 4 F2
Ethnarchou
  Makariou 8 F3
Evangelismos 3 C5
Evangelismos 7 C1
Evangelistrias 2 E4
Evangeliou
  Martaki, Pl 8 D4
Evdoxou 6 E5
Evelpidos
  Rogkakou 3 A4
Evgeniou
  Voulgareos 7 A4
Evmenous 7 B4
Evmenous 7 C5
Evmolpidon 1 A5
Evneidon 1 A5
Evpolidos 2 D4
Evrimedontos 1 A4
Evripidou 1 C4
Evropis 5 B5
Evrostinis 1 B1
Evrou 4 F4
Evrydikis 8 D2
Evrynomis 5 A3
Evzonon 4 D5
Exarcheion,
  Plateia 2 F2
Exikiou 1 C1
Eye Institute 2 F5

F

Faidonos 8 D3
Faidras 5 B1
Faidrou 7 C2
Fainaretis 5 C3
Faistou 2 D1

Falirou 5 C5
Fanarioton 3 C2
Farmaki 6 E2
Farsalon 1 A2
Favierou 1 C2
Feidiou 2 E3
Ferekydou 7 B4
Feron 2 D1
Figaleias 5 B2
Filadelfeias 1 C1
Filasion 5 A2
Filellinon 6 F2
Filetairou 7 B5
Filikis Etairias,
  Plateia 3 B5
Filimonos 4 E3
Filoktitou 7 C5
Filolaou 7 B5
Filopappos Hill 5 B3
Filopappou 5 B4
Filota 5 A3
First Cemetery of
  Athens 7 A4
Flessa 6 E1
Foinikos 7 C5
Foivou 6 F2
Fokaias 8 E2
Fokaias 8 F5
Fokianou 7 B2
Fokionos 6 E1
Fokou 1 A4
Fokylidou 3 A4
Formionos 8 D2
Fotakou 5 C4
Fotiadou 7 A3
Fotomara 6 D5
Frantzi
  Kavasila 3 B2
Frouda 4 D1
Frynichou 6 E2
Frynis 7 C3
Frynonos 7 B5
Fthiotidos 4 F1
Fylis 2 D1
Fyllidos 5 A1

G

Galateias 5 A1
Galinou 5 B4
Gamvetta 2 E3
Gargarettas,
  Plateia 6 D4
Garibaldi 5 C3
Garnofsky 5 C3
Gazias 8 F1
Gedrosias 4 F5
Gelonos 4 E3
Gennadeion 3 C4
Gennaiou
  Kolokotroni 5 A4
George 2 E3
Georgiou B,
  Leoforos V 7 B1
Geraniou 2 D4
Germanikou 1 B4
Gerodimou 4 D2
Geronta 6 E2
Gerostathi 4 D3
Giannetaki 5 C5
Gianni Statha 3 A4
Giatrakou 1 B3
Gkika 5 A3
Gkioni 6D4
Gkoufie 5 C4
Gkoura 6 E2
Gkyzi 3 C2
Gladstonos 2 E3
Glafkou 6 F4
Glykonos 3 B5
Gordiou 1 A1
Gorgiou 6 F3
Granikou 1 B4
Gravias 2 E3
Greek Folk Art
  Museum 6 F2
Grigoriou 8 D2
Grigoriou Labraki 5 A5

Grigoriou
  Theologou 3 C3
Grivogiorgou 4 D5

H

Hadrian's
  Arch 6 E2
Harilaou
  Trikoupi 2 F3
Hephaisteion 5 C1
Hill of the
  Nymphs 5 A2

I

Iakchou 1 A5
Iasiou 4 D5
Iasonos 1 B3
Iatridou 4 D4
Iera Odos 1 A4
Ierofanton 1 A5
Ieronos 8 D3
Ierotheou 1 C3
Ifaistou 5 C1
Ifikratous 8 D3
Igiou 5 A1
Igisandrou 7 B4
Ignatiou 7 C5
Iktinou 2 D4
Iliados 7 B5
Iliodorou 7 B3
Iliou 1 C2
Ilioupoleos 6 F5
Ilision 4 F5
Inglesi 6 E4
Ioanni
  Athanasiadi 4 F2
Ioanni Grypari 5 A5
Ioanni Iakovo
  Mager 2 D2
Ioanninon 1 B1
Ioannou
  Gennadiou 3 D5
Iofontos 8 D2
Iolis 6 F4
Ionias, N 7 C5
Ionon 5 A3
Ionos
  Dragoumi 7 D1
Iosif
  Momferratou 3 B1
Iosif Ton Rogon 6 E3
Ioulianou 1 C1
Ioustinianou 2 F1
Ipeirou 2 D1
Ipitou 6 E1
Ipparchou 6 E5
Ippodamou 7 B3
Ippokrateio 4 F3
Ippokratous 2 E4
Ippomedontos 7 C2
Ipponikou 6 D5
Irakleidon 5 A1
Irakleitou 3 A5
Irakleous 6 D4
Iras 6 E4
Iridanou 4 E5
Iridos 7 B4
Irodotou 3 B5
Irodou Attikou 7 A2
Irofilou 3 C4
Ironda 7 B2
Ironos 7 B3
Iroon,
  Plateia 2 D5
Iroon
  Skopeftiriou 8 E3
Iros Konstanto-
  poulou 8 F4
Isaiou 7 C4
Isavron 3 A2
Isiodou 7 B2
Ivykou 7 B2

J

Jewish Museum	6 F2

K

Kairi	2 D5
Kaisareias	4 F3
Kaisareias	8 E5
Kakourgo Dikeiou	2 D5
Kalaischrou	6 E3
Kalamida	2 D5
Kalamiotou	2 E5
Kalchantos	8 F4
Kalkon	6 D5
Kallergi	1 C3
Kallidromiou	2 F1
Kalliga	3 B1
Kallikratous	3 A3
Kallimachou	7 C2
Kallimarmaro Stadium	7 B3
Kallirois	5 A4
Kallisperi	6 D3
Kallisthenous	5 A3
Kalogrioni	6 D1
Kaltezon	1 A2
Kalvou	3 B1
Kalypsous	1 A4
Kamaterou	2 D2
Kanari	3 A5
Kanari	8 D5
Kanellopoulos Museum	6 D2
Kaningos	2 E3
Kaningos, Plateia	2 E3
Kapetan Petroutsou	4 F2
Kaplanon	2 F4
Kapnikarea	6 E1
Kapnikareas	6 D1
Kapno	2 D2
Kapodistriou	2 E2
Kapsali	3 B5
Karachristos	4 D4
Karaiskaki	1 C5
Karaiskaki, Plateia	1 C3
Karatza	5 C4
Karea	6 F4
Karer	6 E4
Karitsi, Plateia	2 E5
Karneadou	3 C5
Karodistriou	5 A5
Karolou	1 C3
Karori	2 D5
Kartali	4 F4
Karyatidon	6 D3
Karydi	5 A1
Kassianis	3 C2
Katsantoni	3 A1
Katsikogianni	1 C5
Kavalotti	6 D3
Kedrinou	4 E1
Kekropos	6 E2
Kelsou	6 F5
Kennenty	8 E3
Kerameikos	1 B5
Kerameikou	1 A4
Kerameon	1 B2
Kerasountos	4 F4
Keratsiniou	1 A3
Kerkinis	4 E2
Kiafas	2 E3
Kilkis	1 A1
Kimonos	1 A2
Kiou Petzoglou	8 E2
Kioutacheias	8 E4
Kirras	4 F1
Kisamou	8 E5
Kitsiki Nikolaou, Plateia	3 C4
Klada	6 D5
Kladou	6 D1
Klathmonos, Plateia	2 E4

Kleanthi	7 B2
Kleious	1 A1
Kleisouras	8 E1
Kleisovis	2 E3
Kleisthenous	2 D4
Kleitomachou	7 A3
Kleitou	2 E4
Kleomenous	3 B4
Kleomvrotou	1 A4
Klepsydras	6 D2
Kodratou	1 B2
Kodrika	2 D5
Kodrou	6 E1
Koimiseos Theotokou	8 F3
Kokkali	4 E4
Kokkini	6 E4
Kolchidos	4 F1
Koletti	2 F3
Kolofontos	8 D2
Kolokotroni	2 E5
Kolokynthous	1 B3
Kolonakiou, Pl	3 B5
Kolonou	1 B3
Komninon	3 B2
Koniari	4 D3
Kononos	8 D2
Konstantinou Lourou	4 E4
Konstantinou- poleos, Leof	1 A3
Kontogoni	3 C1
Kontoliou	8 D5
Korai	2 E4
Korai	7 C5
Kordeliou	8 E5
Korinis	1 C4
Korinthou	1 A1
Kornarou	6 E1
Koromila	5 C5
Koronaiou	4 F5
Koroneias	4 E2
Koronis	3 A3
Korytsas	8 F5
Koryzi	6 E4
Kosma Aitolou	4 D2
Kosma Melodou	3 B3
Kotopouli, M	2 D3
Kotyaiou	4 E3
Kotzia, Plateia	2 D4
Koukakiou, Plateia	5 C4
Kouma	3 A1
Koumanoudi	3 B1
Koumoundourou	2 D3
Koumpari	7 A1
Kountourioti, Plateia	5 B5
Kountouriotou	2 F2
Koutsikari	4 E1
Kraterou	4 F5
Kraterou	8 F1
Kratinou	2 D4
Kriezi	1 C5
Kriezotou	2 F5
Krinis	8 F5
Krisila	7 B4
Kritis	1 C1
Kritonos	8 D1
Kropias	1 B1
Krousovou	8 E1
Ktisiou	7 C2
Ktisiviou	7 B3
Kydantidon	5 A3
Kydathinaion	6 E2
Kymaion	5 A1
Kynaigeirou	1 B2
Kyniskas	7 A4
Kyprou, Leof	8 D5
Kyriazopoulos Folk Ceramic Museum	6 D1
Kyrillou Loukareos	4 D2
Kyrinis	3 C2
Kyvellis	2 E1

L

Lachitos	4 E4
Laertou	8 E4
Lakedaimonos	4 F1
Lamachou	6 F2
Lamias	4 F2
Lampardi	3 C2
Lampelet	1 B1
Lamprou Katsoni	3 C2
Lampsakou	4 E4
Laodikeias	4 F5
Larissa	1 B1
Larissis	1 B1
Larisis, Plateia	1 C1
Laskareos	3 B2
Laspa	3 B2
Lassani	6 D5
Lavragka	1 B2
Lazaion	5 C4
Lefkippou	8 D4
Lefkotheas	8 D4
Lekka	2 E5
Lempesi	6 E3
Lenorman	1 A1
Leocharous	2 E5
Leokoriou	1 C5
Leonida Drossi	3 C1
Leonidou	1 A4
Leonnatou	1 B3
Lepeniotou	1 C5
Leventi	3 B5
Levidou	8 E2
Limpona	2 D5
Liosion	1 C1
Litous	8 F5
Livini	4 D2
Livvis	4 F5
Lofos Ardittou	7 A3
Lofos Finopoulou	3 B1
Lomvardou	3 B1
Longinou	6 F4
Lontou	2 F3
Louizis Riankour	4 F2
Louka	1 C5
Loukianou	3 B5
Lydias	8 F3
Lykavittos Hill	3 B3
Lykavittou	3 A5
Lykavittou, Plateia	3 A4
Lykeiou	7 B1
Lykofronos	7 B5
Lykomidon	5 B1
Lykourgou	2 D4
Lysikratous	6 E2
Lysikratous, Pl	6 E2
Lysimachias	6 D5
Lysimachou	7 C5
Lysippou	7 B3

M

Madritis, Plateia	7 D1
Maiandrou	4 E5
Maiandroupoleos	4 F1
Mainemenis	4 F1
Makedonias	2 D1
Makedonon	4 E3
Makri	6 E3
Makris	8 E5
Makrygianni	6 E3
Makrynitsas	4 F1
Malamou	6 F4
Mamouri	1 C1
Manis	2 F3
Manoliasis	8 E2
Manou	8 D3
Mantineias	8 F5
Mantzakou	3 A2
Mantzarou	3 A4
Marasli	3 C5
Marathonos	1 B3
Marikas Iliadi	4 E3
Marinou Charvouri	6 F4
Markidi	4 F2

Markou Evgenikou	3 C2
Markou Mousourou	7 A3
Markou Mpotsari	5 C4
Marni	1 C3
Massalias	2 F4
Matrozou	5 B5
Mavili, Plateia	4 E3
Mavrikiou	3 B2
Mavrokordatou	2 E3
Mavrokordatou, Plateia	2 D2
Mavromataion	2 E1
Mavromichali	2 F3
Megalou Alexandrou	1 A4
Megalou Spilaiou	4 E2
Meintani	5 C5
Melanthiou	2 D5
Meleagrou	7 B2
Melidoni	1 B5
Melissou	7 C4
Menaichmou	6 E4
Menandrou	1 C4
Menedimou	1 B1
Menekratous	6 F5
Menonos	6 F5
Merkourie, M	4 D4
Merlie Oktaviou	3 A3
Merlin	3 A5
Mesogeion	8 D3
Mesolongiou	2 F3
Mesolongiou	8 E5
Mesolongiou, Plateia	8 D3
Messapiou	5 A4
Metagenous	6 E5
Metaxourgeiou, Plateia	1 B3
Meteoron	7 A5
Methonis	2 F2
Metonos	1 C4
Metsovou	2 F1
Mexi Ventiri	4 D5
Miaouli	2 D5
Michail Karaoli	8 F2
Michail Mela	4 D3
Michail Psellou	3 A1
Michail Voda	2 D1
Michalakopoulou	4 E5
Mikras Asias	4 F4
Mileon	4 F2
Milioni	3 A5
Miltiadou	2 D5
Mimnermou	7 B2
Miniati	7 A3
Mirtsiefsky	5 A4
Misaraliotou	6 D3
Misountos	8 E3
Misthou	8 D2
Mitromara	6 D3
Mitroou	6 D1
Mitropoleos	6 D1
Mitropoleos, Plateia	6 E1
Mitropoli	6 E1
Mitsaion	6 D3
Mnisikleous	6 D1
Momferratou	3 B1
Monastiraki	2 D5
Monastirakiou, Plateia	2 D5
Monastiriou	1 A3
Monemvasias	5 B5
Monis Asteriou	6 E2
Monis Petraki	4 D4
Monis Sekou	8 D2
Monument of Lysikrates	6 E2
Monument of Philopappus	5 C3
Moraiti, A	3 B3
Moreas, Z	5 C4
Morgkentaou	8 D5
Moschonision	8 F3
Mourouzi	7 B1

Mousaiou	6 D1	Nikolaou Kosti	1 A1	Pappa, A	4 E3	Priinis	8 E2
Mousikis Megaro	4 E4	Nlkomideias	1 C1	Paradesiou	8 E5	Proairesiou	7 B4
Mouson	5 C4	Nikosthenous	7 C3	Paramythias	1 A4	Prodikou	1 A4
Moustoxydi	3 A1	Nikotsara	4 D2	Paraskevopoulou	6 E4	Profiti Ilia,	
Mpalanou	7 A3	Nileos	5 A1	Parmenidou	7 B4	Plateia	7 C4
Mpeles	5 B4	Nimits	4 D5	Parnassou	2 E4	Profitou	
Mpenaki Panagi	3 C2	Niriidon	8 D1	Parthenon	6 D2	Daniel	1 A3
Mperantzofsky	5 A4	Nisyrou	1 B2	Parthenonos	6 D3	Proklou	7 B4
Mpiglistas	8 E2	Nonakridos	4 F1	Pasitelous	7 C3	Promachou	6 D3
Mpotasi	2 E2	Notara	2 F2	Paster	4 F3	Propylaia	5 C2
Mpoukouvala	4 D2	Noti Mpotsari	5 C4	Patousa	2 E3	Propylaion	5 C3
Mpoumpoulinas	2 F2	Nymfaiou	4 F5	patision	2 E3	Protagora	7 B3
Mpousgou	3 A1	Nymfaiou	8 E5	Patriarchou		Protesilaou	8 E4
Municipal Art				Fotiou	3 A3	Protogenous	2 D5
Gallery	1 C4	**O**		Patriarchou		Prousou	4 E2
Museum of				Grigoriou	2 F4	Prytaneiou	6 D2
Cycladic Art	7 B1	Oberlander		Patriarchou		Psallida	3 A1
Museum of Greek		Museum	1B5	Ieremiou	4 D2	Psamathis	5 A3
Popular Musical		Odemisiou	8 E4	Patriarchou		Psaromiligkou	1 B5
Instruments	6 D1	Odysseos	1 B3	Ioakeim	3 B5	Psaron	1 C2
Mykalis	1 A4	Odysseos		Patriarchou		Psiloreiti	1 B1
Mykinon	1 A4	Androutsou	5 C5	Sergiou	3 B3	Psylla	6 F2
Mykonos	1 C5	Ogygou	1 C5	Patron	1 B1	Ptolemaion	7 C2
Myllerou	1 B3	Oikonomou	2 F2	Patroou	6 E1	Ptoou	5 A4
Mylon	1 A1	Oitis	3 A4	Pazikotsika	6 F4	Pylarou	7 B3
Myrinousion	1 B2	Oitylou	4 F1	Peiraios	1 A5	Pyloy	1 A2
Myrmidonon	5 A1	28 Oktovriou	2 E3	Peloponnisou	1 B1	Pyrgotelous	7 C3
Myronidou	1 A4	Olympiados	8 D5	Pelopos	1 B2	Pyrgou	1 B1
Mysonos	6 E5	Olympiou	5 C5	Pentapotamias	4 F5	Pyrronos	7 B4
Mystra	4 D1	Omirou	2 F5	Pentelis	6 E1	Pyrrou	7 C3
		Omonoia	2 D3	Perikleous	2 E5	Pyrsou	1 A2
N		Omonoias,		Perraivou	6 E4	Pytheou	6 E4
		Plateia	2 D3	Pesmatzoglou	2 E4	Pythodorou	1 A3
Nafpaktias	8 F4	Oreon	4 F2	Peta	6 F2		
Nafpliou	1 A2	Orestiados	4 E2	Petmeza	6 D4	**R**	
Naiadon	7 C1	Origenous	3 B3	Petraki	6 E1		
Nakou	6 E4	Orkart	5 A4	Petras	1 A1	Ragkava	6 E2
National		Orlof	5 C4	Petrou Dimaki	3 A4	Ragkavi	3 C1
Archaeological		Orminiou	8 E1	Petsovou	3 A2	Ramnes, Plateia	1 A3
Museum	2 E2	Othonos	6 F1	Pierias	1 A3	Ratzieri	5 C3
National Bank	6 F1	Otryneon	5 B1	Piga, M	7 A3	Ravine	4 D5
National Gallery		Oulof Palme	8 F2	Pindarou	3 A5	Renti	6 D4
of Art	8 D1	Oumplianis	8 E1	Pindou	8 F5	Rethymnou	2 E1
National Gardens	6 F2	Outsika	8 E1	Pinelopis	1 B3	Riga Feraiou	2 F4
National Historical		Ozolon	4 F5	Pinotsi	5 B4	Rigillis	7 B1
Museum	2 E5			Pissa Efstratiou	5 C5	Rizari	7 C1
National Library	2 F4	**P**		Pittaki	1 C5	Roidi	4 D1
National Research				Pittakou	6 E2	Roikou	6 E5
Centre	7 C1	Padova	5 A1	Plaka Square	6 E2	Roma	3 A5
National		Pafsaniou	7 B2	Plapouta	2 F1	Romanou	
Theatre	2 D3	Pagkratiou,		Plastira,		Melodou	3 B3
Navarchou		Plateia	7 C3	Plateia	7 B3	Romvis	2 E5
Apostoli	1 C5	Paianieon	1 B3	Plataion	1 A4	Roumelis	5 A4
Navarchou		Palaiologou, K	1 C2	Platonos	1 A2	Roumelis	8 F1
Nikodimou	6 E1	Palaion Patron		Platypodi	4 D1	Rovertou Gkalli	5 C3
Navarchou		Germanou	2 E4	Plionis	4 F1	Russian Church of	
Voulgari	5 A2	Palamidiou	1 A2	Plithonos	3 B2	St Nicodemus	6 F2
Navarinou	2 F3	Palingenesias	4 D2	Plotinou	7 B4		
Navy Hospital	4 D4	Pallados	2 D5	Ploutarchou	3 C5	**S**	
Nazianzou	7 C5	Pallinaion	5 A2	Pnykos	5 B2		
Nazliou	8 D5	Pamfilis	5 A3	Pnyx	5 B2	Sachini	1 C2
Nearchou	7 C5	Panagi Kyriakou	4 E3	Poikilis	6 D1	Sachtouri	1 C4
Neas Efesou	8 F3	Panagi Tsaldari	1 A5	Polemokratous	7 C2	Salaminos	1 A3
Neofronos	8 E1	Panagi Tsaldari	5 A5	Polemonos	7 C2	Samou	1 C2
Neofytou		Panagi Tsaldari	8 D5	Polydamantos	7 B3	Samouil, K	1 B4
Douka	7 B1	Panagia		Polydorou	1 B2	Sampsountos	4 F1
Neofytou		Gorgoepikoos	6 E1	Polykleitou	2 D5	Santaroza	2 E4
Metaxa	1 C1	Panagiotara	4 D1	Polykleous	6 F5	Sapfous	1 C4
Neofytou		Panaitoliou	5 B4	Polytechneiou	2 E2	Sarantapichou	3 B3
Vamva	7 B1	Panathinaikou	4 E2	Polytechnic		Sarantaporou	5 A5
Neoptolemou	7 C4	Pandrosou	6 D1	School	2 E2	Saripolou	2 F1
Nestou	4 F4	Panepistimiou	2 E3	Polyzoidou	3 C1	Saripolou	5 A5
Nezer	6 E4	Panioniou	8 F3	Polyzoidou	8 F5	Sarri	1 C5
Nika Louka	1 C5	Panormou	4 F2	Pontou	4 E4	Satomis	8 F1
Nikandrou	7 B2	Papadiamanto-		Portas	8 E1	Satovriandou	2 D3
Nikiforidi Nik	8 E4	poulou	4 E5	Potamianou	4 E5	Schina, K	3 B1
Nikiforou	1 C3	Pantazopoulou,		Poukevil	1 C2	Schliemann's	
Nikiforou		Plateia	1 B1	Poulcherias	3 A2	House	2 F5
Lytra	3 C1	Panos	6 D1	Pouliou	4 F2	Scholis, Ev	8 E5
Nikiforou		Papadima	4 D4	Poulopoulou	5 B1	Schou, A	6 E4
Ouranou	3 A3	Papadopoulou	4 E3	Pramanton	5 A4	Secno Despos	6 D4
Nikiou	2 D5	Papagianni	4 D4	Prassa	3 A4	Seirinon	8 E5
Nikis	6 F1	Papanikoli	2 D5	Pratinou	7 C3	Seizani	8 E4
Nikitara	2 E3	Paparrigopoulou	2 E5	Praxitelous	2 E5	Sekeri	7 A1
Nikolaou Dimi-		Paparrigopoulou	3 B1	Premetis	8 E1	Sellasias	1 C2
trakopoulou	5 B5	Papathymiou	4 D2	Presidential		Semelis	4 F5
Nikolaou-Iosif		Papatsori	3 C2	Palace	7 B2	Semitelou	4 E4
Maizonos	1 B2			Priinis	4 E1		

3 Septemvriou	2 D3
Serron	1 A3
Sevasteias	4 F4
Sfakion	1 C1
Sfaktirias	1 A4
Siatistis	1 A3
Sidirodromon	1 B2
Sikelias	5 C5
Sikyonos	1 A2
Sina	2 F5
Sisini	4 D5
Sismani	6 E4
Sithonias	4 F1
Sivrisariou	8 D5
Skaltsa Dimou	4 E1
Skaramagka	2 E1
Skopetea Leonida	4 D3
Skoppa	6 E1
Skoufa	3 A4
Skoufou	6 E1
Skoura	6 E2
Skouze, Plateia	7 B2
Skylitsi	2 F1
Smith, J	5 B2
Smolensky	3 A3
Smyrnis	2 D1
Smyrnis	8 F3
Smyrnis, Plateia	8 D5
Sofokleous	1 C4
Sokratous	2 D4
Solioti	4 E1
Solomonidou	8 F3
Solomou	2 E2
Solonos	2 E3
Sonierou	1 C2
Sorvolou	6 F3
Sosou	7 B5
Sostratou	6 E5
Sotiri Petroula, Plateia	1 A1
Sotiros	6 E2
Souidias	3 C5
Souliou	2 F3
Souliou, Plateia	8 E4
Sourl, G	6 F1
Soutsou	2 D2
Spefsippou	3 B1
Spyridonos Trikoupi	2 F2
Spyrou	7 B4
Spyrou Donta	6 E4
Spyrou Merkouri	7 C3
St Laiou	4 F1
Stadiou	2 E4
Stadiou, Plateia	7 A3
Staikou	2 F4
Stasinou	7 B2
Stathogianni	5 C4
Stavrou, G	2 E4
Steirieon	5 A1
Stenon	8 E1
Stentoros	8 E4
Stilponos	7 B4
Stisichorou	7 B1
Stisikleous	5 A2
Stoa Athinon	2 E4
Stoa Dimosion Ypallilon	2 E4
Stoa Emporiou	2 E4
Stoa Nikoloudi	2 E4
Stoa Of Attalos	5 C1
Stoa Pesmazoglou	2 E4
Stoa Sofokli Venizelou	2 E4
Stoa Spyromiliou	2 F5
Stoa Vyzantiou	2 F5
Stournari	2 D2
Strataion	6 D3
Stratigopoulou	3 B2

Stratigou Dompoli	7 A4
Stratigou Ioannou	7 A4
Stratigou Kontouli	6 D4
Stratiotikou Syndesmou	3 A4
Stratonos	6 E2
Stravonos	8 D3
Strefi Hill	3 A2
Streit	2 D4
Syinis	4 E3
Synesiou	3 C2
Syngrou	8 D1
Syntagma	6 F1
Syntagmatos, Plateia	6 F1
Syrakou	1 B1
T	
Temple of Olympian Zeus	6 F3
Theatrou, Plateia	1 C4
Theokritou	6 D4
Theonos	6 E5
Theopompou	7 B2
Theorias	5 C2
Theotoki	7 A3
Thermopylon	1 A3
Thespidos	6 E2
Thespieon	1 A3
Thesproteos	3 A1
Thesprotias	1 B1
Thessalonikis	1 A5
Thetidos	7 D1
Thironos	8 D2
Thiseio	1 B5
Thiseiou	1 C5
Thiseos	2 E5
Thiseos	5 A5
Tholou	6 E2
Thorikion	5 A1
Thoukldidou	6 E1
Thrakis	1 C1
Thrasyllou	6 E2
Thrasyvoulou	6 D1
Thriasion	5 A2
Thyamidos	1 A1
Tilemachou	3 A3
Timanthous	6 E5
Timoleontos	6 F4
Timotheou	7 C1
Timotheou	8 E4
Timoxenou	6 F5
Tomb of the Unknown Soldier	6 F1
Tompazi	1 C5
Tositsa	2 F2
Tower of the Winds	6 D1
Town Hall	2 D4
Tralleon	8 F3
Trapezountos	3 A3
Trapezountos	8 F5
Trikorfon	2 E1
Trion Ierarchon	5 A2
Tripodon	6 E2
Tritonos	5 A3
Trivonianou	6 F4
Troados	4 F1
Troon	5 A2
Trouman, Plateia	7 B2
Tsakalof	3 A5
Tsamadou	2 F2
Tsami Karatasi	5 C4
Tsangari	6 E2
Tsavella	8 E5
Tseliou Dimou	4 E1
Tsiklitira	7 B3
Tsimiski	3 B3
Tsokri, Plateia	6 E3
Tydeos	7 C4
Tymfristou	6 E1

Tyrnavou	1 A2
Tyrtaiou	6 F4
Tzavella	2 F3
Tziraion	6 E3
U	
University of Athens	2 F4
University of Athens Museum	6 D1
V	
V Sofias	7 A1
Vaindiriou	8 D5
Vakchou	6 E2
Vakchylidou	4 F5
Valaoritou	2 F5
Valavani	5 A3
Valetta	4 F5
Valsamonos	3 C2
Valtetsiou	2 F3
Varnava, Plateia	7 B4
Varoutidi, Plateia	8 E5
Varvaki	3 C1
Vasileiou Laskou	8 E4
Vasileos Alexandrou, Leof	7 D1
Vasileos Georgiou	6 F1
Vasileos Konstantinou, Leof	7 B2
Vasilikis	2 D5
Vasiliki	5 B1
Vasilissis Amalias, Leof	6 F2
Vasilissis Olgas, Leof	6 F2
Vasilissis Sofias, Leof	3 D5
Vassani	5 A3
Vassou Timoleontos	4 E3
Vatatzi	3 B2
Vatheos	4 F2
Vatopediou	4 F2
Vatsaxi	2 D2
Vegoritidos	4 E2
Veikou	5 B5
Veikou, Plateia	6 D4
Velestinou	4 F2
Velissariou	3 B2
Veranzerou	2 D3
Vergas	1 C1
Vergovitsas	4 D1
Vernardaki	4 E1
Versi	7 B3
Victor Hugo	1 C2
Viktoria	2 E1
Vilara	1 C3
Vinkelman	7 A5
Virginias Benaki	1 B3
Vissarionos	2 F4
Vitonos	5 A1
Vlachava	2 D5
Vladimirou Mpensi	4 D5
Vlassopoulou	5 A4
Vogli	6 E2
Voltairou	5 C5
Vonasera	6 E4
Voreou	2 D5
Voreiou Ipeirou	8 D5
Voukourestiou	2 F5
Voulgari	1 C3
Voulgaroktonou	3 A2
Vouli	7 A1
Vouliagmenis, Leof	6 F4
Voulis	6 E1
Vourvachi	6 E4

Voutadon	1 A5
Voutie	5 A4
Vrasida	8 D1
Vrastovou	4 F1
Vrazilias, Plateia	4 E5
Vryaxidos	7 C4
Vrygou	6 D5
Vryoulon	7 C5
Vryoulon	8 F3
Vyronos	6 E2
Vyssis	2 D5
Vyzantiou	6 D4
Vyzantiou	8 E3
W	
War Museum	7 C1
Wemster	5 C3
X	
Xanthippou	3 B5
Xanthis	8 E5
Xanthou	3 B5
Xenias	4 F4
Xenofanous	7 A4
Xenofontos	6 F1
Xenokleous	7 C3
Xenokratous	3 C5
Xifiou	3 C2
Xouthou	2 D3
Xydia	6 E5
Xyniados	4 E2
Xypetis	8 F4
Y	
Ydras	5 A5
Ymittou	7 B5
Ypatias	6 E1
Ypatrou	3 A1
Yperionos	5 A3
Ypsilantou	3 C5
Yvriou	6 F5
Z	
Zacharitsa	5 C4
Zaimi	2 F3
Zalokosta	3 A5
Zalongou	2 F3
Zappeion	6 F2
Zarifi	3 C1
Zefxidos	6 E4
Zinni Anastasiou	5 C4
Zinodotou	8 D3
Zinonos	1 C3
Zitrou	6 D3
Zografou	1 A3
Zonara	3 B2
Zoodochou Pigis	2 F3
Zosimou	3 B2
Zossimadon	2 F2

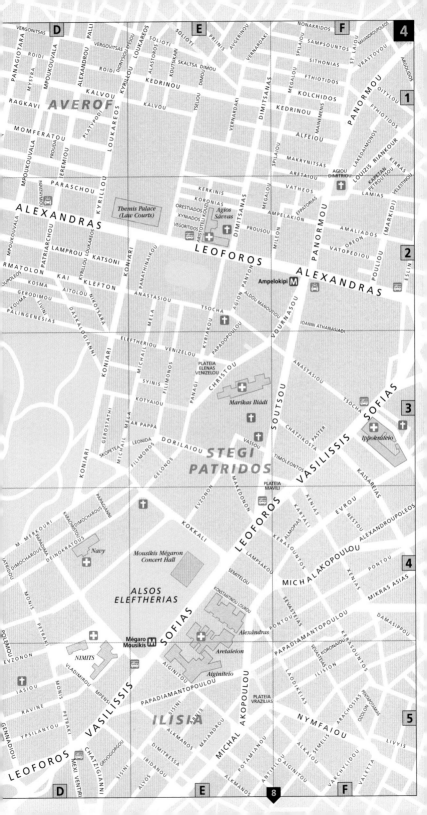

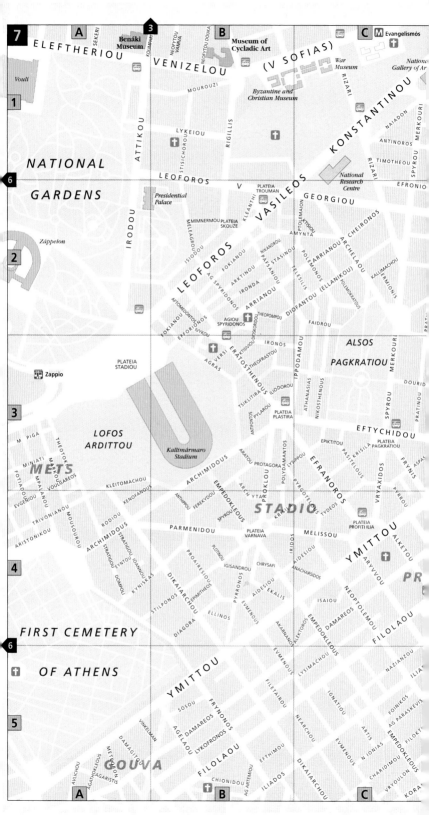

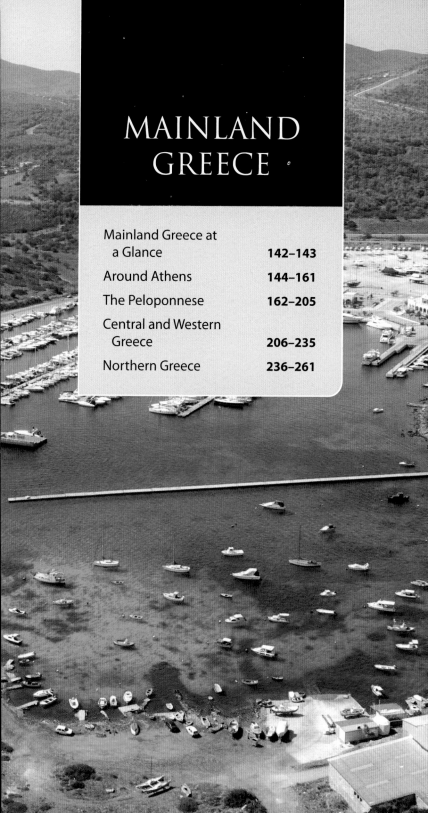

MAINLAND GREECE

Mainland Greece at
a Glance   142–143
Around Athens   144–161
The Peloponnese   162–205
Central and Western
Greece   206–235
Northern Greece   236–261

Mainland Greece at a Glance

The unique attraction of the mainland lies in its wealth of ancient remains, set in landscapes of great natural beauty. Classical sites are most notable in the south, around Athens, and the coasts of Attica and the Peloponnese, while Macedonian remains can be seen in the temperate northeast. Byzantine monasteries and churches are found all over the country, particularly on the holy peninsula of Mount Athos which is governed by its 20 monasteries.

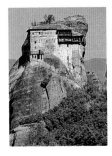

The Metéora area *(see pp220–21)* combines extraordinary sandstone pinnacles with some of the first medieval monasteries in Greece, perched on the rocky peaks.

Delphi *(see pp232–5)* is home to the evocative ruins of an ancient religious complex and theatre situated on Mount Parnassós.

Ancient Olympia *(see pp174–7)* was, from the 8th century BC to the 4th century AD, the site of the Panhellenic Games, forerunner of today's Olympics. One of the best-preserved buildings is the Temple of Hera *(left)*, dating from around the 6th century BC.

Mystrás *(see pp196–7)* is one of the best-preserved Byzantine complexes in Greece, exemplified by this church of Agía Sofía. It is a medieval city, and held out against the Ottomans until 1460.

Florina
Edessa

NORTHERN GREECE
(see pp236–61)

Neápoli
Kozáni
Kate

Kónitsa

Métsovo
Lárisa

Ioánnina

Igoumenítsa
Karditsa

CENTRAL AND WESTERN GREECE
(see pp206–35)

Arta

Lam

Astakós

Galaxidi

Mesolóngi

Pátra

Xilóka

Kyllíni

THE PELOPONN
(see pp162–205)

Pýrgos

Trípoli

Megalópoli

Kalamáta

Areópoli

The Máni peninsula *(see pp198–203)* is dotted with tower houses.

0 kilometres 50
0 miles 25

◀ An aerial view of Marina Lávrio, southeast Attica

Thessaloníki's Archaeological Museum *(see pp250–51)* has spectacular gold finds from the tombs of the Macedonian kings, and this bronze head from around AD 235 of Alexander Severus.

Didymóteicho

Paranéstio

Sidirókastro

Dráma

Komotiní

Kavála

Alexandroúpoli

Thessaloníki

Osios Loukás monastery *(see pp226–7)* is beautifully set in a flowering orchard. The octagonal design of the 11th-century dome was widely copied. Its plain exterior conceals the gold-ground mosaics inside.

Néa Moudaniá

Mount Athos has, since 1060, been entirely occupied by monks *(see pp256–8).*

Ancient Corinth *(see pp166–70)*, capital of the Roman province of Achaia, was renowned for its luxury and elegance, exemplified by this ornate capital.

Vólos

The Monastery of Daphni *(see pp156–7)* is a famous work of Byzantine architecture with outstanding medieval mosaics decorating the interior of the church.

AROUND
ATHENS
(see pp144–61)

Corinth   Athens

os

Mycenae *(see pp182–4)*, one of Greece's oldest sites, dates back to 1550 BC; the Lion Gate was the entrance to the citadel. Mycenae was possibly ruled by Agamemnon.

ranídi

Epidaurus *(see pp188–9)* has one of the best-preserved theatres in Greece.

Monemvasiá *(see pp190–92)* means "one way in", a reference to the strategic advantage of this heavily fortified Byzantine seaport. Its former role as the main port of Byzantine Greece is reflected in the buildings of the old town.

AROUND ATHENS

ATTICA

The area around Athens, known as Attica, is the spiritual heartland of ancient and modern Greece. Its archaeological sites have attracted generations of scholars and plunderers alike, and its mountains and coastline have provided important refuge in times of strife. Today, the golden beaches along the eastern coast attract those simply wishing to escape the bustle of modern Athens.

The land of Attica was the basis of Athenian wealth. The fine marble from the quarries on Mount Ymittós and Mount Pentéli was used for the temples and sculptures of ancient Athens. The silver from Lávrio financed their construction, and the produce from the local agricultural areas fed the population.

Attica has witnessed many significant historical events. The plain of Marathon was the site of one of the greatest battles in Greek history. Piraeus, now Greece's largest and busiest port, was also the port of ancient Athens. The Classical temples at less-known archaeological sites around the countryside, such as Eleusis, Ramnous and Brauron, offer a rural retreat from the overcrowding and pollution of the city.

At Sounion, the majestic, well-preserved Temple of Poseidon on the cape has been a beacon to mariners for centuries.

The Byzantine era also left a great legacy of fine architecture to the region. Two of the best examples of this are the imposing monasteries of Daphni and Kaisarianís, with their ornate mosaics, frescoes and elegant stonework.

Southeast of Athens, the summer heat of the Attic plain is ideal for growing crops. Grapes are a speciality in the Mesógeia (Midland) region, which produces some of the finest *retsína* in the country. North of Athens, Mount Párnitha provides interesting walks and offers superb views over the city from the summit.

The peaceful ruins of the Stoa of the Bear Maidens at Ancient Brauron

◀ The Christ Pantokrátor figure in the dome of the *katholikón* of the Monastery of Daphni

Around Athens

Beyond the endless urban sprawl of Athens, the region around the city, known as Attica, offers the diversity of wild mountains, Byzantine monasteries and churches, evocative archaeological sites and sandy beaches. Not surprisingly, such easy accessibility to the coast and countryside has led to overcrowding in Athens' suburbs, and pollution around Piraeus and Ancient Eleusis. The hills of Mount Párnitha and Ymittós are rich in wildlife, with deserted trails, caves and icy spring water. In the summer months, Athenians move out to the Attic Coast, where the well-kept beaches have every kind of water sport facility, and there are bars and clubs. Towards the cape at Sounion, there are countless fish tavernas by the sea and quiet rocky coves ideal for snorkelling.

Boats moored in Mikrolímano harbour, Piraeus

Key

- ═══ Motorway
- ━━ Major road
- ┄┄┄ Minor road
- ─── Scenic route
- ╌╌╌ Main railway
- ─── Minor railway
- ═══ Regional border

Getting Around

Athens' international airport, Elefthérios Venizélos serves the region. There are two routes out of Athens to southeast Attica: the popular coastal road from Piraeus to Sounion, and the inland road, via Koropí and Markópoulo, to the east-coast towns of Pórto Ráfti and Lávrio. This is also the way for the turn-off to the port of Rafína, where there are ferry connections to Evvoia and the Cyclades. Frequent buses from Athens link all the towns in the area. Mount Párnitha and northern Attica are best reached by taking the A1 (E75) national road.

For hotels and restaurants see p270 and p286

The Temple of Poseidon on the cape at Sounion

Locator Map

Sights at a Glance

1 Amphiareio of Oropos
2 Ramnous
3 Marathónas
4 Rafína
5 *Ancient Brauron pp150–51*
6 Pórto Ráfti
7 Lávrio
8 Sounion
9 Attic Coast
10 Paianía
11 Attica Zoological Park
12 Moní Kaisarianís
13 Kifisiá
14 Mount Párnitha
15 *Monastery of Daphni pp156–7*
16 *Piraeus pp158–9*
17 *Ancient Eleusis pp160–61*

```
0 kilometres        10
0 miles        5
```

The *katholikón* of Moní Kaisarianís

For keys to symbols *see back flap*

The *enkoimitírion* at the Amphiareio

❶ Amphiareio of Oropos

Αμφιαρειο του Ωρωπού

Kálamos, Attica. **Road map** D4. **Tel** 22950 62144. Kálamos. **Open** 8am–3pm Tue–Sun. **Closed** main public hols.

The Amphiareio sanctuary nestles on the left bank of the Cheímarros, a small river surrounded by pine trees and wild thyme bushes. It is dedicated to Amphiaraos, an Arolid hero credited with healing powers whom, according to mythology, Zeus rescued when he was wounded in battle. It is said that the earth swallowed up Amphiaraos while he was riding his chariot, and that he then miraculously reappeared through the sacred spring at this site. In ancient times, visitors would throw coins into the spring in the hope of being granted good health.

The sanctuary came to prominence as a healing centre in the 4th century BC, when its Doric temple and sacrificial altar were built, attracting the sick from all over Greece. Houses erected during the Roman period, when the area became a popular spa centre, are still visible on the right bank of the river. The *enkoimitírion* was the site's most interesting building.

It was a long stoa, the remains of which are still visible today, where the patients underwent treatment by *enkoimisis*. This gruesome ritual entailed the sacrifice of a goat in whose bloody hide the patient would then spend the night. The next morning, priests would prescribe medicines based on their interpretations of the dreams of the patient.

Above the *enkoimitírion* are the remains of an impressive theatre, which has a well-preserved *proskenion* (stage façade) and five sculpted marble thrones, once reserved for the use of priests and guests of honour. On the right bank of the valley, opposite the altar, is a water clock dating from the 4th century BC.

Marble throne from the Amphiareio theatre

❷ Ramnous

Ραμνούς

Attica. **Road map** D4. **Tel** 22940 63477. **Open** 8am–3pm Tue–Sun (Sanctuary of Nemesis only). **Closed** main public hols.

Ramnous is a remote but beautiful ancient town, overlooking the gulf of Evvoia. It is home to the only Greek sanctuary dedicated to the goddess of vengeance, Nemesis. The sanctuary was demolished when the Byzantine Emperor Arcadius decreed in AD 399 that all temples left standing should be destroyed. Thus only the foundations of this sanctuary can be seen today. Within its compound, two temples are preserved side by side. The smaller and older Temple of Themis dates from the 6th century BC. Used as a treasury and storehouse in ancient times, its impressive polygonal walls are all that now survive. Within the cella, some important statues of the goddess and her priestess, Aristonoë, were uncovered. They can now be seen in the National Archaeological Museum (*see pp72–5*).

The larger Temple of Nemesis dates from the mid-5th century BC. It is very similar in design to the Hephaisteion in Athens' Agora (*see pp94–5*) and the Temple of Poseidon at Sounion (*see p152*). Built in the Doric

The remains of the Temple of Nemesis at Ramnous

style, the temple contained a statue of Nemesis by Agorakritos, a disciple of Pheidias *(see p102)*. The statue has been partially reconstructed from fragments, and the head is now in the British Museum.

A ship in the port of Rafína

❸ Marathónas

Μαραθώνας

Attica. **Road map** D4. **Tel** 22940 55155. 🚌 Site & Museum: **Open** Tue–Sun. **Closed** main public hols. 🅿

The Marathon Plain is the site of the great Battle of Marathon, where the Athenians defeated the Persians. The burial mound of the Athenians lies 4 km (2 miles) from the modern town of Marathónas. This tumulus is 180 m (590 ft) in circumference and 10 m (32 ft) high. It contains the ashes of the 192 Athenian warriors who died in the battle. The spot was marked by a simple *stele* of a fallen warrior, Aristion, by the sculptor Aristokles. The original is now in the National Archaeological Museum *(see pp72–5)* in Athens. There is a copy at the site, inscribed with an epigram by the ancient poet Simonides: "The Athenians fought at the front of the Greeks at Marathon, defeating the gold-bearing Persians and stealing their power."

In 1970, the burial mound of the Plataians and royal Mycenaean tombs were found nearby in the village of Vraná. The Plataians were the only other Greeks who sent warriors in time to assist the Athenians already at the battle. The **Marathon Museum** displays archaeological finds from these local sites. There are also some beautiful Egyptian-

Plate discovered in the tomb of Plataians

style statues from the 2nd century AD, found on the estate of Herodes Atticus, on the Marathon Plain. This wealthy benefactor was born and bred in this area. He is known for erecting many public buildings in Athens, including the famous theatre located on the southern slope of the Acropolis *(see p101)* that was named in his honour.

Environs

Just 8 km (5 miles) west of Marathónas is **Lake Marathónas**, which is crossed by a narrow causeway. This vast expanse of water is man-made. The impressive dam, made from white Pentelic marble, was built in 1926. It created an artificial lake that was Athens' sole source of water until 1959. Lake Marathónas is fed by the continuous streams of the Charádras and Varnávas, which flow down from Mount Párnitha *(see p155)* and makes a good setting for a picnic.

❹ Rafína

Ραφήνα

Attica. **Road map** D4. 🏙 8,600. 🚌 🚌

The charm of Rafína is its lively fishing port, packed with caïques and ferries. After Piraeus and Lávrio, it is the third port in Attica. Frequent buses from Athens and the airport bring passengers for the regular ferry connections to some Cyclades islands and Kárystos, opposite in Evvoia.

One of the administrative *demes* (regions) of ancient Athens, Rafína is a long-established settlement. Although there is little of historical or archaeological interest, the town offers a selection of excellent fish restaurants and tavernas. Choose one by the waterside to sit and watch the hustle and bustle of this busy port.

Environs

North of Rafína, a winding road leads to the more picturesque resort of **Máti**. Once a quiet hamlet, it is packed today with trendy cafés and bars, apartment blocks and summer houses owned by Athenians.

The Battle of Marathon

When Darius of Persia arrived at the Bay of Marathon with his warships in 490 BC, it seemed impossible that the Greeks could defeat him. Heavily outnumbered, the 10,000 Greek hoplites had to engage 25,000 Persian warriors. Victory was due to the tactics of the commander Miltiades, who altered the usual battle phalanx by strengthening the wings with more men. The Persians were enclosed on all sides and driven back to the sea. Around 6,000 Persians died and only 192 Athenians. The origins of the marathon run also date from this battle. News of the victory was relayed by a runner, Pheidippides, who covered the 41 km (26 miles) back to Athens in full armour before dying of exhaustion.

Vase showing Greek hoplites fighting a Persian on horseback

❺ Ancient Brauron

Βραυρώνα

Situated near modern Vravróna, Brauron is one of the most evocative sites near Athens. Although little remains of its former architectural glory, finds in the museum reveal its importance as the centre of worship of Artemis, goddess of childbirth and protectress of animals *(see p57)*. Legend relates that it was founded by Orestes and Iphigeneia, the children of Agamemnon, who introduced the cult of Artemis into Greece. Evidence of Neolithic and Mycenaean remains have been found on the hill above the site, but the tyrant Peisistratos brought Brauron its fame in the 6th century BC when he made the worship of Artemis Athens' official state religion.

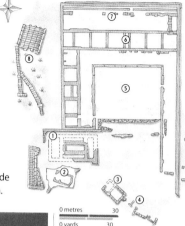

| 0 metres | 30 |
| 0 yards | 30 |

Key to the Sanctuary of Artemis

① Temple of Artemis
② Chapel of Agios Geórgios
③ Sacred House
④ Tomb of Iphigeneia
⑤ Hostel of the Bear Maidens
⑥ Dormitories
⑦ Stoa
⑧ Stone Bridge

The stoa at the Hostel of the Bear Maidens, Brauron

Exploring Ancient Brauron

The centre of this compact site lies just north of the prehistoric acropolis. The 5th-century BC Doric **Temple of Artemis**, of which only the foundations remain, formed the focal point of the sanctuary to the goddess. Beside the temple stands a late Byzantine chapel, dedicated to **Agios Geórgios**.

From here, a path leads southeast to the oldest cult site in the sanctuary. This is said to

be the **Tomb of Iphigeneia**, the high priestess of Artemis. Next to it are the foundations of the **Sacred House**, which was used as a home by the cult's priestesses. The most extensive remains at the site are to the northeast, at the **Hostel of the Bear Maidens**. This courtyard may have been the place where young girls

performed the bear dance. Surrounded by a late 5th-century BC **stoa**, the courtyard had rooms behind that were used as dining areas and **dormitories**. Only the foundations remain, but the stone sleeping couches and bases of statues can still be seen. There is also a 5th-century BC **stone bridge** to the west.

The small Byzantine chapel of Agios Geórgios

Brauronia Ceremony

Held every four years in the spring, the Brauronia festival was celebrated in atonement for the killing of one of Artemis's sacred pet bears. Although little is known about the mysterious rites today, Aristophanes mentions the "bear dance" that initiates had to perform in his play *Lysistrata*. Disguised as bears and adorned with saffron-coloured robes, young girls, aged between five and ten, performed a dance honouring this sacred animal.

Relief showing pilgrims approaching the altar of Artemis at the Brauronia ceremony

VISITORS' CHECKLIST

Practical Information
10 km (6 miles) NE of
Markópoulo, Attica.
Road map D4.
Tel 22990 27020.
Open 8am–2:45pm Tue–Sun.
Museum: **Open** 8am–2:45pm
Tue–Sun. **Closed** 1, 6 Jan, 25 Mar,
Good Fri am, Easter Sun, Mon,
1 May, 25, 26 Dec. ♿ limited
access on site.

Transport
🚌

Mycenaean vase from the Brauron
Museum, 1200–1100 BC

🏛 Brauron Museum
This fascinating museum,
revamped in 2009, has a
wealth of finds from the site.
In Room 1, there are cases
filled with assorted votive
offerings such as miniature
vases and jewellery. In Room 2
are the serene statues of árktoi
("little she-bears"). Room 3
has a fine votive relief of the
gods Zeus, Leto, Apollo and
Artemis, and the remains
of an altar. Rooms 4 and 5
offer a variety of pre-historic
and Mycenaean finds,
including some ornate
Geometric vases.

Retsína
Although many Greeks prefer drinking whisky to wine these days,
retsína is still favoured by millions of tourists. Two large *retsína* vintners,
Kourtakis and Malamatina, claim annual production in
excess of 50 million bottles, of which about half is
exported. The unique, distinctive flavour comes from
the Aleppo pine resin which is added in small
quantities to the grape must during fermentation.
This method has been used since antiquity to
preserve and flavour wine in Greece. Since entry
into the EU in 1981, traditional production areas
have had their own appellations. Aficionados
agree that some of the best *retsína* comes from
the Mesógeia appellation in Attica, where the
Savatiano grape is cultivated. In fact, while several
regions of Greece make *retsína*, purists claim that
only barrelled *retsína* from Attica is the real stuff.

Collection of
pine resin

🔴 Pórto Ráfti
Πόρτο Ράφτη

Attica. **Road map** D4. 🏠 3,300. 🚌

Pórto Ráfti takes its name from
Ráfti island which is visible just
off the headland. On the island
is a colossal marble statue of
a seated female brandishing
shears, made in the Roman
period, known as "the tailor"
(*ráftis*). It was most likely built
to be used as a beacon for
shipping and would have lit up
the harbour. Pórto Ráfti has one
of the best natural harbours in
Greece, although the town
itself has never developed into
an important seafaring port. In
April 1941, during World War II,
6,000 New Zealand troops were
successfully evacuated
from the beach. Today, it is
primarily a pleasant holiday
resort, with tavernas and
bars. The area is rich in
archaeological history.

Many Mycenaean tombs have
been found south of the bay of
Pórto Ráfti, at Peratí, a port that
flourished in the 7th and 6th
centuries BC.

Environs
The remains of a fortress
that was built during the
Chremonidean War (268–
261 BC) between Egypt and
Macedon can be seen on the
southern **Koróni** headland.
The northern coastline of
Peratí is pockmarked with
unexplored caves, and attracts
many people who come to
swim in the clear water and
fish off the craggy rocks.
Markópoulo, a thriving
market town and viticultural
centre 8 km (5 miles) inland,
is famous for its tavernas.
Spicy sausages are for sale in
the butchers' shops and the
bakeries are fragrant with
the smell of fresh bread.

Pórto Ráfti harbour with Ráfti island in the background

One of the many 19th-century Neo-Classical buildings in Lávrio

❼ Lávrio
Λαύριο

Attica. **Road map** D4. 🚶 8,800. 🚌 🚍 🚢 Thu.

Lávrio was famous for its silver mines in ancient times. They were a source of revenue for the Athenian state and financed Perikles's programme of grand public buildings in Athens in the 5th century BC (see p34). They also enabled the general Themistokles to construct a fleet capable of beating the Persians at the Battle of Salamis in 480 BC. It was this excellent naval fleet which established Athens as a naval power. Before their final closure in the 20th century, the mines were also exploited by French and Greek companies for other minerals such as manganese and cadmium.

Originally worked by slaves, over 2,000 mine shafts have been discovered in the surrounding hills, and some are now open to visitors off the road southwest from town. Traces of ore and minerals in the rock face can be seen on tours of the old mines. Since their closure, the area has suffered high unemployment. The old Neo-Classical houses indicate the town's former prosperity. The main sight, at the north edge of town, is **Lavrion Technological and Cultural Park**. The buildings are used during the Athens Festival. The narrow island of Makrónisos opposite the port was used as a prison during the Civil War (see p46).

🏛 Lavrion Technological and Cultural Park
Offroad, NW of town. **Tel** 22920 25316. **Open** daily (bistro: noon till late). 🚲 ♿

❽ Sounion (Soúnio)
Σούνιο

9 km (5.5 miles) from Lávrio, Attica. **Road map** D4. **Tel** 22920 39363. 🚌 to Lávrio. **Open** 8am–sunset daily (winter: from 9:30am). 🚲 🖥

The Temple of Poseidon, built on a site set back from sheer cliffs tumbling into the Aegean Sea at modern Cape Sounion, was ideally located for worship of the powerful god of the sea. Its brilliant white marble columns have been a landmark for ancient and modern mariners alike.

The present temple, completed in 440 BC, stands on the site of older ruins. An Ionic frieze, made from 13 slabs of Parian marble, is located on the east side of the temple's main approach path. It is very eroded but is known to have depicted scenes from the mytho-logical battle of the Lapiths and centaurs, and also the adventures of the hero

The Doric columns of the Temple of Poseidon

Theseus, who was thought to be the son of Poseidon, according to some legends.

Local marble, taken from quarries at nearby Agriléza, was used for the temple's 34 slender Doric columns, of which 15 survive today. The temple also

Ruins of the Temple of Poseidon

possesses a unique design feature which helps combat the effects of sea-spray erosion: the columns were cut with only 16 flutings instead of the usual 20, thus reducing the surface area exposed to the elements.

When Byron carved his name on one of the columns in 1810, he set a dangerous precedent for vandalism at the temple, now covered with signatures. The grounds are also home to many guinea fowl (*fragkókotes*).

A waterside restaurant at Várkiza, along the Attic coast

❾ Attic Coast

Παραλία Αττικής

Attica. **Road map** D4. 🚌

The coastal strip from Piraeus to Soúnio is often called the "Apollo Coast" after a small Temple of Apollo discovered at Vouliagméni. It is covered with beaches and resort towns that are always very busy at weekends, and particularly so in the summer holiday season.

One of the first places along the coast from Piraeus is the tiny seaside resort of **Palaió Fáliro,** which is home to the Phaleron War Cemetery. In this quiet spot is the Athens Memorial, erected in May 1961 to 2,800 British soldiers who died in World War II.

Noisy suburbs near the former Athens airport, like **Glyfáda** and **Álimos** (famous as the birth-place of the ancient historian Thucydides), are very commer-cialized with many marinas, hotels and shopping malls.

At chic **Vouliagméni**, with its large yacht marina, luxury hotels line the promontory. A short

Byron in Greece

The British Romantic poet Lord Byron (1788–1824) first arrived in Greece in 1809 at the age of 21, and travelled around Epirus and Attica with his friend John Cam Hobhouse. In Athens, he wrote *The Maid of Athens,* inspired by his love for his landlady's daughter, and parts of *Childe Harold.* These publications made him an overnight sensation and, when back in London in 1812, he proclaimed: "If I am a poet it is the air of Greece which has made me one." He was received as a hero on his return to Greece in 1823, because of his desire to help fight the Ottomans in the War of Independence (*see pp44–5*). However, on Easter Sunday 1824 in Mesolóngi, he died of a fever without seeing Greece liberated. Proving in his case that the pen is mightier than the sword, Byron is still venerated in Greece, where streets and babies are named after him.

Lord Byron, in traditional Greek costume, by T Phillips (1813)

walk northwards away from the coast, beside the main road, is the enchanting Vouliagméni Lake. This unusual brackish lake lies beneath low, limestone cliffs. The stunning stretch of warm (24°C/75°F), sulphurous water has been used for years to bring relief to sufferers of rheumatism. There are changing rooms and a café close by.

At **Várkiza**, the wide bay is filled with windsurfers. By the main road there is a luxury club-restaurant, *Island.* Open throughout the summer season, it serves cocktails and Asian-fusion cuisine and attracts a glamorous crowd. From Várkiza or Vouliagméni, roads snake inland to **Vári**, renowned for its restaurants serving meat dishes.

The Vári cave is located about 2 km (1 mile) north of the village. Inside is a freshwater spring and some fine stalactites have developed. Some minor Classical ruins remain in the caves, although many have been removed.

There is unrestricted access and no admission charge.

From Várkiza to Soúnio, the coastal road is lined with quiet bathing coves, fish tavernas and luxury villas. **Anávysos** is a thriving market town surrounded by vineyards and fields. In its harbour, caïques sell locally caught fish every day, and there is a small street market every Saturday, with stalls piled high with seasonal fruit and vegetables.

Colourful stall of local produce in Anávysos

Sculpture in the gardens of the Vorrés Museum

two traditional village houses filled with ancient sculptures, folk artifacts, ceramics, Byzantine icons, seascapes and furniture. The second section, housed in a specially built modern building, offers a unique overview of contemporary Greek art since the 1940s, with many excellent works by more than 300 different painters and sculptors, encompassing every major art movement from Photo-Realism to Pop Art.

❿ Paianía
Παιανία

Attica. **Road map** D4. 9,700. Tue.

Just east of Athens, Paianía is a town of sleepy streets and cafés. In the main square, the church of **Zoödóchou Pigís** has some fine modern frescoes by the 20th-century artist Phótis Kóntoglou. The birthplace of the orator Demosthenes (384–322 BC), Paianía is more famous today for the **Vorrés Museum**. Set in beautiful gardens, this features private collector Ion Vorrés's eclectic array of ancient and modern art. The museum is divided into two sections, encompassing 3,000 years of Greek history and heritage. The first is housed in what was the collector's private home:

🏛 Vorrés Museum
Diadóchou Konstantínou 1. **Tel** 210 664 4771. **Open** 10am–2pm Sat & Sun. **Closed** Aug & main public hols. 🅿 🕭 **w** vorresmuseum.gr

Environs
Above Paianía, the **Koutoúki Cave** is hidden in the foothills of Mount Ymittós. It was found in 1926 by a shepherd looking for a goat which had fallen into the 12,200 sq m (130,000 sq ft) cave. There are tours every half hour, with son et lumière effects lighting up the stalagmites and stalactites. The temperature inside is 17°C (62°F).

🏞 Koutoúki Cave
4 km (2.5 miles) W of Paianía. **Tel** 210 664 2108. **Closed** for renovation till end of 2017. 🅿

⓫ Attica Zoological Park
Αττικό Ζωολογικό Πάρκο

Gialoú, Spáta. **Road map** D4. **Tel** 210 663 4725. 319. **Open** 9am–sunset daily. 🅿 🕭 **w** atticapark.com

A popular attraction a short drive east of Athens, this zoo has over 300 species of animal, from white lions and tigers to yellow anacondas and pygmy hippos. It also has one of the largest bird collections in the world. In Cheetah Land, visitors can walk through a tunnel within the cheetah enclosure.

⓬ Moní Kaisarianís
Μονή Καισαριανής

5 km (3 miles) E of Athens, Attica. **Road map** D4. **Tel** 210 723 6619. to Kaisarianís. **Open** 8:30am–3pm Tue–Sun. **Closed** main public hols. 🅿

Moní Kaisarianís was founded in the 11th century. In 1458, when Sultan Mehmet II conquered Athens, the monastery was exempted from taxes in recognition of the abbot's gift to the sultan of the keys of the city. This led to great prosperity until 1792, when it lost these privileges and went into decline. The complex was used briefly as a convent after the War of Independence, until 1855. Its buildings were eventually restored in 1956.

The small *katholikón* is dedicated to the Presentation of the Virgin. All the frescoes date from the 16th and 17th centuries. Those in the narthex, including a

A cheetah at Attica Zoological Park

rare *Holy Trinity* in its dome, are in the best condition, but don't miss the *Baptism, Entry to Jerusalem* and *Pandokrator* in the nave.

Just above the monastery, the source of the River Ilissós has been visited since antiquity, its water reputed to cure sterility. Before the Marathon dam was built *(see p149)*, the spring was Athens' main source of water. This water is no longer potable.

⑬ Kifisiá
Κηφισιά

12 km (7.5 miles) NE of Athens, Attica. **Road map** D4. 🏛 40,000. 🚌 Ⓜ Kifisiá.

Kifisiá has been a favourite summer retreat for Athenians since Roman times. Once the exclusive domain of rich Greeks, it is now full of apartment blocks and shopping malls. Traces of its former tranquillity can still be seen by taking a ride in a horse-drawn carriage. These wait by the metro station offering drives down streets lined with mansions built in a bizarre variety of hybrid styles such as Alpine chalet and Gothic Neo-Classicism.

The **Goulandrís Natural History Museum** is housed in one of these villas. Its collection covers all aspects of Greece's varied wildlife and minerals. There are 200,000 varieties of plants in the herbarium, and over 1,300 examples of taxidermy; the stuffed creatures are carefully displayed in their natural habitats.

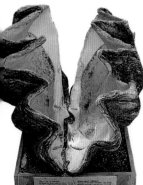

Clam shell outside the Goulandrís Natural History Museum, Kifisiá

The tiny chapel of Agía Triáda on the hillside of Mount Párnitha

🏛 **Goulandrís Natural History Museum**
Levídou 13. **Tel** 210 801 5870. **Open** 9am–2:30pm Tue–Fri, 9:30am–4pm Sat, 10am–4pm Sun. **Closed** main public hols. 🎫 📶 **gnhm.gr**

Environs
In Maroúsi, a suburb of Kifisiá, is the small **Spatháreio Museum of the Shadow Theatre**, which is devoted to the fascinating history of the Karagkiózis puppet theatre. Shadow theatre came to Greece from the Far East, via players who used to travel throughout the Ottoman Empire performing for all strata of society. It was soon transformed into a popular folk art by entertainers who would travel around Greece with their makeshift theatres. The name Karagkiózis refers to the indomitable and impoverished Greek character who is tormented by the other standard theatrical characters such as the rich Pasha and tough guy Stávrakas. The museum displays the history of two generations of the Spathári family, who were the leading exponents of this dying art, along with their home-made sets and puppets.

Puppet from the Spatháreio Museum

🏛 **Spatháreio Museum of the Shadow Theatre**
Mesogeíon & Voreíou Ipírou 27, Maroúsi. **Tel** 210 612 7245. **Open** 9am–2pm Mon–Fri (also 6–8pm Wed), 10am–1pm Sun. **Closed** main pub hols.

⑭ Mount Párnitha
Όρος Πάρνηθα

Attica. **Road map** D4. 🚌 to Aharnés, Thrakomakedónes & Agía Triáda.

In ancient times, Mount Párnitha sheltered wild animals. Today, this rugged range, which extends nearly 25 km (16 miles) from east to west, is rich in less dangerous fauna. Tortoises can be seen in the undergrowth and birds of prey circle the summit of Karampóla at 1,413 m (4,635 ft). Wild flowers are abundant, particularly in autumn and spring when cyclamen and crocus carpet the mountain. There are spectacular views of alpine scenery, all within an hour's drive of the city. At the small town of **Acharnés**, a cable car ascends to a casino perched at over 900 m (3,000 ft). Still little used by hikers, the mountain has plenty of demanding trails. The most popular walk leads from Thrakomakedónes, in the foothills of the mountain, to the Báfi refuge. This uphill march takes about two hours, and offers superb views of the surrounding mountain scenery. Starting with thorny scrub typical of the Mediterranean *maquis*, it follows well-trodden paths to clear mountain air. Once at the Báfi refuge, it is worth walking on to the Flampoúri refuge, which has some dramatic views.

⓱ Monastery of Daphni

Μονή Δαφνίου

The monastery of Daphni was founded in the 6th century AD. Named after the laurels *(dáfnes)* that used to grow here, it was built with the remains of an ancient sanctuary of Apollo, which had occupied this site until its destruction by the Goths in AD 395. The present structure dates from around 1080. In the early 13th century, Otto de la Roche, the first Frankish Duke of Athens, bequeathed it to Cistercian monks in Burgundy, who erected the elegant cloisters just south of the church. Greek Orthodox monks regained the site in the 16th century. Following earthquake damage in 1999, the gold-leaf Byzantine mosaics in the main church have undergone major restoration.

Aerial view of the monastery complex

★ **Esonarthex Mosaics**
These mosaics include depictions of the *Last Supper* and the *Washing of the Feet*. The finest is the *Betrayal by Judas*. Christ stands unmoved as Judas kisses Him.

Entrance

Key to Mosaics in the *Katholikón*

Walls

1. Resurrection
2. Adoration of the Magi
4. Archangel Gabriel
5. Archangel Michael
6. Nativity of the Virgin
8. St John the Baptist
9. Entry into Jerusalem
12. Dormition of the Virgin
13. Last Supper
14. Washing of the Feet
15. Betrayal by Judas
16. Prayer of Sts Anne and Joachim
17. Blessing of the Priests
18. Presentation of the Virgin
20. St Thomas

Ceiling and Dome

3. Nativity
7. Annunciation
10. Christ Pantokrátor
11. Transfiguration
19. Baptism

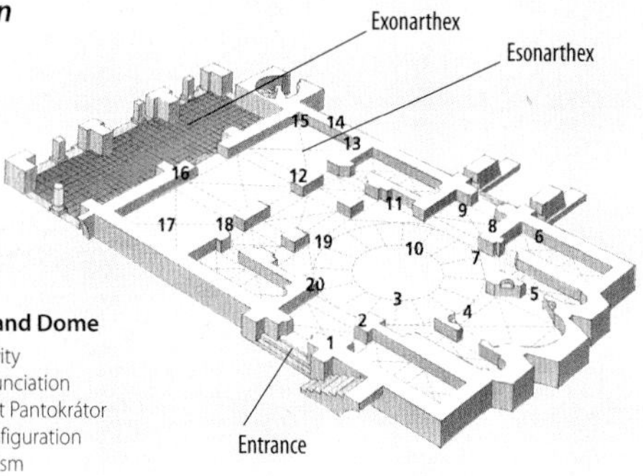

Exonarthex

Esonarthex

Entrance

★ **Christ Pantokrátor**
The Pantokrátor
("Almighty") gazes
sternly down from
the dome of the
katholikón. Around
the central figure
are images of the
16 prophets.

The Transfiguration
This is in the northwest corner
under the dome. Elijah and
Moses are on either side of
Christ and the apostles Peter,
James and John are below.

KEY

① **The cloister** or a covered arcade,
was built in the 13th century by the
Cistercians. On the other side of the
courtyard, above a similar arcade, are
the monks' cells.

② **The symmetry** of the design
makes Daphni one of the most
attractive examples of Byzantine
architecture in Attica.

③ **The Gothic exonarthex** was
built almost 30 years after the
main church.

④ **The dome** is 8 m (26 ft) in
diameter and 16 m (52 ft) high
at the centre.

⑤ **Nave**

⑥ **Museum**

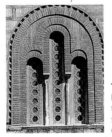

The Windows
Elaborate three-
tiered brickwork
surrounds each
of the windows.

⑯ Piraeus

Πειραιάς

One of the biggest Mediterranean ports, Piraeus is also one of the largest cities in Greece. It has been the port of Athens since ancient times. The Long Walls between Piraeus and Athens were started in 480 BC by Themistokles. However, Sulla destroyed the walls in 86 BC, and by the Middle Ages, Piraeus was little more than a fishing village. When Athens became the Greek capital in 1834, Piraeus was once again revitalized, with Neo-Classical buildings and factories. In 1923, 100,000 refugees came here from Asia Minor, bringing their culture and contributing to the cosmopolitan feel of this port city.

Small boats moored in peaceful Mikrolímano harbour

View across Kentrikó Limáni with ferries in the foreground

Exploring Piraeus

After the Junta (see p47) razed many irreplaceable public buildings in the town centre in the early 1970s, civic pride re-emerged with a vengeance. Beside the Municipal Theatre, there are elegant open-air restaurants and fountains in the shade of Neo-Classical façades. On the streets behind the main banks and ticket offices that rim the **Kentrikó Limáni** (the main ferry port), there are smart restaurants and shops, as well as some fine examples of Neo-Classical architecture, such as the **Town Hall**. For information on ferry departures from Kentrikó Limáni, see p319.

South of the railway station around Navarínou lies the lively market area, including fishmongers', fruit and vegetable stalls, ships' chandlers and hardware stores. On Sunday mornings,

there is also a bustling flea market, which is centred on the antique shops around Plateía Ippodameías, and also on Alipédou and Skylítsi streets.

There are two other harbours in Piraeus, situated east of Kentrikó Limáni. **Zéa** was formerly known as Pashalimáni (Pasha's Port) and used to harbour the Ottoman fleet. Today, however, it is filled with pleasure craft, including large, luxurious gin palaces. Zéa used to be one of Themistokles's major naval ports, with dry docks for 196 triremes. The second harbour, **Mikrolímano** (Little Harbour) was formerly known as Tourkolímano (Turk's Port). It houses many

colourful fishing caïques. It is popular for its waterside fish restaurants and has a more relaxing ambience than the larger harbour.

On the coastal road between Zéa and Mikrolímano, smart bars and clubs occupy the renovated Neo-Classical mansions in the gentrified **Kastélla** neighbourhood. Even traditionally working-class areas, such as Drapetsóna (the most important manufacturing centre in the country), are now popular for their late-night restaurants.

🎭 Municipal Theatre

Iroon Polytechneiou 32. **Tel** 210 414 3300. **Open** Museum: 4–8pm Mon–Wed, 9am–2pm Thu & Fri.

The Neo-Classical façade of this imposing building is one of the delights of Piraeus. Designed by Ioánnis Lazarímos (1849–1913), who based his plans on the Opéra Comique in Paris, it has seating for 800, making it one of the largest modern theatres in Greece.

Façade of the Municipal Theatre

It took nearly ten years to complete and was finally inaugurated on 9 April 1895. Today, it is the home of both the **Municipal Art Gallery** and also the **Pános Aravantinós Museum of Stage Decor**. The Museum of Stage Decor has displays of set designs by the stage designer Pános Aravantinós (who worked with the Berlin opera in the 1920s), as well as general ephemera from the Greek opera.

Statue of Athena in the Archaeological Museum

🏛 Archaeological Museum

Chariláou Trikoúpi 31. **Tel** 210 452 1598. **Open** 8am–3pm Tue–Sun. **Closed** main public hols.

This museum is home to some stunning bronzes. Found by workmen in 1959, large statues of Artemis with her quiver, Athena with her helmet decorated with owls, and Apollo reveal the great expressiveness of Greek sculpture. The Piraeus *koúros* of Apollo, dating from 520 BC,

is the earliest full-size bronze to be discovered. There is also a seated cult statue of the Asiatic goddess Cybele and a fine collection of Greek and Roman statues and grave stelae. Near the museum are the remains of the 2nd-century BC **Theatre of Zéa**; the remains include a well-preserved orchestra.

🏛 Hellenic Maritime Museum

Aktí Themistokléous, Freatýda. **Tel** 210 451 6264. **Open** 9am–2pm Tue–Sat. **Closed** main public hols, Aug.

Behind a park inland, on Aktí Themistokléous, an old submarine marks the entrance to this fascinating museum. Its first room is built around an original section of Themistokles's Long Walls. More than 2,000 exhibits, such as models of triremes, ephemera from naval battleships and paintings of Greek *trechantíri*

(fishing caïques), explore the world of Greek seafaring. From early voyages around the Black Sea by trireme to 20th-century emigration to the New World by transatlantic liner, the museum unravels the complexities of Greek maritime history. Exhibits include models of ships, maps, flags, uniforms and pictures. The War of Independence is well documented with information and memorabilia about the generals who served in it.

Piraeus City Centre

① Town Hall
② Municipal Theatre
③ Theatre of Zéa
④ Archaeological Museum
⑤ Zéa
⑥ Hellenic Maritime Museum
⑦ Mikrolímano
⑧ Kastélla

⓱ Ancient Eleusis

Αρχαία Ελευσίνα

Eleusis was an ancient centre of religious devotion that culminated in the annual Eleusinian Mysteries. These attracted thousands of people from around the Greek-speaking world, for whom the only initial requirement for becoming a *mystes* (or initiate) was to be neither a murderer nor a barbarian. Both men and women were freely admitted. Existing from Mycenaean times, the sanctuary was closed by the Roman Emperor Theodosius in AD 392, and was finally abandoned when Alaric, king of the Goths, invaded Greece in AD 396, bringing Christianity in his wake.

Anaktoron
This small rectangular stone edifice had a single entrance. It was considered the holiest part of the site. Meaning "palace", it existed long before the Telesterion, which was built around it.

Telesterion
Designed by Iktinos, this temple was built in the 5th century BC. It was constructed to hold several thousand people at a time.

The Eleusinian Mysteries

Perhaps established by 1500 BC and continuing for almost 2,000 years, these rites centred on the myth of the grieving goddess Demeter, who lost her daughter Persephone (or Kore) to Hades, god of the Underworld, for six months each year *(see p56)*. Participants were sworn to secrecy, but some evidence of the details of the ceremony does exist. Sacrifices were made before the procession from the Kerameikos *(see pp92–3)* to Eleusis. Here, the priestesses would reveal the vision of the holy night, thought to have been a fire symbolizing life after death for the initiates.

A priestess with a kiste mystika (initiate basket)

KEY

① Roman houses

② Temple of Kore hewn out of rock

③ 4th-century BC shops and bouleuterion (council chamber)

④ One of a pair of triumphal arches

⑤ Temple of Artemis Propylaia

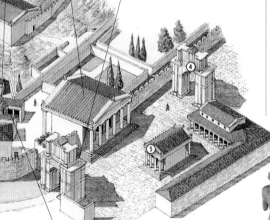

Ploutonion
This cave is said to be where Persephone was returned to the world of the living. It was a sanctuary to Hades, god of the Underworld and the abductor of Persephone.

Greater Propylaia
Built from Pentelic marble in the 2nd century AD by the Roman Emperor Antoninus Pius, this was modelled on the Propylaia of Athens' Acropolis.

Well of Kallichoron
Demeter is believed to have grieved for Persephone here.

Lesser Propylaia
This fragment shows sheaves of grain and poppies, which were used to make *kykeon*, the drink of the initiates.

Ancient Eleusis
This reconstruction is of Eleusis as it was in Roman times (c.AD 150) when the Mysteries were still flourishing. The view is from the east. Although there is little left today, it is still possible to sense the awe and mystery that the rites of Eleusis inspired.

Relief from the Telesterion, now in the museum

🏛 **Eleusis Museum**
This small museum, south of the Telesterion, has five rooms. The entrance hall contains a copy of the famous relief from the Telesterion showing Triptólemos receiving grain from Demeter. Also in this room are a large 7th-century BC amphora and a copy of the Ninnion votive painting, one of the few remaining representations of the Eleusinian Mysteries. The other rooms are arranged on the left of the hall. In the first of these, there is an elegant 6th-century BC *koúros* and a 2nd-century BC Roman statue of Dionysos. In the second room, there are two models of the site. The third room has a Classical period terracotta sarcophagus and a large caryatid from the Lesser Propylaia carrying a *kiste mystika* basket on her head. The last room has a variety of pottery fragments, including examples of unusual terracotta containers that were used to carry foodstuffs in the annual *kernoforía* procession.

Fleeing maiden

THE PELOPONNESE

PELOPONNESE

One of the primary strongholds and battlefields of the 1821–31 Revolution, the Peloponnese is the kernel from which the modern Greek state grew. This enormous peninsula, which falls short of being an island by the mere 6-km (4-mile) width of the Corinth isthmus, also has some of the most spectacularly varied scenery and monuments on the mainland.

The name "Peloponnese" means "island of Pelops", who in legend was fed to the gods by Tantalos, his father. Resurrected, he went on to sire the Atreid line of kings, whose semi-mythical misadventures and brooding citadels were given substance by the discovery of remains at Mycenae. Today, the ancient and medieval sites of the Argolid region, to the south of Corinth, contrast with the elegantly Neo-Classical town of Náfplio.

In the west lies Ancient Olympia, the athletic and religious nexus of the ancient world and inspiration for the games' revival in modern times. The lush coastal plain of Ileía, heart of an early medieval Crusader principality, spawned Frankish-Byzantine architecture, most famously at Chlemoútsi. More purely Byzantine art adorns the churches of Mystrás, Geráki and the remote Máni region, whose warlike medieval inhabitants claimed to be descended from the warriors of ancient Sparta. Imposing Venetian fortifications at the beach-fringed capes of Methóni, Koróni and Monemvasiá allowed the Venetians to play a role here after most of their other Aegean possessions were lost to the Ottomans.

In Arcadia, at the centre of the Peloponnese, lushly cultivated valleys rise to conifer-draped mountains and deep gorges such as the Loúsios; cliff-side monasteries and sombre hill-towns, like Stemnítsa, are a world apart from the popular Mediterranean image of Greece.

Restaurant terrace overlooking the sea, Monemvasiá

◀ Outdoor tables line a flower-strewn street, Náfplio

Exploring the Peloponnese

Ancient and medieval ruins are abundant on the Peloponnese, and provide the main focus of sightseeing. Though there are few highly developed resorts away from the Argolid, Messinía and Ileía, such areas as the Loúsios Gorge and Kalógria attract thousands of trekkers and naturalists. A rural economy is still paramount inland, with Pátra being the only large city. The landscape is dominated by forested mountains and the west coast, between Pátra and Methóni, boasts some of the finest beaches in the Mediterranean.

Karýtaina village, Loúsios Gorge

Key

━━━ Motorway

= = Road under construction

━━━ Major road

⋯⋯ Minor road

━━━ Scenic route

⋯⋯ Main railway

▬▬▬ Regional border

Río

PATRA **7**

8 KALOGRIA
Káto Achaïa

Áigio

Diakc

KALAVRYTA–DIAKOFTO
RAILWAY

Lápas

Káto Vlasiá

Kalávryta

Kyllíni Lechainá

Erýmanthos
2224m

MOUNT CHELMOS

9 CHLEMOUTSI
CASTLE

Gastoúni

Lámpeia

Amaliáda

Ladon

ANCIENT
OLYMPIA
10

Lagkádia

Pýrgos

74

Dimits

Kréstena

LOUSIOS GORGE **11**

Stem

76

Alfeiós

9

ANDRITSAINA

Zacháro

12

Karýtai

A9 Nédas

Megalópoli

P E L O

Kyparissía

Meligalás

Filiatrá

Messinía

30 ANCIENT MES

9

Messíni

29 Chóra

Kalamáta

NESTOR'S
PALACE

82

Karda

Sfaktiría **28** PYLOS

Messiniakós Kólpo

METHONI **27**

26 KORONI

Sapiéntza

Schíza

Getting Around

Major roads link Athens and Pátra via Corinth, and also allow travel from Corinth to Kalamáta. Secondary roads are more interesting, if dangerously narrow. Buses link major towns with their surrounding villages, as well connecting towns with each other. There is only one train line from Athens to the Peloponnese, and it goes as far as Kiáto, to the north of Corinth; from there, you'll have to travel by bus to other destinations. The Rio-Antirio bridge crosses the Gulf of Corinth in the north to link the Peloponnese with mainland Greece, though ferries also make this crossing, if you are travelling without a car.

Gýtheio harbour, Inner Máni

For hotels and restaurants see p270–71 and pp287–8

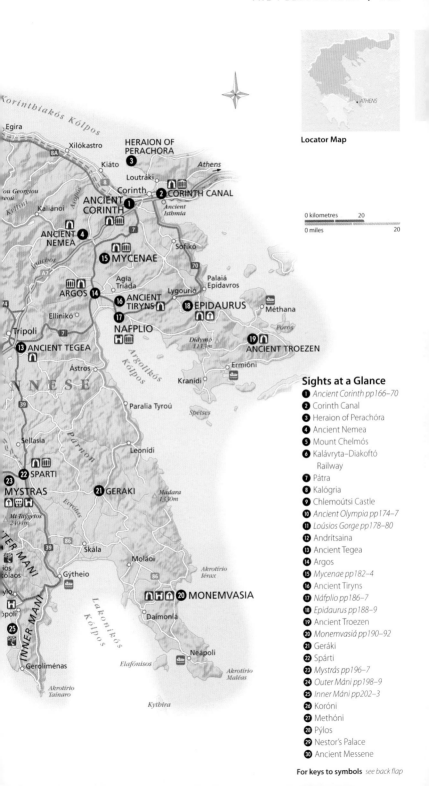

Locator Map

0 kilometres 20

0 miles 20

HERAION OF PERACHORA ③

Sights at a Glance

① Ancient Corinth pp166–70
② Corinth Canal
③ Heraion of Perachóra
④ Ancient Nemea
⑤ Mount Chelmós
⑥ Kalávryta–Diakoftó Railway
⑦ Pátra
⑧ Kalógria
⑨ Chlemoútsi Castle
⑩ Ancient Olympia pp174–7
⑪ Loúsios Gorge pp178–80
⑫ Andrítsaina
⑬ Ancient Tegea
⑭ Argos
⑮ Mycenae pp182–4
⑯ Ancient Tiryns
⑰ Náfplio pp186–7
⑱ Epidaurus pp188–9
⑲ Ancient Troezen
⑳ Monemvasiá pp190–92
㉑ Geráki
㉒ Spárti
㉓ Mystrás pp196–7
㉔ Outer Máni pp198–9
㉕ Inner Máni pp202–3
㉖ Koróni
㉗ Methóni
㉘ Pýlos
㉙ Nestor's Palace
㉚ Ancient Messene

For keys to symbols *see back flap*

❶ Ancient Corinth
Αρχαία Κόρινθος

Ancient Corinth derived its prosperity from its position on a narrow isthmus between the Saronic and Corinthian gulfs. Transporting goods across this isthmus, even before the canal *(see p171)* was built, provided the shortest route from the eastern Mediterranean to the Adriatic and Italy. Founded in Neolithic times, the town was razed in 146 BC by the Romans, who rebuilt it a century later. Attaining a population of 750,000 under the patronage of the emperors, the town gained a reputation for licentious living, which St Paul attacked when he came here in AD 52. Excavations have revealed the vast extent of the city, destroyed by earthquakes in Byzantine times. The ruins constitute the largest Roman township in Greece.

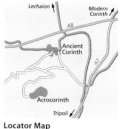

Locator Map

★ **Lechaion Way**
This marble-paved road linked the port of Lechaion with the city, ending at a still-surviving stairway and an imposing *propylaion* (entrance).

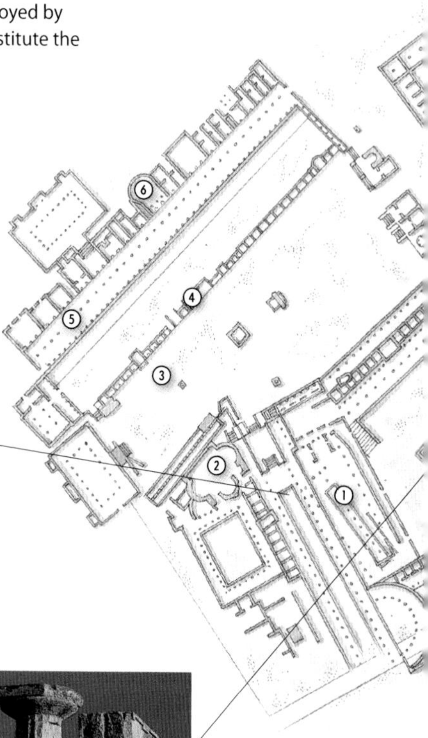

KEY

① **Basilica**

② **The Peirene fountain's** springs still supply the local modern village.

③ **The agora** was the hub of Roman civic life.

④ **The bema** (platform) was where St Paul was accused of sacrilege by the Jews of Corinth.

⑤ **South stoa**

⑥ **Bouleuterion**

⑦ **The northwest stoa** had two series of columns, the outer being Doric and the inner Ionic.

⑧ **The Glauke fountain's** four cisterns were hewn from a cubic monolith and filled by an aqueduct from the hills.

⑨ **The museum** contains artifacts from the site *(see p170)*.

⑩ **The theatre** was modified in the 3rd century AD so water could be piped in and mock sea battles staged.

★ **Temple of Apollo**
The most striking structure of the lower city, this temple was one of the few buildings preserved by the Romans when they rebuilt the site in 46 BC. At the southeast corner, an ingenious stepped ramp leads to the temple terrace.

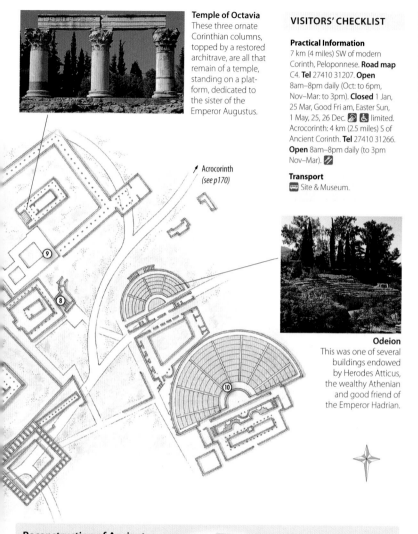

Temple of Octavia
These three ornate Corinthian columns, topped by a restored architrave, are all that remain of a temple, standing on a platform, dedicated to the sister of the Emperor Augustus.

Acrocorinth
(see p170)

(see p170)

Odeion
This was one of several buildings endowed by Herodes Atticus, the wealthy Athenian and good friend of the Emperor Hadrian.

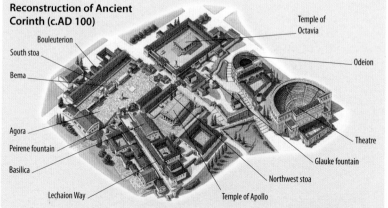

Reconstruction of Ancient Corinth (c.AD 100)

Bouleuterion
South stoa
Bema
Agora
Peirene fountain
Basilica
Lechaion Way
Temple of Apollo
Northwest stoa
Glauke fountain
Theatre
Odeion
Temple of Octavia

Exploring Acrocorinth and the Museum

Excavations of recent years have yielded numerous artifacts now on view in the museum, and have revealed the vast extent of the ancient city, which included the summit of Acrocorinth. Altogether, the ruins constitute the largest Roman township in Greece, since few earlier structures were restored after the Romans destroyed the town in 146 BC. Acrocorinth became one of medieval Greece's most important fortresses and can now be reached by a road which climbs the western face of the hill from the lower town.

🏛 Acrocorinth

Acrocorinth, 4 km (2.5 miles) above the main city, has been held and refortified by every occupying power in Greece since Roman times. Entry is on the west, where the peak's natural defences are weakest, through three successive gateways from different eras. The lowest is mostly Ottoman; the middle, Frankish; and the third and highest, Byzantine, though it and two adjacent towers incorporate abundant ancient masonry. Beyond sprawls a 24-ha (60-acre) terraced wilderness of minaret stumps, Muslim tombs, and lonely mosques or chapels – all that remains of the town abandoned almost two hundred years ago, when its last defenders, the Ottomans, were defeated.

The lower elevation at the southwest corner of the 5-km (3-mile) circuit of walls sports a Venetian tower, while the true, northeast summit bears the scant foundations of an Aphrodite temple, attended in

Mosaic of Bacchus (Dionysos), 2nd century AD, in the museum

antiquity by 1,000 sacred prostitutes. It was against such practices that St Paul wrote his two "epistles to the Corinthians". Today, its attraction is one of the most sweeping views in the whole of Greece, up to 60 km (37 miles) in all directions from the Geráneia range in the northeast to the peaks of Zíria in the southwest. Towards Zíria, a prominent nearby hill, Penteskoúfi, was fortified by the Franks during the 13th century.

Acrocorinth could withstand lengthy sieges owing to the presence of the upper Peirene

spring, on the southeast side of the ramparts. A stairway descends to a vaulted, subterranean chamber pool; in dry seasons, the water recedes to expose a column supporting an ornate Hellenistic pediment.

🏛 Museum

The site museum, just southeast of the odeion, ranks among Greece's best provincial collections. All periods of the ancient town's history are represented, though the Roman gallery in the west wing is particularly rich. Here, pride of place goes to 2nd-century AD mosaics lifted from the floors of nearby villas: a head of Bacchus (Dionysos) set in a circular geometric pattern, a nude shepherd playing his flute to three cows, and a goat napping under a tree. The north doorway is flanked by two columns in the shape of Phrygian prisoners, shown with their arms crossed, their tunics and long hair seeming to prefigure medieval art. Also housed in the west wing are some of the 274 objects stolen from the museum in 1990 and recovered nine years later in Miami. The east gallery features older artifacts. Attic ware from the 5th century BC *(see pp64–5)*, including the famous "Owl" vase, is rarer than the 7th- and 6th-century BC pottery, some painted with fantastic beasts, for which Corinth was noted.

At the shrine of Asklepios, just within the northern boundary of the ancient city walls, votive offerings in the shape of afflicted body parts were found and are on display in a back room, the precursors of the *támmata* or metal *ex votos* left in modern Orthodox churches. Other oddities include a 6th-century marble sphinx and Hellenistic pediments with lion-head spouts.

Stone reliefs in the central courtyard include depictions of the Labours of Herakles *(see p57)*, one of which was performed nearby at the sanctuary of Nemea.

The entrance to Acrocorinth, with its three gateways

Ships passing through the Corinth Canal with the road bridge overhead

❷ Corinth Canal
Διώρυγα της Κορίνθου

Peloponnese. **Road map** C4.
Loutráki.

Stormy Cape Matapan, or Taínaro (see p203), the southernmost point of the Peloponnese, was one of the dreaded capes of antiquity; rather than sail around it, boats would be unloaded on one shore of this isthmus, dragged the 6 km (4 miles) across on the *díolkos* (paved slipway), and then refloated.

The traffic inspired plans for a canal. Emperor Nero began construction, but the project was only completed between 1882 and 1893. The 23-m (75-ft) wide canal is obsolete in an age of giant container ships which easily weather the cape, but small freighters and yachts squeezing through are regularly seen from the road bridge above. Bungee jumping off the pedestrian bridge is a popular activity – and a spectacle, too.

Environs
Near the southern end of the canal is the site of **Ancient Isthmia**, once the major local religious centre (devoted to Poseidon) and location of the biennial Isthmian Games. Today, only foundations of Poseidon's temple (7th century BC) and the remains of a starting gate for track events in the adjacent, vanished stadium are traceable.

The site museum stresses finds from Kechriés, Corinth's eastern port; unique exhibits include panels of painted glass or stone embedded in a resin matrix. They were intended to decorate an Isis temple but were never used.

🏛 Ancient Isthmia
Southern end of Corinth Canal. Site & Museum: **Tel** 27410 37244. **Open** 8:30am–3pm Tue–Sun. **Closed** main public hols. 🦽♿

❸ Heraion of Perachóra
Ηραίον της Περαχώρας

13 km (8 miles) W of Loutráki, Peloponnese. **Road map** C4.

Probably founded during the 8th century BC, the Heraion of Perachóra (a nearby modern village) was primarily a religious centre. Only foundations and column stumps remain of the Archaic temple of Hera Limeneia, plus an altar and a Classical stoa, but the site has a great setting, above a tiny cove on the south shore of Cape Melangávi, close to a 19th-century lighthouse.

Scenic Vouliagméni Lake, 3 km (2 miles) east, is fringed by Aleppo pines, with the best swimming and a selection of tavernas at its west end.

View of the Sanctuary of Hera at Perachóra, Cape Melangávi

❹ Ancient Nemea
Αρχαία Νεμέα

5 km (3 miles) NE of modern Neméa, Peloponnese. **Road map** C4.
Tel 27460 22739. 🚌
Site: **Open** 8:30am–3pm Mon–Fri.
Museum: **Open** 8:30am–3pm Tue–Sun. **Closed** main public hols. 🦽♿

Occupying an isolated rural valley, the site of Ancient Nemea is a local landmark, with the nine re-erected Doric columns of its 4th-century Zeus temple plainly visible from afar. Below them lie the broken remains of column drums toppled by vandals between the 4th and 13th centuries AD. At the west end of the temple's complete floor, the deep *adyton* (underground crypt) has been exposed.

A short walk to the southwest, under a giant modern shelter, are the plunge-pool and feed system of a Hellenistic bathhouse. Excavations in the area have also uncovered the Byzantine village that took root here in the 4th century, including graves, kilns and a basilica built above the ancient pilgrims' inn.

The **museum** has interesting reconstructions and engravings. The Hellenistic stadium, to the southeast, has the earliest known vaulted entrance tunnel. It is used every fourth June for the Nemean Games, revived in part by US archaeologist Stephen Miller, who dug here until 2005.

Three Doric columns of the many re-erected at the Temple of Zeus, Ancient Nemea

One of the natural pools at the Cave of the Lakes

❺ Mount Chelmós

Όρος Χελμός

Peloponnese. **Road map** C4. 🚌 to Kalávryta.

Rising to 2,355 m (7,729 ft), Mount Chelmós is the third highest point of the Peloponnese, its foothills cloaked in extensive forests and divided by deep gorges. The most famous of these is Mavronéri, where the waterfall cascading from the remote north face of the summit is claimed to be the source of the mythical river Styx.

Overlooking the wooded Feneoú valley, on the south-eastern slopes, stands the remote monastery of **Agíou Georgíou Feneoú**, originally founded in 1693, though mostly dating to the mid-18th century. The *katholikón*, with its high dome and transept, offers unusual, vivid frescoes, including some representing the birth and presentation of the Virgin.

Moní Agías Lávras, 6 km (4 miles) from Kalávryta, played a pivotal role in the Greek Revolution. The Archbishop of Pátra raised the standard of revolt here on 25 March 1821, the banner now being the centrepiece of a nationalist shrine in the upstairs treasury *(see pp44–5)*.

Founded in 961, Agías Lávras has been rebuilt after being destroyed by the Germans in 1943. The day before, the Germans had burned the town of Kalávryta, where they perpetrated one of their worst occupation atrocities, massacring nearly 700 civilian of all ages in reprisal for local resistance. The cathedral clock is permanently stopped at the time the killing began.

The **Cave of the Lakes**, near Kastriá, was known in ancient times but was lost until its rediscovery in 1964. Groups can visit the first 350 m (1,150 ft) of the cave, down to the second of 15 lakes. The massive stalactite-hung caverns were formed by an underground river, which still flows during the winter.

🖼 Cave of the Lakes

16 km (10 miles) S of Kalávryta. **Tel** 26920 31633. **Open** 9:30am–4:30pm daily (to 5:30pm Sat & Sun). 🖼

Old steam locomotive at Diakoftó

❻ Kalávryta-Diakoftó Railway

Οδοντωτός Σιδηρόδρομος Καλαβρύτων–Διακοφτού

Peloponnese. **Road map** C4. **Tel** 26920 22245. 🚂 several daily (9am–4pm) Kalávryta–Diakoftó–Kalávryta. 🖥 **W** odontotos.com

The most enjoyable narrow-gauge railway in Greece was engineered between 1889 and 1895 by an Italo-French consortium to bring ore down from the Kalávryta area. Over 22 km (14 miles) of track were laid, over 6 km (4 miles) of which relies on a third rail (a "rack and pinion" system), engaged where grades are up to one in seven. Two of the original steam locomotives, replaced in 1959, are displayed at Diakoftó. For a good view of the mechanism, travel near the driver.

En route there are 14 tunnels and many bridges over the Vouraïkós Gorge. The single station of Káto Zachloroú, with two modest hotels, is roughly halfway. The station is the start of a 45-minute trail up to **Moní Méga Spílaio**, which is believed to be the oldest monastery in Greece.

❼ Pátra

Πάτρα

Peloponnese. **Road map** C4.
🄰 231,000. 🚌 🚆 🚢
ℹ️ Filopimenos 26 (2610 620353).
Open 8am–3pm daily.

Greece's third largest city and second port is no beauty. Tower blocks dominate the few elegantly arcaded streets of this planned Neo-Classical town. Where Pátra excels is in its celebration of carnival – the best in Greece – for which the city's large gay community and student body both turn out in force.

On the ancient acropolis, the originally Byzantine kástro bears marks of every subsequent era. The vast bailey, filled with gardens and orchards, often hosts public events, as does the nearby brick Roman odeion.

At the southwest edge of town, the mock-Byzantine basilica of **Agios Andréas** stands where St Andrew was supposedly martyred, and houses his skull and a fragment of his cross.

Environs

Founded in 1861, the **Achaïa Clauss Winery** was Greece's first commercial winery and is now one of the largest vintners in Greece. It produces 30 million litres (7 million gallons) a year, with grapes gathered from across the country. Tours include a visit to the Imperial Cellar, where Mavrodaphne, a fortified dessert wine, can be tasted.

🏛 **Achaïa Clauss Winery**
Petrotó, 6 km (4 miles) SE of Pátra.
Tel 2610 580100. **Open** 10am–6pm daily (winter: 9am–5pm). **Closed** main pub hols. ♿ 📷 🌐 clauss.gr

❽ Kalógria

Καλόγρια

Peloponnese. **Road map** B4. 🚌 to
Lápas. ℹ️ Lápas town hall (26930 31868).

The entire lagoon-speckled coast, from the Araxos river mouth to the Kotýchi lagoon, ranks as one of the largest wetlands in Europe. Incorporating the Strofyliá marsh and a 2,000-ha (5,000-acre) umbrella pine dune-forest,

Sandy beaches of Kalógria

the area enjoys full protection as a national park. Development is confined to a zone between the Prokópos lagoon and the excellent, 7-km (4-mile) beach of Kalógria. The dunes also support Aleppo pines and valonea oaks, while bass, eels and water snakes swim in the marsh channels.

Migratory populations of ducks, including pintails and coots, live at Kotýchi, while marsh harriers, owls, kestrels and falcons can be seen all year round. A **Visitor Centre** at Lápas documents nature trails through the dunes nearby.

ℹ️ **Visitor Centre**
Kotýchion Strofylliás. **Tel** 26233 60814.
Open 9am–3pm Mon–Fri. **Closed** main public hols. ♿ 📷
🌐 strofylianationalpark.gr

❾ Chlemoútsi Castle

Χλεμούτσι

Kástro, Peloponnese. **Road map** B4.
Open daily.

The most famous Frankish castle in Greece, known also as "Castel Tornesi" after the gold *tournois* coin minted here in medieval times, was erected between 1219 and 1223 to defend thriving Glaréntza port (today, Kyllíni) and the principality capital of Andreville (Andravída). To bolster the weak natural defences, exceptionally thick walls and a massive gate were built; much of the rampart catwalk can still be followed. The magnificent hexagonal keep has echoing, vaulted halls; a plaque by the entry commemorates the 1428–32 residence of Konstantínos Palaiológos, the last Byzantine emperor, while he was governor of Ileía.

Steps lead to a roof for views over the Ionian islands and the coastal plain. Chlemoútsi has been widely reconstructed, with the vast fan-shaped courtyard now used for summer concerts.

The modern Byzantine-style basilica of Agios Andréas, Pátra

⑩ Ancient Olympia

Ολυμπία

At the confluence of the rivers Alfeiós and Kládeos, the Sanctuary of Olympia enjoyed over 1,000 years of esteem as a religious and athletics centre. Though the sanctuary flourished in Mycenaean times *(see pp30–31)*, its historic importance dates to the coming of the Dorians and their worship of Zeus, after whose abode on Mount Olympos the site was named. More elaborate temples and secular buildings were erected as the sanctuary acquired a more Hellenic character, a process completed by 300 BC. By the end of the reign of Roman Emperor Hadrian (AD 117–38), the sanctuary had begun to have less religious and political significance.

Aerial view south over the Olympia site today

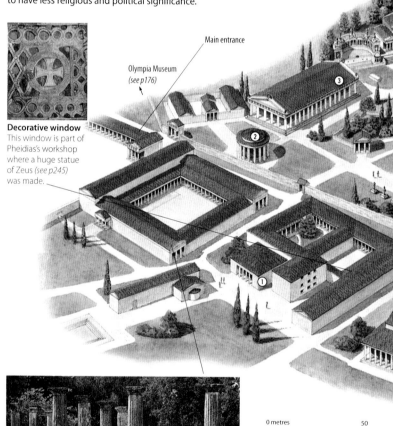

Main entrance

Olympia Museum *(see p176)*

Decorative window
This window is part of Pheidias's workshop where a huge statue of Zeus *(see p245)* was made.

0 metres		50
0 yards		50

Palaestra
This was a training centre for wrestlers, boxers and long-jumpers. Much of the colonnade which surrounded the central court has been reconstructed.

Stadium Entrance
Late in the 3rd century BC, the stadium entrance acquired a vaulted ceiling, part of which survives. The existing stadium was the third laid out at Olympia.

Reconstruction of Olympia (AD 100)

This shows Olympia as it was under the Romans. At that time, the worship of Zeus predominated; the games were dedicated to him, and his temple (containing a huge statue of the god) was at the heart of the Olympian enclosure.

KEY

① **The Heroön** housed an altar dedicated to an unknown hero.

② **The Philippeion,** commissioned by Philip II, honours the dynasty of Macedonian kings.

③ **The Temple of Hera,** begun in the 7th century BC, is one of the oldest temples in Greece.

④ **The Treasuries,** which stored votive offerings from their donor city-states, looked like miniature temples.

⑤ **The Metroön** was a Doric shrine to the pre-Olympian goddess Rhea.

⑥ **South Hall**

⑦ **Altar of Oaths**

⑧ **The Bouleuterion,** or council house, was the seat of the Olympic Senate.

⑨ **Sanctuary entrance**

⑩ **The Leonidaion,** with its clover-shaped water-garden, accommodated distinguished guests.

Temple of Zeus
Though only column bases and tumbled sections remain, they clearly indicate the grandeur of this 5th-century BC Doric temple.

Exploring the Olympia Archaeological Museum

The Olympia Archaeological Museum, built opposite the excavation site to display its many treasures, officially opened in 1982, replacing the old one from 1895. It is one of the richest museums in Greece. Except for the central hall, devoted solely to the pediment and metope sculptures from the Zeus temple, and the corner room dedicated to the games, the exhibits are arranged chronologically over 12 rooms, proceeding clockwise from the entrance hall from pre-history, through the Classical period, to the Romans.

Prehistoric, Geometric and Archaic Galleries

To the left of the entrance hall, room 1 contains finds from the Prehistoric period including pottery and 7th-century BC bronze reliefs. There is also a model of the early Helladic Pelopian Tumulus. Exhibits in room 2 include a bronze tripod cauldron, elongated male figures upholding cauldron handles and griffin-headed cauldron ornaments, popular in the 7th century BC. There are also bronze votive animals from the Geometric period, found in the area surrounding the altar of Zeus. Room 3 has lavishly painted terracotta architectural members from various buildings in the sanctuary.

Classical Galleries

Weapons and helmets made by pilgrims and athletes at Olympia were favourite offerings to Zeus. Two famous helmets used in the Persian Wars (see p33) are shown in room 4: an Assyrian helmet, and that of Miltiades, victor at the Battle of Marathon (see p149). This room also contains a 5th-century BC Corinthian terracotta of *Zeus and Ganymede*, the most humanized of the portrayals of Zeus.

The central hall houses surviving relief statuary from the Temple of Zeus. Unusually, both pediments survive, their compositions carefully balanced though not precisely symmetrical. The more static east pediment tells of the chariot race between local king Oinomaos and Pelops, suitor for the hand of the king's daughter Hippodameia. Zeus stands between the two contestants; a soothsayer on his left foresees Oinomaos's defeat. The two local rivers are personified in the corners. The western pediment, a metaphor for the tension between barbarism and civilization, portrays the mythological *Battle of the Lapiths and the Centaurs*. The centaurs, invited to the wedding of Lapith king Peirithous, attempt, while drunk, to abduct the Lapith women. Apollo, god of reason, is central, laying

Zeus and Ganymede, in terracotta

a reassuring hand on Peirithous's shoulder as the latter rescues his bride from the clutches of the centaur chief. Theseus is seen to the left of Apollo preparing to dispatch another centaur, while the Lapith women watch from the safety of the corners. The interior metopes, far less intact, depict the *Twelve Labours of Herakles*, a hero mythically associated with the sanctuary.

In its own niche, the fragmentary 5th-century BC *Nike* (room 6), by the sculptor Paionios, was a thanks-offering from Messene and Nafpaktos, following their victory over Sparta during the Peloponnesian War (see p34). A plaster reconstruction allows visualization of the winged goddess on the back of an eagle as she descends from heaven to proclaim victory.

The more complete *Hermes*, by Praxiteles, also has a room to itself (room 8), and shows the nude god carrying the infant Dionysos to safety, away from jealous Hera. The arm holding the newborn deity rests on a tree-trunk

Statue of Hermes by Praxiteles

hung with Hermes' cape; Dionysos reaches for a bunch of grapes in the elder god's now-vanished right hand. Room 7 is devoted to Pheidias's workshop and the tools and materials used to create his gold and ivory statue of Zeus.

Hellenistic and Roman Galleries

Room 9 contains late-Classical and Hellenistic finds including the terracotta tiles of the Leonidaion. Rooms 10 and 11 are devoted to a series of statues of Roman emperors and generals and a marble bull dedicated by Regilla, wife of Herodes Atticus. Displays in room 12 include glass from the late-Roman cemetery at ancient Pissa (modern Miráka village), in which athletes and sanctuary officials were buried.

The Origins of the Olympic Games

The establishment of the Olympic Games in 776 BC is traditionally treated as the first certain event in Greek history. Originally, men's sprinting was the only event and competitors were local; the first recorded victor was Koroivos, a cook from nearby Elis. During the 8th and 7th centuries BC, wrestling, boxing, equestrian events and boys' competitions were added. The elite of many cities came to compete and provided victory trophies, although, until the Romans took charge in 146 BC, entry was restricted to Greeks. Local cities disputed control of the games, but a sacred truce guaranteed safe conduct to spectators and competitors. Part of a pagan festival, the Christians did not approve of the games and they were banned by Theodosius I in AD 393.

The ancient pentathlon consisted of sprinting, wrestling, javelin- and discus-throwing and the long jump (assisted by swinging weights). From 720 BC, athletes competed naked and women were excluded from spectating.

Wrestling and boxing are depicted on this 6th-century BC amphora. The boxers are shown wearing *himantes*, an early type of boxing glove made of leather straps wrapped around the hands and wrists.

The Olympic revival came in 1896, when the first modern games were held in Athens *(see p117)*. They were organized by the Frenchman Baron Pierre de Coubertin.

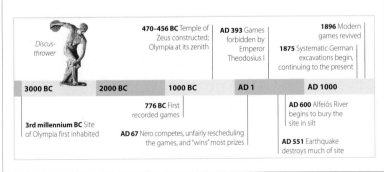

Discus-thrower

3000 BC	2000 BC	1000 BC	AD 1	AD 1000

470–456 BC Temple of Zeus constructed; Olympia at its zenith

AD 393 Games forbidden by Emperor Theodosius I

1896 Modern games revived

1875 Systematic German excavations begin, continuing to the present

3rd millennium BC Site of Olympia first inhabited

776 BC First recorded games

AD 67 Nero competes, unfairly rescheduling the games, and "wins" most prizes

AD 600 Alfeiós River begins to bury the site in silt

AD 551 Earthquake destroys much of site

⓫ Loúsios Gorge

Φαράγγι του Λούσιου

Although merely a tributary of the Alfeiós River, the Loúsios stream in its upper reaches boasts one of the most impressive canyons in Greece. Scarcely 5 km (3 miles) long, the Loúsios Gorge is nearly 300 m (985 ft) deep at the narrowest, most spectacular portion. Because of its remote mountain setting near the very centre of the Peloponnese, the Loúsios region was one of the strongholds of the revolutionaries during the Greek War of Independence *(see pp44–5)*. Medieval monasteries and churches cling to the steep cliffs of the gorge, and hiking trails have been marked, connecting some of the area's highlights. The picturesque villages *(see p180)* of the canyon's east bank make suitable touring bases.

Néa Moní Filosófou
Situated on the west bank amid the narrows, this 17th-century monastery has been renovated and is now home to several monks. Frescoes in the church date from 1693 and illustrate many seldom-depicted biblical episodes, such as the *Gadarene Swine*.

★ Ancient Gortys
The Asklepieion, or therapeutic centre, of Ancient Gortys occupies a sunken excavation on the west bank. It includes the foundations of a 4th-century BC temple to Asklepios, the god of healing.

KEY

① **Agios Andréas,** an 11th-century chapel, stands just below the Loúsios.

② **Paleá Moní Filosófou,** dating to 960, is the oldest monastery of the area. It is now in ruins.

③ **Dimitsána** is the best place to join the path.

④ **Stemnítsa** *(see p180)* is a charming village and a good place to hike out to, having passed through the gorge.

Kókkoras Bridge
This restored medieval bridge once carried the age-old road linking the regions of Arcadia and Ileía. Anglers fish for trout here in the icy river water.

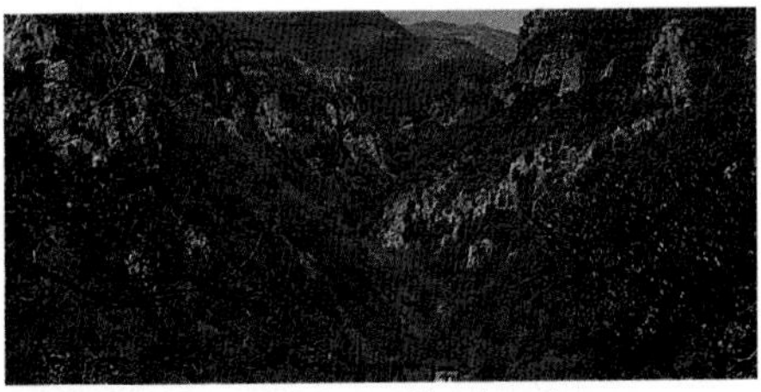

Wooded flanks of the Loúsios Gorge, viewed from the south

VISITORS' CHECKLIST

Practical Information
Peloponnese. **Road map** C4.
All monasteries: **Open** dawn–dusk (often closed for 1–2 hours at midday).
Moní Aimyalón: **Open** daily.
Néa Moní Filosófou: **Open** daily.
Ancient Gortys: **Open** daily.
Trekking: Take walking shoes and maps; paths are not always robust or clearly marked. Do not enter the gorge after heavy rain.

Transport
Dimitsána.

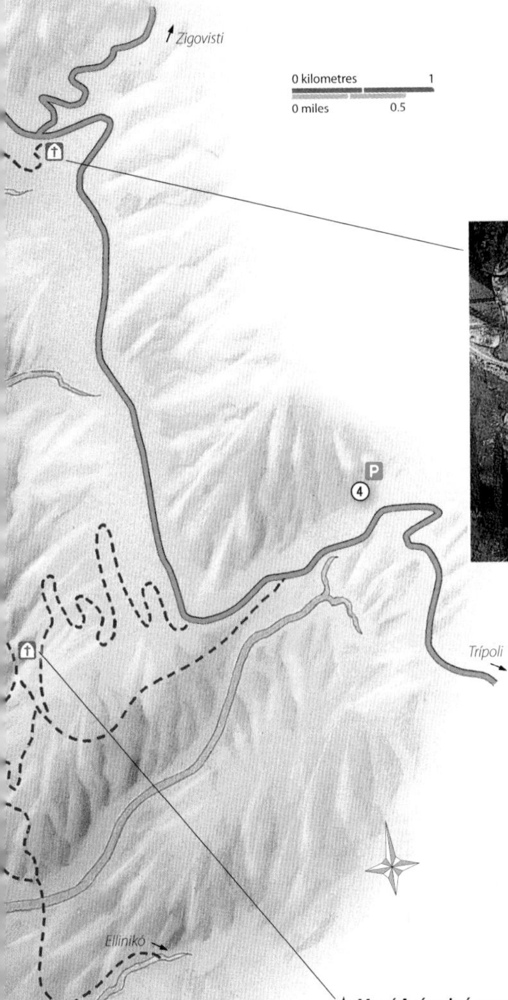
Zigovisti
0 kilometres 1
0 miles 0.5
P
4
Trípoli
Ellinikó

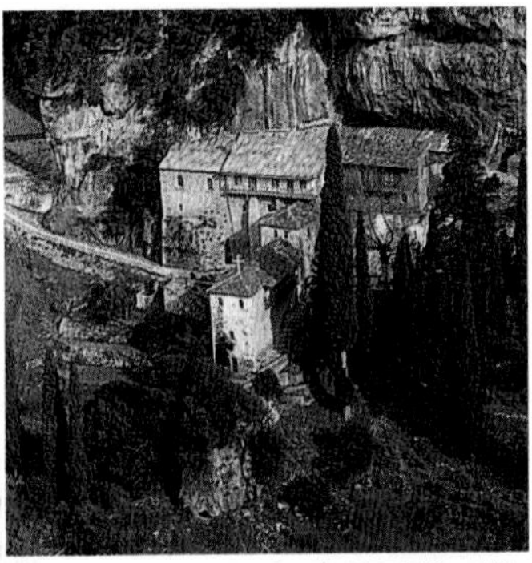

★ Moní Aimyalón
Founded in 1605, Moní Aimyalón is tucked into a side canyon, above garden plots. A passage partly hewn through the rock leads to its barrel-vaulted church with excellent frescoes from 1608.

★ Moní Agíou Ioánnou Prodrómou
Wedged into a palisade on the canyon's east flank, this 12th-century monastery is the most spectacular sight of the Loúsios. There is room for only a dozen monks in the tiny, frescoed church whose shape is dictated by the cliff face.

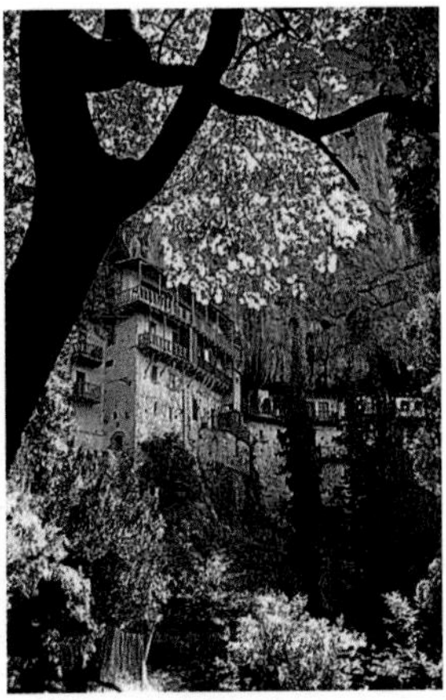

Key
Minor road
Footpath

For keys to symbols *see back flap*

Exploring Around the Loúsios Gorge

Overlooking the gorge are some of the most beautiful hill-towns in the Arcadia region, making good bases for exploring the area. The best-marked trail is between Néa Moní Filosófou and Moní Prodrómou (take water and food). Dimitsána has one bus service daily to Trípoli, while two weekday buses between Andrítsaina and Trípoli can be picked up below Karýtaina. Getting around by car is best, though taxis are available. Winters can be chilly and wet, with snow chains required.

Bridge over the Alfeiós River, below Karýtaina, complete with chapel

The narrow streets of Dimitsána

Dimitsána

Spread along an airy ridge with the River Loúsios on three sides and glorious views down the valley, Dimitsána stands on the Classical site of ancient Teuthis. The town boasts four belfries; that of **Agía Kyriakí** is illuminated at night, while the three-level **Pyrsogiannítiko** bell tower was erected by skilled Epirot masons in 1888.

Two clerics involved in the 1821 revolution against Turkish rule *(see pp44–5)* were born here. The birthplace of Archbishop Germanós of Pátra, who helped instigate the revolution, is marked by a plaque near the summit of westerly Kástro hill. A plaque dedicated to Patriarch Gregory V stands in the market; he was hanged in Istanbul when news of the revolt reached the sultan.

Dimitsána's mansions date from its heyday as a trade centre in the 18th century. There were 14 powder factories here during the

War of Independence – the town's **Water Power Museum** has exhibits on tanning, flour-milling and gunpowder manufacture.

🏛 **Water Power Museum**
Dimitsána. **Tel** 27950 31630. **Open** 10am–6pm (5pm in winter) Wed–Mon. **Closed** main public hols.

Stemnítsa

Situated in a large hollow, the village of Stemnítsa forms a naturally hidden fortress. A main metalworking centre in medieval times, today Stemnítsa boasts a well-respected school for gold- and silversmiths. A **Folklore Museum** re-creates workshops of indigenous craftsmen and local house interiors, and hosts a gallery of weaponry, textiles and ceramics belonging to the Savópoulos family.

The magnificent medieval churches of **Treís Ierárches**, near the Folklore Museum, and 10th-century **Profítis Ilías**, up on Kástro hill, have excellent frescoes. The 12th-century **Panagía Mpaféro** has an unusual portico, while **Moní Zoödóchou Pigís** was where

the revolutionary chieftains held their first convention during the War of Independence; it is for this reason that Stemnítsa was called the first capital of Greece.

🏛 **Folklore Museum**
Stemnítsa. **Tel** 27950 81252. **Open** Oct–Jun: 10am–1pm Mon & Wed–Fri, 10am–2pm Sat & Sun; Jul–Sep: 10am–1pm Mon & Sun, 10am–1pm & 5–8pm Wed, Thu & Sat, 5–8pm Fri. **Closed** Tue (Oct–Jun), main pub hols.

Karýtaina

In a strategic position on a bend of the Alfeiós, Karýtaina is now a virtual ghost town of less than 200 inhabitants. It has a 13th-century **kástro**, dating from the time when the town was the seat of a Frankish barony. The castle was the hideout of Theódoros Kolokotrónis, who survived a long Turkish siege here in 1826. The **Panagía tou Kástrou** boasts restored 11th-century column capitals with intricate reliefs, while the multi-domed **Agios Nikólaos** has excellent medieval frescoes.

Environs

East of Karýtaina, a bridge over the Alfeiós dates to 1439; four of six original arches survive, with a tiny chapel built into one pier.

The town of Dimitsána, seen from the east

⓬ Andrítsaina

Ανδρίτσαινα

Peloponnese. **Road map** C4.
🏔 900. 🚌

The sleepy town of Andrítsaina is hardly touched by tourism. Tavernas and shops around its central square, home to a lively morning produce market, make few concessions to modernity in either their cuisine or their vivid displays. These are echoes of the 18th century, when this was a major market centre. Downhill from the 18th-century fountain of Traní, a **Folk Museum** features local rag-rugs, traditional dress and metalware.

🏛 Folk Museum

Andrítsaina. **Tel** 26260 22430. **Open** daily. **Closed** main public hols.

Environs

The 5th-century BC **Temple of Apollo Epikourios Bassae** graces a commanding knoll, occupying the most remote site of any major ancient sanctuary. Today, it hides under an enormous tent, until 50 million euros (£38 million) can be raised to reinstall the architraves. Without them, winter frost damages the temple's colonnades, now reinforced by scaffolding.

Below Bassae lies the modern village of Figaleía, named after the ancient town to the west. The citizens of Ancient Figaleía built the temple in thanks to Apollo Epikourios for stopping a plague. A path descends to the gorge of the Nédas river.

🏛 Temple of Apollo Epikourios Bassae

14 km (9 miles) S of Andrítsaina. **Tel** 26260 22275. **Open** Apr–Oct: 8:30am–sunset daily (to 3pm Nov–Mar). 🅿 🚻

⓭ Ancient Tegea

Τεγέα

Peloponnese. **Road map** C4. **Tel** 27150 56540. 🚌 Site: **Open** daily (unfenced). Museum: **Open** 8:30am–3pm Tue–Sun. **Closed** main public hols. 🚻
🌐 tegamuseum.gr

About 9 km (5.5 miles) southeast of Trípoli, the remains of the

A quiet street in the traditional town of Andrítsaina

ancient city of Tegea lie near the village of Aléa. The most impressive ruin is the 4th-century BC Doric temple of Athena Alea, with its massive column drums, the second largest temple in the Peloponnese after Olympia's Temple of Zeus *(see p175)*. The site **museum** has sculpture from the city, including a number of fragments of the temple pediment.

⓮ Argos

Αργος

Peloponnese. **Road map** C4.
🏔 20,000. 🚌

One of the oldest settlements in Greece, modern Argos is a busy, rather shabby market town, with its open-air fairground next to a restored Neo-Classical marketplace. To the east of the central square, the **Archaeological Museum** exhibits local finds from all eras. Highlights include a bronze helmet and breastplate, and an Archaic pottery fragment showing Odysseus blinding Polyphemos, as well as a *krater* (bowl) from the 7th century BC.

The most visible traces of Ancient Argos lie on the way to Trípoli, where Roman baths are dwarfed by one of the largest and most steeply raked theatres in the Greek world. From town, a road climbs Lárisa hill, one of Argos's two ancient acropolises.

🏛 Archaeological Museum

E of Plateía Agíou Pétrou. **Tel** 27510 68819. **Closed** for renovation until 2018. 🅿 🚻

Environs

Heading south of Ancient Argos, past the theatre, a minor road leads to the village of **Ellinikó** on the outskirts of which stands an intact pyramidal building. Dating from the 4th century BC, the structure is thought to have been a fort guarding the road to Arcadia.

Lérna, further south, is a 2200-BC palace dubbed the "House of the Tiles" for its original terracotta roofing. It now shelters under a modern protective canopy. Adjacent Neolithic house foundations and two Mycenaean graves, inside the palace foundations, suggest two millennia of habitation. Settlers were attracted by springs which powered watermills and still feed a deep seaside pond. This was the home of the legendary nine-headed serpent Hydra, which Herakles killed as one of his Labours *(see p57)*.

Seating in the ancient theatre of Argos, seen from the stage

⓯ Mycenae

Μυκήναι

The fortified palace complex of Mycenae, uncovered by the archaeologist Heinrich Schliemann *(see p184)* in 1874, is one of the earliest examples of sophisticated citadel architecture. The term "Mycenaean", more properly late Bronze Age, applies to an entire culture spanning the years 1700–1100 BC. Only the ruling class inhabited this hilltop palace, with artisans and merchants living just outside the city walls. It was abandoned in 1100 BC after a period of great disruption in the region.

Secret Stairway
A flight of 99 steps drops to a cistern deep beneath the citadel. A torch is needed to see your way down the steps. Linked to a spring outside, the cistern provided water in times of siege.

KEY

① **Bastion**

② **Northeast gate**

③ **Artisans' workshops**

④ **The megaron** was the social heart of the palace.

⑤ **The "Cyclopean" walls**, up to 14 m (46 ft) wide, were unbreachable. Later Greeks imagined that they had been built by giants, hence the name.

⑥ **The House of Tsoúntas**, named after its discoverer, was a minor palace.

⑦ **The houses of Mycenae** yielded a number of tablets inscribed with an archaic script, known as Linear B, deciphered by Michaïl Ventrís in 1952.

⑧ **Great ramp**

Mycenae Today

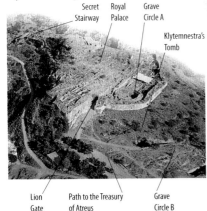

Secret Stairway · Royal Palace · Grave Circle A · Klytemnestra's Tomb · Lion Gate · Path to the Treasury of Atreus · Grave Circle B

Reconstruction of Mycenae

This illustration shows Mycenae as it was in the time of the House of Atreus and the 1250 BC Trojan War (see pp58–9). Most tombs lie outside the walls (see p184).

Royal Palace
Situated at the acropolis summit, only the floors remain of this central structure. Burn-marks dating to its destruction in 1200 BC are still visible on the stone.

Grave Circle A
This contained six royal family shaft graves containing 19 bodies. The 14 kg (31 lb) of gold funerary goods are on display in Athens *(see p74)*.

Lion Gate
The Lion Gate was erected in the 13th century BC, when the walls were realigned to enclose Grave Circle A. It takes its name from the lions carved above the lintel.

VISITORS' CHECKLIST

Practical Information
2 km (1 mile) N of Mykines, Peloponnese. **Road map** C4. **Tel** 27510 76585 **Open** Apr: 8am–7pm daily; May–Oct: 8am–8pm daily; Nov–Mar: 8am–3pm daily. Museum: **Open** as above. **Closed** 1 Jan, 25 Mar, Good Fri am, Easter Sun, 1 May, 25, 26 Dec. Treasury of Atreus & Museum.

Transport
to Mykines village.

Klytemnestra, after murdering her husband, Agamemnon

The Curse of the House of Atreus

King Atreus slaughtered his brother Thyestes's children and fed them to him; for this outrage, the gods laid a curse on Atreus and his descendants *(see p184)*. Thyestes's surviving daughter, Pelopia, bore her own father a son, Aigisthos, who murdered Atreus and restored Thyestes to the throne of Mycenae. But Atreus also had an heir, the energetic Agamemnon, who seized power.

Agamemnon raised a fleet to punish the Trojan Paris, who had stolen his brother's wife, Helen. He sacrificed his daughter to obtain a favourable wind. When he returned, he was murdered by his wife, Klytemnestra, and her lover – none other than Aigisthos. The murderous pair were in turn disposed of by Agamemnon's children, Orestes and Elektra.

Exploring the Tombs of Mycenae

Mycenae's nobles were entombed in shaft graves, such as Grave Circle A (see p183) or, later, in tholos ("beehive") tombs. The tholos tombs, found outside the palace walls, were built using successive circles of masonry, each level nudged steadily inward to narrow the diameter until the top could be closed with a single stone. The entire structure was then buried, save for an entrance approached by a dromos or open-air corridor.

The entrance to the Treasury of Atreus, with a triangular gap over its lintel

Treasury of Atreus

The Treasury of Atreus (see p183) is the most outstanding of the tholos tombs. Situated at the southern end of the site, the tomb dates from the 14th century BC and is one of only two double-chambered tombs in Greece. It has a 36-m (120-ft) dromos flanked by dressed stone and a small ossuary (the second chamber) which held

the bones from previous burials. A 9-m (30-ft) long lintel stone stands over the entrance; weighing almost 120 tonnes (264,550 lb), it is still not known how it was hoisted into place, and is a tribute to Mycenaean building skills.

The treasury is also known as the Tomb of Agamemnon. However, the legendary king and commander of the Trojan expedition (see pp58–9) could not have been buried here, as the construction of the tomb predates the estimated period of the Trojan War by more than 100 years.

Tomb of Klytemnestra

Of the other tholos tombs, only the so-called Tomb of Klytemnestra, which is situated just west of the Lion Gate, is as well preserved as that of Atreus. It is a small, single-chambered sepulchre with narrower and more steeply inclined walls, but the finely masoned dromos and similar

Heinrich Schliemann

Born in Mecklenburg, Germany, Heinrich Schliemann (1822–90) was self-educated and by the age of 47 had become a millionaire, expressly to fund his archaeological digs. Having discovered Troy and demonstrated the factual basis of Homer's epics, he came to Mycenae in 1874 and commenced digging in Grave Circle A. On discovering a gold death mask which had preserved the skin of a royal skull, he proclaimed: "I have gazed upon the face of Agamemnon!" Although archaeologists have since dated the mask to 300 years earlier than any historical Trojan warrior, the discovery corroborated Homer's description of "well-built Mycenae, rich in gold".

triangular air hole over the entrance (which also relieved pressure on the lintel) date it to the same period.

Treasury of Atreus

Unlike their Greek successors, who would cremate their dead, the Mycenaeans buried their deceased in tombs. In the Treasury of Atreus, a Mycenaean king was buried with his weapons and enough food and drink for his journey through the Underworld.

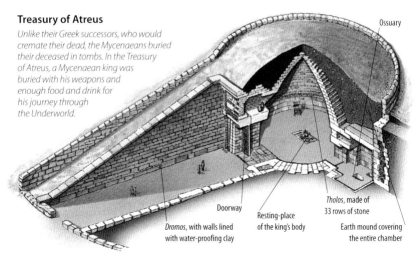

Ossuary

Doorway

Resting-place of the king's body

Dromos, with walls lined with water-proofing clay

Tholos, made of 33 rows of stone

Earth mound covering the entire chamber

⑯ Ancient Tiryns

Τίρυνθα

4 km (2 miles) NW of Náfplio, Pelo-ponnese. **Road map** C4. **Tel** 27520 22657. 🚌 **Open** Apr: 8am–7pm; May–Oct: 8am–8pm Mon–Fri, 8am–3pm Sat & Sun; Nov–Mar: 8am–3pm daily. 🎫

The 13th-century BC citadel of Tiryns confirms Homer's epithet "mighty-walled". A 700-m (2,300-ft) circuit of Cyclopean walls (named after the giants who could be imagined manoeuvering the huge blocks into place) attains a thickness of 8 m (26 ft). The fortifications, over double their present height, were necessarily stronger than those of Mycenae since Tiryns was not on a naturally strong site. The bluff on which it stood was only 18 m (59 ft) higher than the surrounding plain which, in ancient times, was a salt marsh.

An inclined ramp to the east, designed with sharp turns to expose attackers' unshielded sides, leads to the massive middle gate, the lintel of which has long been missing. At the southern end of the complex, beyond and beneath the vanished inner gate, a gallery with a pointed corbel ceiling has had its walls polished by the fleeces of sheep which have sheltered here for centuries. On the west side, a stone stairway between inner and outer walls, leading to a postern gate, has been completely preserved. The lower, northern acropolis was the last to be enclosed and was used to protect commoners, animals and (as at Mycenae) a water supply.

Environs
The early 13th-century Byzantine church of the Panagía rears up startlingly from a cement plaza at **Agía Triáda** (alias Mérpaka), a village 5 km (3 miles) north of Tiryns. The walls are constructed of

The remnants of the Tower of Theseus, Ancient Troezen

ancient masonry to shoulder height; above that, at the southeast corner of the building, the builders have inserted an entire Classical grave *stele*.

Further north, the **Argive Heraion** was the Archaic and Classical religious centre of the Argolid. The most impressive remains are those of a late 5th-century BC temple. Home to the priestesses of Hera, and a huge ivory-and-gold cult statue of the goddess, the temple was flanked by stoas, identifiable by remaining column stumps. Above the temple is the ledge where the Achaian leaders swore loyalty to Agamemnon before sailing for Troy. To the west, complete with drain-gutter,

stands the "Peristyle Building" where *symposia* were hosted.

🏛 **Argive Heraion**
10 km (6 miles) N of Tiryns. **Open** 8am–3pm daily.

⑰ Náfplio

See pp186–7.

⑱ Epidaurus

See pp188–9.

⑲ Ancient Troezen

Τροιζήνα

60 km (37 miles) E of Náfplio, Peloponnese. **Road map** D4. **Open** unrestricted access.

Near the modern village of Troizína are the sparse ruins of ancient Troezen, the legendary birthplace of the hero Theseus and the setting for Euripides' incestuous tragedy *Hippolytus*. Remains from many eras are scattered over a wide area; most conspicuous are three Byzantine chapels known as *Episkopí*, from the time when this was the seat of the Bishops of Damála.

The town was built on a high bluff isolated by two ravines; the westerly Damála Gorge is sheer, and a 15-minute walk up it, a small natural rock arch called the "Devil's Bridge" spans the canyon. Near the lower end of the gorge stands the "Tower of Theseus", Hellenistic at its base, medieval higher up.

Foundations of the Argive Heraion, seen at dawn

⑰ Náfplio

Ναύπλιο

With its marble pavements, looming castles and remarkably homogenous architecture, Náfplio is the most elegant town in mainland Greece. It emerged from obscurity in the 13th century and endured many sieges during the struggles between Venice and Turkey for the ports of the Peloponnese. The medieval quarter, to the west, is mostly a product of the second Venetian occupation (1686–1715). From 1829 until 1834, the town was the first capital of liberated Greece.

View over Náfplio from the stairway to the Palamídi fortress

Exploring Náfplio

Defended to the south by the Akronafplía and Palamídi fortresses and to the north by Boúrtzi castle, Náfplio occupies the northern side of a peninsula at the head of the Argolic Gulf. Since the Venetian period, **Plateía Syntágmatos** has been the hub of public life, and still looks much as it did three centuries ago when a couple of mosques were erected by the victorious Ottomans. One stands at the east end of the square and is now a concert hall; Vouleftikó Mosque, to the south, was where the Greek parliament *(vouli)* first met. West of the bus station, **Agios Geórgios** cathedral was built as a mosque during the first Ottoman occupation (1540–1686). Also converted is the **Catholic church of Metamórfosi**, another early mosque near the top of

President Kapodístrias

Potamiánou, which contains a monument honouring fallen philhellenes, including George Washington's nephew. Four ornate fountains survive from the second Ottoman occupation (1715–1822). The most famous are the scroll-arched one, behind the concert-hall mosque, and another opposite **Agios Spyrídon** on Kapodistríou; this is near where President Kapodístrias was assassinated on 9 October 1831. There are less elaborate Ottoman fountains up the

steps at Tertsétou 9, and at the corner of Potamiánou and Kapodistríou.

🏛 Archaeological Museum

Plateía Syntágmatos. **Tel** 27520 27502. **Open** 8am–3pm Tue–Sun. ♿

Exhibits here largely centre on Mycenaean artifacts from various local sites, including Tiryns *(see p185)*. Noteworthy are a Neolithic *thylastro* (baby-bottle), a late Helladic octopus vase, a full set of bronze Mycenaean armour and a complete Mycenaean boar's tusk helmet. There is also a large selection of Prehistoric, Archaic and Classical pottery.

🏛 Folk Art Museum

Vas. Alexandrou 1. **Tel** 27520 28947. **Open** 9am–2:30pm Mon–Sat, 9:30am–3pm Sun. 🅿 ♿ 🆆 pli.gr

This award-winning museum, established in a former mansion by the Peloponnesian Folklore Foundation, focuses on textiles. Regional costumes are exhibited across two floors with Queen Olga's stunning blue and white wedding gown taking pride of place on the first floor. Also on the first floor are paintings by major Greek artists Yannis Tsarouchis and Theophilos Hatzimihail *(see p222)*. On the second floor are guns and an impressive grandfather clock decorated with revolutionary scenes.

🏰 Boúrtzi

NW of harbour.

This island fortress acquired its appearance during the second Venetian occupation, and until 1930, had the dubious

The fortified isle of Boúrtzi, north of Náfplio harbour

distinction of being the local executioner's residence. It defended the only navigable passage in the bay; the channel could be closed off by a chain extending from the fortress to the town.

Akronafplía
W of Palamídi. **Open** unrestricted access.

Akronafplía, also known as Its Kale ("Inner Castle" in Turkish), was the site of the Byzantine and early medieval town, and contains four Venetian castles built in sequence from west to east. The most interesting relic is the Venetian Lion of St Mark relief over the 15th-century gate just above the Catholic church. The westernmost "Castle of the Greeks" was Náfplio's ancient acropolis, now home to the clock tower, a major landmark.

Palamídi
Polyzoïdou. **Tel** 27520 28036. **Open** Apr–Oct: 8am–7:30pm; Nov–Mar: 8am–4:30pm daily. **Closed** main public hols.

Palamídi, named after the Homeric hero Palamedes, the son of Nafplios and

Palamídi fortress seen from the isle of Boúrtzi

Klymene, is a huge Venetian citadel built between 1711 and 1714. It was designed to withstand all contemporary artillery, though it fell to the Ottomans in 1715 after a mere one-week siege, and to the Greek rebels led by Stáïkos Staïkópoulos on 30 November 1822, after an 18-month campaign.

The largest such complex in Greece, Palamídi consists of a single curtain wall enclosing seven self-sufficient forts, now named after Greek heroes; the gun slits are aimed at each other as well as outward, in case an enemy managed to penetrate the defences. Fort Andréas was the Venetian

headquarters, with a Lion of St Mark in relief over its entrance. The Piazza d'Armi, from where Náfplio assumes toy-town dimensions below you, offers arguably the best views in the country. At the summit, an eighth fort, built by the Ottomans, looks south towards Karathóna beach.

Environs
The 12th-century convent of **Agía Moní** nestles 4 km (2 miles) outside Náfplio; the octagonal dome-drum rests on four columns with Corinthian capitals. Just outside the walls, in an orchard, the Kánathos fountain still springs from a niche decorated with animal reliefs; this was ancient Amymone, where the goddess Hera bathed each year to renew her virginity.

Náfplio Town Centre
① Archaeological Museum
② Plateía Syntágmatos
③ Folk Art Museum
④ Agios Geórgios
⑤ Agios Spyrídon
⑥ Catholic Church
⑦ Akronafplía

0 metres   200
0 yards   200

For keys to symbols *see back flap*

⓲ Epidaurus (Epídavros)

Επίδαυρος

Though most renowned for its magnificent theatre, the Sanctuary of Epidaurus was an extensive therapeutic and religious centre, dedicated to the healing god Asklepios. A physician killed by the gods for reviving a dead patient, he was subsequently deified by Zeus. Asklepios was depicted in his temple here clutching a staff and flanked by a dog and a serpent – common symbols of natural wisdom. This sanctuary was active from the 6th century BC until at least the 2nd century AD, when the traveller-historian Pausanias recorded a visit.

Dusk over Epidaurus during a modern production at the theatre

The Theatre

Designed by Polykleitos the Younger late in the 4th century BC, the theatre is well known for its near-perfect acoustics which are endlessly demonstrated by tour group leaders. Owing to the sanctuary's relative remoteness, its masonry was never pilfered, and it remained undiscovered until the 1870s. It has the only circular *orchestra* (stage) to have survived from antiquity, though the altar that once stood in the centre has now gone. Two side corridors, or *parodoi*, gave the actors access to the stage; each had a monumental gateway whose pillars have now been

Foundations of the *tholos* building in the Asklepieion

re-erected. Behind the *orchestra* and facing the auditorium stand the remains of the *skene*, the main reception hall, and the proskenion which was used by performers as an extension of the stage. Today, the theatre is still the venue for a popular summer festival of ancient drama.

The Asklepieion

Much of the Asklepieion, or Sanctuary of Asklepios, has been re-excavated, with many colonnades re-erected. One of the accessible sites is the *propylaia*, or monumental gateway, at the north edge of the sanctuary, its original entrance. Also preserved are a ramp and some buckled pavement from the Sacred Way which led north from the gateway to the coastal town of ancient Epidavros. At the northwestern end of the

Reconstruction of the Theatre

Surrounding the central orchestra, the north-facing cavea (cavity) of the theatre is 114 m (374 ft) across and is divided into blocks by 36 staircases.

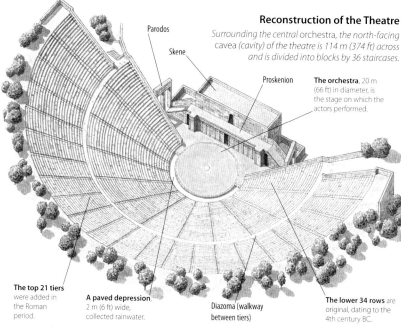

Parodos

Skene

Proskenion

The orchestra, 20 m (66 ft) in diameter, is the stage on which the actors performed.

The top 21 tiers were added in the Roman period.

A paved depression, 2 m (6 ft) wide, collected rainwater.

Diazoma (walkway between tiers)

The lower 34 rows are original, dating to the 4th century BC.

Overview of today's site showing the stadium at the bottom (west)

VISITORS' CHECKLIST

Practical Information
30 km (19 miles) E of Náfplio, Peloponnese. **Road map** C4. **Tel** 27530 22009. Site & Museum: **Open** from 8am (May–Oct: to 8pm; Nov & Dec: 3pm; Jan–Mar: 5pm; Apr: 7pm) (museum opens noon Mon). **Closed** 1 Jan, 25 Mar, Good Fri am, Easter Sun, 1 May, 25, 26 Dec. 🏛 🚹 limited. 📷 💻 🚗 Epidaurus Theatre Festival: Jul–Aug.

Transport
🚌

sanctuary stand the remains of the *tholos* (a circular building of uncertain function, also designed by Polykleitos), whose concentric passages are thought to have been used either as a pit for sacred serpents, or possibly as the locale for rites by the cult's priests. Patients slept in the *enkoimitírion* – a hall north of the *tholos* where they would await a diagnostic dream or a visit from the harmless serpents. Therapeutic mineral springs, which are still on tap beside the museum, also played a part in the curing of patients who were brought here. Only the foundations of Asklepios's temple have survived, lying to the east of the *tholos*.

Another undisturbed point is the late Classical stadium south of the *tholos*. With intact rows of stone benches and a starting line still visible, this was used during the quadrennial festival in honour of Asklepios. The Romans built an odeion inside the Hellenistic gymnasium, to host the festival's musical contests.

Environs
The adjacent village of Lygourió reflects the importance of the region during Byzantine times. There are three Byzantine churches, the most distinguished being the 14th-century **Koímisis tis Theotókou**, which has superb early medieval frescoes.

The Origins of Greek Drama

Greek drama developed from ritual role-play at festivals of Dionysos (*see p56*). First came group dancing – 6th-century BC Athenian vases show groups elaborately costumed, often as animals. In the late 6th century BC, the first Greek theatres appeared: rectangular (later round) spaces with seats on three sides. Singing and dancing choruses were joined by individual actors, whose masks made visible at a distance the various character roles, all played by just three male actors. The depiction of animal choruses on vases suggests humorous presentation, but the earliest plays in Athens were tragedies, staged in sets of three by a single writer (*see p61*), in which episodes from epic poems and mythology were acted out. Historical events were rarely dramatized as they were politically sensitive. Comedy became part of the dramatic festival at Athens only in the 480s BC. Theatre was mass entertainment and had to cater for large numbers – during the Roman period, the theatre at Epidaurus could hold 13,000 people – but it is uncertain whether women were permitted to attend the performances.

Masks were worn by actors to express the personality of the characters they played.

Souvenir statuettes, such as this terracotta figurine of a sinister character from one of the later comedies, could be bought as mementos after performances.

The chorus, though chiefly an impersonal commentator, often spoke directly to the characters, questioning them on the wisdom of their actions.

⑳ Monemvasiá

Μονεμβασιά

A fortified town built on two levels on a rock rearing 350 m (1,150 ft) above the sea, Monemvasiá well deserves its nickname, "the Gibraltar of Greece". A town of 50,000 in its 15th-century prime, Monemvasiá enjoyed centuries of existence as a semi-autonomous city-state, living off the commercial acumen (and occasional piracy) of its fleets and its strategic position astride the sea lanes from Italy to the Black Sea. Exceptionally well defended, it was never taken by force but fell only through protracted siege (*see p192*). Though the upper town is in ruins, most of the lower town is restored.

Pathway to Upper Town
A paved stair-street zigzags up the cliff face from the lower town to the tower gate of the upper town (*see p192*).

★ Agía Sofía
Standing at the summit of Monemvasiá, this beautiful 13th-century church is the only intact remnant of the upper town (*see p192*).

Panagía Myrtidiótissa
The façade of this 18th-century church sports a Byzantine inscription and a double-headed eagle from an earlier Byzantine church.

"The Gibraltar of Greece"
Monemvasiá was severed from the mainland by an earthquake in AD 375, remaining an island until the causeway was built in the 6th century.

VISITORS' CHECKLIST

Practical Information
Peloponnese. **Road map** C5.
🚇 800. 🛈 27320 61210
(number for the tourist police,
available during summer).
Mosque Museum: **Tel** 27320
61403. **Open** 8am–3pm Tue–Sun.
Closed Mon & main public hols.

Transport
🚌 Géfyra.

Christós Elkómenos
Restored in 1697, this 13th-century cathedral with its Venetian belfry is stark inside; the only decoration is the plaque of two peacocks above the door.

★ Walls
The 16th-century walls are 900 m (2,953 ft) long and up to 30 m (98 ft) high. Much of the parapet can be walked.

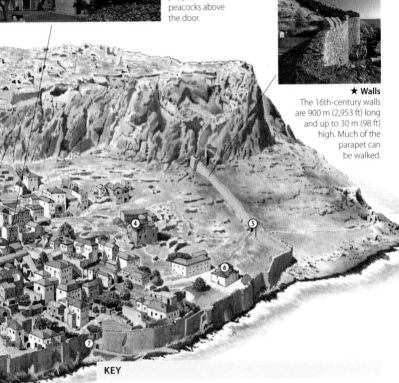

KEY

① **The mosque** has been refurbished as a museum to display local finds, including some fine marble works.

② **Western gate**

③ **The birthplace** of prominent poet and communist Giánnis Rítsos (1909–90) is marked by a plaque and a bust near the front gate of his house.

④ **Agios Nikólaos**, begun in 1703, resembles Myrtidiótissa in its

masonry, cruciform plan and cement-covered dome.

⑤ **The east gate** opens on to a former burial ground known as Leípsana.

⑥ **Panagía Chrysafítissa** has its bell hanging from a cypress tree.

⑦ **The sea, or Portello, gate** gave access to the sea when the main port was threatened.

The cliff-top church of Agía Sofía, at dawn, Monemvasiá upper town

The Siege of Monemvasiá

The siege of Monemvasiá by the Greeks, early in the War of Independence (see pp44–5), began on 28 March 1821. Due to a Greek ruse, the town's Ottoman garrison was badly supplied with food, and reinforcements failed to arrive. By late June, both Christians and Muslims were forced to eat weeds, cats and mice, some even resorting to cannibalism. Turkish civilians in the lower town urged surrender, but the garrison of the upper town refused. The besiegers also seemed set to give up, but one night, the leading Greek civilian inside the town convinced three messengers to swim from the Portello Gate to the revolutionary forces on the mainland, giving them word to persevere. They did, and on 23 July, the Ottoman garrison surrendered to Alexandros Kantakouzenos who was acting for Commander Dimitrios Ypsilantis.

The taking of Monemvasiá by Alexandros Kantakouzenos

Exploring the Upper Town

First fortified in the 6th century as a refuge from raiding Avars, the upper town is the oldest part of Monemvasiá. Largely in ruins, the area is now under the protection of the Greek archaeological service. Though in medieval times it was the most densely populated part of

Ruins of Monemvasiá's 13th-century fortress

the peninsula, the upper town is deserted today, the last resident having departed in 1911.

A path climbs the cliff face above the town's northwestern corner, leading to an entrance gate which still has its iron slats. Directly ahead, a track leads to the summit's best-preserved building, the church of **Agía Sofía**. It was founded by Emperor Andronikos II (1282–1328) in emulation of Daphni monastery (see pp156–7) near Athens. With its 16-sided dome, the church perches on the brink of the northerly cliff and is visible from a considerable distance inland. The west portico is Venetian, while the niche on the south wall dates from its use as a mosque. A few frescoes surviving from the early 14th century are badly faded, but the *Ancient of Days* can be discerned in the sanctuary's vault, as can the *Birth of John the Baptist* in the north vault. Carved ornamentation has

fared better, such as the marble capitals flanking the south windows, depicting mythical monsters and a richly dressed woman.

To the west are the remains of a 13th-century **fortress**. Amid the debris of former barracks, guardrooms and a gunpowder magazine from the Venetian period, a vast **cistern** recalls the times of siege when great quantities of water had to be stored. Food supplies, entirely imported, were more of a problem, as was demonstrated by the siege of 1821.

aisle and narthex added after 1262; a carved marble screen and varied frescoes decorate its interior.

Below the west gate, 13th-century **Zoödóchou Pigís** sports a complete Gothic door and south window, while inside, later frescoes include *Christ on the Road to Calvary*.

At the base of the hill, the domeless, 14th-century church of **Agía Paraskeví** has a fine *Nativity* in its cross vault, plus a painting of the donor family on the west wall.

Environs

Four more churches stand a short drive to the west in **Geráki** village. Both 12th-century Agios Athanásios and 13th-century Agios Sózon share a cross-in-square plan, with a high dome on four piers. Market edicts of the Roman Emperor Diocletian, inscribed on stone, flank the doorway of barrel-vaulted, 14th-century Agios Ioánnis Chrysóstomos, covered inside with scenes from the life of Christ and the Virgin. Tiny Evangelístria has a Pantokrátor fresco in its dome.

Agía Paraskeví, viewed from Byzantine Geráki

❷ Geráki
Γεράκι

Peloponnese. **Road map** C5.
2,000.

Occupying a spur of Mount Párnonas, Geráki is like a miniature Mystrás with its kástro overlooking the frescoed Byzantine churches on the slopes below. The polygonal kástro was built in 1254–5 by the Frank, Jean de Nivelet, though it was ceded in 1262 to the Byzantines, together with Monemvasiá and Mystrás. Inside, 13th-century **Agios Geórgios** is a hybrid Franko-Byzantine church, the third

7th-century BC clay head of a woman, from Spárti acropolis

❷ Spárti
Σπάρτη

Peloponnese. **Road map** C5.
20,000.

Though one of the most powerful of the Greek city-states, ancient Sparta was unfortified and has few ruins dating to its heyday. The acropolis lies 700 m (2,300 ft) northwest of the modern town centre. On the western side of the acropolis is the cavity of the Roman theatre, its masonry largely pilfered to build Mystrás, while directly east stands the long, arcaded stoa which once held shops. Of the Artemis Orthia sanctuary just east of town, where Spartan youths were flogged to prove their manhood, only some Roman seating remains. The most interesting finds are on display in the museum.

The highlight of the rich **Archaeological Museum** is the fine collection of Roman mosaics, including two lions rampant over a vase, Arion riding his dolphin, Achilles disguised as a woman on Skýros, and a portrait of Alkibiades. A Classical marble head of a warrior, possibly Leonidas I (see p228), was found on the acropolis, while bas-reliefs of Underworld serpent-deities hail from a sanctuary of Apollo at modern Amyklés, 8 km (5 miles) south of Spárti. Bizarre ceramic masks are smaller replicas of those used in dances at the Artemis Orthia sanctuary.

Archaeological Museum
Agíou Níkonos & Lykouroú. **Tel** 27310 28575. **Open** 8am–3pm Tue–Sun. **Closed** main public hols.

Life in Ancient Sparta

Rising to prominence around 700 BC, Sparta became one of the most powerful city-states of ancient Greece. Its power was based on rigid social and military discipline, as well as hatred of foreigners, which eventually led to its downfall as it had few allies. The "city" was made up of five villages, where the male citizens lived communally in constant readiness for war. Warriors were selected at the age of seven and subjected to rigorous training – whipping contests, with young boys as the victims, were held in the sanctuary of Artemis Orthia. Sparta was able to support its citizens as professional soldiers because it had conquered neighbouring Messenia, and the enslaved population provided all the food required. Sparta led the Greek forces against the Persians, but ceased to be a major power after defeat by Thebes in 371 BC.

5th-century BC bronze figurine of a Spartan warrior

㉓ Mystrás

Μυστράς

Majestic Mystrás occupies a panoramic site on a spur of the severe Taÿgetos range. Founded by the Franks in 1249, it soon passed to the Byzantines, under whom it became a town of 20,000 and, after 1348, the seat of the Despots of Morea. The despotate acted semi-independently and had become the last major Byzantine cultural centre by the 15th century, attracting scholars and artists from Italy and Serbia as well as Constantinople. One result was the uniquely cosmopolitan decoration of the Mystrás churches – their pastel-coloured frescoes, crowded with detail, reflect Italian Renaissance influence.

Plan of Mystrás

0 metres 100
0 yards 100

KASTRO
UPPER TOWN
LOWER TOWN
Spárti & Néos Mystrás

Key to Plan

① Lower town entrance
② Mitrópoli
③ Moní Perivléptou
④ Moní Pantánassas
⑤ Vrontóchion
⑥ Monemvasiá Gate
⑦ Despots' Palace
⑧ Agía Sofía
⑨ Upper town entrance
⑩ Kástro

Exploring Mystrás

Now in ruins, Mystrás consists of a lower and upper town, linked by the Monemvasiá Gate. The site can be entered from the castle at the top of the upper town or from the base of the lower town. Allow half a day for exploring the monasteries, churches, palaces and houses which line the narrow, winding streets. An unusual northwest-to-southeast alignment of the churches is dictated by the site's steep topography.

🏛 Mitrópoli

The Mitrópoli, situated by the lower town entrance, is the oldest church in Mystrás. It is approached through a double courtyard. Like many Balkan cathedrals, it began life in 1291 as a barrel-vaulted nave flanked by two aisles. The domes were added early in the 1400s in a clumsy attempt to equal the architecture of the Pantánassas and Afentikó churches. Frescoes, mostly early 14th century, show the martyrdom of the church's patron (Agios Dimítrios) in the northeast vaulting, while Christ's miracles begin next to these with the *Healing of the Lepers* and continue on the southwest aisle in such scenes as the *Wedding at Cana*. In the narthex is the *Preparation of the Throne of Judgment*, flanked by angels, a theme repeated in the southwest diaconicon (sacristy). The last Byzantine emperor, Konstantínos Palaiológos, was crowned here in 1449; a double-eagle plaque marks the spot.

The 14th-century fresco of the *Nativity* in the south vault of Moní Perivléptou

🏛 Moní Perivléptou

Squeezed against the rock face, the 14th-century monastery of Perivléptou has a compact, three-aisled church. Its small dome retains a fresco of the Pantokrátor, flanked by the Virgin and prophets, arranged in diminishing order of importance. The 14th-century frescoes, the most refined in Mystrás, focus on the 12 major church feasts. They include a vivid *Nativity* and *Baptism* in the south

◀ Interior of the Byzantine monastic church of Pantánassas, Mystrás

The hillside with remains of Byzantine Mystrás, seen from the south

vault, the *Transfiguration* and *Entry into Jerusalem*, complete with playing children, in the west aisle, and *Doubting Thomas* and the *Pentecost* in the north vault, decorating the wall over the entrance.

⬆ Moní Pantánassas
Dating to 1428, Pantánassas was the last church built at Mystrás. With its decorated apses and the brickwork of its arcaded belfry it imitates Afentikó in the Vrontóchion as an eclectic architectural experiment. The highest frescoes, from 1430, are of most merit, particularly a vivid *Raising of Lazarus* in the northeast vault. Both the *Nativity* and the *Annunciation* in the southwest vault feature animals. The southeast aisle displays the *Descent into Hell*, in which Christ raises Adam and Eve from their coffins, opposite a lively *Entry into Jerusalem*.

⬆ Vrontóchion
A 13th-century monastic complex built by Abbot Pachómios, the Vrontóchion

was the cultural centre of medieval Mystrás – in the 15th century, the Neo-Platonist philosopher Geórgios Gemistós, or Plethon, (1355–1452) taught here. It has two churches; the earliest, Agioi Theódoroi, dates from 1295 and has the largest dome at Mystrás, supported on eight arches. Few frescoes survive. The early 14th-century Afentikó (or Panagía Odigítria) is richly frescoed, with six domes. The galleries and two north-side chapels are shut, but in the west gallery dome, a *Virgin Orans* (praying) and *Prophets* are visible; in the south vault, a crowded *Baptism* includes water monsters. Above the altar, apostles gesticulate towards the aura of the rising Christ in the *Ascension*. The best-preserved frescoes can be found in the north bay of the narthex.

⊞ Despots' Palace
The Despots' Palace consists of two wings which have been reconstructed. The northeast wing was begun by the Franks;

the northwest hall, erected after 1348 and a rare example of Byzantine civic architecture, has the throne room of the rulers of the Kantakoúzenos and Palaiológos dynasties. The square was a venue for public events under the despots and a marketplace under the Ottomans.

The ruins of the Despots' Palace, viewed from the south

⬆ Kástro
Flanked by sheer ravines to the south and west, and crowning the summit of the upper town, the kástro is reached by a path leading from the upper entrance which stands above the church of Agía Sofía. Built by Guillaume de Villehardouin in 1249, the kástro retains its original Frankish design, though it was greatly altered by the Byzantines and Turks. A double circuit of curtain walls encloses two baileys, and a walkway can be taken around most of the structure, affording panoramic views over the lower town.
  It was here that the German writer Goethe, in Part Two of *Faust*, set the meeting of Faust and Helen of Troy, revived after 3,000 years.

Afentikó church, part of the Vrontóchion complex

㉔ Outer Máni
Έξω Μάνη

A harsh, remote region, bounded by mountains to the north, the rocky Máni was the last part of Greece to embrace Christianity, doing so in the 9th century with an enthusiasm borne out by dozens of surviving Byzantine chapels. Though well defended against invaders, the area has a history of internal feuding which led to the building of its many tower houses. A ravine at Oítylo divides Inner Máni, to the south (*see pp202–3*), from the more fertile Outer, or Messenian, Máni which has some of the finest countryside in the Mediterranean.

VISITORS' CHECKLIST

Practical Information
Peloponnese. **Road map** C5.

Transport
🚌 Kalamáta.

Oítylo

Though administratively within the region of Lakonía, by tradition the village of Oítylo (pronounced "Itilo") belongs to the Outer Máni. It affords superb panoramic views over Limeníou Bay and across a flanking ravine, traditionally the border between the Inner and Outer Máni, to Kelefá Castle (*see p202*). Its relatively good water supply fosters a lush setting around and below the village, with cypresses and a variety of orchard trees. Unlike most Mániot villages, Oítylo is not in economic decline. Its many fine houses include graceful 19th-century mansions. The village was capital of the Máni between the 16th and 18th centuries, and was the area's most infamous slave-trading centre; both Venetians and Muslims were sold to each other here. A plaque in the square, written in French and Greek, commemorates the flight, in 1675, of 730 Oítylots to Corsica – 430 of whom were from the Stefanópoulos clan. Seeking refuge from the Turks, the Oítylots were granted passage by the Genoese and, once in Corsica, founded the villages of Paomia and Cargèse. These towns account for the stories of Napoleon's part-Mániot origins.

Environs

From the southwestern corner of Oítylo, a broad path descends west to **Moní Dekoúlou**, nestled in its own little oasis. The 18th-century church features an ornate *témblon* (wooden altar screen) and vivid original frescoes; though they have been preserved by the darkness, a torch is required to see them now. The monastery is only open in the evenings or by prior arrangement with the resident caretakers.

The village of **Néo Oítylo** stands 4 km (2 miles) south of the monastery. Quietly secluded, the village has a pebble beach with fine views.

The Mániot Feuds

By the 15th century, a number of refugee Byzantine families had settled in the Máni, the most powerful forming a local aristocracy known as the Nyklians. Feuding between clans over the inadequate land was rife, though only Nyklians had the right to construct stone towers, which attained four or five storeys and came to dominate nearly every Mániot village.

Pétros Mavromichális

Once commenced, blood feuds could last months, even years, with periodic truces to tend to the crops. Clansmen fired at each other from facing towers, raising them in order to be able to catapult rocks onto opponents' roofs. The hostilities ended only with the total destruction or submission of the losing clan. Historically, the most important clans were those of Mavromichális at Areópoli, Grigorákis at Gýtheio and Troupákis at Kardamýli, whose members boasted of never having been completely subjugated by any foreign power. The Ottomans wisely refrained from ruling the Máni directly, but instead quietly encouraged the clans to feud in order to weaken potential rebellions, and appointed a Nyklian chieftain as *bey* (regional lord) to represent the sultan locally. Under the final *bey*, Pétros Mavromichális, the clans finally united, instigating the Greek Independence uprising on 17 March 1821 (*see pp44–5*).

Oítylo viewed from the northwest, looking towards Kelefá Castle

Agios Spyrídon south window, framed with marble reliefs

Kardamýli

Kardamýli was the lair of the Troupákis family, important rivals of the Mavromichális clan. Nicknamed Moúrtzinos, or "Bulldog", for their tenacity in battle, they claimed to be descended from the Byzantine Palaiológos dynasty.

Olive oil used to be the chief source of income for Kardamýli, but this has now been superseded by tourism.

Inland rises the ancient and medieval acropolis, heralded by twin Mycenaean chamber tombs. In Old Kardamýli (sign posted) are Troupákis-built towers, which stand alongside the 18th-century church of **Agios Spyrídon**. This building is

made of Hellenistic masonry and graced by a pointed, four-storey belfry; the south window and doorway are framed by intricate marble reliefs.

Environs

Two paths lead from Kardamýli, one upstream along the **Vyrós Gorge** where two monasteries shelter beneath the cliffs; the other to the villages of Gourniés and Exochóri. A short drive to the south, **Stoúpa** is popular for its two sandy bays; novelist Níkos Kazantzákis (1883–1957) lived here briefly and partly based his Zorba the Greek character on a mine foreman who worked nearby. The village of **Agios Nikólaos**, a short walk to the south, curls around Outer Máni's most photogenic harbour. It has four tavernas and the closest beach is at **Agios Dimítrios**, 3 km (2 miles) further south.

Mount Taÿgetos

The distinctive pyramidal summit and knife-edged ridge of Mount Taÿgetos, standing at 2,404 m (7,887 ft), divides the regions of Messinía and Lakonía. Formed of limestone and densely clad in black pine and fir, the range is the watershed of the region and

Taÿgetos, seen through the Vyrós Gorge

offers several days of wilderness trekking to experienced, well-equipped mountaineers.

Anavrytí and Palaiopanagiá, on the east, and Pigádia and Kardamýli, on the west, are the usual trailhead villages.

Various traverses can be made by using the Vyrós and Ríntomo gorges which drain west from the main ridge; an unstaffed alpine refuge at Varvára-Deréki, above Anavrytí village, is the best starting point for those wanting to head straight for the summit.

The ridge of Mount Taÿgetos with an olive grove in the foreground

Ⓐ Inner Máni

Μέσα Μάνη

Inner, or Lakonian, Máni is divided into two regions – the "Shadowed", western flank and the "Sunward", eastern shore. The former is famous for its numerous caves and churches, the latter for its villages which perch dramatically on crags overlooking the sea. With its era of martial glory over (*see p198*), Inner Máni is severely depopulated, its only future being as a holiday venue. Retired Athenians of Mániot descent have restored the famous towers as hunting lodges for the brief autumn shoot of quail and turtle dove.

Gýtheio

The lively town of Gýtheio is the gateway to the Máni peninsula and one of the most attractive coastal towns in the southern Peloponnese. It was once the naval base of ancient Sparta (*see p193*), though the main ancient relic is a Roman theatre to the north. The town was wealthy in Roman times, when it exported the purple molluscs used for colouring imperial togas. Until World War II, Gýtheio exported acorns used in leather-tanning, gathered by women and children from nearby valleys.

The town's heart is Plateía Mavromicháli, with the quay extending to either side lined by tiled, 19th-century houses. The east-facing town enjoys sunrises over Cape Maléas and the Lakonian Gulf while snowy Mount Taÿgetos looms beyond a low ridge to the north.

In the bay, and linked to the waterfront by a causeway, lies the islet of Marathonísi, thought to be Homer's Kranaï islet. It was here that Paris of Troy and Helen spent their first night together (*see p56*). It is dominated by the Tzanetakis tower, a crenellated 18th-century fortress which now houses the **Museum of the Máni**. The subject of the exploration of the Máni in medieval times is covered on the ground floor, while the exhibits of the upper storey place the tower houses in their social context.

VISITORS' CHECKLIST

Practical Information
Peloponnese. Road map C5.
🛈 Gýtheio (27330 29032).
Museum of the Máni: Marathonísi
Islet. **Tel** 27330 22676. **Open**
9am–3pm daily. 🅿 Pýrgos
Diroú Caves: 12 km (7 miles)
S of Areópoli. **Tel** 27330 52222.
Open 8:30am–3pm Tue–Sun
(Jun–Sep: to 5:30pm daily). 🅿

Transport
🚌 Gýtheio. 🚌 Areópoli.

Environs

Standing 12 km (7 miles) to the southwest, the **Castle of Passavá** was built in 1254 by the Frankish de Neuilly clan to guard a defile between Kelefá and Oítylo. Its name stems from *passe avant*, the clan's motto, though the present building is an 18th-century Ottoman construction. The Turks left the castle in 1780 after Tzanetbey Grigorákis avenged the murder of his uncle by massacring 1,000 Muslim villagers inside. Today's overgrown ruins are best approached from the southwest.

Areópoli

The Mavromichális (*see p198*) stronghold of Tsímova was renamed Areópoli, "the city of Ares" (god of war), for its role in the War of Independence (*see p44*); it was here that the Mániot uprising against the Ottomans was proclaimed by Pétros Mavromichális. Now the main town of the Shadowed Máni, its central old quarter features two 18th-century churches: **Taxiarchón** boasts the highest bell tower in the Máni, as well as zodiacal apse reliefs, while **Agios Ioánnis**, adorned with naive frescoes, was the chapel of the Mavromichális.

Environs

Ottoman **Kelefá Castle**, standing 10 km (6 miles) north of Areópoli, is the second castle guarding the Máni. It was built in 1670 to command the bays of Oítylo and Liméni and counter the impending Venetian invasion (*see p42*). The bastions of the pentagonal curtain walls are

19th-century houses lining the harbour of Gýtheio

◀ Semi-ruined tower houses of Vátheia village, the architectural jewel of the Máni preserved. The castle can be reached from the Areópoli–Gýtheio road (signposted) and from a footpath from Oítylo.

Pýrgos Diroú Caves

This cave system is one of the largest and most colourful in Greece. During summer, crowds take a 30-minute punt ride along the underground stream which passes through Glyfáda cavern, reflecting the overhanging stalactites. A 15-minute walk then leads to the exit. A nearby chamber, called Alepótrypa cave, is drier but just as spectacular with waterfalls and a lake. Until an earthquake closed the entrance, the cave was home to Neolithic people, and a separate **museum** chronicles their life and death.

The Shadowed Coast

Between Pýrgos Diroú and Geroliménas lies the 17-km (10.5-mile) shore of the Shadowed Coast. Once one of the most densely populated regions of the Máni, it is famous for its numerous Byzantine churches built between the 10th and 14th centuries. The ruins of many Mániot tower houses can also be found.

Among the finest churches is 11th-century **Taxiarchón**, at Charoúda, with its interior covered by vivid 18th-century frescoes. Heading south, the road continues to **Agios Theódoros**, at Vámvaka,

Corner turret of Ottoman Kelefá Castle, near Areópoli

where the dome is supported by carved beams; birds bearing grapes adorn its marble lintel.

Káto Gardenítsa boasts the 12th-century **Metamórfosi tou Sotíros**, with frescoes spanning five centuries, while the 12th-century **Episkopí**, near Stavrí, has a complete cycle of 18th-century frescoes.

Near Ano Mpoulárioi village, **Agios Panteleímon** offers 10th-century frescoes (the earliest and the most primitive in the Máni), while in the village, the 11th-century **Agios Stratigós** bears a set of 12th- and 13th-century frescoes – the *Acts of Christ* is the most distinguished.

Vátheia, 10 km (6 miles) east of Geroliménas, is one of the most dramatically located of the villages; overlooking the sea and Cape Taínaro, its bristling tower houses constitute a showpiece of local architectural history.

Tower houses of Vátheia village, viewed from the southeast

For hotels and restaurants see pp270–71 and pp287–8

㉖ Koróni
Κορώνη

Peloponnese. **Road map** C5.
🏛 1,400. 🚌

One of the "eyes of Venice"
(along with Methóni), Koróni
surveys the shipping lanes
between the Adriatic and
Crete. It stands at the foot of a
Venetian castle, begun in 1206,
whose walls now shelter the
huge **Timíou Prodrómou**
convent. A Byzantine chapel
and foundations of an Artemis
temple stand by the gate of
the convent whose cells and
chapels command fine views.
   The town, lying beneath the
castle and divided by stepped
streets, dates to 1830. Little has
changed here and many houses
retain elaborate wrought-iron
balconies, horizontal-slat shutters
and tile "beaks" on the undulating
roofs. A lively seafront is the sole
concession to tourism.

㉗ Methóni
Μεθώνη

Peloponnese. **Road map** B5.
🏛 1,300. 🚌

Methóni, a key Venetian port,
controlled the lucrative pilgrim
trade to Palestine after 1209.
With the sea on three sides, its
rambling **castle** is defended on
its landward side by a Venetian
moat, bridged by the French in
1828. The structure combines
Venetian, Ottoman and even
French military architecture. The
remains within the walls include
two ruined *hamams* (baths), a
Venetian church, minaret bases

Battle of Navaríno

An unexpected naval engagement which decided the War of
Independence *(see pp44–5)*, the Battle of Navaríno took place on
20 October 1827. Victory here by the French, Russian and English
allies over the Ottoman fleet broke the Greek-Ottoman deadlock
and resolved the problem of the sultan's refusal of an armistice. The
allied fleet of 27 ships, commanded by admirals Codrington, de Rigny
and Heyden, entered Navaríno Bay where Ibrahim Pasha's armada
of 89 lay anchored. The outnumbered allies merely intended to
intimidate Ibrahim into leaving the bay, but were fired upon, and a
full-scale battle ensued. By nightfall, three-quarters of the Ottoman
fleet was sunk, with negligible allied casualties; Greek independence
was now inevitable. The admirals are honoured by an obelisk in their
namesake square (Tríon Navárchon) in Pýlos.

The dramatic *Battle of Navaríno*, painted by Louis Ambroise Garneray (1783–1857)

and the main street. Boúrtzi, an
islet fortified by the Turks, stands
beyond the Venetian sea-gate.

🏰 **Castle**
Open 8:30am–3pm daily.
Tel 27230 28759.

㉘ Pýlos
Πύλος

Peloponnese. **Road map** C5.
🏛 2,500. 🚌

The town of Pýlos, originally
known as Avaríno (later
Navaríno) after the Avar tribes
which invaded the area in the
6th century, is French in design,

like Methóni. Life is confined
to Plateía Trión Navárchon and
the seafront on either side.
   To the west, the castle of
Niókastro, Ottoman and
Venetian in origin, was
extensively repaired by the
French after 1828; their barracks
are now a gallery of antiquarian
engravings by the artist René
Puaux (1878–1938). An institute
of underwater archaeology is
situated in the former dungeons
of the hexagonal keep. The
roof gives views over the outer
bailey, immense Navaríno Bay
and Sfaktiría island, site of a
memorable Athenian victory
over the Spartans in 425 BC.

The fortified islet of Boúrtzi, off the coast at Methóni, with its 16th-century octagonal tower

The former mosque, now Metamórfosi tou Sotíros church, Pýlos

The perimeter walls are dilapidated, but it is possible to walk along the parapet, starting from the imposing west bastion overlooking the mouth of the bay, and finishing above the east gate. The domed and arcaded church of **Metamórfosi tou Sotíros**, once a mosque, is the only medieval survival in the outer bailey.

Niókastro
Town centre. **Tel** 27230 22010. **Open** 8am–3pm Tue–Sun. **Closed** main public hols. limited.

Environs
Boat tours visit a number of memorials on and around **Sfaktiría**, which commemorate those sailors lost in the Battle of Navaríno, foreign philhellenes and revolutionary heroes.

The north end of Navaríno Bay, 11 km (7 miles) north of Pýlos, has excellent beaches, especially **Voïdokoiliá** lagoon, where Telemachos, Odysseus's son, disembarked to seek news of his father from King Nestor. You can walk up the dunes to **Spiliá tou Néstora**, an impressively large cave, which may have been the inspiration for Homer's cave in which Nestor and his father Neleus kept their cows. A more strenuous path continues to Palaiókastro, the ancient acropolis and Franco-Venetian castle, built on Mycenaean foundations.

29 Nestor's Palace
Ανάκτορο του Νέστορα

16 km (10 miles) NE of Pýlos, Peloponnese. **Road map** B5. Site: **Tel** 27630 31437. **Closed** for renovation; may open in 2018. Museum **Tel** 27630 31358. **Open** 8:30am–3pm Tue–Sun. **Closed** public hols. limited.

Discovered in 1939, the 13th-century BC palace of Mycenaean King Nestor was excavated by Carl Blegen from 1952. Hundreds of tablets in the ancient Linear B script were found, as well as a bathtub and olive oil jugs (the contents of which fuelled the devastating fire of 1200 BC). Today, only waist-high walls and column bases suggest the typical Mycenaean plan of a two-storey complex around a central hall. The overstuffed **museum**, 3 km (2 miles) away in Chóra, has gold tomb finds from Peristéria village.

30 Ancient Messene
Αρχαία Μεσσήνη

34 km (21 miles) NW of Kalamáta, Peloponnese. **Road map** C5. **Tel** 27240 51201. Site: **Open** 8am–8pm daily (Nov–Mar: 9am–4pm daily). Museum: **Open** 9am–4pm daily. **Closed** main public hols.

Ancient Messene is now confusingly known as Ithómi – named after the mountain that sits overhead. It is an underrated, intriguing site, still undergoing excavation. The city walls are 9 km (6 miles) long and date from the 4th century BC. They enclose a vast area that incorporates the foundations of a Zeus temple, and the acropolis on Mount Ithómi to the northeast. The massive, double Arcadia Gate situated on the north side is flanked by square towers.

The archaeological zone includes the picturesque village of Mavrommáti, whose water is still supplied by the ancient Klepsýdra fountain at the heart of the site. Below the village, you will find an odeion (amphitheatre), a *bouleuterion* (council hall), stoas and a monumental stairway, all of which surround the foundations of an Asklepios temple. Just a little way further down the hill from here lies a well-preserved stadium.

Remains of the Arcadia Gate, with its fallen lintel, Ancient Messene

CENTRAL AND WESTERN GREECE

EPIRUS · THESSALY · STEREÁ ELLÁDA

Central and Western Greece encompasses many of the lesser-known regions of mainland Greece and is, therefore, less affected by tourism. Though the isolation of Epirus has produced a distinctive and largely autonomous culture, Stereá Elláda has always been of strategic importance, with the pass at Thermopylae and the Vale of Tempe providing invasion routes into the very heart of Greece.

This region of Greece is dominated by the central plain of Thessaly (the former bed of an inland sea), and the sights of interest lie largely on the periphery. Isolated by the Píndos mountains, the Epirus region, to the west, has the strongest of regional identities, having played a minor role in ancient Greece and maintained a large degree of autonomy under the Ottomans. The regional capital, Ioánnina, is thus a fascinating mixture of different architecture and the local traditions of silversmithing and woodcarving.

East of Métsovo, the Egnatía Odós motorway becomes an old road down a steep valley that provides access to the Byzantine Metéora monasteries which soar on the summits of the area's steeply eroded pinnacles.

On the far side of the Thessalian plain, Mount Pílion has forested slopes, charming villages and some of the mainland's best beaches, especially those on the Aegean Sea. In Stereá Elláda, one of Greece's main ancient sights, the ruins of the Delphic Oracle, stands only a short drive away from the Monastery of Osios Loukás, perhaps the finest of late Byzantine buildings, decorated with mosaics.

The Gulf of Corinth has lovely, historic ports at Galaxídi, Náfpaktos and Mesolóngi. Inland towns like Tríkala, Lamía and Arta, while making fewer concessions to tourism, prove of equal interest.

Megálo Pápigko, one of the many remote, once-isolated villages of Zagóri in the Epirus region

◄ The 18th-century Misíou bridge over the Víkos Gorge, Epirus

Exploring Central and Western Greece

Stretching from Attica in the south to Macedonia in the north, the vast expanse of Central and Western Greece has a little of everything, from excellent beaches to the venerable towns of Ioánnina and Métsovo with their craftsmen's guilds and Ottoman heritage. The Pílio offers the best combination of scenery and coastal resorts, while no one should miss the two prime attractions of Ancient Delphi, site of the oracle of Apollo, and the Byzantine splendour of the monasteries of Metéora. Walkers should head north where, in addition to the Víkos Gorge, the Píndos Mountains have several of Greece's highest peaks. The flora and fauna are both splendid here, especially in spring, but wildlife enthusiasts should not miss the wonderful wetlands around Mesolóngi and the beautiful Amvrakikós Gulf, near Arta.

Key

═══ Motorway

= = Road under construction

━━ Major road

┄┄┄ Minor road

━━ Scenic route

╍╍ Main railway

▬▬▬ National border

▬▬▬ Regional border

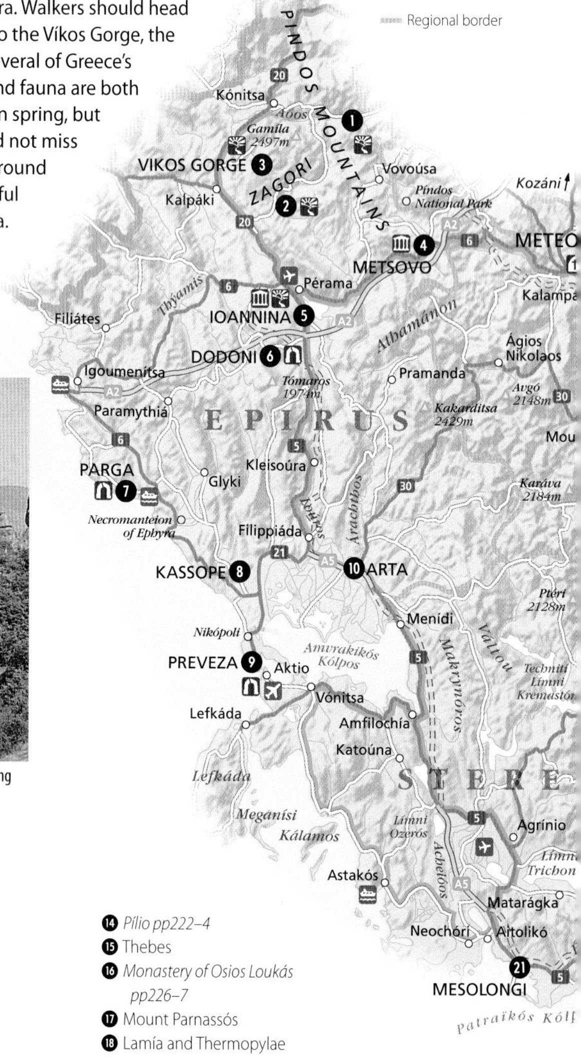

Agíou Nikoláou, one of Metéora's soaring monasteries

Sights at a Glance

1. Píndos Mountains
2. Zagóri
4. Métsovo
5. Ioánnina
6. Dodóni
7. Párga
8. Kassope
9. Préveza
10. Arta
11. *Metéora pp220–21*
12. Tríkala
13. Vale of Tempe
14. *Pílio pp222–4*
15. Thebes
16. *Monastery of Osios Loukás pp226–7*
17. Mount Parnassós
18. Lamía and Thermopylae
19. *Ancient Delphi pp232–5*
20. Gulf of Corinth
21. Mesolóngi

Walks

3. Víkos Gorge

For hotels and restaurants see pp271–2 and pp288–90

Doric columns of the Temple of Apollo, Delphi

Locator Map

Getting Around

There are domestic airports at Préveza, which receives European charter flights in summer, and Ioánnina. Internal flights are fairly inexpensive if travelling from another part of Greece, but within the region, a car is by far the best way to travel. Central Greece's main roads are generally good, though twisting mountain routes can make journeys longer than they seem on the map. Motorways link the west coast with Métsovo, and Thíva with the Vale of Tempe, while an express train connects the Metéora with Athens. Bus connections are good between major towns, with services to smaller villages.

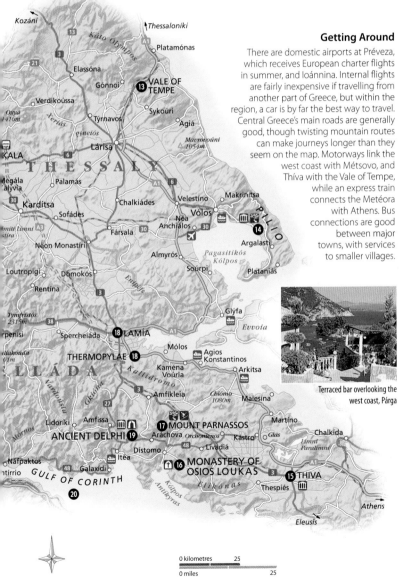

Terraced bar overlooking the west coast, Párga

0 kilometres   25

0 miles   25

For keys to symbols *see back flap*

The Aóös River, flowing through the Píndos Mountains

❶ Píndos Mountains

Οροσειρά Πίνδου

Epirus. **Road map** B2. ✈ 🚌 Ioánnina. ℹ Dodónis 39, Ioánnina (26510 41868). **Open** 8am–3pm Mon–Fri.

The Píndos is a vast range stretching from the Greek border with Albania south to the Corinth Gulf. It extends east into Macedonia, and west towards the Ionian Sea, incorporating two national parks, Greece's second longest gorge and its second highest mountain, Oros Smólikas, standing at 2,637 m (8,652 ft). The Píndos National Park lies entirely within Epirus, between Métsovo and Vovoúsa, while the Víkos-Aóös National Park is a boot-shaped area encompassing the Víkos Gorge *(see p212)* and the Aóös River.

The peaks are snow-covered from November until May, when the melting snows water the ground, producing swathes of purple crocus, gentians, grass-of-Parnassus and many species of orchid *(see p27)*. The protection offered by the parks provides the visitor with an increased chance of seeing roe deer, wild boar and the European wild cat, all of which exist in small numbers.

Smólikas is accessible during summertime for those who are well equipped and prepared for camping out. Slightly easier to reach from the fascinating Zagorian villages via the Víkos Gorge are Gamíla 2,497 m (8,192 ft) and Astráka 2,436 m (7,992 ft), while the two mountain lakes both called Drakolímni are each worth the effort it takes to get to them. One is below Gamíla, near a sheer drop to the Aóös River, while the other stands beneath Smólikas.

Although there are good walking guides and maps of the area, with one wardened mountain hut to stay in and accommodation in most larger villages, visitors should not venture into the mountains unless they are experienced walkers. The weather can change quickly, and in many places you will be a long way from any kind of settlement – though this is one of the main attractions of the Píndos Mountains. They show the rugged side of Greece, offering remote valleys and routes where few visitors venture.

Wildlife of the Píndos Mountains

Visitors to the coastal lowlands are often sceptical when told that wolves and bears still survive in Greece. However, despite the severe degradation of their natural habitat over the last 20 years, both European wolves and European brown bears can be found. The Píndos mountains, and particularly the northern regions towards Albania, continue to harbour the greatest numbers of these endangered and now protected creatures. They are extremely wary of man, having been persecuted by farmers and goatherds down the centuries. Therefore, visitors should consider themselves very fortunate if they see a bear. Wolves are just as hard to see but more evident, as they can often be heard howling at dawn and dusk, and will even respond to imitations of their howls. They pose no real threat to visitors, but are resented locally for eating sheep.

The silver European wolf, a native of the region

One of the 120 European brown bears of the northern Píndos

❷ Zagóri

Ζαγόρι

Epirus. **Road map** B2.

Some of Europe's most spectacular scenery can be found only 25 km (15 miles) north of Ioánnina *(see p214)*, in the area known as Zagóri. Though the soil is largely uncultivable, on the steep hillsides, some 45 traditional Epirot villages still survive; many of them boast imposing *archontiká* (mansions) dating to prosperous 18th- and 19th-century Ottoman times when Zagóri was granted autonomy.

Aroman and Sarakatsan shepherds *(see p213)* make up most of the settled population. Over the winter months, the shepherds used to turn to crafts, forming into guilds of itinerant masons and wood-carvers, who would travel the Balkans selling their trades. This hard and ancient way of life has effectively vanished, as the villagers, and especially the younger generation, prefer to earn their living from tourism.

A series of arched packhorse bridges are among the most memorable monuments to the skills of the local people and are unique features of the region. Two especially fine examples

Vítsa village, by the Víkos Gorge

can be seen at either end of the village of **Kípoi**. Southwestern Zagóri is the busiest area, with a bus from Ioánnina to Monodéndri and **Vítsa** bringing in walkers and climbers. Some of the villages in the east of the region, such as **Vrysochóri**, were refuges for guerrillas during World War II and therefore burnt by the Germans; they have never really recovered.

Near the almost deserted village of **Vradéto**, a 15th-century muletrack zigzags its way up a steep rockface beyond which the path leads to a stunning view of

the spectacular Víkos Gorge *(see p212)*. **Monodéndri**, opposite Vradéto, is the usual starting point for the gorge trail, though another path can be taken from Vítsa. At the far end of the gorge are the villages of **Megálo Pápigko** and **Mikró Pápigko**. They are 4 km (2 miles) apart and their names reflect their sizes, but even "big" Pápigko is no more than a scattering of houses around cobbled streets, with a choice of restaurants, and rooms available in renovated mansions.

Further southeast, though still surrounded by mountains, is the relatively thriving village of **Tsepélovo**. It has a bus service to Ioánnina and many restored mansions providing accommodation, as well as cafés and tavernas. Its cobbled streets and schist-roofed houses provide a perfect portrait of a Zagorian village.

Packhorse bridge near the village of Kípoi

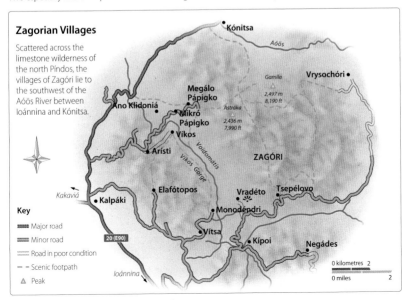

Zagorian Villages

Scattered across the limestone wilderness of the north Píndos, the villages of Zagóri lie to the southwest of the Aóös River between Ioánnina and Kónitsa.

Kónitsa

Aóös

Gamíla
2,497 m
8,190 ft

Vrysochóri

Megálo Pápigko

Áno Klidoniá

Astráka
2,436 m
7,990 ft

Mikró Pápigko

Víkos

Vïdomátis

Arísti

Víkos Gorge

ZAGÓRI

Kakaviá

Kalpáki

Elafótopos

Vradéto

Tsepélovo

Monodéndri

Key

▬▬ Major road

▬▬ Minor road

═══ Road in poor condition

– – Scenic footpath

△ Peak

20 (E90)

Ioánnina

Vítsa

Kípoi

Negádes

0 kilometres 2

0 miles 2

❾ Víkos Gorge Walk

To trek the length of the Víkos Gorge is to undertake what is arguably the greatest walk in Greece, between deeply eroded limestone walls rising to 915 m (3,000 ft). The gorge cuts through the Víkos-Aóös National Park, established in 1975. Cairns and waymarks define the official O3 long-distance route which snakes through the boulder-strewn ravine bed and continues up through stands of beech, chestnut and maple to the higher ground. Egyptian vultures can be seen circling in the thermals, and lizards and tortoises abound. The walk begins at Monodéndri or Vítsa. Landslides and lack of maintenance make the route challenging, and only experienced hikers should attempt it. A shorter 4-km (2-mile) walk between the northern villages of Mikró Pápigko and Víkos passes Panagía Chapel.

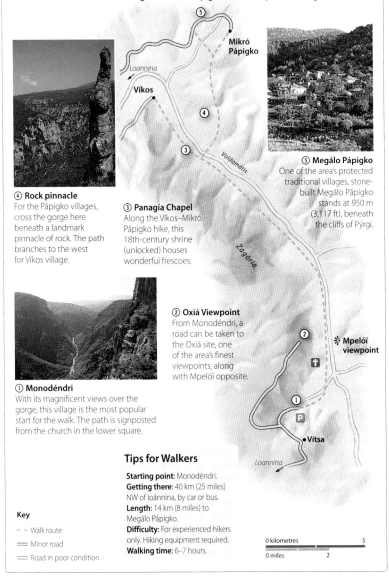

④ **Rock pinnacle**
For the Pápigko villages, cross the gorge here beneath a landmark pinnacle of rock. The path branches to the west for Víkos village.

③ **Panagía Chapel**
Along the Víkos–Mikró Pápigko hike, this 18th-century shrine (unlocked) houses wonderful frescoes.

⑤ **Megálo Pápigko**
One of the area's protected traditional villages, stone-built Megálo Pápigko stands at 950 m (3,117 ft), beneath the cliffs of Pýrgi.

① **Monodéndri**
With its magnificent views over the gorge, this village is the most popular start for the walk. The path is signposted from the church in the lower square.

② **Oxiá Viewpoint**
From Monodéndri, a road can be taken to the Oxiá site, one of the area's finest viewpoints, along with Mpelói opposite.

Mpelói viewpoint

Tips for Walkers

Starting point: Monodéndri.
Getting there: 40 km (25 miles) NW of Ioánnina, by car or bus.
Length: 14 km (8 miles) to Megálo Pápigko.
Difficulty: For experienced hikers only. Hiking equipment required.
Walking time: 6–7 hours.

Key

– – Walk route
═══ Minor road
═══ Road in poor condition

0 kilometres   5
0 miles   2

❹ Métsovo

Μέτσοβο

Epirus. Road map: B2. 🚠 3,500. 🚌
ℹ️ 26560 41233.

Situated below the now disused Katára Pass (the traditional crossing of the Píndos Mountains), Métsovo has a vitality unique among Greek mountain towns. It was originally a small village inhabited by Aroman shepherds, but it became one of the region's most important commercial centres after being granted tax privileges in return for guarding the pass during Ottoman times (*see pp42–3*). Local merchant families invested their new wealth in the town and continue to do so today by providing endowments and grants to encourage industry among the local craftspeople.

One such family was the Tosítsas, and some idea of the size of their wealth can be gained by touring the rebuilt 18th-century **Métsovo Folk Art Museum**. Rising to three floors, the mansion contains an armoury and washroom on the ground floor, with huge wood-panelled reception rooms and bedrooms upstairs, carpeted with beautiful, locally woven *kilim* rugs. Intricate gold- and

Shepherds' crooks, rugs and silverware in a souvenir shop in Métsovo

silverware are on display, as well as collections of traditional Epirot costumes and ornate embroidery. Would-be visitors must wait outside for the half-hourly guided tour.

Another of Métsovo's benefactors was the writer and politician Evángelos Avéroff (1910–90), who founded the **Avéroff Museum**. The core of the gallery is Avéroff's own collection of some 200 paintings and sculptures he acquired over

Interior of the Folk Art Museum, Métsovo

the years, always with the ambition of opening a museum of modern Greek art in his home town. His collection has been expanded to show the work of several dozen Greek artists from the 19th and 20th centuries.

Ancient traditions have survived in the area, from the simple craft of carving shepherds' crooks (from the town's sheep farming days) to embroidery and wine- and cheese-making. Some of the older men (and a few women) still wear traditional costumes; you can see them, dressed in black, sitting in the shelters and cafés around the town square. The shelters are needed during winter when the town, at 1,156 m (3,793 ft), becomes a popular ski resort. The rugs on sale in the souvenir shops also reflect this alpine character.

🏛 **Métsovo Folk Art Museum**
Off main thoroughfare. **Tel** 26560 41084. **Open** 9am–1:30pm & 4–6pm (3–5pm in winter) Fri–Wed. ♿
Ⓦ metsovomuseum.gr

🏛 **Avéroff Museum**
Off central square. **Tel** 26560 41210. **Open** 10am–4pm (to 6:30pm mid-Jul–mid-Sep) Wed–Mon. ♿
Ⓦ averoffmuseum.gr

Environs
Fifteen minutes' walk south, signposted from the centre of town, stands the small and charming 14th-century **Moní Agíou Nikoláou**. Today, it is inhabited only by caretakers who are more than happy to show visitors the church's vivid post-Byzantine frescoes, the monks' living quarters and their own supplies of flowers, fruit and vegetables.

Aroman Shepherds

Of unknown origin, the nomadic Aroman shepherds are today centred in the Píndos Mountains, particularly in and around Métsovo. Their language, which has no written form, is a dialect of Latin origin, and it is thought that they might be descended from Roman settlers who moved through Illyria into the northern Balkans. Traditionally, their way of life has been transhumant – spending summers in the mountains before moving down to the plains of Thessaly with their sheep for six months to avoid the worst of the winter snows. It is a hard way of life which is gradually disappearing, and the shepherds who remain can be found in such villages as Métsovo and Vovoúsa in Epirus, and Avdélla, Samarína and Smíxi in western Macedonia – their traditional summer settlements. Their winter homes lie mainly around Kastoriá (*see p244*).

Zagorian Aroman shepherd

For hotels and restaurants see pp271–2 and pp288–90

⑤ Ioánnina

Ιωάννινα

The capital of the Epirus region, Ioánnina prospered during Ottoman times *(see pp42–3)* when its famous craftsmen's guilds, including the silversmiths', were formed. The Turkish influence is most visible in the fortress area which extends on a small headland into Lake Pamvótis (it was once moated on its landward side). Though dating to the 13th century, the area was rebuilt in 1815 by Ali Pasha, the Albanian Muslim tyrant most closely associated with it. Inside the fortress precinct, a village-like peace reigns, though the bustle of the bazaar and the modern area is a reminder that this is still the region's busiest city.

Aslan Pasha Mosque, housing the Municipal Ethnographic Museum

Ioánnina and the isle of Nisí, seen from the north

🏛 Municipal Ethnographic Museum

Aslan Pasha Mosque. **Tel** 26510 26356.
Open: summer: 8am–8pm daily; winter: 8am–3pm Mon–Fri, 9am–5pm Sat & Sun. **Closed** main pub hols. 🖼

At the northern corner of the fortress, this small museum is housed within a mosque built by Aslan Pasha in 1618. While the mosque itself, which retains original decoration on its dome, is worth a visit, the weapons and costumes on display tell something of Ioánnina's recent past. Ottoman furniture inlaid with mother-of-pearl can also be found, alongside Jewish rugs and tapestries.

🏛 Byzantine Museum

Inner Fortress. **Tel** 26510 25989.
Open Jun–Sep: 8am–8pm Tue –Sun, 1:30–8pm Mon; Oct–May: 8am–5pm. **Closed** main public hols. 🖼

This modern museum contains a few items from local archaeological excavations, but the core is an imaginative display of icons from the 16th to the 19th centuries. Silverware, for which the town is renowned, is displayed in a separate annexe, once the treasury, with a reconstruction of a typical silversmith's workshop.

🏛 Archaeological Museum

Plateía 25 Martíou 6. **Tel** 26510 01051. **Open** 9am–4pm Tue–Sun. 🖼 ♿

Set in a small park, this museum displays various artifacts that include items from the site of Dodóni. Among these is a bronze eagle from the 5th century BC, statuettes of young children and lead tablets inscribed with questions for the oracle.

🏛 Folklore Museum

Michaíl Angélou 42. Tel 26510 20515. **Open** 9am–2pm Tue–Sat (also 5:30–8pm Wed & Sat). **Closed** main public hols. 🖼

Housed in a mansion, this museum has a collection of local crafts. As well as silverwork and traditional costumes, there are woven textiles made by the traditionally nomadic, but now sedentary, Sarakatsans, long rivals of the more numerous Aroman tribe *(see p213)*.

Ali Pasha

Ali Pasha was born in Albanian Tepelene in 1741 and, in 1788, installed himself at Ioánnina as Pasha of Epirus. Though a murderer, he was a great administrator who made the town one of the richest in Greece. His aim was to gain independence from his overlords and by 1820, he had an empire stretching from Albania to the Peloponnese. Once the Greek War of Independence was launched, it became imperative to quash this renegade, and Sultan Mahmud II of Turkey dispatched troops to put him to death. After a long siege within the fortress at Ioánnina, Ali Pasha was lured from the safety of his citadel to the island of Nisí where, on 24 January 1822, he was trapped and killed.

Tapestry of Ali Pasha (centre), Moní Agíou Panteleímonos, Nisí

🚢 Nisí
15 minutes by boat NE from Mólos
quay.

Though its first inhabitants were
the monks who came here in the
early 13th century, the single
village on the isle of Nisí owes
its existence to 17th-century
refugees from Mániot feuds *(see
p198)*. Its main building is Moní
Agíou Panteleímonos, where the
reconstructed room in which Ali
Pasha was shot can be visited,
the bullet holes still visible in
the floor. Other rooms contain
a few of his possessions, some
costumes and period prints.

Stalactites in the Pérama Caves

Environs
Greece's largest cave network,
the **Pérama Caves**, are near the
village of Pérama, 4 km (2 miles)
north of Ioánnina. They were
discovered in 1940 by a shepherd
hiding from the Germans, but
only fully explored years later.
Now, there are regular guided
tours taking visitors along the
1,700 m (5,600 ft) of passages,
where multicoloured lights
pick out the dramatic stalactites
and stalagmites.

🚢 Pérama Caves
Pérama. **Tel** 26510 81521.
Open 9am–sunset daily. 📷

The theatre of Dodona, one of the largest in Greece

6 Ancient Dodona
Δωδώνη

Epirus. **Road map** B2. **Tel** 26510
82287. 🚌 **Open** 8am–3pm Tue–Sun.
Closed main public hols. 📷 free on
Sun. ♿

Dating to at least 1,000 BC,
the Oracle of Zeus at Dodona
is the oldest in Greece and was
second in status only to the
one at Delphi *(see pp232–5)*.
The site is located 22 km
(14 miles) southwest of
Ioánnina in a placid green
valley on the northeastern
slopes of Mount Tómaros.

The oracle focused on a sacred
oak tree ringed with tripods
which held a number of bronze
cauldrons placed so that they
touched each other. Prophecies
were divined from the sound
these made, in harmony with
the rustling of the oak leaves,
when one of the cauldrons was
struck. Petitioners would inscribe
their questions on
lead tablets for the
priestess to read
to Zeus; some of
these have
been found on
the site and can
be seen in the
Archaeological
Museum in
Ioánnina. The
reputed power of
the oak tree was
such that Jason,
before his quest for the Golden
Fleece *(see p224)*, travelled across
from Iolkos (the predecessor
of Vólos) to acquire one of its
branches to attach to his ship,
the Argo. By the 3rd century BC,

a colonnaded courtyard was
built around the tree for
protection; it contained a
small temple of which only
foundations remain. The tree
was uprooted in AD 393 on the
orders of the Roman Emperor
Theodosios (ruled 379–395) in
accordance with his policy of
stamping out pagan practices.

The main feature of ancient
Dodona today is the theatre,
which, with its capacity for 17,000
spectators, is one of the largest in
Greece. Its walls rise to 21 m (69 ft)
and are supported by solid towers
where kestrels now nest. Used by
the ancient Greeks for dramatic
performances, the theatre was
later converted by the Romans
into an arena for animal fights;
bulls and big cats would have
been kept in the two triangular
pens on either side of the stage.
The whole structure was restored
from scattered rubble in the early
1960s but is now off limits to
visitors; summer drama
performances
are held in a
temporary stage
some distance
away. Dodona
also includes the
ruins of a stadium,
acropolis and
Byzantine basilica –
all reminders of
the time when
this valley was
the location of
a flourishing market town.

Dodona was abandoned
during the 6th century AD, when
the Byzantine Emperor Justinian
decided to found the more easily
defendable city of Ioánnina.

Justinian, the last Roman Emperor
to visit Dodona

The tiered, amphitheatre-shaped town of Párga, seen across Kryonéri Bay

❼ Párga
Πάργα

Epirus. **Road map** B3. 🏔 2,000.
🚌 ⛴ Tue.

Párga, the main beach resort of Epirus, is a busy holiday town whose charms are often overwhelmed by the number of summer visitors. The Venetian fortress dominating the west side of the harbour was built in the late 16th century on the site of a building destroyed in 1537 during a brief period of Turkish rule. The Ottomans later returned under the command of Ali Pasha *(see p214)*, who bought the town from the British in 1819. Párga's Christian inhabitants immediately fled to Corfu and Paxoí, though it was regained by the Greeks in 1913.

There are two small beaches within walking distance of the town centre and two larger ones about 2 km (1 mile) away: Váltos, the biggest, is to the north and Lychnos to the southwest. Fish restaurants line Párga's waterfront, affording fine views across the harbour to a group of small islands.

Environs
37 km (23 miles) south of Párga is the **Nekromanteion of Acheron** (Oracle of the Dead), the gateway to Hades, with steps leading to the vaults. In the 4th century BC, drugs and mechanisms may have heightened the sensation of entering the Underworld for visitors who sought advice from the dead.

🏛 Nekromanteion of Acheron
Open summer: 8am–8pm daily; winter: 8:30am–3pm daily. 🏞

❽ Kassope
Κασσώπη

Zálongo, Epirus. **Road map** B3. 🚌
Closed for renovation until 2018.

The Kassopeans were a tribe who lived in this region in the 4th century BC. The remains of their capital city stand on a hillside plateau overlooking the Ionian Sea, from where the island of Lefkáda is plainly visible. Kassope is reached by a walk through a pine grove from the car park. The nearest village is Kamarína.

Greek Orthodox priests in Párga

A site plan illustrates the layout of the once-great city, now the home of birds and lizards.

Just above the ruins is **Moní Zalóngou**, with its monument commemorating the women of Soúli, who threw themselves from the cliffs in 1803 rather than be captured by Albanian Muslim troops.

The remains of the ancient city of Kassope

❾ Préveza
Πρέβεζα

Epirus. **Road map** B3. 🏔 13,000.
✈ 🚌 🚌 🛈 Eleftheríou Venizélou (26820 21078). ⛴ daily (fish).

Often seen as a transit point, the charming town of Préveza repays a longer visit, particularly for the lively atmosphere of the tavernas in its pedestrianized marketplace. It is picturesquely situated on the northern shore of the narrow "Channel of Cleopatra", at the mouth of the Amvrakikós Gulf. It was here that the naval Battle of Actium was fought in 31 BC *(see p38)*.

Two ruined forts, on either side of the straits, recall the town's Venetian occupation in 1499, though in 1798 it passed, via the French, into the hands of Ali Pasha *(see p214)*.

Environs
Seven km (4 miles) north of Préveza stand the ruins of **Nikopolis** ("Victory City"), built by the Roman Emperor Octavian to celebrate his victory at Actium. Later sacked by the Goths, it was finally destroyed by the Bulgars in 1034. Remains include a theatre and the mosaics in the Dometios basilica. A **museum** illustrates Roman and early Christian life here.

Nikopolis
Tel 26820 89892. **Open** Summer: 8am–8pm daily; winter: 8:30am–3pm daily. Museum: summer: 8am–8pm daily; winter: 8:30am–3pm Sun–Fri. **Closed** main public hols. (museum only).

⑩ Arta
`Άρτα`

Epirus. **Road map** B3. 33,000. Krystalli Sq (26810 78551). **Open** 7am–3pm Mon–Fri. Mon–Sat (veg).

Though it is the second largest town in Epirus, after Ioánnina, Arta remains largely untouched by tourism. This traditional Greek market town has a lively, bazaar-like area, established by the Turks who occupied Arta from 1449 to 1881. The **fortress** dates from the 13th century, when the city was the capital of the despotate of Epirus. Stretching from Thessaloníki to Corfu, this was an independent Byzantine state set up after the fall of Constantinople in 1204 *(see p41)*.

Timber-framed houses in the Old Quarter of Tríkala

It lasted until the start of the Ottoman occupation. Some of the town's many 13th- and 14th-century Byzantine churches can be found in the streets near the fortress. The most striking is the **Panagía Parigorítissa**. Built between 1283 and 1296, it is a three-tier building topped with towers and domes. **Agía Theódora**, on Pýrrou, contains the marble tomb of the saintly wife of 13th-century Epirot ruler Michael II.

Approaching from the west, the main road into town crosses the river Arachthos by a 17th-century stone **bridge**. According to local folklore, the builder of the bridge, frustrated by each day's work being ruined by the river at night, was advised by a bird that the problem could be solved by putting his wife in the bridge's foundations. This he did, burying her alive, after which the bridge was successfully completed.

⑪ Metéora
See pp220–21.

⑫ Tríkala
Τρίκαλα

Thessaly. **Road map** C2. 68,000. Mon–Sat.

Tríkala was the home of Asklepios, the god of healing, and today is the market centre for the Metéora area. As such, it is a thriving town with a number of remains from its Ottoman past. One is the **bazaar** area north of the Lethaios River, which bisects the town; another the **Koursoúm (Osman Shah) Tzamí**, a graceful mosque built in 1550 on the south side of the river. Surrounding the **fortress** is the Old Quarter of Varósi. The fortress stands on the site of the ancient acropolis, which was built in the 4th century BC. It is situated in beautiful grounds overlooking the river.

⑬ Vale of Tempe
Κοιλάδα των Τεμπών

Thessaly. **Road map** C2.

As the E75 road approaches Macedonia, it follows the river Pineiós through the Vale of Tempe – the fertile valley where Apollo was said to have purified himself after slaying the serpent Python. Close to the **Wolf's Jaws** or **Lykostómio** (the narrowest point of the gorge) is the **Spring of Daphne**, where a bridge leads to the chapel of **Agía Paraskeví**, carved out of the rock. The impressive **Kástro of Platamónas** at the northern end of the Vale was built after 1204 by Frankish crusaders, atop a pre-existing fort to control the vital route into Thessaly from the north.

Kástro of Platamónas
Tel 23530 44470. **Open** 8:30am–3pm daily.

The arched packhorse bridge of Arta, leading into town from the west

⑪ Metéora

Μετέωρα

The natural sandstone towers of Metéora (or "suspended rocks") were first used as a religious retreat when, in AD 985, a hermit named Barnabas occupied a cave here. In the mid-14th century, Neílos, the Prior of Stagai convent, built a small church. Then, in 1382, the monk Athanásios, from Mount Athos, founded the huge monastery of Megálo Metéoro on one of the many pinnacles. Twenty-three monasteries followed, though most had fallen into ruin by the 19th century. In the 1920s, stairs were cut to make the remaining six monasteries more accessible, and today, a religious revival has seen the return of monks and nuns.

Location of Monasteries of Metéora

Rousánou

Moní Rousánou, perched precariously on the very tip of a narrow spire of rock, is the most spectacularly located of all the monasteries. Its church of the Metamórfosis (1545) is renowned for its harrowing frescoes, painted in 1560 by iconographers of the Cretan school.

KEY

① **Outer walls**

② **Monastic cells**

③ **The refectory** contains a small icon museum.

④ **Ascent Tower**, made in 1536, was used to winch up goods and people by a windlass mechanism.

⑤ **Net descending from tower**

Megálo Metéoro

Also known as the Great Meteoron, this was the first and, at 623 m (2,045 ft), highest monastery to be founded. By the entrance is a cave in which Athanásios first lived. His body is buried in the main church.

◀ Towering sandstone towers with Megálo Metéoro monastery in the foreground, Metéora

Varlaám

Founded in 1518, the monastery of Varlaám is named after the first hermit to live on this rock in 1350. The katholikón was built in 1542 and contains some frescoes by the Theban iconographer Frágkos Katelános.

Entrance

Agios Nikólaos Anapavsás
This monastery houses exceptionally vivid frescoes of 1527 by Theophanes the Cretan, including *Adam Naming the Animals*, *The Dormition of the Virgin* and *The Funeral of St Ephraim of Syria*.

The Building of the Monasteries

Though it is unknown how the first hermits reached the tops of these often vertical rock faces, it is likely that they hammered pegs into tiny gaps in the rock and hauled building materials to the summits. Another theory is that kites were flown over the tops, carrying strings attached to thicker ropes which were made into the first rope ladders.

⓮ Pílio
Πήλιο

The mythological home of the forest-loving centaurs, the Pílio peninsula, with its woods of chestnut, oak and beech, is one of the most beautiful regions of the mainland, and it is always several degrees cooler than the rest of Thessaly in summer. The mountain air is sweet with the scent of herbs which, in ancient times, were renowned for their healing powers. The area became populated in the 13th century by Greeks retreating from the Franks, who had occupied Constantinople, and it flourished, especially given limited autonomy during the 18th century, a time of improved conditions in the Ottoman Empire. But the thick stone walls and narrow windows of a typical Pílio house indicate how uncertain that autonomy really was.

Makrynítsa
Cars are banned from the steep cobbled streets of this traditional village *(see p224).*

Theophilos Hatzimihail

Born on Lésvos in 1873, Theophilos came to the Pílio in 1894 after reportedly killing a Turk in Smyrna. His favoured medium was the mural, though he also painted ceramics and the sides of fishing boats, *kafeneío* counters or horse carts when the mood struck him. He executed numerous mural commissions in the Pílio, notably at the Kontós mansion in Anakasiá. Though unhappily isolated, and mocked by the locals for his strange habits (he dressed in the costumes of his heroes, including Alexander the Great), he had a passion for all things Greek. After Lésvos's unification with Greece in 1912, he returned home destitute and ill. His fortunes changed after meeting his future patron Stratís Eleftheriádis, who provided for the painter's needs until Theophilos's death in 1934.

Konstantínos Palaiológos mural (1899) by Theophilos

Key

▰▰▰ Major road
▬▬▬ Minor road
═══ Non-asphalt road
- - - Ferry route

KEY

① **Vólos** is the capital of the region, straddling the only route into the peninsula. It has an excellent Archaeological Museum *(see p224).*

② **Anakasiá**, now little more than a suburb of Vólos, has a superb museum devoted to the Greek painter Theophilos Hatzimihail.

③ **Agios Ioánnis** has excellent white-sand beaches to either side.

④ **Tsagkaráda** is a delightful mountain village on wooded slopes. In its central square is the largest and oldest (1,000 years) plane tree in Greece.

Agía Kyriakí
Overlooked by the isolated hilltop village of Tríkeri, this small fishing port lacks a beach and hotels but has a working boatyard and good, simple fish tavernas for those very few visitors who take the trouble to travel here.

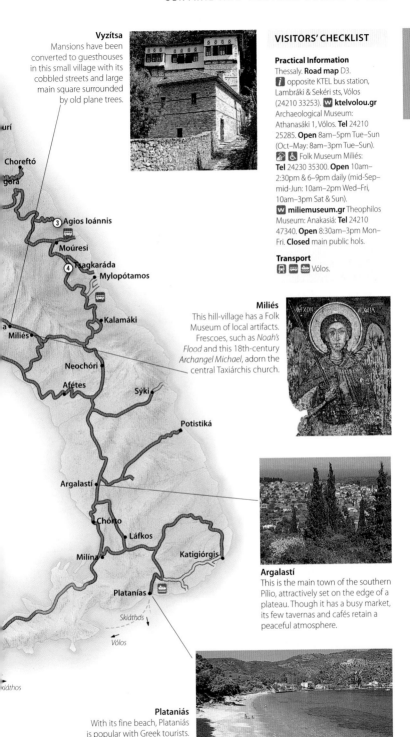

Vyzítsa
Mansions have been converted to guesthouses in this small village with its cobbled streets and large main square surrounded by old plane trees.

VISITORS' CHECKLIST

Practical Information
Thessaly. **Road map** D3.
🛈 opposite KTEL bus station, Lambráki & Sekéri sts, Vólos (24210 33253). 🆆 **ktelvolou.gr**
Archaeological Museum: Athanasáki 1, Vólos. **Tel** 24210 25285. **Open** 8am–5pm Tue–Sun (Oct–May: 8am–3pm Tue–Sun).
📷 ♿ Folk Museum Miliés: **Tel** 24230 35300. **Open** 10am–2:30pm & 6–9pm daily (mid-Sep–mid-Jun: 10am–2pm Wed–Fri, 10am–3pm Sat & Sun).
🆆 **miliemuseum.gr** Theophilos Museum: Anakasiá: **Tel** 24210 47340. **Open** 8:30am–3pm Mon–Fri. **Closed** main public hols.

Transport
🚆 🚌 ⛴ Vólos.

Miliés
This hill-village has a Folk Museum of local artifacts. Frescoes, such as *Noah's Flood* and this 18th-century *Archangel Michael*, adorn the central Taxiárchis church.

Argalastí
This is the main town of the southern Pílio, attractively set on the edge of a plateau. Though it has a busy market, its few tavernas and cafés retain a peaceful atmosphere.

Plataniás
With its fine beach, Plataniás is popular with Greek tourists. A number of fish tavernas provide excellent seafood.

Exploring the Pílio

Travelling by car, a circular tour of the northern villages can be made in a day following the road southeast from Vólos – first to Afétes, then north via Tsagkaráda. The hills in this region rise to 1,650 m (5,415 ft) at the summit of Mount Pílio, and in addition to dense woodlands, the area produces a large number of apples, pears, peaches and olives. While less dramatic, the southern, olive grove-covered Pílio is still hilly enough to ensure that many villages are at the end of "dead end" roads, making travel here time consuming.

Restored traditional mansions on the hillside of Makrynítsa

Vólos

Vólos is one of Greece's fastest growing industrial centres and, since it was devastated by earthquakes in the 1950s, it is difficult to imagine its mythological past. Once the site of ancient Iolkos, the home of Jason, who went in search of the Golden Fleece, Vólos's history is illustrated by what can be found in the excellent **Archaeological Museum**. The museum contains an extensive collection of painted funerary stelae from the 3rd century BC, found at Dimitriás on the far side of the

Gulf of Vólos. Collections of Neolithic pottery from the nearby sites of Sesklo and Dimini can also be found, and there is a room dedicated to the ancient games held in Thessaly, many of which involved horses.

Northern Villages

From Vólos, the road leads southeast, past Ano Lechónia, through the "Vólos Riviera", providing a circular route of the

mountainous northern Pílio. On weekends during summer, a traditional narrow-gauge train runs from Káto Lechónia to Miliés. From the popular inland resorts of **Miliés** and **Vyzítsa** (the latter preserved as a "traditional settlement" by the government), the road turns north past Tsagkaráda to **Agios Ioánnis**. This is the main resort of the east coast; the beaches of Papá Neró and Pláka are particularly fine and are both within easy walking distance. Some of the Pílio's best restaurants can be found in nearby villages.

Returning towards Vólos, take the turning to **Makrynítsa** – a traditional mountain village, regarded as the most important destination for any traveller of the area. Founded in the 13th century by refugees from the first sacking of Constantinople *(see p41)*, the village has beautiful churches, the most impressive being Agios Ioánnis and Panagía Makrynítissa. Many traditional mansions also survive, some functioning as guesthouses. Close to Agios Ioánnis, there is a café with an interior decorated with frescoes painted by the artist Theophilos *(see p222)*.

Anakasiá is the last village before Vólos and home to the delightful Theophilos Museum, which fills the entire Kontós Mansion with his frescoes of heroes and fantastic beasts.

Jason and the Argonauts

According to legend, the Golden Fleece came from a winged ram sent by Hermes, the gods' messenger, to protect two children, Helle and Phrixos, from their evil stepmother. Though Helle drowned, Phrixos was reared in Kolchis, in present-day Georgia, where the ram was sacrificed and its fleece given to the king, Aeëtes. Years later, Jason, Phrixos's cousin, set sail from the kingdom of Iolkos (now Vólos) after his half-brother usurped the throne. Jason was in search of the Fleece, which made its wearer invincible. With a crew of 50, Jason came to Kolchis where King Aeëtes set several tasks before relinquishing the Fleece. After falling in love with the king's daughter, Medea, Jason achieved his tasks and the Argonauts carried the Fleece back to Iolkos in triumph.

Detail from *The Golden Fleece* (c.1905) by Herbert Draper (1864–1920)

Fisherman with his nets at the waterfront, Vólos

Sarcophagus detail outside the
Archaeological Museum in Thíva

⓰ Thíva (Ancient Thebes)
Θήβα

Stereá Elláda. **Road map** D4.
🏙 20,000. 🚉 🚌

Although it was briefly the most powerful city of Greece, in the 4th century BC, the Thebes of today is little more than a quiet provincial town. It played an important role in the power struggles of Classical Greece, until defeated by Philip II of Macedon. Thebes' original acropolis has been built over through the years, but excavations have unearthed Mycenaean walls as well as jewellery, pottery and important tablets of Linear B script which are now in the **Archaeological Museum**. One of the highlights of the museum is the collection of Mycenaean sarcophagi, similar to those found on Crete. The museum's courtyard and well-tended garden stand alongside a 13th-century Frankish tower, all that remains of a castle ruined in 1311 by the Catalans.

A bridge over the river bed, a short walk eastwards from the museum, marks the traditional site of the Fountain of Oedipus,

where the legendary King Oedipus is said to have washed blood from his hands after unwittingly killing his father on his way to the city.

🏛 Archaeological Museum
Plateía Threpsiádou 1. **Tel** 22620 27913. **Closed** for renovation. 🎨 ♿

Environs
About 40 km (25 miles) north is ancient **Orchomenos**, among the wealthiest Mycenaean cities. Visible are a *tholos* tomb, the Treasury of Minyas (Tue–Sun), excavated by Schliemann, a theatre and the Byzantine Panagía Skrípous church.

⓰ Monastery of Osios Loukás
See pp226–7.

The Legend of Oedipus

According to legend, Oedipus was the ill-fated son of Laios and Iokaste, the king and queen of Thebes. Even before his birth, the Delphic Oracle *(see p232)* had foretold that he would kill his father and become his mother's husband. To defy the prophecy, Laios abandoned Oedipus, though the child was rescued and reared by the king and queen of Corinth whom Oedipus believed to be his real parents. Years later, when he heard of the prophecy, Oedipus fled to Thebes, killing a man on his way, unaware that he was King Laios. On reaching Thebes, he found the city gates barred by the Sphinx which he vanquished by solving one of its riddles. The Thebans made him their king and he married the widowed Iokaste. When the truth about his past was revealed, Oedipus blinded himself and spent his final days as an outcast.

Oedipus and the Sphinx, from
a 5th-century BC cup

⓰ Mount Parnassós
Όρος Παρνασσός

Stereá Elláda. **Road map** C3.
🚌 Delfoí. 🛈 Inside the town hall, Delfoí (22650 82900).
Open 8:30am–2:30pm daily.

Rising to a height of 2,457 m (8,061 ft), the limestone mass of Mount Parnassós dominates the eastern portion of Stereá Elláda. The lower slopes are covered with Cephalonian fir, and beneath them, in summer, the wildflower meadows burst into colour. Vultures and golden eagles are commonly spotted.

The village of **Aráchova** is the best base for exploring the area and is renowned for its wine, cheese, noodles and sheepskin rugs. There are many mountain trails for summer hikes, though a detailed walking map is recommended. Reaching the top of Liákoura, the highest peak, involves a long hike and camping overnight on the mountain.

From Aráchova, the two ski centres at **Kelária** and **Fterólakka** are only 23 km (14 miles) and 29 km (18 miles) away respectively. Usually open from mid-December to April, both resorts have top points of about 2,200 m (7,218 ft), served by 14 lifts, half of them bubble-chairs. Fterólakka offers longer, more challenging runs; however, high winds can close either centre at short notice.

Fir-covered foothills beneath the ridge of Mount Parnassós

⑯ Monastery of Osios Loukás

Μονή Οσίου Λουκά

Dedicated to a local hermit and healer, the Blessed Luke of Stíri, Osios Loukás monastery is one of medieval Greece's most important buildings. The first surviving church here was built in c.960 by Emperor Romanos II, who extended an earlier church from AD 944. The octagonal style of the main church became a hallmark of late Byzantine church design *(see pp24–5)*, while the mosaics inside lifted Byzantine art into its final great period. During the time of the Ottoman Empire *(see pp42–3)*, Osios Loukás witnessed a great deal of fighting, as the cannons in the courtyard testify. Here, in 1821, Bishop Isaias declared his support for the Greek freedom fighters.

The monastery seen from the west with the slopes of Mount Elikónas in the background

KEY

① **The narthex** is the western entrance hall; it contains a number of mosaics of Christ's Passion.

② **West portal**

③ **The exterior** is a mixture of dressed poros stone and red brick.

④ **The monastic cells** are small with arched roofs.

⑤ **The north transept** contains medallion-shaped mosaics of saints.

⑥ **Theotókos**, built almost a century before the main church, is a smaller chapel dedicated to the Mother of God; its name means "god-bearing".

⑦ **The apse** has a mosaic of the Virgin and Child pre-dating a devastating earthquake in 1659.

⑧ **The octagonal katholikón**, or main church, dates from around 1040.

⑨ **Frescoes**

⑩ **The refectory** was used as a workshop as well as for meals; it now contains a museum of Byzantine sculpture.

★ **Washing of the Apostles' Feet (Niptir)**
Based on a style dating to the 6th century, this late 11th-century work is the finest of the narthex mosaics. Set on a gold background, it depicts Christ teaching his apostles humility.

Dome

The main dome is decorated with an imposing mural of Christ surrounded by saints and angels, painted in the late 17th century to replace mosaics that had fallen.

VISITORS' CHECKLIST

Practical Information
8 km (5 miles) E of Dístomo.
Road map C4. **Tel** 22670 22797.
Site & Museum: **Open** May–
Sep: 9am–6pm daily; Oct–Apr:
8am–5pm daily.

Transport

★ Crypt

This 10th-century shrine, from the original site, contains the sarcophagus of Holy Luke, and such later frescoes as this *Descent from the Cross.*

Blessed Luke (896–953)

Born in Aegina in 896, Osios Loukás ("Blessed Luke") is known to have been a spiritual child who, in his early teens, left home to seek isolation in central Greece and developed a reputation as a healer. In around 940, he arrived at nearby Stíri on the western slopes of Mount Elikónas, with its glorious view over a peaceful valley of cornfields and groves of almond and olive trees. Here, he settled with some disciples, adding the gift of prophecy to his healing powers. He died in 953, by which time the first monastic cells and the site's first small church had been constructed.

The waterfront houses of Galaxídi in the Gulf of Corinth

❶ Lamía and Thermopylae

Λαμία καί Θερμοπύλαι

Stereá Elláda. **Road map** C3.
🚉 68,000. 🚌 ℹ️ Leof. Kalyvion 14, (22310 32289). 🚆 Sat.

Set in the valley between two wooded hills, Lamía is typical of many medium-sized Greek towns. Although it is little known, it has much to offer, with a lively Saturday market. A 14th-century Catalan **kástro**, built on the site of the town's ancient acropolis, provides excellent views over the roofs to the surrounding countryside.

Lamía is chiefly associated with the Lamian War (323–322 BC), when Athens tried to throw off Macedonian rule after the death of Alexander the Great *(see pp36–7)*. This is recalled at the **Lamía Museum**, which also has finds from the environs of the town spanning all eras.

A short drive east of Lamía, the Athens road crosses the **Pass of Thermopylae**. It was here, in 480 BC, that an army of some 7,000

soldiers, under the command of Leonidas I of Sparta, met an overwhelming force from Persia whose numbers Herodotus *(see p60)* cites as 2,641,610. Though Leonidas held the pass for a number of days, the Persians forced a path through and attacked the remaining 2,300 Greeks from the rear. Only two Greek soldiers survived the ordeal, after which all of central Greece, including Athens, fell to the Persians. The Persian land forces were eventually defeated by Athens and her allies at the Battle of Plataiai in 479 BC *(see p33)*.

An impressive bronze statue of King Leonidas, cast in 1955, stands at the roadside opposite the burial mound of the soldiers who died here. Just to the left of the mound are the famous sulphur springs from

which Thermopylae was given its name, which means the "Hot Gates". Many people bathe for free in the cascades that feed the spa building.

The present landscape has changed considerably from the narrow gorge of old; the coastline to the north has been extended by the silt brought down by the River Spercheiós, pushing the sea back over 5 km (3 miles).

🏛️ **Lamía Museum**
Kástro. **Tel** 22310 29992. **Open** 8am–3pm Tue–Sun. **Closed** main public hols. 🅿️ ♿

❶ Ancient Delphi

See pp232–5.

❷ Gulf of Corinth

Κορινθιακός Κόλπος

Stereá Elláda. 🚌 to Náfpaktos.

The northern coast of the Gulf of Corinth contains several well-known resorts as well as many tiny coastal villages far removed from the usual tourist route. All are served by the main road which, like the resorts, offers fine views across the gulf to the mountains of the Peloponnese.

From Delphi, the main road leads southwards through the largest olive grove in Greece, passing **Itéa**, a busy port. The church of Agios Nikólaos, 17 km (11 miles) southwest, stands on a hill surrounded by the old stone buildings of **Galaxídi**. The history of the town is told in the **Nautical and Historical Museum**, while the 19th-century mansions at the waterfront are reminders of the great wealth brought by the town's shipbuilding industry. Though the industry cleared the region of trees, a reforestation scheme begun early in the 20th century has successfully restored the area to its former beauty. The next major town is **Náfpaktos**. Though perhaps less attractive than Galaxídi, it still possesses plenty of charm and character.

Statue of King Leonidas at the Pass of Thermopylae

A Venetian fortress stands above the town, its ramparts running down as far as the beach. The Venetian name for the town was Lepanto. In 1571, the famous naval Battle of Lepanto *(see p42)*, in which the Venetians, Spanish and Genoese defeated the Ottomans, was fought here. A popular story to emerge from the battle purports that the Spanish author Miguel de Cervantes (1547–1616) lost an arm in the conflict, though in fact only his left hand was maimed.

At **Antírrio**, the coast comes closest to the Peloponnese, and from here, a suspension bridge and regular car ferry cross the stretch of water known as the "Little Dardanelles" to Río, on the southern shore. Beside the harbour stands the Frankish, Venetian and Ottoman Kástro Roúmelis. Another castle can be seen across the water on the Peloponnese.

⚓ Nautical and Historical Museum
Mouseíou 4, Galaxídi. **Tel** 22650 41558. **Open** 10am–1:30pm, 5:30–8:30pm daily (Oct–May: 10am–4:15pm). **Closed** main public hols.

㉑ Mesolóngi
Μεσολόγγι

Stereá Elláda. **Road map** B3.
🏠 12,000. 🚌 🚐 Tue & Sat.

Meaning "amid the lagoons", Mesolóngi is perfectly located for fishing, though the industry is now in decline, aside from its famous eels and pressed cod roe. In 1821, the town became a centre of resistance during the War of Independence *(see pp44–5)*, when a great leader, Aléxandros Mavrokordátos, set up his headquarters here. In January 1824, Lord Byron *(see p153)* came to join the fight, but died of a fever in April. Byron's final resting place is unknown, but a statue in the Garden of Heroes honours him. The nearby Gate of the Exodus commemorates the 9,000 civilians, besieged by the Ottomans for a year, who broke out of Mesolóngi in 1826, leaving behind a small force of defenders who fired their powder magazines rather than surrender, levelling the town. The Ottomans gave up Mesolóngi in 1828, without firing a shot. A small museum chronicles these events.

Statue of Lord Byron at Mesolóngi

Saltpan Birdlife

With its importance for food preservation, the production of salt is a major enterprise in the Mediterranean, the most extensive areas in Greece being around Mesolóngi and the Amvrakikós Gulf. Seawater is channelled into large artificial lakes, or saltpans, which attract a large amount of wildlife. Brine shrimps thrive, providing food for a wide variety of birds. Two of the most striking waders are the avocet and the great egret, though also common is the black-winged stilt with its long red legs. The area is also home to Kentish plovers, stone curlews, and the short-toed lark.

Avocet
Great egret

The fortified harbour of Náfpaktos in the Gulf of Corinth

🔟 Ancient Delphi

Δελφοί

According to legend, when Zeus released two eagles from opposite ends of the world, their paths crossed in the sky above Delphi, establishing the site as the centre of the earth. Renowned as a dwelling place of Apollo, from the end of the 8th century BC, individuals from all over the ancient world visited Delphi to consult the god on what course of action to take, in both public and private life. With the political rise of Delphi in the 6th century BC and the reorganization of the Pythian Games (*see p234*), the sanctuary entered a golden age which lasted until the Romans came in 191 BC. The oracle was abolished in AD 391 with the banning of all vestiges of paganism in the Byzantine Empire by Theodosius I.

Locator Map

The Oracle of Delphi

The Delphic Oracle was the means through which worshippers could hear the words of the god Apollo, spoken through a priestess, or *Pythia*, over the age of 50. Questioners paid a levy called a *pelanos* and sacrificed an animal on the altar. The question was then put to the *Pythia* by a male priest. The *Pythia* would answer in a trance, perhaps induced by vapours from a crack in the ground over which she sat on a tripod. Her incantations were interpreted by the priest, though the answers were often ambiguous. King Croesus of Lydia (r.560–546 BC) came to ask if he should make war against Cyrus the Great of Persia and was told that if he crossed a river, then he would destroy a great empire. In marching on Cyrus, his troops crossed the River Halys and he did destroy an empire, though it turned out to be his own.

To museum
(see p235)

SACRED WAY

The main entrance was once a market place (agora) where religious objects could be bought.

The Sanctuary of Apollo

Also known as the Sacred Precinct, this is at the heart of a complex that also included a stadium and a sacred spring (see pp234–5). It is entered through an agora from which the Sacred Way winds through the ruins of memorials and treasuries.

★ Sacred Way

Leading to the Temple of Apollo, this path was lined with up to 3,000 statues and treasuries, built by city-states to house their people's offerings.

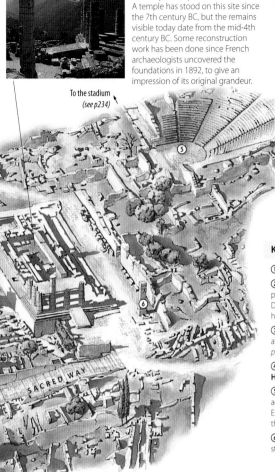

★ **Temple of Apollo**
A temple has stood on this site since the 7th century BC, but the remains visible today date from the mid-4th century BC. Some reconstruction work has been done since French archaeologists uncovered the foundations in 1892, to give an impression of its original grandeur.

To the stadium
(see p234)

VISITORS' CHECKLIST

Practical Information
Mount Parnassós, Stereá Elláda.
Road map C3. **Tel** 22650 82312.
Site & Museum: **Open** 8am–8pm daily (to 3pm Nov–Mar).
Closed main public hols.

Transport

KEY

① **Siphnian Treasury**

② **The Rock of the Sibyl** marks the place where, according to legend, Delphi's first prophetess pronounced her oracles.

③ **The Athenian Treasury** was built after the Battle of Marathon *(see p149)* and reconstructed in 1906.

④ **Vouleuterion (Delphic Council House)**

⑤ **The theatre**, built 2,500 years ago, seats 5,000 people. It rivals Epidaurus *(see pp188–9)* as one of the finest theatres in Greece.

⑥ **A column** once supported a statue of Prusias, King of Bithynia.

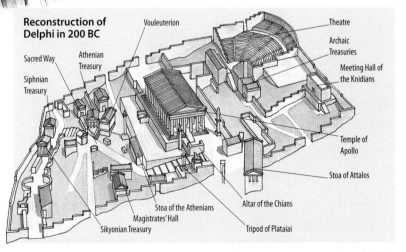

Reconstruction of Delphi in 200 BC

Sacred Way
Siphnian Treasury
Athenian Treasury
Vouleuterion
Theatre
Archaic Treasuries
Meeting Hall of the Knidians
Temple of Apollo
Stoa of Attalos
Stoa of the Athenians
Magistrates' Hall
Sikyonian Treasury
Altar of the Chians
Tripod of Plataiai

Exploring Delphi

The first excavations at Delphi began in 1892, uncovering a much larger area than is apparent now. Though it is most famous for the Sanctuary of Apollo, Delphi also had a sanctuary dedicated to the goddess Athena, whose temple, along with a structure known as the *tholos*, can be seen in a second enclosure to the south. North of the theatre is the stadium where the Pythian Games were held. These, after the Olympic Games *(see p177)*, were the most important sporting event in the Greek calendar, providing an opportunity for strengthening the ethnic bond of the Greek nation which was otherwise divided into predominantly rival city-states.

The Stadium, viewed from the remains of the entrance archway

🔓 Marmaria Precinct

Southeast of the Temple of Apollo, a path leads to the Marmaria Precinct, or "marble quarry", where the Sanctuary of Athena Pronaia can be found. At the sanctuary's entrance stand the ruins of a 6th-century BC temple dedicated to Athena. At the far end of the sanctuary are the remains of a later temple to the goddess, which was built in Doric style in the 4th century BC. Between the two temples stands the Marmaria's most remarkable, and most photographed, monument: the circular *tholos*. The purpose of this structure is still unknown. The rotunda dates from the start of the 4th century BC, and was originally surrounded by 20 columns. Three of these columns, re-erected in 1938, provide some hint of the building's former beauty.

🔓 Stadium

This is one of the best-preserved stadia in the country. Almost 180 m (590 ft) long and partly hewn out of the rocks above the main sanctuary, it held 7,000 spectators who gathered for the field and track events every four years during the Pythian Games. The games grew out of a musical festival, held in the theatre every eight years, to celebrate Apollo's mythical slaying of the serpent Python here. Though poetry and musical recitals remained central to the occasion, from 582 BC, athletic events in the stadium were added and the festival became known as the Pythian Games. All prizes in these tournaments were purely honorary; each winner was awarded the traditional laurel wreath and the right to have his statue in the sanctuary.

Made entirely of limestone from Mount Parnassós, the present structure dates from Roman times and most of the seating (now off-limits) is still intact. The best-preserved seats are the backed benches on the north side, made for the presidents of the games and honoured guests.

🔓 Castalian Spring

Before entering the Sacred Precinct, it is believed that everyone visiting Delphi for religious purposes, including athletes, was required to purify themselves in the clear but icy waters of the Castalian Spring – this process principally involved

The *tholos* beside the Doric Temple of Athena Pronaia, Marmaria Precinct

the washing of their hair. The priestess *Pythia (see p232)* would also wash here before making her pronouncements. The visible remains of the fountain date either from the late Hellenistic or the early Roman period. A number of niches in the surrounding rock once held the votive offerings left for the nymph Castalia, to whom the spring was dedicated.

It is said that the British poet Lord Byron *(see p153)* once plunged into the spring (now cordoned off), inspired by the belief that the waters would enhance the poetic spirit.

The niches of the Castalian Spring

🏛 Gymnasium
Water from the Castalian Spring ran down to the Marmaria to provide cold baths (until the Romans added hot baths in the 2nd century AD) for athletes training for the Pythian Games. The original cold baths, which can be seen in a square courtyard, are some 9 m (30 ft) in diameter. East of the baths lies the Palaestra, or training area, surrounded by the remains of what once were changing rooms and training quarters. As well as an outdoor running track, a covered track 180 m (590 ft) in length was used in bad weather. The gymnasium was built on many levels due to the sloping terrain and was also used for intellectual pursuits – Delphi's poets and philosophers taught here.

🏛 Delphi Museum
The museum at Delphi contains a collection of sculptures and architectural remains of an importance second only to those of the Acropolis Museum *(see pp98–105)*.

There are 13 rooms of exhibits, all on the ground floor. In one of the rooms, there is a scale model that reconstructs the Sanctuary of Apollo in a triumph of limestone whites, blue marble, gold and terracotta. The sanctuary is surrounded by friezes and statues and its size and former beauty is represented vividly.

Votive chapels, or "treasuries", lined the Sacred Way *(see p232)* and contained offerings of thanks, in the form of money or works of art, from towns grateful for good fortune following a favourable prophecy from the Oracle. The Theban Treasury, for example, was established after the victory of Thebes at the Battle of Leuktra in 371 BC. There are two rooms dedicated to the surviving sculpture from the Siphnian and Athenian treasuries, the wealth of the former illustrated by an outstanding frieze depicting the Greek gods waging war on the giants. The colossal Naxian Sphinx was presented by the wealthy citizens of Náxos in 560 BC; it stands 2.3 m (7.5 ft) high and once had its place atop a column reaching over 10 m (33 ft) in height. The most famous of the museum's exhibits is a life-size bronze statue, the *Charioteer*. The statue was commissioned by a Sicilian tyrant named Polyzalos to commemorate a chariot victory in the Pythian Games in 478 BC. Another notable exhibit is the sculpture of *Three Dancing Girls* grouped around a column. The column is believed to have supported a tripod of the kind sat on by the *Pythia* as she went into her oracular trances. The girls are thought to be celebrating the feast of the god Dionysos *(see p56)*, who also resided in the sanctuary. His presence was honoured in the winter months when Apollo was away at his other shrine in Anatolia. Don't miss the Omphalos, or "navel" stone. This is a Hellenistic or Roman copy of the stone that was believed to have marked the place above which Zeus's eagles met, establishing the sanctuary of Delphi as the centre of the earth *(see p232)*.

The bronze *Charioteer*

Detail from the Siphnian Treasury frieze, on display in the Delphi Museum

NORTHERN GREECE

MACEDONIA · THRACE

Macedonia is Greece's largest region and contains the country's second city, Thessaloníki. It is the homeland of Alexander the Great, and the heart of the ancient Hellenistic Empire. In contrast, Thrace has been more influenced by Turkish culture but, like Macedonia, it is an area of comparatively unexplored natural beauty, with many mountain ranges and rivers.

The name Macedonia (Makedonía in Greek) derives from the Makednoi, one of the tribes who first inhabited the region in the late 4th century BC. The legacy of the Macedonian Empire is evident in many ancient sites, including Vergína, the location of King Philip II of Macedon's tomb; Pella, the birthplace of Alexander; and Díon, Philip's city in the foothills of Mount Olympos. During the reign of the Roman Emperor Galerius in the 3rd century AD, many fine monuments were built, including the landmark arch in Thessaloníki. The Byzantine era also left an outstanding legacy of architecture, seen in the many churches throughout northern Greece. Muslim influences remain strong, particularly in Thrace,

where eastern-style bazaars and minarets can still be seen. Macedonia and Thrace (Thráki) have a cooler, damper climate than much of Greece and hence a flourishing flora. Bordering Central Greece is the country's highest mountain, Olympos, and in the northwest lie the beautiful Préspa Lakes. Local produce includes tobacco from Thrace, and wine from Náousa and Dráma.

In contrast to the busy beaches on its two western spurs, the Chalkidikí peninsula in Macedonia has holy Mount Athos to the east. After a purported visit from the Virgin Mary, Byzantine Emperor Konstantínos Monomáchos banished women and children from Athos in 1060. This decree, the *ávaton*, is still valid today.

Villagers at a taverna in the Néstos Valley

◀ One of the monasteries by the sea, Mount Athos

Exploring Northern Greece

Northern Greece offers varied pleasures. The bustle of modern Thessaloníki can be combined with a beach holiday in Chalkidikí, or with an exploration of some of the ancient Macedonian sites. Lovers of natural history will appreciate the National Park around the Préspa Lakes on the borders with Albania and the Former Yugoslav Republic of Macedonia, and the Dadiá Forest and Evros River Delta to the east near Turkey. Walkers will want to explore the paths of Mount Olympos. Kastoriá, Edessa and Kavála, three relatively little-known Greek towns, reward at least an overnight visit as well as making excellent bases for travelling further afield. Kavála straddles the route to the fascinating but little-visited region of Thrace. This region's three main towns – Xánthi, Komotiní and Alexandroúpoli – all offer the attractive combination of Greek and Turkish influence.

A typical stall at the fruit and vegetable market in Xánthi, selling local produce

Reedbeds by the Mikrí Préspa lake

Sights at a Glance

1 Préspa Lakes
2 Kastoriá
3 Siátista
4 Mount Olympos
5 Vergína
6 Véroia
7 Lefkádia
8 Edessa
9 Ancient Pella
10 Thessaloníki pp248–52
11 Northern Chalkidikí
12 Kassándra
13 Sithonía
14 Mount Athos pp256–8
15 Kavála
16 Néstos Valley
17 Xánthi
18 Abdera
19 Komotiní
20 Maroneia
21 Alexandroúpoli
22 Dadiá Forest

Getting Around

Thessaloníki's airport serves both international and domestic routes. Airports at Kastoriá, Kozáni and Alexandroúpoli are for domestic flights only. Ferry connections link Kavála with the northern Aegean islands. Fast trains travel south from Thessaloníki to Athens, and slower ones east into Thrace. The main E75 highway runs south to Athens, while the Egnatía Odós expressway (A2) joins Thessaloníki to Thrace. Buses connect all major points between Kastoriá and Alexandroúpoli.

Locator Map

The harbour of Kavála, in eastern Macedonia

Key

━━ Motorway

━ Major road

┈┈ Minor road

─ Scenic route

┅┅ Main railway

▬▬ International border

▬▬ Regional border

For keys to symbols see back flap

Beautiful landscape of the Préspa Lakes

❶ Préspa Lakes

Εθνικός Δρυμός Πρεσπών

Macedonia. **Road map** B1.
🚌 to Flórina. ℹ️ Agios Germanós
(23850 51211).

This is the only national park in Greece which is made up largely of water. It is one of the mainland's most beautiful and unspoilt places and was little visited in the past because of its rather inaccessible location. The border with Albania runs through the southwest corner of the Megáli Préspa lake, joining the border of the Former Yugoslav Republic of Macedonia. The Greek area of the lake, together with the smaller Mikrí Préspa lake and surrounding countryside, make up the 255 sq km (100 sq miles) of national park, established in 1974. The area is so important for wildlife that Mikrí Préspa and the reed beds that fringe it form a park within a park, a core of some 49 sq km (19 sq miles) regarded as a complete protection area. The boundary of the core area is clearly indicated by signs to prevent accidental trespass.

Over 1,300 species of plant can be found here, including the endemic *Centaurea prespana*, which has small daisy-like flowers. There are over 40 species of mammal, such as bears, wolves, otters, roe deer, wild boar and wild cats. The area is also one of the last remaining breeding refuges in Europe for the Dalmatian pelican, whose numbers are down to less than 1,000 pairs worldwide, with about 150 of these nesting in the Préspa Lakes. Other birds more frequently seen include

Wetland Wildlife

In contrast to the dry and stony terrain found in much of Greece, the north has some outstanding wetlands with a range of different habitats. Reed-fringed lake margins hold large colonies of breeding birds and amphibians, while the open water is home to numerous fish and aquatic insects. The marshes are rich in flowers and full of songbirds; the man-made habitats such as saltpans and lagoons offer sanctuary to nesting waders.

Lake Koróneia is easy to view from nearby villages, most of which have their own colonies of white storks. In spring, terrapins and frogs gather in the shallow margins of the lake.

Kentish plovers nest on the margins of wetlands, such as the Préspa Lakes.

Macedonia

● **Thessaloníki**

● **Kastoriá**

The Préspa Lakes support colonies of rare Dalmatian pelicans. When nesting, they need the peace and quiet this protected area provides.

The Axiós Delta is home to dragonflies and, on the margins, a wealth of spring flowers and bee orchids.

Whipsnakes are common in northern Greece, particularly around Lake Koróneia.

herons, pygmy cormorants, egrets, storks, golden eagles and goosanders.

Scattered around the lakes are several small villages. One of these, on the shore of Megáli Préspa, is **Psarádes**, a picturesque village where fishermen provide a boat service on to the lake. From the boat, you can see

Psarádes village on the banks of Megáli Préspa

hermitages, icons painted on the rocks by the shore, and two frescoed churches: the 15th-century **Panagía Eleoúsa** and the 13th-century **Metamórfosi**. To the east of Mikrí Préspa is **Mikrolímni**. This village has wet meadows to the north that are rich in birdlife. Southwest of Mikrolímni, a path leads to the Ellinikí Etaireía Biological Station, used as a base by research scientists who want to stay in the area while studying.

In summer, the beaches of fine, pale sand that stretch alongside Megáli Préspa can be enjoyed along with a dip in the blue, but rather cold, waters of the lake.

Fresco from Metamórfosi church

Environs

Northeast of the park lies the village of **Agios Germanós**, which has an 11th-century Byzantine church and a number of traditional houses, built in the local architectural style. The village is also home to the **Préspa Information Centre,** which has a permanent exhibition explaining the ecological importance of the Préspa National Park. Guides are available to show visitors around the park, but this must be arranged in advance.

Beyond the village, a road leads up to the summits of Kaló Neró, at 2,160 m (7,090 ft), and Mázi, at 2,060 m (6,760 ft), which give superb views across the lakes below.

Glossy ibises have one of their last remaining European strongholds in the wetlands of northern Greece. Seen in good light, their feathers have a metallic sheen.

Purple herons nest in the reedbeds of the Evros Delta.

Pórto Lágos's lagoons, pools and marshes are a haven for ruddy shelducks.

The Evros Delta lies close to the border with Turkey and access to many of the best areas can be difficult. Numerous water birds, including little egrets, nest and feed in easily viewed locations.

Xánthi

Kavála

Thrace

Alexandroúpoli

Key

- Préspa Lakes
- Axiós Delta
- Lake Koróneia
- Néstos Delta
- Pórto Lágos
- Evros Delta
- — National boundary

The Néstos Delta is one of the finest wetlands in Greece. Many species of birds inhabit the extensive reedbanks and clumps of trees, in particular large breeding colonies of herons and egrets.

```
0 kilometres    50
0 miles            50
```

Ancient Monastery of Símonos Pétras ▶

❷ Kastoriá

Καστοριά

Macedonia. **Road map** B2. 🏔 17,000.
✈ 10 km (6 miles) S of Kastoriá. 🚌
ℹ Plateía Olympiakí Flóga (24670
29630). 🖊 Wed.

Kastoriá is the Greek for "place of beavers". These animals used to live in Lake Kastoriá (also known as Lake Orestiáda) by which the town stands, one of the loveliest settings in Greece. Evidence of a prehistoric settlement was unearthed here in 1940. In 200 BC, the Romans captured the town, then known as Keletron. The beavers first brought the furriers here in the 17th century and, despite the fact that the animals were extinct locally by the 19th century, trading continued. By then, the furriers were also importing unwanted fur scraps, including mink castoffs, and making desirable garments out of them. The fur trade exists today, with the craftsmen still making the fur coats that can be bought in shops here, in Thessaloníki and Athens.

The town prospered as a result of the fur trade, as its several remaining 17th- and 18th-century mansions testify. Most of these are found in the southeast quarter of the town. The elegant Skoútari and Nantzí mansions have interior courtyards and three floors. The ground floor in each case is built of stone; the upper two are made of wood. They have fine timbered rooms fitted with cupboards, hearths and raised platforms. The lower stone floor is used for storage, while the living quarters are in the wooden upper floor which juts out over the street.

The town's **Folklore Museum** is housed in the Aïvazí mansion. Built in the 17th century, it was lived in until as recently as 1972. It now has an eloquent display of the lifestyle of the wealthy fur

The Skoútari mansion in Kastoriá, built in the 18th century

traders. There is typically elaborate woodwork in the salon on the upper floor. The kitchens beneath and the wine cellar have also been restored.

Another notable feature of the town are its many frescoed Byzantine churches. Fifty-four survive, and most are listed as ancient monuments, including the 11th-century **Panagía Koumbelídiki**, situated towards the south end of Mitropóleos. The church is named after its unusually tall dome (or *kubbe*, in Turkish). Some of the churches are tiny and hidden away in Kastoriá's labyrinth of streets, as they were originally private chapels. Many are closed to the public, with some of their icons removed, most of which are now on display in the **Byzantine Museum**. The collection has exquisite pieces on display, including some fine icons.

Apse and cupola of Panagía Koumbelídiki

🏛 **Folklore Museum**
Kapetán Lázou 12. **Tel** 24670 28603.
Open 10am–5pm Tue–Sat,
11am–5pm Sun. **Closed** main
public hols. 🅿

🏛 **Byzantine Museum**
Plateía Dexamenís. **Tel** 24670 26781.
Closed for renovations; call for up-to-date details.

❸ Siátista

Σιάτιστα

Macedonia. **Road map** B2. 🏔 5,000.
ℹ Plateía Tsistopoúlou (24650
21280).

The small town of Siátista was founded in the 1430s, following the Turkish conquest of Thessaloníki. Like Kastoriá, the town flourished initially as a result of the fur trade despite the lack of local fur. Subsequently, Siátista prospered from its role in the wine and leather trades, and especially as a major halt on caravan routes to Vienna.

The wealth that this trade created in the 18th century went into the building of many fine mansion houses. The Ottoman influence in their decoration is strong. The **Nerantzopoúlou** mansion is one of several in the town that can be visited. Keys and directions to the other mansions, including the **Kanatsoúli**, **Manoúsi** and **Poulkídou**, can also be obtained here.

🏛 **Nerantzopoúlou Mansion**
Plateía Chorí. **Tel** 24650 22254.
Open Tue–Sun. **Closed** main
public hols.

View across Siátista, in the Mount Askion range, western Macedonia

View of the Mount Olympos mountain range and Litóchoro village

❹ Mount Olympos

Όλυμπος

17 km (10 miles) W of Litóchoro, Macedonia. **Road map** C2. 🚌 Litóchoro. 🛈 Town Hall: Agíou Nikoláou 17, Litóchoro (23523 50100).

The name Mount Olympos refers to the whole range of mountains, 20 km (12 miles) across. The highest peak in the range, at 2,917 m (9,570 ft), is Mýtikas. The whole area constitutes the Olympos National Park.

Over 1,700 plant species are found here, many of them endemic to the park. Chamois, boars and roe deer also live in this area.

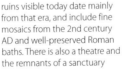

Roman mosaic from Ancient Dion

The base for walkers is the village of **Litóchoro**, a lively place with several hotels and tavernas. Walking maps are available and a marked trail leads up into the national park via the Mavrólogkos Canyon. Mýtikas can be reached in a demanding walk of at least six hours. It is imperative to camp out overnight or stay in one of the two mountain refuges, rather than attempt to get up and down in a day.

Environs

About 10 km (6 miles) north of Litóchoro is the village of Díon, which has an excellent museum showing finds from **Ancient Dion**. This site is near modern Díon village and splendidly set between the coast and the Olympian peaks, its very name deriving from *Díos*, or "of Zeus". To the Macedonians, it was a holy city, and in the 4th century BC, some 15,000 people lived here. The flat plains were used as a military camp and rallying point by King Philip II of Macedon *(see pp36–7)*. Although Dion was a military camp, rather than a civilian city, there was a temple to Zeus, a theatre and a stadium at the site. Later, the Romans built a city here. The ruins visible today date mainly from that era, and include fine mosaics from the 2nd century AD and well-preserved Roman baths. There is also a theatre and the remnants of a sanctuary

dedicated to the Egyptian goddess Isis. She was worshipped by the Romans as a foreign deity, along with many others that were similarly "adopted" into the pantheon. A second temple, dedicated to Zeus, has also been unearthed here.

The bright and modern **Dion Museum** in the village is worth seeing before visiting the site. On display are toys, kitchen utensils and jewellery – all finds from the sanctuary of Isis, along with the star exhibit, a Roman water-organ. Together, they give a vivid picture of life in Ancient Dion.

🏛 Ancient Dion
E of Díon village. **Tel** 23510 53484. **Open** 8am–8pm daily (Nov–Mar: to 3pm). **Closed** main public hols. ♿ 🌐 ancientdion.org

🏛 Dion Museum
Díon village. **Tel** 23510 53206. **Open** 8am–8pm daily (Nov–Mar: to 3pm). **Closed** main public hols. ♿

The Home of Zeus

Zeus, chief and most powerful of the ancient Greek gods, lived on Mount Olympos along with the other immortals and was thought to be responsible for the destinies of men. He was also god of weather and thunderstorms. Many of the myths tell of Zeus's amorous liaisons and his numerous children, some of whom were gods or goddesses and some heroes *(see pp56–7)*. He was worshipped at Olympia and at Dodona in Epirus, site of the oldest oracle in Greece.

❺ Vergína
Βεργίνα

12 km (7 miles) SE of Véroia, Macedonia.
Road map C2. 🚌 Museum: **Tel**
23310 92347. **Open** May–Oct: 8am–
8pm daily (from noon Mon); Nov–Apr:
9am–5pm Tue–Sun. 🎫 (tickets also
valid for Royal Tombs). 🌐 **aigai.gr**

Outside the village of Vergína,
during excavations in 1977,
archaeologist Professor Manólis
Andrónikos found an entrance
to a tomb. The bones inside
included a skull with one eye
socket damaged, evidence that
the tomb belonged to King Philip
II of Macedon, who received such
a wound in the siege of Methóni.
The bones were discovered in
a stunning gold funerary box,
embellished with the symbol
of the Macedonian Sun. The
discovery confirmed that this
area was the site of Aigai, the
first capital of Macedon. The
finds from this tomb, as well as
finds from several other **Royal
Tombs** nearby, are now on
display in the museum here
and are considered the most
important in Greece since
Schliemann's discoveries at
Mycenae (see pp182–4).
A short walk further along
the road from Philip's tomb are
some earlier discoveries, known
as the **Macedonian Tombs**. The
dark interior hides splendid

Terracotta head of a young man,
from the Museum at Véroia

solid marble doors and a
beautiful marble throne.
The **Palace of Palatítsa**
stands beyond on a mound.
It is thought to have been first
occupied in about 1000 BC,
though the building itself
dates from the 3rd century BC.
Today, only low foundations
remain, along with the ruins
of a theatre 100 m (330 ft)
below, thought to be the
site of Philip II's assassination.

🏛 **Royal Tombs, Macedonian
Tombs, Palace of Palatítsa**
Tel 23310 92394. **Open** Apr–Oct:
8am–7:30pm Tue–Sun, 1:30–7:30pm
Mon; Nov–Mar: 8:30am–3pm
Tue–Sun. **Closed** main public
hols. 🎫

The Macedonian Royal Family

The gold burial casket found at Vergína is emblazoned with the
Macedonian Sun, the symbol of the king. Philip II was from a
long line of Macedonian kings that began in about 640 BC
with Perdikkas I. Philip was the first ruler to unite the whole of
Greece as it existed at that time. Also known as the Macedonian
Star, the Sun is often seen on flags within the region, particularly
on that of the Former Yugoslav Republic of Macedonia. Much of
Greece's pride in the symbol lies in the fact that Alexander the
Great used it throughout his empire (see pp36–7). He was just 20
when his father was assassinated at Aigai in 336 BC. He inherited
his father's already large
empire and also his ambition
to conquer the Persians. In
334 BC, Alexander crossed
the Dardanelles with 40,000
men and defeated the
Persians in three different
battles, advancing as far
as the Indus Valley before he
died at the age of 33. With
his death, the Macedonian
Empire splintered.

Burial casket featuring the Macedonian Sun

❻ Véroia
Βέροια

Macedonia. **Road map** C2. 🗺 48,000.
🚌 🚉 🚐 Tue.

The largest town in the region,
Véroia is interesting mainly for
its 50 or so barnlike churches,
the oldest, the frescoed
Christós, dating from the
14th century.
The town's **Byzantine
Museum** is housed in a
converted 19th-century mill,
and the bazaar area bustles on
market days. The old restored
Jewish quarter of Barboúta
deserves a stroll through it.

🏛 **Byzantine Museum**
Thomaïdoú 1. **Tel** 23310 25847.
Open 8am–4pm Tue–Sun.
Closed main public hols. 🎫

Chília Déndra park at Náousa, near Lefkádia

❼ Lefkádia
Λευκάδια

Macedonia. **Road map** C2. **Tel** 23320
41121. 🚌 **Open** 7am–3pm Tue–Fri,
10am–6pm Sat & Sun. **Closed** main
public hols.

The four Macedonian Tombs
of Lefkádia are set in a quiet
agricultural area. The caretaker is
usually at one of the two tombs
that are signposted. The first
of these is the **Tomb of the
Judges**, or Great Tomb. This, the
largest tomb, with a chamber 9
m (30 ft) square and a frescoed
façade portraying Aiakos and
Rhadamanthys, the Judges of
Hades, has been restored.
Beyond is the **Anthemíon Tomb**,
or Tomb of the Flowers, with

Pebble mosaic of the Lion Hunt from the House of the Lion Hunt at Ancient Pella

well-preserved flower paintings on the roof. The key to the **Tomb of Lyson and Kallikles** is sometimes available from the caretaker. The entrance is through a metal grate in the roof. The fourth tomb, called the **Tomb of Kinch** after its Danish discoverer, or the **Tomb of Niafsta** after its one-time occupant, is closed to visitors.

Environs
Renowned for the large park of Chília Déndra (1,000 trees), also known as Agios Nikólaos, and for its lively Carnival, **Náousa** is the home of the Boutari wine-making family. It is situated on the edge of the hills above the plain that extends east to Thessaloníki. Riverside tavernas in the park offer fresh trout as well as the good local wine.

❽ Edessa
Έδεσσα

Macedonia. **Road map** C1. 🚍 16,000.
🚌 🚉 ℹ Parko Katarrákton (23810 20300). **Open** 10am–4pm Mon–Fri, 10am–6pm Sat & Sun. 🛍 Thu.

Edessa is the capital of the modern Pélla region and a popular summer resort. It is renowned for its waterfalls, the largest of which, **Káranos** (24 m/79 ft), has a cave behind it. The surrounding gardens and park are pleasant, with cafés and restaurants. The Varósi old quarter has a Folklore Museum and a Water Museum (open 10am–10pm daily).

❾ Ancient Pella
Πέλλα

38 km (24 miles) NW of Thessaloníki, Macedonia. **Road map** C1. 🚍 **Tel** 23820 32963. Site: **Open** Apr–Oct: 8am–8pm daily (from noon Mon); Nov–Mar: 8am–3pm Tue–Sun. Museum: **Tel** 23820 31160. **Open** same as the site. **Closed** main pub hols. 🏛 ♿

This small site, which straddles the main road, was once the

Káranos waterfall at Edessa

flourishing capital of Macedon. The court was moved here from Aigai (modern Vergína) in 410 BC by King Archelaos, who ruled from 413 to 399 BC. It is here that Alexander the Great was born in 356 BC, and later tutored by the philosopher Aristotle. Some sense of the existence of a city can be gained from a plan of the site, which shows where the main street and shops were located. King Archelaos's Palace is believed to have been north of the main site.

The site has some of the best-preserved and most beautiful pebble mosaics in Greece. The stones are uncut and have been carefully picked not only for their size, but also for their warm, subtle colouring. Dating from about 300 BC, the mosaics include vivid hunting scenes. One of the most famous is of Dionysos riding a panther. The mosaic is protected from the weather in the now-covered House of the Lion Hunt. This was built at the end of the 4th century BC and originally comprised 12 rooms around three open courtyards, the whole structure being 90 m (295 ft) long by 50 m (165 ft) wide.

⑩ Thessaloníki
Θεσσαλονίκη

Thessaloníki, also known as Salonika, is Greece's second city, founded by King Kassandros in 315 BC. The Romans made it capital of their province of Macedonia Prima in 146 BC, and in AD 313, it became the second city of the Eastern Roman Empire. In 1430, it was captured by the Ottomans who held it until 1912. Today, Thessaloníki is a bustling cosmopolitan city. It has a flourishing cultural life and is a major religious centre, with an array of splendid churches *(see p252)*, such as Agía Sofía and Agios Dimítrios, which is the largest church in Greece.

Cafés and fountains in the park near Plateía Ch.An.Th

Exploring Thessaloníki

Greece's second city is also the second port in the Mediterranean, which adds to the bustle and the wealth of this fascinating metropolis. Situated on the Thermaic Gulf, it has an attractive waterfront prom-enade, known as the *paralía*, and a pleasant leafy

Furniture shop in the back streets

park. It also boasts a large number of beautiful Byzantine churches *(see p252)*. In recent years, Thessaloníki has developed its international exhibition facilities and become a major trade fair centre. The city has many museums, including the Archaeological Museum *(see pp250–51)*.

The Great Fire of August 1917 destroyed nearly half the buildings within the medieval walls, including the entire Jewish quarter. Some, however, survived, and many from the original Ottoman bazaar have been restored. One such

building is the **BezestÉni**, once a hall for valuables and now home to plush shops. The **Modiáno**, a covered meat and produce hall, is named after the Jewish family who once owned it. In and around the Modiáno are some of the best *ouzerí*, and **Plateía Aristotélous** is home to many posh cafés.

🏛 Arch of Galerius
Egnatía.

The principal architectural legacy of Roman rule is found at the eastern end of the long main street, Egnatía, which was part of the Roman Via Egnatia road linking Byzantium with Rome. Here stands the Arch of Galerius, built in AD 299 by Galerius (then co-emperor of the Roman Empire) to celebrate his victory over the Persians in AD 298. Its carvings show scenes from the battle. There was once a double arch here, with a palace to the south. Some of its remains can be seen in Plateía Navarínou.

Section of carving from the Arch of Galerius

🏛 White Tower and Paralía
On the waterfront. **Tel** 2310 267832. **Open** 8:30am–3pm Tue–Sun. 🖼

Probably Thessaloníki's most famous sight is the White Tower on the *paralía*. Built in 1430, the Ottomans added three such towers to the 8-km (5-mile) city walls. Today, it functions as an annexe of the Museum of Byzantine Culture on several floors of small circular rooms. The original stone steps climb up to a roof with lovely views of the *paralía*.

🏛 Rotónda
Filíppou. **Open** 8am–7pm daily (winter: to 5pm).

Standing north of the Arch of Galerius is the Rotónda. It is thought that this impressive building was constructed as a mausoleum for Galerius, co-emperor of the Roman Empire AD 305–311. Ultimately, he wasn't entombed here, and the structure was later used both as a church – it is also known as Agios Geórgios – and as a mosque. The minaret nearby is now the only one in Thessaloníki. The Rotónda itself shelters magnificent Byzantine mosaics.

🏛 Museum of Byzantine Culture
Leofórou Stratoú 2. **Tel** 2310 306400. **Open** 8am–8pm daily (Nov–Mar: 9am–4pm). **Closed** main public hols. 🖼 ♿ 🌐 mbp.gr

Behind the Archaeological Museum *(see pp250–51)* is this small, modern museum. Displays include a 5th-century mosaic floor, icons and some fabulous early textiles. There are also temporary exhibitions.

White Tower on the seafront

🏛 Museum of the Macedonian Struggle

Proxénou Koromilá 23. **Tel** 2310 229778. **Open** 9am–2pm Mon–Fri, 10am–2pm Sat. **Closed** main public hols. **w** imma.edu.gr

This is situated in a late 19th-century mansion that originally housed the Greek Consulate when Thessaloníki was under Turkish rule. Photographs, newspapers, weapons and personal items tell the story well. Vivid tableaux depict the struggle and its effect on ordinary people. In one, a Turk with a rifle bursts into a schoolroom while a Greek freedom fighter hides under the floorboards. This was the celebrated Pávlos Melás, who fought to free Macedonia from the Turks but was, ironically, killed by the Bulgarians. Also on display in the museum are his gun and dagger.

🏛 Folklore and Ethnological Museum of Macedonia/Thrace

Vasilíssis Olgas 68. **Tel** 2310 830591. **Open** 9am–3:30pm Fri–Tue, 9am–9:30pm Wed. 🏛 **w** lemmth.gr

This museum is a 20-minute walk from the Archaeological Museum. There are displays of folk costumes, and detailed small models showing rural activities such as ploughing, winnowing, threshing, and children playing. The gruelling life of the nomadic Sarakatsan shepherds is well documented, and a vivid display shows the incredible events at the annual fire-walking ceremony in Lagkadás, a village 20 km (12 miles) northeast of Thessaloníki. The museum also hosts several temporary exhibitions throughout the year and has an extensive archive of fascinating period photography showing the reality of life during the early 20th century.

VISITORS' CHECKLIST

Practical Information
Macedonia. **Road map** C2.
🗺 1,000,000. 🛈 Tsimiskí 136 (2310 254834); Airport (2310 471170). 🎭 Cultural Festival: Oct.

Transport
✈ 25 km (15 miles) SE of Thessaloníki. 🚢 off Koundouriótou. 🚉 Monastiríou. 🚌 78 (local bus to airport), Monastiríou (Intercity buses).

Thessaloníki Town Centre

1. Archaeological Museum
2. Plateía Aristotélous
3. Arch of Galerius
4. White Tower and Paralía
5. Rotónda
6. Museum of Byzantine Culture
7. Museum of the Macedonian Struggle
8. Folklore and Ethnological Museum

For keys to symbols *see back flap*

Thessaloníki Archaeological Museum
Αρχαιολογικό Μουσείο Θεσσαλονίκης

This modern museum, opened in 1963, contains a host of treasures. It concentrates on the finds made within the city and at the many sites in Macedonia. The displays progress chronologically through the ages, giving a clear picture of the area's history. The inner rooms surrounding the courtyard house a number of fabulous gold items from ancient Macedon, including the treasures discovered during excavations at Macedonian cemeteries. The annexe basement contains a small exhibition on the prehistory of Thessaloníki.

Faïence Vase
Found in a 2nd-century BC grave in Thessaloníki, this ornate vase is from Ptolemaic Egypt and is the only such faïence vase in Greece.

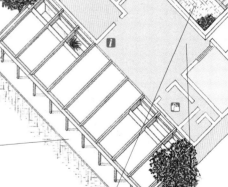

Field House
Garden Grave

★ Floor Mosaics from a Thessaloníki House
These detailed mosaics depicting marine-world mythology are Roman. This mosaic shows a nereid (sea nymph) and a dolphin.

Main entrance

Gallery Guide
An outer circle of rooms surrounds a block of inner rooms housing a collection of Macedonian gold. The outer rooms contain treasures from the first centuries of Thessaloníki and the kingdom of Macedon. The basement of the annexe holds a display of prehistoric antiquities and temporary exhibitions.

Outdoor courtyard with Roman floor mosaic

Marble Sarcophagus
This 2nd- or 3rd-century Roman sarcophagus is decorated with a vivid relief depicting an Amazon battle. The Amazons, a mythical warrior tribe of women, were a favourite subject for artists *(see p59)*.

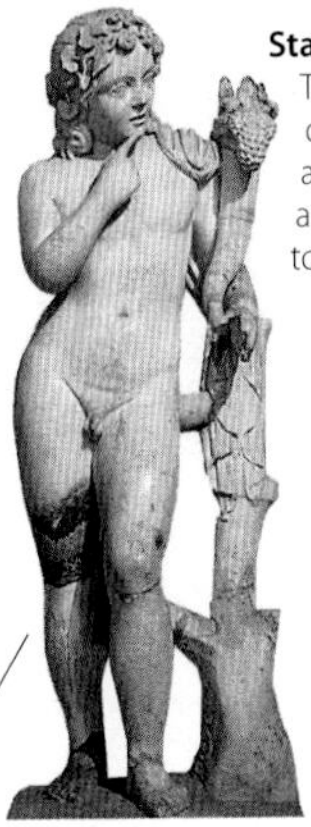

Statue of Harpokrates

The marble statue of Harpokrates, the son of Isis and Osiris, was found in Thessaloníki at the site of a sanctuary devoted to Serapis and other Egyptian gods. It has been dated to the end of the 2nd century AD.

VISITORS' CHECKLIST

Practical Information
Manóli Andrónikou & Leof Stratoú. **Tel** 2310 830538.
Open Apr–Oct: 8am–8pm daily; Nov–Mar: 8am–3pm Tue–Sun, 10am–5pm Mon.
Closed public hols. 🦽 ♿
ⓦ amth.gr

Transport
🚌 3

★ Gold Bracelet from Europos

This gold bracelet is one of the highlights of the collection of Macedonian gold. It dates from the 3rd century BC and is accompanied in the exhibition by other gold finds from the 6th century BC to the 2nd century BC.

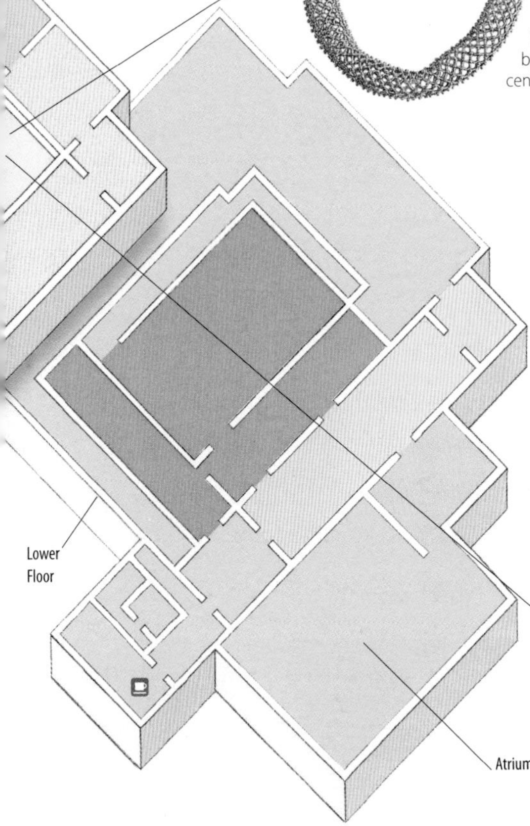

Key to Floorplan

- ▢ Prehistoric collection
- ▢ The Gold of Macedon
- ▢ Macedonia: 7th century BC to late antiquity
- ▢ Thessaloníki: Metropolis of Macedonia
- ▢ Manólis Andrónikos room
- ▢ Towards the birth of cities
- ▨ Temporary exhibitions
- ▢ Macedonia: Fragments to pixels
- ▢ Non-exhibition space

Lower Floor

Atrium

★ Dervéni Krater

Dating from c.300 BC, this bronze wine-mixing vase stands 80 cm (31 in) high. The detailed figures of maenads are exquisite; Dionysos and Ariadne are shown on the front. The volutes at the top are decorated with the head of Herakles.

Exploring Thessaloníki's Churches

Thessaloníki has the richest collection of Byzantine churches in Greece. Of the hundreds of 5th-century basilicas that once stood across the country, only two remain. Both of these, Agios Dimítrios and Acheiropoíïtos, are in Thessaloníki. The 8th-century Agía Sofía is a very significant Byzantine building, both for its mosaics and its role in influencing future architectural development. Three different 14th-century churches – Agios Nikólaos Orfanós, Agioi Apóstoloi and Agía Aikateríni – give an insight into what was a period of architectural innovation.

Agía Sofía church

The mosaic of Ezekiel's vision in Osios David

🏛 Agios Dimítrios

Agíou Dimitríou 97. **Open** 8am–10pm daily. 🚻 Crypt **Open** 8am–3pm Tue–Thu; 8am–1:30pm & 7–10pm Fri; 7:30am–2:30pm Sat & Sun.

This, the largest church in Greece, was entirely rebuilt after the fire of 1917, which destroyed the 7th- and 13th-century fabric of the basilica. The oldest, 3rd-century AD portion is the crypt. Originally a Roman bath, this, according to legend, is the site of the imprisonment, torture and murder in 305 AD of the city's patron saint Dimítrios – a Roman soldier converted to Christianity and martyred on the orders of Emperor Galerius. Six small 5th–7th-century mosaics are found both on the piers flanking the altar and high up on the west side of the church. These mosaics rank among the finest in Greece and include depictions of Dimítrios with young children, or in the company of the church's builders.

🏛 Osios Davíd

Mýronos 1–3, Kástro. **Open** Tue–Sun.

This delightful small chapel was founded some time in the late 5th century as part of a

monastery. Behind the altar is an original vivid mosaic of the *Vision of Ezekiel*, rare in that it depicts a beardless Christ Emmanouel. It owes its marvellous condition to having been concealed beneath plaster and only discovered in 1921. There are also some frescoes from the 12th century, including a fine *Baptism* and *Nativity*. Although the church is usually locked, there is a caretaker who greets visitors and will unbolt the doors.

🏛 Agía Sofía

Plateía Agías Sofías. **Open** 8:30am–2pm, 5:30–8pm daily.

The church of Agía Sofía is dedicated to the Holy Wisdom (Sofiá) of God, just like the church of the same name in Istanbul. It was built in the mid-8th century. In 1585, it became a mosque, but was reconsecrated as a church in 1912. It contains many mosaics and frescoes dating back to the 9th and 10th centuries, including a fine *Ascension* scene in the 30-m (100-ft) high dome. The entrance formerly had a portico, which was obliterated during an Italian air raid in 1941. The imposing nature of the building is emphasized by its location in a partially sunken garden.

🏛 Agios Nikólaos Orfanós

Kástro. **Open** 8am–2:45pm Tue–Sun; key available from warden at Irodhotou 17, opposite the church. 🚻

Situated in a garden plot amongst the lanes of the ancient Kástra district, or upper town, this small, triple-apsed 14th-century church began life as a dependency of the larger Moni Vlatádon, further up the hill. Today, Agios Nikólaos Orfanós retains the richest and best-preserved collection of late Byzantine frescoes in the city. Distributed over the central cella and both aisles, they show rare scenes from the Passion, including Christ mounting the Cross, and Pilate seated in judgment.

Agios Dimítrios, the largest church in Greece

The stretch of sandy beach at Kallithéa on Kassándra

⓫ Northern Chalkidikí
Βόρεια Χαλκιδική

Macedonia. **Road map** D2.
🚌 to Polýgyros.

The north of Chalkidikí is a quiet and delightful hilly region, often overlooked by those whose main interests are the beaches to the south. A glimpse of the hidden interior is given when visiting the **Petrálona Caves**, situated on the edge of Mount Katsíka, 55 km (34 miles) southeast of Thessaloníki. It was in these red-rock caverns in 1960, the year after the caves were discovered by local villagers, that a skull was found. It was believed to be that of a young woman, aged about 25 when she died. A complete skeleton was subsequently discovered, and these are the oldest bones yet to be found in Greece, dating back between 160,000 and 350,000 years. Amid the stalactites and stalagmites, reconstructions of the cave dwellers have been arranged in the caves, along with the bones, teeth and tools that were also found here.

In the northeast of the area is the small village of **Stágeira**, the birthplace of Aristotle (384–322 BC). On a hilltop, just outside the village, is a huge white marble statue of the philosopher, and there are sweeping views over the surrounding countryside.

🏛 **Petrálona Caves**
Mount Katsíka, 55 km (34 miles) SE of Thessaloníki. **Tel** 23730 73365.
Open Apr–Oct: 8am–8pm Tue–Sun; Nov–Mar: 9am–3pm Tue–Sun.
Closed main public hols. 🅿

⓬ Kassándra
Κασσάνδρα

Southern Chalkidikí, Macedonia.
Road map D2. 🚌 to Kassándreia.

Much of this area's population was killed during the War of Independence, and the numbers never really recovered. Little was left on the promontory of Kassándra other than a few fishing villages. However, since the 1960s, many resorts have sprung up. **Néa Poteídaia** straddles the narrow neck of the peninsula, with a good sandy beach, a marina and an attractive town square; nearby, **Ancient Olynthos** deserves a visit. On the west coast, **Sáni**

Statue of Aristotle, Stágeira

has excellent beaches, a summer festival and a luxury resort complex. There are quiet bays around the village of **Possídi**, on a promontory halfway down the west coast. On the east coast, **Néa Fókaia** still functions as a fishing village in spite of the steady invasion of tourism, whereas **Kallithéa**, to the south, is the largest resort on Kassándra.

⓭ Sithonía
Σιθωνία

Southern Chalkidikí, Macedonia.
Road map D2. 🚌 to Agios Nikólaos.

While the peninsula of Sithonía is only marginally larger than Kassándra, it has fewer resorts and a thickly wooded interior. The peninsula begins at **Metamórfosi**, which has a sandy beach shaded by pine trees. **Vourvouroú** is one of the first villages you come to on the north side. A collection of villas spreads along the coast, with a few hotels and a selection of eating places.

To the south of this area is a long undeveloped stretch of coast, with several unspoilt beaches, until you reach the large resort of **Sárti**. At the tip of Sithonía is **Kalamítsi**, little more than a sandy beach and a few bars, while **Pórto Koufó** at the end of the west coast is still a pleasant fishing village set on a bay amid wooded hills. The **Pórto Karrás** resort, halfway down the west coast, was set up by the Karrás wine family. It has three hotels, a marina, a shopping centre, water sports, horse riding, a golf course and tennis.

Boats docked at Pórto Koufó on Sithonía

⑭ Mount Athos

`Άγιον Όρος`

To the Greeks, this is the Holy Mountain, which at 2,030 m (6,660 ft), is the highest point of Chalkidikí's most easterly peninsula. Unique in Greece, Athos is an autonomous republic ruled by the 1,700 monks who live in its 20 monasteries. Only adult males may visit the peninsula, but it is possible to see many of the monasteries from a boat trip along the coast. Together, they include some fine examples of Byzantine architecture and provide an insight into monastic life.

The Monasteries of Athos

--- Ferry route

Mount Athos from the West

This illustration shows the view seen when travelling by boat along the west of Athos. The most northerly monastery on this coast is Zográfou and the most southerly is Agíou Pávlou. The eastern monasteries are covered on p258

Agíou Panteleímonos
Also known as Rosikón (of the Russians), this 11th-century monastery's imposing walls hide many colourful onion-domed churches, evidence of the Russian Orthodox influence on Athos.

```
0 kilometres        15
0 miles          10
```

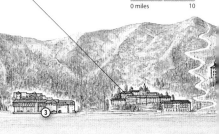

To Ouranoúpoli ←

Docheiaríou
This 10th-century monastery houses a fragment of the True Cross and an icon of the Virgin with healing powers.

Visiting Mount Athos

Only ten non-Orthodox men per day are allowed to visit Mount Athos, with a stay of four nights. To apply, it's best to visit the Pilgrims' Bureau (see address below) in person, with your passport. Alternatively, you may fax a copy of the personal details page in advance, with your desired dates of pilgrimage. Apply well in advance. Once confirmed, you must book the monasteries you wish to visit; the office has the telephone numbers. On the day of your visit, be at the Ouranópoli Pilgrims' Bureau by 8am to collect your *Diamenterion* (official permit); bring your confirmation and passport. Boats leave daily at 9:45am for the monasteries. For more information, contact the Pilgrims Bureau, Egnatías 109, 54622 Thessaloníki, Greece (Tel: 2310 252578; Fax 2310 222424).

Vatopedíou refectory

◀ Coastline of the walled, medieval Panagía quarter, Kavála

Ouranoúpoli
The main town on Athos is where boat trips
around the peninsula start.

Agíou Pávlou
This monastery houses 90 monks,
many from Zákynthos and Kefalloniá,
and has some 13,000 books and
manuscripts in its library.

Grigoríou
Founded in the 14th century,
this monastery was totally
rebuilt after a disastrous fire in
1761, which destroyed all but a
few holy relics. About 40 monks
live here today.

KEY

① **Zográfou** was founded in
AD 971, but the present buildings
are 18th- and 19th-century.

② **Kastamonítou** was founded
in the 11th century by a hermit
from Asia Minor.

③ **Xenofóntos** was founded
in the late 10th century. A
second chapel was built in
1837, using some 14th-century
mosaic panels.

④ **Xiropotámou** was founded
in the 10th century, but the
present buildings date from
the 18th century.

⑤ **Dáfni** is Athos's port and has a
population of 16. A bus goes

from here to the capital, Karyés,
15 minutes away.

⑥ **Símonos Pétras** was named
after Saint Simon who founded
the monastery in the 14th
century AD after seeing a
strange light burning on
this remote ridge one
Christmas night.

⑦ **Agíou Dionysíou** is perched
80 m (260 ft) above the
sea. Its walls conceal
the 16th-century church of
Agios Ioánnis Pródromos.

⑧ **Néa Skíti** belongs to
Agíou Pávlou.

⑨ **Mount Athos**

Exploring Mount Athos

Not all of the 20 monasteries on Athos can be seen from the popular boat trips from Ouranoúpoli, although some boats do go round the whole peninsula. A few are hidden in the mountains and others cling to the eastern coast of the peninsula. In addition to the Greek Orthodox monasteries on Mount Athos, there is one Russian (Agíou Panteleímonos), one Bulgarian (Zográfou) and one Serbian (Chilandaríou). Remote hermitages and monastic villages (*sketes*) in the hills of the peninsula are preferred by some monks, as a quieter alternative to the relatively busy monastery life.

Orthodox Life on Mount Athos

The monks grow their own fruit and vegetables

The East Coast Monasteries

The first monastery to be established on Athos was the **Megístis Lávras** (Great Lavra). It is situated at the southeastern end of the peninsula, on a rocky outcrop (see pp40–41). It was founded in AD 963 by Athanásios the Athonite, and is the only one of the monasteries never to have suffered from fire. It also has the largest font of all the monasteries, which is outside, shaded by a cypress tree said to have been planted over 1,000 years ago by Athanásios himself.

Painting in Megístis Lávras

Halfway along the eastern coast stand the monasteries of Ivíron and Stavronikíta. **Ivíron** was founded in the late 10th century by a monk from Iberia (modern Georgia), hence its name. Its church was built in the early 11th century and restored in 1513. The monastery's main courtyard contains another 16 chapels, one housing a miraculous icon of the Virgin Mary. **Stavronikíta**, to the north, stands on top of a rocky headland. It was first mentioned in a document dated AD 1012.

Moní Vatopedíou, one of the largest monasteries on Athos, is sited on a small promontory at the northern end of the east coast. It was founded in the latter half of the 10th century, and a notable feature is its *katholikón*, or main church, also built in the 10th century. It contains icons dating from the 14th century, though they have been retouched over the years. The refectory is the most imposing on Athos. A wealthy monastery, it is among the best preserved on Mount Athos.

Under the Byzantine time system operating on Athos, midnight is at dawn, and morning services begin about an hour before – around 3 or 4am, secular time. A monk walks around striking a small wooden *símandro* (a carved plank) with a mallet to wake the other monks and call them to prayer. The monks eat two meals a day, consisting mostly of food they grow themselves. There are 159 fasting days in the year when only one meal is allowed which must contain no fish, eggs, cheese, milk or even oil. Meals are eaten after the morning and evening services, and the time in between is spent working, resting and praying.

The Megístis Lávras monastery, with its red *katholikón* in the centre

For hotels and restaurants see pp272–3 and pp290–91

⓯ Kavála
Καβάλα

Macedonia. **Road map** D1.
🏘 56,000. ✈ 35 km (22 miles) SE
of Kavála. 🚢 🚌 🛥 daily.

Kavála's history goes back to its
foundation in the 6th century
BC by settlers from Thássos and
Erétria. It became part of the
Roman Empire in 168 BC, and is
where St Paul first set foot on
European soil in AD 50 or 51 on
his way to Philippi. The biggest
impact, however, was the
Ottoman occupation from 1371
to 1912. It was they who built
the 16th-century aqueduct
here. Mehmet Ali (1769–1849),
the Pasha of Egypt, was born in
Kavála. His birthplace, a well-
preserved house set in gardens,
is marked by a bronze statue of
Mehmet Ali on horseback. The
house is open only sporadically,
but a bar in the grounds
operates during the
summer months.
Kavála is a busy city,
with an industrial
port that also has a
ferry service to the
northeast Aegean
islands. Life
centres around
the harbour
below the
fortified old
Panagía quarter, with a
nocturnally illuminated castle
on top. At its eastern end,
there is a busy fish, fruit and
vegetable market. To the west
is the **Archaeological
Museum**, which has finds from
Amphipolis Abdera *(see p260)*,
including a dolphin mosaic
and a painted sarcophagus.
The **Folk and Modern Art
Museum**, in an old mansion,
highlights works by local
artists, particularly sculptor
Polýgnotos Vágis (1894–1965).
The **Tobacco Museum**
features a unique range of
documents relating to the
cultivation and production of
tobacco, from the agricultural
process to the commercial-
ization of tobacco products.

Sculpture by
Polýgnotos Vágis

🏛 **Folk and Modern Art Museum**
Filíppou 4. **Tel** 2510 222706. **Open**
8am–2pm Mon–Fri, 9am–2:30pm Sat.

The town and harbour of Kavála

🏛 **Archaeological Museum**
Erythroú Stavroú 17. **Tel** 2510 222335.
Open 8am–3pm Tue–Sun.
Closed main public hols. 🚫 ♿

🏛 **Tobacco Museum**
K. Palaiológou 4. **Tel** 2510 223344.
Open 8am–3pm Mon–Fri,
9am–1pm Sat.
🌐 **tobaccomuseum.gr**

⓰ Néstos Valley
Κοιλάδα του Νέστου

Macedonia/Thrace border.
Road map D1. 🚍 🚌 Xánthi (liable
to be cancelled Nov–Apr).

The Néstos river rises high
in the Rodópi mountains in
Bulgaria, and its meandering
course down to the Aegean
near the island of Thássos
marks the boundary between
Macedonia and Thrace. On its
way, it threads through remote
and inaccessible gorges, fed by
other rivers and streams, until
it passes under the
scenic mountain
road which links
Xánthi in Thrace with
the town of Dráma
in Macedonia. This
road, sometimes
closed by snowdrifts
in winter, makes for
a spectacular scenic
drive through the
wooded gorge,
past the valley's
heavy beech forests
and scattering of
small villages.
Stavroúpoli, the
largest of these
villages, has a range
of dining and
lodging options.

⓱ Xánthi
Ξάνθη

Thrace. **Road map** E1. 🏘 25,000. 🚍
🚌 🛥 Sat.

Founded in the 11th century,
it was not until the 1800s
that Xánthi flourished with
the development of the
tobacco industry. Displays on
tobacco are included in the
Folk Art Museum, housed in
two old mansions. The
museum's collection includes
embroidery, jewellery and
costumes. Xánthi's main square
has cafés and fountains, and
east of the square is the bazaar.
This is overflowing on Saturdays,
when people of all ethnicities
and religions visit the busiest
market in the area.

🏛 **Folk Art Museum**
Antiká 7. **Tel** 25410 25421.
Open 8:30am–3pm Tue–Sun. 🚫

The lush landscape of the Néstos Valley

The monastery of Agios Nikólaos, marooned out on the waters of Lake Vistonída

🔞 Abdera

`Άβδηρα`

6 km (4 miles) S of modern Avdira, Thrace. **Road map** E1. 🚐 **Tel** 25410 51003. **Open** Museum: 8:30am–3pm daily. **Closed** main public hols.

The ancient city of Abdera was founded in the mid-7th century BC by refugees from Klazomenae in Asia Minor. The site is quite dispersed and overgrown, and it has been closed for visits for several years. Excavated remains are mostly Roman. The interesting site museum in modern Avdira village is worthwhile, displaying finds from the site ranging from Archaic to Byzantine times, when the town was abandoned.

Environs
Along the minor road from Avdira to Komotiní is **Lake Vistonída**, a haven for wildlife. At one end is Pórto Lágos (*see pp240–41*), an old harbour with the white monastery of Agios Nikólaos.

🔟 Komotiní

`Κομοτηνή`

Thrace. **Road map** E1. 🚹 38,000. 🚆 🚌 🚇 Tue.

Only 25 km (16 miles) from the Bulgarian border to the north, and less than 100 km (62 miles) from Turkey to the east, Komotiní is a fascinating mix of Greek, Slavic and Turkish influence. First founded in the late 4th century AD, it was

taken by the Turks in 1363, and remained part of the Ottoman Empire until 1920 (and, briefly, Bulgaria). Over 500 years of Turkish rule have left their mark on the town, especially since the area's Muslims were excluded from the population exchange following the Greek defeat in Asia Minor in 1922. There is a thriving market with fish, cattle and tobacco for sale, along with a good selection of fresh produce grown in fertile land. The many old wooden shops sell everything from bric-a-brac to genuine, valuable antiques.

A feel of the town's recent past is given in the well-cared-

Finial from a gravestone, Archaeological Museum, Komotiní

for **Folklore Museum**. Its few rooms, in an 18th-century mansion, are crammed with costumes, local copperware and domestic items. There is also a particularly good collection of embroidery, including examples of a type known as Tsevrés, used in Thracian wedding ceremonies. The town's **Archaeological Museum** displays the best of the finds from the sites at ancient Abdera and Maroneia, including gold jewellery found in 4th- century BC graves at Avdira. A 4th-century BC clay mask of Dionysos is on display, found at the god's sanctuary at Maroneia. The museum also has an extensive coin collection, painted sarcophagi, votive reliefs and maps.

Ⅲ Folklore Museum
Agíou Georgiou 13. **Tel** 25310 25975. **Open** 10am–1pm daily. **Closed** main public hols. 🚫 ♿ limited.

Ⅲ Archaeological Museum
Symeonídi 4. **Tel** 25310 22411. **Open** 8am–3pm daily. **Closed** main public hols.

🔟 Maroneia

`Μαρώνεια`

5 km (3 miles) SE of modern Maróneia, Thrace. **Road map** E1. 🚌 to modern Maróneia. **Open** daily. **Closed** main public hols. 🚫 ♿

The road to ancient Maroneia leads through tobacco and

The domed roof and tall minaret of a Turkish mosque, Komotiní

cotton fields, past woodland and small rural communities. A signpost towards Agios Charálampos port points down a track to the ancient remains, in a scenic position overlooking the sea. The city flourished from the 8th century BC until AD 1400, though little is visible under a mantle of olive groves. A small theatre has been refurbished; nearby lie the remnants of a sanctuary, possibly dedicated to Dionysos, whose son, Maron, is credited in legend with founding Maroneia.

Environs
Medieval **Maróneia** is a tiny but attractive farming community with some larger mansions suggesting a more prosperous past.

❹ Alexandroúpoli
Αλεξανδρούπολη

Thrace. **Road map** E1. 🚶 36,000. 🛫 🚌 🚉 🚌 🚢 Tue.

Alexandroúpoli lacks the cultural mix and history of other large Thracian towns, but merits a visit, nevertheless. It was only built up in 1878, under the Turkish name of Dedeagaç (meaning "Tree of the Holy Man"), derived from a group of hermits who first settled here in the 15th century. Prior to that, it was simply an unremarkable fishing village. Alexandroúpoli was renamed in 1919 after the Greek king

The landmark lighthouse in Alexandroúpoli

at the time, Aléxandros I. Today, the city is a thriving market town with a port, its own domestic airport, and train connections north into Bulgaria and west to Thessaloníki.

In the evening, the promenade by the long stretch of beach to the west is thronged with people. The lighthouse, built in 1800, is situated along the seafront. It is the town's most famous feature and is lit up at night.

Inland from the promenade is a warren of narrow streets with junk shops, grocers, cobblers, goldsmiths and fish restaurants. The best eating places are around tiny Plateía Polytechneíou. North from the square, beyond the main road, is the modern cathedral

Old mansion in modern Maróneia

of Agios Nikólaos, notable for the **Ecclesiastical Art Museum** contained in its grounds. This fine collection of more than 400 icons and other religious items is unfortunately seldom open, but those with a particular interest in seeing it may ask for access at the cathedral. The collection predominantly dates from the 18th and 19th centuries, but some artifacts are older. The paintings of a lamenting Mary are of particular note.

🏛 **Ecclesiastical Art Museum**
Palaiológou. **Tel** 25510 82282. **Open** Tue–Sat. **Closed** main public hols.

❷ Dadiá Forest
Δάσος Δαδιάς

27km (17 miles) N of Féres, Thrace.
Road map F1. 🚌 🚌 Féres.
ℹ 1 km (0.5 miles) N, at Dadiá village (25540 32209).

North of the small town of Féres in the Evros valley is the lovely Dadiá pine forest. Covering a series of hills known as the Evros Mountains, it is considered to be one of the best places in Europe for observing raptors. Of special interest is the presence of birds of prey, an indic-

Rare black vulture

ation of the remote location of the forest. There are 39 known species of birds of prey in Europe, 26 of which live and nest in this region.

There is an information centre in the heart of the forest, and observation huts have been placed near feeding stations, built to help preserve the rarer species that nest here. This is one of the black vulture's last refuges in eastern Europe. The forest is home to a huge number of protected and endangered species, including imperial eagles, golden eagles, griffon vultures, sparrowhawks and peregrines. Early morning is the best time to watch the different birds as they fly on the first thermals of the day.

TRAVELLERS'
NEEDS

Where to Stay   264–273

Where to Eat and Drink   274–291

Shopping in Greece   292–293

Specialist Holidays and
  Outdoor Activities   294–297

WHERE TO STAY

Accommodation in Greece has improved vastly since the millennium, helped along by the staging of the 2004 Olympic Games. The spartan box rooms of the 1970s and 80s have been replaced by boutique hotels and luxury holiday resorts, supported by laws that effectively ban simpler grades of lodging. In contrast with commercialized, busy resorts, hospitality off the beaten track can still be warm and heartfelt. Various types of accommodations are described over the next four pages. Information is included for the

network of camp sites and the very limited facilities for hostelling and alpine refuge stays. The listings section *(see pp268–73)* includes over 100 places to stay, ranging from informal *enoikiazómena domátia* (rented rooms) to cutting-edge hotels, either in converted or purpose-built quarters. All-inclusive resorts, especially around coastal areas, are a well-established feature, though not always the best choice. If a half-board option is available at such places, it is wise to choose this until the quality of the food on offer has been tested.

New Malvasia Hotel *(see p271)* at Monemvasiá, restored by the EOT during the 1970s

Hotels

Most Greek hotels have standard Mediterranean concrete architecture, although in many coastal resorts, height limits restrict towering structures. Most hotels, whatever their vintage, have been refurbished since their origins in order to stay competitive. A very few Neo-Classical hotels remain, now benefiting from government preservation orders. Hotels built since the 1990s are generally designed with more imagination and sensitivity to the environment than in the past. The more expensive hotels will have a correspondingly higher level of service, offered by trained personnel.

Chain Hotels

Greece, with its tradition of family business ownership, long resisted the notion of chain hotels. However, both overseas brands, like Hyatt and Best Western, and homegrown chains are now a feature of the landscape. Their main advantage is prime location. The largest local chain, **Grecotel**, comprises 30 luxury and 4-star resort hotels – mostly on the islands, but also in Athens, Attica and the west Peloponnesian coast. Smaller chains, such as **Chandrís** and **Diváni**, offer accommodation in Athens, Thessaloníki and Kalampáka. **Aldemar** is another small chain with two coastal resorts near ancient Olympia. Hipper boutique and restoration hotel groups include **Yes!**, **Tourhotel**, **Domotel** and **Yades**.

Restored Settlements and Boutique Inns

In the 1970s, the EOT (Greek Tourist Office) began sponsoring the restoration of derelict buildings in vernacular style. The completed units offered value for money and an atmospheric environment. All these establishments have passed into private ownership. Surviving properties on the mainland can be found at Areópoli in the Máni, at

Makrynítsa and Vyzítsa on the Pílio, at Megálo Pápigko in Epirus, and at Monemvasiá.

Private entrepreneurs have seized the initiative in such renovation projects, installing small and medium-sized hotels in centuries-old buildings. Particularly successful ventures can be found at Stemnítsa, Kavála, Edessa, Thessaloníki, Ioánnina, Galaxídi, Náfplio, Aráchova and in many villages of the Zagóri region and the Pílio. The better ones combine respect for period features with modern conveniences.

The smallhotelsingreece.com and greatsmallhotels.com websites are excellent sources of information.

Luxury Resorts

Multi-star hotels offer a range of on-site amenities: outdoor or indoor pools; a sauna, hamam or even a full spa; multiple restaurants and bars; tennis courts, water sports or yoga classes; child-minding services and functions rooms.

Façade of the Neo-Classical King Othon 1&2 Hotel, Náfplio *(see p271)*

◀ Outdoor tables at a café in Pláka, Athens

Luxurious interiors of a suite with private garden at Grand Resort Lagonissi *(see p270)*

Enoikiazómena Domátia and Apartments

A large proportion of Greek lodgings is in *enoikiazómena domátia* (rented rooms) or *diamerísmata* (apartments). These are in modern structures, the rooms with a bathroom and usually a self-catering corner or a communal kitchen for guest use. Hot water is provided either by an electric immersion heater or by a solar heating device.

Grading

The EOT grade Greece's hotels, rooms and apartments. Hotel categories range from 1-star up to 5-star, plus deluxe, according to the location and the kind of facilities available. Rooms and apartments vary from 1-key to 4-key. There is supposed to be a direct correlation between amenities and classification, but local deviations mean there are many 3-star hotels that are superior to nearby 4-star ones.

One-star hotels, with basic facilities, are almost extinct. Two-star hotels must have en-suite rooms. A 3-star hotel must have some sort of common area, if only a small combination bar and breakfast room. Four-star hotels have extra amenities such as a full-service restaurant, a more substantial breakfast, and at least one sports facility, such as a pool or tennis court. Five-star hotels are usually at seafront or prime urban locations, and offer all conceivable amenities,

including business facilities. Deluxe category hotels are self-contained resort complexes.

One-key rooms are extinct, supplanted by 2-key blocks of en-suite rooms or studios with a kitchenette or shared cooking facilities. Three-key units consist of furnished apartments with demarcated rooms and superior fittings. A law is due to pass soon requiring all apartments and rooms to meet 4-key standards, with electronic locks, flat-screen TVs and other amenities.

Prices

The price of hotel rooms and *domátia* should correspond to their official category, though this depends on season and location. In Athens, for €60, it is possible to find a 2-star hotel; €75 should cover a 2-key double *domátio* in rural areas, while 3-key *domátia* and 3-star hotels charge €90–100. Four-star hotels ask at least €180 per double room; 5-star hotels typically cost €250–350. Deluxe resorts and restoration projects are exempt from EOT price controls and typically cost in excess of €400.

All of these rate estimations are for high season, including VAT and taxes; prices can

drop by almost 50 per cent in early spring or late autumn. Hotel rates include breakfast. Stays of less than three nights carry a surcharge in high season. In mainland skiing resorts, there is often a vast difference between weekend and mid-week rates.

Opening Seasons

Mainland hotels stay open year-round, except those at seafront resorts, which operate May–October. Hotels in skiing areas, conversely, may open only during the winter period. Rooms and apartments are supposed to shut October–April, but some don't, especially if there are no competing hotels nearby.

Booking

Package holidays on the Greek mainland cover Párga, Pílio, the Messinean Peloponnese and Chalkidikí. City breaks for Athens and Thessaloníki can also be found. If you contact a hotel directly, do so by email, so that there is a written record of the transaction. Most hotels (and many *domátia*) now have direct booking facilities. You usually have to provide credit card details as a deposit for the value of one night's stay.

Conservatory at Grande Bretagne hotel, Athens *(see p269)*

Agiou Pávlou Monastery on Mount Athos *(see p257)*

Youth Hostels

The Greek mainland has three HI (Hostelling International) recognized youth hostels *(xenón neótitos)*, all found in Athens. For more information, contact the **IYHA** (International Youth Hostel Association) in England, or the **YHA** (Youth Hostel Association) in Greece. In addition, a handful of unofficial hostels provide a standard of accommodation that is just as good, if not better. Greek hostels are not nearly as regimented as their northern European equivalents. Even without an IYHF card, you can usually stay if a vacancy is available. However, if there are two of you, a less expensive *domátio* will almost certainly be better value.

Alpine Refuges

The mountains of the Greek mainland are dotted with over 40 alpine refuges *(katafýgia)*. Very few are continuously staffed – two on Mount Olympos *(see p245)* and one on Mount Gamíla, in the Píndos range, being notable exceptions – so you must contact the relevant branch of the **EOS** (Greek Alpine Club) to rent keys for these rooms. This is expensive and not worthwhile unless you muster a large group. The **EOOA** and **SEO** *(see p267)* may also provide information on refuges (SEO for their own one on Mount Olympos). Some of the

mountain huts make wonderful base camps, fully equipped with kitchens, bed linen, and well-designed common areas; others are little more than shacks originally built for shepherds or fire-control personnel. Another complication for the alpine accommodation option is that, as many were built at a time when approaches to the mountain ranges were quite different, today they are often located well away from the preferred hiking routes.

Rural Tourism

Conceived during the 1980s to give women in the Greek provinces a measure of financial independence by renting out rooms in their homes, rural tourism has over time evolved from farm and village stays to include comfortable rural inns and villas. The best selection of such properties is available through the **Hellenic Agrotourism Federation** *(see p303)*.

Mountain refuge, Kóziakas mountain, Tríkala

Monasteries

The less-visited monasteries and convents in Greece operate *xenónes* or hostels, intended primarily for Greek Orthodox pilgrims on weekend visits. Pilgrims will always be a priority, but it is often possible to find a vacancy at short notice. Accommodation is of the spartan-dormitory variety, with a frugal evening meal and morning coffee provided; it is customary to leave a donation in the *katholikón* (main church).

The monasteries on Mount Athos are the most accustomed to non-Orthodox visitors, though these are open to men only. Visits – especially in high season, which also includes Christmas and Orthodox Easter – need to be carefully planned, as the procedure for reserving space and obtaining an entry permit to this semi-autonomous monastic republic can be difficult *(see p256)*.

Camping

The Greek mainland has more than 100 officially recognized camp sites. Most are in attractive seafront settings, and as many cater primarily to caravanners, with limited tent space. Most are privately run; the last few still owned by the EOT, or by the local municipality, are being sold off. All but the most primitive sites have hot showers heated by solar power, shady landscaping and a snack bar or café. Power hookups are generally available for an extra fee. The most luxurious camp sites are miniature holiday villages, with swimming pool, tennis courts, laundry rooms, banking and postal facilities, and bungalows for those without tents. Established sites usually have the advantage of mature shady trees. The ground is often sun-baked and very hard, so short pegs that can be banged in with a mallet are best. You can download a current list of Greek campsites with full descriptions from the **campingingreece.gr** website; a paper booklet is no longer published.

Travellers With Disabilities

Contact Tourism for All (see p303) for an information sheet detailing wheelchair access at hotels, attractions and eateries in Greece, as well as a list of useful contact numbers in the country. The hotel listings in this guide (see pp268–73) indicate which establishments have suitable facilities, such as lifts and ramps, for the disabled.

Swimming pool at Karavostasi Beach hotel (see p272)

Greek information sources for disabled travellers tend to be rudimentary; the EOT only publishes a questionnaire, which can be sent to specific accommodation establishments to assess their suitability.

Further Information

The EOT periodically publishes an informative leaflet entitled *Rural Tourism* detailing the best accomodation to be found in the countryside. Two other hotel manuals, which are both issued by private organizations, are the **Greek Travel Pages** (GTP) and the **Tourist Guide of Greece**. They are not as complete or authoritative as the EOT guides, but they do have the advantage of being published more frequently. The GTP is monthly, offering only skeletal information unless the hotel concerned has purchased advertising space. Similarly, the quarterly publication *Tourist Guide of Greece*

does not detail comprehensive accommodation information.

Recommended Hotels

The hotels in this section have been chosen to reflect their quality and amenities within the themes of Luxury, Historic Restoration, Seaside/Mountain Resort, Rural, Boutique and Value for Money, although some establishments will fall into more than one category. Greece has numerous luxury and historic restoration hotels; we have selected the best. The rural category covers village hotels and inns and those standing in acres of countryside, while the boutique theme is given to hotels that have had a contemporary makeover in recent years. Greece has a wide selection of hotels we consider Value for Money and will stretch the budget a little bit further. The DK Choice hotels are extra special. They may have above-average standards and amenities or a breathtaking location, or simply have a charm that sets them apart.

DIRECTORY

Chain Hotels

Aldemar Hotels
Kifisias 262, 14562 Kifisiá.
Tel 210 628 8400.
W aldemarhotels.com

Chandrís Hotels
Syngroú 377, 17564 Paleó
Fáliron, Athens.
Tel 210 948 4730.
W chandris.gr

Diváni Hotels
Vas. Alexándrou 2, 16121
Athens. **Tel** 210 720 7000.
W divanis.com

Domotel
Tel 210 689 9276
and 2310 647500.
W domotel.gr

Grecotel
Kifissias 64b, Maroúsi,
15125 Athens.
Tel 210 728 0300.
W grecotel.gr

Tourhotel
Tel 210 3232 5605.
W tourhotel.gr

Yades Hotels
Tel 210 364 0441.
W yadeshotels.gr

Yes! Hotels
Tel 210 327 3200.
W yeshotels.gr

Hostels

IYHA (UK)
Tel 01707 324 170.
W hihostels.com

YHA (Greece)
Student & Traveller's Inn,
Kydathinaion 16, Pláka,
10558 Athens.
Tel 210 324 4808.
W studenttravellers
inn.com

Alpine Refuges

**EOOA (Ellinikí
Omospondía
Oreivasías kai
Anarríxisis)**
(Hellenic Federation of
Mountaineering &
Climbing) Milióni 5,
10673 Athens.
Tel 210 364 5904.
W eooa.gr

**EOS (Ellinikós Orei-
vatikós Sýndesmos)**
(Greek Alpine Club)
Ipsilantou 53,
11521 Athens.
Tel 210 321 2355.
W eosathinon.gr

SEO
**(Sýllogos Ellínon
Oreivatón)**
(Association of Greek
Climbers)
Plateía Aristotélous 5,
Thessaloníki.
Tel 2310 224710.
W seoreivaton.gr

Further Information

Greek Travel Pages
Tel 210 324 7511.
W gtp.gr

**Tourist Guide
of Greece**
Tel 210 864 1688.
W tggr.com

Where to Stay

Athens

Exárcheia

Exarchion €
Value **Map** 2 F3
Themistokléous 55, 106 83
Tel *210 380 0731*
W exarchion.com
Well-presented rooms and an
on-site restaurant. Beautiful
rooftop views of the Acropolis.

Ilísia

Hilton €€€
Luxury **Map** 4 D5
Vasilíssis Sofías 46, 115 28
Tel *210 728 1000*
W hiltonathens.gr
This luxury hotel has chic rooms
with all amenities. There is a
thermal spa on site as well as
gourmet restaurants.

Kolonáki

Lion Hotel Apartments €€
Boutique **Map** 4 C5
Evzónon 7, 115 21
Tel *210 724 8722*
W lionhotel.gr
Complex of upmarket, nicely
decorated apartments. Located
near Plateía Syntágmatos, this is a
good base for exploring the city.

Periscope €€
Boutique **Map** 3 B5
Charitos 22, 106 75
Tel *210 729 7200*
W periscope.gr
Smart hotel with wooden floors
and minimalist furniture. Gym,
restaurant and a cocktail bar.

St George Lycabettus €€
Luxury **Map** 3 B4
Kleoménous 2, 106 75
Tel *210 741 6000*
W sglycabettus.gr
Rooms with large windows and
all modern comforts. The rooftop

pool and eatery afford views of the
Acropolis. There is a spa on site.

Koukáki

Art Gallery €
Value **Map** 6 D4
Erechtheíou 5, 117 42
Tel *210 923 8376*
W artgalleryhotel.gr
Housed in a former art gallery, this
family-run hotel has a welcoming
feel. Homely rooms and lounge.

DK Choice

Marble House €
Boutique **Map** 5 C4
Alley off Anastasíou Zínni 35, 117 41
Tel *210 922 8294*
W marblehouse.gr
Located near the Acropolis
Museum, this hotel offers gorgeous rooms with upmarket
fixtures and fittings. Central areas
awash with colour, tasteful
wrought-iron furniture and
plants give the Marble House a
casual but chic feel. Rooms have
furnished balconies or patios.

Makrygiánni

Hera €€
Boutique **Map** 6 E3
Falírou 9, 117 42
Tel *210 923 6682*
W herahotel.gr
Stylish hotel with deluxe suites, a
dome-lit atrium breakfast room
and a rooftop bar-restaurant with
views of the Acropolis.

Herodion €€
Boutique **Map** 5 C3
Rovértou Gálli 4
Tel *210 923 6832*
W herodion.gr
It's the common areas that impress
here: café-restaurant with shaded
seating, roof terrace with two
Jacuzzis and Acropolis views.

Simple but comfortable interiors of a room at Marble House, Koukáki

Price Guide
Prices are based on one night's stay in
high season for a standard double room,
inclusive of service charges and taxes.

€ under €100
€€ €100 to 250
€€€ over €250

Monastiráki

Carolina €
Value **Map** 2 E5
Kolokotróni 55, 105 60
Tel *210 324 3551*
W hotel-carolina-athens.com
A comfortable hotel in a 1936
building. Located within easy
reach of Athens' main attractions
and tavernas. Good breakfast.

Omónoia

Art Athens Hotel €
Boutique **Map** 2 D3
Márnis 27, 104 32
Tel *210 524 0501*
W arthotelathens.gr
Grand Neo-Classical mansion with
hi-tech lighting and cream decor
offset by wooden floors and art.
Rooms come with a Jacuzzi.

The Alassia €€
Boutique **Map** 2 D3
Sokrátous 50, 104 31
Tel *210 527 4000*
W thealassia.com.gr
Welcoming hotel with minimalist
decor. Lots of marble, recessed
lighting and futuristic furniture.

Delphi Art Hotel €€
Historic Restoration **Map** 2 D3
Agíou Konstantínou 27, 104 37
Tel *210 524 4004*
W delphiarthotel.com
A 1930s Neo-Classical building
with lavish rooms, modern
bathrooms and a red foyer.

Pedion Áreos

Radisson Blu Park €€
Boutique **Map** 3 A1
Leofóros Alexándras 10, 106 82
Tel *210 889 4500*
W rbathenspark.com
Lavish rooms with all modern
conveniences. Refined rooftop bar
and an outdoor swimming pool.

Pláka

Phaedra €
Value **Map** 6 E2
*Chairefóntos 16, corner of
Adrianoú, 105 58*
Tel *210 323 8461*
W hotelphaedra.com
Comfortable rooms, larger
ones with balconies. Rooftop

Sweeping views from a room at New Hotel, a boutique property in Pláka

breakfast area with great city views. Located close to the Temple of Zeus.

Student And Travellers Inn   €
Value   Map 6 E2
Kydathinaíon 16, 105 58
Tel *210 324 4808*
🆆 studenttravellersinn.com
Shared and private rooms, some with en suite bathrooms. Garden courtyard. Centrally located.

Acropolis House   €€
Historic Restoration   Map 6 E1
Kódrou 6–8, 105 58
Tel *210 322 6241*
🆆 acropolishouse.gr
Well-preserved 19th-century mansion with many original features and antiques. Free Wi-Fi.

Central   €€
Boutique   Map 6 E1
Apóllonos 21, 105 57
Tel *210 323 4350*
🆆 centralhotel.gr
Conveniently located, with smart designer furniture and marble bathrooms, plus a rooftop bar.

Hermes   €€
Boutique   Map 6 E1
Apóllonos 19, 105 57
Tel *210 323 5514*
🆆 hermeshotel.gr
On a quiet street. Offers stylish renovated rooms, a lounge bar, kids' playroom and a roof garden.

DK Choice

New Hotel   €€
Boutique   Map 6 F1
Fillelínon 16, 105 57
Tel *210 327 3000*
🆆 yeshotels.gr
The award-winning designer duo Campana Brothers have given this hotel a dazzling wood and leather decor. Rooms feature bathrooms with solid brass washbasins. Superb restaurant.

Plaka   €€
Value   Map 6 D1
Kapnikaréas 7 & Mitropóleos St 105 56
Tel *210 322 2706*
🆆 plakahotel.gr
Welcoming rooms here have quiet decor with subtle colours. The roof garden has great Acropolis views.

Ava   €€€
Boutique   Map 6 E1
Lysikrátous 9–11, 105 58
Tel *210 325 9000*
🆆 avahotel.gr
At this all-suite hotel, upper units have courtyard views from their balconies. Bigger suites are good for families.

Electra Palace   €€€
Luxury   Map 6 E1
Navárchou Nikodímou 18–20, 105 57
Tel *210 337 0000*
🆆 electrahotels.gr
Housed in a splendid Neo-Classical mansion, this upscale hotel offers elegant, tasteful rooms with antique-style furniture. Full spa, pool and multiple restaurants on site.

Psyrrí

Arion   €€
Value   Map 2 D5
Agíou Dimitríou 18, 105 54
Tel *210 324 0415*
🆆 arionhotel.gr
Tasteful rooms with marble bathrooms. Excellent rooftop bar and a bright lobby area. A hearty breakfast is available here.

Fresh   €€
Boutique   Map 2 D4
Sofokléous 26 & Kleisthénous, 105 52
Tel *210 524 8511*
🆆 freshhotel.gr
Rooms with minimalist decor in white and vibrant colours. Guests can also enjoy the rooftop pool, wellness suite and a superb restaurant.

O&B Athens Boutique Hotel   €€€
Boutique   Map 1 C5
Leokoríou 7, 105 54
Tel *210 331 2940*
🆆 oandbhotel.com
Very stylish accommodation, with marble bathrooms. Breakfast on the rooftop restaurant.

Sýntagma

Athens Cypria   €€
Value   Map 6 E1
Diomeías 5, 105 63
Tel *210 323 8034*
🆆 athenscypria.com
Quiet and friendly, with stylish rooms in earthy tones; some have balconies with city views.

NJV Athens Plaza   €€
Luxury   Map 6 F1
Plateía Syntágmatos, 105 64
Tel *210 335 2400*
🆆 njvathensplaza.gr
Elegant rooms, superb restaurant and a full spa. The lobby boasts marble walls and chandeliers.

DK Choice

Grande Bretagne   €€€
Luxury   Map 6 F1
Vassiléos Georgíou 1, Plateía Syntágmatos, 105 64
Tel *210 333 0000*
🆆 grandebretagne.gr
Built in 1842, this hotel exudes luxury – from its lavish lobby to its stylish rooms. The Alexander's Bar is famous for its 18th-century tapestry of Alexander the Great.

Thiseío

Phidias   €
Value   Map 5 B1
Apostólou Pávlou 39, 118 51
Tel *210 345 9511*
🆆 phidias.gr
Comfortable rooms – the ones at the front have balconies with great views of the Acropolis.

Chic decor in a brightly lit room at O&B Athens Boutique Hotel, Psyrrí

For more information on types of hotels *see page 267*

A luxuriously furnished suite at the upscale Grand Resort Lagonissi

Around Athens

Kifisiá: Semiramis €€
Boutique **Map** D4
Charílaou Trikoúpi 48, 145 62
Tel *210 628 4400*
W yeshotels.gr
Artistic decor of brilliant white
with candy-inspired colour
themes. Rooms boast futuristic
furniture and hi-tech gadgets.

**Lagoníssi: Grand Resort
Lagonissi** €€€
Seaside Resort **Map** D4
*40th km, Athens–Soúnio road,
190 10*
Tel 22910 76000
W lagonissiresort.gr
Sprawling complex with villas
and bungalows. Top-notch
restaurants, spa and a children's
club on site.

Piraeus: Hotel Mistral €€
Value **Map** D4
*Alexándrou Papanastasíou 105,
185 33*
Tel *210 411 7150*
W mistral.gr
This attractive hotel boasts pictur-
esque views of the Mikrolímano
harbour and the coast from its
rooms and restaurants.

Rafína: Avra Hotel €€
Value **Map** D4
Arafinidón Alón 3, 190 09
Tel *22940 22780*
W hotelavra.gr
Located right next to Rafína's
harbour, this welcoming place
has well-equipped rooms. The
restaurant serves exquisite
Greek fare.

Vouliagméni: The Margi €€
Boutique **Map** D4
Litoús 11, 166 71
Tel *210 892 9000*
W themargi.gr
"Comfy like home" is the well-
deserved motto of this hotel
with eight grades of rooms and
suites; higher floors have great
sea views. The on-site restaurants
source their ingredients from the
hotel's own farm.

The Peloponnese

DK Choice

**Corinth: Prime
Isthmus Hotel** €€
Luxury **Map** C4
Corinth Canal, 201 00
Tel *27410 23454*
W isthmus.gr
The breathtaking location,
just metres away from the
Corinth Canal, is com-
plemented by lush gardens
dominated by a lagoon pool
and a tennis court. Rooms
are in bright summer shades
with patios or balconies. The
restaurant has panoramic
views. Located close to
ancient Corinth and Isthmia.

**Foinikoúnta: Porto
Finissia** €€
Value **Map** C5
Waterfront, 240 06
Tel *27230 71457*
W portofinissia.gr
This hotel is conveniently located
close to the beach. The simple
rooms have large balconies with
ironwork railings. Most have
beach views.

Geroliménas: Tsitsiris Castle €€
Rural **Map** C5
Stavrí hamlet, 23 071
Tel *27330 56298*
W tsitsiriscastle.gr
A complex of stone buildings
with cosy rooms in autumnal
colours. Vaulted breakfast room.
Some rooms look over nearby
tower-houses; others, the well-
tended gardens.

Gýtheio: Gythion €€
Historic Restoration **Map** C5
Vassiléos Pávlou 33, 232 00
Tel *27330 23452*
W gythionhotel.gr
An elegant 1864 Neo-Classical
mansion where modern design
combines with original features.
Overlooks the harbour and the
busy main road.

Kalamáta: Akti Taygetos €€
Seaside Resort **Map** C5
Mikrí Mantineía, 241 00
Tel *27210 42000*
W aktitaygetos.gr
Nestled in lovely gardens with
palm trees and views of the
ocean, this complex has summery
rooms (including family units),
pool and two events rooms.

Kalávryta: Filoxenia €
Luxury **Map** C4
Ethnikís Andistáseos 10, 250 01
Tel *26920 22422*
W hotelfiloxenia.gr
The use of stone and wood
imparts a warm intimacy to this
hotel-spa. Well-equipped rooms
and a spa.

Kalógria: Kalogria Beach Hotel €€
Seaside Resort **Map** B4
Kalógria Metochiou 252 00
Tel *26930 31380*
W kalogriahotel.gr
Set in lush gardens behind the
beach. Well-appointed rooms
and villas. Watersports, pools and
a tennis court, plus a kids' club,
are available.

Kastaniá: Xenonas I Kastania €
Rural **Map** C4
Kastaniá village, Korinthiá
Tel *27470 61289*
W kastania-rooms.gr
This is the best choice for
overnighting in the Stymfalía/
Feneós/Agíou Georgíou
monastery region. Rooms
have stall showers, flat-screen
TVs, winter heating and
mountain or village views.
On-site taverna for all meals.

DK Choice

**Messinía: The Romanos
Resort** €€€
Luxury **Map** B5
*Navaríno Dunes, Costa Navaríno,
240 01*
Tel *27230 96000*
W romanoscostanavarino.com
This beach resort offers every
amenity, from rooms with private
infinity pools and a spa that uses
olive leaves and prickly pears in
its therapies to a health suite and
golf course. Also available are
activities for children and a
choice of 10 restaurants.

Methóni: Castello €
Value **Map** B5
Odós Miaoúli, 240 06
Tel *27230 31300*
W castello.gr
Close to Methóni's huge fortress.
Has tasteful rooms with balconies,
a roof lounge and garden.

Monemvasiá: New Malvasia €€
Historic Restoration   Map C5
Kástro, 230 70
Tel *27320 63007*
W malvasia-hotel.gr
Rooms in warm colours with
stone arches, vaulted ceilings and
antique-style furniture. Fabulous
ocean views from some rooms.

Náfplio: Byron €
Historic Restoration   Map C4
Plátonos 2, 211 00
Tel *27520 22351*
W byronhotel.gr
Elegant hotel in a restored old
mansion overlooking an Ottoman
hamam. Earth-toned decor and
antique furniture. Breakfast terrace.

Náfplio: King Othon 1&2 €€
Historic Restoration   Map C4
Farmakopoúlou 4, 211 00
Tel *27520 27585*
W kingothon.gr
Charming hotel in a century-old
mansion. Rooms have period
decor and wrought-iron beds.

Néos Mystrás: Byzantion €
Value   Map C5
Village Centre, 231 00
Tel *27310 83309*
W byzantionhotel.gr
Spacious rooms with castle and
rural views. Lovely gardens wrap
around a pool and a lounge-bar.

DK Choice

Olympia: Pelops €
Value   Map B4
Varelá 2, 270 65
Tel *26240 22543*
W hotelpelops.gr
Lovely, family-run place offering
well-equipped rooms with
balconies. It has an atmospheric
courtyard and a relaxed lounge.
The restaurant serves authentic
Greek cuisine. Ideal location for
the museums and archaeo-
logical sites of Ancient Olympia.

Pátra: Art Primarolia €€
Boutique   Map C4
Óthonos and Amalías 30, 262 21
Tel *2610 624900*
W primaroliahotel.com
In a converted distillery, this hotel
has subtle decor and original art
on the walls. Fabulous lobby.

Stemnítsa: Xenonas Stemnitsa €
Rural   Map C4
Just off main plateía, 220 24
Tel *27950 81349*
W xenonas-stemnitsa.gr
A great-value inn with four rooms
and one studio. Beamed ceilings,
pointed stonework and plush
furnishings, plus all mod cons.

Zachloroú: Romantzo €
Rural   Map C4
Village centre, 250 01
Tel *26920 22758*
Stone-clad hotel-restaurant by a
stream. The terrace overlooks a
stopping on the Kalávryta-
Diakoftó railway.

Central and Western Greece

Aráchova: Likoria €€
Luxury   Map C3
Filellínon, west of centre, 320 04
Tel *26720 31180*
W likoria.gr
Plush rooms (many with a fireplace
and views), and a sauna/steam
bath. Easy parking, too.

DK Choice

Argalastí: Aspiration €€
Historic Restoration   Map D3
Village centre, 370 06
Tel *6936 497760*
W agamemnon.gr
Housed in a beautiful mansion,
Aspiration has rooms in subtle
colours, stone or wood floors
and antiques. There are three
buildings, one of them with a
pool, bar lounge and restaurant.

Delfoí: Orfeas €
Value   Map C3
Ifigenías & Syngroú 35, 330 54
Tel *26650 82077*
W hotelorfeas.com
Set quite high in the village, the
Orfeas has sweeping views to the
Corinth Gulf from the rear units.

Delfoí: Sun View €
Value   Map C3
Apóllonos 84, 330 54
Tel *22650 82349*
Great views of the Gulf of Corinth
at this pretty pension with rooms
decorated in autumnal shades.

Dílofo: Archontiko Dilofo €€
Historic Restoration   Map B2
Village centre, 440 07
Tel *26530 22455*
W dilofo.com
This inn in a beautiful Zagóri
village has ten colourful rooms,
five with fireplaces. A generous
breakfast is served in the lounge.

Galaxídi: Ganimede €€
Boutique   Map C3
Nikólaou Gourgoúri 20, 330 52
Tel *22650 41328*
W ganimede.gr
Family-run 19th-century mansion
with antique-furnished rooms.
Breakfast features home-made
jams and goodies from the
family's own bakery.

Ioánnina: Politeia €€
Boutique   Map B2
Anexartisías 109, 454 44
Tel *26510 22235*
W etip.gr
Sumptuous rooms and suites with
slightly eccentric furnishings.
Although located in the bazaar,
units face an internal courtyard,
so it's quiet by night.

Kalampáka: Alsos House €
Value   Map B2
Kanári 5, 422 00
Tel *24320 24097*
W alsoshouse.gr
Tasteful rooms and apartments
within a stone inn. Great views
of the Metéora Rocks.

Kalampáka: Doupiani House €
Boutique   Map B2
Kastráki, 422 00
Tel *24320 75326*
W doupianihouse.gr
This excellent-value hotel has a
comfortable lounge, welcoming
host family and good breakfast.
Its deserved popularity means
reservations are mandatory,
especially at weekends. The
well-appointed rooms include
some family units.

Elegant exteriors and rooms with balconies at Pelops, a hotel in Olympia

For more information on types of hotels *see page 267*

Karpenísi: Amadryades €€
Rural **Map** C3
Voútyro village, 361 00
Tel *22370 80921*
W amadryades.gr
Gorgeous stone-and-wood hotel
set on a vast lawn. Upscale rooms
have beamed ceilings, fireplaces,
balconies and art on the walls.
There is a cosy bar and lounge
and a lovely breakfast café.

Kónitsa: Grand Hotel Dentro €
Luxury **Map** B2
Kalpáki to Kónitsa road, 441 00
Tel *26550 29365*
W grandhoteldentro.gr
A façade of stone and wood, with
a similar decor theme in the
rooms, many with balconies.
Suites have Jacuzzis and
fireplaces. Lovely views.

Makrynítsa: Pandora €€
Historic Restoration **Map** C3
Edge of village, 370 11
Tel *24280 99404*
W pandoramansion.gr
Lavish hotel with period charm
and spacious rooms – some with
fireplaces, many with views.

**Megálo Pápigko: Xenonas
Papaevangelou** €€
Rural **Map** B2
Edge of village, 440 41
Tel *26530 41135*
W hotelpapaevangelou.gr
Large rooms and studios in a
stone building in a quiet setting.
Stately country-house ambience.

Métsovo: Kassaros €
Value **Map** B2
Tr Tsoumágka 3, 442 00
Tel *26560 41800*
W kassaros.gr
Rooms offer views of the ravine
at this traditional, cosy inn with
a sauna in the basement.

Moúresi: The Old Silk Store €€
Historic Restoration **Map** D3
Village centre, 370 12
Tel *24260 49086*
W pelionet.gr
This renovated Neo-Classical
mini-mansion, offers rooms
with lovely views. Breakfast
on the garden terrace.

Náfpaktos: Akti €
Value **Map** C3
*Korydaléos 3, Grímpovo Beach,
303 00*
Tel *26340 28464*
W akti.gr
Standard doubles have butler
sinks and marble dresser tables,
while three rooftop suites are
palatial. Gulf views from many
rooms, an antique-crammed
lobby and an airy breakfast salon.

Beautiful views from the hotel Xenonas Papaevangelou

DK Choice

Párga: Karavostasi Beach €€
Seaside Resort **Map** B3
Pérdika, 461 00
Tel *26650 91104*
W hotel-karavostasi.gr
This attractive, family-oriented
resort sits in a secluded spot
with lush gardens. Rooms are
tastefully minimalist, with olive
grove or sea views. It features a
swimming pool, as well as a
restaurant serving international
family meals.

Párga: Lichnos Beach €€
Seaside Resort **Map** B3
Lichnos Bay, 480 60
Tel *26840 31257*
W lichnosbeach.gr
Hillside hotel overlooking Párga's
best beach. Honeymoon suites
have an outdoor Jacuzzi. Free
shuttle to town.

Portariá: Kritsa €
Boutique **Map** C3
Plateía Portariás, 370 11 Portariá
Tel *24280 99121*
W hotel-kritsa.gr
Some of the rooms in this Belle
Epoque building overlook the
square. Cooking courses available.

DK Choice

Tríkala: Panellinion €
Historic Restoration **Map** C2
Plateía Ríga Feraíou, 421 00
Tel *24310 73545*
W hotelpanellinion.com
This landmark 1914 building
has hosted many a Greek VIP;
from its first-floor balcony,
politicians have delivered
speeches for decades. Rooms
are comfortably old-fashioned,
and the lounge bar is a
favourite meeting point.

Tsepélovo: Gouris Inn €
Value **Map** B2
Village centre, 440 10
Tel *26530 81314*
No-frills inn popular with trekkers,
who enjoy the warm welcome
and generous breakfasts.

**Vyzítsa: Archontiko
Karagiannopoulou** €€
Historic **Map** C3
Village centre, 370 10
Tel *24230 86717*
W karagiannopoulou.com
Elegantly restored 18th-century
mansion whose stylish rooms
have stained-glass windows and
painted ceilings.

Zagóri: Porfyron €
Historic Restoration **Map** B2
Ano Pediná, 440 77
Tel *26530 71579*
W porfyron.gr
Stay in antique-furnished rooms
with fireplaces at this mansion.
The on-site taverna means going
half-board is a wise choice.

Northern Greece

**Ammouliani Islet:
Sunrise Hotel** €
Value **Map** D2
Ammouliani, 630 75
Tel *23770 51273*
W sunrise-ammouliani.gr
Outstanding setting, above a
white-sand beach. Modern
rooms and a taverna-style café.

Arnaia: Oikia Alexandrou €
Historic **Map** D2
*Plateía Patriárchou Vartholomaíou
tou Prótou, 630 74*
Tel *23720 23210*
W oikia-alexandrou.gr
A stylish 1812 mansion with
period features, plus fireplace
lounge, gym, spa and restaurant.

Key to Price Guide *see page 268*

DK Choice

Dadiá: Dadiaselo €
Luxury **Map** F1
Dadiá village, 684 00
Tel 25540 32333
W dadiaselo.gr
A modern complex set around
a lagoon pool and terraces,
the Dadiaselo is popular with
visitors keen to explore this
protected region. Its six self-
contained apartments and a
café-bar in a former stable are
attractively presented. Located
close to Dadiá Forest Reserve.

Edessa: Varosi €
Historic Restoration **Map** C1
Archierós Meletiou 45–47, 582 00
Tel 23810 21865
W varosi.gr
An old mansion sensitively
converted into Edessa's most
popular lodging – success has
meant expansion to an annexe.
Small veranda-garden.

Fanári: Fanari Hotel €
Value **Map** E1
Fanári seafront, 691 00
Tel 25350 31300
W fanari-hotel.gr
Beachside hotel with boutique-
standard rooms, a playground
and a cheerful restaurant. A
good base for trips to Xánthi
and Komotiní.

Kastoriá: Chloe €€
Luxury **Map** B2
Antheeon, cnr Giasemión, 521 00
Tel 24670 21300
W hotelchloe.gr
A modern but tasteful hotel
with a mix of rooms and suites,
plus a veranda bar, cheerful
breakfast area and restaurant.

Kavála: Imaret €€€
Boutique **Map** D1
Th. Poulídou 30–32, 651 10
Tel 2510 620151
W imaret.gr
This restored Ottoman-era *imaret*
(a Koranic school) features 26
exquisite rooms and suites, a
restaurant and the original
Turkish bath.

Kerkíni: Oikoperiigitis €
Value **Map** C1
Lake Kerkíni, 620 55
Tel 23270 41450
W oikoperiigitis.gr
Two separate lodgings: a simpler,
rustic, purpose-built inn in wood
and stone, and a more boutique-
like hotel in a 1918-vintage
mansion. Within sight of the
lake, this is Greece's top birdwatching venue.

Litóchoro: Villa Drosos €
Value **Map** C2
Archéllou 20, 602 00
Tel 23520 84561
W villa-drosos.com
Family-run inn opposite a park,
in the village. Bright rooms with
private balconies. Swimming pool.

Maróneia: Roxani Country House €
Value **Map** E1
Edge of village, 694 00
Tel 25330 21501
W roxani.com
Colourful rooms with sea or
mountain views, a pool and a
well-stocked bar and restaurant.

Néos Marmarás: Akrotiri €
Value **Map** D2
Village centre, 630 80
Tel 23750 72191
W akrotirimarmaras.gr
Well-presented studio-style rooms
with their own kitchenettes and
balconies. Stunning sea views.

Néos Marmarás: Kelyfos €€
Luxury **Map** D2
Edge of village, 630 81
Tel 23750 72833
W kelyfos.gr
Charming lodgings amid gardens
full of palm trees. The restaurant
features own-grown ingredients.

Nymféo: La Moara €€
Boutique **Map** B2
Edge of village, 530 78
Tel 23860 31377
Country house-style hotel owned
by the Boutaris family of vintners.
Superb restaurant.

Préspa Lakes: To Petrino €
Value **Map** B1
Agios Germanós village centre, 530 77
Tel 23850 51344
W prespespetrino.com
The interior of this stone-built
inn features rustic furniture and
traditional fabrics.

Préspa Lakes: Prespa Wellness Resort €€
Luxury **Map** B1
Platý village, 531 00
Tel 23850 51400
W prespes-hotelprespaspa.
clickhere.gr
Complex of self-contained studios
with nice decor and balconies.
Gym, spa and a kids' playground.

Symvolí: Faraggi Hotel €
Boutique **Map** D1
Between Kavála, Sérres, Dráma, 620 47
Tel 23240 81667
W faraggihotel.com
Lovely stone-built riverside hotel
near an old bridge. Tasteful
rooms, a fine-dining restaurant
and a spa.

Thessaloníki: Nepheli €
Value **Map** C2
Komninón 1, Panórama, 552 36
Tel 2310 342002
W nepheli.gr
The four-star Nepheli has rooms
and suites and a gourmet
restaurant, but no pool or spa.

Thessaloníki: Orestias Kastorias €
Value **Map** C2
Agnóstou Stratiótou 14, 546 31
Tel 2310 276517
W okhotel.gr
Stay in contemporary rooms in
this budget hotel, a few steps
from Agios Dimítrios church.

DK Choice

Thessaloníki: Electra Palace €€
Luxury **Map** C2
Plateía Artistotélous 9, 546 24
Tel 23102 94000
W electrahotels.gr
Landmark hotel that is superbly
opulent, from the walnut-,
marble- and leather-appointed
lobby to lavish rooms and suites
with all mod cons. Rooftop pool
and garden restaurant, spa and
fitness centre lower down.

Thessaloníki: Makedonia Palace €€
Luxury **Map** C2
Megálou Alexándrou 2, 546 40
Tel 2310 897197
W makedoniapalace.com
Seafront hotel with a mix of rooms
and suites (get a gulf-view unit),
outdoor pool and two restaurants.

Thessaloníki: Le Palace Art €€
Boutique **Map** C2
Tsimiskí 12, 546 24
Tel 2310 257400
W lepalace.gr
Tasteful rooms, good breakfasts
and secure parking in this
refurbished 1920s building.

Boutique-style room in the Fanari Hotel
in northern Greece

For more information on types of hotels *see page 267*

WHERE TO EAT AND DRINK

Greeks consider the best places for eating out to be where the food is fresh, good value and properly cooked, not necessarily where the setting or the cuisine is the fanciest. Visitors, too, have come to appreciate the simplicity and appeal of the traditional Greek kitchen – cheeses, vegetables, a little meat or seafood and some wine or *tsípouro*, always shared with friends. Despite the economic crisis, entire families still dine out together once or twice a month, especially at weekends. The traditional three-hour lunch and siesta – still the daily rhythm of the countryside – is now only a fading memory for most city Greeks, who have adapted to a more Western European routine. But the combination of traditional cooking and outside influences has produced a vast range of eating places in Greece, with something on offer for everyone.

Casual dining at a restaurant in Central Athens

Types of Restaurants

Some restaurants specialize in a particular type of cuisine. In Thessaloníki, for example, and in the suburbs of Athens, where Asia Minor refugees settled after 1923, you may find food to be spicier than the Greek norm, with lots of red peppers.

The menu in a traditional restaurant tends to be short, with no more than a dozen *mezédes* (starters or snacks), eight main dishes, four or five cooked vegetable dishes or salads, plus a dessert of fresh or cooked fruit, as well as local and national wines.

There's some overlap between *oinomageireía* and the taverna. In a traditional *oinomageireío* (literally "wine-cookhouse"), an array of home-style *mageireftá* (pre-cooked casserole dishes) is set out in front of customers.

Foreigners new to Greek fare can simply point to their preferences and may even be invited into the kitchen to see the ingredients. Some *oinomageireía* open only at lunch or close quite early in the evening after being open continuously all afternoon.

An *oinomageireío* usually prides itself on wine from the barrel – known as *chýma* (in bulk) or *me to kiló* (by weight, or litre); it should be at least drinkable if not very good. Many *oinomageireía* have been in the same family for generations and strive to uphold their reputation.

Many hotel restaurants are open to non-residents. Some smaller country hotels have excellent kitchens and also serve good local wines. Check out those near where you are staying.

As part of a general culinary renaissance, many creative Greek tavernas (*koultouriárika*) have sprung up. Chef-owners update traditional recipes and are more daring: less oil, more herbs and spices, unusual flavour juxtapositions, while proudly sourcing local produce.

Exotic cooking has made few inroads except in Athens, Thessaloníki and resorts like Náfplio. Nouvelle French, generic Southeast Asian, bogus Mexican, better Argentine or Spanish and variably successful Middle Eastern cuisines found. But Greeks love Italian food, and good Italian eateries (both pizza joints and full-on *trattorie*) are often busy. Greek-Italian fusion eateries also tend to succeed.

A sign for a taverna in Párga

Tavernas

One of the great pleasures for the traveller in Greece is the tradition of the taverna, a place to eat and drink, even if you simply snack on *mezédes* (Greeks rarely drink without eating).

Athenian restaurant interior fusing classic and contemporary styles

Waiter outside a restaurant in Pláka, Athens

Traditional tavernas are open from mid-evening and stay open late; occasionally they are open for lunch as well. Menus are short and seasonal – perhaps six or eight *mezédes* and four main courses comprising casseroles and dishes cooked *tis óras* (to order), along with vegetables, salads, fruit and wine.

Like traditional restaurants, some tavernas specialize in the owner's home region, a particular style or certain foods.

A *psarotavérna* (seafood taverna) relies on scaly fish, cephalopods like octopus, and shellfish starters. The owner or a family member may bring in a fresh catch each morning. Presentation is usually basic: a whole grilled fish or squid on an oval metal plate, doused in *ladolémono* (olive oil and lemon) and garnished with parsley and a lemon wedge.

Larger, commercial-resort seafood restaurants serve frozen fish. This must be stated on menus but is often done with asterisks or the abbreviation "kat" (for *katapsygméno*, "frozen").

Prestige bream species are often farmed and differ little from north-European supermarket fare. The best seafood in Greece is always caught wild, seasonally: *gónos kalamaráki* (baby squid) in early summer, *gávros* (anchovy) later on, and whole grilled *thrápsalo* (giant deep-water squid) or octopus (one tentacle per portion).

For delicious meat grills head to a *psistariá*, specializing in chops (*mprizóles* are pork and *païdákia* are lamb) or *biftéki* (Greek hamburger). The standard offerings are entire spitted chickens, suckling pig, whole lamb, and *kokorétsi* (offal roulade). The latter, like sheep's head and *glykádia* (sweetbreads), are illegal under EU law but still appear on menus in less supervised locales. After eating, head to a *zacharoplasteío* for sweets and pastries.

Mezedopoleío, Ouzerí and Tsipourádiko

No holiday in Greece is complete without a visit to an *ouzerí*, *mezedopoleío* (*mezédes* shop) or *tsipourádiko*. The terms have become somewhat interchangeable, though the proportions of tipple to food – and type of drink served – vary subtly. They are most fun in a small group, as the idea is to share small platters of meats, seafood and vegetables. More substantial hot mains usually follow, but there is no obligation to order these.

These establishments serve one or more of the following spirits distilled from the grape

Bottle of *ouzo*

residue of wine-making: anise-flavoured *oúzo*, *tsípouro* (also available without anise and less cloying), or Cretan/Cycladic *rakí* (always without anise), along with a bucket of ice and water. Pop the ice in a glass, pour in the spirit, and dilute to taste. All spirits arrive in small sealed bottles or jugs.

Musical *mezedopoleía*, with a fee for acoustic live music, are found in larger centres like Athens, Thessaloníki, Pátra, Ioánnina and Vólos.

Kafeneía and Sweet Shops

Kafeneía (coffee-houses), open dawn till late, were traditionally the hub of Greek life, though they have been eclipsed since the 1990s by trendier cafés and *frappádika*. Besides frappé, you can find Greek coffee, soft drinks, beer and brandy at a *kafeneío*, and all plus espresso and cappuccino at a design-led café.

Those with a sweet tooth should repair to a *zacharoplasteío*, or a confectioner, for syrupy oriental sweetmeats such as *baklavás* or *kataïfi*. A *galaktopoleío* ("milk shop") sells dairy-based desserts like *galaktoboúreko* (custard pie), *ryzógalo* (rice pudding) and *krémes* (custards). Ice cream (*pagotó*) is the perfect summer treat. Along with the biggest towns, the busier mainland resorts like Náfplio, Párga, Galaxídi and Chalkidikí have excellent ice-cream parlours, often run by Italians.

Outdoor tables at the Kritsa restaurant in Portariá *(see p290)*

Enjoying outdoor dining in Pláka, Athens

Fast Food and Snacks

Although American-style fast-food chain outlets dominate town centres and airports – the big Greek chains are Everest, Gregory's and Goody's – they can easily be avoided in favour of more traditional options.

A *souvlatzídiko* provides mostly *sto chéri* (takeaway) *souvláki* – chunks of grilled pork, wrapped in a pitta bread with tzatziki, onion and tomatoes. A *gyrádiko* does the same for *gýros*, thin slabs of compressed pork or chicken cut from a rotisserie cone, and *kebáb*, minced spicy beef treated like *souvláki*. Most stalls offer basic seating and a range of beer and soft drinks.

Most bakeries sell small stuffed savoury turnovers (*pitákia* or *píttes*) or filled croissants. The best cheese pies are the so-called *kouroú* (dry) ones without messy filo pastry. These make ideal on-the-hoof breakfasts, and most *píttes* sell out by noon.

Breakfast

For Greeks, breakfast is the least important meal of the day. Most make do with a coffee, with *paximádia* (sliced barley rusks), *kouloúra* (firm, sesame-seed-sprinkled rolls in rings or S-shapes) or *keik* (pound cake). Any hotel of two stars or more must offer breakfast – sometimes worth taking, sometimes not. If not, cafés offer continental or full English breakfasts.

Reservations

The more popular a restaurant is, the more advisable it is to make a reservation, and it is always worth doing so during weekends. In country areas, and in the suburbs, it is the practice to visit a restaurant or taverna earlier in the day, or a day before, to see what will be served. Good tavernas only cook as much as they can sell on the day; when it's gone, it's gone. The proprietor will reserve any special dish that is in limited supply or requires advance preparation or procurement.

Wine and Beer

Along with renewed pride in regional cuisines has come an interest in fine bottled wine and obscure grape varieties that had almost died out from neglect. Poor economies of scale mean premium wine is expensive, costing well over €30 a bottle in a fancy taverna. More affordable mainland labels include Lazaridi, Tsantali and Neméa. Better island wines also appear on mainland menus.

Bulk or carafe wine is called *chýma* in Greek; it can be great, or it can be terrible. Ask for a glass to sample before you commit – you'll cause no offence by declining it. Alternatively, a drop of soda water added to the wine makes even the harshest drinkable. The best, widespread mainland *chýma* comes from Zítsa in Epirus. Rosé, whether bottled or *chýma*, is often very dark by European standards; taste it before rejecting it on hue alone.

Beer was long the province of centralized mainland breweries with a few bland labels and a stranglehold on national distribution; the best of these are Fix and Alpha, plus Vergina from Komotiní, whose high-alcohol red lager is outstanding. But dozens of microbreweries exist, including Craft in Athens and ZEOS in Argos. Their beers are relatively expensive but very good. Many are unpasteurized so must be kept and served cold. Most other top micro-beers hail from Santoríni, Corfu, Chíos, and Crete.

How to Pay

Greece is still largely a cash society, all the more so since austerity measures mean proprietors have limited access to bank accounts. Fancier eateries in theory accept credit cards but may not on the day, usually blaming malfunctioning card machines. If you need to pay by credit card, check first that the restaurant accepts them and, if so, that they take the card you intend to use – and be prepared to pay cash anyway. Traditional *kafeneía*, modern cafés and bars are cash-only zones; in bars, you pay on being served.

Service and Tipping

Greeks take plenty of time when they eat out and expect a high level of attention. Menu prices include a service charge, but it

Patrons outside a kebab restaurant in Athens

is customary to leave at least 10 per cent of the bill as a tip, and 12–15 per cent if service has been exceptional.

Even at establishments with a reputation for good table service, standards tend to drop between 20 July and 20 August because the wait staff cannot cope with peak-season crowds.

Dress Code

Greeks usually dress to at least smart-casual standard when eating out. For visitors, comfortable cotton clothing is fine, but skimpy tops, shorts or active sportswear are only acceptable at beach tavernas. Restaurants in hotels of three stars and above usually have a no-shorts, no-sandals, no-sleeveless-shirts policy for dinner. During spring or autumn, a cardigan or long-sleeved top is useful for outside dining after dark; in the mainland mountains, this also applies in the summer months.

Children

Greek children become taverna habitués at a very early age – it is an essential part of their socialization – and they are welcome everywhere except the most drink-and-music-oriented *mezedopoleía* or gourmet eateries. Children are expected to behave well; however, in summer, nobody cares if kids play around the outside tables, and indeed some tavernas provide small playgrounds. Facilities such as highchairs are becoming more widespread, and resort diners invariably have children's menus (usually burgers, chicken nuggets and pizza).

Smoking

Since 2010, it has been illegal to smoke inside any bar, restaurant or café, but the law is widely resented and defied. Random inspections can result in hefty fines for proprietors who flout the law. Ashtrays are often not

Interior patio of a restaurant in Thessaloníki

placed on tables, though seashells are universal code that you can ask for one. You can politely ask neighbouring diners to stop smoking, but expect a brusque reaction and to move yourself outside – where smoking is allowed anyway.

Wheelchair Access

Bread ring seller, Athens

In country areas, where room is plentiful, there are few problems for wheelchair users. However, in city restaurants, access is often restricted. The streets have uneven paving, and many eateries have narrow doorways and, possibly, steps. However, more restaurants in Athens and some rural towns are installing ramps and bathrooms with easier access. Restaurants with wheelchair access are indicated in the listings pages of this guide. Also, the organizations listed on page 303 provide information for disabled travellers in Greece.

Outside seating at a café near the lighthouse on Pátra's waterfront

Vegetarians and Vegans

In theory, Greek cuisine includes a great many vegetarian dishes, because of the number of meatless recipes for the fasting days of the Orthodox calendar. However, some of these dishes may still be prepared using meat stock. Vegans will be in for an especially hard time, because dishes topped or stuffed with cheese and other dairy products are ubiquitous.

Picnics

The best time to picnic in Greece is in spring, when the countryside is at its most beautiful and the weather is not too hot. The traditional seasonal foods, such as Lenten olive oil bread, sweet Easter bread, pies filled with wild greens, fresh cheese and charcuterie, are perfect picnic fare. Summer is ideal for eating on the beach. The best foods for summer snacks are peaches and figs, tomatoes and fresh-fruit smoothies.

Recommended Restaurants

The restaurants on pp282–91 have been selected for the quality of their ingredients, recipes, atmosphere and service. Updated Greek or foreign/fusion menus should be creative while still offering value for money. A taverna owned by the same family for generations will likely be traditional, take pride in its work, and not just be interested in the easy money of summer tourism. An entry marked as a DK Choice succeeds notably within its category, by these various criteria.

The Flavours of Greece

The ancient Greeks regarded cooking as both a science and an art. In remoter parts of the mainland, you may find recipes and culinary methods little changed since medieval times. Elsewhere, cookery has been influenced by the Ottoman Empire, with its spicier meat dishes, filled pastries, and vegetable casseroles. Also important were the many fasting days in the Greek Orthodox calendar, requiring meat- and dairy-free recipes – the so-called *nistísima*. Until the 1990s, authentic Greek cuisine was scorned as peasant food, but there has been an upsurge of pride in country cooking and quality, seasonal, local ingredients.

Oregano and thyme

Fisherman returning to harbour with the day's catch

Athens and the Peloponnese

The capital is a city of immigrants from the countryside, the islands and the shores of the eastern Mediterranean. That diversity is reflected in its markets and its cuisine. Street food is key to daily life in Athens. In the Peloponnese, ingredients include fish, sheep, goat and game.

Central and Northern Greece

Mainland Greece, with its long history, has blurred regional food boundaries and varied cooking traditions. The meat and fruit dishes of Thessaloníki show a Jewish influence; the spices, sausages and oven cooking of Ioánnina stem from Ottoman times; and a love of sheep's cheese came with the Aroman shepherds. The spicy food of the North is the legacy of the 1922 immigrants from Asia Minor, while the northern Balkan influence is obvious in the use of pickles, walnuts and yogurt.

Common Menu Items

Oinomageireío menus list as few as four simple salads and six *mageireftá* of the day; at a traditional taverna, add to that a dozen *mezédes* and some grilled dishes. A creative taverna or *mezedopoleío* will have a lot of starters and mains.

Some dishes are ubiquitous year-round. Usual dips include *tyrokafterí* (spicy cheese mash), *melitzanosaláta* (aubergine purée), *fáva* (yellow split-pea mash with onions and lemon) and *taramosaláta* (roe salad, ideally greyish, not pink). *Chórta* (boiled greens, with lemon and oil) are also popular. *Plevrótous* (oyster mushrooms), especially when grilled, are much loved. Every region seems to make its own typical *loukánika* (sausages), which are often grilled, as are *panséttes* (meaty pork spare ribs).

Regional Dishes and Specialities

Sweets such as nougat, *pastéli* (honey-sesame candy), *loukoumádes* (yeast doughnuts in syrup) and *chalvás* (halva, or sweetmeats) have been a part of Greek street life since the days of Aristotle. They are sold in small shops or stalls. *Píttes*, or pies, are a speciality of the western Epirus region. Fillings range from game or offal to cheese and vegetables, often combined with rice or pasta. Reflecting Middle Eastern influences, *soutzoukákia*, a speciality of northern Thrace and Macedonia, are meat patties flavoured with coriander, pepper and cumin. *Choirinó kritikó*, the classic dish of inland Crete villages, is thick pork cutlets baked until tender, while *sýka me tyrí* is a summer *mezés*, dessert or snack, of fresh figs with *mizythra* cheese, made from whey.

Olives

Fakés is a tart wintertime soup of green lentils, lemon juice or wine vinegar, tomatoes, herbs and olive oil.

WHERE TO EAT AND DRINK | **279**

Produce on sale in a typical Greek market

Greece boasts the world's largest variety of olives, grown in vast tracts of the mainland – notably near Spárti, Kalamáta, Lamía, Vólos and Párga – at least for oil if not for eating. Cheese also features on most menus; many are made from blended goat and sheep milk, though single-milk varieties do exist. Pickled capers (*kápari*) sometimes adorn salads, and seafood might be garnished with samphire or glasswort.

Fish and Seafood

The generally warm, sheltered Greek waters support assorted fish, cephalopods and shellfish. Fish are served with heads on to indicate the variety; Greeks like the cheek flesh especially.

Scaly fish in restaurants are often of the bream or grouper families. Late spring sees squid spawn (*gónos kalamáráki*), while summer brings *sardélla*

A plate of moussaka with salad garnish at a Greek restaurant

(sardine), *gávros* (anchovy), pelagic tuna and swordfish. Mussels are always farmed, and prawns are often imported.

Desserts

A menu may include a separate section for desserts (*epidórpia*), but some tavernas offer a *kérasma*, or sweet, on the house. Depending on the location and season, this might be *simigdalísio chalvás* (halva made from semolina, butter and sugar), *ekmek kataïfi* (bread pudding and custard) or *glykó koutalioú* ("sweet spoon", often candied grapes, figs or cherries).

WHAT TO DRINK

Wine-making in Greece has a millennial, ongoing history, with wineries on the mainland and islands. That said, most tavernas stock labels from premier mainland wine regions: Peloponnesian Neméa, Macedonia (including Chalkidikí) and Epirus. *Retsína* (pine-resin-flavoured wine) is bottled in several places, but purists claim only barrelled Attica *retsína* is genuine.

Distilled spirits include *oúzo*, *tsípouro* and *rakí*. Brandy and fortified dessert wines may also be offered. "Greek" (oriental) coffee is made from ground robusta beans boiled in a long-handled *mpríki* pot and served in tiny cups.

Spetzofáï, from Mount Pílio, is a spicy stir-fry of sliced country sausage, peppers, onions, garlic and tomatoes.

Barboúnia, or red mullet, has been esteemed since antiquity; *koutsomoúres* are a smaller, cheaper variant, equally tasty.

Loukoumádes are a street-stall snack of deep-fried beignets drizzled with syrup and sprinkled with cinnamon.

The Classic Greek Menu

The menu begins with a selection of *mezédes* (appetizers) – first the cold ones, then hot. Many are light and vegetarian; others, like *loukánika* (sausages) or *apáki* (cured pork), can be combined to create a main dish. Salads then make their appearance. Next up are meat and seafood main courses, the former usually with a side serving of rice or fried potatoes, the latter unadorned. Bread arrives in a basket as part of the *servítzio* (cutlery and napkins). Formerly, taverna bread was perfunctory, but now many establishments serve healthier whole-grain, olive or corn breads.

Round Greek bread loaves

Tiganiá are small chunks of meat, often pork, flavoured with lemon, herbs and olive oil, grilled on skewers.

Choriátiki saláta, Greek salad, combines tomatoes, cucumber, onions, herbs, capers and feta cheese.

Psária plakí is a whole fish baked with vegetables in a tomato, onion, garlic and olive oil sauce.

Olives — **ΜΕΖΕΔΕΣ** / *MEZÉDES*

Ελιές / *Eliés*

Salted mullet roe dip — **Ταραμοσαλάτα** / *Taramosoláta*

Yogurt, garlic and cucumber dip — **Τζατζίκι** / *Tzatíki*

Τιγανιά / *Tiganiá*

Chickpea (garbanzo) purée — **Κεφτέδεσ** / *Keftédes*

Aubergine (eggplant) purée — **Χούμουσ** / *Choúmous*

Vine leaves stuffed with rice — **Μμελιτζανοσαλάτα** / *Melitzanosaláta*

Stuffed baked aubergines (eggplant) — **Ντολμάδες** / *Ntolmádes*

Μελιτζάνες ιμάμ μπαϊλντί / *Melitzánes imám baïldí*

Vegetables and salads often use wild produce — **ΛΑΧΑΝΙΚΑ ΚΑΙ ΣΑΛΑΤΙΚΑ** / *Lachaniká kai salatiká*

Χωριάτικη σαλάτα / *Choriátiki saláta*

Fried aubergines (eggplant) and courgettes (zucchini) — **Μελιτζάνες και κολοκυθάκια τηγαν** / *Melitzánes kai kolokythákia tiganitá*

Artichokes with potatoes, carrots, dill, lemon and oil — **Αγκινάρες α λα πολίτα** / *Agkináres a la políta*

Tis scháras means "from the grill". The term can be applied to meat or fish, or even vegetables. Here, a swordfish steak has been marinated in lemon juice, olive oil and herbs before being swiftly chargrilled.

Mezédes

Mezédes are eaten as a first course or as a snack with wine or other drinks. *Taramosaláta* is a purée of salted mullet roe and breadcrumbs or potato. Traditionally a dish for Lent, it is now on every taverna menu. *Melitzanosaláta* and *choúmous* are both purées. *Melitzanosaláta* is grilled aubergines (eggplant) and herbs; *choúmous* is chickpeas (garbanzos), tahini, cumin and garlic. *Melitzánes imám baïldí* are aubergines filled with a purée of onions, tomatoes and herbs. *Ntolmádes* are vine leaves stuffed with pine nuts, rice and herbs.

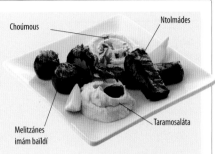

Choúmous

Ntolmádes

Taramosaláta

Melitzánes imám baïldí

Typical selection of mezédes

ΨΑΡΙΆ
PSÁRIA

Πλακί
Plakí

Της Σχαρας
Scháras

Καλαμαράκια Τηγανιτά
Kalamarákia Tiganitá

ΜΑΓΕΙΡΕΦΤΑ
Mageireftá

Μουσακάς
Mousakás

Σουβλάκια
Souvlákia

Xoirino σουβλάκι
Choirinó souvláki

Κλέφτικο
Kléftiko

ΕΠΙΔΌΡΠΙΑ
EPIDÓRPIA

Τιραμισού
Tiramisu

Παγοτά
Ice-cream

Χαλβάς
Chalvás

Γλυκά του κουταλιού
Glyká tou koutalioú

Fish are at their best around the mainland coast near river mouths and lagoons

Fried squid

Moussakás (layered lamb, potato slices and aubergine, baked)

Desserts are simple affairs of pastry, fruit or yogurt.

Keftédes are fried balls of minced beef, or a beef/lamb blend, egg and breadcrumbs, flavoured with mint and parsley.

Kléftiko is chunks of lamb (sometimes goat) wrapped in parchment paper to seal in the juices and flavours while cooking.

Sweet pastries filled with nuts and honey are made at *zacharoplasteía* but sometimes figure as taverna desserts. The most famous are *baklavás*, with layers of filo pastry and nuts, and *kataïfi*, similar, but with the filo shredded into filaments.

Giaoúrti kai méli (yogurt with honey) is a common component of hotel breakfasts or offered as a taverna dessert.

Where to Eat and Drink

Athens
Exárcheia

I Kriti (O Takis) €
Cretan **Map** 2 E3
Inside stoa at Veranzérou 5, Platéia Kánigkos, 106 77
Tel *210 382 6998* **Closed** *Sun*
Expect typical dishes at this popular hangout: *apáki* (cured pork), two kinds of sausage (opt for the Sfakian), *stamnagáthi* greens, fennel pie and *ntákos* salad, plus, of course, plenty of *rakí* from Sitía province. Cretan music accompanies your meal.

Rakoumel €
Cretan **Map** 2 F3
Emmanouíl Mpenáki 71, 106 81
Tel *210 380 0506* **Closed** *Sun; Aug*
A favourite among several Cretan eateries in Athens, with delicacies like fennel pie, Sfakian sausages and seasonal Cretan greens. There is also *paximádia* (hard rusks) instead of bread, and Cretan *rakí* by the small vial. Street or indoor tables.

DK Choice
Rozalia €
Traditional Greek **Map** 2 F2
Valtetsíou 54, 106 81
Tel *210 330 2136*
Housed in a beautiful Neo-Classical building with a garden full of vines, olive trees and flowers, this taverna has been attracting diners with its signature dish, *tiganiá* (pork in a peppery sauce), as well as classics like *spanakóryzo* (spinach rice) and *ouzo*-marinated fish and seafood for over 35 years. Superb wine list and choice of *ouzo* blends.

A tempting dish of grilled cuttlefish with spinach at the restaurant Yiantes

Peinaleon €€
Mezedopoleío **Map** 3 B2
Mavromicháli 152, 114 72
Tel *210 644 0945* **Closed** *Jun–mid-Sep*
Reserve ahead at this local favourite famous for its *mezédes* and home-made red wine. Retro lamps, old photos and *rempétiki* music complete the scene.

Rififi €€
Mediterranean Fusion **Map** 2 F3
Emmanouíl Mpenáki 69 & Valtetsíou, 106 81
Tel *210 330 0237* **Closed** *Aug*
Rififi serves traditional dishes made with unusual ingredients. Don't miss the lamb cooked for 24 hours with *stamnagáthi* greens, or the skewer of chicken breast grilled with sweet chilli sauce and yogurt. Quirky decor.

Salero €€
Mediterranean Fusion **Map** 2 F3
Valtetsíou 51, 106 81
Tel *210 381 3358*
A vibrant restaurant with a wide-ranging menu despite the Spanish name. Choose from over 20 *tapas*-style dishes or mains and home-made desserts. Excellent wine cellar (including Argentinian labels) and cocktails.

Yiantes €€
Mediterranean **Map** 2 F3
Valtetsíou 44, 106 81
Tel *210 330 1369*
Yiantes serves delectable Greek and Mediterranean dishes such as zucchini croquettes, couscous with pancetta and grilled liver with caramelised onions. Dishes in the seasonal menus are prepared with organic produce. There is also a good selection of wines and *ouzo*.

Ilísia

DK Choice
Galaxy Restaurant €€€
International **Map** 4 D5
Hilton, Vasilíssis Sofías 46, 115 28
Tel *210 728 1402*
Everything about Galaxy is tasteful – from the cocktails and finger food served at the bar to the upscale Japanese *teppanyaki*. Gourmet dishes and fine wines are served at dark wooden tables. The highlight of this rooftop restaurant is the view of the Acropolis through the floor-to-ceiling windows.

Price Guide
Prices are based on two diners having three courses, a bottle of house wine, plus extra for a tip.
€ under €45
€€ €45 to €65
€€€ over €65

Kerameikós
Funky Gourmet €€€
Fine Dining **Map** 1 B4
Paramythiás 13, crn of Salamínos, 104 35
Tel *210 524 2727* **Closed** *lunch; Sun & Mon*
There is no à la carte at this Michelin-starred minimalist restaurant, merely three degustation menus. The wine list features both foreign and top Greek microwineries.

Kolonáki
To Kioupi €
Traditional Greek **Map** 3 A5
Platéia Kolonakíou 4, 106 73
Tel *210 361 4033* **Closed** *dinner (summer); Sun; Aug*
A local favourite since the 1950s, this *mageireio* makes for an ideal lunch stop after visiting the nearby museums. Typical dishes include *gída vrastí* (stewed goat) and *ntolmádes*. Good bulk wine.

Il Postino €€
Italian **Map** 3 A4
Grivaíon 3 & Skoufá 64, 106 73
Tel *210 364 1414* **Closed** *Sun*
Osteria-style restaurant with authentic Italian cuisine in the heart of Athens. Choose from delicious antipasti, meat dishes like veal in wine, and home-made pasta and desserts.

Prytaneion €€
International **Map** 3 A5
Milioni 7–9, 106 73
Tel *210 364 3353*
Spread over three floors, this restaurant is decorated in earthy colours and wall art. The menu tempts with Mediterranean meat and pasta dishes and Aegean fish, as well as Italian desserts.

Kiku €€€
Japanese **Map** 3 A5
Dimokrítou 12, 106 73
Tel *210 364 7033* **Closed** *Sun; Aug*
An award-winning restaurant that serves exquisite cuisine in minimalist surroundings. There's a superb sushi bar, while sashimi and tempura dishes are presented like works of art. Good wine list.

Magnificent views of the Acropolis from Orizontes Lykavittou

Orizontes Lykavittou
Fine Dining €€€ Map 3 B4
Summit of Lykavittós Hill, 106 75
Tel *210 722 7065*
The views of Athens don't get much better than at this elegant venue near the hill's summit, popular with the local trendy set. Access is via funicular or a pathway through the pines. Upmarket appetizers, imaginative salads as well as fish and pasta dishes are artfully plated. Meat dishes include delicious steak from central Greece. Exemplary desserts and wines.

Koukáki

Mikri Venetia
Mediterranean Fusion €€ **Map** 5 C5
G. Olympíou 15, 117 41
Tel *213 025 9158* **Closed** *lunch Mon–Fri*
There is nothing particularly Venetian about "Little Venice" – Venetia is actually the name of one of the partners. The wide-ranging menu combines Greek with world tastes in such dishes as Cretan *kalitsoúnia* turnovers and green-curry shrimps. Their motto is "tastes and distillations"; accordingly, there's a good choice of *rakí, tsípouro* and *ouzo*.

Makrygiánni

Strofi
Modern Greek €
Map 6 D3
Rovertou Gkalli 25, 117 42
Tel *21092 14130* **Closed** *Mon*
Open since 1975, this eatery serves creative Mediterranean and Greek fare. Try the delicious fried feta cheese with honey and sesame for the starter, followed by lamb wrapped in vine leaves stuffed with cheese for your main. Great views of the Acropolis from the rooftop terrace. Reserve ahead.

DK Choice

Mani Mani
Modern Greek €€€
Map 6 D3
Falírou 10, 117 42
Tel *210 921 8180* **Closed** *dinner Sun*
Stylishly occupying the top floor of a graceful interwar townhouse, this established restaurant serves nouvelle-Grecque cuisine which takes hints from the Peloponnese. Menu items include *sýgklino* (streaky pork) and Messinian *talagáni* cheese, but there are also various pan-Hellenic *mezédes*, salads and creative desserts. Just a few steps from the Acropolis Museum.

Metaxourgeio

Aleria
Modern Greek €€
Map 1 B3
Megálou Alexándrou 57, 104 35
Tel *210 522 2633* **Closed** *lunch; Sun*
Located in a beautiful renovated house, this restaurant features a lovely bar and indoor and outdoor dining areas. Choose between the à la carte menu or a very reasonable degustation menu; likely dishes include bergamot-marinated amberjack tartare, red pumpkin mousse or couscous *bourdeto*, with Ios-island cheesecake to finish. Extensive wine and beer list.

Alexander The Great
Traditional Greek €€
Map 1 C3
Megálou Alexándrou 3–7, 104 37
Tel *210 522 7990*
This wooden-beamed restaurant also offers outdoor dining in a garden. The authentic Greek and Cypriot cuisine features *afélia* (pork in wine) and *spetzofáï* (Pilion sausage with sautéed peppers).

Monastiráki

Thanasis
Grill/Psistariá €
Map 6 E1
Mitropóleos 69, 105 55
Tel *210 324 4705*
Three grill stalls cluster at the Plateía Monastirakioú end of this street, and the queues proclaim which is the best. Thanasis's trademark dish is Oriental kebab: minced beef blended with onion and spices. Eat in or take away.

Athinaïkon
Modern Greek €€
Map 6 E1
Mitropóleos 34, 105 55
Tel *210 325 2688*
This restaurant is a trendy mid-town venue. The menu is Greek with contemporary flourishes. Superb dishes include veal liver and smoked eel.

Café Avissinia
Café €€
Map 5 C1
Kinétou 7, Plateía Avyssinías, 105 55
Tel *210 321 7047* **Closed** *Mon*
A menu of seasonally changing *mezédes* platters and heartier mains has made this café one of the trendiest places in Athens. The atmosphere is warm, and there is live music on weekends.

Omónoia

Black Duck Multiplarte
Mediterranean Fusion €€ Map 2 E5
Chrístou Ladá 9a, 105 61
Tel *210 323 4760*
This bistro serves imaginative dishes like beef *kavourmás* and lentils or grilled shrimp with wild black rice. The real selling point is the ground-floor bar, always packed, with a 1960s rock 'n 'roll playlist (open late Fri–Sat).

Klimataria
Traditional Greek €€
Map 2 D4
Plateía Theátrou 2, 105 52
Tel *210 321 6629*
This is the place for hearty, meat-based dishes like leek-laced *tiganiá* or mature lamb fricassee with *stamnagáthi* greens. There are also vegetarian and seafood options, plus live acoustic music Thursday night through to noon on Sunday.

Olive Garden
Mediterranean €€€
Map 2 E3
Titania Hotel, Panepistimíou 52, 106 78
Tel *210 383 8511*
This award-winning rooftop restaurant combines elegant decor with a menu of delicious Mediterranean gourmet cuisine. Enjoy a romantic meal here with fine dining and great views of the Acropolis.

For more information on types of restaurants *see page 274*

Fine dining outside the Neo-Classical Spondi

Pangráti

Colibri
American   €
Map 7 B4
*Empedokléou 9–13, down from
Plateía Varnáva, 116 36*
Tel *210 701 1011*
The habitually packed tables
in the pedestrian lane tell you
that this is the best local place
for thin-crust pizza, burgers
and a few pasta dishes. There
is a small interior for cooler days,
though there are heaters outside.
Wash the food down with the
rather decent *chýma* wine.

Karavitis
Traditional Greek   **Map** 7 B2   €
*Arktínou 33, crn of Pafsaníou 4,
116 35*
Tel *210 721 5155*   **Closed** *lunch
Mon–Fri*
Karavitis is the last surviving
taverna from the 1920s-era.
It dishes out *mageireftá* and
a few *mezédes* and grills, plus
carafe wine from the Mesógeia.
The slightly elevated prices for
this kind of eatery are offset by
the seriously large portions.
Traditional desserts include
baked quince and semolina
halva. Diners can enjoy outdoor
seating in a garden just across
the street, or choose to stay
indoors, amid the decorative
wine barrels.

Vyrinis
Traditional Greek   **Map** 7 B3   €
Archimídous 11 & Arátou, 116 36
Tel *210 701 2153*   **Closed** *dinner
Sun*
This classic neighbourhood
taverna is now managed by the
Anglo-Greek grandsons of the
founder. They have updated the
decor while retaining some
period features. Reliable fare
encompasses salads, *mezédes*
and creative mains. Good red
and white carafe wine.

DK Choice

Spondi
Fine Dining   **Map** 7 B4   €€€
Pýrronos 5, 116 38
Tel *210 756 4021*
Housed in a Neo-Classical
building with a lovely interior
of natural stone, the Michelin-
starred Spondi serves exquisite
food prepared by an expert
French chef. Menu classics
include terrine of *foie gras*,
venison with wild mushrooms,
polenta and spinach, and duck
in a vanilla and bitter chocolate
sauce. Tasting and dessert
menus are available. The wine
cellar boasts a comprehensive
list of 1,300 labels.

Pedion Áreos

St'Astra
Mediterranean   **Map** 2 F1   €€€
Leofóros Alexándras 10, 106 82
Tel *210 889 4500* **Closed** *Sun & Mon*
This designer-furnished rooftop
restaurant of the Radisson Blu
Park Hotel is a city favourite.
Enjoy superb cocktails with
gourmet dishes such as
salmon quinoa and pork
with mango chutney.

Petrálona

Askimopapo
Traditional Greek   **Map** 5 A3   €
Iónon 61, 118 51
Tel *210 346 3282* **Closed** *lunch Tue–
Fri; Mon; mid-Jun–Sep*
The decor at the long-running
"Ugly Duckling" comprises archival
theatre photos and original art
donated by patrons. Dishes – a
mix of meaty *mageireftá* and
veggie *mezédes* – is plainly
presented but delicious. White
and red *chýma* wines hail from
Límnos and Neméa.

Santorinios
Traditional   **Map** 5 A3   €
Doriéon 8, 118 52
Tel *210 345 1629*   **Closed** *Mon;
some of the summer*
Seating is in small rooms or in
the enchanting courtyard at
this cult taverna inside a former
refugee compound. Sensibly
limited menu of Santoríni
specialities, and island carafe
wine (opt for the red). If the
odd dish is only three-and-
a-half stars, the atmosphere,
service and low prices rate five.

Oikonomou
Traditional Greek   **Map** 5 A3   €€
Tróön 41, crn of Kydantidón, 118 51
Tel *210 346 7555*   **Closed** *lunch; Sun*
There's no sign outside, but
busy sidewalk tables announce
that you've reached this historic
oinomageireio, long the haunt
of artistic types. Big portions
of meat stews and vegetable-
based *mageireftá* are their
stock in trade, and there is
good barrelled red wine and
retsína. Inside are antiquarian
engravings and caricatures.

Pláka

Bakalarakia O Damigos
Traditional Greek   **Map** 6 E2   €€
Kydathinaíon 41, 105 58
Tel *210 322 5084*   **Closed** *Mon*
This rustic restaurant is famous
for its *bakalarákia* – battered cod
in a fiery garlic sauce that has,
to go by legend, been served
here since 1864. There are
plenty of other dishes besides
cod. Look for the photo of
Josephine Baker, who ate
here when she visited Athens.

Platanos
Traditional Greek   **Map** 6 D1   €€
Diogénous 4, 105 56
Tel *21032 20666*
Platanos takes its name from
the plane tree outside and has
been serving classic *mageireftá*
dishes like *pastítsio* (baked pasta
with ground beef and white
sauce) and meat platters for
decades. Wash it all down the
decent barrelled *retsína* or red
wine. The lovely pink-washed
courtyard covered with bou-
gainvillea is a major attraction.

Psyrrí

Nikitas
Traditional Greek   **Map** 1 C5   €
Agíon Anargýron 19
Tel *210 325 2591* **Closed** *dinner; Sun*
The oldest surviving taverna in
Psyrrí, Nikitas (founded 1967)
relies on a small but perfectly

formed daily changing menu of Greek favourites, along with beer, *ouzo* and a limited wine choice. Seating is indoors or (more popular) out on the pedestrian street – if you're lucky, right next to the Agioi Anárgyroi church. Arrive early or be prepared to wait for a table.

Taverna Tou Psyrri €
Traditional Greek **Map** 1 C5
Aischýlou 12, 105 54
Tel *210 321 4923*
Housed in an old stone building, this traditional taverna is another of the few good-value options in trendy Psyrrí. The menu emphasizes fish and seafood, as well as the usual starters. There's a lovely garden out back, while the interior sports old photos and engravings of Athens.

Hytra €€€
Fine Dining **Map** 1 C5
Syggroú 107-109, 117 45
Tel *210 331 6767* **Closed** *Wed & Thu*
Enjoy the views from this stylish Michelin-starred eatery on the sixth floor of the Onassis Cultural Centre. The menu has a short if slightly wacky à la carte section – think mung bean soup with smoked eel and yogurt, or mesclun salad with island goat's cheese – plus a more extensive choice of tasting menus.

Sýntagma

Noodle Bar €
International **Map** 6 E1
Apóllonos 11
Tel *210 331 8585*
This fun, minimalist eatery has a menu that focuses on salads featuring mango, wasabi and wontons, mains of authentic Chinese and Asian dishes, and creative desserts. There is a kid's menu and a good selection of beers and wines.

Avocado €€
Café **Map** 6 F1
Nikis 30, 105 57
Tel *210 323 7878*
A vegetarian/vegan/gluten-free eatery and juice bar, Avocado is renowned for its creative salads, entrées, pizzas and desserts. The bread is home-made. Wash down the delicious food with a smoothie or organic wine.

Furin Kazan €€
Japanese **Map** 6 E1
Apóllonos 2
Tel *210 322 9170*
Furin Kazan is considered the best-value Asian restaurant in Athens – groups of Japanese tourists think so, anyway, making advance reservations prudent. Sushi to the fore, plus a few tempura platters, salmon teriyaki and appetizers like miso soup.

Mama Roux €€
International **Map** 6 D1
Aiólou 48, 105 64
Tel *21300 48382* **Closed** *Sun*
Food from all over the world, in unique combinations of ingredients, is served here in a friendly ambience. The wide-ranging menu features dishes such as burgers, tandoori chicken, burritos, tacos, kebab, falafel and soups. Don't miss the hummus or the delectable cheesecake.

GB Roof Garden €€€
Fine Dining **Map** 6 F1
Hotel Grande Bretagne, Vasiléos Georgíou tou Prótou 1, Plateía Syntágmatos, 105 64
Tel *210 333 0766*
The rooftop restaurant of the Hotel Grande Bretagne offers a sophisticated menu of gourmet dishes inspired by Mediterranean cuisine. Diners enjoy the exquisite cooking accompanied by fine wines and beautiful, uninterrupted views of the Acropolis.

DK Choice

The Tudor Hall €€€
Fine Dining **Map** 6 F1
King George Palace, Vasiléos Georgíou tou Prótou, Plateía Syntágmatos, 105 64
Tel *210 333 0265*
Located on the 7th floor of the luxury hotel, this restaurant serves enticing creations like roasted scallops with celery cream, mushrooms and garlic, and rabbit *stifado* (stew). Other platters might be slow-cooked octopus with smoked peppers and bean purée, duck breast with kumquat, sweet potato and turnips, and sweetbreads with garlic cream and parsley.

Thiseío

Thissio View €€
Mediterranean **Map** 5 B1
Apostólou Pávlou 25, 118 51
Tel *210 347 6754*
This restaurant is great for meals, coffee or drinks in a lively space with superb views of the Acropolis. Try the steamed mussels with *ouzo* and the pepper beef fillet. Great cocktails. Friendly atmosphere.

To Steki Tou Ilia €€
Traditional Greek **Map** 1 A5
Eptachálkou 5 & Thessaloníkis 7, 118 51
Tel *210 345 8052* **Closed** *lunch Tue–Sat, dinner Sun; Mon*
These two premises of the same outfit are the prime spots in central Athens for grilled lamb chops and lamb liver. Starters like *fáva* mash, *chórta* and *tzatzíki* are toothsome, and the carafe wine is okay; service could be better. Outdoor seating for Eptachálkou is on a terrace across the way, above the metro tracks; tables for Thessaloníkis 7 are on the pavement.

Simply furnished dining area at Avocado, an eatery in Syntagma serving vegetarian food and juices

For more information on types of restaurants *see page 274*

Around Athens

Kessariani: Trata O Stelios €€
Seafood **Map** D4
Plateía Anagenísseos 7–9, 161 21
Tel *21072 91533* **Closed** *Sun eve*
This lively eatery dominates the central square and is popular with the locals. On the menu are delicious seafood dishes, the speciality being the calamari, prawns and fish soup. Superb Sunday lunches.

Kifisiá: Rakkan €€
Japanese **Map** D4
Leofóros Kifisiás 238-240, 145 62
Tel *210 808 7941*
A stylish bar-lounge-restaurant that offers a varied Japanese menu, including sushi, sashimi, tempura and teriyaki dishes.

Kifisiá: Berdema by Lakis €€€
Fine Dining **Map** D4
Skiáthou 3, 145 64
Tel *210 620 1108*
Berdema means "confusion", and so it is here with a fusion of Greek and international flavours, like chicken fillet inside a Parmesan crust with parsley pesto, melted cheese and roast vegetables.

DK Choice

Kifisiá: Eleas Gi €€€
Fine Dining **Map** D4
Dexamenís & Olimpionikón 4, Politeía, 145 63
Tel *210 620 0005* **Closed** *Sun eve*
Housed in a stone mansion, this charming restaurant welcomes diners through a corridor decorated with wine bottles. No à la carte, just two tasting menus of 14 and 24 "flavours" ranging from starters to dessert. Great wine list. The elegant dining area boasts crisp linens, high ceilings and a dining terrace.

Piraeus: Achinos €€
Seafood **Map** D4
Akti Themistokléous 51, 185 34
Tel *210 452 6944* **Closed** *Mon; winter*
A local favourite specializing in top-notch fish and seafood platters. Built against a cliff with great sea views and access to Freatýda beach.

Piraeus: Ta Katsarolakia €€
Greek **Map** D4
Akti Moutsoupoúlou 21, Zéa marina, 185 34
Tel *210 410 0609*
This waterside eatery is always buzzing. Standard taverna fare is enlivened by oddities like *goúlbasi* (lamb baked in parchment with vegetables and cheese).

Sweeping views from the lovely outdoor dining area at Eleas Gi, a restaurant in Kifisiá

Piraeus: Jimmy's Fish and the Sushi Tavern €€€
Seafood **Map** D4
Akti Koumoundoúrou 46, Mikrolímano, 185 33
Tel *210 412 4417*
A nautical theme and a deck by Mikrolímano's harbour provide the setting for a superb menu of creative dishes based on sea produce. There is also a full range of sushi and sashimi.

DK Choice

Piraeus: Kollias €€€
Seafood **Map** D4
Syggroú 303 and Dimosthenous, 175 64
Tel *210 462 9620* **Closed** *Sun*
This legendary restaurant has some unusual seafood options on the menu – appetizers such as sea-urchin spaghetti and battered mussels *souvláki*, as well as mains of salt-crusted seabream, red mullet and bass. Extensive dessert menu.

DK Choice

Piraeus: Vassilenas €€€
Fine Dining **Map** D4
Aitolikoú 72, 185 45
Tel *210 461 2457* **Closed** *Sun*
Founded in 1920, Vassilenas claims to be the oldest taverna in Attica. Tastefully decorated, it relies on the set-menu concept. The nine-plate degustation offer must be one of the best bargains in Greece, but it doesn't have the breadth of the à la carte menu. Expect to find gilt-head bream ceviche, beef cheeks with *myzíthra* cheese, pumpkin soup or *mylokópi* (sea trout) with buckwheat and marsh samphire. Fine wines, too.

Pórto Ráfti: Psaropoula Mpimpikos €€
Seafood **Map** D4
Leofóros Avlakíou 118, 190 09
Tel *22990 71292*
Enjoy a range of delicious seafood *mezédes* as well as decadent desserts. With a separate menu for children, this is an ideal place for family dining, just metres away from the beach.

Rafína: Kavouria Tou Asimaki €€
Seafood **Map** D4
Limáni Rafína (harbour), 190 09
Tel *22940 24551*
Established in 1952, this is one of the oldest and best seafood eateries in Rafína. Try the fisherman's spaghetti, made with mussels, squid and octopus in a rich tomato sauce or, in season, the *atherína* (sand smelts).

DK Choice

Rafína: Ioakeim €€€
Seafood **Map** D4
Limáni Rafína (harbour), 190 09
Tel *22940 23421*
Popular with Athenians, Ioakeim has been a part of Rafína's picturesque harbour for decades. Try the fish flavoured with *krítamo* (rock samphire), and oysters or barracuda with herbs. Dine on the terrace while watching ferries come and go.

Soúnio: Syrtaki €€
Seafood **Map** D4
2 km (1 mile) N of Temple of Poseidon, 195 50
Tel *22920 39125*
Frequented more by local than international tourists, Syrtaki excels at *mezédes* and (mainly) seafood mains, including some unusual ones, like mussels in saffron sauce. There are great views from its terrace.

Key to Price Guide *see page 282*

The Peloponnese

Ancient Corinth: Archontiko €€
Greek   Map C4
Paralía Kantaré, 20 100
Tel *27410 27968*
Situated between ancient and
modern Corinth, on the shore.
The house speciality, *kokkinistó
Archontiko* (Greek beef stew),
made with the taverna's own
meat in red wine, is a must try.

DK Choice

Giálova: Chelonaki   €€
Seafood   Map B5
Limáni Giálova, 240 01
Tel *27230 23080*
This informal waterside taverna
looks out on to Navaríno Bay,
with a small beach out front.
The daily catch is artfully served,
dressed either with lemon and
herbs or a creamy home-made
sauce. Sunset views from the
terrace are legendary. Features
live music on most weekends.

Gýtheio: I Trata   €
Traditional Greek   Map C5
Paralía Gýtheio, 232 00
Tel *27330 24429*
An excellent seaside option
for enjoying traditional dinner
and delicious *mezédes* made
with the freshest ingredients.
Friendly staff. Great atmosphere.

Gýtheio: Saga   €€
Seafood   Map C5
Odós Tzanní Tzannetáki, 232 00
Tel *27330 21358*
This excellent family-run eatery
serves home-made fish soup
and stuffed squid, along with
chargrilled meats. Dishes come
in generous portions. Sit at one
of the outdoor tables set on
the pavement by the sea.

Kalamáta: Krini   €€
Seafood   Map C5
Evangelistrías 40, 241 00
Tel *27210 24474*
Krini's menu features seafood
in *saganáki* (melted cheese)
sauce, *ouzo*-drenched prawns
and chargrilled sea bass. There
are also grilled meats and good
local wines on offer.

Koróni: Peroulia   €
Traditional Greek   Map C5
*Peroulia Beach, 2 km (1 mile) N of
town, 240 04*
Tel *27250 41777*
Enjoy meals of the freshest fish
and ingredients, along with extra
virgin Messinian olive oil. The
Peroulia Beach Bar offers exotic
cocktails and coffee on the beach.

DK Choice

Kosmas: Navarchos   €
Greek   Map C5
Central plateía, 210 52
Tel *27570 31489*
This taverna in the picturesque
village of Kosmas, on Mount
Párnon, offers great value and
excellent fare. Sit under the
giant trees while tucking into
sausages, goat stew, *tzatzíki* and
chórta, the kitchen's reliable
perennials. Good bulk wine.

Loúsios Gorge: Drymonas   €
Traditional Greek   Map C4
South end of Dimitsána, 220 07
Tel *27950 31116*
Expect country-style dishes at
Drymonas, the best of several
tavernas in this historic stone-built
town: *kounéli ladorígani* (rabbit),
fresh beets served with their
greens, and baked aubergine,
plus good house wine.

Loúsios Gorge: Georganta   €
Traditional Greek   Map C4
Main road, Ellinikó village, 220 22
Tel *27931 31009*
It's worth driving some distance
to tuck into the meat platters
here. There are also cheese-based
recipes and *trahanás* (sourdough
soup), all washed down by strong
bulk wine. Alluring wood-and-
stone interior.

Loutrá Ellénis: To Pefko   €
Traditional Greek   Map C4
*National road between Isthmía and
Palaiá Epídavros, 201 00*
Tel *27410 33801*
Travelling along the coastal road
between Corinth and Epidaurus,
be sure to lunch here. Tables on
the pebble beach (ideal for a dip)
are soon laden with excellent
seafood or meat platters, and
affordable drinks.

A dessert of Greek yoghurt with honey and
walnuts at Chrisovoulo in Monemvasía

DK Choice

Methóni: Klimataria   €
Traditional Greek   Map B5
Odós Miaoúli, 240 06
Tel *27230 31544*
Klimataria excels in *mezédes*,
mageireftá and vegetarian dishes.
The delectable food is served
artfully on tables laid out in
crisp linens. Dine in the courtyard shielded from the sun by
a vine-covered pergola, featuring tubs of flowers and its own
bar. The wine list has something
to go with every dish.

Monemvasiá: Matoula   €€
Greek   Map C5
Kástro, 230 70
Tel *27320 61660*
Matoula has been serving diners
since 1950. The setting, inside
the castle, is the main draw.
The walls of the eatery are
lined with old photographs.

Monemvasiá: Skorpios   €€
Traditional Greek   Map C5
Géfyra coast road, 230 70
Tel *27320 62090*
Situated on a waterside spot
with a terrace overlooking the
rock. Diners flock to this eatery
to enjoy marinated fish dishes
of *gávros* (anchovies) and
atherína, and a daily *mageireftá*.

DK Choice

Monemvasiá: Chrisovoulo €€€
Fine Dining   Map C5
Kástro, 230 70
Tel *27320 62022*
This fashionable eatery inside
the castle tempts diners with
appetizers such as *saíti* pie
(traditional turnover filled with
wild greens), mains of veal
with Malvasia wine sauce, as
well as feta cheese ice cream.
Superb wine list. The decor
complements the stone walls,
while a terrace looks over the
rooftops to the sea.

Mystrás: Chromata   €€
Fine Dining
*Pikouliánika village, 3 km (2 miles)
past the ruins, 231 00*
Tel *27310 23995*
In a renovated stone building –
and boasting great views of
the Lakonian plain (but not the
ruins) – Chromata does updated
Greek and continental dishes
with great flair. Sticking to house
wine controls the bills. If you
want to sit inside, you need
to book as there are less than
a dozen tables.

For more information on types of restaurants *see page 274*

Náfplio: Aiolos €
Traditional Greek Map C4
Vasilíssis Olgas 30, 211 00
Tel *27520 26828*
Expect *mezédes*, meat grills
and a few seafood plates, plus
affordable *chýma* wine or
tsípouro at this lively taverna.
Book ahead at weekends.

Náfplio: Omorfo Tavernaki €€
Traditional Greek Map C4
Vassilísis Ólgas 1, 211 00
Tel *27520 25944*
Charming eatery in a Neo-
Classical building on a beautiful
street. Try the home-made
tyrokafterí (spicy cheese dip)
and the signature dish
kolokotroneiko (pork in wine).

Palaiá Epídavros: Akrogiali €€
Traditional Greek Map D4
Limáni, Palaiá Epídavros 210 59
Tel *27530 41060*
Enjoy dishes such as aubergine
in wine sauce, and *soupióryzo*
(cuttlefish in rice). Both audience
and thespians come here after
summer-festival events at the
nearby Little Epidaurus theatre,
making booking mandatory.

Pátra: Istopoïkos Omilos €€€
Seafood Map C4
*Iroön Polytechníou 8, corner of
Terpsithéas, 262 22*
Tel *2610 435905*
The diner of the local sailing
club is considered the best
in the city for seafood of all
varieties. Come in summer,
when it is possible to eat
outdoors on the water, since
the interior can get smoky.

Pýlos: Gregory's €
Traditional Greek Map B5
Pýlos
Tel *27230 22621*
A local favourite for its hearty
mageireftá menu, which includes
kokkinistó (beef stew) and
spetzofáï. Tables are set out
under the *plateía* trees for
alfresco dining.

DK Choice

Rio: Naut-oiko €€
Seafood Map C4
Poseidonos 12, 265 04
Tel *2610 995992*
Imaginative fresh fish and
seafood with fine Peloponnese
wines is the deal at this elegant
restaurant. There are pergolas
and subtle lighting outside.
Add an idyllic location right
next to the beach and it's easy
to see why Naut-oiko is popular
with locals and tourists alike.

Spárti: Remo €
Pizza & Pasta Map C5
Dinekous 8, 231 00
Tel *27310 89089*
With its bright red decor,
Remo is something of a Spárti
landmark. It offers pizza, tasty
pasta dishes and meat grills.

Central and Western Greece

DK Choice

**Agios Ioánnis (Pílio):
Poseidonas** €€
Seafood Map D3
Coast road, 370 12
Tel *24260 31222*
The ready supply of fish at this
charming taverna on the Pílio's
coast appears in the menu in
the form of tasty creations.
Kakaviá (fish soup) and *baroúnia*
(red mullet) cooked with lemon
are house specials. Dine indoors
or alfresco.

Aráchova: Panagióta €€
Fine Dining Map C3
Opposite Agios Geórgios, 320 04
Tel *22670 32735*
An elegant little place, way up
in the village (it is best to drive
there), with Greek-continental
fusion cuisine on the menu.
Their steak (for two) is notable.
Reservations are best made in
person. Great views over the
church from window tables.

Delfoí: Vakhos €
Greek Map C3
Apóllonos 31, 330 54
Tel *22650 83186*
A charming family-run taverna
serving dishes prepared from

A traditional Greek meal of calamari, olives,
bread and fish

fine Mount Parnassós produce.
Superb selection of wines. There's
a lovely veranda from where the
view can be enjoyed.

Diáva: Neromylos €
Greek Map B2
*Pigí Goúra, top end of Diáva village, 5
km (3 miles) out of Kalampáka, 421 00*
Tel *24320 25224* **Closed** Sun eve
Housed in an old watermill, this
rustic taverna has a large local
following. The house special is
trout from the farm on site, but
all other Greek dishes (especially
starters) are also present.

DK Choice

Eláti: Sta Riza €
Traditional Greek Map B3
Village centre, 440 07
Tel *26530 71550* **Closed** Wed &
Thu
One of Eláti's best kept secrets,
Sta Riza offers spectacular views,
with delicious food to match.
The speciality is *lachanópita*
(vegetable pie with feta cheese),
served with home-made bread
and salad. Choose to dine on
the sun terrace, with views of
Mount Gamíla.

Galaxídi: Albatross €
Traditional Greek Map C3
Konstantínou Sathá 36, 330 52
Tel *22650 42233*
The limited daily menu at this
lovely *mageireío* specializing in
home-style dishes might include
octopus or rabbit stew, oven pies,
taramosaláta or their special,
samári (savoury pancetta).

DK Choice

Ioánnina: Stoa Louli €
Mezedopoleio Map B2
Anexartisías 78, 454 44
Tel *26510 71322*
This eatery takes advantage of
Ioánnina's bazaar's architectural
heritage. The fare is creative
Greek, but one comes mainly
for the atmosphere and the
excellent live music (after
10pm several nights a week).

Ioánnina: Fysa Roufa €€
Traditional Greek Map B2
Avéroff 55, 452 21
Tel *26510 26262*
This durable *mageireío* offers a
vast menu (including tripe soup,
baked fish and suckling pig),
quick friendly service, upmarket
decor (including archival photos)
and, most remarkably, 24-hour
service, which accounts in part
for the slightly elevated prices.

Kalampáka: Skaros €
Grill/Psistariá **Map** B2
Road to Tríkala, west edge of town, 422 00
Tel 24320 24152
A bit out of the way, but worth the detour for the meat platters: kebab, *splinántero* (spitted offal) and chops – plus wild greens or vegetables from their own patch. Book at weekends.

Karpenísi: To Spiti Tou Psara €€
Traditional Greek **Map** B3
Gavros village main road, 360 75
Tel 22370 41202
Tasty Greek fare and mountain views from the veranda attract diners to this taverna. *Tyrokafterí* (spicy cheese dip), *chortópita* (greens pie) and grilled trout are menu highlights.

Kastráki: Gardenia €
Traditional Greek **Map** B2
Village centre, 422 00
Tel 24320 22504
A great taverna offering grills, *moussakás*, fried courgettes and salads, plus friendly service and great terrace views of the Metéora pinnacles.

DK Choice

Katigiórgis: Floisvos €€
Seafood **Map** D3
On the beach, 370 06
Tel 24230 71071
Some diners drive all the way from Vólos to this family-run eatery, attracted by fresh fish (ask for the *tsitsíravla* topping) and honest *mageireftá*. Dine on the sand if you wish – wind and waves permitting.

Kípoi: Stou Mihali €€
Modern Greek **Map** B2
Main road through village, 440 10
Tel 26530 71630
Breathtaking views from its terrace and a superb menu of contemporary cuisine have put Stou Mihali on the map. The emphasis is on using Zagorian produce. Try the dishes of wild boar roasted in a claypot or the venison *stifádo*, accompanied by a local red wine.

Kissós: Synantisi €
Modern Greek **Map** C3
Plateía Kissoú, 370 12
Tel 24260 31620
Creative takes on traditional pan-Hellenic and Pílion recipes, the local tipple *tsípouro* and a warm welcome draw crowds of diners to this attractive village eatery poised on the northeast flanks of the mountain.

Neatly arranged tables in the sheltered veranda at Vakhos, a restaurant in Delfoí

Kónitsa: To Dendro €
Greek **Map** B2
Approach road, 441 00
Tel 26550 22055
To Dendro has a daily-changing menu that features dishes such as *gástra* (baked goat) and wild boar cooked in wine until tender. The wine is local and plentiful.

DK Choice

Koronisiá: Myrtaria Patentas €€€
Seafood **Map** B3
Coast road, 471 00
Tel 26810 24021
Looking out over the picturesque Amvrakikós Gulf, this laidback taverna has garnered a reputation for its exquisitely cooked and pre-sented fresh fish and seafood dishes. The specialities here are prawns (caught straight from the gulf), sole and *makaronáda* with smoked eel. Superb wine list. There's an outdoor dining area on a terrace.

Lamía: Periklis €
Grill/Psistariá **Map** C3
Ypsilántou 132, 351 00
Tel 22310 39001
Periklis is a much-loved spot offering every variety of roast beast. It has both indoor and outdoor patio seating, but it can get booked out for functions, so it is wise to reserve ahead.

Lamía: Araxovoli €€
Seafood Ouzeri **Map** C3
Megálou Alexándrou 21, 351 00
Tel 22310 33091
In this meat-mad part of Greece, it's good to find a seafood-biased *ouzerí* – the nearby Maliakós Gulf ensures freshness. Friendly service and live music some nights (usually Fridays), when booking is advisable.

Mesolóngi: Dimitroukas €€
Traditional Greek **Map** B3
Razikótsikas 11, 302 00
Tel 26310 23237
The Mesolóngi area is famous for its eels, and this is the best place to try them. The eel-phobic will find plenty of other choices, too.

Mikró Pápigko: Dias €
Traditional Greek **Map** B2
Village centre, 440 04
Tel 26530 41257
This long-running taverna offers local specialities like *píttes* (turnovers), stews and grills, plus views of the Pýrgoi palisades.

DK Choice

Miliés: To Salkimi €€
Traditional Greek **Map** D3
Central plateía, 37 010
Tel 24230 86010
In a smart wooden building, this buzzing eatery serves classic dishes made with fresh local produce. Its signature dish is *salkimi* – veal, aubergines and courgettes in a brandy and *béchamel* sauce. Outdoor dining is accompanied by views across the Pagasitikos Gulf.

Milína (Pílio): Sakis €
Seafood **Map** D3
Waterfront, 370 06
Tel 24230 66078
An established, inviting taverna offering outdoor seating on the waterfront. Excellent *mezédes*, plus a range of seafood dishes.

Náfpaktos: Papoulis €
Mezedopoleío
Sismáni, cnr Formionos, 303 00
Tel 6996 555111
With an outdoor section on a waterside balcony, this restaurant offers standard *ouzerí* platters with a stress on seafood, like *gardiopílafo* (prawns in rice).

Néo Mikro Horió: To Horiatiko €
Traditional Greek Map C3
Central plateía, 360 75, near Karpenísi
Tel *22370 41257*
Welcoming taverna in a stone
building offering home-made
food in generous portions. Try the
kokoretsi (a dish of lamb or goat
intestine) and lamb *souvlákia*.

Párga: Golfo Beach €
Traditional Greek Map B3
Píso Kryonéri cove, 480 60
Tel *26840 32336*
This 1970s time-capsule taverna
excels at dishes like *moussaká*,
stifádo and stuffed vegetables,
plus home-made desserts. Live
Greek music three nights a week.

Párga: Sakis €
Greek Map B3
*Tourkopázaro, by the fountain and
plane trees, 480 60*
Tel *26840 32262*
One of the oldest tavernas in
town (founded 1954), this is the
place for cheap and cheerful
grills and *mageireftá*, but no
seafood. Good red wine.

DK Choice

Párga: Filomila €€
Fusion Map B3
Patatoúka, Tourkopázaro, 480 60
Tel *26840 31265*
Established, romantic restaurant
with great sea views and food
to match: pasta dishes, mussels
in *ouzo* sauce, then tiramisu or
pannacotta to finish off. Good
wine list, too.

DK Choice

Portariá: Kritsa €€
Fine Dining Map C3
Hotel Kritsa, Central plateía, 370 11
Tel *24280 90006*
Atmospheric place in a former
grocery shop. The elegant
ambience, crisp linens and
good wine make it the local
favourite for special occasions.
Unusual specialities include
grilled smoked *talagáni*
cheese and pickled aubergine,
as well as *píttes* and *spetzofáï*.
Booking advised.

Préveza: Skaloma €€
Seafood Map B3
Limáni Lygiás, 481 00
Tel *26820 56240*
Prawn *saganáki*, fried *kalamári* and
seafood *mezédes* top the crowd
favourites at this harbourside
taverna with famously fresh
fare and a good wine list. Great
views of Paxoí from its terrace.

**Sarakíniko Bay: Taverna
Tou Christou** €€
Traditional Greek Map B3
15 km (9 miles) NW of Párga, 480 60
Tel *26840 35207*
Own-grown vegetables, prime
seafood, a few selected meat
platters, good service and labels
from top local microwineries
combine for a winner. You can
take a boat to the bay from Párga.

Tríkala: Diachroniko €
Modern Greek Map C2
Hatzipétrou, crn Ypsilántou, 421 00
Tel *24310 77522*
This traditional taverna must be
visited if only for the ambience.
The food is good too, with a wide
menu that will satisfy vegetarians
and carnivores equally.

Tríkala: Palaia Istoria €€
Modern Greek Map C2
Ypsilántou 3, 421 00
Tel *24310 77627*
Authentic flavours, but with a
touch of the modern, at this
popular alleyway *ouzerí*. Pork and
lamb with creamy sauces and
garnishes like *ftéri* (fried fern) are
a must-try. One of the few Old
Bazaar places open for lunch.

Tsagkaráda: Agnanti €
Traditional Greek Map D3
Plateía Agíon Taxiarchón, 370 12
Tel *24260 49210*
All standard dishes are prepared
with flair at this long-running
taverna. Sit on the square, under
the plane trees, in summer,
or inside, by the fire, during
the winter months (there is
an enforced no-smoking
policy). Good *chýma* wine.

Tsagkaráda: Dipnosofistis €€€
Fine Dining Map D3
*Old road to Mylopótamos beach,
370 12*
Tel *24260 49825*
Delights such as salmon risotto
and blueberry cheesecake are
complemented by an excellent
wine list at this upscale bar-
restaurant. Appealing seating
under trees. Call first, since
they do not open every day
except in midsummer.

**Vólos: I Marina
Tsipourádiko** €
 Map C3
Magnisías 13, Néa Ionía, 384 46
Tel *24210 66245*
Vólos is famous for its legendary
400 *tsipourádika*, mostly on the
seafront and mostly touristy.
This, however, is the real deal:
each vial of *tsípouro* arrives with a
random platter – some scallops,
an octopus tentacle, hot peppers,
fluffy meatballs. Unmissable.

Charming outdoor dining area at Kritsa,
a restaurant in Portariá

Northern Greece

Alexandroúpoli: Nea Klimataria €
Greek Map E1
Plateía Kyprou 8, 681 00
Tel *25510 26288*
Rest your feet and people watch
while enjoying superb Greek
food in one of the town's busiest
squares. House specials include
kótsi (pork shank) and *sarmadákia*
(the local version of *ntolmádes*).

Alexandroúpoli: To Nisiotiko €€€
Seafood Map E1
Zaríki 3, 681 00
Tel *25510 20990*
An upmarket fish taverna with
a nautical decor located a block
inland. All fish dishes are present
and correct, starting with proper
white (not pink) *taramosaláta*
and continuing to less usual
recipes like seafood *kritharotó*
(orzo risotto). Very popular, so
you have to book in advance.

Fanári: O Faros €€
Seafood Map E1
Fanári seafront, 691 00
Tel *25330 31311*
Typical salads and *mezédes*
(including some dishes for the
fish-averse) pave the way for
creditably fresh seafood at this
hangout with great sea views.

DK Choice

Kastoriá: Doltso €€
Macedonian Map B2
Plateía Ntoltsoú, 521 00
Tel *24670 23777*
In a refurbished 18th-century
mansion in the old town, Doltso
doesn't just rely on its setting.
The menu features regional
dishes like *sarmádes* (cabbage
leaves stuffed with lamb offal),
pork hotpot with raisins and
plums, bean recipes and, in
winter, wild boar. Extensive
wine list, biased towards reds.

Kavála: To Araliki €
Traditional Greek   Map D1
Poulídou 33, 653 02
Tel *6984 718521*
At the edge of the old Panagía quarter, this taverna draws both locals and visitors with its big portions of pork dishes and chicken sautéed in mustard sauce. No seafood.

Kavála: Savvas €€
Seafood   Map D1
Thásou 29, shore E of centre 65201
Tel *2510 225505*
The go-to diner for fish in Kavála, Savvas sits on a relatively quiet spot with small boats moored in front. Creative salads precede the mains. Open all year.

Komotiní: Sultan Tepe €
Turkish   Map E1
Vasiléos Pávlou 10, 691 00
Tel *25310 30003*
Eastern Thrace has a significant Turkish minority, and this is one of the more accessible places to try their cuisine – mostly starters and various kinds of kebabs. Service can be haphazard.

DK Choice

Litóchoro: Gastrodromio "En Olympo" €€€
Fine Dining   Map C2
Agíou Nikoláou 36, 602 00
Tel *23520 21300*
The place to enjoy alfresco dining and renowned gourmet fare. The menu surprises with creations like octopus salad with peppers and saffron, or 12-hour-braised rosemary rabbit. Good wine list, salad selection and almost 30 Greek cheeses.

Psarádes: I Syntrofia €
Greek   Map B1
Village centre, 530 77
Tel *23850 46107*
Dine indoors at this welcoming hotel taverna, or on the summer terrace looking out over Megáli Préspa Lake. The menu features *grivádi* and *tsiróni* lake fish, the famous local beans and peppers, and home-made wine.

Thessaloníki: Ta Koumparakia €
Mezedopoleío   Map C2
Egnatía 140, 546 22
Tel *2310 271905*
Hidden behind a tiny Byzantine church, this place has a steadily improving menu that includes veggie platters (mushrooms, courgettes, grilled aubergines) and seafood delights (smoked mackerel, hake, swordfish) besides the older meat recipes.

Thessaloníki: Vrotos €
Modern Greek   Map C2
Skra 3, 546 22
Tel *2310 222392* Closed Mon & Sun
A tiny taverna (with only about 10 tables) with a sensibly short menu, in which titbits like *pastourmadopitákia* (cured meat turnovers) and *lachanontolmádes* stand out. Book ahead.

DK Choice

Thessaloníki: Aristotelous €€
Ouzerí   Map C2
Aristotélous 8, 546 23
Tel *2310 230762*
Classic spot, tucked away from the bustle of the eponymous *plateía* in a little passageway behind iron gates. Seafood includes *galéos skordaliá* (small shark with garlic sauce) and *mydopílafo*. Arcaded interior with vintage Greek tourism posters.

Thessaloníki: Dia Choiros €€
Creative Greek   Map C2
Valaorítou 25, 546 25
Tel *2310 235960*
The name – meaning "by pork" – is a pun on the soundalike *dia cheiros* ("by hand"). Pork is prominent, but not dominant, and there are also plenty of cheese and vegetable dishes. Sit in the quirky interior or in the secluded courtyard.

Thessaloníki: Ergon Agora €€
Fine Dining   Map C2
Pávlou Melá 42, 546 22
Tel *2310 288088*
This is the flagship branch of a chain of deli-bistros run by a Greek celebrity chef. The changing menu might have such delights as quinoa tabouleh or wild mushroom pilaf, and decadent chocolate *mpaklavás* for pudding. Brunch, offering assorted egg dishes and sweet or savoury pastries, is a highlight.

Thessaloníki: Kamares €€
Mezedopoleío   Map C2
Plateía Agíou Georgíou 11
Tel *2310 219686*
Outdoor tables face a grassy area. On the menu is standard but well-executed fare: beets, *chórta*, pulses, seafood bites and grilled chops, plus a full array of *ouzo* and *tsípouro*.

Thessaloníki: Kitchen Bar €€
International   Map C2
Limani Thessaloníki, 546 27
Tel *2310 502241*
A fun, trendy place in a restored warehouse on the jetty. The open kitchen allows diners to watch European and Mediterranean food being prepared by the chefs.

Thessaloníki: Ouzou Melathron €€
Modern Greek   Map C2
Stoá Karýpi 21, 546 24
Tel *2310 275016*
The "Palace of *Ouzo*" is a full-on taverna serving huge portions of everything from grilled octopus to pickled vegetables. Live music many nights. Warm-weather seating in a courtyard.

Thessaloníki: To Yenti €€
Mezedopoleío   Map C2
Paparéska 13, 54634
Tel *2310 246495*
One of the oldest, and still the best, of the Kástra eateries. Signature dishes include buffalo kebab, *mydopilafo* (mussels in rice), grilled mushrooms and *coq au vin*. Live music most nights.

Xánthi: Ta Fanarakia €
Traditional Greek   Map E1
Georgíou Stávrou 18, 671 00
Tel *25410 73606*
Both the premises and the menu at this old favourite taverna have had a revamp. Food quality can vary, but dishes always come in big portions; service and atmosphere are also reliable.

Food shop selling local and organic products at Ergon Agora, in Thessaloníki

For more information on types of restaurants *see page 274*

SHOPPING IN GREECE

Shopping in Greece can be entertaining, particularly when you buy directly from the producer. There is a wide range of shops and boutiques, as well as corner stores and department stores. Markets provide a colourful shopping experience, whether you are looking for olives, sugary sweets or traditional handi-

crafts. In smaller villages, embroiderers, lace makers and potters can often be seen at work. Leather goods, carpets, rugs and jewellery are also widely available, as are religious icons. Most other goods in Greece have been imported and carry a heavy mark-up. For information on shopping in Athens, see pages 118–19.

VAT and Tax-Free Shopping

Almost always included in the price, FPA *(Fóros Prostitheménis Axías)* – the equivalent of VAT – is about 23 per cent in Greece.

Visitors from outside the EU who stay less than three months may claim this money back on purchases over €120. A "Tax-Free Cheque" form must be completed in the shop, a copy of which is then given to the customs authorities on departure. You may be asked to show your receipt or goods as proof of purchase.

Opening Hours

Allowing for plenty of exceptions, shops and boutiques are generally open on Monday, Wednesday and Saturday from 9am to 2:30pm, and on Tuesday, Thursday and Friday from 9am to 2pm and 5:30 to 8:30pm (6–9pm in summer). Department stores remain open Monday to Friday from 9am to 9pm and Saturday from 9am to 6pm. Supermarkets, found in all but the smallest communities, are often family-run and open long hours, typically Monday to Friday from 8 or 9am to 9pm, and Saturday

from 9am to 8pm. Sunday shopping is possible in most tourist resorts and also in some of the suburban shopping malls in Athens. The corner *períptero* (street kiosk), found in nearly every town, is open from around 7am to 11pm or midnight, selling everything from aspirins to ice cream, as well as phonecards.

Markets

Most towns in Greece have their weekly street market *(laïkí agorá)*, a colourful selection of fresh fruit and vegetables, herbs, fish, meat and poultry – often juxtaposed with shoes and underwear, fabrics, household items and sundry electronic equipment. In the larger cities, the street markets are in a different area each day, usually opening early and packing up by about 2pm, in time for the siesta. Prices are generally cheaper than in the supermarkets, and a certain amount of bargaining is also acceptable, at least for non-perishables. This guide gives market days in the information under each town entry.

In Athens, there is a famous Sunday-morning flea market

that is held around Plateia Avyssinías and its radiating streets, which should not be missed if you are in the city *(see p91)*.

"Brettos" distillery and liquor store, in Athens

Food and Drink

Culinary delights to look out for in Greece include honey – the best varieties coming from the mountain villages – a wide selection of cured olives, high quality olive oil, and fresh and dried herbs and spices (especially Kozáni saffron, cheaper than Spanish saffron and just as good). A great selection of nuts is also available, including pistachios, hazelnuts and sunflower seeds.

The famous Greek feta cheese is widely available, and delicious in a salad or with rustic bread. Sweet breads and biscuits from a *foúrnos* (bakery) are another must. Oriental pastry fans should instead head to a *zacharoplasteío* (confectioner or patisserie).

Greece is also renowned for several alcoholic drinks, including *oúzo* (an aniseed-flavoured spirit), *retsína* (a resinated wine), brandy and the firewaters *tsípouro* and *rakí* (distilled from grape-press residue every autumn).

Souvenir shop window in Párga, central Greece

What to Buy in Greece

Traditional handicrafts, though not particularly cheap, do offer the most genuinely Greek souvenirs. Handicrafts cover a range of items from finely wrought gold reproductions of ancient pendants to rustic pots, wooden spoons and handmade sandals. Some of the country's best ceramics can be found in the markets and shops of Athens' northern suburb, Maroúsi. Brightly coloured embroidery and wall-hangings are produced in many villages throughout Greece, where they are often seen hanging out for sale, along with thick *flokáti* rugs, which are handwoven from sheep or goat's wool. *Flokátia* are made mainly in the Píndos Mountains and can also be found at Aráchova, near Delphi *(see p225)*. In the small, rural communities, crafts are often cottage industries, earning the family a large chunk of its annual income. Here, there is room to engage in some bartering over the price. The *Shopping in Athens* section, on pages 118–19, indicates places within the capital where traditional crafts may be bought.

Gold jewellery is sold in larger towns or cities. Modern designs are found in jewellers such as Lalaounis, and reproductions of ancient designs in museum gift shops.

Icons are generally sold in shops and monasteries. They range from very small portraits to substantial pictures. Some of the most beautiful, and expensive, use only age-old traditional techniques and materials.

Ornate utensils, such as these wooden spoons, are found in traditional craft shops. As here, they are often hand-carved into the shapes of figures and produced from the rich-textured wood of the native olive tree.

Kombologiá, or worry beads, the best ones made from amber, bone or coral, are counted as a way to relax. They are sold in souvenir shops and jewellers.

Kitchenware is found in most markets and in specialist shops. This copper coffee pot *(mpríki)* is used for making Greek coffee.

Leather goods are sold throughout Greece. Bags, wallets, purses, satchels and sandals make useful and good-value souvenirs.

Ornamental ceramics come in many shapes and finishes. Traditional earthenware, often simple, functional and unglazed, is frequently for sale by the roads on the outskirts of Athens and the larger towns.

SPECIALIST HOLIDAYS AND OUTDOOR ACTIVITIES

Many organized tours and courses cater for the special interests of visitors to Greece. You can follow in the footsteps of the apostle Paul or take a train ride through history; you can visit ancient archaeological sites with a learned academic as your guide, or learn to cook traditional recipes while sampling microwinery products. Sailing and windsurfing holidays are available, as are walking tours and botanical and birdwatching expeditions. There are also plenty of opportunities to watch sporting events. Many organized holidays include food and accommodation in the price.

A scenic railway journey through the Greek countryside

Archaeological Tours

For those interested in Greece's ancient past, a tour to some of the famous archaeological sites can make a fascinating and memorable holiday. You can choose from an array of destinations and itineraries, all guided by qualified academics or archaeologists. As well as visiting ancient ruins, many tours also take in Venetian fortresses, Byzantine churches and frescoes, museums and monasteries en route to the archaeological sites. The leading organizers

An archaeological guided tour

of such tours are **Andante Travels**, **Martin Randall** and **ACE Cultural Tours**.

Cooking Lessons and Wine Tasting

The growth in the reputation and popularity of traditional Greek country cuisine and microwineries has resulted in the rise of cooking and wine-tasting courses. **Athens Walking Tours** organizes three-hour evening cooking courses in the city, plus dinner time to eat your creations. The chef at the luxury **Kinsterna Hotel**, near Monemvasiá, does short courses on vegetable *píttes* and seafood, as well as sweets. Similar courses are offered through **Taverna Kritsa**, in Portariá village of Mt Pílio.

Near Métsovo in Epirus, the respected **Katogi Averoff** winery offers several tasting tours. The two wineries of **Niko Lazaridi**, near Dráma and Kavála in east Macedonia, also welcome visitors. The **Lafazanis**, **Lafkiotis** and **Semeli** wineries, in the Neméa region of the Peloponnese, are also happy to show visitors around.

Great Rail Journeys

The rail network in Greece is not extensive, nor is it used much by visitors, who tend to prefer the country's excellent bus system. It does, however, have one of the greatest railway journeys in Europe, on the narrow-gauge track to the mountain town of Kalávryta *(see p172)* from Diakoftó. There is another miniature train ride on Mount Pílio. A 60-km (37-mile) line linking Vólos with Miliés operated regular services until 1971. Today, the surviving section of the route between Ano Lechónia and Miliés runs as a tourist attraction (weekends and holidays Easter–Oct; daily

Beautiful spring wildflowers

Jul–Aug), using one of the original steam locomotives and providing views of impressive bridges, tunnels and buttressing.

Another superb railway trip is the journey from Athens to the Metéora, which passes over the spectacular Gorgopótamos viaduct, which was dynamited in 1942, to hamper resupplying of the Germans in North Africa.

At present, no rail tours are offered to Greece, but it's easy enough to secure information and tickets locally.

A horse-riding holiday along the azure coast

Nature Tours

Much of the Greek countryside is rich in birdlife and noted for its spring flowers. Specialist tour operators that include mainland Greece in their programmes are **Limosa Holidays**, with a trip to Lake Kerkíni in winter, and **Naturetrek**, which offers autumn tours for butterflies on mounts Chelmós and Parnassós, or wildflowers in the Peloponnese. It is worth consulting the website of the **Hellenic Ornithological Society** for coverage of the best birding areas.

Walking and Cycling

Greece is a paradise for walkers, particularly in the spring, when the countryside is at its greenest and the wildflowers are in bloom. The best locations are on the Pílio peninsula *(see pp222–4)* and the Píndos mountain range in western Greece *(see p210)*. **Trekking Hellas** has walking programmes (guided or self-guided) in the Píndos and on Mount Olympos. **Bikegreece** offers a week of mountain biking around Messinía, based at the Costa Navarino resort.

Rafting, Canoeing and Canyoning

Trekking Hellas is the prime organizer of rafting trips on the lively rivers of the central mainland and the Peloponnese, particularly the Karpenisiótis and the Loúsios. Rafting on the Voïdomátis River, exiting the Víkos Gorge, is the province of small local operators. There is also more gentle canoeing amid the wildlife-rich islets of the Amvrakikós Gulf in western Greece. The Kalypsó Gorge on Mount Kíssavos, between mounts Pílio and Olympos, sees organized canyoning expeditions.

Skiing on Mount Parnassós

Horse Riding

The Pílio peninsula *(see pp222-4)*, home to the legendary Centaurs – half-man and half-horse – is an ideal place for a riding holiday. **Ride World Wide** offers two different riding itineraries. One follows a route along the Pagasitic Gulf coast, while the other involves day-rides around the lovely south-easterly resort of Katigeórgis.

Skiing

There are more than a dozen ski resorts around the mainland mountains. The closest to Athens are those on Mount Parnassós and Tymfristós in central Greece, and Mount Chelmós near Kalávryta. You'll find better snow in northern Greece at Mount Vorrás (Kaïmaktsalán), near Edessa, and Mount Vérmion, near Véroia. The season runs between Christmas and mid-April. No foreign operators offer tours to Greece, and lift pass and equipment rental costs are in line with those of the Alps or Pyrenees. Northern Greek skiers save money by going to Bulgaria.

For more information on skiing in Greece, pick up a copy of the EOT's booklet entitled *Mountain Refuges and Ski Centres;* it is free from tourist offices and describes all the major ski centres. During the winter, **weather.gr** maintains a page (with an English option) titled "Ski Centers", detailing real-time conditions at the most popular resorts, though nothing on the snowpack – for that, you will have to go to the individual resorts' sites.

Windsurfing in the Peloponnese

Watersports

All along Greece's coastline, facilities for watersports are numerous. Visitors will find everything from windsurfing and water-skiing to jet-skiing and parasailing in the larger resorts. Many of the shops and beach huts that rent equipment also offer instruction. The best venues for windsurfing are Sývota and Páliros on the west mainland coast, Giálova in Messinía, Epanomí near Thessaloníki and Psakoúdia on the Chalkidikí peninsula.

An excellent resource for keen windsurfers is **windguru.cz**, which gives real-time wind-condition reports for all main resorts in Greece and beyond. The only UK tour operator to offer packages to the Greek mainland is **Neilson**.

Snorkelling and Scuba Diving

Thanks to Greece's amazingly clear waters, snorkelling can be enjoyed almost anywhere along the coast, though scuba diving is restricted due to many submerged ancient artifacts. Greece is highly protective of its antiquities, and it is forbidden to remove them.

A list of places where scuba equipment may be used is available from the Greek National Tourism Organization

Scuba diver exploring the submarine life

(GNTO) *(see p303)*. The Athens-based **Athina Diving** organizes diving trips along the Attica coast, and tuition is available for those with no previous diving experience. Another reliable scuba operator is **Atlantis** in Chalkidikí, on Sithonía peninsula.

Sailing Holidays

Sailing is a great way to explore Greece's vast coastline. Sailing holidays can be booked through charter companies either in Greece or abroad. The season runs from April to late October, and itineraries range from a few days to several weeks.

Charters fall into four main categories. Bareboat charter, without a skipper or crew, is available to anyone with sailing experience (most companies require at least two crew members to have a basic skipper's licence). Crewed charters range from the services of a paid skipper, assistant or cook to fully crewed yachts with every imaginable luxury. Chartering a yacht as part of a flotilla – typically in a group of six to 12 yachts – provides the opportunity for independent sailing with the support of a lead boat contactable by radio. **Nautilus**, **Sunsail** and **Neilson** offer this kind of holiday out of a few mainland ports like Zéa (Athens) and Páliros (west mainland), as well as holidays that mix cruiser sailing with shore-based dinghy sailing and windsurfing.

A sailboat under power along the Corinth Canal in the Peloponnese *(see p171)*

Cruises and Boat Trips

Running April to October, cruise options range from the luxury of a large liner or handsome tall sailing ship to inexpensive mini-cruises and boat trips. The former, with a limited number of Greek mainland ports of call, can be booked through the big operators such as **Swan Hellenic**, while the tall ships belong to **Star Clippers**. Mini-cruises and boat trips are best booked at a travel agent on site.

The Cruise Lines International Association (www.cruiseexperts.org) has a list of cruise companies sailing to Greece.

A luxury cruise ship

Spas and Hot Springs

The Greek mainland is not as well served with spas as some of the islands, but several of the resort hotels on Chalkidikí *(see p253)* do have excellent facilities. Many tour operators feature them, particularly **Eden Collection** in the UK.

If you don't require luxury, the Greek mainland is dotted with outdoor hot springs and covered thermal baths open to all day-visitors. The best are in the central mainland at Kámena Voúrla, Loutrá Kotséki and Ypáti (near Lamía); in the western Peloponnese at Kaïáfa and Kyllíni; and in Macedonia at Agkistro (Sérres) and, best of all, Loutrá Pózar (Edessa), which is close to the Vorrás ski resort.

Unusual Activities

Not everyone wants to do a bungee-jump into the Corinth Canal, but for those highly-adventurous travellers who do, it can be arranged direct through the sole operator, **Zulu Bungy**. While in Athens, take a

load off your feet by arranging an excursion with **Athens Segway Tours**, which offers four themed itineraries around the historic centre. Its affiliate, **Thessaloniki Segway Tours**, has a similar programme for the northern metropolis.

DIRECTORY

Archaeological Tours

ACE Cultural Tours
Babraham, Cambridge, CB22 5BP, UK.
Tel 01223 841 055.
W aceculturaltours.co.uk

Andante Travels
The Clock Tower, Unit 4, Southampton Road, Whaddon, Salisbury SP5 3HT, UK.
Tel 01722 713800.
W andantetravels.co.uk

Martin Randall
Voysey House, Barley Mow Passage, London W4 4GF, UK.
Tel 020 8742 3355.
W martinrandall.com

Cooking Lessons and Wine Tasting

Athens Walking Tours
Tel 210 884 7269.
W athenswalkingtours.gr/Cooking-Lessons

Katogi Averoff
Métsovo, 44200.
Tel 26560 31490.
W katogihotel.gr

Kinsterna Hotel
Monemvasiá, Agios Stéfanos 23070.
Tel 27320 66300.
W kinsternahotel.gr

Lafazanis
Neméa, Kefalári, 20500.
Tel 27460 31450.
W georgioslafazanis.gr

Lafkiotis
Neméa, Kleonai, 20500.
Tel 27460 31000.
W lafkiotis.gr

Niko Lazaridi
Chateau Lazaridi, Agorá Drámas 66100.
Winery Makedon, Platanotópou Kaválas.

Tel 25210 62049.
W chateau-lazaridi.com

Semeli
Neméa, Koútsi 20500.
Tel 27460 20361.
W semeliwines.gr

Taverna Kritsa
Portariá, 37011.
Tel 24280 90006.
W hotel-kritsa.gr

Great Rail Journeys

Diakoftó–Kalávryta Narrow Gauge
Diakoftó station.
Tel 26910 43206.
Kalávryta station.
Tel 26920 22245.
W odontotos.com

Pílio Trenáki
W trenose.gr

Nature Tours

Hellenic Ornith-ological Society
Themistokléous 80, 10681 Athens.
Tel 210 822 7937.
W ornithologiki.gr

Limosa Holidays
West End Farmhouse, Chapel Field, Stalham, Norfolk, NR12 9EJ, UK.
Tel 01692 580623.
W limosaholidays.co.uk

Naturetrek
Mingledown Barn, Wolf's Lane, Hants, GU34 3HJ, UK.
Tel 01962 733051.
W naturetrek.co.uk

Walking and Cycling

Bikegreece
Karaiskáki 13, 10554 Athens.
Tel 210 453 5567.
W bikegreece.com

Trekking Hellas
Athens. **Tel** 210 331 0323.
Loúsios Gorge.
Tel 27910 25978.
Karpenísi.
Tel 22370 25940.
Kissavos.
Tel 24940 51809.
Parnassós.
Tel 22670 31901.
Ioánnina.
Tel 26510 71703.
Mt Olympos.
Tel 24620 87999.
W trekking.gr

Rafting, Canoeing and Canyoning

Trekking Hellas
See Walking and Cycling

Horse-Riding

Ride World Wide
Staddon Farm, North Tawton, Devon, EX20 2BX, UK. **Tel** 01837 82544.
W rideworldwide.co.uk

Watersports

Neilson
Tel 0333 014 3351.
W neilson.co.uk

Snorkelling and Scuba Diving

Athina Diving
38th km Coastal Road, Lagoníssi, Attica, 19010.
Tel 22910 25434.
W athinadiving.gr

Atlantis Diving
Nikití, 63088 Sithonía.
Tel 6978 165361.
W atlantis-scuba diving.com

Sailing Holidays

Nautilus
The Watermill, 87 High Street, Edenbridge, Kent, TN8 5AU, UK.

Tel 01732 867 445.
W nautilusyachting.com

Neilson
See Watersports

Sunsail
DST House, St Marks Hill, Surbiton Surrey, KT6 4BH, UK.
Tel 020 3797 2567.
W sunsail.co.uk

Cruises and Boat Trips

Star Clippers
Olympus House, 2 Olympus Close, Ipswich, Suffolk, IP1 5LN, UK.
Tel 0845 200 6145.
W starclippers.co.uk

Swan Hellenic Cruises
Compass House, Rockingham Rd, Market Harborough, Leics, LE16 7QD, UK.
Tel 01858 898 439.
W swanhellenic.com

Spas and Hot Springs

Eden Collection
Tel 01244 567 000.
W edencollection.co.uk

Unusual Activities

Athens Segway Tours
Tel 210 322 2500.
W athenssegwaytours.com

Thessaloniki Segway Tours
Tel 2311 242975.
W thessaloniki segwaytours.com

Zulu Bungy
Tel 27410 49465.
W zulubungy.com

SURVIVAL GUIDE

Practical Information   **300–309**

Travel Information   **310–323**

PRACTICAL INFORMATION

Greece's appeal is both cultural and hedonistic. The country's physical beauty, hot climate and warm seas, together with the easy-going outlook of its people, are all conducive to a relaxing holiday. It does pay, however, to know something about the nuts and bolts of Greek life – when to visit, what to bring, how to get around and what to do if things go wrong –

to avoid unnecessary frustrations. Greece is no longer the cheap holiday destination it once was, though public transport, vehicle hire, eating out and hotel accommodation are still slightly less expensive than most west European countries. The many tourist offices *(see p303)* offer information on all the practical aspects of your stay.

Boats near the Greek coast in high summer

When to Go

High season – July and August – is the hottest *(see p53)* and most expensive time to visit Greece; it is also very crowded on the coast. December to March are the coldest and wettest months, with many hotels and restaurants closed for the winter.

Skiing in Greece is possible from January to April, with around a dozen mainland resorts to choose from *(see p295)*.

Spring (late Apr–May) is one of the loveliest times to visit – the weather is sunny but not debilitatingly hot, there are relatively few tourists about, and the countryside is ablaze with wild flowers *(see pp26–7)*.

Visas and Passports

Visitors from EU countries need a valid passport or ID card to enter Greece and do not need a visa. Some non-EU citizens such as those from the US, Canada, Australia and New Zealand, do not need a visa, but do need a valid passport for a stay of up to 90 cumulative days within any 180-day period (there is no

maximum stay for EU visitors). For longer stays, you must obtain a resident's permit from the **Aliens' Bureau** or the local police. Visitors of other nationalities should check visa requirements with a Greek embassy before travelling.

Non-EU citizen planning to work or study in Greece should contact their Greek consulate about visas and work permits.

Travel Safety Advice

Visitors can get up-to-date travel safety information from the Foreign and Commonwealth Office in the UK, the State Department in the US and the Department of Foreign Affairs and Trade in Australia.

Customs Information

EU residents can import alcohol, perfumes and tobacco without limits so long as they are for personal use. Visitors entering Greece from non-EU countries should check http://greece. visahq.com/customs for details of quantities they can import free of charge.

The unauthorized export of antiquities and archaeological artifacts from Greece is a serious offence punished with hefty fines and even prison sentences.

Any prescription drugs should be brought into Greece in the original container *(see pp304–5)*.

Tourist Information

Tourist information is available in many towns and villages in the form of government-run EOT offices (*Ellinikós Organismós Tourismoú*, also often referred to as **Greek National Tourism Organization, GNTO**), municipal tourist offices, the local tourist police *(see p304)* or travel agencies. Many of these offices operate only in summer. The GNTO publishes an array of tourist literature and brochures, but be aware that not all of this information is always up to date.

The addresses and phone numbers of the GNTO and municipal tourist offices are listed throughout this guide. A list of major Greek festivals and cultural events is given on pages 48–52, but it is also worth asking your nearest tourist office about what's happening locally.

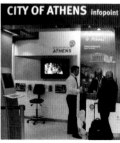
Getting information at a City of Athens infopoint

Ticket for the National Archaeological Museum

Admission Prices

Most state-run museums and archaeological sites charge an entrance fee of €3–€12. Visitors aged 18 or under from EU countries are entitled to free admission, as are EU travellers carrying an International Student Identity Card (ISIC) (see p302). Reductions of around 25 per cent are granted to EU citizens aged 65 and over (use your passport as proof of age), and reductions of 50 per cent to non-EU students with an ISIC card.

Though most museums and sites are closed on public holidays (see p52), the ones that do stay open are free of charge. Admission to all state-run museums and archaeological sites is free on Sundays between November and April.

Opening Hours

Opening hours tend to be vague in Greece, varying from day to day, season to season and place to place. In addition to this, the financial crisis that the country has been experiencing since 2010 is having significant impact on many attractions, causing staff budget cuts and reduced opening hours. The opening times in this book have been checked at the time of going to print, but it is advisable to use them as a rough guideline only and to check with local information centres before visiting a sight.

Most attractions usually close on Mondays and main public holidays. Small and private museums may be closed on local festival days in addition to main public holidays. On the nights around the August full moon, there is free admission to major archaeological sites –

including the Parthenon and the Poseidon Temple at Sounion. Sites stay open until 2am or so.

Monasteries and convents are open during daylight hours but will close for a few hours in the afternoon.

Most shops and offices are also closed on public holidays and local festival days, with the exception of some shops in tourist resorts. The dates of major local festivals are included in the Visitors' Checklists in each main town entry in this guide.

Social Customs and Etiquette

For a carefree holiday in Greece, it is best to adopt the local philosophy: *sigá, sigá* ("slowly, slowly"). Within this principle is the ritual of the afternoon siesta, a practice that should be taken seriously, particularly during the hottest months, when it is almost a physiological necessity.

Like anywhere else, common courtesy and respect are appreciated in Greece, so try speaking a few words of the language, even if your vocabulary covers only the basics (see pp344–8).

Though formal attire is rarely needed, modest clothing (trousers for men and skirts for women) is de rigueur for churches and monasteries. Topless sunbathing is generally tolerated, but nude bathing is officially restricted only to a few designated beaches.

In restaurants, the service charge is always included in the bill, but tips are still appreciated – the custom is to leave at least 10 per cent if you were satisfied with the service. Public toilet attendants should also be tipped. Taxi drivers do not expect tips, but they are not averse to them either; likewise, hotel porters and chambermaids.

In 2010, Greece introduced a law officially banning smoking

in enclosed public spaces, including in restaurants, bars and cafés. An estimated 40 per cent of Greeks smoke, and many ignore this law. Restaurant and café owners prefer to turn a blind eye to this, for fear of losing custom. Many bar staff smoke too. All the same, visitors should avoid smoking in enclosed public spaces; smoking in outdoor areas such as café terraces is permitted.

Note that Greek police will not tolerate rowdy or indecent behaviour, especially when fuelled by alcohol consumption; Greek courts impose heavy fines or even prison sentences on people who behave indecently.

Religion

About 97 per cent of the population is Greek Orthodox. The symbols and rituals of the religion are visible everywhere. Saints' days are celebrated throughout Greece (see p52), sometimes on a local scale and sometimes across the entire country.

Greek Orthodox monasteries and churches, many dating back centuries, are among the country's top cultural attractions. Visitors to these sacred places should dress respectably (shoulders and legs covered for both men and women) and refrain from taking photographs or shooting videos (this is officially forbidden, though rules do vary).

Regarding religious minorities, the largest group are the Muslims of Thrace, which constitute only about 1.2 per cent of the country's total population. Many immigrants from Muslim countries such as Bangladesh, Pakistan, Afghanistan and Somalia, as well as Albania, now live in Athens. In addition, there is a sizeable community of Roman Catholics, including ethnic Greeks and immigrants from Poland and the Philippines, who are catered for by the Roman Catholic Archdiocese of Athens.

A Greek priest

Sign for disabled parking

Travellers with Special Needs

There are few facilities for the disabled in Greece, so careful advance planning is essential; sights that have wheelchair access will have a wheelchair symbol at the start of their entry in this guide. In the United Kingdom, **Tourism for All** has a useful section about foreign travel on its website. Agencies such as **Accessible Travel and Leisure** and **Responsible Travel** arrange holidays specifically for disabled travellers, though at present neither includes Greece in their programmes.

Travelling with Children

Children are welcomed just about everywhere, including restaurants, where children's menus are often available. Babysitting facilities are provided by some hotels on request, but always check before booking. Some coastal resorts also have special amenities such as playgrounds, children's pools and even Kids' Clubs with organized activities.

Those aged 18 or under from EU countries enjoy free entry to state-run museums and archaeological sites, as do children aged five and under from non-EU countries. Concessions of up to 50 per cent are offered on most forms of public transport for children aged ten and under (in some cases, eight and under). Big hotels often let kids aged five and under sleep for free, and charge reduced rates for five- to 12-year-olds, as long as they are not occupying a separate room.

Swimming in the sea is generally safe for kids, but keep a close eye on them, as lifeguards are rare in Greece. Choose sandy beaches in sheltered bays with shallow water. Be aware of the hazards of overexposure to the sun and dehydration (see p305).

Student and Youth Travellers

Concessions are offered on train, metro and bus travel in Greece to students below the age of 25 with a valid **International Student Identity Card (ISIC)**. They may also need to show their passport. There are plenty of deals to be had getting to Greece, especially during low season. Agencies for student and youth travel include **STA Travel**. Before setting off, it is worth joining **Hostelling International** to enjoy discounts in Greek hostels. Most state-run museums and archaeological sites are free to EU students with a valid ISIC card; non-EU students with an ISIC card are usually entitled to a 50 per cent reduction.

An International Student Identity Card

There are no youth concessions available, but occasional discounts are possible with an International Youth Travel Card (IYTC), which can be obtained from any STA office by travellers under the age of 31.

Women Travellers

Greece is by and large a very safe country, and local communities are generally welcoming. Foreign women travelling alone are usually treated with respect, especially if they are dressed modestly. Although local men openly display their interest in women, making it clear that you are not interested in them is usually

enough to curtail any flirtation. Like elsewhere, hitchhiking alone in Greece carries potential risks and is not advisable.

Time

Greece is 2 hours ahead of Britain, 1 hour ahead of countries on Central European Time (such as France and Italy), 7 hours ahead of New York, 10 hours ahead of Los Angeles and 8 hours behind Sydney.

Greece puts the clock forward to summertime, and back again to wintertime, on the same days as other EU countries, in order to avoid any confusion when travelling around Europe.

Electricity

Greece, like other European countries, runs on 220–240 volts/50 Hz AC. Plugs have two round pins. Newer wall outlets are of the earthed type, while older ones, not intended for heavy-load appliances, have narrower, unearthed holes.

Adaptors for North American appliances are easy to find, while adaptors for UK gadgets are less common so bring your own.

Conversion Chart

Greece uses the metric system, with two small exceptions: sea distances are expressed in nautical miles and land is measured in *strémmata*. One *strémma* equals 0.1 ha (0.25 acre).

Kids enjoying the shallow waters at a sandy beach

Imperial to Metric
1 inch = 2.54 centimetres
1 foot = 30 centimetres
1 mile = 1.6 kilometres
1 ounce = 28 grams
1 pound = 454 grams
1 pint = 0.6 litres
1 gallon = 4.6 litres

Metric to Imperial
1 millimetre = 0.04 inches
1 centimetre = 0.4 inches
1 metre = 3 feet 3 inches
1 kilometre = 0.64 miles
1 gram = 0.04 ounces
1 kilogram = 2.2 pounds
1 litre = 1.8 pints

Responsible Tourism

Greece is lagging behind most other EU countries when it comes to issues of environmental awareness – recycling is scarcely practised, illegal dumping in rural areas is the norm, and waste management is a major problem.

However, there is much interest in renewable energy sources. Greece has great potential for developing solar energy – many families already have solar panels for heating water (they can sell the surplus to the National Grid), and there have been talks about producing solar power on a far larger scale. Wind energy is already used to some extent on the islands, but here too there is potential for further exploitation in the future.

Agrotourism (working farms that offer accommodation and meals to visitors) has been slow to take off in Greece, though there is a growing number of properties on the Peloponnese, the central mainland, Epirus and Macedonia. You can find them through the **Hellenic Agrotourism Federation** or **Guest Inn**.

Visitors can support local communities by shopping for local produce at the Central Market in Athens (see p121) and Modiáno Market in Thessaloníki (see p248), as well as the open-air street markets held weekly in various neighbourhoods of Athens. In some areas, you can buy local specialities directly from the producers – for example, formaella cheese in Aráchova (near Delphi) and metsovone cheese in Métsovo – and visit vineyards for wine tastings and direct purchases.

The Athens-based **Ecotourism Greece** is a useful source of ideas for ethical and sustainable tourism to rural destinations, as well as activities and small family-run hotels.

DIRECTORY

Visas and Passports

Aliens' Bureau
Pétrou Rálli 24, Távros, Athens.
Tel 210 340 5828.

Travel Safety Advice

Australia: Department of Foreign Affairs and Trade
W dfat.gov.au
W smarttraveller.gov.au

UK: Foreign and Commonwealth Office
W gov.uk/foreign-travel-advice

US: Department of State
W travel.state.gov

Embassies

Australia
Level 6, Thon Building, Kifissías & Alexándras avenues, Ambelókipoi, 11523 Athens.
Tel 210 870 4000.
W greece.embassy.gov.au/athn/home.html

Canada
Ethnikís Andistáseos 48, 15231 Chalándri, Athens.
Tel 210 727 3400.

Ireland
Vassiléos Konstantínou 7, 10674 Athens.
Tel 210 723 2771
W dfa.ie/irish-embassy/greece

United Kingdom
Ploutárchou 1, 10675 Athens. **Tel** 210 727 2600.
W ukingreece.fco.gov.uk/en

United States
Vasilíssis Sofías 91, 11521 Athens. **Tel** 210 721 2951.
W athens.usembassy.gov

Tourist Information Offices

Greek National Tourism Organization (GNTO)
Head office: Tsoha 7, 11521 Athens.
Tel 210 870 7000.
W visitgreece.gr
Information centre:
Dionysíou Areopagítou 18–20, 11742 Athens.
Tel 210 331 0392.

GNTO Australia and New Zealand
Underwood House, Suite 307, 37–49 Pitt St, Sydney, NSW 2000.
Tel (2) 9241 1663.

GNTO United Kingdom and Ireland
4 Great Portland St, London, W1W 8QJ.
Tel 020 7495 9300.

GNTO USA
305 E 47th Street, New York, New York 10017.
Tel (1212) 421-5777.

Travellers With Special Needs

Accessible Travel and Leisure
Tel 01452 729 739.
W accessibletravel.co.uk

Responsible Travel
Tel 01273 823 700.
W responsibletravel.com

Tourism for All
Tel 0845 124 9971.
W tourismforall.org.uk

Student Travellers

Hostelling International
Tel 01707 324 170.
W hihostels.com

International Student Identity Card (ISIC)
W isic.org

STA Travel
Tel 0333 311 0099.
W statravel.co.uk

Responsible Tourism

Ecotourism Greece
Tel 211 710 0050.
W ecotourism-greece.com

Guest Inn
Tel 210 960 7100.
W guestinn.com

Hellenic Agrotourism Federation (SEAGE)
Tel 6936 500 670.
W agroxenia.net

Personal Health and Security

Strikes and protest marches have always been regular features of Greek life. However, the rise in unemployment and in the cost of living caused by the ongoing economic crisis have led to higher levels of public unrest. Despite this, Greece remains a safe country to visit, although it is best to avoid protest marches and demonstrations, which can turn violent – especially in Athens, and most notably on Plateía Syntágmatos, in front of the Greek Parliament. Crime is rare outside Athens, where the biggest danger is the road – Greece has one of the highest accident rates in Europe. Considerable caution is recommended, for both drivers and pedestrians.

Police

Regular Greek police officers wear blue uniforms and keep a relatively low profile. However, there are several special units, the most conspicuous being the riot police (MAT), who wear a khaki military-type uniform and a helmet with a visor. The MAT are usually only seen at unruly demonstrations.

The tourist police combine normal police duties with dispensing advice to tourists. They wear a cap with a white band, a white belt and white gloves, as well as a "Tourist Police" badge on their shirt. Should you suffer a theft, lose your passport or have cause to complain about restaurants, shops, taxi drivers or tour guides, your case should first be made to them. Tourist police officers speak several languages and each office claims to have at least one English speaker, so they can also act as interpreters if the case needs to involve the local police.

What to be Aware of

Most crime-related problems centre on Athens. Visitors are advised to avoid public demonstrations, in particular those in Athens' Plateía Syntágmatos, which have become increasingly violent due to widespread public discontent. Gangs of pickpockets around Plateía Syntágmatos and Monastiráki target tourists arriving from the airport on public transport. They are adept at removing wallets and other valuables from outer trouser and backpack pockets, especially as you alight. It's advisable to get off one stop before or after Plateía Syntágmatos or Monastiráki and walk to your destination. There has also been a rise in muggings, especially around Omónoia Square, which is a gathering point for drug addicts, the homeless and other people on the margins of society. Burglaries are also more common than they once were.

Take sensible precautions such as keeping an eye on your bags in public, especially in crowded places, and keeping important documents and valuables in the hotel safe. If you do have anything stolen, contact the police or tourist police.

In an Emergency

In case of emergencies, the appropriate services to call are listed in the directory on the opposite page. For accidents and other medical emergencies, a 24-hour ambulance service operates within Athens, as well as in every provincial capital on the mainland, but due to the state of the roads, ambulances can take some time to arrive at remote locales. If necessary, patients can be transferred from local ESY (Greek National Health Service) hospitals or surgeries to a main ESY hospital in Athens by ambulance or helicopter.

A list of ESY hospitals, private hospitals and clinics is available from the tourist police.

Hospitals and Pharmacies

Emergency medical care in Greece is free for all EU citizens in possession of a **European Health Insurance Card (EHIC)**. All the main hospitals are in Athens, so if you have more serious issues, you will probably need to be taken to the capital. Also in Athens, **SOS Doctors** is a good service that carries out emergency home visits for a fee. Public hospitals are often understaffed, and it is not unusual for relatives to help feed and provide basic nursing care for patients. Corruption is rife within the Greek healthcare system, and it is considered perfectly normal to offer doctors under-the-table payments for priority treatment. There is now a codified, non-bribe fee for clinic appointments of €3–5.

Greek pharmacists are highly qualified and can not only advise on minor ailments, but also dispense medication not usually available over the counter back home. Their premises, *farmakeía*,

Greek police officers wearing typical blue uniforms

Ambulance

Police car

are identified by a green cross on a white background. **Pharmacies** are open 8:30am–2pm Monday to Friday, and they are usually closed in the afternoon and at weekends. However, in larger towns, a rota system is usually in place to maintain a daily service from morning to night. Details of on-duty pharmacies are posted in pharmacy windows.

Be sure to bring an adequate supply of any medication you may need while away, as well as a copy of the prescription with the generic name of the drug – this is useful not only in case you run out, but also for the purposes of customs when you enter the country.

Pharmacy sign

Several international pharmaceutical companies have stopped selling to Greece due to delayed payments, so some drugs are now in short supply. Also be aware that codeine, a painkiller commonly found in headache tablets, is illegal in Greece. However, this law has not been enforced in years.

Minor Hazards

The most obvious thing to avoid is overexposure to the sun; always wear a hat and good-quality sunglasses, as well as a high-factor suntan lotion. Heat stroke is a real hazard for which medical attention should be sought immediately; heat exhaustion and dehydration are also serious. Be sure to drink

plenty of water, even if you don't feel thirsty; if in doubt, invest in a packet of electrolyte tablets (a mixture of potassium salts and glucose) to replace lost minerals. These are available at any Greek pharmacy.

Tap water in Greece is generally safe to drink, but in remote communities, it is a good precaution to check with the locals. In mountain villages, water from springs and fountains is safe and delicious unless otherwise signposted. Bottled spring water, for sale in shops and kiosks, is reasonably priced and often has the advantage of being chilled.

When swimming in the sea, hazards to be aware of are weever fish, jellyfish and sea urchins. The latter are not uncommon and are extremely unpleasant if trodden on. If you do tread on one, the spine will need to be extracted using olive oil and a sterilized needle. Jellyfish stings can be relieved by applying vinegar, baking soda or various remedies sold at Greek pharmacies to the affected area. The sand-dwelling weever fish (*drákaina*) has a powerful sting, its poison causing extreme pain. The immediate treatment is to immerse the affected area in hot (over 40° C) water to dilute the venom's strength. Victims should then be taken to the nearest public clinic for an antivenin injection. The same applies to stingrays, which also like the sandy sea floor.

No inoculations are required for visitors to Greece, though your doctor may recommend tetanus and typhoid boosters.

Travel and Health Insurance

EU citizens should carry a European Health Insurance Card (EHIC) to receive free emergency medical care. Private

medical insurance is needed for all other types of treatment. Visitors are strongly advised to take out comprehensive travel insurance – available from travel agents, banks and insurance brokers – covering both private medical treatment and loss or theft of personal possessions. Be sure to read the small print – not all policies, for instance, will cover you for activities of a "dangerous" nature, such as motorcycling and trekking; not all policies will pay for doctors' or hospital fees direct, and only some will cover you for ambulances and emergency flights home. Paying for your flight with a credit card such as VISA or American Express will provide limited travel insurance, including reimbursement of your air fare if the agent happens to go bankrupt.

DIRECTORY

Countrywide Emergency Numbers

Ambulance
Tel 166.

Coastguard patrol
Tel 108.

Emergencies
Tel 112.
w sos112.info

Fire (Forest)
Tel 191.

Fire (Urban)
Tel 199.

Police
Tel 100.

Tourist Police (Athens)
Tel 171.

Athens Emergency Numbers

European Health Insurance Card (EHIC)
w ehic.org.uk

Pharmacies
Tel 14944 (information on 24-hour pharmacies).

Poison treatment centre
Tel 210 779 3777.

SOS Doctors
Tel 1016.
w sosiatroi.gr

Banking and Currency

Greece adopted the euro in 2002. Hit by the economic crisis of 2010, the country procured massive loans, but it soon emerged that it might be unable to repay them and therefore be forced to declare bankruptcy. In 2011, Greece's future within the Eurozone began to look uncertain. The impact of this situation on visitors remains to be seen. At the time of going to press, the economy had been stabilized thanks to yet more loans. Prices have risen, as many tax concessions to popular holiday areas have been abolished. If Greece did leave the Eurozone and readopt the drachma, foreign exchange rates would make the country a more competitive destination.

Visitors changing money at a foreign exchange bureau

Banks and Bureaux de Change

Towns throughout Greece, as well as tourist resorts, have the usual banking facilities, including 24-hour cash machines (ATMs). Alternatively, you can change foreign currency into euros at a bureau de change. Some travel agents, hotels, tourist offices and car-hire agencies are also willing to do this.

The main banks in the country are Ethniki Trapeza tis Ellados (National Bank of Greece), Alpha Bank, Pireaus Bank and Eurobank. Banks are open 8am–2:30pm Monday to Thursday and 8am–2pm on Friday. They are closed on public holidays (see p52) and may also be closed on any local festival days.

ATMs

Easily found in all Greek towns and resorts, ATMs can be used to withdraw cash using internationally recognized credit and debit cards. There has been a rise in ATM crime the world over, so exercise caution when using one, and always shield your PIN from passers-by.

Many ATMs will give you the option to levy a transaction in euros. This option often incurs a terrible exchange rate so it is best to make the withdrawal in your home currency.

Credit and Debit Cards

VISA and **MasterCard** are the most widely accepted credit cards in Greece; **American Express** less so, and Diners Club not at all. A credit card is the most convenient way to pay for air tickets, international ferry journeys, car hire, some hotels and large purchases. Keep your phone switched on when you make an expensive purchase, since somebody may ring you to confirm your identity before authorizing the transaction. Some small tavernas, shops and hotels do not take credit cards, so be sure to have cash with you when visiting these establishments. Some shops and travel agencies may charge up to 3 per cent extra for card use.

Unless your bank account offers free or reduced foreign currency transactions, all use of credit or debit cards in ATM machines attracts commissions totalling about 5 per cent of the withdrawn sum's value, usually itemised as a "foreign exchange fee" and a flat "transaction charge." This is taken out of your bank account, not out of the amount delivered at the ATM. All Greek ATMs take just about any type of debit card, except Visa Electron.

Prepaid debit cards brought from home in the currency of your choice are a good option, given the high commissions levied on credit/debit card use.

Be sure to tell your bank that you are travelling to Greece, so that your card is not blocked while you are away. This can usually be done through your bank's internet banking system.

DIRECTORY

Lost Credit Cards

American Express
Tel 00 44 1273 696 933.

MasterCard
Tel 001 636 722 7111 (call collect).

VISA
Tel 00 800 11638 0304 (toll-free).

Queueing at an ATM

The Euro

The euro (€) is the common currency of the European Union. It went into general circulation on 1 January 2002, initially for 12 participating countries, including Greece. EU members using the euro as sole official currency are known as the Eurozone. Several EU members have opted out of joining this common currency. Euro notes are identical throughout the Eurozone countries, each one including designs of fictional architectural structures and monuments. Each Eurozone member mints its own coins; the value side is identical everywhere, but the other ("heads") side features a national hero or the current sovereign. Both notes and coins are exchangeable in each of the Eurozone countries.

Bank Notes

Euro bank notes have seven denominations. The €5 note (grey in colour) is the smallest, followed by the €10 note (pink), €20 note (blue), €50 note (orange), €100 note (green), €200 note (yellow) and €500 note (purple). All notes show the stars of the European Union.

€5

€10

€20

€50

€100

€200

€500

€2

€1

50 cents

20 cents

10 cents

Coins

The euro has eight coin denominations: €2 and €1; 50 cents, 20 cents, 10 cents, 5 cents and 1 cent. The €2 and €1 coins are both silver and gold in colour. The 50-, 20- and 10-cent coins are gold. The 5-, 2- and 1-cent coins are bronze.

5 cents

2 cents

1 cent

Communications and Media

The Greek national telephone company is OTE (Organismós Tilepikoinonión Elládos), with several private providers utilising the OTE infrastructure. Telecommunications in Greece are good, and there are direct lines to all major countries. Mobile phones are ubiquitous and telecom companies compete for customers. Internet cafés have mostly been replaced by Wi-Fi zones. Greek post is fairly reliable and efficient, especially from the larger towns and resorts. The Greeks are avid newspaper readers. There are no longer any local English-language newspapers printed, but foreign newspapers are available in Athens, Thessaloníki and major mainland resorts, often the same day.

International Telephone Calls

Public telephones are ever more rare on the streets of Greece as more and more people now have mobile (cell) phones.

Making long-distance calls from a hotel can be very expensive. The best deals on long-distance calls are to be found at privately run call centres, which have sprung up in all the larger cities (often close to the train or bus station) to serve Greece's immigrant communities. Each call centre displays specific rates, as well as information about peak and cheap times, which vary depending on the country you are phoning. You can also buy a prepaid card with an access code that you scratch off and a toll-free number. These may not work from hotel phones but should work from a public telephone or private line.

Mobile Phones

The main mobile phone network providers are **Cosmote**, **Vodafone Greece** and **WIND Hellas**. To reduce the cost of calls while in Greece, it might be a good idea to purchase a Greek SIM card from one of these companies; however, this will work only if your phone is unlocked. Alternatively, you could use your network's roaming facility, which within the EU is set to plunge in cost to much the same as calling on a Greek SIM. All Greek mobile phone numbers begin with "69", and have ten digits in total.

Internet

Wi-Fi zones in cafés, restaurants, hotels and even some public spaces (including some Athens metro stations) are now widespread. Speed and bandwidth are often woeful, however, and any operation other than checking your email is likely to be frustrating.

A sign advertising free Wi-Fi at a bar/restaurant in Greece

Postal Services

The Greek postal service is run by **ELTA**. Greek post offices (*tachydromeía*) are generally open 7:30am–2:30pm Monday to Friday, with some main branches, especially in larger towns or cities, staying open as late as 8pm. Major branches are also occasionally open for a few hours on Saturday morning. All post offices are closed on public holidays (*see p52*). If you require assistance, take a queue number from the machine as soon as you enter a post office to prevent unnecessary waiting.

(see p52)

Useful Dialling Codes

- Directory enquiries for calls within Greece: 11888
- International operator and directory assistance: 139
- For reverse-charge call instructions, call the international operator
- For international calls from Greece, dial 00, followed by the country code (see the list below), the local area code (usually minus the initial 0), then the number.
  Australia 61
  Ireland 353
  New Zealand 64
  UK 44
  USA & Canada 1
- To call Greece from abroad, dial the international access code (see list below), followed by 30 (country code for Greece), then the 10-digit number.
  Australia: 0011
  Ireland, New Zealand & UK: 00
  USA & Canada: 011

Post boxes are usually bright yellow; some have two slots, marked *esoterikó* (domestic) and *exoterikó* (overseas). Bright-red post boxes are reserved for express mail, both domestic and overseas. Express is a little more expensive, but it cuts delivery time by a few days. Airmail letters take three to six days to most European countries, and anywhere from five days to a week or more to North America, Australia and New Zealand.

Stamps (*grammatósima*) can be bought at post offices and occasionally from vending machines inside post offices. In small towns where there is no post office, local independent shops sometimes sell stamps and offer mailing services.

The poste restante system – whereby mail can be sent to, and picked up from, a post office – is widely used in Greece, especially in more remote regions. Mail should be clearly marked "Poste Restante", with the recipient's surname underlined so that it gets filed in the right place.

A standard Greek bright-yellow post box

Proof of identity is needed when collecting the post, which is kept for a maximum of 30 days before being returned to the sender. If you are sending a parcel to a non-EU country, do not seal it before heading to the post office – its contents will need to be inspected by security before it is sent.

The main post offices in central Athens – on Plateía Syntágmatos and at Aiólou 100 (just off Omónoia Square) – are indicated on the Street Finder maps *(see pp126–39)*.

International courier services such as **ACS**, **Speedex** and **DHL** have offices in Athens and other major cities. They offer the best solution for express deliveries.

Newspapers and Magazines

The trusty corner *períptera* (kiosks), bookshops in larger towns and tourist shops in the resorts often sell foreign newspapers and magazines. These papers are expensive, however, as the mark-up on them is substantial. The rise of the Internet, combined with the continuing economic crisis, has cut a clean swathe through the former forest of English-language print publications in Greece. Currently, no English-language print media survives in Greece.

The most popular Greek-language newspapers are **Kathimerini**, *Eleftherotypía* and *Ta Néa*. The weekly Greek-language **Athinorama** *(see p122)* details cultural events in Athens.

Television and Radio

There are three state-run and several private TV channels, plus a host of cable and satellite stations from across Europe available in the country. The state-owned TV and radio broadcasting corporation is **ERT** (**EPT** in Greek). It was revived by the Syriza government in 2015. Most Greek stations cater to popular taste, with a mix of dubbed foreign soap operas, game shows, sport and films. Foreign-language films tend to be subtitled rather than dubbed. Satellite stations CNN and Euronews have international news in English around the clock. Guides detailing the coming week's television programmes are best accessed online.

With three state-owned radio channels and a plethora of local stations, the airwaves are positively jammed in Greece, and reception is not always dependable. Many stations are devoted exclusively to Greek music, either traditional or contemporary. ERT's Deeftero Prógramma (102.9 or 103.7 FM) plays quality Greek music. There are also classical music web stations, such as ERT's Tríto Prógramma (90.9 or 95.6 FM), one of the three state channels, and modern music stations such as **Rock FM** (96.9 FM). For the daily news in English, you can pick up the BBC World Service (90.2 FM in the Greater Athens area; frequency varies in other parts of Greece). The BBC can also be received over the Internet. Athens International Radio (AIR; 104.4 FM) broadcasts news bulletins, current affairs discussions and local information in English, German, French and a dozen more languages. It is therefore very easy to keep up to date with global affairs.

DIRECTORY

Mobile Phones

Cosmote
Tel 13838. [W] cosmote.gr

Vodafone Greece
Tel 13830. [W] vodafone.gr

WIND Hellas
Tel 13800. [W] wind.gr

Postal Services

ACS
Tel 210 819 0000.
[W] acscourier.net

DHL
Tel 210 989 0000.
[W] dhl.gr

ELTA
[W] elta.gr

Speedex
Tel 210 340 7000.
[W] speedex.gr

Newspapers and Magazines

Athinorama
[W] athinorama.gr (Greek only)

Kathimerini
[W] ekathimerini.com

Television and Radio

ERT
[W] ERT.gr

Rock FM
[W] rockfm.gr

A typical street kiosk, selling a wide variety of newspapers and magazines

TRAVEL INFORMATION

Reliably hot, sunny weather makes Greece a popular destination for holiday-makers, particularly from northern Europe. From mid-May to early October, there are countless flights to Greece. For those with more time, it is also possible to reach the country by car, or car plus ferry from Italy. Travelling on the mainland is easy enough. An extensive bus network reaches even the tiniest communities, with frequent services on all major routes. Greece's rail network is skeletal by comparison, and aside from the intercity expresses, service is much slower. Travelling by car offers the most flexibility, allowing visitors to reach places that are not accessible by public transport. However, road conditions are variable, and in remoter parts can be rough and dangerous *(see p316)*. Some of the larger cities and popular tourist destinations can also be reached by plane from Athens and Thessaloníki. Note that strikes (a regular occurrence in Greece) can cause disruption to public transport both to and within the country, and that demonstrations in the capital often see the roads of central Athens closed to all traffic.

Green Travel

To limit smog and traffic congestion in central Athens, driving restrictions apply – cars with registration numbers ending in an even number may drive in the city centre only on even dates of the month; cars with registrations ending in an odd number may drive in the city centre only on odd-numbered dates of the month *(see p322)*. However, these restrictions do not apply to foreign-reg and rental vehicles.

The city buses run on natural gas, while trolley-buses are powered by electricity, making them both environmentally friendly transport options.

Cycling in Athens is only for the brave. Local drivers have little respect for bicycles, and cycle lanes are non-existent. However, more people have started to use bicycles in the capital, and cyclists are now allowed to ride in the bus lanes.

For long-distance travel, Greeks have always preferred buses to trains. This has been even more true since 2011, when the already limited rail network suffered further cuts as a result of the economic crisis *(see p314)*. The only fast and reliable railway lines are the ones linking Athens to Thessaloníki and the Metéora.

In rural areas (notably the Peloponnese), cycling and hiking holidays are ever more popular; visitors relish the glorious unspoilt landscapes.

Arriving by Air

The main airlines operating direct scheduled flights from London to Athens are **Aegean Airlines** and **British Airways**; Aegean also flies in direct from Birmingham and Manchester. In addition, several budget airlines – including **easyJet** (from London Gatwick, Manchester and Edinburgh to Athens; and from London Gatwick and Manchester to Thessaloníki) and **Ryanair** (from London Stansted to Thessaloníki and Pátra) – also connect the UK to the Greek mainland. The Irish airline **Aer Lingus** runs scheduled flights from Dublin to Athens, while all the major European carriers such as **Air France** and **Alitalia** also operate scheduled flights.

There are about 15 international airports around Greece that can be reached directly from Europe; however, most of these are located on the islands. On the mainland, Athens and Thessaloníki handle most scheduled flights. The other mainland international airports – such as Préveza, Kavála and Vólos – can be reached directly mainly by charter flights; Kalamáta is now served seasonally by British Airways.

All scheduled long-haul flights to Greece land in Athens although many are not direct and will require changing at a connecting European city. There are direct flights to Athens from New York with **Delta** and from Philadelphia with **American Airlines**; **Air Transat** flies from Montreal and Toronto. **Air China** flies directly from Beijing to Athens. Although there are no direct flights to Athens from Australia or New Zealand, there are more than five flight routes daily from that part of the world that involve changing to a connecting flight at hubs in the Middle East.

Athens Elefthérios Venizélos International Airport

Light and spacious interior of Elefthérios Venizélos International Airport

Charter Flights and Packages

Charter flights to Greece are nearly all from within Europe, and mostly operate in the summer between the months of May and October. They are usually the cheapest option during peak season (Jul–Aug), when air fares rise steeply, and increasingly the differences between them and no-frills scheduled airlines are vanishing.

Tickets are sold through airline websites and, to a lesser extent, by travel agencies either as part of an all-inclusive package holiday or as a flight-only deal. **Thomson Airways** flies from London Gatwick and Manchester to Kávala all summer, while **Thomas Cook Airlines** links Manchester with Kalamáta and Préveza, plus Gatwick with Préveza.

Some real bargains can be found by buying tickets through price comparison websites such as **Kayak**, **Momondo** and **Skyscanner**. **Flycheapo** is a useful website that tells you which budget airline flies where.

Athens Airport

Greece's largest and most prestigious infrastructure development project for the millennium, **Elefthérios Venizélos – Athens International Airport** opened to air traffic in 2001. Located at Spáta, 27 km (17 miles) southeast of the city centre, the airport handles the majority of Greece's international and

domestic flights, as well as all of Athens' passenger and cargo flights.

It has two runways, designed for simultaneous, round-the-clock operation, and a Main Terminal Building for all arrivals and departures. Arrivals are located on the ground floor (Level 0) and departures on the first floor (Level 1). Security checks are often lengthy, so passengers are advised to check in as early as possible and to contact their airline in advance to find out the recommended time to arrive at the airport for their flight.

Service facilities include a shopping mall, restaurants and cafés in the Main Terminal Building and a five-star Sofitel hotel in the airport complex. Car-rental firms, banks, bureaux de change and travel agencies are all located in the arrivals area. There is also a small museum displaying archaeological findings from digs carried out in the airport area.

Transport from Athens Airport

Metro line 3 (blue line) links the airport to Sýntagma and Monastiráki from 6:33am until 11:33pm while the Proastyiakós suburban rail service runs from 5:26am to 9:44pm from the airport to Ano Liosia, just north of Athens (every 20 mins) and to Kiáto (every hour). You may have to take the Proastyiakós service as far as Doukíssis Plakentías station and change to the metro. Tickets for both metro and suburban rail journeys from the airport to the city centre cost €8 (single) and €14 (return); discounts are available for couples and groups.

Visitors who prefer to use the road (for those travelling between 11:30pm and 5:30am this is the only option) can take a bus, taxi or hired car. The X95 bus runs from the airport to Plateía Syntágmatos, in the city centre, every 10–15 minutes (journey time: about 70 mins). Bus X96 runs to Piraeus port every 20–25 minutes (journey time: about 90 mins). Bus X93 runs to Kifissós and Liosíon intercity bus stations in Athens every 25–30 minutes (journey time: about 65 mins). Bus X97 runs to Ellinikó metro station every 45–60 minutes (journey time: about 70 mins). All four buses run 24 hours a day, and a single ticket costs €5. A taxi ride to the centre costs €35 by day and €50 between midnight and 5am (fixed prices). A six-lane toll motorway links the airport to the Athens ring road. Several car hire companies are also based at the airport (see p316).

Bus outside Athens Elefthérios Venizélos International Airport

Thessaloníki and Other International Airports

Makedonia-Thessaloníki Airport is located 15 km (9 miles) southeast of Thessaloníki, in the north of the country. It handles a number of inter-national scheduled flights, but only from the rest of Europe.

The number 78 bus, which runs 24 hours a day, links Thessaloníki airport to the city's central train station, a journey of about 45 minutes, costing €0.90. A taxi covering the same route takes about 20 minutes depending on traffic, but is considerably more expensive (€15–€20).

Greece's other mainland international airports (such as Vólos, Kavála and Préveza) are served by charter flights only, mostly from the United Kingdom, Germany, the Netherlands and Scandinavia, during the summer season (May through September). Kalamáta is served by **easyJet** and **British Airways** as well, and Pátra-Araxos has a **Ryanair** service.

Domestic and Connecting Flights

Greece's domestic airline network is fairly extensive. The majority of internal flights are operated by three Greek airlines: **Aegean Airlines** and its subsidiary **Olympic Air**, based in Athens, and **Astra Airlines**, based in Thessaloníki but with a growing hub in Athens.

As well as having the largest number of international flights in Greece, Athens has the most connecting air services to other

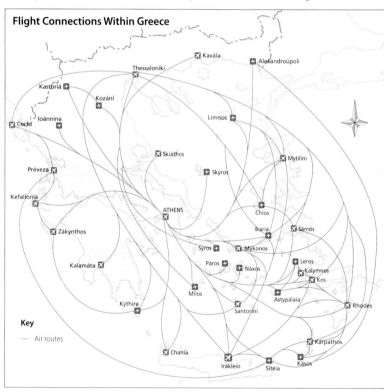

Flight Connections Within Greece

Key

— Air routes

Island	Distance	Flying Time	Island	Distance	Flying Time
Corfu	381 km (237 miles)	40 minutes	Crete (Chaniá)	318 km (198 miles)	45 minutes
Rhodes	426 km (265 miles)	45 minutes	Santoríni	228 km (142 miles)	40 minutes
Skýros	128 km (80 miles)	40 minutes	Kos	324 km (201 miles)	45 minutes
Skiáthos	135 km (84 miles)	30 minutes	Mykonos	153 km (95 miles)	30 minutes
Límnos	252 km (157 miles)	45 minutes	Páros	157 km (98 miles)	35 minutes

For keys to symbols *see back flap*

An Aegean Airlines plane on an airport runway

parts of the country. Both international and domestic flights use the city's Elefthérios Venizélos airport *(see p311)*.

Both Aegean Airlines and Olympic Air operate direct flights from Athens to four mainland destinations (Thessaloníki, Ioánnina, Alexandroúpoli and Kavála); in addition, Olympic runs services to more than two dozen island airports. Astra Airlines links Athens with Kastoriá and Thessaloníki to Kalamáta, as well as running services to many islands from both airports.

Other domestic and international Greek airlines come and go, but they are often unprofessional and best avoided.

Fares and Tickets

Fares for domestic flights are often at least double the equivalent of a bus journey or deck-class ferry trip. Timetables and tickets are available from the websites of the three major domestic airlines.

If you buy from a high-street travel agency or airport office, you will pay a huge commission; not so with a smartphone or iPad. Affordable seats sell out far in advance for the summer season and other busy periods, such as Easter, official holidays (like Pentecost) that form a three-day weekend, Christmas, New Year, the start of school term, the end of term, and election time (when Greeks travel back to their home villages to cast their vote).

Airport and Departure Taxes

Any and all applicable airport and departure taxes are included in the price of your air ticket at the time of purchase, so you can happily spend your last euro at the airport shops.

DIRECTORY

Arriving by Air

Aegean Airlines
Viltanioti 31,
14564 Athens.
Tel 801 112 0000.
🔲 aegeanair.com

Aer Lingus
🔲 aerlingus.com

Air China
Tel 210 722 0630.
🔲 airchina.com

Air France
Tel 210 998 0222.
🔲 airfrance.com

Air Transat
🔲 airtransat.com

Alitalia
Tel 210 998 8888.
🔲 alitalia.com

American Airlines
🔲 aa.com

British Airways
Tel 0800 4414 6798.
🔲 britishairways.com

Delta
Tel 211 180 9475.
🔲 delta.com

easyJet
Tel 210 353 0300.
🔲 easyjet.com

Ryanair
🔲 ryanair.com

Charter Flights and Packages

Fly Cheapo
🔲 flycheapo.com

Kayak
🔲 kayak.co.uk

Momondo
🔲 momondo.com

Skyscanner
🔲 skyscanner.net

Thomas Cook Airlines
🔲 thomascookairlines.com

Thomson Airways
🔲 thomson.co.uk

Athens Airport

Elefthérios Venizélos – Athens International Airport
5th km Spáta–Loútsa Ave,
19019 Spáta.
Tel 210 353 0000.
🔲 aia.gr

Thessaloníki Airport

Makedonia – Thessaloníki Airport
PO Box 22605, GR-55103
Kalamaria, Thessaloníki.
Tel 2310 985 000.
🔲 thessalonikiairport.com

Domestic Flights

Aegean Airlines
See Arriving by Air.

Astra Airlines
12 km Thessaloníki
Moudania Road/
Airport Area, GR 57001
PO Box 608 04,
Thermi Thessaloníki.
Tel 801 700 7466.
🔲 astra-airlines.gr

Olympic Air
Tel 210 355 0500.
🔲 olympicair.com

Travelling by Train

Greece's rail network is limited to the mainland and was always fairly skeletal by European standards. However, in 2011, as part of the restructuring of the vastly overstaffed and debt-ridden Greek railways, train services were cut even further and some routes completely suspended.

Except for the intercity express trains linking Athens to Thessaloníki (a trip of about five and a half hours), services tend to be extremely slow. On the plus side, non-express tickets are not expensive (cheaper than coach fares), and some lines allow you to experience Greece's rugged and beautiful countryside. An overnight sleeper service is available on the Athens–Thessaloníki route.

First- and second-class carriages of a non-express train

Arriving by Train

Travelling to Greece by train is expensive and difficult. This is largely because of the reduction in cross-border rail services, which are currently either suspended or functioning unreliably. However, travelling to Greece by train may be a good option if you wish to make stopovers en route. From London to Athens, the main route takes around three days. The journey is through France, Switzerland and Italy, then by overnight ferry from an Italian port such as Ancona or Bari to the Greek port of Pátra, followed by a bus to Athens.

In 2011, due to the critical state of the Greek railways' finances, all international overland train services into and out of the country were suspended. However, in 2014, one daily service between Thessaloníki and Sofia, Bulgaria resumed.

An alternative option is the rail-coach service that runs from Thessaloníki to Belgrade in Serbia.

Travelling Around Greece by Train

Greece's railway infrastructure is owned by **OSE** (Organismós Sidirodrómon Elládos), and train services are run by **TrainOSE**. Athens forms the principal hub of the system. A north-bound line from Laríssis station connects Athens to Thessaloníki, with branch lines to Vólos from Lárissa, and to Kardítsa, Tríkala and Kalampáka from the rather obscure Palaiofársalos junction.

From Thessaloníki, there is a line travelling west to Flórina (through Véroia and Edessa) and another travelling east to Alexandroúpoli (passing through Xánthi and Komotiní).

Destinations on the Peloponnese are no longer served by train, with the exception of Corinth. Trains depart from Laríssis station on the **Proastyakós** network, stopping at Corinth shortly before terminating at Kiáto. Passengers heading for Pátra then have to change to a TrainOSE bus service to reach their final destination. There are plans to build a new standard-gauge line from Kiáto to Pátra, but no dates have been set for this project. Proastyakós also runs a service from Athens' airport to Kiáto via Nerantziotissa (see p311).

There are two picturesque heritage routes: the rack-and-pinion line between Diakoftó and Kalávryta on the Peloponnese (see p172), and the trenáki on Mount Pílio (see p294).

Train Tickets

Train tickets can be bought at an OSE office, railway station or through the TrainOSE website.

There are two basic types of ticket: first and second class. Tickets for intercity express trains on the Athens–Thessaloníki line are more expensive, but worth it for the time they save.

When booking through the TrainOSE website there is a 10 per cent reduction on ticket prices, a 15 per cent reduction if you buy tickets at least two days

Laríssis station, the main railway station in Athens

Train station ticket window

before the beginning of your journey and a 20 per cent reduction on all return journeys. With the Intercity 6+1 ticket, you get six intercity train tickets plus an extra ticket for free.

Travellers aged over 65 are entitled to a 25–50 per cent reduction on tickets. Children up to age four travel free; those aged 4–12 get a 50 per cent reduction, while teenagers and students below the age of 25 receive a 25% discount with an International Student Identity Card.

Rail passes issued by **Interrail** (a global pass for European residents that covers 30 countries) and **Eurail** (a global pass for non-European residents that covers 23 countries) are valid in Greece, though supplements are charged on some lines. The passes also allow reductions on some ferries between Italy and Greece. Interrail pass holders travel free of charge with Superfast (see p319) from Ancona to Pátra, while Eurail pass holders can travel free with both Superfast and Minoan (see p319) on the same route. There may be a small surcharge in high season (Jun–Sep) and a port tax.

Railway Stations in Athens and Thessaloníki

Athens has one main terminal, **Laríssis Station**, which is located a 15-minute walk northwest of Omónoia Square and is served by metro Line 2 (red line). There are baggage storage facilities inside the station.

Thessaloníki Station is located a 15-minute walk west of the city centre. There are plans to build a one-line metro system in Thessaloníki (running from the east to the west of the city), with a stop at the train station. This project is already underway and will be completed by the year 2018.

A modern commuter train run by Proastyakós, linking Athens with Corinth

Greek Rail Network

0 km   100
0 miles   100

Díkaia

Sidirókastro
Kilkís   Sérres   Dráma   Xánthi   Komotiní
Edessa
Flórina   Thessaloníki   Alexandroúpoli
Véroia
Kateríni
Litóchoro
Kalampáka
Lárisa
Trikala   Vólos
Kardítsa
Lamía
Livadiá   Chalkída
Thebes
Kiáto   ATHENS
Corinth

Key
— Principal Rail routes

Travelling by Road

Travelling by car allows you to explore at your own pace. Greece's express highways (motorways) are the A1/E75 (north–south from Thessaloníki to Athens, passing Lárisa en route); the A2/ Vía Egnatía (east–west from Evros to Igoumenítsa, passing Thessaloníki en route); the A8 (east–west from Athens to Pátra, passing Corinth en route); and the A7 (north–south from Corinth to Kalamáta, passing Trípoli en route). The A5/Iónio Odós, from Ioánnina to the Kalamáta area, is barely half-completed, mostly between Vónitsa and Pýrgos near ancient Olympia. Some stretches of these motorways are being upgraded, and roadworks may cause delays. However, the roads are designed to be fast, and tolls are charged for their use – it cost nearly €30 to travel on the A1/E75.

You have priority	You have right of way

Do not use car horn	Wild animals crossing

Hairpin bend ahead	Roundabout ahead

Arriving by Car

The most direct overland routes to Greece are from Hungary, and then onwards via either Serbia or Former Yugoslav Republic of Macedonia (mostly on excellent motorways), or through Bulgaria (again, mostly new motorways). Many visitors choosing to drive from the UK to Greece head for Italy, then catch an overnight ferry from Ancona port to Pátra.

For a small fee, the **AA** and **RAC** will compile individual itineraries for motorists. They can also supply up-to-date information on route closures and potential hotspots. It is also worth asking their advice on insurance needs and on any special driving regulations for those countries en route.

In order to drive in Greece, you will need to have a full, valid national driving licence and insurance cover (at least third party is compulsory). **ELPA** (the Automobile and Touring Club of Greece) offers useful information on driving in Greece.

Rules of the Road

Driving is on the right in Greece. Road signs conform to European norms and are usually in both Greek and Roman scripts. However, on rural back roads, the names of villages are sometimes signposted in Greek only.

The speed limit for cars on national highways is 120 km/h (75 mph), on country roads it is usually 80–90 km/h (50–55 mph) and in towns 50 km/h (30 mph). For motorbikes, the speed limit on national highways is 90 km/h (55 mph), while on country roads it is 70 km/h (45 mph).

The use of seatbelts in cars is required by law, and children under the age of ten are not allowed to sit in the front seat. Using a mobile phone (without hands-free) while driving is prohibited, although many Greeks ignore this law. Parking and speeding tickets must be paid at the local police station or at your car-hire agency.

Tolls

Tolls – usually very high and frequent – are payable on all Greek motorways and on the Attiki Odos (the Athens ring road). There are also tolls for crossing the spectacular Rion-Antirio bridge (close to Pátra), and through the Artemission tunnel (on the Corinth–Trípoli motorway) and the Aktion undersea tunnel (close to Préveza). On major public holidays, be prepared for long tailbacks (and a lot of irate drivers) at busy toll booths on the motorways.

Car Hire

There are scores of car-hire agencies in every major city and resort, all offering a full range of cars and four-wheel-drive vehicles. International companies such as **Budget**, **Avis**, **Hertz** and **Europcar** (which have offices at Athens airport, as well as in the city centre) tend to be more expensive than their local counterparts, though the latter are generally just as reliable. Advance booking online via a consolidator agency is highly recommended.

The car-hire agency should have an agreement with an emergency recovery company, in the event of a vehicle break-down. Also, be sure to check the insurance policy cover: third party is required by law, but personal accident insurance is also strongly recommended. A valid driving licence held for at least one year is necessary, and there is a minimum age, ranging from 21 to 25 years.

Car hire kiosks at an airport

Rack of bicycles for hire at a coastal resort

Motorbike, Scooter and Bicycle Hire

Motorbikes and scooters are readily available for hire in all the tourist resorts. Scooters (dubbed *michanákia* or *papákia* –"little ducks" – in Greek) are ideal for short distances on fairly flat terrain, but for travel in more remote or mountainous areas, a motorbike is essential.

Always make sure the vehicle you hire is in good condition before you set out, and that you have adequate insurance cover; also check whether your own travel insurance covers you for motorbike accidents (many do not). Speeding in Greece is penalized by fines, drink-driving laws are strict, and helmets are compulsory.

Though less widely available, bicycles can be hired in some tourist resorts. The hot weather and tough terrain make cycling extremely hard work, though. On the positive side, bikes can be transported for free on most Greek ferries, and for a small fee on trains.

Petrol

Petrol stations are plentiful in urban centres, but few and far between in rural areas – always set out with a full tank to be on the safe side. Fuel is sold by the litre, and the price is comparable to most other European countries. There are currently three grades available: regular (95 octane), super (98 octane) and diesel, which is confusingly called *petrélaio*.

Filling stations are generally open from around 7am or 8am to between 7pm and 9pm daily but closed on Sundays in many areas. Some in the larger towns or along the busiest motorways are open 24 hours a day.

Taxis

Taxis provide a reasonably priced way of making short trips around Greece. All taxis are metered, but for longer journeys, a price can usually be negotiated per day or per trip. Also, drivers are generally amenable to dropping you off somewhere and returning to pick you up a few hours later.

In Athens, taxis are plentiful and can simply be hailed on the street. In smaller towns, it is best to find a taxi rank, which is likely to be either in the centre or by the bus or train station. Most rural villages have at least one taxi, and the best place to arrange for one is at the local *kafeneío* (café).

Although taxis are metered, it is worth getting a rough idea of the price before setting out. Round up to the nearest euro as a tip; luggage and entering a port or airport will incur an additional charge. In Greece, taxis are often shared with other passengers, each paying for their part of the journey.

Hitchhiking

Greece is a relatively safe place for hitchhiking but, like anywhere else, there are potential risks. Women especially are advised against hitching alone. If you do hitchhike, finding a lift is usually easier in the less populated rural areas than on busy roads heading out from major towns and cities. It is illegal to hitchhike on motorways.

Maps

Visitors who intend to do much motoring around the country are advised not to rely on maps issued by local travel agents and car-hire agencies, since these are rarely detailed enough. Instead, they should come prepared with maps procured overseas, in particular the Marco Polo whole-country map (1:300,000) or the Freytag Berndt (1:500,000). Freytag Berndt also produces regional mainland maps at 1:150,000. Two excellent Greek map publishers are **Anavasi** and **Terrain**. Both do large-scale maps of individual mainland regions. In the UK, **Stanfords** stocks a variety of useful maps to Greece.

Δράμα
Drama 36
Θεσσαλονίκη
Thesaloniki 161

Dual-language road sign, found on most routes

Travelling by Coach and Bus

Time permitting, bus travel is a good way of experiencing the country. Greece's bus system is operated by KTEL (Koinó Tameío Eispráxeon Leoforeíon), a syndicate of dozens of regional private companies. The network is comprehensive in that it provides every community with services of some sort: in rural villages this may be once a day; in remoter places, once or twice a week. Services between the larger centres are frequent and efficient.

International coaches also connect Greece with some of its neighbouring countries; these services are used mainly by immigrants who work in Greece.

Domestic coach, run by KTEL

Travelling by Coach

The Greek coach system is operated by a network of regional private companies under the umbrella of **KTEL**. It is extensive, with services to even the remotest destinations and frequent express coaches on all the major routes. Larger cities – Athens, Thessaloníki and Lamía, for example –have more than one terminal, each serving a different set of destinations.

Ticket sales are computerized for all major routes, with reserved seating on modern, air-conditioned coaches. It is wise to purchase your ticket in advance, since seats often sell out on popular routes and Greek coaches tend to leave a few minutes early.

In country villages, the local *kafeneío* (café) often serves as the coach station. You can usually buy your ticket from the owner; if not, it is possible to buy a ticket upon boarding.

Coach Tours

In the resort areas, travel agents offer a wide range of excursions on air-conditioned coaches accompanied by qualified guides. These trips include visits to major archaeological and historical sites, other towns and seaside resorts and special events. Be aware that coach tours are best booked a day in advance.

In Athens, **Key Tours** and **Fantasy Travel** offer a range of mainland excursions, including one- to four-day coach tours to places like Mycenae, Delphi, Epidaurus or Metéora.

Coach Services from Athens & Thessaloníki

From Athens, there are frequent coach services to all the larger towns on the mainland, apart from those in Thrace, which are served by coaches departing from **KTEL Thessaloníki** rather than the capital.

Athens' **Terminal A** is situated 4 km (2 miles) northeast of the city centre. The terminal serves Epirus, Macedonia and the Peloponnese, as well as the Ionian islands of Corfu, Kefalloniá, Lefkáda and Zákynthos (ferry crossings are included in the price of the ticket). It takes 6 hours to reach Thessaloníki, and 2 hours 30 minutes to the port of Pátra.

Terminal B is situated north of Agios Nikólaos metro station, but it is most easily reached by taxi. It serves most destinations in central Greece, including Delphi (3 hours) and Vólos (6 hours). Coaches to destinations around Attica (Soúnio, Lávrio, Rafína and Marathónas) leave from the Mavrommataíon coach terminal, on the corner of Leofóros Alexándras and 28 Oktovríou (Patisíon).

Be sure to check that you are heading to the correct terminal for the journey that you want to make.

DIRECTORY

Coach Tours

Fantasy Travel
Filellinon 19,
10557 Athens.
Tel 210 331 0530.
🆆 fantasy.gr

Key Tours
Athanasíou Diákou 26,
11743 Athens.
Tel 210 923 3166.
🆆 keytours.gr

Coach Services from Athens & Thessaloníki

KTEL Thessaloníki
Giannitsón 244,
Thessaloníki.
Tel 2310 500 111.
🆆 ktelthes.gr

Terminal A
Kifissoú 100,
Athens.
Tel 210 512 4910.

Terminal B
Liosíon 260,
Athens.
Tel 210 831 7096.

Travelling by Sea

The sea has always played an important role in the life and history of Greece. Today, the sea is a major source of revenue for the country, with millions of tourists descending each year for beach holidays on the Mediterranean and the Aegean, and thousands coming here for yacht-charter sailing holidays too. The Greek mainland and islands are linked by a vast network of ferries, catamarans and hydrofoils that serves the local population all year round, as well as tourists through the summer.

Arriving by Sea

There are ferry crossings from the Italian ports of Ancona, Bari, Brindisi, Venice and Trieste to Igoumenítsa in Epirus and Pátra in the Peloponnese. **Minoan**, **ANEK** and **Superfast** are the main Greek companies on these routes. In summer, it is advisable to book, especially if you have a car or want a cabin.

Greek Ferry Service

Athens' port, **Piraeus**, is the largest passenger port in Europe and one of the world's busiest. There are frequent ferry services (run by several private companies) to the islands of the Argo-Saronic, the Cyclades, the Dodecanese, the Northeast Aegean and Crete. Northeast of Athens, the smaller port of Rafína sees ferry departures for Evvia, plus some islands

in the Cyclades. Southeast of Athens, Lávrio has more services to the Cyclades and many to the northeast Aegean.

The crisis has culled several of the less sound shipping companies, leaving **Hellenic Seaways**, **ANEK** and **Blue Star** as the main operators in the Aegean. Their fleets comprise a limited number of conventional ferries and hydrofoils, plus many more high-speed ferries and catamarans. Hydrofoils get cancelled in adverse weather, so they are confined to relatively sheltered routes.

Tickets can be bought online or from travel agents in Athens. Advanced bookings are recommended for ferries in high season and essential for high-speed catamarans and hydrofoils. Out of season, services (and, to a lesser extent, prices) are reduced. **Greek Travel**

Pages is the most accurate and comprehensive source of information on ferry departures.

Cruises

Most cruise ships sailing the Mediterranean stop at Piraeus to give passengers a day in Athens. The port can accommodate even the largest vessels.

Piraeus Port Map

This shows where you are likely to find ferries to various destinations. A free shuttle service operates from in front of the metro station to the very remote berths for the Dodecanese, Northeast Aegean islands and Crete.

Key to Departure Points

- Argo-Saronic Islands
- Northeast Aegean Islands
- Dodecanese
- Cyclades
- Crete
- International cruise ships
- Hydrofoils and catamarans

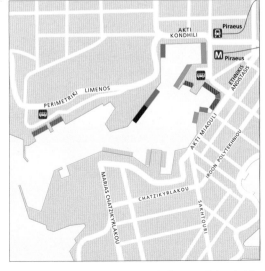

For keys to symbols *see back flap*

Getting Around Athens

The sights of Athens' city centre are closely packed, and almost everything of interest can be reached on foot. Walking is the best way of sightseeing in the city, especially in view of the traffic congestion, which can make both public and private transport slow and inefficient. The bus and trolleybus network provides the majority of public transport in the capital for Athenians and visitors alike; the three-line metro system offers a good alternative to the roads for some journeys, though the rudimentary tram is too slow to be very useful. Taxis are another option and, with the lowest tariffs of any EU capital, they are worth considering even for longer journeys.

One of the fleet of yellow, blue and white buses

Bus Services

Athens is served by an extensive bus network. Buses are white, yellow and blue. The network covers over 300 routes, connecting various districts to each other and to the city centre. All buses are ecologically friendly and run on natural gas.

Bus journeys are inexpensive but can be slow and uncomfortably crowded, particularly in the city centre and during rush hours; the worst times are from 7am to 8:30am, from 2pm to 3:30pm and from 7:30pm to 9pm.

Note that to reach Piraeus port, metro Line 1 (green line) is infinitely faster and more convenient than the bus. Timetables and route maps (only in Greek) are available from **OASA**, the Athens Urban Transport Organization.

Tickets must be purchased in advance from a metro station or a *períptero* (street kiosk); metro stations are more reliable sources, since very few *períptera* stock them any longer. Tickets can be bought individually or in a book of ten. The same ticket can be used on any bus, trolleybus, metro or tram, but must be validated in a ticket machine upon boarding. There is a penalty fine for not holding a validated ticket, and tourists who are unfamiliar with this may be caught out by inspectors who board buses to carry out random checks. Tickets are valid for 70 minutes from the time of validation.

Trolleybuses

Athens has a good network of trolleybuses, which are yellow and purple in colour and run on electricity. There are more than 20 routes that criss-cross the city centre and connect many of the main sights. Routes 7 and 8 are useful to reach the National Archaeological Museum from Plateía

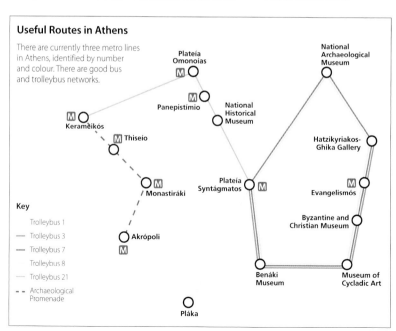

Useful Routes in Athens

There are currently three metro lines in Athens, identified by number and colour. There are good bus and trolleybus networks.

Key
— Trolleybus 1
— Trolleybus 3
— Trolleybus 7
— Trolleybus 8
— Trolleybus 21
- - Archaeological Promenade

Plateía Omonoias
Panepistímio
National Historical Museum
Keramēikós
Thiseío
Monastiráki
Akrópoli
Plateía Syntágmatos
National Archaeological Museum
Hatzikyriakos-Ghika Gallery
Evangelismós
Byzantine and Christian Museum
Benáki Museum
Museum of Cycladic Art
Pláka

An Athens trolleybus

Syntágmatos, while route 1 links Laríssis railway station with Omónoia and Sýntagma.

Tickets can be bought at ticket machines or windows at metro stations, plus a few street kiosks. They must be validated upon boarding the trolleybus.

Trams

Athens' tram system, a project inaugurated for the 2004 Olympics, connects the city centre and the coast. There are just three lines, confusingly numbered 3, 4 and 5. Line 3 runs along the coast between Néo Fáliro and Voúla; Line 4 runs from Sýntagma to Néo Fáliro; and Line 5 runs from Sýntagma to Voúla. The trams operate 5am–1am Sun–Thu (24 hours on Fridays and Saturdays).

Tickets can be bought at ticket machines at tram stops and must be validated at a machine at the tram stop before entering the tram.

Metro

The metro is fast and reliable. It was a key element in the restructuring of urban public transport for the 2004 Olympics, leading to the reduction in the number of private cars, as well as buses, in the city centre.

The metro has three lines: Line 1 (green line) runs from Kifissiá in the north to the port of Piraeus in the south, with central stops at Thiseío, Monastiráki, Omónoia and Victória. Most of the line is overland and only runs underground between Attikí and Monastiráki stations. The green line is used mainly by commuters who live in the northern suburbs, but it also offers visitors the fastest way of reaching Piraeus.

Line 2 (red line) and Line 3 (blue line) form part of a huge expansion of the system, most of which was completed in time for the 2004 Olympic Games. These two lines, which intersect at Sýntagma, were built 20 m (66 ft) underground in order to avoid interfering with material of archaeological interest. Panepistímio, Sýntagma and Akrópoli stations feature impressive displays of archaeological finds uncovered during construction work.

Line 2 (red line) runs from Anthoúpoli in northwest Athens to Ellinikó in the southeast. Line 3 (blue line) runs from Agía Marína to Doukíssis Plakentías in the northeast, with some trains continuing on to Elefthérios Venizélos airport.

One ticket allows travel on any of the three lines, as well as surface public transport, and is valid for 70 minutes in one direction. You cannot exit a station and then go back to continue your journey with the same ticket. Tickets must be validated before boarding the train – use the machines at the entrances to all platforms. Trains run every five minutes, 5am–midnight on Line 1, and 5:30am–midnight on Lines 2 and 3. At weekends, trains run from 5am to 2am.

Walking

The centre of Athens is very compact, and most major sights and museums are within a 25-minute walk of Plateía Syntágmatos, which is regarded as the city's centre.

Since the 2004 opening of the Archaeological Promenade, Athens has become infinitely more pleasant to navigate on foot. A broad car-free walkway running 4 km (2.5 miles), the promenade skirts the foot of the Acropolis to link the city's main ancient sites, as well as four metro stations. The streets of Dionysíou Areopagítou and Apostólou Pávlou run between Akrópoli metro station and Thiseío metro station (passing the Acropolis and the New Acropolis Museum); Adrianoú street runs from Thiseío metro station to Monastiráki station (passing the Ancient Agora); and Ermoú runs from Thiseío metro station to Kerameikós metro station (passing the Kerameikos archaeological site).

By day, Athens is still one of the safest European cities in which to walk around. However, it pays to be vigilant at night.

Evangelismós metro sign

Archaeological remains on display at Sýntagma metro station

A yellow taxi on a street in Athens

Taxis

Swarms of yellow taxis can be seen cruising the streets of Athens at most times of the day or night. However, trying to persuade one to stop can be a difficult task, especially between 2pm and 3pm, when taxi drivers usually change shifts. Then, they will only pick you up if you happen to be going in a direction that is convenient for them.

To hail a taxi, stand on the edge of the pavement and shout out your destination to any cab that slows down. If a cab's "taxi" sign is lit up, then it is definitely for hire (though often a taxi is also for hire when the sign is not lit). It is common practice in Athens for drivers to pick up extra passengers along the way, so it is worth flagging the occupied cabs too. If you are not the first passenger on board, make a note of the meter reading immediately; there is no fare sharing, so you should be

No parking on odd-numbered months (Jan, Mar, etc)

No parking on even-numbered months (Feb, Apr, etc)

charged for your portion of the journey only.

Despite a rise in prices, Athenian taxis are still very cheap by European standards – depending on traffic, you should not have to pay more than about €5 to travel to any destination within the downtown area, and between €6 and €9 from the centre to Piraeus. Higher tariffs come into effect between midnight and 5am and for journeys that exceed certain distances from the city centre. Fares to the airport, which is out of town at Spáta, are now fixed at €35 in the daytime and €50 at night (midnight–5am).

There are also small surcharges for extra pieces of luggage weighing more than 10 kg (22 lbs), and for journeys from the ferry or railway terminals. Taxi fares are increased during holiday periods, such as Christmas and Easter.

For an extra charge (€3.50–€6), you can make a phone call to a radio taxi company and arrange for a car to pick you up at an appointed place and time. Radio taxis are plentiful in the Athens area. Telephone numbers of a few companies are listed in the Directory box.

Driving

Driving in Athens can be a nerve-racking experience and best avoided, especially if you are not accustomed to Greek road habits. Many streets in the centre are pedestrianized, and there

are also plenty of one-way streets, so you need to plan your route carefully.

Finding a parking space can be very difficult too. Despite appearances to the contrary, parking in front of a no-parking sign or on a single yellow line is illegal. There are pay-and-display machines for legal on-street parking, as well as underground car parks, though these usually fill up quickly.

In an attempt to reduce dangerously high air pollution levels, there is an "odd-even" driving system in force. Cars that have an odd number at the end of their licence plates can enter the central grid, also called the *daktýlios*, only on dates with an odd number, and cars with an even number at the end of their plates are allowed into it only on dates with an even number. To avoid being unable to access the *daktýlios*, some people have two cars – with odd and even plates. The "odd–even" rule does not apply to foreign cars; however, if possible, avoid taking your car into the city centre.

Sign for a pedestrianized area

DIRECTORY

Public transport

Metro
Tel 210 519 4012.
W amel.gr

OASA (buses/trolleybuses)
Metsovou 15.
Tel 111 85.
W oasa.gr

Trams
Tel 210 997 8000.
W tramsa.gr

Taxis

Athina 1
Tel 210 921 2800
(central Athens).

Ermis
Tel 210 411 5200
(Piraeus).

Hellas
Tel 210 645 7000 (central Athens).
Tel 210 801 4000 (north Athens).

Athens Transport Links

The hub of Athens' public transport is the area around the two squares of Sýntagma and Omónoia. From this central area, the metro and various buses can be taken to Elefthérios Venizélos International Airport, the port at Piraeus and Athens' Laríssis train station. In addition, three tram lines connect the city centre with the Attic coast.

Bus X95 runs between the airport *(see p311)* and Plateía Syntágmatos, and bus X96 links the airport to Piraeus *(see p319)*. The airport is also served by Line 3 (blue line) of the metro, from Sýntagma and Monastiráki.

Metro Line 1 (green line, from Omónoia and Monastiráki) extends to Piraeus; the journey from the city centre to the port takes about half an hour. Trolleybus route 1 goes past Sýntagma metro station and Laríssis train and metro stations. Laríssis train station is also served by metro Line 2 (red line), from both Sýntagma and Omónoia.

Tram line 3 runs along the coast from Néo Fáliro to the seaside suburb of Voúla; tram line 4 runs from Sýntagma Square in the city centre to Néo Fáliro; and tram line 5 runs from Voúla to Sýntagma. These lines

are especially useful if you are staying in a hotel along the coast, or if you wish to have a day on the beach.

Though more expensive than public transport, the most convenient way of getting to and from any of these destinations is by taxi. Journey times vary greatly, but if traffic is free-flowing, the journey from the city centre to the airport takes about 40 minutes; the journey from the city centre to Piraeus takes around 30 minutes; and the journey from Piraeus to the airport, via the coast takes about an hour.

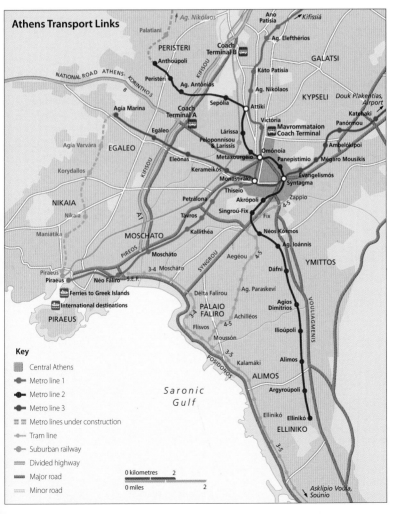

Athens Transport Links

Key
- Central Athens
- Metro line 1
- Metro line 2
- Metro line 3
- Metro lines under construction
- Tram line
- Suburban railway
- Divided highway
- Major road
- Minor road

0 kilometres 2
0 miles 2

For keys to symbols *see back flap*

General Index

Page numbers in **bold** refer to main entries

A

Abdera 15, **260**
Accessories
  shopping in Athens **120**, 121
Accommodation **264–73**
Achaïa Clauss Winery (Pátra) 173
Acharnés 155
Achilles 58–9
"Achilles Painter" 75
Acrocorinth **170**
Acropolis (Athens) 12, 68,
  98–105, 110–11
  around the Acropolis **104–5**
  map 98
  Parthenon **102–3**
  temple architecture 62
  timeline 99
  Visitors' checklist 99
Acropolis Museum (Athens) 12,
  104
Actium, Battle of (31 BC) 38, 216
Admission prices 301
Aeëtes, King 224
Aegeus, King 100
Aeneas 59
Aeschylus 34, 61
  Eumenides 105
  Theatre of Dionysos (Athens)
  101
Agamemnon 31, 185
  The Curse of the House of
  Atreus 183
  Mask of Agamemnon 73, 184
  Mycenae 143
  Treasury of Atreus (Mycenae)
  184
  Trojan War 58, 59
Agiá 14
Agía Kyriakí 222
Agía Marína 50
Agía Moní (Náfplio) 187
Agía Paraskevi 50
Agía Sofía (Monemvasiá) 190
Agía Sofía (Thessaloníki) **252**
Agía Triáda 185
Agioi Apóstoloi Pétrus kai Pávlos
  50
Agios Andréas (Pátra) 173

Agios Andréas (St Andrew's Day)
  51
Agios Dimítrios (Athens) **105**
Agios Dimítrios (festival) 51
Agios Dimítrios (Outer Máni) 199
Agios Dimítrios (Thessaloníki) 15,
  252
Agios Geórgios (Athens) 76
Agios Geórgios (St George's Day)
  49
Agios Germanós 241
Agios Ioánnis (Pílio) 222, 224
  restaurants 288
Agios Ioánnis (St John's Day) 50
Agios Konstantínos kai Agía Eléni
  49
Agios Nikólaos (Outer Máni) 199
Agios Nikólaos (St Nicholas's Day)
  52
Agios Nikólaos Anapavsás 221
Agios Nikólaos Orfanós
  (Thessaloníki) **252**
Agios Nikólaos Ragkavás (Athens)
  112
  Street-by-Street map 107
Agios Panteleímon 51
Agios Vasíleios 52
Agíou Dionysíou (Mount Athos)
  257
Agíou Georgíou Feneoú 172
Agíou Nikoláou 208
Agíou Panteleímonos (Mount
  Athos) 256
Agíou Pávlou (Mount Athos) 257
Agíou Pnévmatos 50
Agora (Athens) 68
Agorakritos 149
Aigisthos 59, 183
Air travel **310–13**
  airport and departure taxes 313
  arriving in Greece **310–12**, 313
  Athens airport **311**, 313
  charter flights **311**, 313
  domestic and connecting
  flights **312–13**
  fares and tickets 313
  package deals **311**, 313
Akronafplia (Náfplio) **187**
Alaric, King of the Goths 160
Albania 23, 43
Alcaeus 60

Alcman 60
Alcohol 301
Alexander II, Tsar 115
Alexander the Great 29, 35, 222,
  246
  death 36, 228
  Hellenistic Greece **36–7**
  Macedonia 237
  Pella 15, 237, 247
Alexandria 36
Aléxandros I, King 261
Alexandroúpoli **261**
  restaurants 290
Alfeiós River 174, 177, 178
Ali Pasha 43, **214**
  death 215
  Párga 216
  Préveza 217
Álimos 153
Alkibiades 193
Alónissos 30
Alpine refuges **266**, 267
Amalía, Queen
  Mitrópoli (Athens) 112
  Museum of the City of Athens
  81
  National Gardens (Athens)
  116
  National Historical Museum
  (Athens) 84
Ambulances 304, 305
American School of Classical
  Studies 94
Ammouliani Islet
  hotels 272
Amphiareio of Oropos **148**
Amphitrite 56
Anafiótika (Athens) **112–13**
  Street-by-Street map 107
Anakasiá 222, 224
Análipsi 49
Anávysos 153
Ancient Agora (Athens) 12,
  94–5
Ancient Brauron 13, 145,
  150–51
Ancient Corinth 13, 37, 143,
  166–70
  hotels 270
  restaurants 287
  Roman Greece 38–9

Ancient Delphi 10, 14, 142, 230–31, **232–5**
  Sanctuary of Delphi 34–5, 232
Ancient Dion 15, 237, 245
Ancient Dodona 14, **215**
Ancient Eleusis 13, 145, **160–61**
Ancient Gortys 178
Ancient Greece **55–65**
  The development of Greek sculpture **74–5**
  Gods, goddesses and heroes **56–7**
  Greek writers and philosophers **60–61**
  National Archaeological Museum (Athens) **72–5**
  Temple architecture **62–3**
  The Trojan War **58–9**
  Vases and vase painting **64–5**
Ancient Isthmia 171
Ancient Messene **205**
Ancient Nemea 13, **171**
Ancient Olympia 13, 142, 163, **174–7**
  Olympia Archaeological Museum **176**
  The origins of the Olympic Games **177**
  Visitors' checklist 175
Ancient Olynthos 253
Ancient Pella 15, 36, 237, **247**
Ancient Tegea 13, **181**
Ancient Thebes see Thíva
Ancient Tiryns 13, 31, **185**
Ancient Troezen **185**
Andrew, St 173
Andrítsaina 13, **181**
Andronikos II, Emperor 192
Andrónikos, Manólis 246
ANEL 47
Anogianákis, Phoivos 108
Anthemíon Tomb (Lefkádia) 246–7
Antiochus IV, King 105
Antiques shops
  Athens **118–19**, 121
Antírrio 229
Antoninus Pius, Emperor 161
Antony, Mark 38
Apartments, staying in 265
Aphrodite 56, 57

Apókries 48
Apollo 57
  Delphi 232, 235
  Monastery of Daphni 156
  Vale of Tempe 217
Apotomí Kefalís Ioánnou Prodrómou 51
Aráchova 13, 14, 225
  hotels 271
  restaurants 288
Aravantinós, Pános 159
Arcadia 163
Arcadius, Emperor 148
Arch of Galerius (Thessaloníki) **248**
Archaeological Museum (Argos) 181
Archaeological Museum (Ioánnina) **214**
Archaeological Museum (Kavála) 259
Archaeological Museum (Komotiní) 260
Archaeological Museum (Náfplio) **186**
Archaeological Museum (Piraeus) **159**
Archaeological Museum (Spárti) 193
Archaeological Museum (Thíva) 225
Archaeological Museum (Vólos) 13, 224
Archaeological tours **294**, 297
Archaic Period **32–3**
Archelaos, King 247
Archer, A 104
Archilochus 60
Archimedes 37
Architecture
  Athenian Neo-Classical architecture **85**
  Byzantine architecture **24–5**
  Temple architecture **62–3**
Areopagos Hill (Athens) **105**
Aréopoli **202**
Ares 88, 105
Argalastí 13, 223
  hotels 271
Argive Heraion 185

Argolid 163
Argonauts 224
Argos 23, **181**
Argyrós 77
Aristeides the Just 95
Aristion 149
Aristokles 149
Aristonoë 148
Aristophanes
  Frogs 76
  Lysistrata 150
  Theatre of Dionysos (Athens) 101
Aristotle 34, 40
  birthplace 253
  death 36
  Lyceum 61
  tutors Alexander the Great 247
Arnaia
  hotels 272
Aroman shepherds 211, **213**
Art
  The development of Greek sculpture **74–5**
  Greek myths in Western art **59**
  Icon painters in Pláka **113**
  Icons in the Orthodox Church **80**
  shopping in Athens **118–19**, 121
  Vases and vase painting **64–5**
  see also Museums and galleries
Arta 14, 207, **217**
Artemis 57, 58
  Ancient Brauron 150
  Theatre of Dionysos (Athens) 101
Arts and crafts see Crafts
Asklepieion (Epidaurus) **188–9**
Asklepios 188, 189, 217
Aslan Pasha 214
Athanásios 220
Athanásios the Athonite 258
Athena 56, 57, 59
  Acropolis (Athens) 98
  Erechtheion (Athens) 100–101
  Lykavittós Hill (Athens) 76
  Parthenon (Athens) 102, 103

Athena Lemnia (Pheidias) 35

Athens **67–139**
  airport **311**, 313
  Around Athens: Attica **145–61**
  Central Athens North **71–85**
  Central Athens South **87–117**
  climate 53
  coach services **318**
  emergency numbers 305
  entertainment **122–5**
  The flavours of Greece **278**
  history 34
  hotels 268–70
  map 68–9
  Neo-Classical architecture **85**
  railway station 315
  restaurants 282–6
  shopping **118–21**
  Street finder 126–39
  travel **320–23**
  Two days in Athens 12
Athens Academy 85
Athens Festival 50
Athens Memorial (Palaió Fáliro)
  153
Athos, Mount *see* Mount Athos
ATMs 306
Atreid kings 163
Atreus, King 59, 183
Attalos, King of Pergamon 95
Attic Coast **153**
Attica **145–61**
  Five days in Attica and the
    Peloponnese 11, **12–13**
  map 146–7
Attica Zoological Park 13, **154**
Atticus, Herodes 176
  Kallimármaro Stadium (Athens)
    117
  Marathon Museum 149
  Odeion (Ancient Corinth) 167
  Theatre of Herodes Atticus
    (Athens) 98, 101
Augustus, Emperor (Octavian)
  167, 217
Autumn in Greece 51
Avars 40
Avéroff, Evángelos 213
Avéroff, Geórgios 117
Avéroff Museum (Métsovo)
  213
Avramídis, Minás 90
Axiós Delta 240

B

Balkan Wars 45
Balkans 23
Bank notes 307
Banks **306**
Barber shop in Marousi
  (Tsaroúchis) 46
Barnabas 220
Basil the Bulgar Slayer 41
Basketball
  Athens 124
Beavers
  Kastoriá 244
Beer **276**
Benáki Museum (Athens) 12, 69,
  82–3
Benákis, Antónis 82
Benákis, Emmanouíl 82
Beulé, Ernest 100
Beulé Gate (Athens) 98, **100**
Bezesténi (Thessaloníki) 248
Bicycles **295**, 297
  hiring **317**
Birds
  Dadiá Forest 261
  Préspa Lakes 240–41
  Saltpan birdlife **229**
  see also Wildlife
Blegen, Carl 205
Boats **319**
  cruises and boat trips **296**, 297,
    319
  Hellenic Maritime Museum
    (Piraeus) **159**
  sailing holidays **296**, 297
Bonastro 84
Book shops
  Athens **120**, 121
"Bosanquet Painter" 75
Bost 81
Botanical Museum (Athens) 116
Boulanger, François 84, 112
Boúrtzi **186–7**
Boutique inns 264
Bowling
  Athens 124
Braque, Georges 77
Brauron *see* Ancient Brauron
Brauron Museum (Ancient
  Brauron) **151**
Brauronia ceremony **150**
Breakfast **276**
Briseis 58

Bronze Age 29, 30, 56, 182
Brueghel, Pieter 77
Bulgaria 23
Bulgars 40
Bureaux de change 306
Buses **318**
  in Athens **320**
  from Athens airport 311
Byron, Lord **153**
  Castalian Spring (Delphi) 235
  Childe Harold 113, 153
  death 44, 229
  Gennádeion (Athens) 77
  Mesolóngi 229
  National Historical Museum
    (Athens) 84
  Plateía Lysikrátous (Athens) 107,
    113
  statue of 229
  Temple of Poseidon (Sounion)
    153
Byzantine and Christian Museum
  (Athens) **80**
Byzantine Greece 39, **40–41**
  architecture **24–5**
Byzantine Museum (Ioánnina)
  214
Byzantine Museum (Kastoriá)
  244
Byzantine Museum (Véroia)
  246

C

Caesar, Julius 38
Calatrava, Santiago 124
Camping **266–7**
Canoeing **295**, 297
Canyoning **295**, 297
Cape Matapan 171
Caravaggio 77
Carnivals 48
Cars **316–17**
  driving in Athens **322**
  driving to Greece **316**, 317
  hiring 311, **316**, 317
  motoring maps **317**
  motorway tolls **316**
  petrol **317**
  rules of the road **316**
  vintage car rallies 124
Cash machines 306
Castalian Spring (Delphi)
  234–5

Castles and fortresses
  Arta 217
  Chlemoútsi Castle **173**
  Karýtaina 180
  Kástro (Mystrás) **197**
  Kástro of Platamónas 217
  Kelefá Castle 202–3
  Koróni 151
  Methóni 204
  Monemvasiá 192
  Niókastro (Pýlos) 204–5
  Palamídi (Náfplio) **187**
  Pasavá 202
Cathedrals
  Agios Geórgios (Náfplio) 186
  Christós Elkómenos
    (Monemvasiá) 191
  Mitrópoli (Athens) 106, **112**
  see also Churches; Monasteries
Caves
  Cave of the Furies (Athens) 105
  Cave of the Lakes 172
  Koutoúki Cave 154
  Pérama Caves 215
  Peratí 151
  Petrálona Caves (Northern
    Chalkidikí) 253
  Pýrgos Diroú Caves 203
  Spiliá tou Néstora 205
  Vári 153
Cem, Prince 42–3
Cemeteries
  First Cemetery of Athens **117**
  Kerameikos (Athens) 92–3
  Phaleron War Cemetery (Palaió
    Fáliro) 153
Central and Western Greece
  207–35
  Ancient Delphi **232–5**
  Aroman shepherds **213**
  climate 53
  The flavours of Greece **278–9**
  hotels 271–2
  Ioánnina **214–15**
  map 208–9
  Metéora **220–1**
  Monastery of Osios Loukás
    226–7
  One week in Central and
    Western Greece 10, 13–15
  Pílio **222–4**
  restaurants 288–90
  Víkos Gorge walk **212**

Ceramics
  Kerameikos Museum (Athens)
    93
  Kyriazópoulos Folk Ceramic
    Museum (Athens) 89, **90**
  Vases and vase painting
    64–5
  What to buy in Greece 293
Cervantes, Miguel de 229
Cézanne, Paul 77
Chain hotels **264**, 267
Chaironeia, Battle of (338 BC) 29,
  35
Chalepás, Giannoúlis 117
  Sleeping Beauty 46
Chalkidikí see Northern Chalkidikí
Chateaubriand, François René,
  Vicomte de 113
Chatzidákis, Mános 46
Children **302**
  in restaurants 277
Chíos, massacre at (1822) 44
Chlemoútsi Castle 163, **173**
Chremonidean War (268–261 BC)
  36
Christós Elkómenos
  (Monemvasiá) 191
Christoúgenna 52
Churches
  Byzantine architecture **24–5**
  Thessaloníki **252**
  see also Cathedrals; Monasteries
    and individual towns and cities
Churches in Athens
  Agios Dimítrios **105**
  Agios Geórgios 76
  Agios Nikólaos Ragkavás 107,
    112
  Kapnikaréa 84
  Panagía Gorgoepíkoös (Athens)
    12, 69, 106, **109**
  Pantánassa church 89
  Russian Church of the Holy
    Trinity **115**
Churchill, Winston 46
Cinema
  Athens **123**, 125
  Thessaloniki Film Festival 51
Cistercians 156–7
Civil War (1946–49) 46
Classical Greece **34–5**
Cleopatra, Queen of Egypt 38
Climate **53**, 300

Clothes 301
  in restaurants 277
  shopping in Athens **120**, 121
Clubs
  Athens **124**, 125
Coach travel **318**
Coastguard 305
Coffee-houses **275**
Coins 307
Colossus of Rhodes 37
Communications **308–9**
Communists 46
Constantine, Emperor 38, 39, 41,
  49
Constantine I, King 45
Constantine II, King 46
Constantinople 29, 38, 40, 42
Constitution 44
Convents
  opening hours 301
  Agía Moní (Náfplio) 187
  Timíou Prodrómou 204
  see also Monasteries
Conversion chart 302–3
Cooking lessons **294**, 297
Corfu
  air travel 312
Corinth see Ancient Corinth
Corinth, Gulf of see Gulf of
  Corinth
Corinth Canal 13, 45, **171**
Corinthian architecture 63
Coubertin, Baron Pierre de 177
Crafts
  shopping in Athens **119**, 121
  What to buy in Greece 293
Credit cards 306
  in restaurants 276
Cretan School 42, 83, 220
Crete
  air travel 312
  icons 42
  Minoan culture 30–31
  Mycenaean culture 30–31
Crime 304
Croesus, King of Lydia 232
Cromek, Thomas Hartley 81
Cruises **296**, 297, 319
Crusades **40–41**
Currency **306–7**
The Curse of the House of Atreus
  183
Customs information 300

Cycladic art 30–31
  Museum of Cycladic Art
  (Athens) **78–9**
Cycling **295**, 297
  hiring bicycles **317**
Cyprus 46, 47
Cyrus the Great, King of Persia
  232

D

Dadiá
  hotels 273
Dadiá Forest **261**
Dáfni (Mount Athos) 257
Dance
  Athens **122**, 125
Daphni, Monastery 13, 143, 145,
  156–7
Darius I, King of Persia 33, 149
Darius III, King of Persia 36
Dark Ages **32–3**
De Neuilly clan 202
Debit cards 306
Delacroix, Eugène 77
  Scènes de Massacres de Scio 44
Delfoí
  hotels 271
  restaurants 288
Delian League 34
Deligiánnis, Theódoros 84
Delos 39
Delphi *see* Ancient Delphi
Delphi Museum **235**
Delphic Oracle 207, 225
Demeter 56
  Eleusinian Mysteries 160, 161
Demosthenes 61
  Pnyx Hill (Athens) 105
  birthplace 154
Department stores
  Athens **118**, 121
Despots of Morea 196
Despots' Palace (Mystrás) **197**
Dexileos 93
Dialling codes 308
Diáva
  restaurants 288
Dílofo
  hotels 271
Dimítrios, St 252
Dimitsána 178, **180**
Dimotikí (everyday speech) 21
Diocletian, Emperor 193

Diogenes the Cynic 36, 61
Díon *see* Ancient Dion
Dion Museum 245
Dionysios the Areopagite 105
Dionysios of Kollytos
  tomb of 92
Dionysos 56
  Delphi 235
  The origins of Greek drama
  189
  Vases and vase painting 65
Disabled travellers **302**, 303
  in hotels **267**
  in restaurants 277
Discounts
  student and youth travellers
  302
Diving **296**, 297
  Athens 124
Docheiaríou (Mount Athos) 256
Doctors 304, 305
Dodecanese 46
Dodona *see* Ancient Dodona
Dodwell, Edward 81
Doric architecture 63
Drama **61**
Dráma (Northern Greece) 237
Draper, Herbert
  The Golden Fleece 224
Dress code, in restaurants 277
Drinks *see* Food and drink; Wines
Dupré, Louis 28
Dürer, Albrecht 77

E

Easter **48–9**
Ecclesiastical Art Museum
  (Alexandroúpoli) 261
Economy **21–2**, 47
Edessa 15, **247**
  hotels 273
Egnatía Odós 207
Eisódia tis Theotókou 51
Eláti
  restaurants 288
Electricity 302
Eleftheriádis, Stratís 222
Eleftheríou, Mános 21
Elektra 59, 183
Eleusinian Mysteries **160**
Eleusis *see* Ancient Eleusis
Eleusis Museum (Ancient Eleusis)
  161

Elgin, Lord
  Elgin Marbles 43, 104
  Plateía Lysikrátous (Athens)
  113
Elgin Marbles 43, 47, 102, **104**
Ellinikó 181
Embassies 303
Emergencies 304, 305
Emigration 19
Enoikiazómena domátia
  (rented rooms) 265
Entertainment
  Athens **122–5**
Ephialtes 34
Epidaurus (Epídavros) 13, 143,
  188–9
Epidaurus Festival 50
Epikouros 61
Epirus 207, 214, 217
Erechtheion (Athens) 63, 86,
  96–7, **100–101**
Erechtheus, King 101
Eris 56
Eros 57
Etiquette **301**
Euclid 61
Euripides 34, 61
  Hippolytus 185
  Theatre of Dionysos (Athens)
  101
European Central Bank 47
European Commission 47
European Union 21–2, 29, 46, 47
Euros 307
Eurystheus, King of Tiryns 57
Evangelismós 48
Evans, Arthur 45
Evros Delta 241
Evros Mountain 261
Exárcheia (Athens) **76**
  hotels 268
  restaurants 282
Exekias 56, 65

F

Fanári
  hotels 273
  restaurants 290
Fast food **276**
Ferries **319**
Festivals **48–52**
Fethiye Mosque (Athens)
  Street-by-Street map 89

Figaleía 181
Filikí Etaireía 43, 45
Film *see* Cinema
Filopáppou Hill (Athens) **105**
Filothéi, Agía 112
Finlay, George
 tomb of 117
Fire services 305
First Cemetery of Athens **117**
Flea Market (Athens) 12, **91**
 Street-by-Street map 88
Flora-Karavia 77
Flórina 15
Flowers **27**
Foinikounta
 hotels 270
Folk and Modern Art Museum
 (Kavála) 259
Folk art
 shopping in Athens **119**, 121
Folk Art Museum (Náfplio) **186**
Folk Art Museum (Xánthi) 259
Folk Museum (Andrítsaina) 181
Folklore and Ethnological
 Museum of Macedonia/Thrace
 (Thessaloníki) **249**
Folklore Museum (Ioánnina) **214**
Folklore Museum (Kastoriá) 244
Folklore Museum (Komotiní)
 260
Folklore Museum (Stemnítsa)
 180
Food and drink
 The classic Greek menu **280–81**
 cooking lessons **294**, 297
 Easter 49
 The flavours of Greece **278–9**
 picnics 277
 shopping **120**, 121, **292**
 what to drink 279
 see also Restaurants; Wines
Football
 Athens 124
Franks 40
Frescoes
 Byzantine churches **25**
Freud, Sigmund 59
Frissiras, Vlassis 114
Frissiras Museum (Athens) **114**
 Street-by-Street map 107
Fterólakka 225
Fur trade
 Kastoriá 244

G

Galaxídi 14, 207, 228
 hotels 271
 restaurants 288
Galerius, Emperor 39, 237
 Arch of Galerius (Thessaloníki)
 248
 Rotónda (Thessaloníki) 248
 and St Dimítrios 252
Galleries *see* Museums and
 galleries
Gardens *see* Parks and gardens
Gátsos, Níkos 21
Gemistós, Geórgios (Plethon) 197
Gennádeion (Athens) **77**
Gennádios, Ioánnis 77
Génnisis tis Theotókou 51
George I, King 85
Geráki 163, **193**
Germanós, Archbishop of Pátra
 45, 180
Geroliménas
 hotels 270
Gialova
 restaurants 287
Glyfáda 153
Gods, goddesses and heroes **56–7**
Goethe, Johann Wolfgang von
 197
Golden Fleece 224
The Golden Fleece (Draper) 224
Golf
 Athens 124
Gortys *see* Ancient Gortys
Goths 39
Goulandris, Nikolaos and Dolly 78
Goulandris Natural History
 Museum (Kifisiá) 155
Government **22–3**
"Great Idea" 29, 44, 45
Great Lavra (Mount Athos) 40–41,
 258
El Greco 77
Greco-Turkish War (1919–22) 29
Greek Orthodox Church 20, 301
 Easter **48–9**
 Icons in the Orthodox Church
 80
 Mount Athos **256–8**
 Orthodox life on Mount Athos
 258
 see also Churches; Convents;
 Monasteries

Greek War of Independence
 (1821–32) 28, 29, **44–5**
 Mesolóngi 229
 The siege of Monemvasiá **192**
Green travel **310**
Gregory V, Patriarch of
 Constantinople
 Dimitsána 180
 tomb of 112
 University of Athens 85
Grigorákis, Tzanetbey 202
Grigorákis clan 198
Grigoríou (Mount Athos) 257
Gulf of Corinth 14, 207, **228–9**
Gýtheio **202**
 hotels 270
 restaurants 287
Gýzis, Nikólaos 77, 81
Gymnasium (Delphi) **235**
Gynaikokratía 52

H

Hades 56
 Eleusinian Mysteries 160, 161
 Nekromanteion of Acheron
 216
Hadjikyriakos-Ghikas, Nikólaos 77,
 81
Hadjikyriakos-Ghikas Gallery
 (Athens) **81**
Hadrian, Emperor 38, 167
 Ancient Olympia 174
 statue of 95
 Temple of Olympian Zeus
 (Athens) 115
Hadrian's Library (Athens)
 Street-by-Street map 88
Halikarnassos, Mausoleum of 36
Hansen, Christian 85
 Municipal Art Gallery (Athens)
 92
 University of Athens 85
Hansen, Theophil 85
 Athens Academy 85
 Hill of the Nymphs (Athens) 105
 Mitrópoli (Athens) 112
 National Library (Athens) 85
 Záppeion (Athens) 116
Harpokrates 251
Haseki, Hadji Ali 115
Hatzimihail, Theophilos **222**
 Folk Art Museum (Náfplio)
 186

Hazards 305
Health **304–5**
Health insurance 304, 305
Heat stroke 305
Hector 58
Hegeso 75, 92
Helen, St 41, 49
Helen of Troy 93, 183
  Marathonísi 202
  Trojan War 31, 56, 58
Helios 57
Hellenic Maritime Museum (Piraeus) **159**
Hellenistic Greece **36–7**
  Macedonia 237
Hephaistos 88
Hera 56, 57, 187
Heraion of Perachóra **171**
Herakles 56
  The Labours of Herakles **57**
Hermes 57, 58, 224
Hermes (Praxiteles) 176
Herodotus 34, 60, 228
Heruli tribe 99, 100
Hesiod 60
Hill of the Nymphs (Athens) **105**
Hippodameia 176
Hipponax 60
Hiring
  cars **316**, 317
  motorbikes, scooters and bicycles **317**
Historical and Ethnological Society of Greece 84
History **29–47**
Hitchhiking 302, **317**
Hockney, David 114
Holidays, public 52
Home life **23**
Homer 184
  Ancient Tiryns 185
  Gýtheio 202
  Iliad 33, 58, 60
  Odyssey 33, 59, 60
  Spiliá tou Néstora 205
Homeric kingdoms 32
Horse riding **295**, 297
Hospitals 304
Hostels **266**, 267
Hot springs **296**, 297

Hotels **264–73**
  Athens 268–70
  booking 265
  Central and Western Greece 271–2
  chain hotels **264**, 267
  grading 265
  luxury resorts 264
  Northern Greece 272–3
  opening seasons 265
  The Peloponnese 270–71
  prices 265
  restaurants in 274
  restored settlements and boutique inns 264
  tipping in 301
House of Atreus **183**
House of Masks (Delos) 39
Hydra 181

I

Icons
  Icon painters in Pláka **113**
  Icons in the Orthodox Church **80**
  Virgin Mary **25**
  What to buy in Greece 293
Ida, Mount 56
Ifaístou (Athens) 88
Iktinos 102, 160
Iliad (Homer) 33, 58, 60
Ilías Lalaoúnis Jewellery Museum (Athens) **108**
Ilisia (Athens)
  hotels 268
  restaurants 282
Ilissós, River 155
Independence Day 48
Inner Máni 13, **202–3**
  map 202
Inoculations 305
Insurance 304, 305
International Monetary Fund 47
Internet **308**
Ioánnina 14, 207, **214–15**
  hotels 271
  restaurants 288
Iokaste 225
Ionian Islands 43
Ionic architecture 63
Iphigeneia 58, 59, 150
Ipsus, Battle of (301 BC) 36
Irene, Empress 40, 84

Isaias, Bishop 226
Isis 245
Islam *see* Muslims
Issus 36
Isthmia *see* Ancient Isthmia
Itéa 228
Ithómi *see* Ancient Messene
Ivíron (Mount Athos) 258

J

Jason 215, **224**
Jazz
  Athens **123–4**, 125
Jellyfish stings 305
Jewellery
  Ilías Lalaoúnis Jewellery Museum (Athens) **108**
  shopping in Athens **119**, 121
  What to buy in Greece 293
Jewish Museum of Greece (Athens) **114**
John, Don of Austria 42
Jung, Carl 59
Junta 47
Justinian, Emperor 215

K

Kafeneía (coffee-houses) **275**
Kalamáta
  hotels 270
  restaurants 287
Kalamítsi 253
Kalampáka
  hotels 271
  restaurants 289
Kalávryta
  hotels 270
Kalávryta-Diakoftó Railway **172**
Kallikrates 100, 102
Kallimármaro Stadium (Athens) **117**
Kallithéa 253
Kalógria **173**
  hotels 270
Kanellópoulos Museum (Athens) **108**
  Street-by-Street map 106
Kantakouzenos, Alexandros 192
Kantakoúzenos dynasty 197
Kapnikaréa (Athens) **84**
Kapodístrias, Ioánnis 44
  assassination 44, 186
Karamanlís, Konstantínos 23, 47

Káranos waterfall (Edessa) 247
Kardamýli **199**
Karpenísi
  hotels 272
  restaurants 289
Kartsonákis, Nikólaos 92
Karýtaina **180**
Kassándra **253**
  festivals 50
Kassandros, King 248
Kassope 14, **216**
Kastamonítou (Mount Athos)
  257
Kastaniá
  hotels 270
Kastélla (Piraeus) 158
Kastoriá 15, **244**
  hotels 273
  restaurants 290
Kastráki
  restaurants 289
Kástro (Mystrás) **197**
Kástro of Platamónas 217
Katelános, Frágkos 221
Katharí Deftéra 48
Katigiórgis
  restaurants 289
Kavála 15, 239, 254–5, **259**
  hotels 273
  restaurants 291
Kazantzákis, Nikos 199
Kelária 225
Kelefá Castle 202–3
Kentrikó Limáni (Piraeus) 158
Kerameikos (Athens) 64, 68,
  92–3
  restaurants 282
Kerameikos Museum (Athens)
  93
Kerkíni
  hotels 273
Kerkíni, Lake 15
Kéros-Sýros culture 30
Kessariani
  restaurants 286
Kifisiá **155**
  hotels 270
  restaurants 286
Kípoi 211
  restaurants 289
Kissós
  restaurants 289
Kitaj, RB 114

Kitchenware
  shopping in Athens **120**,
    121
Kládeos River 174
Kleánthis, Stamátis 80
Klymene 56, 187
Klytemnestra 59, 183, 184
Knights of St John 42–3
Knosós 45
Koímisis tis Theotókou 51
Kókkoras Bridge 178
Kolokotrónis, General Theódoros
  Karýtaina 180
  National Historical Museum
    (Athens) 84
  statue of 84
  tomb of 117
  War Museum (Athens) 77
Kolonáki (Athens)
  hotels 268
  restaurants 282–3
Komotiní **260**
  restaurants 291
Kónitsa
  hotels 272
  restaurants 289
Konstantinidis, Aris 81
Konstantínos Monomáchos,
  Emperor 237
Konstantínos Palaiológos,
  Emperor 173, 196
Kóntoglou, Phótis 77, 84,
  154
Koroibos of Melite 92
Koroivos 177
Koróneia, Lake 240
Koróni 151, 163, **204**
  restaurants 287
Koronisiá
  restaurants 289
Kos
  air travel 312
Kosmas
  restaurants 287
Koukáki (Athens)
  hotels 268
  restaurants 283
Koutoúki Cave 154
Kyriazópoulos Folk Ceramic
  Museum (Athens) **90**
  Street-by-Street map 89
Kyriazópoulos, Vasíleios 90
Kyrrestes, Andrónikos 89, 90

L
Labour Day 49
The Labours of Herakles **57**
Lagoníssi
  hotels 270
Laios, King 225
Lalaoúnis, Ilías 108
Lamía 13, 207, **228**
  restaurants 289
Lamía Museum 228
Lamian War (323–322 BC) 228
Landscape **26–7**
Language **20–21**
  phrase book 344–8
Lausanne, Treaty of (1923) 45
Lávrio 13, 145, **152**
Lavrion Technological and
  Cultural Park 152
Lazarímos, Ioánnis 158
League of Corinth 35
Lear, Edward 77, 81
Lefkádia 15, **246–7**
Leighton, Lord 59
Leo III, Pope 40
Leo IX, Pope 41
Leonidas I, King of Sparta 193,
  228
Lepanto, Battle of (1571) 42, 229
Lérna 181
Leuktra, Battle of (371 BC) 35, 235
Libraries
  Gennádeion (Athens) **77**
  Hadrian's Library (Athens) 88
  National Library (Athens) 85
Lighthouses
  Alexandroúpoli 261
Limnos
  air travel 312
Linear B script 31, 182, 205
Literature **60–61**
Litóchoro 15, 245
  hotels 273
  restaurants 291
Loúis, Spyrídon 45
Loúsios Gorge 13, 163, 164,
  178–80
  restaurants 287
Loutrá Ellénis
  restaurants 287
Ludwig I, King of Bavaria 84
Luke, Blessed 226, **227**
Luxury resorts 264
Lýtras, Nikifóros 77

Lýtras, Nikólaos 77
Lygourió 189
Lykavittós Hill (Athens) **76**
Lykavittós Theatre (Athens) 76
Lykodímou family 115
Lykostómio 217
Lykourgos 33
  Panathenaic Stadium (Athens)
  117
  Theatre of Dionysos (Athens)
  98, 99, 101
Lysanías 93
Lysias 61
Lysikrates 113

M

Macedonia 237
Macedonian Royal Family **246**
Macedonian Tombs (Vergína) 246
Magazines **309**
  shopping in Athens **120**, 121
Mahmud II, Sultan 214
Makedonia-Thessaloníki Airport
  312, 313
Makrigiánnis, General 84
Makrygiánni (Athens)
  hotels 268
  restaurants 283
Makrynítsa 222, 224
  hotels 272
Máni peninsula 142, 163
  see also Inner Máni; Outer Máni
Mániot Feuds **198**
Manousakis, Yorgos 81
Maps
  Ancient Corinth 166–7
  Ancient Delphi 232–3
  Around Athens 146–7
  Athens 68–9
  Athens: Acropolis 98
  Athens: Central Athens North
  71
  Athens: Central Athens South
  87
  Athens: Monastiráki 88–9
  Athens: Pláka 106–7
  Athens: Street finder 126–39
  Athens transport links 323
  Byzantine architecture 24
  Byzantine Greece 40
  Central and Western Greece
  208–9
  Classical Greece 34

Maps (cont.)
  The climate of Mainland Greece
  53
  Dark Ages and Archaic Period
  32
  Europe and North Africa 17
  flight connections within
  Greece 312
  getting around Athens 320
  Greece 10–11, 16–17
  Hellenistic Greece 36–7
  Inner Máni 202
  Loúsios Gorge 178–9
  Mainland Greece 142–3
  Metéora 220
  Modern Greece 44
  motoring maps 317
  Mount Athos 256
  Mystrás 196
  Náfplio 187
  Northern Greece 238–9
  Outer Máni 198
  The Peloponnese 164–5
  Pílio 222–3
  Piraeus 159, 319
  Prehistoric Greece 30
  rail network 315
  Roman Greece 38
  Thessaloníki 249
  Venetian and Ottoman Greece
  42
  Víkos Gorge walk 212
  Zagorian villages 211
Maquis 26–7
Marathon, Athens 124
Marathon, Battle of (490 BC) 33,
  145, **149**
Marathon Museum 149
Marathónas **149**
Marathónas, Lake 149
Marcellinus, Flavius Septimius
  100
Markets **292**
  Athens **118**, 121
  Flea Market (Athens) 12, 88, **91**
Markópoulo 151
Marmaria Precinct (Delphi) **234**
Maroneia **260–61**
  hotels 273
Mary, Virgin **25**, 237
Máti 149
Mausoleum of Halikarnassos 36
Mavrokordátos, Aléxandros 229

Mavromichális, Pétros 198, 202
Mavromichális clan 198, 199,
  202
Medea 224
Media **308–9**
Megáli Evdomáda 49
Megálo Metéoro 218–19, 220
Megálo Pápigko 207, 211
  hotels 272
  Víkos Gorge walk 212
Megístis Lávras (Mount Athos)
  258
Mehmet II, Sultan 42
  Fethiye Mosque (Athens) 89
  Moní Kaisarianís 154
Mehmet Ali, Pasha of Egypt 259
Melás, Pávlos 249
Meletzis, Spyros 81
Menelaos, King of Sparta 56, 58
Menus **280–81**
Merkoúri, Melína 47
  Elgin Marbles 104
  tomb of 117
Mesógeia 145
Mesolóngi 14, 44, 207, **229**
  restaurants 289
Messene *see* Ancient Messene
Messinía
  hotels 270
Metamórfosi 51, 241, 253
Metaxás, Anastásios 117
Metaxás, Yanni 29, 46
Metaxourgeio (Athens)
  restaurants 283
Metéora 14, 142, 207, **220–21**
  map 220
Methóni 163, **204**
  hotels 270
  restaurants 287
Metro (Athens) 311, **321**
Métsovo 14, **213**
  hotels 272
Métsovo Folk Art Museum 213
Mezédes **281**
Mezedopoleío **275**
Michael II of Epirus 217
Mikrí Préspa lake 238, 240
Mikró Pápigko 211
  restaurants 289
Mikrolímano (Piraeus) 12, 158
Mikrolímni 241
Miliés 13, 223, 224
  restaurants 289

Milina (Pílio)
    restaurants 289
Miller, Stephen 171
Miltiades 149, 176
Minoan culture 29, 30–31
Minotaur 100
Miss T K (Mitarákis) 92
Mitarákis, Giánnis
    Miss T K 92
Mithridates 38
Mitrópoli (Athens) **112**
    Street-by-Street map 106
Mitrópoli (Mystrás) **196**
Mnesikles 100
Mobile phones **308**, 309
Modern Greece **44–7**
Modiáno (Thessaloníki) 248
Modigliani, Amedeo 78
Monasteries (general)
    opening hours 301
    accommodation in **266**
Monasteries (individual)
    Agías Lávras 172
    Agios Nikólaos Anapavsás 221
    Agíou Dionysíou (Mount Athos)
        257
    Agíou Georgíou Feneoú 172
    Agíou Ioánnou Prodrómou 179
    Agíou Nikoláou 208
    Agíou Panteleímonos (Mount
        Athos) 256
    Agíou Pávlou (Mount Athos)
        257
    Aimyalón 179
    Daphni 13, 143, 145, **156–7**
    Dekoúlou (Outer Máni) 198
    Docheiaríou (Mount Athos) 256
    Great Lavra (Mount Athos)
        40–41, 258
    Grigoríou (Mount Athos) 257
    Ivíron (Mount Athos) 258
    Kaisarianís 13, 145, 147, **154–5**
    Kastamonítou (Mount Athos)
        257
    Méga Spílaio 172
    Megálo Metéoro 218–19, 220
    Megístis Lávras (Mount Athos)
        258
    Metéora 207, **220–21**
    Mount Athos **256–8**
    Néa Moní Filosófou 178
    Osios Loukás 14, 143, 207,
        226–7

Monasteries (individual) (cont.)
    Perivléptou (Mystrás) **196–7**
    Rousánou 220
    Símonos Pétras (Mount Athos)
        242–3, 257
    Stavronikíta (Mount Athos) 258
    Vatopedíou (Mount Athos) 258
    Xenofóntos (Mount Athos) 257
    Xiropotámou (Mount Athos)
        257
    Zográfou (Mount Athos) 257
    Zoödóchou Pigís (Stemnítsa)
        180
    see also Convents
Monastiráki (Athens) 12
    hotels 268
    restaurants 283
    Street-by-Street map 88–9
Monemvasiá 13, 18, 143, 163,
    190–92
    history 42
    hotels 271
    restaurants 287
    The siege of Monemvasiá **192**
Money **306–7**
Moní Agías Lávras 172
Moní Agíou Ioánnou Prodrómou
    179
Moní Agíou Nikólaou (Métsovo)
    213
Moní Aimyalón 179
Moní Dekoúlou (Outer Máni) 198
Moní Kaisarianís 13, 145, 147,
    154–5
Moní Méga Spílaio 172
Moní Pantánassas (Mystrás)
    194–5, **197**
Moní Perivléptou (Mystrás) **196–7**
Moní Vatopedíou (Mount Athos)
    258
Moní Zalóngou 216
Moní Zoödóchou Pigís
    (Stemnítsa) 180
Monodéndri 211
    Víkos Gorge walk 212
Moore, Henry 72, 78
Moralis, Yiannis 77, 81
Moreas, Jean 116
Morosini, General Francesco 102,
    105
Mosaics
    Agios Dimítrios (Thessaloníki)
        252

Mosaics (cont.)
    Ancient Pella 247
    Monastery of Daphni 156–7
    Monastery of Osios Loukás
        226–7
    Osios David (Thessaloníki) 252
    Thessaloníki Archaeological
        Museum 250
Mosques
    Fethiye Mosque (Athens) 89
Motorbikes
    hiring **317**
Motorways 316
Mount Athos 15, 143, 236, 237,
    256–8
    Great Lavra 40–41, 258
    map 256
    Orthodox life on Mount Athos
        258
    visiting Mount Athos 256
Mount Chelmós **172**
Mount Katsíka 253
Mount Olympos 15, 174, 237,
    245
    The Home of Zeus **245**
Mount Parnassós 13, **225**
Mount Párnitha 145, **155**
Mount Pentéli 145
Mount Pilion 207
Mount Taÿgetos **199**
Mount Ymittós 145
Moúresi
    hotels 272
Mpraésas, Dímos 92
Municipal Art Gallery (Athens) **92**
Municipal Art Gallery (Piraeus)
    159
Municipal Ethnographic Museum
    (Ioánnina) **214**
Municipal Theatre (Piraeus) **158–9**
Museum copies
    shopping in Athens **119**, 121
Museums and galleries (general)
    admission prices 301
    opening hours 301
Museums and galleries
    (individual)
    Acropolis Museum (Athens) 12,
        104
    Ancient Nemea 171
    Ancient Tegea 181
    Archaeological Museum (Argos)
        181

Museums and galleries
(individual) (cont.)
Archaeological Museum
(Ioánnina) **214**
Archaeological Museum
(Kavála) 259
Archaeological Museum
(Komotiní) 260
Archaeological Museum
(Náfplio) **186**
Archaeological Museum (Spárti)
193
Archaeological Museum (Thíva)
225
Archaeological Museum (Vólos)
13, 224
Avéroff Museum (Métsovo)
213
Benáki Museum (Athens) 12, 69,
82–3
Botanical Museum (Athens) 116
Brauron Museum (Ancient
Brauron) **151**
Byzantine and Christian
Museum (Athens) **80**
Byzantine Museum (Ioánnina)
214
Byzantine Museum (Kastoriá)
244
Byzantine Museum (Véroia) 246
Chatzikyriakos-Ghikas Gallery
(Athens) **81**
Delphi Museum **235**
Dion Museum 245
Ecclesiastical Art Museum
(Alexandroúpoli) 261
Eleusis Museum (Ancient
Eleusis) **161**
Folk and Modern Art Museum
(Kavála) 259
Folk Art Museum (Náfplio) **186**
Folk Art Museum (Xánthi) 259
Folk Museum (Andrítsaina) 181
Folklore and Ethnological
Museum of Macedonia/Thrace
(Thessaloníki) **249**
Folklore Museum (Ioánnina) **214**
Folklore Museum (Kastoriá) 244
Folklore Museum (Komotiní) 260
Folklore Museum (Stemnítsa)
180
Frissiras Museum (Athens) 107,
114

Museums and galleries
(individual) (cont.)
Goulandris Natural History
Museum (Kifisiá) 155
Hellenic Maritime Museum
(Piraeus) **159**
Ilías Lalaoúnis Jewellery
Museum (Athens) **108**
Jewish Museum of Greece
(Athens) **114**
Kanellópoulos Museum
(Athens) 106, **108**
Kerameikos Museum (Athens)
93
Kyriazópoulos Folk Ceramic
Museum (Athens) 89, **90**
Lamía Museum 228
Marathon Museum 149
Métsovo Folk Art Museum
213
Municipal Art Gallery (Athens)
92
Municipal Art Gallery (Piraeus)
159
Municipal Ethnographic
Museum (Ioánnina) **214**
Museum (Acrocorinth) **170**
Museum of Byzantine Culture
(Thessaloníki) **248**
Museum of the City of Athens
81
Museum of Cycladic Art
(Athens) 12, 69, **78–9**
Museum of Greek Folk Art
(Athens) **114**
Museum of Greek Popular
Musical Instruments (Athens)
106, **108**
Museum of the Macedonian
Struggle (Thessaloníki) **249**
Museum of the Maní (Inner
Maní) 202
National Archaeological
Museum (Athens) 12, 69, **72–5**
National Gallery of Art (Athens)
77
National Historical Museum
(Athens) **84**
Nautical and Historical Museum
(Galaxídi) 228
Olympia Archaeological
Museum (Ancient Olympia)
175

Museums and galleries
(individual) (cont.)
Pános Aravantinós Museum of
Stage Decor (Piraeus) 159
Spatháreio Museum of the
Shadow Theatre (Kifisiá) 155
Stoa of Attalos (Athens) 94, **95**
Theóphilos Museum (Anakasiá)
224
Thessaloníki Archaeological
Museum 15, **250–51**
Tobacco Museum (Kavála) 259
University of Athens Museum
106, **108**
Vorrés Museum (Paianía) 154
War Museum (Athens) **77**
Water Power Museum
(Dimitsána) 180
Music
Athens **123–4**, 125
Museum of Greek Popular
Musical Instruments (Athens)
106, **108**
Muslims 301
Northern Greece 237
Mycenae 13, 29, 30–31, 44, 143,
163, **182–4**
National Archaeological
Museum (Athens) 74
Tombs **184**
Trojan War 58
Mygdalinós, Dimítrios 90
Mykonos
air travel 312
Mystrás 13, 142, 163, **196–7**
history 40, 41, 42
map 196
restaurants 287
wildlife 26
Myths
Gods, goddesses and heroes **56–7**
The Trojan War **58–9**

N

Náfpaktos 14, 207, 228–9
hotels 272
restaurants 289
Náfpaktos, Peace of (217 BC) 37
Nafpliios 187
Náfplio 13, 21, 22, 162, 163, **186–7**
hotels 271
map 187
restaurants 288

Name days 52
Náousa 237, 247
Napoleon I, Emperor 198
National Archaeological Museum
(Athens) 12, 69, **72–5**
National Gallery of Art (Athens) **77**
National Gardens (Athens) 12, **116**
National Historical Museum
(Athens) **84**
National Library (Athens) 85
National parks
Kalógria **173**
Olympos 245
Píndos 210
Préspa Lakes **240–41**
Vikos-Aóös 210
National Theatre (Athens) 85
NATO 46
Nature tours **295**, 297
Nautical and Historical Museum
(Galaxídi) 228
Navaríno, Battle of (1827) 44, 205
Néa Fókaia 253
Néa Moní Filosófou 178
Néa Poteídaia (Kassándra) 253
Néa Skíti (Mount Athos) 257
Neílos, Prior of Stagai 220
Nekromanteíon of Acheron 216
Nelly's 81
Nemea see Ancient Nemea
Nemesis 148–9
Neo-Classical architecture
Athens **85**
Néo Mikro Horió
restaurants 290
Néo Oítylo 198
Neolithic 30
Néos Marmarás
hotels 273
Néos Mystrás
hotels 271
Nerantzopoúlou Mansion
(Siátista) 244
Nero, Emperor 38, 101
Corinth Canal 171
Olympic Games 177
Nestor, King 205
Nestor's Palace **205**
Néstos Delta 241
Néstos Valley 15, **259**
New Democracy 47
Newspapers **309**
shopping in Athens **120**, 121

Nikopolis 217
Niókastro (Pýlos) 204–5
Nisí **215**
Nivelet, Jean de 193
Normans 41
Northern Chalkidikí 237, **253**
Northern Greece **237–61**
climate 53
The flavours of Greece **278–9**
hotels 272–3
map 238–9
Mount Athos **256–8**
One week in Northern Greece
11, 15
restaurants 290–91
Thessaloníki **248–52**
Wetland wildlife **240–41**
Notitia Dignitatum 38
Nyklians 198
Nymféo
hotels 273

O

Oberlander, Gustav 93
Ochi Day 51
Octavian (Augustus), Emperor
167, 217
Odeion (Ancient Corinth) 167
Odysseus 205
Odyssey (Homer) 33, 59, 60
Oedipus **225**
Oinomageireío (restaurants) 274
Oinomaos, King 176
Oítylo **198**
Olga, Queen 186
Olympia
hotels 271
see also Ancient Olympia
Olympia Archaeological Museum
(Ancient Olympia) **175**
Olympic Games 33
1896 Games 117
history 39, 45
The origins of the Olympic
Games **177**
Olympos, Mount see Mount
Olympos
Olympos National Park 245
Olynthos see Ancient Olynthos
Omónoia (Athens)
hotels 268
restaurants 283
Onassis, Aristotle 46, 47

Opening hours 301
shops 118, 292
Opera
Athens **123**
Oracle of Delphi **232**
Oratory **61**
Orchomenos 225
Orestes 59, 150, 183
Orlandos, Athanasios 81
Ortelius, Abraham 29
Orthodox Church see Greek
Orthodox Church; Russian
Orthodox Church
Osios David (Thessaloníki) **252**
Osios Loukás, Monastery of 14,
143, 207, **226–7**
Otto, King
Athenian Neo-Classical
architecture 85
Mitrópoli (Athens) 112
Museum of the City of Athens
81
National Historical Museum
(Athens) 84
Royal Palace (Athens) 44
University of Athens 85
Otto de la Roche, Duke of Athens
156
Ottoman Greece 19, 29, 40,
42–3
Ouranoúpoli 257
Outdoor activities **294–7**
Outer Máni 13, **198–9**
Mániot Feuds **198**
map 198
Ouzerí **275**
Oxiá Viewpoint
Víkos Gorge walk 212

P

Pachómios, Abbot 197
Paianía **154**
Palace of Knosós (Crete) 31
Palace of Palatítsa (Vergína) 246
Palaiá Epídavros
restaurants 288
Palaió Fáliro 153
Palaiológos dynasty 197, 199
Palamedes 187
Palamídi (Náfplio) **187**
Palonios 176
Panagía Chapel
Víkos Gorge walk 212

Panagía Eleoúsa 241
Panagía Gorgoepíkoös (Athens)
  12, 69, **109**
  Street-by-Street map 106
Panagía i Spiliótissa (Athens) 98,
  101
Panagía Myrtidiótissa
  (Monemvasiá) 190
Pangráti (Athens)
  restaurants 284
Panhellenic Socialist Movement
  (PASOK) 20, 23, 47
Pános Aravantinós Museum of
  Stage Decor (Piraeus) 159
Pantánassa church (Athens)
  Street-by-Street map 89
Papandréou, Andréas 22–3, 47
Papandréou, George the Younger
  47
Papandréou, Geórgios 22, 46
Paralía (Thessaloníki) **248**
Párga 14, 209, **216**
  hotels 272
  restaurants 290
Paris 56, 183
  Marathonísi 202
  Trojan War 56, 58, 59
Parks and gardens
  Chília Déndra (Náousa) 247
  National Gardens (Athens) 12,
  116
Parliament (Athens) 44
Parnassós, Mount *see* Mount
  Parnassós
Páros
  air travel 312
Parthénis, Konstantínos 92
Parthenon (Athens) 12, 34, 99,
  102–3
  Acropolis Museum (Athens) 12,
  104
  Elgin Marbles 43
  history 43
  The illusion of perfection
  103
PASOK (Panhellenic Socialist
  Movement) 20, 23, 47
Pass of Thermopylae 13, **228**
Passports **300**, 303
Pátra **173**
  hotels 271
  restaurants 288
Patroklos 58

Paul, St 38
  Corinth 166, 168
  Kavála 259
  sermon on Areopagos Hill
  (Athens) 99, 105
Pausanias 39, 60, 188
  Guide to Greece 117
Pédion Áreos (Athens)
  hotels 268
  restaurants 284
Peirithous, King 176
Peisistratos 33
  Ancient Brauron 150
  Temple of Olympian Zeus
  (Athens) 115
Pélla region 247
  see also Ancient Pella
Pelopia 183
The Peloponnese 47, **163–205**
  Ancient Corinth **166–70**
  Ancient Olympia **174–6**
  climate 53
  Epidaurus (Epídavros) **188–9**
  Five days in Attica and the
  Peloponnese 11, 12–13
  The flavours of Greece **278**
  history 43
  hotels 270–71
  Inner Máni **202–3**
  Loúsios Gorge 178–80
  map 164–5
  Monemvasiá **190–92**
  Mycenae **182–4**
  Mystrás **196–7**
  Náfplio **186–7**
  Outer Máni **198–9**
  restaurants 287–8
Peloponnesian War (431–404 BC)
  34, 60
Pelops 176
Penthesileia 59
Pentikostí 50
Pérama Caves 215
Peratí 151
Perdikkas I, King of Macedon 246
Perikles 34
  Acropolis (Athens) 98, 99
  Lávrio 152
  Pnyx Hill (Athens) 105
  Tomb of the Unknown Soldier
  (Athens) 116
Persephone 56
  Eleusinian Mysteries 160, 161

Persian Empire 36–7
Personal security **304–5**
Petrálona (Athens)
  restaurants 284
Petrálona Caves (Northern
  Chalkidikí) 253
Petrol **317**
Phaleron War Cemetery (Palaió
  Fáliro) 153
Pharmacies 304–5
Pheidias 74, 149
  Ancient Olympia 174
  Athena Lemnia 35
  Olympia Archaeological
  Museum (Ancient Olympia)
  176
  Parthenon (Athens) 62, 102
  Temple of Olympian Zeus
  (Athens) 115
Pheidippides 149
Philip II, King of Macedon 36, 61,
  246
  Ancient Olympia 175
  Ancient Pella 46
  assassination 35, 246
  Battle of Chaironeia 29, 34, 35
  Dion 245
  League of Corinth 35
  Thebes 225
  tomb 35, 237, 246
  Tower of the Winds (Athens) 90
Philip V, King of Macedon 37
Phillips, Thomas
  Lord Byron 153
Philopappus, Caius Julius
  Antiochus 105
Philosophers **61**
Phones **308**, 309
Phrase book 344–8
Phrygana 26–7
Picasso, Pablo 77, 78
Picnics 277
Pikionis, Dimitris 81
Pílio 13, **222–4**
  map 222–3
Píndos Mountains 20, 207, **210**
  Wildlife **210**
Píndos National Park 210
Piraeus 12, 145, 146, **158–9**
  hotels 270
  map 159, 319
  restaurants 286
Plaisance, Duchesse de 80

Pláka (Athens) 12
  hotels 268–9
  Icon painters in Pláka **113**
  restaurants 284
  Street-by-Street map 106–7
Plataiai, Battle of (479 BC) 33, 228
Plataniás 223
Plateía Kolonakíou (Athens) **81**
Plateía Lysikrátous (Athens) **113**
  Street-by-Street map 107
Plateía Syntágmatos (Athens) 12,
  116
Plato 34
  Athens Academy 35, 40, 61, 85
  Kritías 76
  statue of 35
Plethon (Geórgios Gemistós) 197
Pnyx Hill (Athens) **105**
Poetry **60**
Poisonous creatures 305
Police 304, 305
Poliorketes, Demetrios 105
Polýchoroi
  Athens **124**, 125
Polykleitos the Younger 188, 189
Polyzalos 235
Poros, King 37
Portariá
  hotels 272
  restaurants 290
Pórto Karras 253
Pórto Koufó 253
Pórto Lágos 241
Pórto Ráfti 13, **151**
  restaurants 286
Poseidon 56, 98
  Erechtheion (Athens) 100–101
Possídi 253
Postal services **308–9**
Pottery *see* Ceramics
Praxiteles 74
  Hermes 176
Prehistoric Greece **30–31**
Presidential Palace (Athens) **116**
Préspa Information Centre 241
Préspa Lakes 15, 237, **240–41**
  hotels 273
Préveza 14, **216–17**
  restaurants 290
Priam, King of Troy 58, 59
Profitis Ilías 50
Propylaia (Athens) 12, 98, **100**
Protomagiá 49

Prusias, King of Bithynia 233
Psarádes 23, 241
  restaurants 291
Psyrrí (Athens)
  hotels 269
  restaurants 284–5
Puaux, René 204
Public holidays 52
Puppets
  Spatháreio Museum of the
    Shadow Theatre (Kifisiá) 155
Pýlos 58, **204–5**
  restaurants 288
Pýrgos Diroú Caves 203
Pydna, Battle of (168 BC) 37
Pyrrhos, King of Epirus 36
Pythia 232, 235
Pythian Games 232, 234, 235

Q

Qadiri sect 91

R

Radio **309**
Rafína 13, **149**
  hotels 270
  restaurants 286
Rafting **295**, 297
Railways *see* Trains
Ramnous 145, **148–9**
Raphael
  The School of Athens 61
Refugees 22, 47
Regilla 176
Rego, Paula 114
Religion **20**, **301**
  Easter **48–9**
  festivals **48–52**
  see also Greek Orthodox Church
Rembrandt 77
Responsible tourism 303
Restaurants **274–91**
  Athens 282–6
  breakfast **276**
  Central and Western Greece
    288–90
  children in 277
  The classic Greek menu **280–81**
  dress code 277
  fast food and snacks **276**
  The flavours of Greece **278–9**
  in hotels 274
  how to pay 276

Restaurants (cont.)
  mezedopoleío, ouzerí and
    tsipourádiko **275**
  Northern Greece 290–91
  The Peloponnese 287–8
  reservations 276
  service and tipping 276–7
  smoking in 277, 301
  tavernas **274–5**
  tipping 301
  types of restaurants 274
  vegetarian and vegan food 277
  wheelchair access 277
  wine and beer **276**
  see also Food and drink
Restored settlements,
  accommodation in 264
Retsína **151**
Rhodes
  air travel 312
  Ottoman Greece 42–3
Rio
  restaurants 288
Rítsos, Giánnis 191
Road signs 322
Road travel **316–17**
Rock music
  Athens **123–4**, 125
Rockefeller, John D, Jr 95
Roman Catholic Church 301
Roman Greece 29, 37, **38–9**
  Theatre of Herodes Atticus
    (Athens) 99, **101**
Romanos II, Emperor 226
Rotónda (Thessaloníki) **248**
Rousánou 220
Roxane 37
Royal Tombs (Vergína) 246
Rufa'i sect 91
Running
  Athens 124
Rural tourism **266**
Russian Church of the Holy Trinity
  (Athens) **115**
Russian Orthodox Church 256, 258

S

Safety **304–5**
  hitchhiking 317
  swimming 302, 305
  travel safety advice **300**, 303
  women travellers 302
Sailing holidays **296**, 297

Salamis, Battle of (480 BC) 33
Salonika *see* Thessaloníki
Saltpan birdlife **229**
Samaras, Antonis 47
Sanctuary of Apollo (Delphi) 232, 234
Sáni 253
Sani Festival (Kassándra) 50
Santoríni 31
    air travel 312
Sappho 33, 60
Saracens 40
Sarakatsan shepherds 211
Sarakíniko Bay
    restaurants 290
Sárti 253
Savópoulos family 180
Scènes de Massacres de Scio (Delacroix) 44
Schliemann, Heinrich **184**
    Mycenae 44, 73, 182
    Orchomenos 225
    tomb 117
Schliemann's House (Athens) 85
Schmidt, Friedrich 116
The School of Athens (Raphael) 61
Scooters
    hiring **317**
Scuba diving **296**, 297
    Athens 124
Sculpture
    The development of Greek sculpture **74–5**
    see also Art; Museums and galleries
Sea travel **319**
Sea urchin stings 305
Seféris, Giórgos
    tomb of 117
Seven Wonders of the Ancient World 36
Severus, Alexander 143
Sèvres, Treaty of (1920) 45
Sfaktiría 205
Shadowed Coast **203**
Shepherds, Aroman **213**
Shopping **292–3**
    Athens **118–21**
    food and drink **292**
    markets **292**
    opening hours 292, 301
    VAT and tax-free shopping 292
    What to buy in Greece **293**

Siátista 15, **244**
Signs, road 316, 322
Silenus 99
Simítis, Kóstas 47
Simon, St 257
Simonides 149
Símonos Pétras (Mount Athos) 242–3, 257
Sínas, Georgios 105
Sithonia 15, **253**
Skiáthos
    air travel 312
Skiing **295**, 297
Skopje 23
Skýros 312
Slavs 40
Sleeping Beauty (Chalepás) 46
Smoking 301
    in restaurants 277, 301
Smyrna 44, 45
Snacks **276**
Snorkelling **296**, 297
Sóchos, Lázaros 84
Social customs **301**
Socrates 34
    Ancient Agora (Athens) 94
    Athens Academy 61, 85
    death 35
    Tower of the Winds (Athens) 90
Solomós, Dionýsios 116
Solon 32
Sophokles 34, 61
    Theatre of Dionysos (Athens) 101
Sotiríou, Geórgios 80
Sounion (Soúnio) 12–13, 145, 147, **152–3**
    restaurants 286
Sparta 33, 34, 35, 37, 163
    life in Ancient Sparta **193**
Spárti **193**
    restaurants 288
Spas **296**, 297
Spatháreio Museum of the Shadow Theatre (Kifisiá) 155
Special needs travellers *see* Disabled travellers
Specialist holidays **294–7**
Speed limits 316
Spiliá tou Néstora 205
Spirits 275, 279
Sports **294–7**
    Athens **124**, 125
    see also Olympic Games

Spring of Daphne 217
Spring in Greece 48–9
Stadium (Delphi) **234**
Stágeira 253
Staïkópoulos, Stáïkos 187
Stathátos, Otto and Athína 79
Stavronikíta (Mount Athos) 258
Stavroulákis, Nikólaos 114
Stavroúpoli 15, 259
Stefanópoulos clan 198
Stemnítsa 163, 178, **180**
    hotels 271
Stereá Elláda 207
Stoa of Attalos (Athens) 68, 94, **95**
Stoúpa 199
Stréfi Hill (Athens) **76**
Student travellers **302**, 303
Stymfalía, Lake 27
Sulla 38, 158
Summer in Greece 50–51
Sun protection 305
Supermarkets
    Athens **118**, 121
Susa 37
Sweet shops **275**
Swimming
    safety 302, 305
Symvolí
    hotels 273
Sýntagma (Athens)
    hotels 269
    restaurants 285
Sýnaxis tis Theotókou 52
SYRIZA 23, 47

T

Tantalos 163
Tavernas **274–5**
Taxes
    airport and departure taxes 313
    tax-free shopping 292
Taxis 311, **317**
    in Athens **322**
    tipping 301
Tegea *see* Ancient Tegea
Telemachos 205
Telephones **308**, 309
Television **309**
Temples
    architecture **62–3**
    Temple of Apollo (Ancient Corinth) 62, 166, 168–9
    Temple of Apollo (Bassae) 62

Temples (cont.)
  Temple of Apollo (Delphi) 62,
    209, 233
  Temple of Apollo Epikourios
    Bassae (Andrítsaina) 181
  Temple of Artemis (Ancient
    Brauron) 62
  Temple of Athena Aléa (Tegea) 62
  Temple of Athena Nike (Athens)
    12, 98, **100**
  Temple of Hera (Ancient
    Olympia) 33, 62, 175
  Temple of Octavia (Ancient
    Corinth) 167
  Temple of Olympian Zeus
    (Athens) 12, 62, **115**
  Temple of Poseidon (Ancient
    Isthmia) 62, 171
  Temple of Poseidon (Sounion)
    13, 62, 145, 147, 152–3
  Temple of Zeus (Olympia) 62
Tennis
  Athens 124
Thássos 11
Theatre
  Ancient Dodona 215
  Athens **122**, 125
  Epidaurus **188**
  Greek drama **61**
  Lykavittós Theatre (Athens) 76
  Municipal Theatre (Piraeus)
    158–9
  National Theatre (Athens) 85
  The origins of Greek drama **189**
  Pános Aravantinós Museum of
    Stage Decor (Piraeus) 159
  Theatre of Zéa (Piraeus) 159
Theatre of Dionysos (Athens) 12,
  101
Theatre of Herodes Atticus
  (Athens) 99, **101**
Thebes see Thíva
Theft 304
Themistokles 95
  Lávrio 152
  Piraeus 158, 159
  Pnyx Hill (Athens) 105
Theodosius I, Emperor
  Ancient Delphi 232
  Ancient Dodoma 215
  Ancient Eleusis 160
  bans Olympic Games 39, 177
Theofánia 52

Theophanes the Cretan 221
Theóphilos 77, 224
Theóphilos Museum (Anakasiá)
  224
Thermopylae, Battle of (480 BC) 33
Thermopylae, Pass of 13, **228**
Theseus 56, 100
  Ancient Troezen 185
  Temple of Poseidon (Sounion) 152
Thessaloníki 15, 23, 143, 237,
  248–52
  airport **312**, 313
  Arch of Galerius 39, 248
  churches **252**
  coach services **318**
  hotels 273
  map 249
  railway station 315
  restaurants 291
  Saracens capture 40
Thessaloníki Archaeological
  Museum 15, **250–51**
Thessaloníki Film Festival 51
Thessaly 207
Thiersch, Ludwig 115
Thiseio (Athens)
  hotels 269
  restaurants 285
Thíva (Ancient Thebes) **225**
Thoukydídou (Athens) 106
Thrace 237
Thucydides 60, 106, 153
Thyestes 183
Tickets
  air travel 313
  entertainment in Athens 122
  trains 314–15
Time zone 302
Timíou Prodrómou 204
Tipping
  in restaurants 276–7, 301
Tiryns see Ancient Tiryns
Tloupas, Takis 81
Tobacco Museum (Kavála) 259
Tolls, motorway **316**
Tombs
  Macedonian Tombs (Lefkádia)
    246–7
  Macedonian Tombs (Vergína) 246
  Mycenae **184**
  Royal Tombs (Vergína) 246
  Tomb of Klytemnestra
    (Mycenae) 184

Tombs (cont.)
  Tomb of the Unknown Soldier
    (Athens) 116
Ton Taxiarchón Archangélou
  Michaíl kai Gavriíl 51
Tosítsas family 213
Tourist information **300**, 303
Tower of the Winds (Athens) 12,
  68, **90–91**
  Street-by-Street map 89
Trains **314–15**
  Athens 311
  Great rail journeys **294**, 297
  Kalávryta-Diakoftó Railway **172**
  tickets 314–15
Trams
  in Athens **321**
Travel **310–23**
  air **310–13**
  around Athens 146
  in Athens **320–23**
  buses 311, **318**, **320**
  cars **316–17**, **322**
  Central and Western Greece 209
  coaches **318**
  green travel **310**
  hitchhiking 302, **317**
  Metro (Athens) 311, **321**
  Northern Greece 239
  The Peloponnese 164
  sea **319**
  taxis 311, **317**, **322**
  trains 311, **314–15**
  trams **321**
  trolleybuses **320–21**
Travel insurance 305
Travel safety advice **300**, 303
Travlós, Giánnis 81
Treasury of Atreus (Mycenae) **184**
Trebizond 40
Triantafyllídis, Theófrastos 92
Tríkala 14, 207, **217**
  hotels 272
  restaurants 290
Trikoúpis, Chárilaos 84
Troezen see Ancient Troezen
Trojan Horse 59
Trojan War **58–9**
Trolleybuses **320–21**
Troupákis clan 198, 199
Troy 31
Tsagkaráda 222
  restaurants 290

Tsaroúchis, Yannis 77
 Barber shop in Marousi 46
 Folk Art Museum (Náfplio) 186
Tschumi, Bernard 104
Tsepélovo 211
 hotels 272
Tsipourádiko **275**
Tsipras, Alexis 23, 47
Turks *see* Ottoman Greece
Tzistarákis, *voivode* 90

U

University of Athens 70, 85
University of Athens Museum **108**
 Street-by-Street map 106
Utrillo, Maurice 77

V

Vágis, Polýgnotos 259
Valaorítis, Aristotélis 116
Vale of Tempe **217**
Van Dyck, Sir Anthony 77
Van Pelt and Thompson 77
Vári 153
Várkiza 153
Varlaám 221
Vases and vase painting **64–5**
VAT and tax-free shopping 292
Vátheia 200–201, 203
Vegan food 277
Vegetarian food 277
Venetian Greece 40, 41, **42–3**
Venizélos, Elefthérios 22, 45, 84
Ventrís, Michaïl 182
Vergína 15, 237, **246**
Véroia 15, **246**
Vikos-Aóös National Park 210
Víkos Gorge 14, 206
 Víkos Gorge walk **212**
Villehardouin, Guillaume de
 197
Virgil
 Aeneid 58
Vírvos, Kóstas 21
Visas **300**, 303
Vistonída, Lake 260
Vítsa 211
Vlachopanagía 51
Voïdokoiliá lagoon 205
Vólos 222, 224
 restaurants 290
Vorrés, Ion 154
Vorrés Museum (Paianía) 154

Vouliagméni 153
 hotels 270
Vourvouroú 253
Vradéto 211
Vrontóchion (Mystrás) **197**
Vrysochóri 211
Vyrós Gorge 199
Vyzítsa 13, 223, 224
 hotels 272

W

Walking **295**, 297
 in Athens **321**
 Víkos Gorge walk **212**
War of Independence *see* Greek
 War of Independence
War Museum (Athens) **77**
Washington, George 186
Water, drinking 305
Water Power Museum
 (Dimitsána) 180
Water-skiing
 Athens 124
Waterfalls
 Káranos (Edessa) 247
Watersports **296**, 297
 Athens 124
Watteau, Antoine 77
Weather **53**, 300
Weever fish stings 305
Western Greece *see* Central and
 Western Greece
Wetland wildlife **240–41**
Wheelchair access *see* Disabled
 travellers
"White Terror" 46
White Tower (Thessaloníki) **248**
Wildlife
 Kalógria **173**
 nature tours **295**, 297
 Píndos Mountains **210**
 Saltpan birdlife **229**
 Wetland wildlife **240–41**
 see also National parks; Zoos
Windsurfing 296
 Athens 124
Wines **276**, 279
 Achaïa Clauss Winery (Pátra) 173
 retsína **151**
 wine tasting **294**, 297
Winter in Greece 52
Wolf's Jaws 217
Women travellers **302**

Wooden Horse of Troy 59
World War I 45
World War II 29, 46
 Athens Memorial (Palaió Fáliro)
 153
 Jewish Museum of Greece
 (Athens) 114
 Mount Chelmós 172
Writers **60–61**

X

Xánthi 11, 15, 238, **259**
 restaurants 291
Xenofóntos (Mount Athos) 257
Xiropotámou (Mount Athos) 257

Y

Youth hostels **266**, 267
Youth travellers **302**, 303
Ypapantí 52
Ypsilantis, Dimitrios 192
Ypsosis tou Timíou Stavroú 51
Yusuf Aga 105

Z

Zachloroú
 hotels 271
Záchos, Aristotélis 80
Zagóri 14, **211**
 hotels 272
 map 211
Záppas, Evángelos and
 Konstantínos 116
Záppeion (Athens) 116
Zéa (Piraeus) 158
Zeus 56
 Amphiareio of Oropos 148
 Ancient Olympia 174–6
 Delphi 232, 235
 The Home of Zeus **245**
Zézos, Dimítrios 112
Ziller, Ernst 85
 Frissiras Museum (Athens) 114
 Kallimármaro Stadium (Athens) 117
 National Theatre (Athens) 85
 Presidential Palace (Athens) 116
 Schliemann's House (Athens) 85
 Stathátos Mansion (Athens) 79
Zográfou (Mount Athos) 257
Zoödóchou Pigís 154
Zoos
 Attica Zoological Park 13, **154**
 see also Wildlife

Acknowledgments

Dorling Kindersley would like to thank the following people whose contributions and assistance have made the preparation of this book possible.

Main Contributors
Marc Dubin is an American expatriate who divides his time between London and Sámos. Since 1978 he has travelled in every province of Greece. He has written or contributed to many guides to Greece.

Mike Gerrard is a travel writer and broadcaster who has written several guides to various parts of Greece, which he has been visiting annually since 1964.

Andy Harris is a travel and food journalist based in Athens. He is the author of *A Taste of the Aegean*.

Tanya Tsikas is a Canadian writer and travel guide editor. Married to a Greek, she has spent time in Crete and currently lives in Oxford.

Deputy Editorial Director Douglas Amrine

Deputy Art Director Gillian Allan

Managing Editor Georgina Matthews

Managing Art Editor Annette Jacobs

Additional Illustrations
Richard Bonson, Louise Boulton, Gary Cross, Kevin Goold, Roger Hutchins, Claire Littlejohn.

Design and Editorial Assistance
Emma Anacootee, Hilary Bird, Julie Bond, Elspeth Collier, Michelle Crane, Catherine Day, Mariana Evmolpidou, Jim Evoy, Emer FitzGerald, Jane Foster, Michael Fullalove, Emily Green, Lydia Halliday, Emily Hatchwell, Leanne Hogbin, Kim Inglis, Despoina Kanakoglou, Lorien Kite, Esther Labi, Maite Lantaron, Felicity Laughton, Delphine Lawrance, Nicola Malone, Alison McGill, Andreas Michael, Rebecca Milner, Ella Milroy, Lisa Minsky, Robert Mitchell, Adam Moore, Jennifer Mussett, Tamsin Pender, Marianne Petrou, Rada Radojicic, Jake Reimann, Ellen Root, Simon Ryder, Collette Sadler, Sands Publishing Solutions, Rita Selvaggio, Ellie Smith, Susana Smith, Claire Stewart, Claire Tennant-Scull, Amanda Tomeh, Helen Townsend, Dora Whitaker, Maria Zygourakis.

Revisions and Relaunch Team
Ashwin Adimari, Dipika Dasgupta, Rebecca Flynn, Carole French, Mohammad Hassan, Bharti Karakoti, Rupanki Kaushik, Zafar Khan, Sumita Khatwani, Rahul Kumar, Darren Longley, Anwesha Madhukalya, Deepak Mittal, Tanveer Abbas Zaidi.

Dorling Kindersley would also like to thank the following for their assistance: The Greek Wine Bureau, Odysea.

Additional Research
Anna Antoniou, Garifalia Boussiopoulou, Anastasia Caramanis, Michele Crawford, Magda Dimouti, Shirley Durant, Jane Foster, Panos Gotsi, Zoi Groummouti, Peter Millett, Eva Petrou, Ellen Root, Tasos Schizas, Linda Theodora, Garifalia Tsiola, Veronica Wood.

Additional Photography
Stephen Bere, Mariana Evmolpidou, John Heseltine, Ian O'Leary, Steven Ling, Tony Souter, Clive Streeter, Jerry Young.

Artwork Reference
Ideal Photo S.A., The Image Bank, Tony Stone Worldwide.

Photography Permissions
Dorling Kindersley would like to thank the following for their assistance and kind permission to photograph at their establishments:

Ali Pasha Museum, Ioannina; City of Athens Museum; Museum of Greek Folk Art, Athens; V Kyriazopoulos Ceramic Collection; Kavala Modern Art Gallery; National Gallery of Art, Athens; National War Museum, Athens; Nicholas P Goulandris Foundation Museum of Cycladic and Ancient Art, Athens; Theatrical Museum, Athens; University of Athens Museum; Polygnotos Vagis Museum, Thassos. Also all other cathedrals, churches, museums, hotels, restaurants, shops, galleries, and sights too numerous to thank individually.

Picture Credits
a = above; b = below; c = centre; f = far; l = left; r = right; t = top.

Works of art have been reproduced with the permission of the following copyright holders: Vorres Museum *Water Nymph* (1995) Apostolos Petridis 154tl.

The publisher would like to thank the following individuals, companies and picture libraries for permission to reproduce their photographs:

123RF.com: Elena Duvernay 27c; Dariya Maksimova 240cr; preckas 149tr.

AKG, London: Antiquario Palatino 57bl; *Bilder aus dem Altherthume*, Heinrich Leutemann 232cla; British Museum 99bc; Edward Dodwell 91cr; Erich Lessing Akademie der Bildenden Künste, Vienna 58cr; Musée du Louvre 57tc; Museum Narodowe, Warsaw 149br; Mykonos Museum 59tr; National Archaeological Museum, Athens 30–1(d), 31tc; Staatliche Kunstsammlungen, Dresden 35crb; Liebighaus, Frankfurt/Main 37crb; Staatliche Antikensammlungen und Glyptotek, München 4tr, 56bl; **Alamy Images:** Ancient Art & Architecture Collection Ltd 56tr, 215cb; Arco Images GmbH 221cr; The Art Archive 8-9, 28; Art Directors & TRIP/Bob Turner 311br; Fero Bednar 241bl; CW Images/Chris Warren 294bl; David Crousby

302tl; Greg Balfour Evans 308c; Everett Collection Inc 42c; FAN Travelstock/Katja Kreder 276tl; Fine Art 47ca; funkyfood London - Paul Williams 194-5; Bob Gibbons 27bl; Greece 162; Andrew Holt 279tl, 294cla; Just Greece Photo Library/Terry Harris 51bl; Terry Harris 81tl, 276br, 301tl 316br; INTERFOTO 46bc, 102br; Hercules Milas 172t, 181tr; Rolf Nussbaumer Photography 27br; Werner Otto 294crb; Peterforsberg 114tl; Photo Researchers, Inc 57cr; Picpics 295br; Kostas Pikoulas 305tl; Prisma Archivo 36tc, 61cl, 65bl; Peter Titmuss 305cla; Aristidis Vafeiadakis 123br; World History Archive 61b; **Ancient Art and Architecture**: 33crb, 38ca, 39cb, 41tl, 60cb, 60bc(d), 250cl, 258c; **Antikenmuseum Basel and Sammlung Ludwig**: 64–5c(d), 189br(d); **Aperion**: John Hios 188c; **Apollo Editions**: 189tl; **Argyropoulos Photo Press**: 49t, 49c, 51c, 51tr, 52crb; **Centre for Asia Minor Studies**: Museum of Greek Popular Musical Instruments Fivos Anoyianakis Collection 108tr; **Athens International Airport**: 310bl, 311tl; **Athens Urban Transport**: 320cl; 321tl; **Athinaïkon**: 284tl; **Avocado**: 285b.

Beau Brummel Restaurant: 274br; **Benaki Museum**: 29b, 40cl, 43tl, 43crb, 45cra, 69br, 82–3 all; **Paul Bernard**: 37tc; **Bibliotheque National**, Paris: Caoursin folio 179 42–3(d); **Bourazani**: 289tr; **Bridgeman Art Library**, London: Birmingham City Museums and Art Galleries *Pheidias Completing the Parthenon Frieze*, Sir Lawrence Alma-Tadema 62tr; Bradford Art Galleries and Museums *The Golden Fleece* (c.1904), Herbert James Draper 224br; British Museum, London *Cup, Tondo, with Scene of Huntsmen Returning Home* 33cb, *Black-necked Amphora, Depicting Boxers and Wrestlers* (c.550–525 BC) Nidosthenes 177cra; Fitzwilliam Museum, University of Cambridge *Figurine of Demosthenes*, Enoch Wood of Burslem (c.1790) (lead glazed earthenware) 61tl; House of Masks, Delos *Mosaic of Dionysus Riding a Leopard* (c.AD 180) 39t; Guildhall Art Library *Clytemnestra*, John Collier 183cr; National Archaeological Museum, Athens *Bronze Statue of Poseidon* (c.460–450 BC) photo Bernard Cox 56cl; Private Collection *Two-tiered Icon of the Virgin and Child and Two Saints, Cretan School* (15th century) 42cl; Kunsthistorisches Museum, Vienna 38clb; © **The British Museum**: 30clb, 31cb, 34cb, 35clb, 57tr(d), 57br, 59cl(d), 65tc, 65ca, 104br, 177cla(d), 189bl.

Camera Press, London: Anag 47bl(d); Wim Swaan 247t; **Chrisovoulo**: 287bc; **Courtesy of the City of Athens Development and Destination Agency**: 300br; **Corbis**: John Heseltine 278cl; JAI/Walter Bibikow 245t.

Dreamstime.com: Costas Aggelakis 254-5; Airphoto 15br; Alanesspe 26bl; Georgios Alexandris 14tl, Anastasios71 218-9; Michael Avory 168-9; Pietro Basilico 140-1; Olena Buyskykh 210bc; Byvalet 229cr; Cmarkou 124tr; Costas1962 202bl; Dimaberkut 2-3; Dudau 306bl; Elgreko74 154b; Emicristea 10bl; Enmanja 11tl; Flaviano Fabrizi 27bc; Alexandre Fagundes De Fagundes 86; Freesurf69 66-7; Kristie Gianopulos 262-263; Milan Gonda 277bc; Imagin.gr Photography 96-7; Gabriela Insuratelu 210t; Kalousp 300cla; Andreas Karelias 204b; Gilles Malo 241cl; Jeroen Mikkers 261cr; Milosk50 100cl; nehru 240bl; Ollirg 11crb,

241cr; Dmitry Ometsinsky 266tl; Pajche 298-9; Yiannis Papadimitriou 54-5, 253tl; Lefteris Papaulakis 13bc, 211cr; Picturefan1414 13tl; Preisler 14b; Sborisov 110-1, 152b; Nikolai Sorokin 230-1; Ferdinand Steen 279c; Stockbksts 200-201, 205t; Nikifor Todorov 25crb; Valery109 12br; Dejan Veljkovic 236; Vasilis Ververidis 295c; Leon Viti 27cb; Ivonne Wierink 190cl; Witr 31cr; Wiktor Wojtas 313tl; **Marc Dubin**: 23tl, 172bc, 212cr, 257cl, 256br.

Ecole Nationale Superieure Des Beaux Arts, Paris: *Delphes Restauration du Sanctuaire Envoi Tourn-aire* (1894) 34–5; **ECB**: 307 all; **Ekdotiki Athinon**: 25br, 30crb; **Eleas Gi**: 286tr; **Ergon**: 291br; **ET Archive**: British Museum 189cr; National Archaeology Museum, Naples 36cl; **Mary Evans Picture Library**: 245br.

Fanari Hotel: 273br; **Ferens Art Gallery**: Hull City Museums and Art Galleries and Archives *Electra at the Tomb of Agamemnon* (1869), Lord Frederick Leighton 59br; **FLPA**: Martin B Withers 27cr; **Folk Art Museum**, Athens: 114bl; **Frissiras Museum**: 107tc.

g7ahn/Flicker: 315c; **Getty Images**: © Dimitris Sotiropoulos Photography 242-3; Lonely Planet 122cra; Print Collector 36cb; Lizzie Shepherd 206; George Tsafos 50bl; **Giraudon**, Paris: Laruros Versailles Chateau *Le Batille de Navarin*, Louis Ambroise Garneray 204tr; Louvre, Paris 64cl, *Scene de Massacres de Scio*, Delacroix 44ca(d); Musee Nationale Gustave Moreau *Hesiode et Les Muses* Gustave Moreau 60cla; Musee d'Art Catalan, Barcelona 99br; National Portrait Gallery, London *Portrait of George Gordon Byron*, Thomas Phillips (1813) 153tr(d); **Grande Bretagne Hotel**: 265br; **Grand Resort Lagonissi**: 265tl, 270tl; **Greek National Tourist Organization**: 300tc; **Nicholas P Goulandris Foundation Museum of Cycladic and Ancient Greek Art**: 69cr, 78–9 all.

Robert Harding Picture Library: David Beatty 48br; Tony Gervis 48cl, 48bl; Mel Longhurst 309tl; Nico Tondini 49bl; Adam Woolfitt 50c; **Helio Photo**: 258b; **Hellenic Post Service**: 47tl; **Hotel Kritsa**: 275br, 290tr; **Hotel Pelops**: 271br; **Hulton Getty Collection**: 45crb(d); Central Press Photo 46clb(d); **Hutchison Library**: Hilly Janes 102tr.

Ideal Photo SA: N. Adams 120clb; T Dassios 49br, 179tl, 256cl, 256bl, 257bl, 266bc; C. Vergas 52bl,182bl; **Images Colour Library**: 103bl.

Karavostasi Beach Hotel: 267cl; **Kostos Kontos**: 30ca, 46cra, 46cla, 49crb, 124br, 144, 156tr, 156cla,157tl, 157cra, 174tr, 179cra, 183bc, 188tr, 193tr, 321br; **KTEL Bus**: 318cla.

Ilias Lalaounis: 293cla; **Lampropoulos**:118c.

Mansell Collection: 56–7; **Marble House**: 268bl; **Melissinos Art - The Poet Sandalmaker**: 119tc; **Municipal Art Gallery of Athens**: *Despinis TK* Mitarakis Yannis 92tl.

National Gallery of Victoria, Melbourne: Felton Bequest (1956) *Greek by the Inscriptions Painter Challidian* 58bl;

National Historical Museum, Athens: 44–5(d), 45tl, 46bl, 177clb, 192cr(d), 198crb; New Acropolis Museum: 104cl.

O&B Athens Boutique Hotel: 269br; Octopus Sea Trips: Peter Nicolaides 296tr; Orizontes Lykavittou: 283tl.

Romylos Parisis: 18t, 108bl, 222cr; City of Athens Museum 44clb; Pictures Colour Library: 20bl, 48crb; Michalis Pornalis: 222br, 223crb, 223br; Private Collections: 221tc, 221br.

Ride World Wide: 295tl; Rex Features: 21cr; Sipa/Argyropoulos 52t; Sipa/C.Brown 47tr; Rex by Shutterstock: Universal History Archive 184tr.

Scala, Florence: Gallerie degli Uffizi 32clb; Museo Archeologico, Firenze 33tl; Museo Mandralisca Cefalu 34cl; Museo Nationale Tarquinia 65bc; Museo de Villa Giulia 32-3, 64tr; Spathario Shadow Theatre Museum: 155c; Spectrum Colour Library: 248bl; STA Travel Group: 302c; STASY/Attiko Metro Operation Company S.A. (AMEL): 321cr; Maria Stefossi: 122b; Theodoros-Patroklos Stellakis: 158br; Carmel Stewart: 277c; Sunvil: 296bl; SuperStock: age fotostock / Wolfgang Kaehler 64br; Album / Oronoz 40clb; Album / Oronoz 225cra; Iberfoto 58tr; Swan Hellenic: 296cr.

Ta Fanaria: 288bc; Tap Service Archaeological Receipts Fund Hellenic Republic Ministry of Culture: A Epharat of Antiquities 9b, 47cb, 62br, 98clb, 98br, 99tl, 99cb, 100br, 101c, 101tl, 102cl, 103crb; Ancient Corinth Archaeological Museum 170c; B Epharat of Antiquities 145b, 148 all, 150 all, 151cla, 152cr; Byzantine Museum, Athens 80 all; D Epharat of Antiquities 143c, 143br, 166–7 all, 171bl, 181br, 182tr, 183tl, 183ca, 184cla; Delphi Archaeological Museum 234tl, 235c, 235br; E Epharat of Antiquities 178cb; Elefis Archaeological Museum 160cb; 11th Epharat of Byzantine Antiquities 241tr; 5th Epharat of Byzantine Antiquities 25cla, 25c, 41ca, 196bc; 1st Epharat of Byzantine Antiquities 143cra, 157bl, 226–7 all; I Epharat of Antiquities 142ca, 209tl, 232br, 233tl, 234tr, 234bl; IB Epharat of Antiquities 215tr, 216c; IO Epharat of Antiquities 260c; IST Epharat of Antiquities 245c; Keramikos Archaeological Museum 93t, 93cr, 93br, 95t, 95car; Marathon Archaeological Museum 149c; National Archeological Museum, Athens 1, 7c, 32tr, 69tr, 72-3 all, 74–5 all, 103tl, 161cr; 9th Epharat of Byzantine Antiquities 252c, 252b; Pireaus Archaeological Museum 159tl; 2nd Epharat of Byzantine Antiquities 25cra; 6th Epharat of Byzantine Antiquities 17t, 7th Epharat of Byzantine Antiquities 25bl, 223ca; Thebes Archaeological Museum 225tl; Thessaloníki Archaeological Museum 35tl, 143tc, 246bl(d), 250tr, 250br, 251 all; I Epharat of Antiquities 92ca, 92cb, 93tc, 93c, 93bl, 94-5 all, 160tr, 160cla, 161 all; Z Epharat of Antiquities 142clb, 174cl, 174bl, 175tc, 175bc, 176 all, 205b; Yannis Tsarouhis Foundation: Private Collection Barber Shop in Marousi (1947) 46tr.

Wadsworth Atheneum, Hartford Connecticut: T Pierpont Morgan Collection 193bc; Peter Wilson: 63bl, 98cla, 101br, 220clb; Woodfin Camp & Associates: John Marmaras 258tr; Adam Woolfitt 49clb.

Xenonas Papaevangelou: George Papaevangelou 272tr.

YES! Hotels: 269tl; Yiantes: Kamilo Nollas 282bl.

Front Endpaper: Alamy Images: Greece Lbl; Dreamstime.com: Freesurf69 R bc; Dejan Veljkovic Rcr; Getty Images: Lizzie Shepherd cla.

Map Cover: Getty Images: Jean-Pierre Lescourret.

Jacket
Front and Spine top: Getty Images: Jean-Pierre Lescourret.

All other images © Dorling Kindersley. For further information see: www.dkimages.com

Phrase Book

There is no universally accepted system for representing the modern Greek language in the Roman alphabet. The system of transliteration adopted in this guide is the one used by the Greek Government. Though not yet fully applied throughout Greece, most of the street and place names have been transliterated according to this system. For Classical names, this guide uses the k, os, on and f spelling, in keeping with the modern system of transliteration. In a few cases, such as Socrates, the more familiar Latin form has been used. Classical names and ancient sites do not have accents. Where a well-known English form of a name exists, such as Athens or Corfu, this has been used. Variations in transliteration are given in the index.

Guidelines for Pronunciation

The accent over Greek and transliterated words indicates the stressed syllable. In this guide, the accent is not written over capital letters (except for diaeresis, eg, "ϊ") nor over mono-syllables, except for question words and the conjunction ή (meaning "or") in the right-hand "Pronunciation" column below, the syllable to stress is given in bold type.

On the following pages, the English is given in the left-hand column with the Greek and its transliteration in the middle column. The right-hand column provides a literal system of pronunciation and indicates the stressed syllable in bold.

The Greek Alphabet

Α α	A a	**a**rm
Β β	V v	**v**ote
Γ γ	G g	**y**ear (when followed by e and i sounds); otherwise, **g**(love)
Δ δ	D d	**th**at
Ε ε	E e	**e**gg
Ζ ζ	Z z	**z**oo
Η η	I i	sk**i**
Θ θ	Th th	**th**ink
Ι ι	I i	sk**i**
Κ κ	K k	**k**id
Λ λ	L l	**l**and
Μ μ	M m	**m**an
Ν ν	N n	**n**o
Ξ ξ	X x	ta**xi**
Ο ο	O o	t**o**ad
Π π	P p	**p**ort
Ρ ρ	R r	**r**oom
Σ σ	S s	**s**orry (**z**ero when followed by μ or ν)
ς	s	(used at end of word)
Τ τ	T t	**t**ea
Υ υ	Y y	bare**l**y
Φ φ	F f	**f**ish
Χ χ	Ch ch	lo**ch** in most cases, but **h**e when followed by a, e or i sounds
Ψ ψ	Ps ps	ma**ps**
Ω ω	O o	t**o**ad

Combinations of Letters

In Greek, there are two-letter vowels that are pronounced as one sound:

Αι αι	Ai ai	h**ey**
Ει ει	Ei ei	sk**i**
Οι οι	Oi oi	bel**ie**ve
Ου ου	Ou ou	t**ou**rist

There are also some two-letter consonant clusters that yield predictable or unusual results:

Μπ μπ	Mp mp	**b**ut if initial; nu**mb**er in the middle of a word
Ντ ντ	Nt nt	**d**esk if initial; u**nd**er in the middle of a word
Γκ γκ	Gk gk	**g**o if initial; bi**ng**o in the middle of a word
Γξ γξ	Nx	a**nx**iety
Τζ τζ	Tz tz	ju**dge**
Τσ τσ	Ts ts	hi**ts**
γγ	gg	bi**ng**o in the middle of a word

In an Emergency

Help!	Βοήθεια!	vo-e**e**-theea
	Voïtheia	
Stop!	Σταματήστε!	sta-ma-te**e**-steh
	Stamatíste	
Call a doctor!	Φωνάξτε ένα γιατρό	fo-n**a**k-steh **e**-na ya-tr**o**!
	Fonáxte éna giatró	
Call an ambulance/ the police/the fire brigade!	Καλέστε το ασθενοφόρο/την αστυνομία/την πυροσβεστική!	ka-l**e**-steh to as-the-no-**fo**-ro/teen a-sti-no-m**i**a/teen pee-ro-zve-stee-k**ee**
	Kaléste to asthenofóro/tin astynomía/tin pyrosvestikí	
Where is the nearest telephone/hospital/ pharmacy?	Πού είναι το πλησιέστερο τήλεφωνο/νοσοκο-μείο/φαρμακείο;	poo e**e**-ne to plee-see-**e**-ste-ro tee-**le**-pho-no/no-so-ko-me**e**-o/far-ma-ke**e**-o?
	Poú eínai to plisiés-tero tiléfono/nosoko-meío/farmakeío?	

Communication Essentials

Yes	Ναι	neh
	Nai	
No	Όχι	**o**-chee
	Ochi	
Please	Παρακαλώ	pa-ra-ka-l**o**
	Parakaló	
Thank you	Ευχαριστώ	ef-cha-ree-st**o**
	Efcharistó	
You are welcome	Παρακαλώ	pa-ra-ka-l**o**
	Parakaló	
OK/alright	Εντάξει	en-d**a**k-zee
	Entáxei	
Excuse me	Με συγχωρείτε	me seen-cho-re**e**-teh
	Me synchoreite	
Hello	Γειά σας	yeea sas
	Geiá sas	
Goodbye	Αντίο	an-d**ee**-o
	Antío	
Good morning	Καλημέρα	ka-lee-m**e**-ra
	Kaliméra	
Good night	Καληνύχτα	ka-lee-nee**ch**-ta
	Kalinýchta	
Morning	Πρωί	pro-e**e**
	Proí	
Afternoon	Απόγευμα	a-p**o**-yev-ma
	Apógevma	
Evening	Βράδυ	vr**a**th-i
	Vrádi	
This morning	Σήμερα το πρωί	se**e**-me-ra to pro-e**e**
	Símera to proí	
Yesterday	Χθές	chth**e**s
	Chthés	
Today	Σήμερα	se**e**-me-ra
	Símera	
Tomorrow	Αύριο	**a**v-ree-o
	Avrio	
Here	Εδώ	ed-**o**
	Edó	
There	Εκεί	e-ke**e**
	Ekeí	
What?	Τι;	tee?
	Tí?	
Why?	Γιατί;	ya-te**e**?
	Giatí?	
Where?	Πού;	poo?
	Poú?	
How?	Πώς;	pos?
	Pós?	
Wait!	Περίμενε!	pe-re**e**-me-neh
	Perímene!	

Useful Phrases

How are you?	Τι κάνετε; *Ti kánete?*	tee **ka**-ne teh
Very well, thank you	Πολύ καλά, ευχαριστώ *Polý kalá, efcharistó*	po-lee ka-**la**, ef-cha-ree-**sto**
How do you do?	Πώς είστε; *Pós eíste?*	pos ees-te?
Pleased to meet you	Χαίρω πολύ *Chaíro polý*	**che**-ro po-**lee**
What is your name?	Πώς λέγεστε; *Pós légeste?*	pos **le**-ye-ste?
Where is/are…?	Πού είναι; *Poú eínai?*	poo **ee**-ne?
How far is it to…?	Πόσο απέχει…; *Póso apéchei…?*	po-so a-**pe**-chee?
How do I get to?	Πώς μπορώ να πάω….; *Pós mporó na páo…?*	pos bo-**ro**-na pa-o?
Do you speak English?	Μιλάτε Αγγλικά; *Miláte Angliká?*	mee-**la**-te an-glee-**ka**?
I understand	Καταλαβαίνω *Katalavaíno*	ka-ta-la-**ve**-no
I don't understand	Δεν καταλαβαίνω *Den katalavaíno*	then ka-ta-la-**ve**-no
Could you speak slowly?	Μιλάτε λίγο πιο αργά παρακαλώ; *Miláte lígo pio argá parakaló?*	mee-**la**-te lee-go pyo ar-**ga** pa-ra-ka-**lo**?
I'm sorry	Με συγχωρείτε *Me synchoreíte*	me seen-cho-**ree** teh
Does anyone have a key?	Έχει κανένας κλειδί; *Échei kanénas kleidí?*	**e**-chee ka-**ne**-nas klee-**dee**?

Useful Words

big	Μεγάλο *Megálo*	me-**ga**-lo
small	Μικρό *Mikró*	mi-**kro**
hot	Ζεστό *Zestó*	zes-**to**
cold	Κρύο *Krýo*	**kree**-o
good	Καλό *Kaló*	ka-**lo**
bad	Κακό *Kakó*	ka-**ko**
enough	Αρκετά *Arketá*	ar-ke-**ta**
well	Καλά *Kalá*	ka-**la**
open	Ανοιχτά *Anoichtá*	a-neech-**ta**
closed	Κλειστά *Kleistá*	klee-**sta**
left	Αριστερά *Aristerá*	a-ree-ste-**ra**
right	Δεξιά *Dexiá*	dek-see-**a**
straight on	Ευθεία *Eftheía*	ef-**thee**-a
between	Ανάμεσα / Μεταξύ *Anámesa / Metaxý*	a-**na**-me-sa/me-tak-**see**
on the corner of…	Στη γωνία του… *Sti gonía tou…*	stee go-**nee**-a too
near	Κοντά *Kontá*	kon-**da**
far	Μακριά *Makriá*	ma-kree-**a**
up	Επάνω *Epáno*	e-**pa**-no
down	Κάτω *Káto*	**ka**-to
early	Νωρίς *Norís*	no-**rees**
late	Αργά *Argá*	ar-**ga**
entrance	Η είσοδος *I eísodos*	ee **ee**-so-thos
exit	Η έξοδος *I éxodos*	ee-**ex**-o-dos
toilet	Οι τουαλέτες /WC *Oi toualétes / WC*	ee-too-a-**le**-tes
occupied/engaged	Κατειλημμένη *Kateiliméni*	ka-tee-lee-**me**-nee
unoccupied/vacant	Ελεύθερη *Eléftheri*	e-**lef**-the-ree
free/no charge	Δωρεάν *Doreán*	tho-re-**an**
in/out	Μέσα /Έξω *Mésa/ Exo*	me-sa/**ek**-so

Making a Telephone Call

Where is the nearest telephone booth?	Πού βρίσκεται ο πλησιέστερος τηλεφωνικός θάλαμος; *Poú vrísketai o plisiésteros tilefonikós thálamos?*	poo **vrees**-ke-teh o plee-see-**e**-ste-ros tee-le-fo-ni-**kos** tha-la-mos?
I would like to place a long-distance call	Θα ήθελα να κάνω ένα υπεραστικό τηλεφώνημα *Tha íthela na káno éna yperastikó tilefónima*	tha ee-the-la na ka-no **e**-na ee-pe-ra-sti-**ko** tee-le-**fo**-nee-ma
I would like to reverse the charges	Θα ήθελα να χρεώσω το τηλεφώνημα στον παραλήπτη *Tha íthela na chreóso to tilefónima ston paralípti*	tha ee-**the**-la na chre-**o**-so to tee-le-**fo**-nee-ma ston pa-ra-**leep**-tee
I will try again later	Θα ξανατηλεφωνήσω αργότερα *Tha xanatilefoníso argótera*	tha ksa-na-tee-le-fo-**ni**-so ar-**go**-te-ra
Can I leave a message?	Μπορείτε να του αφήσετε ένα μήνυμα; *Mporeíte na tou afísete éna mínyma?*	bo-**ree**-te na too a-**fee**-se-teh **e**-na mee-nee-ma?
Could you speak up a little please?	Μιλάτε δυνατότερα, παρακαλώ; *Miláte dynatótera, parakaló*	mee-**la**-teh dee-na-**to**-te-ra, pa-ra-ka-**lo**
Local call	Τοπικό τηλεφώνημα *Topikó tilefónima*	to-pi-**ko** tee-le-**fo**-nee-ma
Hold on	Περιμένετε *Periménete*	pe-ri-**me**-ne-teh
Phone box/kiosk	Ο τηλεφωνικός θάλαμος *O tilefonikós thálamos*	o tee-le-fo-ni-**kos** tha-la-mos
Phone card	Η τηλεκάρτα *I tilekárta*	ee tee-le-**kar**-ta

Shopping

How much does this cost?	Πόσο κάνει; *Póso kánei?*	**po**-so **ka**-nee?
I would like….	Θα ήθελα… *Tha íthela…*	tha ee-**the**-la…
Do you have….?	Έχετε…; *Echete…?*	**e**-che-teh
I am just looking	Απλώς κοιτάω *Aplós koitáo*	a-**plos** kee-**ta**-o
Do you take credit cards?'	Δέχεστε πιστωτικές κάρτες; *Décheste pistotikés kártes?*	**the**-ches-teh pee-sto-tee-**kes** kar-tes?
What time do you open/close?	Πότε ανοίγετε/ κλείνετε; *Póte anoígete/ kleínete?*	**po**-teh a-nee-ye-teh/ klee-ne-teh?
Can you ship this overseas?	Μπορείτε να το στείλετε στο εξωτερικό; *Mporeíte na to steílete sto exoterikó?*	bo-**ree**-teh na to **stee**-le-teh sto e-xo-te-ree **ko**?
This one	Αυτό εδώ *Aftó edó*	af-**to** e-**do**
That one	Εκείνο *Ekíno*	e-**kee**-no

expensive	Ακριβό *Akrivó*	*a-kree-v**o***
cheap	Φθηνό *Fthinó*	*fthee-n**o***
size	Το μέγεθος *To mégethos*	*to m**e**-ge-thos*
white	Λευκό *Lefkó*	*lef-k**o***
black	Μαύρο *Mávro*	*m**a**v-ro*
red	Κόκκινο *Kókkino*	*k**o**-kee-no*
yellow	Κίτρινο *Kítrino*	*kee-tree-no*
green	Πράσινο *Prásino*	*pra-see-no*
blue	Μπλε *Mple*	*bleh*

Types of Shop

antique shop	Μαγαζί με αντίκες *Magazi me antikes*	*ma-ga-zee me an-dee-kes*
bakery	Ο φούρνος *O foúrnos*	*o foor-nos*
bank	Η τράπεζα *I trápeza*	*ee tra-pe-za*
bazaar	Το παζάρι *To pazári*	*to pa-za-ree*
bookshop	Το βιβλιοπωλείο *To vivliopoleío*	*to vee-vlee-o-po-lee-o*
butcher	Το κρεοπωλείο *To kreopoleío*	*to kre-o-po-lee-o*
cake shop	Το ζαχαροπλαστείο *To zacharoplasteío*	*to za-cha-ro-pla-stee-o*
delicatessen	Μαγαζί με αλλαντικά *Magazi me allantiká*	*ma-ga-zee me a-lan-dee-ka*
department store	Πολυκατάστημα *Polykatástima*	*Po-lee-ka-ta-stee-ma*
fishmarket	Το ιχθυοπωλείο/ ψαράδικο *To ichthyopoleío/ psarádiko*	*to eech-thee-o-po-lee-o/psa-ra-dee-ko*
greengrocer	Το μανάβικο *To manáviko*	*to ma-na-vee-ko*
hairdresser	Το κομμωτήριο *To kommotírio*	*to ko-mo-tee-ree-o*
kiosk	Το περίπτερο *To períptero*	*to pe-reep-te-ro*
leather shop	Μαγαζί με δερμάτινα είδη *Magazi me dermátina eidi*	*ma-ga-zee me ther-ma-tee-na ee-thee*
street market	Η λαϊκή αγορά *I laikí agorá*	*ee la-ee-kee a-go-ra*
newsagent	Ο εφημεριδοπώλης *O efimeridopólis*	*O e-fee-me-ree-tho-po-lees*
pharmacy	Το φαρμακείο *To farmakeío*	*to far-ma-kee-o*
post office	Το ταχυδρομείο *To tachydromeío*	*to ta-chee-thro-mee-o*
shoe shop	Κατάστημα υποδημάτων *Katástima ypodimáton*	*ka-ta-stee-ma ee-po-dee-ma-ton*
souvenir shop	Μαγαζί με "souvenir" *Magazi me "souvenir"*	*ma-ga-zee meh "souvenir"*
supermarket	Σουπερμάρκετ/ Υπεραγορά *"Supermarket"/ Yperagorá*	*"Supermarket"/ee-per-a-go-ra*
tobacconist	Είδη καπνιστού *Eídi kapnistoú*	*Ee-thee kap-nees*
travel agent	Το ταξειδιωτικό πρακτορείο *To taxeidiotikó praktoreío*	*to tak-see-thy-o-tee-ko prak-to-ree-o*

Sightseeing

tourist information	Ο ΕΟΤ *O EOT*	*o E-OT*
tourist police	Η τουριστική αστυνομία *I touristiki astynomia*	*ee too-rees-tee-kee a-stee-no-mee-a*
archaeological	αρχαιολογικός *archaiologikós*	*ar-che-o-lo-yee-k**o**s*

art gallery	Η γκαλερί *I gkalerí*	*ee ga-le-ree*
beach	Η παραλία *I paralia*	*ee pa-ra-lee-a*
Byzantine	βυζαντινός *vyzantinós*	*vee-zan-dee-n**o**s*
castle	Το κάστρο *To kástro*	*to ka-stro*
cathedral	Η μητρόπολη *I mitrópoli*	*ee mee-tro-po-lee*
cave	Το σπήλαιο *To spilaio*	*to spee-le-o*
church	Η εκκλησία *I ekklisia*	*ee e-klee-see-a*
folk art	λαϊκή τέχνη *laiki téchni*	*la-ee-kee tech-nee*
fountain	Το συντριβάνι *To syntriváni*	*to seen-dree-va-nee*
garden	Ο κήπος *O kípos*	*o kee-pos*
gorge	Το φαράγγι *To farággi*	*to fa-ran-gee*
grave of….	Ο τάφος του… *O táfos tou…*	*o ta-fos too*
hill	Ο λόφος *O lófos*	*o lo-fos*
historical	ιστορικός *istorikós*	*ee-sto-ree-k**o**s*
island	Το νησί *To nisí*	*to nee-see*
lake	Η λίμνη *I límni*	*ee leem-nee*
library	Η βιβλιοθήκη *I vivliothíki*	*ee veev-lee-o-thee-kee*
mansion	Το αρχοντικό *To archontikó*	*to ar-chon-di-ko*
monastery	Μονή *moní*	*mo-nee*
mountain	Το βουνό *To vounó*	*to voo-no*
municipal	δημοτικός *dimotikós*	*thee-mo-tee-k**o**s*
museum	Το μουσείο *To mouseio*	*to moo-see-o*
national	εθνικός *ethnikós*	*eth-nee-k**o**s*
park	Το πάρκο *To párko*	*to par-ko*
river	Το ποτάμι *To potámi*	*to po-ta-mee*
road	Ο δρόμος *O drómos*	*o thro-mos*
saint	άγιος/άγιοι/αγία /αγίες *ágios/ágioi/agia/agies*	*a-yee-os/a-yee-ee/a-yee-a/a-yee-es*
spring	Η πηγή *I pigí*	*ee pee-yee*
square	Η πλατεία *I plateía*	*ee pla-tee-a*
stadium	Το στάδιο *To stádio*	*to sta-thee-o*
statue	Το άγαλμα *To ágalma*	*to a-gal-ma*
theatre	Το θέατρο *To théatro*	*to the-a-tro*
town hall	Το δημαρχείο *To dimarcheío*	*To thee-mar-chee-o*
closed on public holidays	κλειστό τις αργίες *kleistó tis argíes*	*klee-sto tees aryee-es*

Transport

When does the …. leave?	Πότε φεύγει το ….; *Póte févgei to…?*	*po-teh fev-yee to…?*
Where is the bus stop?	Πού είναι η στάση του λεωφορείου; *Poú eínai i stási tou leoforeíou?*	*poo ee-neh ee sta-see too le-o-fo-ree-oo?*
Is there a bus to…?	Υπάρχει λεωφορείο για ….; *Ypárchei leoforeío gia…?*	*ee-par-chee le-o-fo-ree-o yia…?*
ticket office	Εκδοτήριο εισιτηρίων *Ekdotírio eisitirion*	*Ek-tho-tee-ree-o ee-see-tee-ree-on*
return ticket	Εισιτήριο με επιστροφή *Eisitírio me epistrofi*	*ee-see-tee-ree-o meh e-pee-stro-fee*
single journey	Απλό εισιτήριο *Apló eisitírio*	*a-plo ee-see-tee-reeo*

bus station	Ο σταθμός λεωφορείων *O stathmós leoforeíon*	*o stath-mos leo-fo-ree-on*
bus ticket	Εισιτήριο λεωφορείου *Eisitírio leoforeíou*	*ee-see-tee-ree-o leo-fo-ree-oo*
trolley bus	Το τρόλλεϋ *To trólley*	*to tro-le-ee*
port	Το λιμάνι *To limáni*	*to lee-ma-nee*
train	Το τρένο *To tréno*	*to tre-no*
railway station	σιδηροδρομικός σταθμός *sidirodromikós stathmós*	*see-thee-ro-thro-mee-kos stath-mos*
motorbike	το μηχανάκι *To michanáki*	*to mee-cha-na-kee*
bicycle	Το ποδήλατο *To podílato*	*to po-thee-la-to*
taxi	Το ταξί *To taxí*	*to tak-see*
airport	Το αεροδρόμιο *To aerodrómio*	*to a-e-ro-thro-mee-o*
ferry	Το φερρυμπότ *To "ferry-boat"*	*to fe-ree-bot*
fast ferry	Το ταχυπλοΰ *To tachyplŏ*	*to ta-hee-plo*
hydrofoil	Το δελφίνι / Το υδροπτέρυγο *To delfíni / To ydroptérygo*	*to del-fee-nee/To ee-throp-te-ree-go*
catamaran	Το καταμαράν *To katamarán*	*to catamaran*
for hire/rent	Ενοικιάζονται *Enoikiázontai*	*e-nee-kya-zon-deh*

Staying in a Hotel

Do you have a vacant room?	Έχετε δωμάτιο *Echete domátio?*	*e-che-teh tho-ma-tee-o?*
double room with double bed	Δίκλινο με διπλό κρεβάτι *Díklino me diplό kreváti*	*thee-klee-no meh thee-plo kre-va-tee*
twin room	Δίκλινο με μονά κρεβάτια *Díklino me monά krevátia*	*thee-klee-no meh mo-na kre-vat-ya*
single room	Μονόκλινο *Monόklino*	*mo-no-klee-no*
room with a bath	Δωμάτιο με μπάνιο *Domátio me mpánio*	*tho-ma-tee-o meh ban-yo*
shower	Το ντους *To douz*	*To dooz*
key	Το κλειδί *To kleidí*	*to klee-dee*
I have a reservation	Έχω κάνει κράτηση *Echo kánei krátisi*	*e-cho ka-nee kra-tee-see*
room with a sea view/balcony	Δωμάτιο με θέα στη θάλασσα/μπαλκόνι *Domátio me théa sti thálassa / mpalkóni*	*tho-ma-tee-o meh the-a stee tha-la-sa/bal-ko-nee*
Does the price include breakfast?	Το πρωινό συμπεριλαμβάνεται στην τιμή; *To proinό symperilamvánetai stin timí?*	*to pro-ee-no seem-be-ree-lam-va-ne-teh steen tee-mee?*

Eating Out

Have you got a table?	Έχετε τραπέζι; *Echete trapézi?*	*e-che-te tra-pe-zee?*
want to reserve a table	Θέλω να κρατήσω ένα τραπέζι *Thélo na kratíso éna trapézi*	*the-lo na kra-tee-so e-na tra-pe-zee*
The bill, please	Τον λογαριασμό, παρακαλώ *Ton logariasmό parakaló*	*ton lo-gar-yaz-mo pa-ra-ka-lo*
I am a vegetarian	Είμαι χορτοφάγος *Eímai chortofágos*	*ee-meh chor-to-fa-gos*
What is today's special?	Πιό είναι το πιάτο ημέρας; *Piό eínai to piáto iméras?*	*pyό ee-neh to-pi-a-to ee me-ras?*

waiter/waitress	Κύριε / Γκαρσόν / Κυρία (female) *Kýrie/Garson/Kyría*	*Kee-ree-eh/Gar-son/Kee-ree-a*
menu	Ο κατάλογος *O katálogos*	*o ka-ta-lo-gos*
cover charge	Το κουβέρ *To "couvert"*	*to koo-ver*
wine list	Ο οινοκατάλογος *O oinokatálogos*	*o e-no-ka-ta-lo-gos*
glass	Το ποτήρι *To potíri*	*to po-tee-ree*
bottle	Το μπουκάλι *To mpoukáli*	*to bou-ka-lee*
knife	Το μαχαίρι *To machaíri*	*to ma-che-ree*
fork	Το πηρούνι *To piroúni*	*to pee-roo-nee*
spoon	Το κουτάλι *To koutáli*	*to koo-ta-lee*
breakfast	Το πρωινό *To proinό*	*to pro-ee-no*
lunch	Το μεσημεριανό *To mesimerianό*	*to me-seer-mer-ya-no*
dinner	Το δείπνο *To deípno*	*to theep-no*
main course	Το κύριο πιάτο *To kýrio piáto*	*to kee-ri-o piato*
starters/first courses	Τα ορεκτικά *Ta orektiká*	*ta o-rek-tee-ka*
dessert	Το γλυκό *To glykό*	*to ylee-ko*
dish of the day	Το πιάτο της ημέρας *To piáto tis iméras*	*to pya-to tees ee-me-ras*
bar	Το μπαρ *To "bar"*	*To bar*
taverna	Η ταβέρνα *I tavérna*	*ee ta-ver-na*
café	Το καφενείο *To kafeneío*	*to ka-fe-nee-o*
fish taverna	Η ψαροταβέρνα *I psarotavérna*	*ee psa-ro-ta-ver-na*
grill house	Η ψησταριά *I psistariá*	*ee psee-sta-rya*
wine shop	Το οινοπωλείο *To oinopoleío*	*to ee-no-po-lee-o*
dairy shop	Το γαλακτοπωλείο *To galaktopoleío*	*to ga-lak-to-po-lee-o*
restaurant	Το εστιατόριο *To estiatório*	*to e-stee-a-to-ree-o*
ouzeri	Το ουζερί *To ouzerí*	*to oo-ze-ree*
meze shop	Το μεζεδοπωλείο *To mezedopoleío*	*To me-ze-do-po-lee-o*
take away kebabs	Το σουβλατζίδικο *To souvlatzídiko*	*To soo-vlat-zee-dee-ko*
rare	Ελάχιστα ψημένο *Eláchista psiménο*	*e-lach-ees-ta psee-me-no*
medium	Μέτρια ψημένο *Métria psiménο*	*met-ree-a psee-me-no*
well done	Καλοψημένο *Kalopsiménο*	*ka-lo-psee-me-no*

Basic Food and Drink

coffee	Ο καφές *O Kafés*	*o ka-fes*
with milk	με γάλα *me gála*	*me ga-la*
black coffee	σκέτος *skétos*	*ske-tos*
without sugar	χωρίς ζάχαρη *chorís záchari*	*cho-rees za-cha-ree*
medium sweet	μέτριος *métrios*	*me-tree-os*
very sweet	γλυκύς *glykýs*	*glee-kees*
tea	τσάι *tsái*	*tsa-ee*
hot chocolate	ζεστή σοκολάτα *zestí sokoláta*	*ze-stee so-ko-la-ta*
wine	κρασί *krasí*	*kra-see*
red	κόκκινο *kόkkino*	*ko-kee-no*
white	λευκό *lefkό*	*lef-ko*
rosé	ροζέ *rozé*	*ro-ze*

raki	Το ρακί	to ra-ke**e**
	To raki	
ouzo	Το ούζο	to o**o**-zo
	To ouzo	
retsina	Η ρετσίνα	ee ret-se**e**-na
	I retsina	
water	Το νερό	to ne-r**o**
	To neró	
octopus	Το χταπόδι	to chta-p**o**-dee
	To chtapódi	
fish	Το ψάρι	to psa-re**e**
	To psári	
cheese	Το τυρί	to tee-re**e**
	To tyrí	
mastello	Το μαστέλο	to mas-**te**-lo
	To mastélo	
feta	Η φέτα	ee **fe**-ta
	I féta	
bread	Το ψωμί	to pso-me**e**
	To psomí	
bean soup	Η φασολάδα	ee fa-so-l**a**-da
	I fasoláda	
houmous	Το χούμους	to choo-moos
	To houmous	
halva	Ο χαλβάς	o chal-v**a**s
	O chalvás	
thin meat slabs	Ο γύρος	o y**ee**-ros
	O gýros	
Turkish delight	Το λουκούμι	to loo-ko**o**-mee
	To loukoúmi	
baklava	Ο μπακλαβάς	o bak-la-v**a**s
	O mpaklavás	
kleftiko	Το κλέφτικο	to kl**e**f-tee-ko
	To kléftiko	

Numbers

1	ένα	**e**-na
	éna	
2	δύο	the**e**-o
	dýo	
3	τρία	tree-a
	tría	
4	τέσσερα	t**e**-se-ra
	téssera	
5	πέντε	p**e**n-deh
	pénte	
6	έξι	**e**k-si
	éxi	
7	επτά	ep-t**a**
	eptá	
8	οχτώ	och-t**o**
	ochtó	
9	εννέα	e-n**e**-a
	ennéa	
10	δέκα	th**e**-ka
	déka	
11	έντεκα	**e**n-de-ka
	énteka	
12	δώδεκα	tho-the-ka
	dódeka	
13	δεκατρία	de-ka-tre**e**-a
	dekatría	
14	δεκατέσσερα	the-ka-t**e**s-se-ra
	dekatéssera	
15	δεκαπέντε	the-ka-p**e**n-de
	dekapénte	
16	δεκαέξι	the-ka-**e**k-si
	dekaéxi	
17	δεκαεπτά	the-ka-ep-t**a**
	dekaeptá	
18	δεκαοχτώ	the-ka-och-t**o**
	dekaochtó	
19	δεκαεννέα	the-ka-e-n**e**-a
	dekaennéa	
20	είκοσι	ee-ko-see
	eíkosi	
21	εικοσιένα	ee-ko-see-**e**-na
	eikosiéna	
30	τριάντα	tree-**a**n-da
	triánta	
40	σαράντα	sa-r**a**n-da
	saránta	
50	πενήντα	pe-n**ee**n-da
	penínta	
60	εξήντα	ek-s**ee**n-da
	exínta	
70	εβδομήντα	ev-tho-me**e**n-da
	evdominta	

80	ογδόντα	og-th**o**n-da
	ogdónta	
90	ενενήντα	e-ne-ne**e**n-da
	eneninta	
100	εκατό	e-ka-t**o**
	ekató	
200	διακόσια	thya-k**o**s-ya
	diakósia	
1,000	χίλια	cheel-ya
	chília	
2,000	δύο χιλιάδες	the**e**-o cheel-y**a**-thes
	dýo chiliádes	
1,000,000	ένα εκατομμύριο	**e**-na e-ka-to-mee-ree-o
	éna ekatommýrio	

Time, Days and Dates

one minute	ένα λεπτό	**e**-na lep-t**o**
	éna leptó	
one hour	μία ώρα	mee-a o-ra
	mía óra	
half an hour	μισή ώρα	mee-see **o**-ra
	misí óra	
quarter of an hour	ένα τέταρτο	**e**-na t**e**-tar-to
	éna tétarto	
half past one	μία και μισή	mee-a keh mee-se**e**
	mía kai misí	
quarter past one	μία και τέταρτο	mee-a keh t**e**-tar-to
	mía kai tétarto	
ten past one	μία και δέκα	mee-a keh th**e**-ka
	mía kai déka	
quarter to two	δύο παρά τέταρτο	the**e**-o pa-ra t**e**-tar-to
	dýo pará tétarto	
ten to two	δύο παρά δέκα	the**e**-o pa-ra th**e**-ka
	dýo pará déka	
a day	μία μέρα	mee-a m**e**-ra
	mía méra	
a week	μία εβδομάδα	mee-a ev-tho-m**a**-tha
	mía evdomáda	
a month	ένας μήνας	**e**-nas mee-nas
	énas mínas	
a year	ένας χρόνος	**e**-nas chro-nos
	énas chrónos	
Monday	Δευτέρα	thef-t**e**-ra
	Deftéra	
Tuesday	Τρίτη	tree-tee
	Tríti	
Wednesday	Τετάρτη	te-t**a**r-tee
	Tetárti	
Thursday	Πέμπτη	pemp-tee
	Pémpti	
Friday	Παρασκευή	pa-ras-ke-ve**e**
	Paraskeví	
Saturday	Σάββατο	sa-v**a**-to
	Sávvato	
Sunday	Κυριακή	keer-ee-a-ke**e**
	Kyriakí	
January	Ιανουάριος	ee-a-noo-**a**-ree-os
	Ianouários	
February	Φεβρουάριος	fev-roo-**a**-ree-os
	Fevrouários	
March	Μάρτιος	m**a**r-tee-os
	Mártios	
April	Απρίλιος	a-pree-lee-os
	Aprílios	
May	Μάιος	m**a**-ee-os
	Máios	
June	Ιούνιος	ee-oo-nee-os
	Ioúnios	
July	Ιούλιος	ee-oo-lee-os
	Ioúlios	
August	Αύγουστος	av-goo-stos
	Avgoustos	
September	Σεπτέμβριος	sep-t**e**m-vree-os
	Septémvrios	
October	Οκτώβριος	ok-t**o**-vree-os
	Októvrios	
November	Νοέμβριος	no-**e**m-vree-os
	Noémvrios	
December	Δεκέμβριος	the-k**e**m-vree-os
	Dekémvrios	

Livewire Warrington

3 4143 11019129 1

A & H	01-Jun-2017
914.95 TP	£15.99
WES	

5414558